"GIMMICKRY"

"GIMMICKRY"

In the Search for More Money
[Whatever Works in the Scheme of Things]

Jay Wenderoth

Jay Wenderoth

To order additional copies of this book, contact:
Xlibris Corporation
1-888-795-4274
www.Xlibris.com
Orders@Xlibris.com
64175

CONTENTS

In framing a Government for posterity as well as ourselves, we ought in those provisions which are designed to be permanent, to calculate not on temporary, but permanent causes of expense. If this principle be a just one, our attention would be directed to a provision in favor of State Governments for an annual sum of 200,000 pounds, while the exigencies of the union could be susceptible of no limits, even in imagination.

—Alexander Hamilton
Federalist Paper no. 34

CHAPTER ONE

The Civil War

The United States of America is the great experience. The United States, among nations, has generated great wealth, a wealth system created in a little over two centuries. How did this wealth materialize? It was pure capitalism in a new republic with immeasurable resources, astounding growth, and escalating debt amid social and monetary pain along the way. Some countries, impoverished a thousand years ago, are still impoverished. It is unthinkable that a civil war occurred; a fourth- and fifth-generation America was crippled. Southern states were devastated. The Civil War was a correction. There was emancipation and the Thirteenth Amendment; the federal government ballooned. State sovereignty took more hits; industrialization emerged, escalated. A most dramatic immediate change was the nation's money. Modern money creation and debt funding had been in evidence since the beginning of the eighteenth century. The Bank of England launched the British Empire and influenced the United States in its financial beginnings. The legislative connection between government and the banks in the money scheme escalated in the United States because of the Civil War.

In April of 1861, the South fired on Fort Sumter, and the North invaded the South. The North blamed the war on slavery. The South claimed states rights. Lincoln, in his way, simply said, "Without slavery, the rebellion could never have existed, without slavery, it could not continue."

The South believed in state sovereignty. When Virginia finally came on line, secession was complete. The South quickly formed the Confederate States of America with a central government in Richmond, Virginia. The Southern states quickly united, formed a constitution although they believed in state sovereignty. The South formed a central government in Richmond although they didn't believe in a central government in Washington. Lincoln called their action an ingenious sophism. There was a national debt in 1861. Lincoln said, "If one State may secede, so may another; and when all shall have seceded, none is left to pay the debts. Is this quite just to creditors? Did we notify them of this sage view of ours when we borrowed their money?"

In April 1861, there were thirty-four states, twenty-three in the North and eleven in the South. Separate state paper currencies was the norm issued by approximately 1, 500 chartered banks in the thirty-four states. Counterfeiting was rampant and would continue. If one traveled from Wisconsin to New York or from South Carolina to New York, a traveler's paper money may be discounted from 25% to 30%. A state bank paper currency or financial transaction may not be accepted in another state. The paper money the banks circulated was redeemable in state stock or assets and a specie reserve if it existed. Specie, or gold and silver coin, was supposedly the legal tender money; but for the most part, it was exchange outside the domain. It was bank reserve. Paper money was apparently created against a specie reserve, stock, or other forms of security. State banks were banks of issue. The dollar amount of circulated paper money, on average, may extend to several times the dollar amount of specie or state stock held in reserve. The security of state bank issues varied from state to state.

The United States government spent about $80 million in 1860. The national debt was $90 million. U.S. government revenue came from the tariff (duties on imports) and public land sales. Duties were paid in coin or bullion. Property taxes and excise taxes furnished state revenue. This was supposedly the revenue setup since the ratification of the Constitution. State financial sovereignty changed dramatically when the Constitution was ratified. First, it was Confederation and then the Constitution. The states took the hits when sources of state revenue were reduced. Federal revenue was in the form of "indirect taxation," and the state revenue source was a "direct taxation." The states took another hit when Hamilton's excise tax caused the Whiskey Rebellion in 1794. The United States had existed for eighty-five years, and a federal income tax did not exist, yet. There were no laws governing interstate commerce. At that time in 1860, government revenue and public debts paid were in specie. An 1860 census counted 32 million people in the United States. The normal collection of import duties and postal connections extended from Maine to New Orleans. Approximately 80% of the United States Navy was in foreign ports.

The Civil War changed everything. For starters, the South confiscated import duties at all Southern ports, such as Norfolk, Savannah, Charleston, New Orleans, etc. Import duty, the tariff, primarily gold, was taken by the South. These import duties, the indirect taxation, belonged to the United States government; the duties did not belong to the states, in this case the Southern states (one of the reasons for the Blockade). Postal connections were cut off. The South destroyed coastal navigational systems from Norfolk to New Orleans. The war and restoration of the Union would cost an enormous amount of money. Government spending, annually, increased four times in 1861. Spending increased twenty times by 1865. There was just $2.3 million in the Treasury in April of 1861. At the beginning of the Civil War, federal government spending represented about 5% of a national product. That 5% figure would increase dramatically to approximately a third of a national product. The Treasury went from a yearly $80 million expenditure to hundreds of millions of dollars. Where did all the money come from? Money was created.

Lincoln called a special session of Congress to begin July 4, 1861. Vice President Hannibal Hamlin called the Senate to order. Galusha A. Grow was elected Speaker of the House.

Lincoln asked the Congress for "four hundred thousand men, and $400,000,000." Lincoln stressed that the loan would be less per capita than the War of Independence. In July 1861, Lincoln was thinking a "short and decisive" war.

A loan bill was passed on July 17, 1861. The secretary of the Treasury, Salmon Chase, was authorized to borrow $250 million within a twelve-month period. Fifty million dollars of the loan was paper money printed and issued by the government. This paper currency was originally called demand notes because the notes were redeemable in coin. Later in 1862, paper currency printed and issued by the United

States government would be called greenbacks. The initial demand note currency was non-interest-bearing currency printed in $5, $10, $20, and $50 denominations. It was the advent of the first United States circulating paper currency approved by Congress. Secretary Chase introduced this measure in his message to the Congress. Chase said the issue of the non-interest-bearing currency would be "convenient." A portion of this currency was not circulated; it was kept in the Treasury. The government had very little coin. The government paid all its debts in coin. An immediate Treasury stock was a currency redeemable in coin.

So why, after eighty-five years, did the federal government print a circulating paper currency? Hopefully, a simple answer is in this writing. The issue of this non-interest-bearing currency was a spark that initiated one of the biggest debates in American political economic history. There was Civil War, but a currency tug-of-war would begin as well.

The remaining $200 million of the loan would be obtained through the proposed sale of twenty-year bonds at 6% interest payable semiannually and the issue or sale of interest-accruing Treasury notes, payable three years from issue. The Treasury notes were called seven-thirties because the interest was 2¢ per day per 100 for 365 days or 7.3 dollars. The Treasury could pay bills with these Treasury notes, but the notes were interest accruing. Once received, they would be held; they wouldn't circulate as currency. The Treasury had issued this type of Treasury note on many previous occasions. The new laws included changes to the collection of import duties and the collection of direct taxation. Chase was going to vie with the states for a share of the excise taxes. Chase needed an additional $80 million from duties and taxation. Chase recommended various tax rates "on the real and personal property of the States not under insurrection," which would produce about $22 million. He estimated the property value in the North at $11 billion. An income tax was considered based on an income in excess of $800 at "3% per annum."

The loan also stipulated that Chase could sell bonds "in any foreign country." The amount could not "exceed one hundred millions of dollars."

The total revenue projected for the coming year was $330 million, 250 million in loans and 80 million in taxation. The nation's projected debt would increase to $340 million in the first year, $ 90 million on the books, plus the $250 million loan.

There is no evidence in the *Congressional Record* of substantial debate on appropriations in this special session. There were differences to administration policy, but action by Congress was swift. The first loan bill was passed and signed by the president in fourteen days. Anyway, there was a general feeling that the war wasn't going to last very long.

Lincoln had his detractors. Congressman Vallandigham of Ohio was one of his harshest critics. The congressman called Lincoln's message "a labored and lawyerly vindication of his own course and policy; that his message omitted the origins of the secession; and called Lincoln's political party a sectional organization . . . which sooner or later would precipitate a revolution and the dissolution of the Union." He also said that Lincoln's actions were "infractions of the Constitution and usurpation of power, such as the suspension of *Habeas Corpus*, the calling up the volunteers, the blockade etc." Vallandigham did not approve of and voted against the loan bills in this first session.

Why the Vallandigham remark "which would sooner or later precipitate a revolution and the dissolution of the Union" when secession was complete? Vallandigham did make interesting points about the "origins of the secession," principally, the nineteenth-century tariff ; the tariff was high in the United States. It was a protective policy favored by the Northeastern states and hated by the South. South Carolina, the first to secede, threatened separation from the Union in 1828 unless there was a change in the tariff. The South's economy depended on trade with England; the South's agricultural products, textiles, and tobacco went to England. South Carolina was a force in the South and, apparently, could be a problem child of the Union. South Carolina controlled her economic destiny and states around her. She had Charleston; imports and exports went through Charleston.

Senator Polk from Missouri and Senator Powell of Kentucky were critical of Lincoln. President Lincoln had words for Kentucky and Maryland. Kentucky and Maryland were the "border States" or "middle States." They were neutral at the time of secession. Lincoln called their "armed neutrality" disunion completed.

The Sub-Treasury Act of 1840 was repealed. The government had been depositing its revenue in its own depositories. Bank failures in the past brought this about. Because of the new loan, Chase would be leaving the money in the bank from where it was borrowed. Most of the money borrowed was in New York, Philadelphia, and Boston, the money centers of the country. Bills were passed that appropriated expenditures for the expansion of the army, navy, and the Marine Corps. The cost of five hundred thousand men and ordinance was $189 million. The bills provided for the expansion of government departments, offices, clerks, and secretaries. Thousands of new jobs were created to collect internal taxes and to affect the collection of duties on the water or their "redirection." There was a need for men to weigh, gaugers, measurers, inspectors, and paymasters for the army and navy. The states would be indemnified for the call-up of the militia. There was the law passed allowing the president to confiscate rebel property. The tariff had been increased in an earlier session. Sixty-five acts were passed in this session. Assessors and collectors would eventually be needed for the vast collection of taxes.

There was government business as usual. Appropriations were made for the governments of the Dakota, Nevada, and the Colorado territories, public land sales, new settlements, the Indian nations, the postal service, the railroads, new canals, the Union Pacific Railroad and connection to the Pacific, and world trade and commerce.

Congress adjourned on August 6. This first session of the Thirty-seventh Congress responded to the Lincoln administration. Lincoln got five hundred thousand men for the army. He had asked for a loan of $400 million; Congress gave him 250 million. Chase had asked for thirty-year bonds at 7% interest; Congress gave him twenty-year bonds at 6% interest.

The best feature of the loan bill was the $50 million in demand notes. There was virtually little money in the Treasury. The demand notes were an immediate infusion to the Treasury. The response was favorable. The demand notes that were circulated initially paid government and troop salaries. Demand notes were exchangeable for interest-accruing Treasury notes or Exchequer bills and twenty-year bonds at 6% interest. Demand notes paid into the Treasury could be reissued by the secretary. But circulation could not exceed $50 million.

In August of 1861, the nation's varied principal money and notes included the following:

- Specie—gold bullion and coin, primarily silver bullion
- State bank paper currencies
- U. S. Treasury notes or exchequer bills, interest accruing at 7.3%, maturity in three years
- U.S. demand notes, non-interest-bearing, redeemable in specie
- "Fractional currency," which included nickels, dimes, quarters, and half-dollars

From 1791 until the Civil War, state banks printed the circulating paper currency. Because of the Civil War, the United States Treasury joined the fray. The Treasury started printing circulating paper currency. The banks continued issuing their paper currency, and specie would begin to vanish, disappear. The demand note and its substitute, the eventual greenback, was another forerunner to a future national uniform currency in the United States.

CHAPTER TWO

Suspension of Specie Payment:

The Greenbacks

Lincoln and his special session of Congress did well in July and August of 1861. The Army of the Potomac was an embarrassment. This army lost the first major battle of the war. It was the First Battle of Manassas [Bull Run] in Virginia.

On December 2, 1861, the second session of the Thirty-seventh Congress was in order. Hannibal Hamlin and Galusha Grow remained as president of the Senate and Speaker of the House. Lincoln and cabinet messages again addressed the Congress.

Since August, railroad and bridge destruction had been repaired in Maryland. In the beginning, normal movement of Northern troops through Maryland had been impossible. The famous Thomas Viaduct across the Patapsco River Valley was spared; a Northern army detachment guarded this bridge during the Civil War. This bridge, built in 1832, is used today by the CSX railroad. There was a Confederate victory in Missouri. The North controlled the western part of Virginia. The North maintained Fort Hatteras and Port Royal that enabled the Union to withstand blockade-runners from Savannah and Charleston. After Manassas, things were quiet in Virginia and Kentucky.

The most troubling event for the North was the Trent Affair. In November, the Union Navy prevented the Confederate commissioners John Slidell and James Mason from proceeding to Europe. Their purpose was to ask for Confederate aid from France and England. They were intercepted off Cuba aboard the British ship *Trent*. and imprisoned in Boston. The act was shown to be a violation of freedom of the seas. England protested; the United States apologized, and the two men were released. The two men proceeded to Europe. An apparent threat of war between the United States and England was diminished.

General George McClellan had replaced Winfield Scott as general of the army of the North. Business in the General Land Office had stopped; there were no public land sales in the South. "Ordinary channels of trade and commerce" and "sources of income" were reduced according to the secretary of the Interior, Caleb B. Smith. Fewer people were migrating westward; many volunteered for the army.

Some of the first actions of the Congress were recognizing the provisional governments of Tennessee, North Carolina, and Virginia. In August, Senator Breckinridge returned to Kentucky and accepted a commission in the Confederate Army. The Senate expelled Mr. Breckinridge; the vote was 36-0. There was an official congressional thank-you to Captain Wilkes of the U.S. Navy for his role in intercepting the British ship *Trent*.

Lincoln's message in December 1861 omitted the Trent Affair. Lincoln covered capital and labor; he wrote, "Labor is prior to, and independent of capital. Capital is only the fruit of labor, and could never have existed if labor had not first existed. Labor is superior of capital, and deserves much the higher consideration." He concluded his message, "There are already among us those who, if the union be preserved, will live to see it contain two hundred fifty millions."

Since August, Chase had borrowed $197 million. Of that amount, there was in circulation and on deposit in the Treasury $25 million in $5, $10, $20, and $50 demand notes. Chase said "this money may be regarded as a loan from the people, payable on demand without interest." The Treasury, by way of the comptroller, printed, lent, borrowed, and issued, in one fell swoop, $50 million, without interest, a pretty neat trick; and the authority to do so had always been there?

Chase mentioned the paper circulation in the country.

In January of 1861, the total money in circulation in the United States was 202 million dollars, 150 million of which was in the North. The whole of this circulation constitutes a loan without interest from the people to the banks, costing them nothing, except the expense of issue, and redemption and the interest on specie, kept on hand for that purpose. And it deserves consideration whether sound policy does not require that the advantages of this loan be transferred, in part at least, from the banks, representing only the interest of the stockholders, to the Government, representing the aggregate interest of the people.

Secretary Chase's statement from the past is noteworthy. Chase simply said that it cost the banks practically nothing to print and issue their paper money. The paper money was interest free to the banks, but the paper money was not interest free to the people. The banks, by constitutional law, had been doing their pretty neat trick for years. Chase planted a seed, a beginning, whereby the government, in the future, through legislation, would be printing the paper money—a national paper currency. The beginning was in 1863. The secretary talked of two plans, a possible continuation of demand notes or an issue of United States Notes, a "National Uniform Currency" backed by U.S. stocks or bonds. Chase preferred a uniform currency plan or the second plan. Chase called the uniform currency plan a credit circulation. He said, "The Secretary entertains the opinion that if a credit circulation in any form be desirable, it is most desirable in this."

Putting Chase's statement another way, it was a way of funding a debt. A credit circulation and funding a perpetual debt, as we shall see, is one and the same thing. From the record, this new plan was not a Chase plan. "In August of 1861, O. B. Potter of New York," a banker financier, presented the scheme to Secretary Chase. Chase spent a lot of time with the banks, principally with Jay Cooke, a banker from Philadelphia. Jay Cooke was the principal government agent in the distribution and sale of government bonds and securities in the United States during the Civil War. Chase's plan was partly of a Thomas Jefferson principle but primarily of an Alexander Hamilton principle, as in shareholders and a future private banking system.

Although the Constitution originally said no to the "states," state banks did print and issue paper currency. Chase mentioned that the state bank issue would have to be eliminated to realize a "National Uniform Currency." He mentioned that placing a tax on the state paper currencies would encourage their withdrawal from circulation.

What Chase recommended would be difficult to do, establishing a uniform currency in thirty-four states, eleven of which had seceded, and in the territories with a war going on. In looking back, the separate paper currencies within each state demonstrated the extent of state financial sovereignty in the nineteenth century. But state banking and exchanges, apparently, could be most cumbersome in settling business transactions between towns and states.

The atmosphere was different in this session. There was realization that the war was going to go on. Chase's message on December 3, reflected the reality. He mentioned revenue from customs and taxes was far short of expectations. His projections went into 1863; he wanted $200 million immediately. He asked for an additional $655 million in 1862. If the war continued into 1863, the debt would climb to 900 million.

It was in the House of Representatives where a second money bill, a tax bill, and a uniform currency plan were paramount. The money bill centered mostly on the issue of *legal tender* paper currency issued by the United States government.

A $650 million loan bill was passed on February 25, 1862, 150 million in United States Notes and $500 million in bonds. The notes were to be lawful money, *legal tender*, non-interest-bearing for all debts in the United States, public and private, *except duties on imports*. Demand notes would be discontinued. On December 30, 1861, the banks suspended specie payment. Suspension of specie by the banks meant that 50 million of the new notes were to replace the existing demand notes "as soon as practicable." The total of all new United States Notes could not exceed $150 million. The notes were printed by and under the guidance of the comptroller of the Treasury.

The suspension of specie was a repeat of the past. President Jackson shut down the Second Bank of the United States in 1832-1836. Since that time and up to the Civil War, the government accepted coin only in all transactions and expenditures. Part of the first loan of 1861 (150 million) was to be paid in coin. The banks rescinded after the first 100 million. A final installment of $50 million would be paid in bank paper currency. According to Thadeus Stevens, the currency was discounted at a loss of $5 million. Thadeus Stevens was chairman of the Ways and Means Committee in the House. Discounted means interest charged up front for money borrowed. The banks also took the 7.3% short-term Treasury notes (the first 100 million), not the 6% twenty-year bonds. These short-term Treasury notes were payable in three years in gold. This was understandable; the banks would hopefully get their gold back quickly with interest.

Mr. Stevens said,

> Before the last $50,000,000 were due all the banks in the United States suspended specie payments, and it was paid in paper currency at a loss to the Government of over $5,000,000. This gave such a shock to public credit that it was found impossible to negotiate a loan in coin at any price. The financiers of New York [bankers and brokers] were consulted and gave it as their opinion that a loan of $50,000,000 put on the market would not produce over eighty per cent, payable in the irredeemable paper currency of the Banks; that a specie loan was impracticable.

If an irredeemable paper currency was going to be used by the government, "it had better use its own notes."

What did "not produce over eighty per cent" mean? It meant the banks would gladly lend the government $40 million of bank paper money for a payback by the government of $50 million.

During the War of 1812, the banks suspended specie payment. In the money game, it was never expected that specie meet exhaustive payment. Accepted money before that war was bank paper circulation representing gold coin. In 1812, money was needed, a lot more money than the ordinary circulation; more money was needed to support the increased demand for goods and services. More money did come forth because the banks increased the money supply by printing more paper currency. The Bank of England suspended specie payment during and after the Napoleon Wars. The Bank of England issued an irredeemable paper currency for a period of twenty-five years (1797-1822). History was repeating itself during the Civil War in America. Specie was suspended, and the banks would expand their paper currency again.

It took two months to pass the $650 million loan bill. Substitute bills and / or amendments quickly followed. Vallandigham spoke gloom and doom. But his substitute bill contained the $150 million in United States Notes and the discontinuance of the demand notes. Vallandigham wanted a "temporary" money measure. Vallandigham wanted "to support and float these $150,000,000, with a nearly equal amount of taxation and revenue, payable of course in these notes." He mentioned that the government had no gold and silver. There could be no demand notes; specie had been suspended. Speaking of his "substitute" bill, he said, "Its purpose is to provide a new but temporary medium, receivable for the public dues, and sufficient only to meet the increased fiscal action of the Government." There were two significant changes to Vallandigham's bill. The United States Notes were made a legal tender, and the notes would not be acceptable for duties on imports. The legal tender clause and the payment of duties on imports were debated aggressively. The legal tender clause became a contested constitutional issue.

Vallandigham didn't like Chase's uniform currency plan. It was a plan for the long term. In referring to a "permanent" plan, he concluded, "I cannot and I will not vote to bring down upon the wretched people of this once happy and prosperous country, the triple ruin of a forced currency, enormous taxation, and a public debt never to be extinguished."

Roscoe Conkling of New York submitted a substitute bill that stipulated that the United States Notes should not be accepted for duties on imports.

Congressman Spaulding of New York debated approvingly for the issue of legal tender United States Notes. He emphasized taxation

($150,000,000) to support the United States Notes. Did Congress have the power to print and issue legal tender paper currency? Spaulding referred to Alexander Hamilton's words that he felt would support his argument. Congress, he felt, did have the power to print legal tender paper currency. Alexander Hamilton had been aide-de-camp to George Washington; he became the first secretary of the Treasury of the United States.

Spaulding submitted words from the Federalist No. 23. Hamilton wrote of "no limitation of that authority" in matters of the "NATIONAL FORCES." Hamilton wrote, "It rests upon two axioms as simple as they are universal. The *means* ought to be proportional to the *end;* the persons, from whose agency the attainment of any *end* is expected, ought to possess the *means* by which it is to be attained."

Spaulding mentioned Great Britain's specie suspension (1797-1822). "As a measure of necessity, she made the Bank of England Notes virtually a legal tender by suspending the specie restriction. During all this time the people of Great Britain advanced in wealth, population and resources."

Congressman Crisfield of Maryland favored a national currency plan; he didn't want the legal tender note issue in the bill. He didn't offer any substitute bills either. He said, "This Government has no power to declare anything but gold and silver coin a legal tender in the discharge of debts." Concerning the "precious metals," he said,

> We must have a larger and more abundant currency than we have heretofore found to be necessary . . . The business of the Government and the business of the country require some substitute for coin. We must therefore create a new or vastly enlarge the existing currency. We must therefore create a public debt, establish a currency, and impose new taxes.

Crisfield said he was "brought up in the old Whig school." The Whig Party was in opposition to Andrew Jackson policies. The Whig Party opposed Jackson's abolishment of the Second Bank of the United States.

Congressman George Pendleton of Ohio called the government legal tender notes unsound and illegal. The government had "no power except that which is granted." Pendleton introduced the "Madison Papers" to support his position.

The Madison Papers include the original and final drafts of the Constitution and debates by the Framers. The original draft stated, "To borrow money and emit bills on the credit of the United States." The final draft omits the words "emit bills"; the final draft states, "To borrow money on the credit of the United States." The Framers voted 9-2 to strike the words "emit bills." Pendleton presented the discussions of Gouverneur Morris, James Madison, and others.

Gouverneur Morris was a Pennsylvania delegate to the convention in 1787. He served in the Continental Congress during the Revolutionary War. The more celebrated James Madison became the fourth president of the United States. Morris and Madison contributed greatly to the wording of the Constitution.

Debates are controversial contests. Only those words supporting an argument are usually presented. Pendleton presented the words of Gouverneur Morris and James Madison. The papers show Morris moving to strike out "and emit bills on the credit of the United States." Morris said, "If the United States had credit such bills would be unnecessary; if they had not, unjust and useless." Madison responded to Morris, "Will it not be sufficient to prohibit the making them a *tender*? This will remove the temptation to emit them with unjust views." Pendleton did not present Morris's response to Madison, which was, "Striking out the words will leave room still for notes of a *responsible* minister which will do all the good without the mischief."

Spaulding "solicited" the constitutional opinion of the attorney general, Edmund Jennings Randolph. In 1790, the attorney general emphasized "Section 10" of Article I and the absence of "inferential prohibition." Section 10 states, "No State shall emit bills of credit." The attorney general stated, "Treasury notes are bills of credit. This applies to a State only, and not to the nation, and thus it has always been understood."

Spaulding favored the issue of legal tender Treasury notes; Pendleton was against. Yet both used the words of Alexander Hamilton to support their arguments.

Pendleton referred to Hamilton's famous bank reports of 1790. Hamilton stated, "The emitting of paper money by the authority of the Government is wisely prohibited to the individual States by the national Constitution; and the spirit of that prohibition ought not to be disregarded by the Government of the United States." About "government paper emissions," Hamilton used the word "advantages." And then he used the words "disadvantages, abuse, dangerous an expedient"; and then he used the words "have no ill consequence and productive of good." Then Hamilton stressed the avoidance "as much as possible" of the government emitting paper currency in his banking report.

In his bank reports, Alexander Hamilton did not write that the emission of paper currency by the government of the United States was strictly prohibited. It was 1790; the Constitution was agreed upon. The second session of the First Congress was in progress. Did the Constitution, as written, strictly prohibit the emission of bills of credit by the federal government? If it had, Hamilton would have said so. Hamilton did suggest the role of government and the role of a proposed bank, the eventual First Bank of the United States. This proposed new bank, fashioned by Hamilton and modeled after the Bank of England, would print the paper currency. The Bank of England was inaugurated in 1694. The British Empire was well on its way in 1790 propelled by the Bank of England. Alexander Hamilton wanted the young nation, the United States, to follow a similar path.

Alexander Hamilton showed great interest in banking during the Revolutionary War. He prepared another bank report as early as 1781. He wanted to assist Robert Morris, who, at the time, was formulating the Bank of North America. That bank opened in 1782. Robert Morris was "superintendent of Finance of the United States from 1781 to 1784." Robert Morris, reportedly with great success, helped finance the American Revolution. Morris did not accept Hamilton's invitation.

Alexander Hamilton was right there with Washington, Jefferson, and Madison, all presidents. But Hamilton couldn't become president; he was born in the West Indies.

Alexander Hamilton, John Jay, and James Madison wrote the Federalist Papers. John Jay, a lawyer, was minister to Spain and the first chief justice of the Supreme Court. The Federalist Papers have been referred to as propaganda. The papers were articles published in New York newspapers to promote the Constitutional Convention. The papers were written under the name "Publius." It was hoped the states of New York and Virginia would join the rest of the states and ratify the Constitution. Every imaginable topic pertaining to the Articles of Confederation and the Constitution is in the papers. The banking practice, literally, is excluded. Public debt, taxation, indirect taxation, direct taxation, state revenue, federal revenue, borrowing of money are included. Hamilton articulated expenditures, taxes, and public debt. Madison mentions gold and silver coin, paper currency, and bills of credit. The words "bank," "a national bank," "a United States bank," "any bank" are not in the papers. The states believed in sovereignty. The states feared central power. A bank, a United States bank, a central bank, was central power. Alexander Hamilton, a Federalist, wanted central power.

In the Federalist Papers, when referring to federal and state expenditures, debt, and taxation, Hamilton wrote,

> In framing a Government for posterity as well as ourselves, we ought in those provisions which are designed to be permanent, to calculate not on temporary, but on permanent causes of expense. If this principle be a just one, our attention would be directed to a provision in favor of the State Governments for an annual sum of about 200,000 pounds; while the exigencies of the union could be susceptible of no limits, even in imagination.

Hamilton may not have written about a central bank in the literal sense, but he was probably thinking one when he wrote those words. Hamilton had referred to "state expenses being permanent and fixed."

He referred to federal expenses as being permanently unlimited, "even in imagination."

It is more than probable Alexander Hamilton waited. He would not write a bank, a national or central bank in the Publius. It was after the ratification. There was now a United States of America with a central government; now was the time. It was after he became the first secretary of the Treasury. The First Congress was in session. Hamilton was asked by the House of Representatives to prepare a report on the "Public Credit." He then submitted his bank reports. Alexander Hamilton was clever. He had to be most clever. Thomas Jefferson and James Madison, two future presidents, were against his plan for a central bank. Jefferson was secretary of state, and Madison was a senator in Congress. Responding to a request from the president, Jefferson and Madison each submitted reports to George Washington. Jefferson and Madison, citing the Constitution, opposed the proposed bank. Their reports cited that the Constitution did not expressly grant Congress the power to charter a private banking corporation. Attorney General Edmund Randolph's response to Washington was also negative. Although Thomas Jefferson and James Madison opposed him, Alexander Hamilton won the bank battle. George Washington and a majority in Congress apparently wanted the central bank.

The First Congress assembled in New York on March 4, 1789. Those first days of the First Congress were spent establishing protocol and the various departments, one of which was the Treasury. There was the debt, the "Public Credit." There were members of Congress who wanted no part of debt funding. There were public lands to the West. There were members who wanted to swap public lands for Revolutionary War debt.

In 1789, the Revolutionary War debt was more than $10 million; interest on the debt had grown to "$1,640,071." The money was owed to France, the Dutch [Amsterdam], and to Spain. It was necessary that Hamilton negotiate the payment of these debts.

Congressman Hooper stressed the importance of the tax bill. Taxation was the "security" for the United States Notes and the government bonds. "This tax bill will give to the bonds of the United States the character so much desired by capitalists, that of a sure interest-paying security." Hooper mentioned that the capitalist didn't care if the principal was never paid. It was the interest-paying "revenue" that was desired. Bonds could always be sold for the "principal"; it was the same as a "transfer" of the principal.

Referring to Great Britain, Hooper said, "The amount of debt of the British Government is so great that the most sanguine political economist can devise no method by which it can be extinguished; but yet the bonds representing that very debt are of great value." The bonds were of great value because the "interest is sure" were Hooper's words.

Hooper spoke of a meeting between Chase, the banks, and the boards of trade. The meeting was in Washington. The boards of trade and the banks wanted the government to use bank paper currency. The record indicates that the secretary "declined." The "effect" would be a negative one. The government would have to sell bonds at "the rate or terms" of the banks and receive "the notes of suspended banks in payment of these bonds." During the War of 1812, government bonds "were then negotiated in some instances at twenty per cent less than their par value." The government received depreciated "bank currency—from twenty to twenty-five percent discount, as compared with coin." Hooper said, "To render the Government financially more independent, it is necessary to make the United States notes a legal tender."

The House received a message from Secretary Chase; it was January 29, 1862. His message contained the following points:

- Chase demanded immediate action on the money bill, House Bill 240.
- There was no money in the Treasury.
- The war had caused heavy expenditures.
- There was no coin; banks had suspended specie.

- The issue of United States Notes was necessary, and they should be a legal tender as recommended by the Ways and Means Committee.
- The legal tender note would place all citizens on an equal footing and neutralize those who won't accept them.
- The Treasury would provide the security for the notes by funding them in interest bearing bonds, adequate legislation, and taxation.[1]
- The circulation would eventually return to a currency of coin

Congressman Morrill of Vermont said the bill "should not pass." He said the "national credit would be damaged." It would "reduce our standard of legal tender already sufficiently debased, because it will inflate the currency." Also, "it will banish all specie from circulation."

Wouldn't it be correct to state that specie had already been banished by the banks?

Morrill had a sense of humor. In referring to the war, Morrill stated, "But General McClellan must harvest *some* of the glories of this war within the next ninety days, or be gazetted 'an accomplished gentlemen, but no General.'" Probably one of Lincoln's biggest frustrations during the Civil War was McClellan's failure to move against Lee's Army of Northern Virginia.

At this point in the debate, two substitute bills had been presented. There were amendments to the substitute bills and amendments to the amendments. Vallandigham, Spaulding, Pendleton, Morrill, and Stevens were the most active in presenting amendments to the original bill. The original committee bill and the substitute bills stipulated "six percent interest on the bonds." The bills and amendments did not stipulate interest paid, in what? The original intent in the House was to pay the interest in United States Notes, a view supported by Thadeus Stevens. Mr. Morrill and Mr. Hooper wanted interest paid in specie.

---

[1]   As part of the future "National Uniform Currency Plan," the secretary would be asking for the funding of United States Notes, "a credit circulation," in future legislation.

Mr. Hooper said, "It is now proposed in this bill to limit the Secretary to par for six percent bonds, the principal and interest to be payable in specie or its equivalent." Hooper mentioned, in the summer of 1861, the banks wanted 7% interest, but the law stated 6%. The banks balked. It may be the loans could not be negotiated unless interest on the bonds was paid in coin. The banks didn't take the bonds anyway; they took the 7.3% Treasury notes payable in three years. The Vallandigham bill stated that import duties would be paid with United States Notes. Mr. Morrill stated, "We do not propose to receive these notes for duties on imports, for the reason, that it is desirable to leave the tariff stable amid all fluctuations, and, also, that we may secure the coin we promise to pay out as interest on the bonds."

The Ways and Means bill did not stipulate specie payment for interest on bonds and specie payment for import duties. The secretary was not specific about specie payment in his first and latest messages to the Congress. The final bill would stipulate coin for the payment of interest on bonds and coin for the payment of import duties.

Congressman Morrill, following several members, also spoke of England's specie suspension. But Morrill talked about specie resumption. He elaborated on the "pains to be suffered" when specie payment would resume. He mentioned England's return to specie payment in 1824. It "convulsed the whole country," affecting two generations of people. The effect of return to specie was wipeout time for the unaware, the unfortunate. Payment of inflated debt had to be paid in gold or the equivalent in paper money; it was good-bye time for paper money.

Morrill expanded on the nation's wealth, coal, minerals, agriculture, and manufacturing, its vast resources. "The agricultural and manufacturing capabilities of our land and people are sufficient to carry us through any war, offensive or defensive." He wanted no loans extended to foreigners. "We strike out all words in relation to any foreign loan." This didn't happen; England would later get the gold-paying bonds.

Roscoe Conkling of New York said the government had declared "war" on the banks. He said there were 1,200 banks, $350 million, and 200,000 stockholders. Should the government "make the banks its fiscal enemies, or its fiscal friends?"

He mentioned the banks of New York, Philadelphia, and Boston. These banks loaned the government 100 million of their total capital of 119 million. No other interest in the country "put so nearly its whole capital into the war"?

Conkling would vote "against the attempt by legislation to make paper a legal tender." Conkling talked about intrinsic value on the value of paper versus the value of gold or coin. Gold had "a value equal to the cost of producing it." Conkling centered on gold, gold in and of itself, being the absolute value. He put down the "prohibition" argument. "Has the power been given; is it there? Can you put your finger upon it among the grants of the Constitution? If not, if it is not there at all, you have not the power, and there is an end of the whole matter." Conkling mentioned the wealth of the nation. There was $300 million of gold "more than ever before, and if we deserve it we can have it."

According to Congressman Conkling, sufficient gold was in supply. But the banks suspended specie payment; they were not making payment on their paper currency.

Morrill talked about the wealth of the nation in terms of its people and resources. Conkling talked about the nation's wealth in terms of gold.

John Bingham of Ohio had the floor. He chided Mr. Pendleton for using Alexander Hamilton's words whereby "Hamilton denied the power to issue Treasury notes."

Bingham explained that Hamilton "showed the propriety of establishing a national bank authorized to issue currency, and he gave certain reasons therefore." Bingham continued, "My colleague is a most excellent lawyer. He knew well, and so did Hamilton know well when he made that argument, that what the Government does by another it does by itself—*qui fecit per alium fecit per se.*" Pendleton responded, saying his "remarks" did not assert that "Hamilton denied the power to issue Treasury Notes." Bingham was "much obliged . . . This avowal saves me a great deal of trouble. It is what I expected from the ingeniousness of my colleague." There was laughter in the House when Pendleton said, "I am very much flattered by what my colleague says but I object to his putting it upon that footing exactly."

Bingham referred to Daniel Webster. Daniel Webster had been a congressman, a senator, and a secretary of state. He was most famous as an orator. When in the Senate, Webster opposed President Jackson in 1832 on the renewal of the charter of the Second Bank of the United States. Bingham mentioned Webster's three strong opinions in 1816, 1836, and his last in 1837. In 1816, Webster spoke "against any but a metallic or specie currency." His famous "specie circular" in 1836 was a reaffirmation of coin. Bingham said his last opinion in 1837 "was his matured opinion." Webster said,

> I am for no new experiments; but I am for a sound currency
> for the country. And I mean by this a convertible currency,
> so far as it consists of paper . . . Congress has authority to
> regulate, and must regulate and control, any and all paper
> which either States or individuals might desire to put into
> circulation purporting to represent coin, and to take its place
> in the uses of trade and commerce.

Bingham referred to a "remarkable essay of Hume" when asked the question, "What is Money?" David Hume was an eighteenth-century philosopher from Scotland. Hume wrote, "Money is that which is authorized by the sovereign, and agreed upon among men [speaking, of course, through their sovereign] as the standard of value, and the medium for the exchange of commodities."

In his *Writings on Economics*, Hume wrote, "It is indeed evident, that money is nothing but the representation of labour and commodities, and serves only as a method of rating or estimating them." Also,

> we find, that, in every kingdom, into which money begins
> to flow in greater abundance than formerly; everything
> takes a new face. Labor and industry gain life; the merchant
> becomes more enterprising; the manufacturer more diligent
> and skillful; and even the farmer follows his plow with
> greater alacrity and attention.

Mr. Bingham emphasized sovereignty. That sovereignty was "the Government of the United States." That sovereignty has "the power to determine what shall be money, what shall be the standard of value." He went on to mention that power was granted by the Constitution. The Constitution has granted the power to the "Congress of the United States to determine what shall be money everywhere within the jurisdiction of the United States."

Mr. Bingham stirred things up when he said, "I stand here to assert that the Constitution of the United States has nowhere declared what shall be a legal tender. Your Constitution, I repeat, never made gold and silver a legal tender. It never made anything a legal tender in the discharge of debts." He said, "Acts of Congress" have made it so. Mr. Bingham was right; it is nowhere stated in the Constitution.

Bingham was for the issue of legal tender United States Notes approved by the Congress redeemable eventually at a prescribed time in the coin of the United States. Bingham reminded the House that the secretary felt that legal tender notes were unavoidable. Certain railroads and banks had refused to accept them. The secretary said, "Such discriminations should, if possible, be prevented; and the provision making the notes a legal tender, in a great measure at least, prevents it, by putting all citizens, in this respect, on the same level, both of rights and duties."

Roscoe Conkling had a question for Mr. Bingham. "It is true always, and certainly it has been true since 1857, that the debtor interest immensely preponderates over the credit interest, numerically and otherwise." Would there be an

> inducement to form all combinations possible for the purpose of bearing down and keeping down to the lowest depreciation that medium in which debts shall be paid? And therefore I ask him the practical question, whether this idea of legal tender, so far from imparting value to these notes, is not offering a reward and bounty to the greatest interest in the country, numerically and otherwise, to make them of the least value possible?

Bingham answered "with all frankness that I do not see that we present any inducement to the people to undertake to undermine their own fabric of Government, to destroy their own credit, to paralyze their own arms." Mr. Conkling clarified that he was suggesting only an "inducement" and not necessarily a deliberate attempt by financial interests to depreciate the notes.

During the War of 1812, the government and the people took the hits when the banks depreciated bank paper currency; the consequence was the inflation of the debt incurred.

Mr. Bingham mentioned the Joint Resolution, which had just been agreed upon by both houses of Congress. The resolution imposed "upon the two Houses of Congress, the obligation of raising $150,000,000 annually by taxation, direct and indirect." The Congress had pledged the security for the issue of $150,000,000 in United States Notes.

Congressman William P. Sheffield of Rhode Island was against the legal tender clause; he said, "It is dishonest." The Treasury note was "paper." "By this bill, it is proposed that we shall give them paper. They ask us for bread, and we give them a stone." Thadeus Stevens asked Mr. Sheffield, "Will the gentleman tell me what currency he proposes to pay them in, and where he will get it?" Mr. Sheffield would not vote for the bill with legal tender clause in it. Mr. Sheffield said, "Bring forward your banking scheme." Mr. Sheffield would vote for a national uniform currency bill.

Over in the Senate, Mr. Carlile of Virginia had jumped the gun. He submitted a resolution, which he called "bringing to the attention of the Senate the necessity of early action upon the financial policy that is to be adopted by the Government."

The House was nowhere near approval of House Bill 240 and a tax bill. The House of Representatives prepare the money bills and the tax bills. The Senate makes amendments to those bills. Mr. Carlile apparently didn't wait for those bills. From his comments, he wanted Senate attitude geared for the impending bills. "We may be induced to adopt a system that will be ruinous to the interests of the country, if not in violation of the Constitution of the land."

Mr. Carlile's resolution called for the following:

- Raise direct taxation on real property of every kind, liquors, luxuries, etc.
- Enough taxation to pay 7% interest and 8% interest on up to $800,000,000 in bonds.
- The government would pledge the public lands as security for the bonds, a security worth $1,000,000,000.
- The Government would authorize the creation of a fiscal agent or agency in New York. This would be a department of the government? The resolution was vague.
- The secretary would deposit each time $25 million in specie and $75 million in bonds from time to time. The total coin to be deposited would be $200 million.
- The secretary would receive from the agency $100 million in demand notes for each deposit of the above.

In effect, the secretary would be borrowing $100 million each time. Who was going to print the demand notes? The agency, probably, or representatives of banks?

- Over time, the secretary would deposit a total of $200 million in specie and a total in bonds of $800 million, a total worth of $1,000,000,000. The minimum amount of specie could not be less than $25 million.
- The government would pay 7% and 8% interest on ten-year and thirty-year bonds sold by the agency, 200 million in ten-year and 800 million in thirty-year bonds.
- The government would have the right to redeem the ten-year bonds after five years and the thirty-year bonds after ten years.
- The agency would be authorized to sell enough bonds necessary to enable the redemption of notes issued by the agency.

The resolution didn't specify that coin would purchase the bonds. It did specify that demand notes could purchase the bonds.

- Interest would be paid in coin by the agency semiannually.
- Specie on hand shall not be less than a 1:4 proportion against the circulation. If less, the agency would call upon the secretary for an additional deposit of bonds.
- All payments by the government would be made in the demand notes issued by the agency.

Apparently, all spending by the government would be in agency notes.

Mr. Carlile said, "Whenever you assure the capitalist that certain provision is made for the prompt payment of his interest in coin, and the return of the principal at maturity, you will be able to command all the coin that you may want." Mr. Carlile mentioned the specie deposit would guarantee that government notes would be received at par everywhere. Apparently, Mr. Carlile was looking out for the capitalist.

"All the coin you may want" may have sounded pretty good, but the primary circulation by banks before the war was paper currency. Coin, apparently, was a reserve. This plan by Mr. Carlile would ensure a continued paper currency circulation, but the government would not do the printing and circulating. The banks would be assured of receiving interest payments in coin, and the coin would primarily stay in reserve in the banks. This new agency, apparently, would be a bank of issue similar to the present-day Federal Reserve? Mr. Carlile's plan would require the government to supply the reserve in the new agency. The reserves in the Federal Reserve bank today are provided by the member Federal Reserve banks.

Mr. Carlile wanted to place an entity between the government and the banks. Mr. Carlile wanted the government to tax real estate. Property taxes were reserved for the states. Mr. Carlile wanted government public lands used as collateral for the bonds. Mr. Carlile wanted this new entity to issue the paper currency. The resolution was vague; it did not specify which entity would print the demand notes. The government would receive and spend the demand notes. This was a credit circulation of a different form. The government's credit circulation would operate through an agency in New York. The government under a Carlile plan would fund its debt by borrowing money from an authorized agency set up in New York City. Mr. Carlile wanted the banks to receive 7 and 8% interest. The Congress had set a limit of 6% interest on bonds.

The secretary said in his message to the Congress that there was no money in the Treasury. This deficiency included coin. Starting an agency would be difficult to do. How could the secretary deposit coin in this agency when the government had little coin?

At the beginning of the war, the government dealt in specie payment. Why did the banks stop lending the government the needed coin in 1861? Why did the banks suspend specie payment? Gold was deficient in supply. Capitalization in the banking scheme could never work if dependent upon the specie supply; only an inexhaustible supply of paper currency would do.

Mr. Carlile's plan would guarantee coin to the capitalist. The government would receive demand notes to spend. We can say Mr. Carlile's plan had merit for the banks. The government would not issue a paper currency. The banks would not issue a paper currency. A separate entity or agency would issue the paper currency. Would this agency have government connections but be run privately? The Federal Reserve System today is a government connection but with private control and interests. Mr. Carlile may have been ahead of his time. The Senate approved Mr. Carlile's resolution. It was too soon though; this resolution, some of its ideas, would surface at a later time.

The Civil War was not a year old. Military needs were pressing but so was westward expansion. A bill was passed giving President Lincoln control of the railroads for troop movements. Mr. Rollins of Missouri introduced a bill; the bill would aid in the construction of a railroad and telegraph line from the Missouri River to the Pacific Ocean. The bill would secure for the government the use of the railroad for postal, military, and other purposes. Another resolution was presented and agreed that the secretary of war "report to this House as early as practicable what arrangements can be made, and the terms of the same, with the railroad corporations on the line between Washington and New York, by way of Baltimore and Philadelphia."

Mr. Spaulding informed the House that the secretary was unable to issue more of the Treasury note seven-thirties "without a discount." And so it would go, the discounting, the depreciation. Mr. Kellogg of Illinois said,

> The opponents of this bill were the banks and their friends in Congress. Issuing the Treasury notes and keeping the value of the currency would be difficult. What will be the result? Why, the bankers and the brokers of the country will have a direct interest to depreciate it. The country owes them. The debts of the country are fixed in amount; and if they can force this currency down, they thereby comparatively force their debts up. They make you pay a good currency what you owe, and they depreciate the currency you have to pay in. Why will they depreciate it? Because they propose to furnish the currency themselves. They propose to depreciate, and speculate in a depreciated currency. And, Sir, they can do it by their hold on the commerce of the country . . . They will try to depreciate it and they will succeed.

Mr. Edwards talked about the exception placed on the United States Note. The exception was payment on duties on imports or the nonpayment of duties on imports. Mr. Edwards said,

> If you look at the phraseology of the bill, you will see that the Government itself is not to receive them at par for all its dues. It is proposed to make an exception, a discreditable exception, against them at their very outset. They are not to be accepted in payment of duties on imports. They are to be barred of ingress into the Customhouses of the country. Branded with this exclusion, where should they find admission? For this, and other reasons equally sufficient, they will at once be depreciated, and no one will take them as currency, for nobody will be able to pass them as such. They will not pass at par among individuals, and they will not be received at the counters at the banks.

Thadeus Stevens wanted the interest on U.S. bonds paid in the lawful money of the United States. By law, the United States Note was declared lawful money. But apparently, the deal was made. Interest on the bonds would be paid in coin. The government had no coin. The banks had suspended specie. The only way the government could obtain the coin was through the tariff, duties on imports. So backed into a corner, the government "repudiated" its own currency. But United States Notes were printed. They did become legal tender; they would be called greenbacks, and the banks did take them. The banks bought government securities with the "repudiated" currency, held them as reserve for suspended coin for redemption in gold, and collected the interest on the bonds in gold.

Mr. Kellogg of Illinois had the floor; he talked about the First Bank of the United States. Why was it started? "It was to make a currency for commerce; it was to aid commerce in the means of exchanging commodities; it was to make a circulating medium; it was to make a representative value. That is all it was. In other words, it was to make money."

Alexander Hamilton created the First Bank of the United States, which created paper currency. The paper currency was bank currency payable in gold!

Thadeus Stevens mentioned that Congress had established the First Bank of the United States by law.

> The Supreme Court pronounced it constitutional. In short, whenever any law is necessary and proper to carry into execution any delegated power, such law is valid. Now, it is for this Congress to determine whether this bill is necessary . . . The value of legal tender notes depends on the amount issued compared with the business of the country. If a less quantity were issued than the usual and needed circulation, they would be more valuable than gold.

Stevens referred to the writer McCulloch when he made that statement.

Mr. Stevens continued that the "$150,000,000" issue of United States Notes would meet the demands of government. "In the rapid circulation of money, $100 in a year is turned so often as to purchase ten times its value." He mentioned that the United States Notes would serve the country better than the "suspended paper of the banks."

At the time of this writing (early 2002), the gross domestic product in the United States was approximately $10 trillion. The dollars in circulation was approximately $800 billion. In the modern money scheme, where ample money supply pumps a viable economy, the ratio of circulation to product generally remains a constant. It was 1:10 or more in the eighteenth century and in 1862. It was 1:10 or more in early 2002.

Mr. Riddle of Ohio called the money bill "shameless." Mr. Blake of Ohio said that "the money-shavers of the city of New York" wanted to defeat the bill. Mr. Pike of Maine called the money bill a "venture." If the venture would not work, he said, "There are other remedies in our saddle bags besides bleeding, and we must try them." Mr. Pike had a sense of humor. Mr. Alley of Massachusetts said if Hamilton and Webster were here, they would "favor this bill." Mr. Thomas of the same state hoped the debt would be on "this generation . . . and not by their heirs." Mr. Wright was for taxation and the national currency bill. And so on and on it went, members for the legislation, those against and those members for a complete overhaul, the national uniform currency plan.

The debate in the House was winding down. There were changes offered to the bill. There were amendments to the amendments. In the middle of all this, there was Samuel Shellabarger of Ohio.

The opponents of the bill cried "disaster," "inflation," and "bankruptcy." Mr. Shellabarger said that "the cry of alarm" was "unreasonable." Shellabarger presented a "parallel to it." He presented a history of England's national debt. It began early in the eighteenth century, five warring periods between 1713 and 1820. The national debt grew from $250 million to $4 billion. During the first period, "not pot-house politicians merely, but profound thinkers, declared the Government permanently crippled." And later, during the next period as the debt grew, "historians, statesmen, and economists concurred in declaring that the case of England was certainly now desperate; but now the nation persisted, although demonstrated by the books to be bankrupt, in becoming far richer than any period of her history." And then by 1760, "the National debt came to be $700,000,000. Adam Smith, the father of political-economic science, thought the limit had been reached, and an increase in the debt would be fatal."

"David Hume, the profoundest man of his age, declared it would have been better that England had been conquered and crushed by Prussia and Austria than by debts for which all the revenues of the kingdom north of Trent and west of Reading were mortgaged. He said the madness of England exceeded that of the Crusaders. Richard Coeur de Lion and St. Louis had not gone in the face of arithmetic. England had. You could not prove that the road to national ruin was through a national debt. But still, in defiance of Hume and Smith, and even Burke, the Nation would live and grow richer, and pay the interest on the national debt. Then the next period was the taxing of the Colonies, the American Revolution; and the debt grew to 1.2 billion dollars; then the wars with Napoleon and a debt of four billion. But the interest on the debt continued to be paid."

Shellabarger quoted "a great historian and a great commoner of England."

> Cries of bankruptcy and ruin were based on a double fallacy. They who raised these cries imagined that there was an exact analogy, between the case of an individual who is in debt to another, and the case of a society, which is in debt to part of itself. And they also forgot that other things grew as well as the debt.

In the case of Great Britain, it was the empire.

And that was Shellabarger's parallel. The cries of alarm were similar to England's past when there was no need for alarm. He didn't want to "show that a national debt was a blessing." He mentioned that the opponents of the bill wanted to devalue the Treasury notes "so that out of the blood of their sinking country they may be enabled to coin the gains of their infamy."

Thadeus Stevens put things in perspective; he presented some numbers. The present debt was "at least $ 180,000,000." The secretary had been unable to negotiate the total $250 million loan of August 1861. The government daily expense had risen to $2 million a day. He mentioned that 700 million more dollars was needed before the next session of Congress. The total debt would rise to $1,050,000,000. How was the money to be raised? It would be disastrous to go into the market negotiating more bonds. "I have no doubt they would sell as low as sixty per cent." He estimated having to sell 1.5 billion in bonds to achieve $1.1 billion that would "carry us to the end of the next fiscal year. This sum is too frightful to be tolerated."

And again, there was Mr. Morrill of Vermont and Roscoe Conkling of New York. They were in opposition to the money bill. They opposed the chairman of the Ways and Means Committee. They both referred to Thadeus Stevens as a man of sneers. Conkling said, "He devoted one or two of them to me."

Mr. Hooper, bringing up the notes again, mentioned that many of the banks were not accepting the notes. Without the

> legal tender clause from this bill would make it useless to the Secretary of the Treasury. The proposed issue of Government notes guards against this effect of inflating the currency by the provision to convert them into Government bonds, the principal and interest of which, as stated before, are payable in specie.

Hooper, Morrill, and Conkling kept stating that the payment of the principal and interest on the bonds would be in specie. The bill, approved by the House and sent to the Senate, did not specify specie; it specified the lawful money of the United States.

Thadeus Stevens pressed the Committee of the Whole in the House to close the debate and have the House vote on the bill. After last-minute amendments to the bill, House Bill 240 was passed by the House on February 6, 1862. The vote was 95-55. One hundred fifty million dollars of legal tender Treasury notes were approved for issue. The $50 million of demand notes approved in the first session, half of which had been issued, would be taken out of circulation. The bill was referred to the Committee on Finance in the Senate.

The SENATE

Mr. William P. Fessenden of Maine had House Bill 240 read twice and referred to the Committee on Finance. Mr. Fessenden was chairman of the Senate Finance Committee.

Secretary Chase sent an urgent message to the Senate. The Treasury had "immediate" needs. Chase wanted an extension of the 1861 act. He wanted an immediate issue of $10 million in United States Notes in addition to the $50 million authorized. The Senate responded. Senate Bill 190 authorized the issue, and the secretary would get his money. And presto, just like that, $10 million was printed for the secretary.

The Senate approved an amended bill on February 13, 1862. The Senate knew what was coming. The Senate was ready. The amended bill was done in quick time. The House took two months putting the bill together. The Senate added nineteen amendments to the bill in eight days. The vote was 30-7 in favor. The amended bill was sent back to the House. The significant changes and/or additions amended by the Senate are the following:

- All interest on bonds and notes shall be paid in coin (gold).
- Keep the $50 million of demand notes in circulation.
- The secretary should sell the bonds for the market price of coin.
- The seven-thirty Treasury notes of July 1861 were to be declared legal tender.
- The government could redeem the bonds after five years and pay the bonds after twenty years.
- Sell two-year bonds at 7.3%
- Minimum amount of bond or short-term deposit shall be $100.
- A section 4 was added. Short-term certificates of deposit could be sold up to a total of $25 million, 5% interest in coin.

- A section 5 was added. A sinking fund was set up to pay the principal on the debt. The sale of public lands, import duties, and the sale of seized rebel property in coin would pay the interest on the debt.

Senator Fessenden, chairman of the Finance Committee, spoke to the Senate before the amendments were presented. He made the following points from a senator's view:

- During the War of 1812, government stocks depreciated 60%. The government took depreciated bank currency to pay its bills. But the government didn't then issue a legal tender paper currency. The government was doing it now only out of "extreme reluctance."
- The interest on the public debt shall be paid in coin. "According to our amendment, the Government will be obliged to provide itself with coin for the payment of the interest." The Secretary will "provide himself with coin . . . and be obliged to do it at whatever sacrifice may be necessary in order to accomplish that purpose." The people who take government paper will receive more in return than just paper. Specie had been suspended, but coin could be available or could be had at the right price. "Money in the market is always worth what it will sell for."
- The 1861 loan crippled the banks; the loan "took all the capital they have." We should have gone into the market when our credit was high. "We resorted to the banks." The Senate will give the secretary the authority to get the funds needed. "We have abandoned the idea of adhering to the notion of putting our paper in the market at par when it is not entitled to command it."

Fessenden said the loan took all the capital from the banks. The capital he referred to was coin. The amount of coin in the loan was $100 million. Previously in the House, Conkling mentioned that 300 million in gold was available. Where was the 200 million in gold the banks didn't have? Apparently, other sources were dealers, brokers, foreign banks, the people? Specie payment was suspended because it wasn't there?

- What is the public credit? It is the ability of the people to pay. Prior to the war, the foreign debt had been greatly reduced. The country was "one of the richest . . . on the globe." There was great wealth in the land, production, agriculture, manufacture, and commerce. "We must be entitled to credit for our ability to pay." The Framers of the "Constitution considered the best capital that a nation could have" was what? "Labor, the power and the will to work." And the country had grown rapidly as a result.

- There was the public creditor. He "looks not to the principal" but "his investment." The public creditor "wants to know what his interest will be." England will never pay its debt, but "her stocks are always sound" because of "security." As long as we pay the interest "for a series of years," we will "satisfy the public creditor, either at home or abroad."

- News had been received from London that the government's paper "could be negotiated there on favorable terms." Our rate of interest was much better than there, and if our paper was acceptable to them, the investment by them "would be sought for with avidity."

- "How is our credit to be sustained. We must tax; tax speedily, strongly, vigorously. The people can bear it, and will bear it with cheerfulness and hope."

- About the addition of Section 4, the section was added as an inducement for the banks to take the United States Notes. It would be under the control of the secretary. "It will allow the Sub-Treasuries to be used as places of deposit. It is an argument by which the banks themselves are controlled. They live by deposits. The banks of your great cities are not banks of great circulation. Their money is made on deposits. We want to induce them to take these notes on deposit; and if we provide a place where, if they do not take them on deposit, they can be deposited by individuals. It is a strong pressure to bear upon the banks to give the notes a currency by taking them and passing them themselves." Section 4 was a "highly important one," he said, "It will give force to these notes." Section 4 was the short-term certificate at 5% interest.

- The twenty-year bonds should be redeemable at the pleasure of the United States after five years and payable after twenty years.

- The only argument against the legal tender clause was that certain banks wouldn't accept the notes unless they were legal tender. A main obstacle was the clearinghouse in New York. Banks, which cannot meet their balances, must borrow at 7% until balances are met. Banks, accepting the notes, would be at a disadvantage because the notes may not be accepted at the clearinghouse. The best financial minds in the country were undecided about the legal tender clause. The constitutional question was not raised; let the courts decide. There was indecision whether the notes should be legal tender.

Senator Fessenden could not make up his mind; should the notes be legal tender or not? A bit later, Senator Sherman would make up his mind for him.

Senator Pearce from Maryland wanted to know what Fessenden was implying concerning the twenty-year bonds. "Redeemable" and "payable" mean the same thing. "The terms are the same; they are convertible." What was the "necessity"? Did he mean at the pleasure of the government after five years and the pleasure of the creditor after twenty years? Fessenden said he would check on the "phraseology."

Making the bonds redeemable after five years would allow the Treasury to control the country's debt. After five years, the Treasury could buy back the bonds by refunding at possibly a better rate of interest. This was done during a period after the Civil War was over. It's a continued practice to borrow long to pay short.

Senator Jacob Collamer of Vermont was so negative about the bill, he provoked Senator Wilson of Massachusetts to say, "It seems the argument made by the Senator from Vermont is an argument against issuing these Notes as a currency at all." Senator Wilson said, "I venture to express the opinion that ninety-nine of every hundred of the loyal people of the United States are for this legal tender clause. Collamer did not want the legal tender clause; he did not want the notes to be used for private debts."

There was Senator Sherman of Ohio. Senator Sherman was brother to William Tecumseh Sherman, general of the Northern Army. General

Sherman was known for his infamous march through the South and the burning of Atlanta. Senator Sherman was on the Senate Finance Committee. He would later become secretary of the Treasury. Much later in the nineteenth century, he would author the Sherman Antitrust Act.

Sherman said the House bill was "evidently imperfect. The Committee on Finance, have so improved it, as materially to change its character." Sherman was to the Senate, the same as Thadeus Stevens was to the House. Both were pragmatic. Sherman didn't waste any time; he got right to the point:

- As of July next, the Treasury has to pay out over $300 million.
- One hundred million is due now.
- Where do we get the money?
- We don't have a tax bill yet; there will be no tax money for six months.
- Put our bonds on the world market now?
- England did that at a great sacrifice. She sold bonds valued at 420 million pounds, for 260 million pounds. It was pointed out earlier that England issued a paper currency to finance the Napoleon Wars. The sale of securities was insufficient.
- The United States has to pursue the same course.
- The major banks have no money; the banks can't help us.
- We have to borrow elsewhere.
- The law says the government can accept coin only for our bonds.
- Where do we get the coin? It is stowed away. Suspension did that.
- The buyer of our bonds must go to a broker first to buy the coin. This exchange would determine the market price of our bonds.
- Opponents of the bill want to use bank paper currency to purchase our bonds, an irredeemable inflated currency of the worst character.

Sherman went on and on for an hour. The following by Sherman tells us where he was coming from. If coin was insufficient to form a medium of exchange for the increased wants of the country, then Congress may establish another medium of exchange, another standard of value. This was twice done, by establishing a Bank of the United States. I much prefer the credit of the United States, based, as it is, upon all the productions and property of the United States, to the issues of any corporation, however well guarded and managed [the future uniform currency plan, the permanent credit circulation].

Alexander Hamilton started the First Bank with congressional approval, a scheme to create a paper currency pyramidal in function to augment the commerce of the country. Congressman Bingham reminded us earlier that what the government does by another, it does by itself. In his statement above, Senator Sherman was referring to a similar scheme. The next scheme would be the beginning of a future uniform currency plan, which would unfold in 1863.

Senator Timothy Howe of Wisconsin disagreed with Sherman's acceptance of government "sacrifices" in the open market. He said, "If you notify the capital of the country that you are prepared to pay for money whatever it is pleased to exact, it will be hoarded to await the extremity of your distress."

Senator Howe made significant comments. "The Government may be able to borrow of the banks, but the Government cannot borrow specie of the banks. If it borrows anything of them it must borrow, not their money, but their promises to pay money." About the banks issuing the paper currency, Howe said,

> The banks will loan the Government one hundred of its promises each to pay ten dollars on demand, without interest, in exchange for the Government's promise to pay $1000, with interest, in ten or twenty years. No man believes that those one hundred promises can ever be redeemed until the banks have raised the money upon the Government's promise.

What was Howe saying? The banks would print the paper money at no interest to the banks and lend the paper to the government at interest. The interest would be paid over a period of time. The interest paid to the banks would be in gold or silver or coin. After accumulating the gold over a long period, then, and only then, could the banks begin to pay any money on demand. The money in this instance was gold, which the opponents of House Bill 240 and the banks insisted was the legal money. But the way to achieve the coin was through paper; the bankers were a clever bunch.

Senator Howe continued, "Until that time the people must hold the bank notes, and pass them from hand to hand as money, and must pay interest upon the note of their own Government. The Government should issue that paper, because its promises are safest to take and surest to hold." Howe emphasized the security of the Treasury note compared to a bank note. He finished this thought, saying, "It has the largest estate pledged to its redemption, and survives the death of generations."

Senator Doolittle, also of Wisconsin, placed emphasis on the tax bill. He wanted to have a tax bill prior to House Bill 240. He wanted a guarantee of revenue before indebtedness. He said, "This Government must assert its Constitutional authority over the currency of the country in some practical way."

Senator Doolittle expanded on Howe's words about the banks. Doolittle said,

> While upon that subject, allow me to say that the real truth is, that these paper money banks, with few exceptions, are far from lending money to anybody, are mere borrowers themselves. They give nothing but their credit in exchange for other men's promises, with this remarkable difference that they give their notes without interest and take the peoples notes on interest, and with good security. It is a simple and ingenious contrivance, such as the philosophers of old could never discover, to turn nothing into gold, by which certain shrewd and clever men get interest on what they owe. Other people have to pay interest on what they

owe; but the banks of issue are contrivances to get interest not on the money they lend, but on what they owe the community.

More of the meaning here we get later in chapter 4 from Thomas Jefferson.

Senator Charles Sumner of Massachusetts agreed with the plan of legal tender United States Notes. Although "emit bills" was stricken from the Constitution, he said there were no words stating that Congress could not emit bills. Sumner was a staunch supporter of Lincoln. Prior to the Civil War, Sumner spoke strongly against Southern senators in the Congress and against slavery most aggressively. In 1856, Sumner directed negative remarks toward a senator from South Carolina. He was severely beaten in the Senate as a result. Many months of recovery were required before Sumner returned. It would appear that congressional deportment could be quite brutal in the nineteenth century. Maybe it was expected in those days. It hadn't been that long since dueling had been officially banned in the United States. In the early days, did members bring their firearms into the chambers?

Apparently, the Carlile resolution or plan was not considered in immediate plans. There was nothing in the record to indicate otherwise. Some of his ideas did appear in the senate amendments, such as interests on bonds and notes paid in coin, five-year redemption on bonds, and the public land consideration. Carlile's agency, an entity to interact between government and the banks, was to come much later down the road.

The approved Senate version of the bill was sent back to the House. Thadeus Stevens "reported back the bill." He called the Senate changes "very pernicious." Before the House voted on the Senate's amended bill, Chairman Stevens would have his say "with more depression of spirits than I ever before approached any question." About the House bill, Stevens said,

> Congratulations from all classes—merchants, traders, manufacturers, mechanics and laborers poured in upon us from all quarters. The Boards of Trade from Boston,

New York, Philadelphia, Cincinnati, Louisville, St. Louis, Chicago and Milwaukee approved its provisions, and urged its passage as it was. Stevens had a "dispatch" from the Cincinnati Chamber of Commerce "urging the speedy passage of the bill as it passed the House."

Stevens continued, "From the caverns of bullion brokers, and from the saloons of the associated banks, their cashiers and agents were soon on the ground, and persuaded the Senate, with but little deliberation, to mangle and destroy what it had cost the House months to digest, consider and pass." Stevens brought laughter to the House when he mentioned the bill was so "disfigured" and "deformed, that its very father would not know it."

Apparently, the Senate was for the banks; the House was for the people.

Stevens declared the amended bill was now "mischievous" with "bad qualities." The amended bill made "two classes of money—one for the banks and brokers and another for the people." The banks will have the gold, and the people will have the paper. Stevens said the amended Senate bill was designed in principle to depreciate the legal tender United States Notes. It was unfortunate; the government had already "purposely discredited" the United States Notes. Stevens mentioned, as an example, the discounted bank paper currency lent to the government in 1861 ($50 million discounted to $44.5 million). The Senate wanted the interest on that paper to be paid in coin, not on $44.5 million but on $50 million, the amount of the bond. The $44.5 million, received by the Treasury, was irredeemable bank paper currency. Stevens called the financiers harpies. He said, "I suppose these men act from instinct." Also, the $100 minimum short-term certificate of deposit favored the financier, not the working class. The financier would get the coin; the working class would get the paper.

Stevens did not like the change in the twenty-year bonds. The Senate wanted the bonds to be redeemable in five years and payable in twenty years. Stevens insisted that the government could not possibly meet the redemption stipulation in five years. Besides, the investors would be buying twenty-year bonds with the five-year stipulation in mind.

The five-twenty bond was more attractive; the government could refinance in five years.

Thadeus Stevens felt that House Bill 240 was a bill for the people; the amended Senate version was a bill to satisfy the financial interests of the country. The House went over the nineteen Senate amendments and "concurred" in twelve, voted "non-concurrence" in seven.

It was February 21, 1862, when these deliberations were taking place. The previous day, President Lincoln's son Willie died. The message was received in the House. Mr. Knapp made the following resolution:

> Entertaining the deepest sentiments of sympathy and condolences with the President of the United States and family in their present affliction, by the death of his son.
>
> Resolved that this House do now adjourn.

On February 24, proceedings resumed on the bill. A committee of conference was ordered between the two bodies. Three managers each from the Senate and the House resolved the differences. The managers were the following:

SENATE
    W. P. Fessenden
    John Sherman
    John Carlile
HOUSE
    Thadeus Stevens
    V. B. Horton
    C. B. Sedgwick

President Lincoln signed House Bill 240 on February 25, 1862. Highlights of the bill were the following:

- One hundred fifty million dollars in United States Notes, non-interest-bearing, legal tender for all debts, public and private, is to be received the same as coin for all taxes, all claims and demands, etc., except duties on imports. The 50 million in demand notes were to be replaced when eventually received by the Treasury. The demand notes were held by banks and brokers. The minimum denomination of the new notes was $5.

- Total United States Notes in circulation is 150 million.
- Interest on bonds and notes is to be paid semiannually in coin.
- U.S. bonds could be purchased with United States Notes, $50 minimum.
- U.S. bonds or securities were exempt from state taxation.
- Five hundred million in five-twenty U.S. bonds were to be issued or sold by the secretary for whatever the market price in coin dictated.
- Short-term deposits of $100 in United States Notes for a minimum of thirty days and accepted by the secretary would pay an interest of 5% in coin. The maximum amount of the aggregate deposit could not exceed $25 million.
- Duties on imports shall be paid in coin.
- A sinking fund was to be set up to pay the principal of the debt.
- An appropriation of $300,000 would pay for the engraving, printing, etc.

The secretary could now sell bonds in the marketplace for whatever price the coin would bring. The second money bill had been passed and signed by President Lincoln. It was February 26, 1862. Let's look at the total approximate projected debt to July 1863:

- The national debt beginning in 1861 was $90,000,000.
- The loan bill of July 17, 1861, was $250,000,000.
- The loan bill of February 25, 1862, was $650,000,000.
- The additional notes requested by Chase was $10,000,000.
- Total approximate projected debt was $1 billion

In February of 1862, The nation's principal money included the following:

- Gold coin and bullion, silver bullion primarily (suspended)
- State bank paper currencies

- U.S. Treasury notes or exchequer bills, interest accruing at 7.3%, maturity in 1864
- U.S. demand notes, non-interest-bearing, originally redeemable in specie
- "Fractional currency"
- The soon-to-be-issued legal tender, non-interest-bearing United States Notes, they would soon be referred to as greenbacks.

In February of 1862, there was approximately $60 million of demand notes in circulation. It would be awhile before these notes were replaced by legal tender United States notes, the greenbacks. banks, brokers, and individuals held the demand notes. The demand notes were "good as gold." The demand notes and subsequent greenbacks were non-interest-bearing. Why did the Treasury issue *non-interest-bearing* currency in 1862? The banks wanted the government to borrow bank paper money during the Civil War. Bank paper was a costly move by government during the War of 1812; it wasn't going to be repeated. What is most consistent in the record when reading the history of money is the inconsistencies and the contradictions. The proponents of specie, the opponents of the greenbacks, the banking scheme, which created the bill of credit since the Bank of England, had suspended specie many times when it was time to pay; they couldn't pay! The banks suspended again in 1861. There was no promise to pay by the banks on their depreciating bank bill of credit.

On page 6 in chapter 2, there is a paragraph that describes how Secretary Chase articulated the paper circulation of the banks. The banks did their trick; they printed their paper money. The banks created their interest-bearing currency (to the people) against stock held in reserve in the banks. The paper currency the banks created cost the banks nothing except the cost of printing. The bank's paper currency comprised its circulation. A bank's beginning may be by charter, a charter granted by the sovereign, a head of state, or government. The First Bank of the United States was granted a charter by the Congress. The Congress granted the charter applying constitutional implication with an assist from Alexander Hamilton. The bank's value was its stock or reserve. Seventy-five percent of the stock consisted of commercial paper, war debts, and 25% specie. Commercial paper is a contract of indebtedness, a note of credit, government debt funding, money owed to the bank, assets of the bank. The approved bank may issue its paper currency to their customers for a fee. The fee was in the form of the discount, a discounted paper currency, or interest was charged. The bank paper money was supposedly redeemable in specie. After the Civil War started (December 1861), the banks suspended specie payment. The banks did not make payment or redeem for the currency they issued. The bank's paper currency was no longer redeemable in coin. Mr. Lovejoy of Illinois stated that a bank that does not make payment on currency issued is a "broken bank." Bank-printed paper money was never legal tender.

Beginning in June 1861, the U.S. Treasury issued a non-interest-bearing currency, which represented a valuable stock. The valuable stock was the people, taxation revenue, the government's public lands and sales, duties on imports, customs revenue. The government's charter was by congressional legislation. The Congress, applying constitutional implication, granted the power to the Treasury to print and issue the non-interest-bearing United States Notes. Section 8 of Article I of the Constitution grants this power to the Congress. The non-interest-bearing legal tender currency the government issued didn't cost the government or the people anything except the cost of printing. The government issued the non-interest-bearing currency to the people for a fee. The fee was in the form of taxation. The people's tax in the amount of the circulation would support the circulation. The cost of the currency to the people in this form, at the time, was less than the cost of a bank circulation. United States currency consisted of demand notes replaced with United States Notes. This currency, which became known as the greenbacks, was not redeemable in coin. A depreciating government paper currency was more attractive than immanent depreciating bank paper circulation. That premise, a currency that may be less costly to the people, appears to have been the perspective of the majority in the Congress during the Civil War. At that time in the money scheme, the banks created its paper currency on its basis of wealth, which was commercial paper, specie paid in by others, etc. The United States government created its paper currency based on its representation of wealth, which were the people, taxation, public land sales, customs in specie, and internal revenue. *Tit for tat*

The greenbacks, according to the opponents, were not secure; but the banks bought Treasury bonds with greenbacks, the banks receiving gold for the bonds. But the banks didn't pay gold for their paper currency. The battle for control of the money scheme would continue. After the Civil War, greenback opponents contested the legislation by the Congress whereby the Treasury was granted the authority by the Congress to issue non-interest-bearing United States currency. The constitutionality of the legal tender greenback would be taken to the Supreme Court in 1870. In the meantime, the war would continue, and the printing of the greenbacks would continue. The private and state banks continued the printing and issue of their paper money.

If the United States Treasury would have accepted a depreciating private banking paper currency to finance the war, it is probable the financial hardships inflicted upon the people would have been worse. A total of $450 million in greenbacks were issued to pay for the Civil War. However, the greenbacks didn't fully circulate. Bankers, brokers, and individuals, apparently, held the greenbacks; they purchased securities with the greenbacks. Banks circulated their paper currency in place of the greenbacks. The greenbacks became bank reserves, substitutes for coin suspension. It was a Civil War financial impasse between the money interests and government. The normal free flow of money from creditor to debtor and back again, apparently, in the case of the greenbacks, didn't happen. They were held, once received, like the seven-thirties, mainly by the banks. The banks bought the government bonds with the greenbacks. Thadeus Stevens felt that a $150 million circulation in greenbacks was all that was necessary. In a pyramidal banking deposit scheme, $150 million in a greenback currency may have accounted for an approximate $1.5 billion product, enough to finance a major part of the war. Unfortunately, according to Stevens, the greenback was "hoarded."

What would have been better during the Civil War, the depreciated greenback or a depreciated private banking paper currency? The Congress chose the greenback. According to a majority in Congress, the country, the people took the hits previously in 1812 with depreciated bank paper currency. Most definitely, a paper currency was necessary. Capitalization was never achieved with gold; it could never happen. The money interests suspended coin during the Civil

War. The banks did not accept payment on their paper currency. It was the same repeated ploy, but necessary for the banks. American banks were always short on gold. Gold was constantly shipped abroad. America was the debtor in the nineteenth century.

Coin was deficient in quantity; it always was! When Alexander Hamilton started his bank, he knew the rapid creation of money and resultant capitalization could not be achieved with gold and silver; it had to be, could only be, achieved with paper, paper currency. The hypocrisy went on; coin was suspended during the Napoleon Wars, the War of 1812, in 1837, in 1857. Apparently, the banks did not want to make payment on their currency during any of those periods. Coin suspensions and subsequent money panics would continue throughout the nineteenth century. From all appearances, gold and silver, the supposed real money, the difference in exchange for foreign commodities, was, in time of emergency, in time of war, in time of suspension, in the banking money scheme, when the loans were called, within the domain, a necessary contradiction. The banks, always short on the gold, demonstrated the periodic necessity when specie was suspended. When payment in gold was demanded by the bankers or creditors, payment had to be made in gold or its equivalent in paper money; this demand extinguished the paper currency circulation. The resultant demand in gold held "a veto on the action of money."

CHAPTER THREE
The Legal Tender Greenbacks

On June 17, 1862, the second session of the Thirty-seventh Congress was nearing an end.

Almost four months had passed since House Bill 240. The war had become more intense. Several major battles were fought in the first months of 1862. There was some geographic change between North and South. The North gained territorial advantage. The Civil War was one year old.

In February, General Grant won a strategic victory at Fort Donelson. The South would lose control of Tennessee and Kentucky as a result of that action. In March, the *Monitor* and the *Merrimack* fought their famous battle in Hampton Roads. The battle was a standoff, but the *Merrimack* would no longer be a factor. The South destroyed its *Merrimack*. In April, the Battle of "Shiloh or Pittsburgh Landing" claimed almost twenty-four thousand in losses, both from the North and the South; there was no substantial gain for either side. Northern forces seized New Orleans on April 29. President Lincoln went to Fort Monroe in May to view federal troop movements in Virginia. The Virginia campaign was a total frustration to Lincoln. McClellan failed to move on Richmond. The North had made gains in Tennessee, Kentucky, Louisiana, and North Carolina. But Lee's Army of Northern Virginia continued to perplex McClellan and his army of over one hundred thousand men.

During this period, Lincoln was moving toward emancipation. In April, the president signed a bill that prohibited slavery in Washington, DC In May, President Lincoln signed the Homestead Act. The Homestead Act was most important in the development of the West. There was a

resolution in the Senate to "encourage enlistment in the regular Army."
Secretary Chase mentioned earlier that the navigational systems off
the coast were being repaired or replaced. The state of Minnesota
gained authorization to change branch railroad alignments on public
lands.

On March 1, Congress approved a "Certificates of Indebtedness" act.
This act gave the secretary the credit needed to pay for "munitions,
supplies and transportation." Because of a lack of funds, certificates
of indebtedness, bearing 6% annual interest, were printed and given
to contractors as payment for service and work performed. This act
helped to "prosecute the war." The certificates were payable in full
in one year plus interest. Certificates worth $50 million had been
expended at 3 million in interest.

Also, on June 17, Bill 391 "was laid before the House." The bill
concerned polygamy in the "territory of Utah and other areas." Later
in this session, the bill would become law. Anyone accused of bigamy
could be punished by a fine of $500 and five years imprisonment or
both.

On June 17, another money bill was considered before the House, bill
187. The secretary of the Treasury was coming back for more United
States Notes. The secretary wanted an additional $150 million in
United States Notes. Why was the secretary asking for more money?
The secretary had been authorized to borrow $650 million more in
February. There was a problem. Five hundred million dollars of the loan
was in the form of bonds. The secretary couldn't sell the bonds at 6%
interest. But the short-term certificates were popular. The secretary
sold $45 million worth although the limit was 25 million. You take the
money where you can get it, but it wasn't enough. One hundred fifty
million dollars of United States Notes were printed.

Commenting on the additional issue, Spaulding in the House said
that the

> United States notes, without interest, has given the country
> a sound national currency, in which the people have had
> entire confidence. Every man, woman and child having a

five-dollar legal tender "Green-back" note in possession, has directly or indirectly loaned to the Government that amount, and becoming thereby interested in the perpetuity of the Government, is a strong advocate for a vigorous prosecution of the war.

The people liked the greenback; it was currency the people didn't have to pay for before issue. There was an income tax. The banks continued to issue their paper currency, a discounted paper currency. Because of escalation, both currencies would depreciate.

Spaulding wasn't enthralled with the request for more notes, however. He hoped the secretary would issue the additional notes only when necessary. It was the first time in the public record that the government currency was referred to as the greenback. Spaulding also referred to the notes as a sound national currency. The ultimate goal was a national uniform currency. A uniform currency was not a totally new idea. It was supposedly the ultimate plan of the first two central banks of the United States.

Secretary Chase's message included the following requests and comments:

- He wanted a part of the new issue to include currency in small denominations less than $5. Twenty-five million dollars in this currency was asked for. The burdens of the people would be lessened. The people would realize tax savings of $1.5 million.
- The smaller notes would be more convenient to the soldiers. The need for fractional state bank currencies would be lessened.
- There was awareness of the objections to currency less than $5. This type of currency is absorbed, their force is lost, and the currency disappears from circulation. There is inconvenience to the government.
- But legal tender notes of both large and small denominations will help to restore the resumption of specie payment. It would lessen the circulation of non-specie-paying corporations, solvent and insolvent.

- The new issue would only replace withdrawn or canceled notes. The new notes will only offset revenue not received from taxes, revenue not received from deposits, and revenue not exchanged for five-twenties.
- The short-term deposits were popular. But a reserve of notes in the Treasury was necessary to cover interest and early withdrawals. The requested reserve would not be less than one-third the temporary deposits.

When asked by Mr. Thomas of Massachusetts why the need for more United States Notes, Thadeus Stevens said he only wanted $150 million in United States Notes; "It is all I would have asked; but they spoiled the bill, and I don't know how long it will go on." Also, the hoarding of the United States Notes had begun.

Mr. Baker of New York was positive the Treasury didn't need another $150 million in United States Notes. He said the Treasury was averaging a million dollars per week from customs, and after the tax bill goes into effect, 2 to 3 million more per week will fill the Treasury. Imports were pouring into the country. He said more Treasury notes "will bring disaster and ruin upon our country." Debates in the Congress could be puzzling. Each member had his own platform or agenda. Mr. Baker cited "the banking scheme of John Law." John Law was a financier from Edinburgh, Scotland. Baker mentioned the eighteenth-century John Law scheme as a "warning." John Law is described in *World Book* as a banker and a gambler. Mr. Baker didn't mention that customs would be needed to pay the gold to the banks for the bonded debt.

Congressman Baker referred to a "recent magazine article" that covered John Law's expansion of bank notes in "excess of gold and silver. A Plutus had come among them, and enraptured the nation with his skill in creating debt and converting it into money." This happened in France. The period was 1716 to 1720; prices rose four times. John Law started a bank; its paper currency issue totaled $540,000,000. The paper money was supposed to be redeemable in specie. According to the article, other "nations poured their commodities" into France for the "kingdom's" gold and silver. The exchange was "ruinous to

France." The article Baker referred to didn't mention the "Mississippi Scheme." John Law's "Mississippi Company" was tied to "business operations in French held Louisiana and Canada." John Law's company flopped, and most investors lost everything. Specie, in and of itself, was considered the wealth; the loss of an insufficient quantity meant disaster in France. John Law, another genius from Scotland, almost three hundred years ago, created paper money out of a possible projected growth, equity, and ensuing debt, which is the basis of modern-day money creation.

It was June 23. How many United States Notes were in circulation?

- Fifty-six million dollars in demand notes were held by the banks and by individuals. These notes were supposedly held for specie payments on imports. Four million in demand notes had been paid into the Treasury.
- Approximately $94 million of United States Notes had been issued. The 94 + 56 = 150 represented the number of United States Notes in millions authorized by the February 25, 1862, bill.

A new bill would authorize 150 million additional notes. The bill would also extend the limit of short-term certificate investment to $100 million in deposits. These certificates were popular; they paid 5% interest.

Mr. Hooper hoped the secretary would circulate but $200 million, holding 100 million for the payment of interest and withdrawal of short-term certificate deposits. Mr. Hooper praised the banks for their past patriotism. He realized their power of the currency had been lessened. But he hoped they would "sustain the value of the Government issues, whether of currency or of bonded debt" during the "great emergency like the present." At the same time, he said, "I have long since expressed the opinion that the currency should be guarded and controlled by national law, and that the banks should be the servants and not the masters of the currency." Because of the legal tender clause, the notes for a while were approximately at par with gold. That had since changed; gold was at a 7% premium.

Hooper said,

> Mr. Chairman, to provide a suitable currency for the trade
> and commerce of the country, and carefully to guard
> its security and purity, has been deemed by all political
> writers and statesmen to be one of the highest duties and
> highest privileges of a National Government. This duty is
> performed, and this privilege is exercised by every civilized
> country other than the United States, either directly by
> the Government itself, in furnishing coin or paper for
> the currency; or indirectly, by conferring the power on
> banks established by the Government, and more or less
> under its control. The Government of the United States
> is the only exception, the only Government that has not
> claimed this to be its exclusive privilege and duty. [By the
> Constitution, the government had this "exclusive right
> and privilege."]

Hooper had no kind words for England. "The recent increase in the
demand for gold has been to remit for stocks sent here for sale from
England. It was done in no friendly spirit."

Mr. Watts of New Mexico chided Mr. Baker. Watts called the bankers
of New York John Laws. Mr. Watts said the banks would hold the
United States Notes to buy United States bonds. The banks would
then circulate their own notes.

Mr. Holman of Indiana brought laughter to the House. He hoped
that Mr. Watts hadn't referred to his "colleague, Mr. Law." Watts
responded, "Not in the slightest degree. The John Law that I
am referring to was an outlaw, and not an in law in this House."
There was a John Law in the House of Representatives. John Law,
a representative from Indiana, was "not in his seat" during these
proceedings.

Mr. Morrill of Vermont was back with more opposition. He mentioned
the demand notes were good for customs, and the Treasury notes
were good for all debts, public and private. And now the country will
have no demand for gold.

And now, Sir, if you inaugurate this new issue of Treasury notes, you will make gold and silver useless to the country, and it will be exported, as a matter of course. We are too poor to hoard it. We shall trade to the amount of our ability to pay with our exports of grain, flour, cotton, tobacco, and whiskey, we must pay the difference in gold and silver.

The country would be stripped of gold. Although he didn't make the comparison, Mr. Morrill's scenario appeared similar to the past events in France, to John Law, and the Mississippi Scheme. Away with the gold, the country is left holding paper. Kaput!

Mr. Lovejoy of Illinois said the banks were "broken." He spoke of the banknote and the bank's promise to pay. But when returning to the bank, "I ask them to pay their note, and am told they have suspended specie payments, a very soft way of saying the bank is broken, for when a Bank refuses or fails to pay according to promise, that is on demand; it is a broken Bank."

Thadeus Stevens spoke about notes less than $5; Stevens made the following observations:

- Banks are excellent things; a dollar bank note is not known beyond its local circulation.
- He had a Pennsylvania bank note and couldn't pass it at all.
- Our soldiers get these bank notes, and they can't pass them when they go home.
- We should issue these government notes less than $5 to the soldiers. The notes can be redeemed everywhere.

Small notes would be issued in 1's, 2's, and 3's. Two- and three-dollar bills were issued in 1862. In addition, $5, $10, $20, $50, $100, $500, and $1,000 bills completed the issue. A section would be added to the bill whereby the government would engrave and print the new United States Notes. The printing would be done at the Treasury Department at considerable savings. The cost of printing the currency less than $5 was about 8¢ per $100. The cost of printing the currency greater than $5 was about 7¢ per $100. The "American and National Bank Note Company's" price was about 20¢ per $100 of printing.

The House agreed on several amendments and approved Bill 187. The bill was sent to the Senate. On July 5, a Senate-amended bill was soon agreed upon by both houses after a committee of conference. The bill was signed into law on July 11, 1862.

Highlights of Bill 187 were the following:

- The secretary was authorized to issue an additional $150 million in United States Notes. (The United States Notes were the greenbacks.)
- Thirty-five million of the issue would be in notes less than $5 (1's, 2's and 3's).
- Seventy-five million dollars or half of the new issue would not be circulated but kept in reserve. The reserve would pay interests and withdrawals on short-term certificate deposits.
- The limit of short-term certificate deposits was increased to $100 million.
- A big change in this bill—if the secretary so directed, Treasury notes issued may be paid in coin instead of exchanged for certificates of deposit or bond equivalent.[2]
- Treasury notes may be exchanged for five-twenty bonds at 6% interest.
- The secretary may borrow any sum of the original $250 million loan that may not have been negotiated.
- Engraving and printing of the United States Notes was by the Treasury Department.

The certificates of indebtedness began in March, and Bill 187 would increase the projected debt to $1,200,000,000 as of July 1863. Money borrowed since July 1861 was about $450 million. Circulating currency included 56 million in demand notes, 94 million in United States Notes, and approximately $150 million in state bank currencies.

---

[2]   Specie payment was suspended; however, the secretary would sell bonds at the market price of coin. Interest on bonds would be paid in coin, and Treasury notes may be exchanged for coin if so directed by the secretary. The Treasury notes were the interest-accruing seven-thirty notes. The bankers preferred gold rather than exchanging them for bonds.

Approximately $300 million in paper currency was circulating in the Northern states in July 1862. The Treasury paid bills with greenbacks, interest-bearing Treasury notes, and certificates of indebtedness. The Treasury had to pay interest in gold coin on bonds. Bonds could be purchased with greenbacks and certificates of deposit.

The second session of the Thirty-seventh Congress adjourned on July 17, 1862. It was a productive session. More than two hundred acts became law.

To name a few:

- Duties on tea, coffee, and sugar were increased.
- The president was authorized to take control of railroads and telegraph in certain cases.
- Appropriations for just about everything, money couldn't be spent without appropriations.
- Expenditures for all the Western territories and the surveys of the public lands.
- Regulating trade and intercourse with the Indian nations.
- A new mint in Denver, Colorado.
- Provision for the appointment of sutlers in the volunteer service.
- Judicial proceedings—captured property. Polygamy was outlawed.
- Public education in primary schools—District of Columbia.
- The biggest, most enormous act of all—the Internal Revenue Act. As a comparison, the money bill in the public record covered two-thirds of a page. The tax bill included eighteen pages of the record. A commissioner of Internal Revenue was nominated by the president and confirmed by the Senate. The president divided the states and the territories into districts. Assessors and collectors were hired in each district. Anyone not declaring all private property could be fined $500. There was an income tax, appropriations, expenses for the Indian department, property tax, license fees, taxes on ale, beer, and porter, etc.
- The Department of Agriculture was established.
- The Homestead Act.

The nation's currency, loans, notes, and bonds as of July 1862 included the demand notes; the lawful money greenbacks; Treasury notes at 7.3% interest held by the banks, maturity in 1864; certificates of deposit (short-term borrowing); certificates of indebtedness at 6% interest payable in twelve months; gold coin and bullion, suspended; silver bullion, suspended; twenty-year bonds at 6% interest payable in gold; fractional currency; and circulating private state banking paper currency.

CHAPTER FOUR
The Credit Circulation

The third session of the Thirty-seventh Congress began on December 1, 1862. In his message to the Congress, Lincoln mentioned the war's effects at home and abroad. There were positives and negatives. There was "the treaty with Great Britain for the suppression of the slave trade." The blockade was productive, but there were "violations of neutral rights" on the seas. Lincoln favored the project for connecting the United States with Europe by Atlantic Telegraph. He mentioned the need for the United States Notes; the details were left to Salmon Chase. He spoke of "the great interior region" of the United States. He had thought of deportation and colonization of American slaves, but an audience with Frederick Douglas may have altered his thinking. Emancipation would begin in 1863. The debt had grown to almost 500 million, but population and growth could handle the debt. There were Indian nations favorable to the North and those nations overpowered by "insurgents" who favored the South.

There was improvement in the postal system, but expenses still exceeded receipts by more than $2 million. "The public land sales had ceased to be a source of revenue." Lincoln mentioned that the Homestead Act would help, but it would not be enough to "meet the expenses of the General Land Office, the cost of surveying and bringing the land into market." There were problems in the territories. The "Sioux Indians" had raided white settlements in Minnesota. There was progress made on the Pacific Railroad "enterprise." Canals in New York and Illinois would be enlarged. Based on the act "of the 15th of May last, I have caused the Department of Agriculture of the United States to be organized."

"The great interior region" was the middle part of the country. Lincoln said,

Its people and produce were cut-off. This region has no seacoast; touches no ocean anywhere. As part of one Nation, its people now find and forever find, their way to Europe by way of New York, to South America and Africa by New Orleans, and to Asia by San Francisco. But separate our common country into two nations, as designed by the present rebellion, and every man of this great interior region is thereby cut off from some one or more of these outlets, not, perhaps by a physical barrier, but by embarrassing and onerous trade regulations. These outlets, east, west and south, are indispensable to the well being of the people inhabiting and to inhabit this vast interior region. Which of the three may be the best is no proper question. All are better than either; and all of right belong to that people, and to their successors forever.

Enough said!

Emancipation was a moral, strategic, and economic move. Morally, it was the thing to do. Strategically, it was necessary; it was done in the South. The war was not going well. Lincoln's generals were useless; a positive move was necessary, and Lincoln made it. Emancipation would gain favor in the North. Would it have the crippling effect in the South? "Without slavery, the rebellion could never have existed, without slavery, it could not continue."

Emancipation would greatly reduce the cost of the war because the war would end sooner. At least, it was Lincoln's hope. Slavery was considered property; there would be compensation for lost property. And compensation was a North and South responsibility. Emancipation was only a beginning. Freedom for the African American people came in 1865 with the Thirteenth Amendment. But it took one hundred years, almost one-half of the country's existence, before positive civil rights legislation was enacted in 1965.

Lincoln was pragmatic. Lincoln mentioned that emancipation would take time. The money needed to pay for compensation would come from the sale of government bonds. The country was going to grow in population. American citizens of the future would help to pay the debt of compensation. Lincoln was thinking of the 100 million people in the future, not just the 31 million population of 1862. In terms of the war debt as well, Lincoln projected the population growth of the country to the year 1930 (250 million). He was projecting the population growth at a greater rate than the interest on the debt. Lincoln said, "Thus time alone relieves a debtor Nation, so long as its population increases faster than unpaid interest accumulates on its debt." A lot of people would disagree with Lincoln's "Don't pay now, pay later" philosophy, leaving a debt to future generations. Lincoln said, "In a word, it shows that a dollar will be much harder to pay for the war than will be a dollar for emancipation on the proposed plan. And then the latter will cost no blood, no precious life. It will be a saving of both."

The United States was a debtor nation during the nineteenth century. The debt accelerated with the Louisiana Purchase, a great purchase at the time. A very young, financially deficient nation possessed the most important ingredient in the modern money scheme, and that was a vast growth potential. The Louisiana Purchase almost doubled the size of the country in 1803. A lot of real estate had become public lands of the United States. The purchase occurred during the first session of the Eighth Congress, recorded in the public acts of Congress, October 17, 1803. The Louisiana Territory was purchased from Napoleon who was desperate for funds; his war with England had been costly. The cost of the purchase was in two installments; the first was a $11.25 million loan bearing an interest of "six per centum per annum." The remainder was paid out of the Treasury. The total principal was $15 million. The proprietor of the $11.25 million of "stock" delivered to the French government was not mentioned in the public act. It was the House of Barings in England.

It was December 1863. Secretary Chase asked for legislation that would establish a uniform currency and banking associations throughout the United States. The war was a deterrent and also a catalyst. It was a time when the United States would never look back. A civil war, emancipation, currency, banking, industry, commerce, the railroads, westward expansion, trade, etc. The country was moving ahead, bursting almost, in spite of the war and because of it.

Chase mentioned that because the war had not gone well, there was less confidence in government bonds and securities. According to Chase, the reduced confidence "made it impossible for the banks and capitalists, who had taken the previous loans, to dispose of the bonds held by them except at ruinous loss, and impossible for the Government to negotiate new loans of coin except at like or greater loss." And so, according to Secretary Chase, the banks suspended specie payment. The government then suspended specie; the demand notes were in circulation.

Chase began his reasoning and necessity for the Congress to adopt a national uniform currency. He mentioned the circulating currencies, United States Notes, and "notes of corporations" (the banks). He disagreed with "experienced opinion" that United States Notes alone and United States Notes and bank notes together in circulation were in "excess of legitimate demands for its employment." Chase said there was very little change in the circulation since specie was removed. In November 1861, there was $355 million in circulation; and in November 1862, there was 377 million. It appeared that United States Notes had replaced coin, which had been removed from circulation. Chase mentioned that the price of consumer goods changed little over the same period. Bank deposits had increased. "The augmentation of deposits always accompanies increase in circulation." If any currency depreciation had occurred, "it was attributed to the increase of bank circulation and deposits and not to Treasury note circulation." Continuing, he said, "It was only when United States notes, having been made a legal tender, were diverted from their legitimate use as currency and made the basis of Bank circulation, that the great increase of the latter began." What did Chase mean by that?

Chase said the U.S. Notes (the greenbacks) "were diverted from their legitimate use," which meant they were taken out of circulation. "Made the basis of bank circulation" meant the banks substituted their notes for the government notes. Chase stated that the banks had used legal tender United States Notes as reserve instead of coin, which had been suspended. The banks then circulated their own notes.

Chase went on to mention the suspension of coin, the "extension" of Treasury note circulation to allow loans "from holders" of the notes, congressional limitation on the increases of the Treasury notes, "which makes the notes receivable for loans," and interest being paid in coin. Chase said, "Under these circumstances, the path of wisdom and duty seems very clear. It leads to the support of a United States note circulation, and to the reduction of the bank circulation." Initially, the reduction of bank notes would be slow and then increase. The gradual substitution "would be stimulated by a moderate corporate tax" imposed by the secretary. The corporate tax was a bank tax. Chase, most of the time, referred to banks as "corporations" and "associations."

Chase mentioned the time was right for the change to a uniform currency. The banking associations were integral to the plan. The plan would "be entirely voluntary." Chase proceeded to detail how United States currency would be furnished by the government and issued by the private banking associations. The associations would be required to

- invest the required capital in U.S. bonds,
- deposit the bonds with a U.S. officer,
- then receive U.S. currency in denominations desired,
- use the U.S. currency as money in discounts and exchanges,
- transfer stockholders' capital from old banks to the new associations.
- Until specie was resumed, the new currency would be payable in U.S. Notes.
- After specie resumption, the new currency would be payable in coin.
- If any association should fail, the U.S. Treasury would "pay the notes and cancel the public debt held as security."

"The Secretary does not yield to the fantasy that taxation is a blessing and debt a benefit; but it is the duty of public men to extract good from evil whenever it is possible." Chase went on to mention how wise tax legislation could promote "public and private security and welfare."

The national uniform currency plan was a permanent plan, a "credit circulation." The federal government, after 1863, would begin to print the nation's paper currency. The government would print the currency for the banks and fund its expenditures while paying for the debt and the new circulation in gold. It was the new neat trick. It was a credit circulation the people would pay for, eventually, forever. Taxation was its redemption; the people would pay for their currency initially by being taxed. Taxation was part of the revenue the government needed to fund and back the new uniform currency for the "public and private security and welfare." The Treasury would print the new currency, and the banks would issue the new currency. The plan would be gradual; forming the new banking associations would take time.

The third session of this Civil War Congress enacted the plan. There was also the immediate need. Chase wanted another $277 million for the current fiscal year till July 1863. If the war went another year, till July 1864, another 630 million would be needed. The popular short-term certificate limit would be extended to 125 million.

Chase continued; a total of $65 million in gold and silver coin had been minted in 1861. Chase recommended another mint for the Nevada Territory. The restoration of lighthouses, beacons, and buoys was continuing along the coast. "The Light-House Board" had been directed by Chase to repair the coastal navigational systems. Forty-five million dollars was due the troops in the army. Some soldiers hadn't been paid for six months. Five hundred million in bonds (the five-twenties) still hadn't been sold.

The Congress approved a uniform currency bill on February 24. President Lincoln signed the bill on February 25, 1863. The act would eventually be called the National Bank Act. The act was six pages long containing sixty-four sections in the Congressional Globe record. Senate Bill 486, directed by Senator Sherman, was the adopted and approved bill. There was a House bill presented by Ways and Means. It was House Bill 656. The House bill was apparently changed. There was little record of debate and action on the House bill. The final bill was a Chase/Jay Cooke/Senate plan from the beginning, spearheaded in the Senate by Sherman. The demand notes, the greenbacks, the legal tenders came from Ways and Means in the House. The demand notes, the greenbacks came first, started in 1861 and 1862. A war was on; currency was needed. But the Chase/banking/Senate combo got the gold for the money interests. Jay Cooke became the agent for the Treasury in the selling of government securities. The circulation was paper currency, but the Treasury had to pay its debt to the banks in gold.

The bill in brief:

- New associations or national banks were required to buy United States bonds.
- The minimum capital to start a bank was $50,000. One-third of that stock was paid immediately, the remainder in fourteen months.
- The bonds would pay 6% interest semiannually in coin. The bonds at maturity would pay the full value of the bond in coin (maturity—twenty years).
- The bonds purchased was the security for the new national uniform currency.
- Purchased bonds would be kept at the Treasury.
- The United States Treasury printed and issued the new currency to the banks.
- Bonds may be purchased with the new currency.
- The new currency was good for all transactions, public and private, except duties on imports.
- The new banks would receive the new currency from the Treasury up to 90% of the market value of the bonds. Bonds sold at 50¢ to 60 ¢ on the dollar.
- A $10,000 bond sold for $6,000 in gold, the market price. Fifty-four hundred dollars in currency would be issued—or 10% less than the market value of the bond. The currency was in $5, $10, $20, $50, $100, $500, and $1,000 denominations. The currency issued could not exceed the bank's capital stock paid in.
- Apparently, the 10% reduction in currency took the form of a discount. There was the cost of printing and issue, etc. Sherman said it accounted for depreciation.
- The new banks would then issue the new currency discounted at 6% interest.
- The new currency may be used to purchase the United States bonds.
- Banks not in the new system would be taxed 2% on their currency issue. The purpose was to eventually remove all state bank issue.

- Each association or bank must have a minimum of five members.
- The maximum limit of issue was to be $300 million.

Senator Sherman, pushing the bill, emphasized the following:

Great sums of money were needed for the war and after the war. The army would be needed in the South to maintain the peace. Specie was suspended. The banks took the U.S. legal tenders, but didn't circulate them; the banks bought U.S. securities with them. The banks then circulated their own notes. The U.S. government didn't accept bank notes. The banks effectively reduced the circulation of U.S. legal tenders. But bank and government paper money was circulating, inflating the currencies. Something had to be done. A tax may stem the state bank circulation. The banking community would oppose the tax. Then bring the government and the banks together with a "uniform common system." A recent *Times of London* article stated, "The different States were, as to their bank notes, so many foreign nations, each refusing the paper of the others, except at varying rates of discount." The article belittled the financial condition of the country.

The wealth of the people in the North was $12 billion; a system was needed to direct it. The new uniform currency will expedite tax collection; the government didn't take state bank paper money. A table was presented that listed 1,500 state banks. More than 1,200 of the banks had been counterfeited; a new uniform currency would supposedly, in time, correct the problem, hopefully.

Senator Sherman probably chafed states rights people in and out of Congress. He said,

> All private interests, all local interests, all banking interests, the interests of individuals, everything, should be subordinate now to the interests of the Government; and whenever I see anything whatever standing in the way, of what I believe is demanded by the good of the United States at large; I will seek, if possible, without doing them any injury; to make them harmonious with the system, adopted by the Federal Government.

One couldn't be more for a dominant central government than Sherman was at the time. Senator Collamer was a critic of Sherman and the bill. Both men spoke of the financial interests in the country, but Collamer's remarks appeared to concern more directly the interests of the people. Sherman and Collamer spiced the debate!

Collamer mentioned how the small community banks would be crippled. Farmers "endorsed" their sons through these banks. State bank currencies would have to be totally "withdrawn" for the plan to work. Collamer brought up the famous French writer Montesquieu. "We have new illustrations of the principle laid down by Montesquieu that power was always at war with its own boundaries; it is always restless with its own limitations." Collamer's point was whether the government had the power to "extinguish the State banks" through taxation. Collamer mentioned that the Supreme Court ruled the states couldn't tax the First Bank of the United States. Then the Supreme Court ruled the states could issue a paper currency. "Hence, I say the United States has no more power to tax a State Institution out of existence than a State has to tax a United States Institution out of existence."

Montesquieu was a French philosopher (1689-1755). "His major work, 'The Spirit of the Law' [1748] influenced the writing of many constitutions, including the Constitution of the United States."

State banks were taxed by the states. State funding for schools and the like derived its revenue through bank taxation. The destruction of state banks would end the funding of state institutions. Collamer made these points. Collamer was convinced that state property would not be invested in U.S. stocks. But Sherman was right; state banks were already buying tax-free U.S. securities.

Collamer wanted to know why this new scheme? The Treasury had issued $250 million of non-interest-bearing currency, the greenbacks. This currency hadn't cost the people anything. Now this new uniform currency scheme was going to cost the people "12 million dollars in gold."

The banks were going to pay a 2% tax on the $300 million circulation. The Treasury would pay 6% interest on the bonds. Six minus two equals four or the equivalent of 4% interest on $300 million or 12 million in gold annually. And thus, Collamer's assertion that the new money scheme would cost the people "12 million dollars in gold." each year. The Senate was always looking out for the banks.

Collamer continued,

> There is all there is about it. You may discuss it as you please and use a great many expressions and schemes; but that is the English of it; that is the simple common sense of it. Instead of circulating that amount of our currency upon our own responsibility and paying nothing, we are to hire them to circulate that amount of our currency, and pay them $12,000,000 a year in gold for doing it; and we are to be responsible after all. That is all there is of it.

But there was a problem. The United States non-interest-bearing currency was not circulating because of the banks, and the banks were not buying the twenty-year bonds. Something had to be done. Sherman's message was getting the circumstances across to the Senate.

Sherman had presented an inducement to the banks:

- There was 167 million in bank currency in circulation.
- Induce the banks to withdraw 100 million. The government does not accept bank notes. The bank notes only benefit the banks.
- If the banks are induced to withdraw their notes and buy government bonds and then accept United States Notes, one can see the advantage to the country. U.S. Notes are in circulation, and the bank's notes are removed. The banks do the patriotic thing, and the country moves toward a uniform currency. "That is the object of the bill. If it fails, as a matter of course it does no harm." The crux was paying the interest on the bonds in gold and gold in full at maturity. Was that possible?

The state banks in New England came to the government's rescue early in the war. Now this bill would cause "calamities" to the community banks in Vermont. The business community was in good shape. Taxes had been raised to pay the interest on the debt. Government stock was not below par. The country did not need this bill. These were the words of Senator Collamer. The state banks would pay a 2% tax to the government and pay state taxes also. The new associations would pay a 2% tax on the circulation but would not pay state taxes.

About Collamer's emotional appeal for the local bankers, Sherman said,

> If he can refer to their interests, and appeal to us in eloquent terms to protect them from the doom that the sons of Jacob believed was about to fall upon Benjamin; and almost excite our sympathy to tears in view of the afflictions we are about to put upon local banks; if he can cite the opinions of those who have charge of them, surely I may cite the opinions of grave and honorable men who are charged with the responsibilities of administrating the Executive Departments of the Government.

Sherman mentioned that the people who put this bill together did so with full consideration of the subject. "I have no doubt" the banks were going to make money. The banks made 12% on their money the past year. As far as Sherman was concerned, the banking scheme would not fail.

Sherman was probably right. The banks were going to make money. The banks could buy U.S. bonds with legal tenders, with the new currency, and for the market value of the bonds. The banks would be paid interest in gold semiannually and the full value of the bond at maturity in gold. The banks would receive 90% of the market value of the bond in the new currency. The banks would discount that currency at 6% interest. The banks received this currency at no cost except a 2% tax on the circulation, later changed to 1%.

The approved currency or banking bill, as recorded in the statute, accentuated "the transfer of bonds." Starting at Section 16, the bill mentions the transfer of U.S. bonds by banking associations to the Treasury. The bill didn't include the buying or purchasing of bonds; a transfer was emphasized. During the debate, emphasis was placed on the purchase of bonds. But the banks already held U.S. interest-bearing

Treasury notes. Apparently, the idea then was to immediately transfer bonds held by banks. The bill was written emphasizing the transfer of bonds to the Treasury. It would appear the initial cost to the banks was a transfer; an exchange in currencies would take place. Sherman was confident that bonds held in the market would be transferred to the Treasury, and the new U.S. currency would gradually replace the varied paper currencies. Sherman used a figure of $50 million within six months. In his rebuttal to Collamer, Sherman said the banking business was "hazardous"; most banking systems were either "wound up by the States or wound up by bankruptcy" in about twenty years anyway. Collamer loved that! "Is that common candor?" Collamer admitted most bank charters are for twenty years, but now they want "to wind up the whole of them in one year." Collamer was quick in his replies to Sherman.

Senators Powell and Howard wanted the new banks to put up a gold and silver reserve equal to one-third of the currency issue. They wanted gold and silver somewhere in the bill. Sherman got Howard to admit that he wouldn't take United States Notes. That was the end of that! The Powell and Howard amendments were voted down.

Powell introduced another amendment whereby the banks would redeem 50% of the circulation within twelve months and a complete return to specie payment within two years. Sherman mentioned that England waited five years after the war with Napoleon. Revulsion still occurred. Powell's amendment was rejected. Senator Wilson of Massachusetts cited the people in the agricultural areas, Kentucky and the West, lost "hundreds of millions of dollars" after the War of 1812.

Senator Carlile was back. He couldn't understand how the Senate could vote for the bill. Why the banks could just reinvest the currency into bonds and make a killing doing it? Carlile said the premium on gold was 60%. An initial investment of $6,000 in gold would buy $9,600 in bonds and a cash return of $8,640. Successive currency investments in bonds would add up quickly. "Mr. President, run the calculation out, and you will find that upon an investment of $6,000 you can be the owner of $100,000 of these bonds." Mr. Carlile said that in one year, an individual could be drawing interest equal to the original investment of $6,000 (6% interest). Mr. Carlile felt the bill was flawed. Why do the business of banking when the banks were going to be paid in gold? There was no recorded response to Mr. Carlile's calculation.

Senator Doolittle did not want to debate the bill; he would just take "five minutes." He brought up the Supreme Court case involving the State of Kentucky and paper currency issue by state banks. The Supreme Court in the "case of Briscoe" (1837) allowed "the State of Kentucky to incorporate a bank that could issue paper currency without violating the Constitution of the country." Senator Davis objected, saying the bank in question was "based not upon specie at all, but, like the present *projet,* based entirely on the credit of the State." Doolittle continued, "Justice Story . . . in very strong language, that the issuing of paper money by banks was not the emission of bills within the meaning of the Constitution, and therefore not prohibited." Doolittle's point was that as a result of the decision, "fifteen hundred or two thousand Banks" arose that issued their own paper money, which was the currency of the country at the start of the Civil War. Specie was then suspended, and if the war was to be carried on with a paper issue, it had better be a uniform government issue.

Doolittle made his point; there was a proliferation of state banks issuing paper currency. What was more significant was the Supreme Court decision. The bank in Kentucky was issuing a paper currency based on the wealth in the state. That wealth was the people and the state's resources. The creation of the greenbacks was based on a similar principle.

The Senate approved the currency bill on February 12, 1863. The vote was a narrow one, twenty-three yeas and twenty-one nays. On February 20, the House approved the currency bill. The vote was 78-64.

Spaulding of New York liked the bill. He mentioned New York City as a potential banking "agent" for government expenditures, loans, taxes, and customs. He cited other principal cities. He talked of the Bank of England as being the "fiscal agent of the British Government." He mentioned the greatness of the first two banks of the United States.

> It is now apparent that the policy advocated by Alexander Hamilton, of a strong central Government, would most likely have been able to avert this rebellion; but if not able to prevent it entirely, it would have been much better prepared, to have met and put down the traitorous advocates of secession and states rights; who have forced upon us this unnatural and bloody war.

There were those people who believed in states rights.

What happened to the first two central banks of the United States? The banks were located in Philadelphia. How long did they last? The First Bank's charter was for twenty years. The charter was granted in 1791, to be renewed in 1811. The Congress did not renew the charter. Why didn't the Congress renew the charter?

In 1810, there was a bill before the House. The bill would renew the First Bank's charter and also increase the stock from the original 10 million to "twenty or thirty millions." Mr. Love, speaking on the bill, mentioned a report presented by Treasury Secretary Albert Gallatin in March 1809. Gallatin "alluded" to information, "which demanded an investigation before the Nation." In 1809, foreigners owned 75% of the stock in the bank. More recent U.S. bank stock in 1810 showed prices much higher in London "than in our own markets." Because of those reports, Mr. Love felt that they owned more than 75% of the bank stock. "King George the Third, or the Emperor Bonaparte, may send their men, the ostensible owners of the stock, who may easily find among the citizens of our Republic the friends and advocates of crowned heads." Ten million in gold had been shipped to foreign stockholders since the bank's beginning. The amount had risen to 1 million in gold each year. Mr. Love submitted a resolution whereby he wanted the Congress to obtain the "names and Titles of the stockholders of the Bank of the United States." There was also a minority of domestic stockholders. The resolution was amended to read "foreign stockholders." Treasury Secretary Gallatin favored the continuance of the bank. He felt the public money was handled safely; loans were always made to the government when needed. When money was needed by the government, the bank probably printed new currency, and new debt went on the books.

Let's step back to 1791 and Hamilton's bank report. Banks "have a tendency to banish gold and silver from the country." Hamilton covered the "advantages and disadvantages" of banks. In his report, Hamilton alluded to the investments in stock in lieu of "bank-lending" because "the profits of bank stock exceed the legal rate of interest" in lending.

Tripling the stock through capitalization (bank notes), there had to be a projected immediate profit in the stock. Hamilton probably knew who the subscribers of the bank might be: the United States government, the state governments, entities, and individuals who profited from the Revolution and foreign governments, individuals, and merchants. Past oft-used bank practices were reflected in Hamilton's report as a prognostication.

In the report, Hamilton wrote,

> It ought not to escape without a remark, that as far as the citizens of other countries become adventurers in the bank, there is a positive increase of the gold and silver of the Country. It is true, that from this a half-yearly rent is drawn back, accruing from the dividends upon the stock. But as this rent arises from the employment of the capital, by our citizens, it is probable, that it is more than replaced by the profits of that employment. It is also likely, that a part of it is, in the course of trade, converted into the products of our Country: And it may prove an incentive, in some cases, to emigration to a country, in which the character of the citizen is as easy to be acquired, as it is estimable and important. This view of the subject furnishes an answer to an objection, which has been deduced from the circumstance here taken notice of, namely the income resulting to foreigners from the part of the stock, owned by them, which has been represented as tending to drain the country of its specie. In this objection, the original investment of the capital, and the constant use of it afterwards seem both to have been overlooked.

There was benefit to the foreign stockholders and benefit to the United States. There was indebtedness, but there was occurrence, a most important happening, and that was growth in the United States. With that growth, there was increased equity, more indebtedness, money creation, capitalization and profits, a proliferation and expansion of commerce and trade.

It was August 1789 before Hamilton's report. The First Congress had been in session since March. The president and the Congress received a letter from the public creditors of the state of Pennsylvania. The letter concerned the public credit. When was the Congress going to do something? The public creditors had "waited in anxious suspense for some evidence of the disposition of Congress upon this interesting subject . . . American character" could not be preserved, "should Congress adjourn without any more decisive act for the restoration of public credit . . . that public credit is the vital spark of modern policy." The letter stated that "procrastination" was fatal. But *"to pay off the public debt, principal and interest, if not impracticable, would be greatly inconvenient, and is certainly unnecessary."* What was important was the *"punctual payment of the interest,"* which would *"enable the public creditor to enjoy, by the facility of a transfer, all the advantages of the principal, without injuring the credit of the country, or restraining her resources."* There was a *"national benefit"* to a *"funded debt."* There would be *"creation of a new species of money by this means"* after the revolution in England, *"a funding system was there encouraged as the best means of attaching the great and powerful body of stockholders to the Government."*

So what was the letter asking? The above is the crux of the government funding scheme and subsequent riches. The public creditors wanted to make money at public expense. The letter was asking President Washington and the Congress to get on with it. Let's get on with funding the debt of the United States. Let's get on with it; there was a lot of public investing to do, a lot of money to be made. It was Hamilton and the bank in 1791-1792, then the trading in New York and Philadelphia, the money centers. There was "a new species of money" to be created, to be obtained. Apparently, to this day, it is the way of things in the United States. Money is created to the delight of an attached "powerful body of stockholders" to government debt.

What constituted the First Bank of the United States? From the statute, the bank started with an authorized stock of $10 million. The smaller portion of the stock was gold and/or silver to be paid within a twelve-month period. An amount of 7.5 million dollars of the stock was in subscriptions of public debt. The debt included the Revolutionary War debt of the states. This indebtedness went into the bank as assets or stock; call it commercial paper. But its value was $7.5 million, and the creation of bank paper money became reality. Hamilton's First Bank would print paper currency and issue the currency at a discount. The new currency did not cost the bank anything except the cost of printing. The value of the bank, hopefully, would augment rapidly. Notes were paid on the indebtedness of $7.5 million at varying rates of interest. There was the capitalization of new bank notes issued at a discount of 6% interest and the interest to be paid the creditors on the public debt. The new United States government received a loan of $2 million of the new paper currency. Although non-legal tender paper money, the first Treasury accepted this paper money. The bank was authorized from time to time to purchase bullion or gold. The purchase of gold, apparently, with paper money augmented the capital of the bank. This became a profitable reality. The First Bank sent 10 million in gold to its foreign stockholders during its twenty-year history. The scheme of this First Bank of the United States, modeled from the British bank, was the Hamilton bank. Alexander Hamilton was the pure capitalist; he knew what he was about. He and the rest of his people knew money was at hand. The Congress gave this bank the power to print paper money, a substitute for specie; it was not legal tender paper. But the currency was made redeemable in specie; this was the crux of the scheme, to capitalize with paper and accumulate gold. Redemption was the key; it gave the bank the power to purchase gold, a principal purpose. This creation of paper money and the purchase and accumulation of gold with that paper money was an important goal "to make gold out of nothing."

There is the factor of ignorance when reading the bank act, approved March 2, 1791. Was it ever the intention that the people, "the gulls," including members of Congress, would ever understand the money scheme? The words "money," "bills," and "notes," when referred to in that first statute, appear in abstract. Hamilton's bank was started to print money, to create paper currency. Explanation of capitalization in simple terms, in the creation of paper currency, discounting, the printing of paper money, by whom, plates for printing, penalties for counterfeiting, etc., is nonexistent or vague. There is the nuance of banking, which comes with those who practice. We may try to understand if we could get past banking jargon. The biggest pyramid scheme is the nation's paper money creation scheme. The scheme continues and is lasting because growth and taxation is its redemption. Our great-great-grandchildren and their children will be subjected to taxation's infinite oppressive payment.

In 1810, there were members in the Congress who felt the First Bank was not in the interests of the United States. Did foreigners own it? The Europeans (England and France) owned 75% of the stock! The new bill to renew a second charter would at least double the stock of the First Bank to "nearly $20,000,000, affording a circulation to three times the amount if they choose, which must influence every part of society." These were the words of Mr. Love. Jefferson and Madison were originally against the bank. The Congress did not renew the charter in 1811. The United States went to war again with England in 1812.

———————————

When Spaulding was concluding his remarks, he mentioned that Thomas Jefferson opposed all banks.

———————————

Jefferson said, "We are an agricultural Nation." Hamilton wanted a mercantile nation. Thomas Jefferson differed with Hamilton in principle in the matters of money. In a letter to John Wayles Eppes in 1813, Jefferson said, "Let us have banks; but let them be such as are alone to be found in any country on earth, except Great Britain." Jefferson mentioned that all the banks in Europe lent "cash" on credit except Great Britain. The cash Jefferson spoke of was coin or its equivalent. John Wayles Eppes of Virginia was a member of the Ways and Means Committee in the House of Representatives. John Wayles Eppes was Jefferson's son-in-law. The Bank of England lent paper, and Hamilton's First Bank of the United States dealt in paper money. Hamilton modeled the United States bank after the Bank of England. In the same letter, Jefferson said, "It is from Great Britain we copy the idea of giving paper in exchange for discounted bills." In another letter to Eppes, he called the United States the unfortunate copyist of Great Britain. Jefferson felt the practice would be ruinous for the United States, eventual bankruptcy. The debt of Great Britain at the time was huge and growing but so was the empire.

Before 1764, Benjamin Franklin toyed with the idea of a bank similar to the Bank of England. Franklin said it wouldn't work because of "present circumstances of the colony trade." The trade "draws all the cash [gold] to Britain, and would soon strip the bank."

In 1813, the United States was at war with England. There was a new bill in Congress, a bill to grant a bank charter to a Second Bank of the United States to run forty to fifty years. Thomas Jefferson wrote letters to John Wayles Eppes about the new bill. In a November 6, 1813, letter, Jefferson analyzed the bill. "This is a summary of the case as I understand it; but it is very possible I may not understand it in all its parts, these schemes being always made unintelligible for the gulls who are to enter into them." Jefferson said he would "disentangle it as much as we can." Jefferson's description was pages and pages, but it is listed here in brief because the writer didn't fully understand all of Jefferson's disentangle. Maybe Jefferson included himself as one of the "gulls"?

Jefferson wrote that the government, the states, and individual subscribers would collectively contribute 30 million in 6% stock; he stated that the Congress would have no say as to the management by the directors of the bank. The individual subscribers would be the sole beneficiaries of any "future augmentations." The bank would be authorized by Congress to issue $90 million in paper money (three times the value of the stock). Of the issue, Jefferson said,

> This bank oligarchy or monarchy enters the field with ninety millions of dollars, to direct and control the politics of the Nation; and of the influence of these institutions on our politics, and into what scale it will be thrown, we have had abundant experience. Indeed, England herself may be the

real, while her friend and trustee here shall be the nominal
and sole subscriber

and "no relief for forty or fifty years." The $90 million, "which increases
our circulation medium fifty per cent, depreciates proportionately the
present value of a dollar, and raises the price of all future purchases
in the same proportion."

(If there are ten commodities and $10, each commodity may cost $1. If
there are ten commodities and $20, each commodity may cost $2.)

Thomas Jefferson was for banks. Jefferson was for banks that dealt
in coin or cash. The Constitution directed that the states should deal
in coin. Jefferson didn't like the Bank of England or Hamilton's bank
of the United States and their paper money scheme. But it was 1813;
Napoleon eventually would be deposed. The paper money scheme
continued in England; its debt was huge, but the vast British Empire
was becoming more vast.

Thomas Jefferson wrote, "It is said our paper is as good as silver,
because we may have silver for it at the Bank where it issues. This
is not true. One, two or three persons might have it; but a general
application would soon exhaust their vaults." Jefferson called it a
fallacious pretense. Jefferson was critical of "the English practice of
perpetual funding." The redemption scheme was simply "fiction." But
it was for the gold!

It was the War of 1812. Specie had been suspended. Jefferson wrote,

> As to the public, these companies have banished all our
> gold and silver medium, which before their institution, we
> had before interest, which never could have perished in our
> hands, and would have been our salvation now in the hour
> of war; instead of which they have given us two hundred
> million of froth and bubble, on which we are to pay heavy
> interest, until it shall vanish into air, as Morris' notes did.

Robert Morris, the financier who reportedly saved the Revolution,
wound up in debtor's prison. Robert Morris died a pauper.

Jefferson said the nation's greatest fear was "Public Debt." Jefferson believed that public debts should be paid in full, principals and interests, within each generation's time period. Referring to mortality rates from Buffon's tables, Jefferson arrived at the figure of nineteen years, the extent of a contract. Buffon was a "French naturalist" (1707-1788). Jefferson wrote about circulation and its proportion to annual produce; from different references, the numbers varied.

The time of this writing, in the year 2003, a couple of articles appeared in the *Wall Street Journal* about the velocity of money. The velocity of money equation was illustrated. How much product does the circulation buy? What propels a viable economy? It boils down to the 10:1 ratio, which has been around for a while, two, three centuries? In the money circulation process, $100 approximately purchases ten times its value.

Jefferson wrote about a "public debt, being a public blessing." The proponents of the national debt expounded the phrase. Jefferson called the stock of the debt a paradox, and "the gulls" were swept up in it. *"Private* debts" he called bank notes. He wrote, "The bank notes become active capital, and aliment the whole commerce, manufactures, and agriculture of the United States." Jefferson wrote that this bank would not be responsible for the debt. Individuals, unbeknown to the Congress and the public, would control the original stock and reap the benefits of three times that amount ($90 million). The bank notes would be the $90 million created by the bank from the original stock out of nothing. Jefferson felt that this bank should be responsible for all the debt (the original stock plus the 90 million). That adds up to 120 million. But the people were "blessed" for the convenience of the public debt. The people (Congress) therefore "exempted by law" the bank's responsibility for all of the debt. Jefferson wrote,

> And to fill up the measure of blessing, instead of paying, they receive an interest on what they owe from those to whom they owe; for all the notes, or evidences of what they owe, which we see in circulation, have been lent to somebody on an interest which is levied again on us through the medium of commerce.

According to Jefferson, the "augmentations" of the bank that were to materialize would only benefit the individuals of the bank. There would be more commerce, more debt, and more capital or bank notes. "More active capital was created." The bank was a paper money creation scheme. Hamilton put it into being. Thomas Jefferson objected to it. Abundant paper money was circulated. The cost of everything inflated; there was depreciation of the bank notes. Specie was gone, and it was the War of 1812. Entities holding paper when specie returned paid a heavy price. More than $200 million in wealth was lost (and gained) after the war according to the *Congressional Record*.

At this point, we must step back again. Things can get confusing. What was the money scheme during the War of 1812? The first United States bank and its branches were no longer operating. The first central bank had been a depository of the federal government. Specie had been suspended. The state banks dealt in cash (specie) or paper? What was the legal money and by whom? From 1791 to 1811, the federal government accepted the paper money issued by the defunct first United States bank. What was the acceptable exchange during the War of 1812?

The specie-paying state banks, which adopted the same scheme of the first United States bank, were dealing in paper currency. The legal tender money was specie, but it was gone. The federal government accepted the notes of state banking institutions. The government issued Treasury notes. These notes were interest-bearing notes. These notes were like currency, but the notes were also bills of credit or bonds. These notes would not circulate; they were held, cashed in at maturity. The Treasury notes were payable in specie or its equivalent at maturity in principal and interest. The government paid bills with these notes. These notes also became subscriptions to banks in the form of loans. The market price of the Treasury notes went as low as 75%. The government accepted bank notes in exchange and paid 5.5% to 5.25% interest on the Treasury notes. During this period, the Congress approved several loans authorizing the Treasury to sell Treasury notes for bank paper money. Apparently, it was a necessary course of action. It was a chaotic period, and the accepted money was depreciated bank paper currency. Treasury Secretary Dallas recalled these circumstances in a financial report to the Congress in 1816. He mentioned the suspension of specie and the different exchange rates between the "institutions of the different States." The conditions "deprived the Treasury of all facilities of transferring its funds from place to place." He stated, "Public funds in one part no longer affords the evidence of a fiscal capacity to discharge a public debt in any other part of the Union." It was at that time that Dallas was pushing the need to start a Second Bank of the United States. A standard currency was needed across the nation. At the beginning of the year 1817, the national debt was $110 million.

Jefferson wrote, "Bank paper must be suppressed, and the circulating medium must be restored to the Nation to whom it belongs." Jefferson wanted the Treasury to issue Treasury notes that would represent gold and silver. He continued,

> Treasury bills, bottomed on taxes, bearing or not bearing interest, as may be necessary, thrown into circulation will take the place of gold and silver, which last, when crowded, will find an efflux into other countries, and thus keep the quantum of medium at its salutary level. Let banks continue if they please, but let them discount for cash alone or for the Treasury notes. They discount for cash alone in every other country on earth except Great Britain, and her too often unfortunate copyist, the United States.

Jefferson wanted the United States government to produce and control the paper issue. It didn't happen.

Treasury notes were issued during the war; the banks issued their notes. The Treasury took the bank's notes for the Treasury notes. The Treasury notes were discounted; the bank notes were discounted. The bank notes depreciated. At maturity, the Treasury paid a steep price in specie when the Treasury notes were redeemed. The government and the people took the hits during the War of 1812. The Congress, apparently, enacted the greenbacks during the Civil War mainly, for good reason, to counter a repeat of 1812 coin suspension, depreciating bank paper currency, excessive debt, and property loss.

In a letter to John Adams in 1819, Jefferson wrote,

> Certainly no nation ever before abandoned to the avarice
> and jugglings of private individuals to regulate, according
> to their own interests, the quantum of circulating medium
> for the nation, to inflate, by deluges of paper, the nominal
> prices of property in the pound, having first withdrawn the
> floating medium which might endanger a competition in
> purchase.

Jefferson called their action the schemes of plunder and spoliation. Benjamin Franklin knew the banking scheme when he said "strip the bank." His awareness of the "Colony Trade" was a trade imbalance, which continued a seesaw into the twentieth century. There was consistent delinquency of specie reserve at home. There was no delinquency in the periodic demand for payment in specie by the money interests, which resulted in consistent currency contractions and panics.

A banking system in cash, one Jefferson would have preferred, didn't happen. Jefferson wanted a specie bank that dealt in specie. Hamilton wanted a specie bank that dealt in paper. The United States went the way of Hamilton. It was the British way; it was the American way. Alexander Hamilton wanted an engine to augment the commerce of the country. Specie was insufficient in quantity. Full payment or redemption was never there. Paper/specie was the arrangement within the domain. After goods for goods were traded, didn't specie simply satisfy the duties in payments between nations? Wasn't specie merely the difference in payments between merchants and for purposes of trade, the purchase of foreign commodities? Specie was simply the crank that started the Hamilton engine; capitalization would be achieved with paper.

The War of 1812 ended officially in 1815. It was a "peculiar" war. Was President Madison pressured into declaring war against England? England continually baited the United States, harassed her on the seas. The United States was in no posture to cope with British power. New England withdrew its support; Jefferson's earlier embargo didn't help. English purpose must have been the destruction of Washington. Virtually unopposed, the British sailed up the Chesapeake Bay and burned the Capitol buildings in Washington, probably at the pleasure of King George III. The burning of the Capitol occurred in August of 1814. The British sailed to Baltimore. On September 13, 1814, the British were repelled there at Fort McHenry and North Point. Baltimore's strong effort inspired "The Star-Spangled Banner." From this viewpoint, it seems incredible that Congress convened six days later in Washington on September 19, 1814. This young country, the United States, was destined. It was the third session of the Thirteenth Congress; one of their first actions was a resolution whereby the Congress debated on the "the Removal of the Seat of Government." Previous battles along the Canadian border were a standoff. The British were routed at New Orleans. Unfortunately, the New Orleans battle occurred after the war was over. Although defeated at Washington, the young nation somehow survived against a powerful enemy. The British fleet blockaded but never ventured into New York, Philadelphia, and Boston, the money capitals.

Thomas Jefferson's ten-thousand-volume library helped restore the Library of Congress. The Library of Congress was one of the Capitol buildings destroyed by the British. On September 21, 1814, Jefferson wrote to the Congress, "I learn from the Newspapers that the Vandalism of our enemy has triumphed at Washington, over science as well as the arts, by the destruction of the public library, with the noble edifice in which it was deposited." Jefferson called the British action a barbarism, which does not belong to a civilized age. Much of Jefferson's writings reflected little fondness of Great Britain. There are invaluable government records made available because of Thomas Jefferson. Jefferson sold his vast library collection to the government.

The British burning of Washington in 1814 was probably as infamous as Sherman's burning of Atlanta in 1865. The British destroyed the government buildings, which was the center, the heart of the new free republic. The United States was a contrast to British monarchy and a bit of irony. The young United States was a political economic reflection of the British Empire and also her debtor. The United States recovered quickly; James Monroe flexed the country's muscles with the Monroe Doctrine in 1823.

The Congress granted a new bank charter in 1816. President James Madison, who objected to the First Bank, signed the second bank bill into law. The Second Bank of the United States began operations in

1817. It was another twenty-year charter. An "Outline of a Plan for a National Bank" was presented to the Congress by the secretary of the Treasury, A. J. Dallas.

The Second Bank was authorized a reserve of $35 million. The United States would subscribe one-fifth of the stock or 7 million to be paid in over a seven-year period. The stock was to be 25% gold or silver and 75% public debt at 6% interest. The Congress, by law, in the future, could authorize an increase of the reserve to 50 million. This addition to the stock was reserved for the states. The states would be allowed subscriptions of 15 million in public debt or stock. Investors were of a similar nature. Twenty-eight million was subscribed to the bank by individuals, corporations, foreign entities, etc. The 28 million in reserve was to be paid within an eighteen-month period. Individuals, corporations, and foreign entities would subscribe 7 million in gold and silver and 21 million in public debt. Again, the smaller portion of the stock was in specie. As soon as 1.4 million in gold and silver was paid in, the bank may begin operation. The bank would have a stock value of $35 million. In this charter, bank notes (paper circulation) would be at least 35 million; it would grow to 80 million, doubling the reserve of the bank. The financial power of this Second Bank was more formidable than the First Bank.

Presumably, there would be more administrative control by the president of the United States and the Treasury secretary in this second edition. The president of the United States picked five directors of this Second Bank. One of the five directors was always a president-designate of the bank. The bank was located in Philadelphia; branch banks were located in the states. The government was paid a bonus of $1.5 million for granting the charter. The charter was considered "exclusive"; substantial profit was to be made by the bank. This bank was authorized again to use its capital to purchase bullion or coin. This bank would accumulate gold, the same as the First Bank. The bank's paper notes was the accepted currency of the United States government. The bank act was approved on April 10, 1816. More voluminous wording in this second bank act covered subscription of stock and the regulation thereof, the selling of funded debt for specie. Also covered were loans, dividends, appointment of officers, directors, penalties for counterfeiting, etc. Specifics of capitalization, the plates, the printing of bank notes or paper currency, by whom, was not in the bill. Except for the minimum $5 bill, bank note denominations were not specified. This bank, again, would print non-legal tender paper money good for gold.

The bank opened in 1817. The war was over. There was a resolution in Congress; specie payment was to be resumed, but why? There was little specie in the country. Subsequently, a contraction of paper currency ensued; the country experienced a recession until 1823. Jefferson's letter to Adams in 1819 reflected the period. The fate of the Second Bank matched the death knell of the First Bank.

President Andrew Jackson terminated the charter. The Second Bank charter of the United States ended in 1836. Two years were allowed by law to wind up all affairs. Officially, the bank ceased operations in 1838. An ample majority in the Senate wanted the bank; Jackson did not. In his first message to the 1829-1830 session of Congress, President Jackson said, "Both the constitutionality and the expediency of the law creating this bank are well questioned by a large portion of our fellow citizens; and it must be admitted by all that it has failed in the great end of establishing a uniform and sound currency."

The Supreme Court had ruled that the grant of a charter by the First Congress to the First Bank of the United States was constitutional. The Constitution was not the question when another Congress disallowed the charter in 1811. The Constitution, apparently, was not the question when the Congress granted a charter to the Second Bank in 1816. President Jackson made the Constitution an issue when he vetoed the bank bill in 1832. Senator Smith from Maryland criticized the president because Jackson "thought lightly of the authority of Congress . . . and . . . still more lightly of the Supreme Court." Smith continued that what was "deemed necessary and proper are no longer to be regarded, and therefore the bank is unconstitutional." Maybe it wasn't the constitutionality at inception but the unconstitutionality in practice that killed the Second Bank.

There were abuses. In 1832, in the Senate, Senator Thomas H. Benton, senator from Missouri, presented a joint resolution. He wanted the currency of the bank suppressed. The Second Bank had issued an

"Illegal and Vicious Currency." Benton stated that the Second Bank had taken up a "contrivance of European Origin." The scheme originated in Scotland (the boys from Scotland were a most active and clever bunch). Notes in small denominations were issued in outlying provinces. The notes were payable but in London, a great distance away. The practice spread to Ireland. The notes in small denominations were handled by the laboring classes. The mass of the people could not negotiate the distance for payment. The English parliament ruled the practice "vicious." It was stopped in 1826. Mr. Benton's resolution stated that the Second Bank of the United States had adopted the same practice in America. The bank issued large volumes of notes in the western branches, which were not payable there. The notes issued were in denominations less than $5. A $5 note was the allowable note by statute. The notes became a "local currency" payable at Philadelphia. "The greatest quantity was usually issued at the most remote and inaccessible branches, the payment of the drafts were well protected by distance and difficulty."

Benton listed fourteen abuses, which included nonpayment where issued. The notes weren't protected by the Treasury. There was no corporate seal; there was no signature by the president of the bank. There was no specie restriction protection; there was no double interest for nonpayment. They weren't transferable by delivery, by endorsement only; they were not payable at other branches. They weren't payable for public dues, etc. Benton called the currency a bastard issue. It was unfortunate, and usually the case, that the laboring classes were more subjected to the abuses.

The majority in the Senate was friendly to the bank. Benton's joint resolution was delayed and then considered at a later time. When congressional debate did surface on the "recharter," the Senate "acknowledged that the currency was illegal." There was "a clause put into the new charter to suppress it." Although efforts were made to correct the abuses, there did not exist a two-thirds majority in the Congress to save the bank. State banks would continue the "practice" after the Second Bank went out of business.

Daniel Webster voted against the charter in 1816; he was for the recharter in 1832. In 1816, Webster was a congressman and represented New Hampshire in the House. He had been a federal leader (National Republican). The National Republicans became the Whigs after the Second Bank was finished. Webster supported the bank, but he acknowledged the abuses. There was no gold during the tenure of the bank. He blamed it on "over-trading." There were "excesses" and "revulsions." There was "twenty-two millions in silver," mostly bullion in the bank vaults. He mentioned that too much small denominational paper money was in circulation. "The paper will take the place of the gold and silver." Webster estimated about 80 million in paper circulation. He opposed the bonus paid to the government. He said the interest of 6% on the paper issue was excessive. Discount the paper at 5% and give no bonus to the government. The people would get the benefit. These were better "terms" for a recharter. The Second Bank was supposed to correct the "debased evils of the local banks." Instead, "this great bank was itself to be the most striking exemplification of all the evils."

What were the debased evils of the local or state banks? In February of 1816, Daniel Webster before the House, said, "There had grown up in different States a currency of paper issued by banks, setting out with the promise to pay gold and silver, which they had been wholly unable to redeem." The War of 1812 came along. Specie was suspended. There was no gold and silver. The government needed funds. Webster said, "The Government had been obliged, in direct violation of existing statutes, to receive the amount of their taxes in something which was not recognized by law as money of the country, and which was, in fact, greatly depreciated. This was the evil." The evil was the depreciated paper money of the banks. Webster wanted a specie bank; he wanted to reduce the stock from 35 million to 20 million in this Second Bank. The stock reduction would subsequently reduce the capitalization in paper money. Congressman Cuthbert said "that to become and remain a specie bank, the institution must be slow in its operations, and directors and stockholders be content with small gains on their capital."

The Bank of England and the bank of Hamilton were not meant to operate slowly. The design was to perpetuate a rapid increase in growth, an increase in equity, allowing the proliferation of indebtedness, the vast creation of paper money, capitalization. The modern banking principle or design, the paper money scheme, could never be accomplished with specie.

The Second Bank was a "monopoly" the same as the First Bank, much central power. The condition occurred because of a restriction placed in the charters. Mr. Benton made these points in the Senate. The acts stated that no succeeding Congress could charter another bank during the continuance of the present charter. If one Congress can establish a charter, then by the Constitution, all succeeding congresses "have the right to charter banks. Mr. Madison was express in his opinions in the year 1791, that, if there was one bank chartered, there ought to be several!" Madison made the point that the American government "required the diffusion of wealth and power." England, on the other hand, centralized power. Benton continued, "The establishment of branches did not satisfy the principle of diffusion." The Second Bank "pervaded the whole Union, drawing wealth from every part . . . convulsed the country with expansions and contractions of paper currency." The expansions and the contractions were effectively the excesses and the revulsions. Convulsions were caused by the movements of specie out of the country.

President Jackson felt the bank was "dangerous," more formidable than the government with its political, social, and economic power. Jackson wanted a bank "as a branch of the Treasury Department, based on the public and individual deposits, without power to make loans or purchase property." Jackson wanted a bank not to be "a corporate body, having no stockholders, debtors, or property, and but few officers." Such a bank "would be shorn of the influence which makes that bank formidable." President Jackson didn't want to extend more "privileges" to the "present stockholders." Jackson felt the bank stock and its "full market value" was a "privilege." If the Congress assumed the role of a bank, then the "premium" from those privileges would go into the "Treasury."

The political platform of Henry Clay stated, "Another institution is recommended as a substitute, which, so far as the description given of it can be understood, would be no better than a machine in the hands of the Government for fabricating and issuing paper money without check or responsibility." Clay opposed Jackson in the election of 1832.

In 1832, Daniel Webster answered the president's objections to the bank bill. In 1832, Daniel Webster was a senator from Massachusetts. President Jackson had given "his reasons for refusing to approve and sign the same." A bank veto was imminent. Webster said, "The Bank has fallen, or it is to fall." Webster mentioned that the main objections related to the Western states. The largest debt to the bank was in the West, around $30 million. The stockholders were predominately from the East and the South and foreigners. There were little dividends going west, only interest payments going east, to the bank, about $1.8 million yearly. President Jackson stated that the bank should wind up its affairs in four years. Webster said it couldn't be done without distress, about 8 million per year plus interest, and money in the West was worth 2% less in value. Was that because of distance, transfer, and exchanges? The president "has pointed out nothing, he has suggested nothing . . . if the pressure be heavy, the fault will be the bank's." Webster said, "A great majority of the people are satisfied with the bank as it is, and desirous that it should be continued. They wished no change." Webster talked about the positives. The bank "secured the safe collection and convenient transmission of public moneys, to maintain the circulation of this country . . . Congress has sought fit to provide for its continuance." Webster mentioned the "privileges," the benefit to the stockholders. "The stockholders received their charter not gratuitously, but for a valuable consideration in money, prescribed by Congress, and actually paid. The objection lies against all banks." But there were the foreign stockholders. They represented about 25% of the stock. The dividends to foreigners amounted to "two to five millions of specie every year." The foreigner was "exempt from taxation" but "taxed by his own Government."

Webster said that the president's objections were "injurious to the credit and character of the country abroad, because it manifests a jealousy, a lurking disposition not to respect the property of foreigners invited hither by our own laws."

Senator White of Tennessee refuted Webster's distress call. It was "the old argument used in 1811" (the First Bank). "The capital employed in the bank was not annihilated." Senator White mentioned that debtors will seek "accommodations elsewhere." The capital of the bank in 1811 "was applied to the uses of the community." Senator White called

Webster on his "frankness." According to White, Webster wanted to wait the bank bill till before the election because if the president rejected the charter, "he ought to be turned out, and another put in his place. I thank the Senator for the candid avowal, that unless the President will sign such a charter as will suit the directors, they intend to interfere in the election, and endeavor to displace him."

Senator Thomas Ewing mentioned positives. The bank sent the capital to the West where it was "deficient. It loaned extensively where it found capital deficient, and the means of employing it abundant." Thirty million dollars had been invested in the "Valley of the Mississippi." There was "public improvement and general prosperity." There was $30 million invested in the West, and there was $30 million of debt. It was the name of the game. There was indebtedness, but significantly, there *was* growth in the Western states.

In spite of the abuses, the bank "has proved beneficial to the country." Senator Ewing also mentioned an inequality. The bank act allowed "a bond of union among the banking establishments of the nation, erecting them into an interest separate from the people." President Jackson objected as in the following:

> If a State bank in Philadelphia owe the bank of the United States, and have notes issued by the St. Louis branch, it can pay the debt with those notes; but if a merchant, mechanic, or other private citizen, be in like circumstances, he cannot, by law, pay his debt with those notes, but must sell them at a discount, or send them to St. Louis to be cashed.

Ewing called the practice odious. There was not "equal justice to the high and the low, the rich and the poor." It was "one prominent objection to the bill extending the charter" by the "executive." It was the period of "laissez-faire" in the growing United States.

Webster had commented earlier that there was no gold during the bank's tenure. Did Webster mean that the bank had no gold during the period because at least 3 million in gold each year was going across the Atlantic? The bank had been operating for sixteen years. Considering its last ten years, did the bank send at least 30 million in gold to foreign stockholders during its tenure? Webster mentioned that expansions and contractions occurred. Did the expansions occur when the specie was in the vault? Did the contractions occur when the specie was sent abroad? Expansions and contractions relate to the paper currency in circulation. Expanding the currency meant putting more money in circulation. Contracting the currency meant taking money out of circulation. Capitalization cannot occur during contraction. When the bank stopped "discounting" (lending the paper money), payments were made amid the banishment of specie? People, unsuspecting, are held to a note by the bank, and a contraction occurs. There is no money, what then? The bank removed the specie "so as to produce a scarcity of money, and to collect into the hands of the stockholders of the said bank almost the whole of the money which remains amongst us." Jefferson articulated "froth and bubble," and all the notes "shall vanish into air, as Morris' notes did."

In his December 1836 message, President Jackson said,

> On the establishment of a National Bank it became the interests of its creditors that gold should be superseded by the paper of a bank as a general currency. A value was soon attached to the gold coins, which made their exportation to foreign countries as a mercantile commodity, more profitable than their retention and use at home as money.

Jackson said, "The bank became, in effect, a substitute for the mint of the United States." Jackson blamed the flood of state bank paper issues on the bank of the United States. He said, "Such was the origin of a national bank currency, and such the beginning of those difficulties which now appear in the excessive issues of the banks incorporated by the various States." The excess of state bank paper issues occurred after the Second Bank was dissolved. On June 23, 1836, the Congress passed the Deposit Act. All public revenue would be placed in selected state "Deposit Banks."

In December 1836, Jackson spoke of the "excesses" that occurred in the public land sales. Speculators bought up the public lands with state bank paper issues, driving the prices to three times the value. Jackson said the currency was paid "out again and again" to the speculators. With each purchase, the money returned to the banks, and currency reissued; there was a proliferation of debt and currency, land value appreciation. The transactions were "mere instruments to transfer to speculators the most valuable public land, and pay the Government by a credit on the books of the banks." The "credits on the books . . . usually called deposits . . . were beyond immediate means of payment." The practice was "alarming." The "Specie Circular" of 1837 ended the practice. Only gold and silver coin became the official exchange for public land sales. President Jackson wanted settlers to buy the land at a reasonable cost, people who would settle, cultivate the land, and inhabit the West. It was supposedly a positive period. Jackson's Treasury claimed a substantial surplus during this time. The public land sales were a major part of the surplus.

The 1836 Treasury report showed $120 million of paper money in circulation; 28 million was the specie circulation. Forty-five million in specie, of which 20 million in silver bullion, was in the bank vaults. Levi Woodbury was the secretary of the Treasury. Treasury receipts totaled $48 million, and $24 million came from public land sales. The receipts exceeded expenditures by $16 million. President Jackson had eliminated the public debt. Jackson said, "The experience of other nations admonished us to hasten the extinguishment of the public debt." No doubt! President Jackson, apparently, had cut off the public creditor, domestic and foreign; no more public funds to feed on. Nasty business! Down the road, the country would pay the price. In 1836, the federal government began placing surplus revenues in selected bank institutions and dealing in specie exclusively. President Martin Van Buren started an independent sub-Treasury depository in 1840. This was done to protect the revenue.

President Jackson preferred a specie bank an arm of the Treasury that dealt in specie. Jackson was of the "Jeffersonian School." Jackson wasn't totally correct either? After 1837, the state banks continued to issue tons of their paper currency. They had no specie; many failed in the forthcoming panic. The U.S. Treasury dealt in specie payment. The fate of the Second Bank accentuated the power of a presidential veto. Jackson's veto was not popular in Congress; it wasn't popular with the friends of the central bank and also the business community.

But Jackson's veto didn't deter a majority of the voting public; he was elected to a second term in 1832. Jackson carried 55% of the vote to Clay's 42%. The Union comprised twenty-four states at the time, about twenty million people.

The Second Bank became an incorporated bank in Pennsylvania. The stockholders acquired the Pennsylvania charter before the federal charter expired. Jackson said,

> The old Bank had no right to issue or re-issue its notes after the expiration of its charter . . . Instead of proceeding to wind up their concerns, and pay over to the United States, the amount due on account of the stock held by them, the President and directors of the old bank appear to have transferred the books, papers, notes, obligations, and most or all of its property, to this new corporation, which entered upon business, as a continuation of the old concern.

Jackson stated that the bank's notes after expiration should have been "paid up as presented . . . canceled and destroyed." Jackson called their action fraudulent. But it was 1837, and state financial sovereignty was still in vogue.

A money panic happened soon after Martin Van Buren took office in early 1837. Why did that happen? The Specie Circular didn't help. Western and Southern state banks dealt in paper. The people wanting the land could only borrow paper. There was an imbalance of trade. Specie was leaving the country. Banks in England and Ireland failed. Loans were called, and when payment is demanded, it had to be in coin or its equivalent in depreciated paper. The banks in "New York" suspended specie; other banks soon followed. The period of abundant paper money and easy credit ended. It was 1837 and the beginning of an economic depression lasting seven years. Van Buren blamed the downturn on the banks, but nine hundred banks went out of business.

Nicholas Biddle was supposedly at the forefront of the money panic and the subsequent depression starting in 1837. Biddle was the head of the Second Bank of the United States. Apparently, there was no love lost between Biddle and Jackson. Biddle called in the circulation; he stopped the money supply in response to Jackson moving federal money out of the Second Bank to selected state "pet" banks. All loans had to be paid. It was a difficult time, gold leaving the country, payment in specie demanded, a lot of it attributed to Biddle. In 1834, according to Senator Benton, $3,500,000 was transferred to the house of Barings in London; this after the removal of U.S. deposits from Biddle's bank. The Barings Bank was an agent of the second United States bank. The Senate censured President Jackson; he was later vindicated. The Senate, Mr. Biddle, the Second Bank, the money interests—these entities, apparently, opposed Andrew Jackson.

The widespread use of credits and deposits, a voluminous "vicious" paper currency, its capitalization, and political opposition was apparently too much for President Jackson. Growth and debts were going west while dividends and profit were coming east. Andrew Jackson was right about the tremendous power of the Second Bank; the Second Bank of the United States was history and so was an abundant money supply for seven years. Jackson may have won the bank battle, but at what cost? President Van Buren was treated to a dried-up money supply.

Direction was westward and "Manifest Destiny." The country expanded from the Atlantic to the Pacific. Spain, Mexico, and the Indian nations kept the United States busy between the War of 1812 and the Civil War. There were the Seminole Wars in Spanish-controlled Florida. Florida became a state in James Monroe's administration. There was the Black Hawk War in Illinois and Wisconsin. Abraham Lincoln took part in that one; he was twenty-three years old. Andrew Jackson moved the Cherokee Nation from Georgia to Oklahoma in the journey known as the Trail of Tears. The Mexican-American War of 1846-1848 was significant. The country gained the Southwest Territory, California, Nevada, Utah, Wyoming, Colorado, Texas, and New Mexico. The cost was a negotiated $15 million deal with the Mexican government by treaty of 1848. Thomas Jefferson acquired the Louisiana Territory in 1803. The Lewis and Clark expedition was unequaled, more than two years in length. Jefferson's instructions to Captain Lewis was extensive. Jefferson's instructions to Lewis covered survey, agronomy, native tribes and languages, animal life, celestial observations, minerals, metals, limestone, plant life, etc. The annexation of Mexican land completed the territorial boundary of the western half of the nation. President James K. Polk "accepted the terms" with Mexico. The expansion and annexation was inevitable and complete. The country had obtained tremendous growth establishing the northwest border with Canada. It was a "destined" westward advance and takeover to the Pacific during the Polk administration. The French, the Spanish, the Indian nations, and the Mexicans were swept aside. All the territories, the expansion, the Indian reservations, initially, as always and as before, were public land.

As the Civil War approached, the country's territorial boundary was defined. There were thirty-four United States and the Western territories. The nation's continental expansion in just eighty-five years was complete, and it was accomplished during a varied and complex money period. The federal government and its quest for central banking had failed. The first two central bank charters were not renewed. Each sovereign state had its own paper currency, and the federal Treasury was accepting only gold and silver.

According to the record of the first session of the Eighth Congress, the money needed for the Louisiana Purchase was approved in two acts on October 31 and on November 10, 1803. The first in the amount $11,250,000 in certificates of stock was delivered to the French government. The proprietors of said stock, an English bank, were paid an interest of 6%. The English bank was the house of Barings. The second act in the amount of $3,750,000 was to be paid out of the Treasury. Fifteen million dollars was paid to the government of France. Section 2 of the first act stipulated that interest if paid in London would be "at the rate of four shillings and six pence sterling for each dollar" and "two guilders and one-half guilder for each dollar" if paid in Amsterdam. The 15 million-plus interest was paid in specie. During those first years, Alexander Hamilton borrowed from the Dutch (Amsterdam) to pay indebtedness to France and Spain.

The Treaty of Guadalupe Hidalgo in February of 1848 stipulated two methods of payment. The Mexican government was to decide after the ratification of the treaty which method of payment was most desirable to them. After a first payment, "four annual" payments were made "with interest at 6%." The payments were in Spanish gold or silver coin. The agreed-upon initial cost of $15 million was the second largest purchase by the United States.

On June 30, 1848, the United States made the first payment of $3,000,000. Subsequent payments were the following:

1. $3,720,000 on May 30, 1849
2. $3,540,000 on May 30, 1850
3. $3,360,000 on May 30, 1851
4. $3,180,000 on May 30, 1852

According to the record, a total payment for the Southwest Territory was $16,800,000.

There was a money panic in 1857. It occurred during James Buchanan's administration. The panic was blamed on "the failure of the Life Insurance Company of Cincinnati in August of 1857." There were "bank runs" across the country. A depression ensued that "lasted until the Civil War." Supposedly, the causes of the depression were bank failures; over expansion of the railroads; the California gold rush, which dropped the price of gold; a decline in exports; and the Crimean War ended (the Charge of the Light Brigade). But why did the insurance company fail? The insurance company had "large liabilities to Eastern Institutions; a panic occurred in New York, followed by a suspension of specie payments." The famous ship *Central America* was carrying California gold to New York; the ship went down in the Atlantic, taking all the gold and people with her. There was the Tariff Act of 1857, a reduction in duty. Gold left the country; a panic ensued. Between 1845 and 1857, the paper circulation had been more than ample; there was great industrial expansion. Credit was abundant again until the panic; the result was soaring indebtedness. A suspension of specie occurred; there was another crash. It was 1857. Treasury deficits increased during the period 1858 through 1860. There was a surplus in the Treasury in 1836. At the start of the Civil War in 1861, a national debt of $90 million existed.

The debate was winding down in the House. Spaulding had concluded his presentation.

Mr. Baker said the currency bill was flawed. The currency would have to be redeemed at the same banking counter. The currency was issued in blank, to be signed by the officer of the particular bank. How can the currency have the same value all over the country? It would be discounted as before. And how about a possible future unconstitutional ruling on the legal tender clause? Havoc would be caused on associations loaded up with legal tenders then having to buy coin at "sixty, seventy, or eighty per cent."

Mr. Alley's amendment, voted in the affirmative, changed the 2% currency tax to 1%. The associations (the new national banks) would pay only 1% tax on the new circulation. The state banks would still pay 2% on their paper circulation. Congressman Hooper wanted to get on with it; the bill was voted on and passed. President Lincoln signed Senate Bill 486 on February 25, 1863. Lincoln didn't like the bill, but he signed the bill. President Lincoln had wanted an audience after the war. "I will settle with these Gentlemen after the War is over"; his assassination killed that. Bill 486 was a Senate bill. It is unclear why the initiative on this bill was established in the Senate. All money bills originate in the Ways and Means Committee in the House. There was a House Bill 656 reported by Thadeus Stevens from Ways and Means. This House bill found no meaning in the record; it just wasn't there. The *Congressional Record* does not show otherwise. Senator Sherman referred to the bill as the bank bill. The National Bank Act became law in 1863 without a national or central bank becoming a part; there was great opposition.

> In August, 1861, O.B. Potter, of New York, submitted to the Secretary of the Treasury a scheme to permit State banks and bankers to issue notes secured by the United States bonds, saying: *"None of the objections justly urged against a United States Bank lie against this plan. It gives to the Government no power to bestow favors and does not place a dollar in its hand to lend."* (Sixty-first Congress, session 2, pp. 46-48)

Congressman Hooper said, "Thus are secured all the benefits of the old
United States Bank without many of those objectionable features which
aroused opposition." It was another beginning. Of most importance,
the bankers were getting the bonds and the gold; the bankers would
have to wait until 1913 before getting their third central bank.

It was another beginning, and it would take time. What did it mean?
Before the Civil War, state banking schemes from the record issued
paper currencies and accumulated specie directly or indirectly, and
that wouldn't change. Before the Civil War, the cost of money to the
people was a direct discount from a bank. The state banks issued paper
money at a discount. There was little cost to the banks, and the initial
cost of money to the people was the discount or interest. A uniform
currency plan would change that. A uniform currency plan was a credit
circulation, the start of a permanent plan, which the people would pay
for initially, several times, and forever. A uniform currency plan was a
federal plan. There would be federal taxation to support the circulation.
Part of the cost of the currency issue was the payment in gold to the
new national banks. The currency would be discounted not once but
several times from the government through the banking system to the
people. It would be a dramatic change in the money scheme.

What was the impact of the change? The people would pay much more
initially for their money, the gold to the banks, additional discounts,
and the income tax. After these inflicted costs of money, there is
depreciation, property taxes, excise taxes, etc., and the cost of living. It
was a new scheme. The federal government would print the currency,
borrow the same currency, and fund a national debt in one fell swoop,
a coincident process; this was the credit circulation. A credit circulation
was a plan out of financial impasse. It was only a beginning; partial
"end of the beginning" would occur in 1913. In 1863, it was a plan in
infancy. It was a plan in infancy because the nation's currency would
become "varied" and fiercely contested. Counterfeiting continued in
the old and the new currency; a government secret service agency
was formed in 1865 to counter the problem.

There were the forces that wanted to contract the paper currency
after the war, mainly the greenbacks. And the West was beginning
to open up, and there was hoped for reconstruction in the South. An

adequate money supply was necessary. But there were the forces for resumption of specie payment as soon as possible. The debt would be refunded. There was the famous gold sale by Gould and Fisk. There were the proponents of gold who didn't want silver. Demonetization of silver occurred. The Indians were most formidable in the West amid the Homesteaders; George Armstrong Custer was wiped out at Little Bighorn in Montana. There was the greenback party, more money panics, strikes, unemployment, the advent of Communism in America. Alaska was purchased; ten new states were added to the Union. There was another intended correction: woman's suffrage was introduced in the Congress. The telephone and the electric light were invented amid industrial expansion, favorable trade, trade imbalance. President Garfield was assassinated. There was the Interstate Commerce Act and the Interstate Commerce Commission for the regulation of "competition between railroads," vast immigration. The population doubled, the Gold Standard Act and the Spanish-American War, to mention a few of the events before the turn of the century.

At the start of all this, President Johnson had a rough term in office; he had many enemies in Congress. A Lincoln "mild Reconstruction" policy needed the Southern gentleman, Andrew Johnson. But Southern segregationists, Northern hard-liners, the carpetbaggers, property raiders from the North killed any possibility of a Lincoln policy. Reconstruction failed! Slavery was officially abolished in 1865 by the Thirteenth Amendment. But the Ku Klux Klan in 1866 "was founded" in Tennessee. A meaningful beginning of human rights wouldn't begin to affect until 1965, one hundred years later. Northern money interests ravaged the war-torn South. Growth and turmoil marked nineteenth-century America.

There had to be a plus to an eventual conclusive uniform currency. The discounting of currency between states would end. Non-accepted currencies between townships and states would also end. But there would be another hit. The states would begin to lose financial independence; state sovereignty would weaken some more. State banks would pay a 2% tax on their paper currency. There was going to be a central power currency, a dramatic financial change coming because of the Civil War. The United States would grudgingly unify its currency, its collection system, over time.

The federal government was always connected to the banking scheme, a necessary coalition. The connection was created when a charter was granted the First Bank of the United States. Congressman Bingham reminded us that "what the Government does by another it does by itself." The uniform currency plan of 1863 brought even closer, a contested political economic connection. Apparently, the money interests needed government; the government needed the money interests.

A debt-funding scheme began with Alexander Hamilton; the scheme was stopped in 1811. The scheme resumed in 1816 with the Second Bank. President Jackson stopped that scheme in 1832-1836. A central bank was more "formidable" than government. There was the interim period when the government dealt strictly in specie, and a resultant seven-year economic thud resulted, the big bankers' backlash. The next scheme was brought on by the Civil War impasse. It was called the National Bank Act, but it was also a new idea; it was a seedling, the start of a permanent credit circulation, debt-funding scheme in the United States but undefined. Alexander Hamilton's federal expenses as being permanently unlimited, "even in imagination," would begin slowly to unfold.

A credit circulation was in embryo. Because of the Civil War, the banks would not in total, until 1913, control the money supply. Prior to the Civil War, the banks printed and issued the paper and, hopefully, accumulated gold. The bank act of 1863 would gradually remove bank-printed paper money from circulation. It was a currency swap; it was Treasury currency for bank currency. The U.S. Treasury would direct the printing of a national currency in exchange for United States bonds purchased by the banks. The banks would make 5% net interest on issues of the national currency. The banks would be paid 6% interest in gold on the bonds. Senator Sherman, in the Senate, said the banks were going to make money. State banks who continued issuing their paper currency would have to pay a 2% tax on their circulation.

The new credit circulation was a "national Currency." This paper currency was called circulating notes. The notes would be printed and issued to new national banks by the Treasury of the United States. The national currency could not be exchanged for duties on imports. The national currency was not payable on the public debt. The national currency was not legal tender. The notes were issued in blank to be signed by the president of each bank. Although the government printed this new currency, the currency was a national bank currency; private bank paper currency was never legal tender. The government could not pay its debt to the banks with this bank paper currency.

The greenback, also printed by the Treasury, was non-interest-bearing legal tender. The new national currency was interest bearing and was "equal in amount to ninety per centum of the current market value of the United States bonds." It would appear the 1863 bank act was the beginning of a rediscount system in the United States. It was the beginning of interest-bearing currency forever; the public creditor was back in business.

At that time, government bonds were selling for 50¢ on the dollar. If a bank made a bid of $50 on a $100 bond, the Treasury issued $45 in new currency to the bank. This new currency replaced bank paper money. Considering 6% interest on a bank issue of national currency, minus a 1% tax and payment in gold at 6% for the bonds according to Senator Sherman, the banks were going to make plenty of money. It was a currency swap, Treasury money for bank money. Bank currency was received and apparently destroyed. In the future, after bank currency was removed from circulation, an apparent exchange of currency was no longer needed. The banks were apparently issued new currency based on a bid price of the bond. Before the turn of the century, the banks were issued the new currency based on 100% of the bid price of the bond. The banks, apparently, purchased the bonds with currency the Treasury printed.

CHAPTER FIVE

The Gold Bill

The Civil War ended April 9, 1865. General Lee of the Confederate Army of Northern Virginia surrendered to General Ulysses S. Grant at Appomattox. Six days later, President Lincoln was murdered by actor John Wilkes Booth. Booth shot Lincoln at Ford's Theater in Washington on the evening of April 14. President Lincoln died the following morning, April 15, 1865.

The Civil War had not gone well for the Union. It had not gone well until July 1863. That summer, General Lee's Army of Northern Virginia and its northern advance was stopped, defeated at Gettysburg in Pennsylvania. General George Meade marked the first major success of the Union Army. At almost the same time, General Grant took the vital city of Vicksburg in the West. The Union now controlled the entire Mississippi River Valley to New Orleans. The South's supply line from the West was cut off. Lincoln had stressed the importance of controlling the Mississippi since the beginning of the war. The favorable turn of events enabled Lincoln's election to a second term in 1864. But the war went on.

The many Americans who died, a cream of early American youth, would never claim their American heritage, both North and South. The Civil War was fought in the South and the West. Military engagement did reach Pennsylvania, but there was another kind of warfare that reached the North; it was civil strife. The racial riots in New York City, brought on by the Conscription Act, resulted in death and destruction, which lasted four days. Three hundred dollars could buy your way out of military service.

Emancipation had been in effect, but to what extent? Lincoln said, "The General Government had no lawful power to affect emancipation in any State." Maryland and Missouri, two states who wanted no part, had relented, changed their ways. After emancipation, one hundred thousand former slaves had served in the Union Army; fifty thousand were bearing arms. The blockade had captured more than a thousand ships, the value, "thirteen million dollars." There were more "open ports" for "foreign merchants," namely, "Norfolk, Fernandina and Pensacola."

The Civil War prevailed, but other things were happening. A telegraph line between America and Russia was undertaken through the "Bering Straits." The design of an Atlantic Telegraph crossing was in the works. Lincoln mentioned these things in his last annual message to Congress. "Conditions" in the territories were "generally satisfactory." There were the rich mineral resources in "Colorado, Nevada, Idaho, New Mexico and Arizona." There was a shortage there of all industries. Lincoln had asked for the "encouragement of immigration." He said, "Tens of thousands of persons, desperate of remunerative occupation, are thronging our foreign consulates."

Lincoln mentioned Japan; conditions had worsened. A fire occurred at the legation in Yedo. The U.S. foreign minister "complained of damages he sustained in the destruction." Lincoln said, "Our relations with Japan have been brought into serious jeopardy, through the perverse opposition of the hereditary aristocracy of the Empire to the enlightened and liberal policy of the Tycoon, designed to bring the country into the Society of Nations." Hopefully, things would improve.

Great Britain had cooperated by "preventing the departure of new hostile expeditions from leaving British ports." There were "disloyal citizens of the United States" involved in "inexcusable insurrection." Also, a treaty had been ratified with Great Britain suppressing the "African Slave Trade."

Land sales had picked up. More than four million acres of public land had been "disposed of," more than 1 million under "the Homestead Law," also "for military bounties . . . for Railroad and for other purposes." Settlements had increased although the war was going on. The secretary of the Interior recommended that the Homestead Act be changed to favor veterans from the war; Lincoln agreed.

As of November 1864, "five hundred and eighty four National Banks had been organized, a considerable number of which were conversions from State banks." Lincoln spoke favorably of the new system. Lincoln briefly mentioned the national debt. The debt had grown to more than $1.7 billion "as of July last" (1864). Lincoln wanted the debt to be owned "by our own people . . . persons of limited means." It was up to Congress to "provide that a limited amount of some future issue of public *securities* might be held by any *bona fide* purchaser exempt from taxation and from seizure from debt." Continuing, he said, "The great advantage of citizens being creditors as well as debtors, with relation to the public debt, is obvious. Men readily perceive that they cannot be much oppressed by a debt which they owe to themselves."

> The condition of our foreign affairs is reasonably satisfactory. At the request of the States of Costa Rica and Nicaragua, a competent engineer has been authorized to make a survey of the river San Juan and the port of San Juan. Mutual claims had been settled between the United States and Peru. Our relations are of the most friendly nature with Chile, the Argentine Republic, Bolivia, Costa Rica, Paraguay, San Salvador and Hayti.

In his December 1863 message, Lincoln presented a proclamation. It was about "the present and the future." He was looking toward the end of the war. The "National Authority" had to be reestablished in the Southern states within the limits of the "Constitution." The secessionists would be pardoned; an oath to the Constitution was part of it. The "political framework of the States" would not be jeopardized. There would be "reconstruction . . . without danger of harm." In December 1864, Lincoln maintained his position on emancipation. He would not change his mind. Emancipation was an aid in ending the war.

Lincoln's last annual message to the Congress was December 6, 1864. One of his last public addresses was his second inaugural. The date was March 4, 1865. Before the war ended, the first and second sessions of the Thirty-eighth Congress amended the Uniform Currency Act in 1864 and 1865. The Congress passed a "Gold Bill" joint resolution in 1864. Ways and Means in the House appropriated $900 million in 1863 and $211 million more in 1864. These appropriations covered more loan bills approved by the Congress. The Internal Revenue Act was amended in 1864 and 1865.

The secretary in December of 1864 asked the Congress for 470 million in new loans. The debt projection to July 1865 was $2.2 billion. The debt was more than twenty times greater than when the war started in 1861.

The loans and indebtedness took many forms. Introduced were more interest-accruing Treasury notes payable in not less than three years; the certificates of indebtedness, the short-term certificates of deposit; the five-twenty bonds; the ten-forty bonds. The ten-forties were the latest bonds payable in forty years, redeemable in ten years, and the non-interest-bearing greenbacks. Twenty million dollars of interest-bearing Treasury notes in small denominations were issued to the troops. The remaining demand notes had been paid and disposed of.

A gold bill would authorize the Treasury secretary to sell gold in the open market. Imports had flooded the East Coast during the war. Resulting duties had swelled the Treasury with coin. The amount of gold "was beyond the demands of the Treasury for the payment of interest and for all disbursements which by law are required to be made."

Congressman Kasson of Iowa was presenting a joint resolution before the House. The Treasury had become the "bull in the New York market." Merchants and importers in New York were short on gold. Speculators drove up the price of gold because of it. The purpose of the resolution was to allow the secretary to sell surplus coin, get the specie back into the normal "channels of the city." This was the opinion of the majority of the Committee of Ways and Means.

Mr. Pendleton disagreed; he wasn't buying it. The secretary of the Treasury or the "head of any Department" should not have the power to buy and sell gold "at his pleasure to raise or depress the market." Mr. Pendleton pointed out that the "government acknowledged that its credit is below par." The merchants and bankers and brokers were buying U.S. bonds at 50¢ to 60¢ on the dollar, and now Chase would sell gold for the government's depreciated legal tender notes. "No honorable man would do so in his own private affairs." Mr. Pendleton said the government should "not seek to control the money market instead of allowing the laws of trade to control it. Private interests are at the bottom of this movement."

There was 18 million in gold in the Treasury. There would be 37 million by June 1864. The government had to pay out 24 million in gold in interest payments, leaving a surplus of 13 million. This was the surplus. The resolution would allow Chase to dispose of this surplus. But Pendleton said the Treasury surplus was less than one-third of the 60 million on deposit in New York. The government should not become a "bull" or "bear."

Mr. Brooks's opinion was let the price of gold ascend. Maybe imports would slow down. Let the price of gold rise high enough to stop the imports; it would be for the best.

Congressman James Garfield of Ohio (the future twentieth president) mentioned that $500 thousand in gold was coming into the Treasury every day; he was for the resolution. Garfield mentioned there was gold in "stockings, trunks, bureaus, bed heads and bank vaults, 200 million of it." He said if the "Treasury didn't get rid of it, the Government would have one-quarter of the country's gold locked up . . . the price of gold would rise . . . the Government's credit would go down." Mr. Garfield said he was "ashamed." A "charge" had been made on the other side of the isle. "If we did not pay our sailors and soldiers in gold, their wives would become prostitutes."

How much gold was there? Mr. Garfield mentioned 200 million. Pendleton said there was 60 million. The numbers varied. During this debate, no one mentioned silver; it was about gold. But what was the total specie in the country? In 1836, Secretary Levi Woodbury stated 73 million in specie was circulating, which was gold and silver. Of that amount, the people held 28 million. The people held approximately one-third of the specie circulation. How much specie did the people hold during the Civil War? It's not mentioned in the record. But people held the coin just like the banks. People didn't spend any coin, and the banks didn't circulate any coin. It was "Gresham's Law" all over the place. Gresham's law is where bad money drives out good money. The gold was either hoarded or exported, according to Thadeus Stevens. Gresham's law isn't physics or mathematics; these are the true sciences. People drive out the money, in this case, the gold.

Mr. Boutwell of Massachusetts disagreed with Garfield; there was no guarantee a surplus would continue. Boutwell asked Garfield about the 85 million in interest payments due by July 1865. Revenues would total only 70 million. If the Treasury in the future couldn't make its interests payments; if it had to go into the market to buy gold, then the premium on gold may go as high as "200 per cent." There was a 60% premium on gold at the time.

Mr. Boutwell changed the premise of the gold bill. A Boutwell amendment was significant. It stated "that the Secretary of the Treasury be authorized to anticipate the payment of interest upon the public debt from time to time, upon a rebate of interest by the holder of coupons at the rate of six per cent, per annum in gold." Boutwell said a merchant would be allowed to convert his coupon into gold ahead of time, then satisfy his custom requirements. The transaction would be reciprocal. Customs are paid; the Treasury pays its interest, and the credit is maintained. Instead of interest being paid in "July," the interest would be paid "now." Mr. Boutwell's bill would allow a merchant "to go into the market and buy coupons payable in July and January next, and convert them into gold." The merchant would satisfy his custom payment, and the gold comes back into the Treasury.

Mr. Brooks of New York wanted the secretary to apply the excess gold to the sinking fund. "Let him create the sinking fund there provided. Let him diminish the public debt. There is the way to get rid of the coin, and not in the way proposed by the Committee of Ways and Means." Mr. Brooks said the secretary should not have control of the gold. He was surrounded by "thieves and robbers."

The act of February 1862 stated that excess funds would be paid into the sinking fund. The proponents of this joint resolution weren't talking sinking fund.

In the Senate, John Sherman said the idea was to control the price of gold and bring the Treasury's paper currency closer to the value of gold. Currency depreciation happens in time of war as it did to France and England (It happened to the United States during the War of 1812; it was the same story happening during the Civil War). Sherman said that the secretary could control the speculators, having 20 million in gold at his disposal. One argument against the bill was the secretary having too much power. Sherman said Chase was already wielding a "debt of $1,500,000,000." The additional power would not be significant.

Senator Hendricks of Indiana wanted to pay the contractors with the excess gold. Senator Sherman shot back; of all the people to be paid out in gold, Hendricks "selected the contractors, the men who have been cheating the Government, according to the declarations I have so often heard from his side of the House." Hendricks presented an amendment. He wanted the secretary to give ten days' notice prior to going into the market. Sherman felt that ten days' notice was not a good idea. During the ten-day period, the speculators would run up the price of gold thus depreciating the government's currency more so. Hendricks would change his amendment to five days. Sherman said that five days was not a good idea either.

Hendricks and Sherman went at it pretty good. Sherman said that Hendricks forgot about the "soldier" when he singled out the contractor. Hendricks countered with a rhetorical proposition. The soldiers were paid $13 a month at enlistment. The premium on gold was now 60% and going up. Hendricks wanted "the pay of the soldier equal to what the Government promised him." Hendricks asked Sherman to support a "measure" that would pay the soldier "$1.60 for every one of the thirteen dollars promised." If Sherman would support the measure, he would support the measure. That was the end of that!

Senator Sherman didn't like the House bill as amended by Mr. Boutwell. Sherman said,

It is an absurd proposition while we are borrowing
$2,000,000 per day, to authorize the Secretary to anticipate
the payment of a portion of the debt, thus losing the
interest, and not relieving at all the pressure upon the
market in New York.

Was it a question of preference because of political constituency?
Senator Sherman and the Senate wanted the secretary to get the
gold back into the market by selling it. The House version would get
the gold back into the market with the secretary "buying up interest
coupons." The House version would allow a merchant to convert
coupons into gold that the Treasury had, which the Treasury would
receive back again when the merchant paid customs. Boutwell's
version passed in the House by a vote of 90-34, a popular majority.
Was Sherman right? Was the House right? The biggest argument
against the original resolution was the granting of too much power
to the secretary. Sherman's argument was that the government was
borrowing 2 million per day. *The banks bought the majority of the
government bonds, securities, etc., with government-printed currency
at 50¢ to 60¢ on the dollar.* The Treasury paid its bills in legal tender
paper currency but had to pay its debt to the banks in gold. What a
deal! The Treasury had a surplus of gold because of excessive imports.
It would appear of most importance at the time the gold was needed
to pay interest on the public debt. The Treasury had been borrowing
paper currency every day. But the Treasury was accumulating a lot
of gold, and the private money interests wanted it. The way to get it
was through Congress.

The debate on the gold bill went on for a month. The bill opened in
the House on February 17, went to the Senate on March 9, and was
signed into law on March 17, 1864. The House bill went to the Senate
as the "the Gold Bill." In the Senate, it would be called interest on the
public debt. The purpose of the resolution was the same, whether
from Ways and Means in the House or the Finance Committee in the
Senate. The purpose was to restore surplus gold to the import-export
exchanges in New York. The House bill, apparently, would have
relieved the secretary of directly marketing the gold; and why the
difference in terminology? The House called the resolution for what
it was, a gold bill. When the bill was signed into law, it was called

"a Joint Resolution—to authorize the Secretary of the Treasury to anticipate the Payment of Interest on the Public Debt, and for other purposes." The Senate version went beyond the House version. The Senate version, the final version, allowed the secretary "to dispose of any gold in the Treasury of the United States not necessary for the payment of interest on the Public debt." A sinking fund consideration was placed in the resolution. The money bills may have originated in the House, but Senator Sherman and the Senate held sway. Apparently, there was more power on the Senate side of Congress. There were compromises, but significant changes had to be accepted by the House. There would be no money bills without amendments more suitable to the Senate.

When the bill came back from the Senate, Congressman Kernan of New York said, "I presume no one will be deceived by the attractive name given to this bill—a bill to sell *surplus* gold in the Treasury." This act, at a later time, allowed President Grant to counter the direction of "Black Friday" (Gould and Fisk, chapter 7).

On February 28, 1865, Thadeus Stevens spoke before the House. Stevens was "making another effort to resist the present financial policy of the Government." There was yet another loan bill. His speech read like a lament. Starting at the beginning, he said that after the first loan of 250 million, there was the fight to make the first 150 million in greenbacks a legal tender. The greenbacks were legislated in the House as lawful money. The House wanted all interest on loans to be paid in the lawful money, not gold. "The House saw the absurdity of declaring by law a circulation which they had just created and declared lawful money and made a legal tender to be of less value than gold, thus depreciating its value. The New York brokers and bankers" descended on Washington and "persuaded the Secretary of the Treasury and the Senate to adopt that fatal policy," the paying of interest in gold. The duties on imports policy followed; duties would be "paid in specie." Later, the principal of bonds, securities, etc., although purchased with paper currency, would be paid in gold. Stevens called it unwise discrimination, creating two kinds of currency. The greenbacks were automatically inferior to gold. To this, "I attribute most of the trouble which has arisen from the high price of everything, the enormous and unnecessary expense of the war, and the constant fluctuation in the market." It was Stevens's contention that since gold was suspended, gold was no longer money; it was a commodity. But "Congress made gold, when no longer money, no longer a circulating medium, the standard of value." The government "depreciated its own money." The yellow metal, gold, was made the standard of value.

Stevens said, "Had all our loans been for lawful money there would have been no difficulty in having them taken at six per cent at par. All 'lawful money' being received for duties and interest." The fact that the lawful money would not have been accepted "abroad," Stevens said, "That to me would have been a merit." Stevens said the United States could have paid all its loans without foreigners. "The annual net earnings of this country would have been sufficient to absorb all our loans and pay all our expenses of the war." Stevens said that prices in America had escalated but stayed the same in Europe. American products "sold abroad at forty dollars on the hundred, and we immediately pay $100 dollars in coin for it as interest, and must ultimately pay for every $40 received when specie payments are resumed. What an immense sacrifice to a foolish theory."

On March 3, 1865, the war was still going on, and another loan bill was approved. The secretary was authorized to borrow 600 million more in five-forty bonds and/or 6% interest-bearing Treasury notes. The Treasury notes would mature in five years and then be transferable into bonds. Payment of interest and principal at maturity was paid in gold. The Treasury notes were more useful than bonds. The notes were initially currency. Bills were paid. The notes were then held as investment with interest paid semiannually and maturity in five years. Interest in gold was at 6%. Interest was 7.3% if paper currency was desired.

There was a reason in the latest bill why the Treasury notes would pay interest in currency. The government was paying $56 million interest in gold on the debt annually. Sherman said, "We dare not therefore increase it to any considerable extent. Then how must we borrow this money?" Sherman said, "We must borrow it on the Currency Bonds." Sherman called the interest-accruing Treasury notes currency bonds. Another reason the government would pay its bills with the notes; the notes would then be held for the interest, and inflation may be curbed. After maturity, the notes may be transferred into long-term bonds. The issue of more non-interest-bearing greenbacks would inflate the currency. Sherman did not want to issue more greenbacks.

Senator McDougall of California objected. He said the "measure complicates our financial system." The government didn't have a "policy." There were too many "changes." Mr. Sherman has "a new form of Government bonds payable in currency; that is, using our credit to pay our debts, and then our credit to pay our interest—a thing false in all political economy." Maybe an economist would call it innovative finance.

Interest-accruing Treasury notes or currency bonds was not new. Their latest planned innovative use, critically described by McDougall, was new. The bill would be approved as outlined by Sherman all bonds, notes, securities, etc., exempt from state and municipal taxation. There was opposition to the nontaxation clause. Sherman pointed out, very simply, that securities would not sell unless nontaxable. Between 1812 and 1865, more than twenty acts were passed by the Congress, whereby Treasury notes or currency bonds were authorized for issue.

It was discussed in the Congress that the country could return, hopefully, to specie payment within a five-year period.

In 1865, the nation's currency included the following:

- Non-interest-bearing greenbacks, circulating, many held as reserves.
- Interest-accruing Treasury notes, interest payable in gold, maturity in three years, not circulated. The banks held 150 million in these notes, the original loan in 1861.
- Interest-accruing Treasury notes, interest payable in gold and currency, maturity in five years, not circulated.
- Circulating notes as part of the uniform currency plan.
- Circulating state bank paper currency.
- Circulating fractional currency.
- Gold and silver, suspended.

Thadeus Stevens estimated approximately $600 million was the circulation in 1865, maybe less. "A large portion of the legal tenders are hoarded," which were the greenbacks. Stevens said the circulating medium at the start of the war was $400 million. The $400 million would have included paper currency and coin. Stevens estimated that the 600 million in circulation was "no more than is necessary to carry on the increased business of the Nation." The annual product of the North, during the latter part of the war, was, say, $6 billion? During the war, West Virginia (1863) and Nevada (1864) were added to the Union.

By April 15, 1865, the Civil War had ended. Lincoln was gone, and Andrew Johnson was sworn in. Andrew Johnson became the sixteenth president of the United States. Secretary Chase resigned in 1864. William Fessenden assumed the Treasury duties until 1865; he then returned to the Senate.

CHAPTER SIX

The Legal Tenders and the Supreme Court

Salmon Chase resigned as secretary of the Treasury in 1864. Chase had threatened to resign earlier; Lincoln didn't want him to leave. Later, Abraham Lincoln appointed Chase to the Supreme Court. Chase became chief justice. In December of 1870, the legal tender cases were before the Court. Salmon Chase presided on the constitutionality of the legal tender greenbacks. There was a dissenting opinion and then a concurring opinion of the Court. The legal tender greenback was affirmed constitutional on January 15, 1872. The opinion of the Court emphasized probable economic calamity if a dissenting opinion was reached. The Court stated that there would occur "great business derangement, widespread distress, and the rankest injustice." In both opinions, Salmon Chase as chief justice declared the issue of legal tender greenbacks unconstitutional.

Salmon Chase, when secretary of the Treasury, was granted the authority by the Congress to issue legal tender greenbacks during the Civil War. Four hundred fifty million dollars of legal tender lawful money, the greenbacks, were issued.

On January 29, 1862, Chase had sent an urgent message to the House. The message urged the immediate action on the bill containing the greenbacks. Mr. Spaulding in the House had

> the Clerk read an extract from that letter . . . Immediate action is of great importance. The Treasury is nearly empty. I have been obliged to draw from the last installment of the November loan. So soon as it is paid, I fear the banks generally will refuse the United States notes, unless made

a legal tender. You will see the necessity of urging the bill
through without more delay.

The Ways and Means Committee was for legal tender. The words
in Chase's letter indicated the banks were for legal tender? Did the
words indicate Chase's intent or the bank's intent? Secretary Chase
indicated in his letter the absolute necessity for legal tender. In the
letter, Chase also expressed his "aversion to making anything but
coin a legal tender in payment of debts." Thadeus Stevens said that
Chase was "hostile to the scheme." At that time, the Congress did
what was "necessary and proper" in making the greenbacks legal
tender money. Although opponents said no, it was "necessary and
proper." Was it necessary and proper because the second decision
by the Supreme Court in 1872 was decided in the affirmative? The
greenbacks were constitutional because the Congress had the power
to make them so (Section 8 of Article I of the Constitution). One of
the initial efforts after the Civil War was to remove the greenbacks
from circulation (chapter 7).

In his dissenting opinion, Salmon Chase wrote, "In no report made by
him to Congress was the expedient of making the notes of the United
States a legal tender suggested." Literally, in his message, Salmon
Chase didn't "suggest"; he merely expressed urgency, a necessity for
legal tender. Was it one of the many reasons Chase wanted to resign
in 1862 over the legal tender issue? When Chase was secretary of
the Treasury, the greenbacks were necessary; as chief justice, the
greenbacks were unconstitutional.

The arguments for and the arguments against were abundant,
voluminous. The many arguments are not presented here. What
currency or money scheme is constitutional in a political economy?
Daniel Webster said the government accepted state bank paper
currency during the War of 1812, which, he said, was against
constitutional law. Madison and Jefferson were against the First Bank.
Those past presidents wrote that the First Bank incorporation charter
was unconstitutional. But the Framers left out the incorporation of
private entities. Because incorporation was left out, there was reason
why a First Bank corporation was considered. The First Bank was
granted a charter because it was "necessary and proper." "Bills of

credit" were left out of the Constitution. "Bills of credit" were left out because in the future, it may be "necessary and proper" that bills of credit may be printed. This was Gouverneur Morris's contention in his conversation with Madison in 1787. Attorney General Amos Akerman wrote in the legal tender case, "It is not given to man, when framing a Constitution, to foresee all the cases to which the conferred powers will properly extend. And in this very matter, notwithstanding, that the power to emit bills of credit was struck out, this court has held that the power exists."

The first and second central banks of the United States printed paper currency. The United States Treasury accepted this paper currency in the payment of debts. This paper currency printed by the first two banks was not legal tender. State or private bank paper currency never was and never could be legal tender. Only the Congress of the United States has the power to make a currency a legal tender. But the United States government accepted the paper currency of the first and second banks of the United States. The first Supreme Court declared the practice constitutional in the eighteenth century; John Jay was the chief justice. In 1812, the government of the United States accepted the paper currency of the state banks. Daniel Webster called the practice unlawful. Was it unlawful? Maybe it was! President Andrew Jackson didn't accept the constitutionality of the Second Bank in 1832. What is constitutional in a political economy as may be determined by the Supreme Court, a Court that may, in action, be more political than judicial? The power that may be in power will determine what will be the lawful power?

The Constitution did not allow the "states" to emit bills of credit. The Constitution did not state that private banking institutions within a state cannot emit bills of credit. State banks adopted the same principle as the First Bank of the United States. The state banks adopted "specie-paying" institutions, which printed and issued paper currency.

The opponents of the Legal Tender Act of 1862 said this act was unconstitutional. The opponents within and outside the Congress said the Congress did not have the power to create legal tender paper currency in the payments of debts. It was coin, gold and silver; the opponents of government legal tender paper money were simply proponents of gold coin or specie. It was constitutional when the Congress created the First Bank that printed paper currency, which was not legal tender, a paper money, which the government accepted in the payments of debts. This paper money, which was not legal tender, was declared the money; it was legislated to be backed by coin. But the primary design of the first two banks of the United States was gold accumulation and swift capitalization against stock with bank notes, a pyramidal bank paper currency. The money scheme today is pyramidal paper "fiat" currency supported by a mounting tax burden, and it is now constitutional. Since the beginning, the banks were allowed to purchase gold with their non-legal tender paper money.

In 1862, the Treasury, authorized by Congress, printed and issued a non-interest-bearing legal tender greenback. The experts stated there was no promise to pay with the greenback; the statement is not entirely correct. A promise to pay did exist, indirectly, with the greenback. The greenback purchased government securities payable semiannually in gold. A promise to pay did not exist with bank paper money. Bank paper currency, which previously purchased gold, was not redeeming or paying in gold. The banks suspended during the Civil War. The government repudiated its greenbacks because of customs; the banks repudiated its paper money during suspension, but the greenbacks indirectly paid in gold. Bank paper money did not pay in gold. The banker's premise was, in contradiction, the unending contradiction in money. The banker's premise, from the record, appeared a promise to pay when convenient to do so.

It seems there is a time, a place, a mentality, a design, and acceptance by the Congress and the controlling money interests for a specific constitutional money scheme in a political economy in the United States. The Federal Reserve Act of 1913 enacted by the Congress is constitutional. All laws passed by the Congress are constitutional. The Constitution of the United States granted that power to the Congress. The Congress is, by the Constitution, the most powerful body in the United States. Congressional legislation is lasting unless amended by an Act of Congress or unless contested by opponents and then rendered unconstitutional by a Supreme Court decision, which can be overturned. In 1913, a new money scheme appeared acceptable; it was approved. It appeared politically and financially acceptable; the money interests liked it. They didn't contest it; they made a lot of money as a result. Is it constitutional because the Congress made it so or because the money interests didn't contest it?

CHAPTER SEVEN
The Nation's Currency

At the turn of the century, approximately $360 million in greenbacks were still part of the paper circulation. One hundred million had been redeemed and destroyed. The lovers of the "soft money" greenback had somewhat prevailed; $360 million in greenbacks survived, but to what extent? The money interests fought the greenback issue, never wanted them. Imagine borrowing a dollar in 1862 and in 1900, the debt was still a dollar. The banks couldn't make money with a greenback circulation; the greenbacks were interest free. The greenbacks were lawful money legal tender but also a "fixed" circulation. The money scheme, the private banking money creation scheme, would not function with a fixed circulation. Supreme Court decisions ruled in the greenbacks' favor in 1872 and 1884. Banks may not have liked them, but banks found the greenbacks useful as a reserve, payable for customs and redeemed them for gold. The greenbacks, because of later legislation, were on a par with gold; they were at last formidable, no longer technically "repudiated" in the latter nineteenth century and into the twentieth century. The greenbacks were legal tender "lawful money" of the United States. The Treasury held them as part of the gold redemption process.

In December 1865, Hugh McCulloch was the new secretary of the Treasury. Hugh McCulloch was a banker from Indiana. He was comptroller of the Treasury and was there in the beginning of the new banking system. He said,

> The National system of banking has been devised with a wisdom that reflects the highest credit upon its author to furnish to the people of the United States a *national-bank note circulation without the agency of a national bank.*

> It is not to be a mammoth corporation, at the will of its
> managers, thus enabling a board of directors to control the
> business and politics of the country.

In other words, McCulloch said it was a banking system without an objectionable third central bank. The objectionable would be created later in 1913.

McCulloch stressed three priorities: the national debt, the paper circulation, and the revenue. The total public debt was $2.8 billion. The greenback issue, as part of the total debt, was $454 million. The new national bank issue was $185 million. State banks were still doing their thing; their issue was 65 million. The total paper currency in circulation was about $704 million. The paper currency had to be contracted. McCulloch, for starters, wanted to contract or eliminate as much as 200 million in greenbacks. The country should return to specie payment, hopefully without trauma, in a reasonable period of time. Contraction was necessary. The war was over; expenditures were down. The circulation should balance the needs of employment. Get rid of the greenbacks—this was McCulloch's policy. Reduce the paper circulation eventually to be at par with gold and refund the debt.

About the debt, McCulloch said, "The Public debt of the United States represents a portion of the accumulated wealth of the country. While it is a debt of the nation, it becomes the capital of the citizen." A most significant statement from the past, it articulates the essence of capitalism, the control of money. Indebtedness is wealth.

The first two central banks of the United States were started with subscriptions of indebtedness. The bulk of the original bank stock was owned indebtedness. Entities, who profited from the eighteenth-century revolution and the War of 1812, owned the indebtedness of the United States; they were the profiteers, the stockholders, the creditors of the first central banks. Seventy-five percent of the stock of the first two banks was owned indebtedness subscribed to the banks in the form of commercial paper. Specie went along for the ride; specie represented the small portion of the stock. In 1811, foreigners owned 75% of the stock of the First Bank. Foreigners owned about 25% of the Second Bank. McCulloch earnestly hoped that the people of the United States would retain ownership of all the present national debt, the Civil War debt. It didn't happen!

An act of April 12, 1866, accomplished refunding, payment of debt, and contraction. More than $800 million in short-term seven-thirties would be converted into five-twenty bonds at 6% interest. These Treasury notes or currency bonds were part of the short-term non-funded debt. These currency bonds were maturing (imagine paying off these notes to the tune of 800 million in gold and currency, it couldn't be done; refunding was done). The short-term (one year) certificates of indebtedness were also due; they were paid. Interest on the bonds would be paid semiannually in gold.

People are refunding today. People are constantly refinancing mortgages at lower interest rates. People are also taking out equity loans to pay off credit card debt, a bad deal; it shouldn't be done. The big fish continue to eat the little fish. Perpetual funding, borrowing, the way of things should primarily occur, equity for equity. In the commercial world in the United States, unfortunately, this is not primary in the schools.

An act in1866 started the contraction of the greenbacks. "Ten millions of dollars may be retired and canceled within six months from the passage of this act, and therefore not more than four millions of dollars in any one month" after that. The act would stay in force unless amended. Banks bought the bonds with the greenbacks. The Treasury received the greenbacks and destroyed them. This was the beginning of the contraction. Interest on the bonds was paid in gold. Banks received interest in gold twice a year and the principal, if paid to the owner, in gold at maturity. The Treasury was retiring the short-term Treasury notes or currency bonds by borrowing. It was costing the Treasury gold to retire the greenbacks. The banks and the Treasury apparently shortchanged the people in the refunding process, taking the greenbacks out of circulation.

The national debt was 2.8 billion. But the interest-bearing debt was 2.35 billion. The $0.45 billion greenback part of the debt was non-interest-bearing. The greenback circulation was not an interest-bearing burden to the people. McCulloch's greenback priority appeared a negative trade-off, ridding the country of interest-free debt while creating interest-bearing debt to accomplish contraction. McCulloch's refunding of the interest-bearing debt would save the country about 26 million in interest each year. But if 450 million of the greenbacks were eventually destroyed and replaced by bank paper, the people would lose a minimum saving of 27 million in interest each year. The opponents of the greenback, the banks, did not wave any flags or emphasize this saving of interest to the people over a period of more than thirty years. Senator Sherman, in 1890, before the Senate, did mention the savings to the people over a ten-year period. Sherman estimated the savings to the people from $120 to $160 million. McCulloch's main strategy was to fund the greenbacks out of existence, a double whammy on the people.

There was the faction for the free circulation of the greenback currency and no contraction. The country was growing; reconstruction in the South required a great deal of money. This faction favoring the greenback circulation would grow and later become the Greenback Party. The Greenback Party, which included "many farmers from the West and South," was formidable between 1876 and 1884. The party believed that abundant money supply was coincident with good times; this certainly wasn't startling news. David Hume stated as much in his writings. The party came into power after the money panic in 1873.

Secretary McCulloch launched a period of currency contraction. At a time when the railroads, steel, oil, the telephone were industrializing the nation, the masses were being left behind. Between 1865 and 1885, the currency circulation per capita reduced by more than three times. A tremendous disparity was being created between the wealth in the country and American labor.

The greenback contraction was temporarily stopped in January of 1868, but not before 44 million had been destroyed. President Johnson received the act for his approval on January 23, 1868. Johnson didn't return the approved bill within the required ten days; there was no explanation. The act "to suspend further reduction of the Currency" became law although not signed by the president (from the Constitution, Article I, Section 7, "If any bill shall not be returned by the President within ten days [Sundays excepted], after it shall have been presented to him, the same shall become law.").

The rest of the debt, the bonds, was the funded debt. The bonds were refunded by the act of July 14, 1870. Previous bond issues allowed the Treasury to redeem after five years. This five-year redemption thing allowed the Treasury to negotiate new debt at less interest. European debt instruments were less costly than the Civil War indebtedness incurred by the United States. An amount of 1.5 billion in bonds were converted into ten- and thirty-year instruments paying from 5% to 4% to 3% in interest. All interests and principal on the converted bonds were payable in gold. So after 1870, the $2.35 billion debt was funded debt at an average interest payment of approximately 4%, a considerable saving in interest payments.

Ulysses S. Grant succeeded Johnson as president in 1868. Grant's presidency was marred by scandal. The most famous was "Black Friday." James Fisk and Jay Gould "set out to corner the gold market." Fisk and Gould, two wealthy businessmen, were also speculators. The pair within four days drove "up the price of gold sharply." Secretary of the Treasury Boutwell, by order of President Grant, sold Treasury gold to help stabilize the market. Many investors and businesses took the hit anyway. The date was "Black Friday," September 24, 1869. The gold bill was there in this case.

During this period, the Forty-first Congress was in session. This session was momentous for reasons other than the currency, the national debt, and business as usual. It was the first time since before the Civil War in which there was, once again, a complete representation in the Congress from all the states. Georgia, Mississippi, Texas, and Virginia were the last of the seceding states to return senators and congressmen to Washington. Virginia was the last. The return took five years. The year was 1870; the full complement of the Congress had been restored.

Demonetization of silver took place on February 12, 1873. This act "amended the laws of the mints" and "coinage of the United States." This act created controversy. From time to time, the Treasury amended the weights and measures of alloy to silver and gold in the minting of the nation's coins. All the existing coins were mentioned in this bill except the silver dollar. The silver dollar was simply not mentioned. At the time, the United States was producing more than 50% of the world's silver. From the beginning, it was gold and silver; specie represented gold and silver. In 1873, the silver dollar was eliminated from domestic circulation; a trade dollar was introduced for trade use. Section 15 of the bill stated "that the silver coins of the United States shall be a trade dollar, a half dollar, or fifty cent piece, a dime, or ten cent piece." In this act, the words "silver dollar" were not mentioned in the bill. By omission, coinage of the silver dollar was discontinued. The payment of interest on bonds, in the future, would be in gold. Payment of interest was always in gold anyway. A new trade dollar was minted. The trade dollar was used exclusively in Asian foreign trade, primarily with China. The trade dollar could be spent in the United States only up to a total value of $5. Another law in 1876 nullified the $5 amount. One couldn't spend a trade dollar in the United States for anything. Opponents, the friends of silver, felt the government had "dishonored" the silver dollar. At the time the 1873 act was passed, many in Congress didn't know the full content of the bill. They didn't know that the silver dollar was not mentioned in the bill. All the bills in Congress, apparently, although voted on by most of the members, are not always read by most of the members.

During the Civil War period in the Congress, silver was not a topic; it was never brought up. The debate centered on legal tender currency and gold. Davis Rich Dewey stated that silver was not a part of the monetary exchange. Dewey also mentioned a general ignorance on the part of many members in Congress concerning money matters; there was no determined effort on the part of the Congress to discontinue the silver dollar. President Grant himself was oblivious to the new law, the discontinued silver dollar. This business didn't matter; the proponents of silver would carry on.

Action was later taken to bring back the silver dollar. Congressman John E. Kenna of West Virginia voiced approval for the remonetization of the silver dollar. It was the first session of the Forty-fifth Congress; the date was February 9, 1878. Kenna in the House, said, "Such an act is not only an act of justice—it is an act of restitution as well."

Kenna cited that Alexander Hamilton and Thomas Jefferson agreed on bimetallism. Kenna repeated Hamilton's words,

> To annul the use of either of the metals as money is to abridge the quantity of circulating medium, and is liable to all the objections which arise from a comparison of the benefits of a full with the evils of a scanty circulation . . . Neither could the exclusion of either of them be deemed in other respects favorable to commerce.

Kenna noted a letter from Jefferson to Hamilton, "I concur with you that the unit must stand on both metals." The proponents of silver hoped the return of the silver dollar would ease the currency crunch. The country had been in the throes of a depression.

It was the "bondholders"; they wanted to rid the country of silver. The bondholders wanted gold for the bonds, not silver. There had to be a conspiracy, first the greenbacks, then the silver; this was the feeling of the proponents of silver. As for the bondholders, they defied the interest-free greenbacks; silver was not the specie of choice. After the Contraction Act, there was the Coinage Act of March 18, 1869. The Coinage Act stipulated gold and silver payment for all debt instruments. It was Senator Sherman who in 1865 pushed for the currency bonds (interest-bearing Treasury notes) to be paid in paper money; then later in 1869, he recanted and pushed for coin. The banks bought bonds with legal tenders, the government's paper currency. The 1869 act preceded the refunding act in 1870; whereby all the currency bonds would be paid in specie, which, after the act of 1873, would be paid in gold, silver being eliminated. All of this appeared to be gymnastics. The Treasury, primarily, was paying interest in gold anyway. All money discussions during Civil War legislation in Congress centered on gold.

There was the private debt. During the period of the Civil War, the private debt increased by $1.5 billion. American industry had borrowed heavily amid foreign investment. The private debt was owed to England and Europe. England and Europe dealt primarily in gold. Payments made to that part of the world by the United States and private industry was paid in gold. Before the Civil War, the public debt represented less than 5% of the country's total debt. After the Civil War, it was at least 25% of the total.

In 1873, there was a money panic. A depression lasted five years. Many reasons for the panic have been documented. There was the Chicago Fire in 1871; the insurance business took the hits. Many businesses failed; there were losses because of railroad construction. Four million people were out of work. According to Dewey, because of private debt and exports, gold was going to England and Europe every year; the total exceeded hundreds of millions of dollars.

United States bonds were transferred to Europe as payment for private debt. The bonds were good as gold; this occurred because of the Civil War. In effect, ownership of the public debt was being transferred by private entities, the big banks in New York, to foreigners. Secretary McCulloch estimated in 1868 foreigners owned $600,000,000 in government bonds. That means foreigners (England and Europe) owned more than 50% of the funded Civil War debt of the United States. That means that the people of the United States did not retain ownership of the Civil War debt. Then after the war, gold was demanded; there was the drain of gold to England and Europe. The accumulation of gold in that direction continued into the twentieth century. England was the creditor of all nations. Before 1914, England controlled or owned 70% of the world's gold. This is why England was the world power. In the nineteenth century, money panics occurred in the United States when there was a deficiency of specie. The panics precipitated the convulsions, contractions, and resulting depressions. It is part of the record. The population of the United States as of 1873 had increased to forty million. The adult male population dominated the workplace at the time. The male unemployment rate during the depression of the 1870s reached 14%.

> It follows that whoever can get control of the specie of the world can rule the markets with despotic hand, and may work his will upon communities and nations; and, also that such a monopoly of the circulating medium can be effected with an ease almost infinitely greater than a monopoly of any other article of general use. And thus specie money,

> from being a convenient medium of circulation, has become the tyrant of both the production and consumption of the world.

This is from the book *Solution of the Social Problem* written by Joseph Proudhon (1809-1865), nineteenth-century France. Proudhon "was a French socialist and reformer." Proudhon expounded on usury; he felt "the banker's discount should be just enough, [1%], to defray the expenses of the bank and pay for the metal unproductively employed of which the money is made." Proudhon started a "Peoples Bank." There were "27 thousand subscribers to his bank"; response was favorable, but the bank didn't last. Politics was Proudhon's undoing; Proudhon was an anarchist. Proudhon and Karl Marx corresponded in the mid-nineteenth century. It is not a wonder that Communism was rearing its ugly head; it was fermenting in the 1870s and 1880s in the United States amid the unemployment, the strikes, and unrest among labor-class America.

Why was silver supposedly de-monetized in 1873? There was more political power behind gold. Congressman Voorhees of Pennsylvania, in January 1878, said,

> From 1792 to 1873, from the coinage of the American silver dollar to the day of its insidious destruction, eighty-one years, gold and silver never fluctuated in their relation to each other but a fraction over 3 per cent; and during most of that time silver money ranked higher than gold money and did so the day it was destroyed.

The minting of gold in the United States did outdo silver by about four to one in the nineteenth century. In Europe, gold was also de-monetized. Gold was discovered in California and then in Australia. "The whole world rejoiced with one exception . . . The creditor class dreaded it." Gold was demonetized in Europe in 1857 "in order to maintain the scarcity of money." Gold was too abundant. There was a creditor fear in Europe that the debtor class may have too much access to gold. The United States was affected by the scarcity of money but not to the extent felt in Europe. Mr. Voorhees stated there was

no great creditor class in this country; we had no stupendous
national debt held as an investment for fixed incomes; no
such State, Municipal, and corporation debts as have since
filled all the stock markets with interest bearing bonds, and
which are now a draining tax on all the labor and production
of the country.

A "stupendous national debt" did occur; it was the Civil War debt.
Congressman Voorhees continued, "The creditor class is not so much
concerned what coin or other material shall constitute money, as it is
there shall be *no redundancy* after its demands are paid."

Secretary McCulloch stated the importance of a "home debt." Also,
there was the importance of an "equal distribution" of government
securities among the people. He mentioned these things in his 1868
message to the Fortieth Congress. "If the bonds of the United States
were equally distributed among the people of the different States
there would be less complaint of the debt than is now heard." There
would be no burden "if the interest upon a public debt is paid out
where the taxes to provide for it are collected." But there was a wide
gap between creditor and debtor. The creditor class, the money
interests were predominate in the eastern states and in the European
countries during the nineteenth century. The United States was a
debtor nation throughout the nineteenth century. McCulloch's words
may have sounded encouraging, but it was a period of dominant
capitalism.

The Resumption Act of January 14, 1875, demanded that specie
payment resume in 1879. Specie payment would be accomplished by
"enforcing the contraction of the non-interest bearing currency of the
country." In the words of Mr. Voorhees, it was "the destruction of all
money except gold." The enforced contraction of the greenbacks, how
was that to be done? The greenbacks were turned in for gold by banks
via the debt-funding process, and the greenbacks were destroyed by
the Treasury. But a fierce debate ensued in the Congress in 1878. The
destruction of all the greenbacks didn't happen.

Mr. Voorhees mentioned the year 1877; 44 million in gold had been
minted in the United States. The bulk of the gold was going abroad.

Since 1793, 984 million in gold had been minted in the United States, a period of eighty-four years. Voorhees mentioned "that amount of gold would not pay for one single crop of agricultural products in the western States." He mentioned eleven states; they were "Ohio, Kentucky, Indiana, Illinois, Michigan, Wisconsin, Missouri, Minnesota, Iowa, Kansas and Nebraska." Nine hundred eighty-four million in gold was a small amount "in the long space of eighty-four years, nearly the whole life-time of the American Republic." The Voorhees example illustrates in the scheme what a small fixed quantity gold really was. There wasn't but one-tenth of gold in the country in 1878 compared to currency circulation. How was the country "to do business on a specie basis"? How was 70 million in gold going to buy up the paper circulation? Secretary McCulloch in 1868 stated that since 1848, the United States had "parted with" $1.1 billion in gold and silver for the payment of foreign production. The departed coin was the product of "California and the territories."

Congressman Voorhees estimated the public and private debt to be $6 to $9 billion. After January 1879, by act of 1875, indebtedness was paid in gold but with a contracted currency. That was the problem; total cost of the indebtedness remained the same, and the circulating currency would begin to vanish. The people piled on the debt with an expanded or inflated currency. The money interests call for the note in gold; the smoke clears, and the debt number remains fixed. But the payoff must be done with a resultant contraction of less currency. "A thousand-dollar bond for which only $600 in gold was realized by the Government, in its distress, at the time of its issue, has now to be taken up and paid for with over a thousand dollars in gold by the tax-payers." This was the insidious contrivance, the trend in the nineteenth century, the money panics and resultant loss of money and property. A similar trend continued into the twentieth century.

The circulation of money was the topic and continuation of the debate in early 1878, the members of Congress who represented the West and the South, who favored the greenback circulation, restoration of the silver dollar, the maintenance of an ample money supply. There was the opposition, the members in Congress who favored gold, the national uniform currency, currency contraction, and a return to specie payment.

The Greenback Party was against the Resumption Act. This party didn't want government bonds sold to foreigners; they were for "limiting" the uniform currency circulation. The Greenback Party was successful in legal tender survival. The Resumption Act of 1875 called for the cancellation of the greenback currency to be effective in 1879. It didn't happen!

The Forty-fifth Congress Second session stopped the destruction of the greenback. The act became law on May 31, 1878. See Chap. 146 on page 87 in the Book of Statutes, in the Library of Congress, Jefferson and Madison Buildings.

> An Act to forbid the further retirement of United states legal tender notes . . . And when any of said notes [United States legal tender notes] may be redeemed or be received into the Treasury under any law from any source whatever and shall be belong to the United States, they shall not be retired canceled or destroyed but they shall be re-issued and paid out again and kept in circulation.

The non-interest-bearing part of the national debt remained in circulation, $360 million worth of a much-needed circulating currency.

The government's policy since McCulloch (1866) was contraction of the currency. The paper circulation in 1866 was $705 million. In 1878, the circulation was $710 million, an increase of 1%. But the U.S. population increased almost 40% since the Civil War. Contraction of the currency did the job; available money per person decreased from approximately $45 to $15 per person. In 1878, Congressman Giddings in the House, said, "England has a money circulation of $28 *per capita*; France, $44 *per capita*; and Germany $24 *per capita*." It would appear that maybe the "inflationist successes" was an attempt by the Greenback Party to keep a living standard in the United States on a par with England and Europe. Mr. Giddings said the United States was "so vast a territory we require at least $30 *per capita*." But there was a problem. Giddings mentioned insufficient gold in the country to support an increased circulation. On top of that, the proponents of gold wanted to return to specie payment in 1879 upon "the single standard." Silver wasn't wanted. The proponents of gold wanted to destroy the greenbacks, reduce the national currency, and diminish the circulation. The Bland-Allison Act of 1878 restored the silver dollar; it was the advent of the Morgan silver dollar. The proponents of silver had won the day? Silver was again part of the specie base? Legal tenders and other paper instruments may again be exchanged for silver? Not really! The bankers, the bondholders, the U.S./England/ European connection, those who preferred gold for their bonds would still get the gold; they preferred gold at redemption, and the U.S. Treasury secretaries apparently accommodated.

A money panic and depression occurred in 1837, 1857, 1873, and 1884. There was a money panic and depression in 1893, another money panic and depression in 1907. The 1907 panic lead to the Federal Reserve Act in 1913. The Federal Reserve Act was supposedly the cure for the nation's financial ills. But the same elements persisted; there was a depression in 1921. The stock market crash of 1929 followed; the Great Depression followed that. World Wars I and II interrupted the apparent perpetrated trends.

Hugh McCulloch, in his December 1884 message to the Congress, emphasized the pay down of the national debt since 1865, the national banking system, and the over accumulation of silver in the Treasury. The debt in 1865 was $2.8 billion. The debt in 1884 had been reduced to $1.4 billion. During the period, the annual interest payments were reduced from 6% to 3%. The refunding act of 1870 reduced the interest rates. The sinking fund was a concerted effort during the period. The debt principal was reduced by $47 million during the year 1884 alone, a remarkable effort. "It is true all this has been effected by heavy taxes, but it is also true that these taxes have neither checked enterprise or retarded growth." There was plenty of growth; it was the great industrial period. But 1884 also saw "industrial unrest . . . many mines shut down . . . there was a large 'army' of the unemployed." McCulloch, in his report, didn't address the money panic or the unemployed. The interest-bearing national debt was $1 billion; $400 million of debt was the non-interest-bearing greenback circulation.

The Resumption Act (1879) stated that the greenback would be accepted at all customhouses, thus making the greenback equal to gold. The Treasury on receiving the United States Notes or legal tenders or greenbacks held them for gold redemption. The greenbacks were saved, made equal to gold, and the cost of their use would be more payment in gold or its equivalent paid to the banks.

There was a problem with the national bank circulation. In November of 1884, there were 2,672 national banks. "Since the establishment of the National Banking System, on February 25, 1863, there have been organized 3,261 National Banks." Four hundred eighty-nine banks had failed; presently, one hundred were in receivership. There were $290 million of the national currency in circulation and $1.2 billion in loans and discounts. "Individual deposits" totaled almost a billion dollars. Bank specie totaled 129 million, and the U.S. "bonds to secure circulation were 327 million dollars." And here was the impending problem. The national uniform currency circulation was based on the purchase of bonds. The bonds securing the circulation were coming due. "In as much as about $ 135,000,000 of the circulation of banks is based upon our 3 per cent bonds, which are now redeemable and being rapidly redeemed, remedial action cannot be postponed beyond the present Session if a rapid reduction of our bank-note circulation is to be avoided." McCulloch went on to laud Secretary Chase for starting the national system. "Its preservation is a matter of national importance; its discontinuance would be a national calamity." President Chester Arthur, in his message, said, "The probable effect of such an extensive retirement of the securities [bonds] which are the basis of the national-bank circulation would be such a contraction of the volume of the currency as to produce grave commercial embarrassments." McCulloch recommended eliminating the tax on the circulation and the issue of the currency to 100% of the face value of the bonds. New twenty-year bonds would be sold to secure the circulation temporarily. The currency to 100% face value of the bonds would, hopefully, take place in 1895. An issue to 100% face value of the bonds meant eliminating the government's initial discount of 10% on the national currency.

In 1884, the government was faced with maturing bonds in the amount of 135 million dollars. These bonds, payable in gold, were purchased with paper money. Paying off the bonds would eliminate the circulation, a dilemma, to say the least.

The demand for commodities and services should be coincident with the natural growth of the country with the increase in population and employment. The increase in the money supply should meet that demand. It would appear that this "purchase" of United States bonds by private banks was not totally responsive to business, to money supply, nor did it guarantee a continuance of a future credit circulation. Nineteenth-century 20 year bonds for currency would end in 1913. In 1913, a new elastic currency would be introduced, a government obligation, and a bond to secure the obligation became a debt in perpetuity. The national bank currency would remain in place.

"We now hold $ 147,573,221.89 in Silver." McCulloch called the amount "so large as to become burdensome, and additional vaults must be soon constructed if the coinage is to be continued." Silver was accumulating in the Treasury; there was a lack of silver in circulation. The banks didn't want silver, and as written by Dewey, the people didn't want the silver dollars either. "The people were not accustomed to use coins of heavy weight, and under the original Act, no provision was made for the issue of silver certificates in denominations of less than ten dollars."

According to Dewey, the final resting place for the silver dollars was in the government Sub-treasuries. That is where the silver dollars stayed for more than a hundred years. A vast reserve of silver dollars never circulated. After one hundred years, in the 1990s, vaulted Morgan silver dollars were made available to collectors.

In 1872, silver was more valuable than gold. Germany in the 1870s "demonetized" silver, "throwing upon the market the large amount, which up to that time, had constituted her metallic currency." Other European nations also restricted its coinage. "In 1874 the decline commenced, and it has been continued until the silver dollar is worth only about 85 cents in gold; and further depreciation is prevented by its having been made receivable by the United States for all public dues and the coinage at the rate of $28,000,000 a year." McCulloch emphasized the demonetization of silver by Germany and Europe in his message, but the United States demonetized silver as well in 1873. From the recorded events, it would appear the United States and Europe, almost at the same time, depreciated silver. The silver advocates in the United States stopped the demonetization with the Bland-Allison Act of 1878. There would be free coinage of silver, and the issue of silver certificates and the surplus started. McCulloch said the silver certificates would increase by $50 million with coinage continuing. By law, the certificates were "receivable for duties." But "neither standard silver dollars nor silver certificates have been or are now offered in settlement of balances at the clearing-house." The "clearing house" was the clearinghouse in New York, which didn't accept silver. Transactions were done in gold or notes representing gold. The result was there was a drain of gold from the Treasury. The gold drain was 40 million, and the silver increase was 20 million in 1884. The U.S. Treasury was a member of the New York clearinghouse. McCulloch felt it imperative that the coinage of silver be stopped, or silver would replace gold as the primary specie.

The United States Notes or legal tenders or greenbacks were saved in 1878 but for a price. The Treasury had to have gold. The 1875 Resumption Act took effect in 1879. Specie payment returned; suspension was over. The Treasury had to maintain a minimum surplus of 100 million in gold to redeem or pay for legal tenders held by banks. That was the deal; the greenbacks were saved, but the banks would receive gold at redemption and semiannual interest in gold for the bonds. The $100 million gold surplus in the Treasury appeared to belong to the banks. The price was 4 million in gold per year in interest or almost 100 million to the banks by the turn of the century. But the cost of 346 million in greenbacks if replaced by bank paper at 6% interest would have cost about $500 million to the people. The greenback in the latter part of the nineteenth century was on a par with gold. The greenback was no longer a "repudiated" currency. As the gold supply lessened, the Treasury had to sell bonds from time to time to replenish the reserve.

It was gold. The banks wanted the gold, needed the gold. England and Europe demanded gold when payment was due, and at the time of export, silver was jeopardizing that. McCulloch said,

> Many persons regard legal tenders as being money, and hold that no means should be provided for their redemption. That this is a delusion will be shown whenever there is

a large demand for gold for export. They are not money,
but merely promises to pay, and the Government must be
prepared to redeem all that may be presented or forfeit its
character for solvency.

McCulloch wasn't enamored with the greenbacks. Whether McCulloch
accepted it or not—and apparently, he didn't—the greenbacks were
part of the nation's currency by law, legal tender money. They were
an established currency by Act of Congress.

The paper currency that McCulloch said could not be money, was
money. McCulloch said the legal tender greenback was not money,
only a promise to pay. He mentioned panic time if gold left the country.
Proudhon's opinion appeared in tune; because of the structured
money scheme, the controllers and owners of specie held "a veto
on the action of money." Did the proponents of gold control the
mentality, or was it simply the mentality? In the beginning, the first
United States bank's non-legal tender paper currency was a promise
to pay. McCulloch said the government would "forfeit its character"
if it didn't pay on its paper currency. Since the beginning, did the
banks forfeit their character when they refused to pay on their paper
currency during all the suspensions, all the emergencies, and all the
panics? What kind of paper money scheme by the banks, based on
specie, was not suspect when the periodic demand for payment and
export of the specie, to the beat of the drum, extinguished their
own paper money, which preceded the panics? Benjamin Franklin
and Thomas Jefferson were skeptical and disapproved of the specie/
paper money scheme.

There was the promise to pay, and there was depletion of specie,
which dried up the promise to pay. Why a promise to pay? Gold and
silver was the real money? Specie was nonperishable; it was intrinsic.
Specie, the money in and of itself, was the established value and also
the problem. There was so little of it. Hamilton's bank printed the
paper money, which was not real money; it only represented the
real money? But this paper money, which was not the real money,
was an acceptable abundant exchange for public and private debts,
property, commodities, and government dues. John Jay and the
Supreme Court said it was OK; it was constitutional. This pyramidal

paper money scheme, based on commercial paper and specie reserve, and deposits upon deposits, escalated prices multiple times beyond actual values. There was capitalization, and there was growth, which precipitated the creation of more paper money. It was neat, a most clever money scheme, and the country grew not because of specie but in spite of it. At apparent scheduled intervals, the money interests demanded payment in gold; but after, whoops, there was insufficient gold. And then there was no gold and no money. The inflated cost of indebtedness through paper remained the same. Payment would have to be made at the escalated price of gold. If not, there was the eventual takeover and property loss, "no redundancy," partners to the end; but it was the end. Why were two exchanges necessary for the purchase of one commodity? Having to pay in gold established gold as the value above all other values. Paper currency and the promise to pay the establishment of gold as the money and the security was clever, the perfect trick; it allowed the proponents to purchase gold, to accumulate gold, to demand gold, and, with that gold, extinguish currencies and control the economies of countries.

"Every fair and legal effort has been made by the Treasury Department to distribute this currency among the people." This was President Grover Cleveland's silver message to the Congress in December 1886. "The Director of the Mint again urges the necessity of more vault room for the purpose of storing these silver dollars which are not needed for circulation by the people." There was a $73 million silver surplus in the Treasury, 167 million in circulation. Silver included silver dollars and $10 silver certificates. Ten-dollar silver certificates were issued to entities depositing silver dollars in the Treasury. The price of silver had fallen from 94¢ (1878) to 78¢ in 1886. The 1878 act was a compulsory coinage act, free coinage. Cleveland called for the suspension of the silver coinage; there was ample circulation among the people. Also, there had been "significant increase of our gold exportations during the last year."

The silver glut mounted in the 1880s. The "1890 Sherman Silver Purchase Act" was an effort to change things. The Silver Act of 1890 repealed the "monthly purchase and Coinage clause" of the Bland-Allison Act of 1878. After 1878, the secretary could purchase up to $4 million in silver bullion and "coin the same" in silver dollars per month. Bimetallic parity of silver with gold was to be established with all countries. After 1890, the secretary purchased silver by the ounce "from time to time" as required. Treasury notes were printed and issued by the Treasury to pay for the silver. The notes were in denominations of $1 to $1,000. The $1, $2, $5 silver certificates were a currency circulation for the people. The notes were legal tender for all public dues, customs, taxes, etc., and redeemable for gold and silver. Unlimited silver coinage was out although all mined silver would be purchased.

"After July 1, 1891, standard silver dollars were to be coined only when necessary for the redemption of notes." The Treasury notes could be used as reserves in national banks as well as redemption for gold and silver coin. This was Senator Sherman's bill. "For substituting the measurement of purchases by ounces instead of by dollars, Senator Sherman has the credit, and its importance becomes obvious in view of the subsequent fall in the value of Silver." According to Dewey, Sherman's 1890 bill reduced silver additions, thereby lessening the surplus in the Treasury while the 1878 act increased the surplus. Silver fell in value in either case.

If an entity-redeeming Treasury notes after July 1891 asked for silver coin, silver coins would have to be coined. But in most cases, gold was wanted and requested; silver would not be coined. Thus, silver coinage was reduced. What angered the opponents of gold was that the creditors were allowed by the Treasury to make the choice of gold rather than silver. Democrats claimed it was the fault of the secretaries of the Treasury. The act of 1890 stated that the Treasury notes would be issued by the Treasury for the purchase of silver, but the law also stated that the Treasury notes could be redeemed in both gold and silver. It was a clever bill by Senator Sherman. It led to the open demand for more gold at redemption, "keeping silver out of use"; there would be less silver coinage. The friends of silver expected "parity"; it wasn't happening. Because of opposing clamor, "the purchasing clause of the Sherman Law of 1890 was repealed" in November 1893.

In 1894, Grover Cleveland was the twenty-fourth president of the United States. "Underlying causes of the depression were rapidly dwindling gold reserves, industrial over expansion, poor crop harvests in the South and West, and an economic slump in Europe." Dewey recorded the collapse of the house of Barings in 1990. The Barings's collapse contributed to the drain of gold from the United States. Businesses and railroads failed; "hundreds of millions of dollars" were lost. The Pullman Strike occurred during the period, which affected the railroads and business. Almost six hundred national, state, private, and savings banks and trust companies failed amid strikes, riots, and a march in Washington.

Grover Cleveland was a proponent of gold. Cleveland wanted a "stable currency" for the people maintained by gold, and the gold was leaving the country. Great! This appeared to be another frustrating admission and stance in the vast array of apparent continuing contradictions. The money exchanges included gold and silver coin, gold and silver certificates, greenbacks, currency certificates, Treasury notes, and the national currency. On the surface, it would appear to be a government/banking varied currency issue constituting a contracted money supply, which continued as the United States neared the twentieth century.

Secretary of the Treasury J. G. Carlisle presented a currency plan to the Congress in December of 1894. Secretary Carlisle sought the "permanent retirement of United States legal-tender notes of both classes." Both classes meant the greenbacks and the Treasury notes of 1890. Carlisle wanted to "secure within a reasonable time a safe and elastic National and State bank currency." As far as Mr. Carlisle was concerned, because of the redemption process, the greenbacks and Treasury notes were a "constant menace to the gold reserve." The notes are repeatedly "reissued and are now outstanding." Secretary Carlisle stated that the redemption/reissue process "endangers the entire volume of our currency, discredits the obligations of the Government and the people, increases the public debt, and seriously embarrasses the administration of our financial affairs." Carlisle wanted "to repeal all laws providing for the deposit of United States bonds as security for circulation" (That made sense). Also, state bank issues would be exempt from federal taxation. Senator John S. Carlile from Virginia, during the Civil War, wanted to start an agency in New York to run the country's money, its financial affairs.

What is an "elastic currency"? From the dictionary, in the figurative sense, "elastic" means "easily changed to suit conditions, flexible, adaptable." In the banker's vernacular, elastic currency meant to contract or expand the currency to meet the conditions of business and employment. Secretary Carlisle and the bankers wanted the issue of the paper currency to be controlled exclusively by state and national banks. Carlisle said the country's currency was "fixed." He said,

> Under our present currency system, so far as it consists of notes issued by the United States Government, the volume of circulation was intended to be, and is, in fact, unchangeable; it is unalterably fixed at a certain amount and, no matter how great the emergency may be, it can neither be enlarged or diminished.

Carlisle mentioned that the only currency with any elasticity was the national currency (2.5 billion deposits/325 million circulation), but this currency amount was only "twelve per cent of the whole." The whole was the gold coin, silver coin, gold certificates, silver certificates, the greenbacks, the Treasury notes, etc. The nation's currency situation was a "failure." Carlisle mentioned "three principal causes," namely, "the large volume of United States currency of various kinds kept constantly outstanding"; the ineffective national currency as a result of the whole; and the deposit of bonds for security of the circulation. When expansion of the currency was needed, it couldn't be provided. The deposit of long-term bonds was required prior to issue of the currency, and the issue of the currency required "thirty to sixty days." Emergencies could not be met. Also, the bonds were at a premium, above par during those periods; and the currency issue was 90% of the par value of the bond, a loss for the banks, according to the banks. The banks were not paying currency for these bonds; the banks received currency from the Treasury based on the market value of the bonds. This maneuver carried over when the Federal Reserve Act came to being as we shall see.

What was the significance of the "large volume of United States currency of various kinds kept constantly outstanding?" What did it mean? The proliferation of money—the creation of money, the expansion of the money supply, and then contraction—was not working. Carlisle wanted the banks to control the currency issue and no bonds as security. The "outstanding" currency was out there for redemption in gold and maybe silver. And the gold was needed in the Treasury, and the "outstanding currency" would be redeemed again. And the gold was needed in the Treasury, and on and on it went. The banks collected interest on the gold during this exercise. The "outstanding" currency was not expanding/contracting; it was not meeting commercial/industrial demands. It was stagnant? Secretary Carlisle said the "outstanding" currency was "fixed" and "unchangeable." The currency could not be "enlarged or diminished." The only currency that may expand or contract was the national currency. The silver certificates were supposedly in circulation and there for redemption in silver. The gold certificates were there for redemption in gold. The greenback issue totaled approximately 450 million after the Civil War; it totaled 360 plus million in the year 1900. During a period of thirty-five years, the greenbacks were basically "fixed"; gold was kept in the Treasury for their redemption. In the banking scheme, there could be no capitalization based on a greenback circulation. Capitalization is an integral function of an elastic currency. Secretary Carlisle said the national currency was the only part of the whole with elastic capability. The national currency was the credit circulation idea; it was too small a part of an entire picture. The post-Civil War financial complexities and impasse between the federal government and the banks had continued and was working quite well as the country entered the twentieth century. Secretary Carlisle was right about the fixed circulation thing. Secretary Carlisle proposed a twelve-part plan. The Carlisle plan would become "the Carlisle Bill." The bill, prepared in 1895, was vigorously debated in the Congress; and it didn't pass as such. Carlisle's plan became part of the Gold Standard Act in 1900.

> The Currency—Volume controls price and prices control profits, prosperity, and the equity of all time payments—Who then should control volume.

This was the premise of Congressman Henry Coffeen of Wyoming; he debated the Carlisle bill in the House on January 8, 1895. "We demand the suppression of all bank issues and the future issuance of all forms of money, whether coin or paper, by the Federal Government, making all issues full legal tender, and controlling and regulating the volume in strict accord with the interests of industry and the maintenance of equity." Congressman Coffeen lumped the American Bankers Association with the European moneyed interests into one description. He called them the money power. Coffeen felt the money power was concealing "their main purpose in all the proposed legislation before us." Coffeen also called them the money dealers. Their purpose for "themselves" was to have "the power to expand or contract the volume of currency suddenly and entirely at their own option, so to control the value of money and credits in their relation to property and profits."

Coffeen, a Democrat, presented an interesting statistic. The money dealers had been "raiding" the Treasury of gold. The "raiding" was by design. Beginning in 1891, $50 million in Treasury notes were redeemed for gold in a two-year period. The Sherman clause of the 1890 Silver Act was repealed to stop the "raid." Remember; the Treasury notes were redeemable for gold and silver. The act was passed to achieve silver parity with gold. Senator Sherman was acclaimed for not allowing that to happen. The clause was repealed, but the "raid" continued with greenbacks. In 1894, $124 million in greenbacks were redeemed for gold. Coffeen said the money power were "retiring greenbacks to secure the issue of bonds." Coffeen showed a table; more greenbacks were redeemed in the year 1894 than in the previous thirteen years. D. N. Morgan, treasurer of the United States, upon request, presented the table to Congressman Coffeen. With reference to the exporting of gold, Coffeen said, "Much of the gold that was drawn on Treasury notes and others while the scare was being worked up against Treasury notes and to secure the repeal of the Silver-Purchase Clause, was shipped back again from Europe in the same kegs that contained the gold when exported." Coffeen accused the money power of using the Carlisle bill "to turn over the issuance of all paper currency to both State and Federal banks." This could be done by "discrediting the Greenback and preparing an excuse for the Secretary to sell more bonds to the raiders, to get the looted gold back again." The secretaries of the Treasury were accused of being too cooperative in relinquishing gold to creditors instead of the silver in the Treasury, a claim and a sore spot with the Democrats. This as reported by Coffeen in the *Congressional Record*.

One gets a different slant when reading Dewey. "There was a reversal of Treasury practice." In 1890, there was a subsequent dearth of gold in the banks. According to Dewey, the banks needed gold for trade purposes. The banks went to the Treasury with their "government notes" for gold; the banks apparently had the lawful money greenbacks, which were good for gold. There was this huge exchange of greenbacks at the Treasury, and the gold went to Europe.

Congressman Coffeen called it a "raiding" of the Treasury. Dewey said a Treasury reversal practice started in August of 1890. The Sherman Silver Purchase Act became law in July of 1890. But Dewey also mentioned the Barings collapse of 1890; there was the drain of gold from the United States. The banks and dealers apparently used the Treasury notes and the greenbacks to get the gold for foreign accounts due and not just for trade? In any event, there was a foreign collapse, and gold was shipped out.

Congressman Coffeen mentioned the "'Scare Word' of 'Fiat Money.'" It is now generally seen and conceded, and no member on this floor will deny that money cannot be coined or issued or otherwise sufficiently certified for general circulation without the authority of law. And the right and force of money as such, whatever it may be, are legal rights—not natural. In short, money is the creature of law. All genuine money, whether coin or paper, is in this sense fiat money. The term "fiat money" is another scare word or "bogeyman" with which "the cunning bank syndicate would scare people out of the right to exercise their own authority to issue legal tender notes. Bank notes cannot and do not circulate in this country except by the fiat of law. They are the joint creation or "fiat of the banks and the Government."

In the Gold Standard Act of March 1900, legislation favored the national banking associations. Secretary Lyman Gage, in his December summary report, mentioned the positive: there would be more maintenance of the gold standard by the government. There was more gold in the Treasury than at any time in history. The National Bank Note issue had been "liberalized." The banks would now receive 100% of the bond security in paper money issue. There were already "$77,000,000" additional notes in circulation. This would account for the upswing in individual bank deposits in 1900.

The "purchasing" of bonds as security remained an essential part of the system. But Secretary Gage added that there was

> no assurance whatever that the volume of bank currency
> will be continuously responsive to the country's needs,
> either by expanding as such needs require or by contracting
> when superfluous in amount. The truth is that, safe and
> desirable as is our currency system in many respects, it is
> not properly related. The supply of currency is but remotely,
> if at all, influenced by the ever-changing requirements of
> trade and industry. It is related most largely, if not entirely,
> to the price of Government bonds in the market.

Secretaries of the Treasury McCulloch, Carlisle, and Gage—their policies appeared in concert with the bankers, the bondholders, the England/European connection, the "Money Power." The money power wanted the banks to control the paper currency issue and gold lurking behind the scenes.

Thomas Jefferson said,

> I have never been the enemy of banks, not of those
> discounting for cash [gold], but of those foisting their own
> paper into circulation and thus banishing our cash. My
> zeal against those institutions was so warm and open at
> the establishment of the bank of the United States that I
> was derided as a maniac by the tribe of bank mongers who
> were seeking to filch from the public their swindling and
> barren gains.

Jefferson's legacy was enduring. William Jennings Bryan echoed Jefferson's words when speaking in the House in December 1894. Bryan was in opposition to the money power. Bryan was a proponent of a government-controlled issue of the currency. William Jennings Bryan arrived in Washington in 1891. Bryan was a champion of silver. Bryan was elected to the House of Representatives. He was born in Illinois; he went to school there, and he settled in Nebraska. Bryan represented Nebraska in Congress and was a leader for the Western and the Southern States. He was for the greenback, free coinage of silver, and an ample money supply. The tariff and the currency needed to be changed; they were the big issues. Bryan was in favor of a federal income tax based on wages. Bryan felt an income tax was fairer to the workingman than a protective tariff. It was Bryan's contention that the protective tariff favored the money interests. Bryan said that 80% of customs went into the pockets of big business; the Treasury received only 20%. Bryan, as a Democrat and Populist, ran for the presidency twice against the Republican William McKinley in 1896 and 1900. Bryan was tabbed a radical, a demagogue, a socialist. McKinley, backed by the industrial East, defeated Bryan both times. In 1908, Bryan ran against William Howard Taft and lost again.

In December of 1894, in the House, William Jennings Bryan answered President Grover Cleveland's endorsement of the Carlisle plan. In his message to the Fifty-third Congress, Cleveland said, "The absolute divorcement of the Government from the business of banking is the ideal relationship of the Government to the circulation of the currency of the country." Bryan refuted President Cleveland's remarks; he said,

> Mr. Jefferson thought that the issue of paper money was more a function of the government; and that the banks ought to go out of the governing business; and I am not ashamed to say that I would rather stand with Thomas Jefferson and drive the banks out of the governing business, than to stand with Grover Cleveland and drive the Government out of the business of issuing paper money.

There was applause in the House. Bryan gained prominence swiftly. When Bryan ran against William McKinley in 1896, he was just thirty-six years old. It was at the convention in Chicago when he made his famous "Cross of Gold" speech. Speaking of the proponents of the "gold standard," he said, "You shall not press down upon the brow of labor this crown of thorns, you shall not crucify mankind upon a cross of gold." The speech won him the nomination. He didn't return to Congress after losing his presidential bid. While in Congress, he debated against the "protective tariff." Bryan maintained that the protective tariff money went into the pockets of industry and not to the American worker as promised.

The tariff act of 1890 (July 1) was enacted during the same period as the Sherman Silver Purchase Act (July 14). It was another "Protectionist Measure." William McKinley, heading the Ways and Means Committee, spearheaded the bill; it was appropriately called the McKinley Tariff. McKinley's protection of American industry inflated the cost of domestic goods; it didn't help the American consumer or commercial interests. Between 1890 and 1894, receipts from customs reduced by $100 million; Treasury gold reserves plummeted. "In June of 1893, the British Government closed the mints in India to the free coinage of silver." Dewey records that "the price of silver bullion fell rapidly . . . public opinion, at least in the Eastern States, was aroused to a belief that the entire financial problem was associated with the coinage of silver." The Panic of 1893 followed. But there was a great movement of gold, a demand for payment by the foreign money interests. And out of the country went the gold, and when that happened, there was the contraction of the money supply; it lasted four years. A new tariff act in 1894, although not signed by President Cleveland, lowered the McKinley Tariff. Included in the bill was an income tax of 2% on annual wages above $4,000. The income tax was never enforced. The following year, the Supreme Court declared the income tax unconstitutional.

In December 1897, McKinley, as president, asked the Congress to remedy the great "evil." The great evil was the nation's currency. Before getting into the evil, McKinley emphasized that the interest-bearing national debt was down to $850 million, and yearly expenditures had been reduced by almost 300 million from the previous year. McKinley mentioned the $900 million of government circulating currency. This currency included the greenbacks, the Treasury notes of 1890, the silver certificates, and the silver dollars. By law, this currency had to be kept "at par with gold." McKinley continued,

> Nobody is obliged to redeem in gold but the Government. The banks are not required to redeem in gold. The Government is obliged to keep equal with gold all its outstanding currency and obligations, while its receipts are not required to be paid in gold. They are paid in every kind of money but gold, and the only means by which the Government can with certainty get gold is by borrowing. It can get it in no other way when it needs it most.

The government had to continuously "increase its bonded debt" to maintain "the gold reserve." According to McKinley, "the Government should be relieved from the burden of providing all the gold required for exchanges and export . . . The banks do not feel the strain of gold redemption." McKinley was critical of the greenbacks. He said the greenbacks should be set aside after redemption for gold and not reissued. Why should the "government issue an interest-bearing debt to provide gold for the redemption of United States Notes—a non-interest-bearing debt"? McKinley urged the Congress to adopt the plan of the secretary of the Treasury Lyman Gage. Gage's plan was simply an extension of the Carlisle plan, parts of which ultimately became the Gold Standard Act of 1900. The Carlisle plan reflected a plan adopted by the "American Bankers' Association" in Baltimore, Maryland. The plan became known as the Baltimore Plan. Carlisle wanted to do away with the purchase of bonds as security and substitute the deposit of greenbacks and Treasury notes. This never came to pass. After becoming president, Republican William McKinley restored the protective tariff, but it was "inadequate." The 1894 tariff was replaced by the "Dingley Tariff Act of 1897," a more revenue-oriented tariff to restore Treasury deficits.

On December 14, 1899, Congressman James T. McCleary, a Republican from Minnesota, in the House of Representatives, favored a bill that would eventually become the Gold Standard Act of 1900. McCleary talked down to the Democrats, the Populists, and silver. He emphasized the need for "the liberalization of our system of bank-note issues."

SILVER HAS NOT BEEN DEMONITIZED IN THIS COUNTRY.

This was McCleary's observation. McCleary explained, "The so called 'Free Coinage' of silver means the coinage of silver on private account." In other words, anyone, a citizen, a private entity could have their silver bullion minted into silver dollars without charge at the mint. A citizen or private entity would have control of its minted money. The Populists' "platform" was the free coinage of silver, which would allow the private entity to control its money. But the Populists also wanted the government to control the issue of the nation's currency. The Populists also did not want the private banks to control the currency issue. How can that be? This was McCleary's directory to the "other side" of the aisle. There had to be a contradiction in their political philosophy.

McCleary went on; he said there was no "crime" in 1873. How could Silver ever be demonetized when it really was never used? McCleary said that before 1873, "in all This Century we have not coined a single silver dollar on private account for use as money." He mentioned that all the mints were open, "open to the free coinage and unlimited coinage of silver . . . during all that time."

McCleary explained the beginnings of the American silver dollar and gold dollar. He referred to the Coinage Act of 1792. The British units were impractical: "Shillings, Pence, Farthings." The "Old Spanish Milled Dollar" was adopted; "it was in circulation" at the time. The Spanish dollar was a silver dollar.

McCleary continued that it was decided that "371 and ½ grains of Silver would make up the dollar." This was decided after weighing an average number of new and used Spanish dollars in circulation. Hamilton and Jefferson decided that a "market proportion" would determine the gold dollar. "Upon investigation it was found that at that time the commercial ratio of gold to silver was 15:1. This was adopted as the legal ratio, Section 11 of the Mintage Act of April 2, 1792. The gold dollar at 24.75 was the number of grains to the gold dollar," 371.5 divided by 15 equals 24.8. The "eagle" or $10 gold piece was chosen as the minimum-size gold coin. The "gold dollar piece was too small a coin for practical money uses." Fractional silver coins followed, dimes, quarters, and half-dollars in different "degrees of fineness" of the silver dollar. "By the year 1833 the commercial ratio of silver to Gold had fallen to 15.93" The ratio was changed to 16:1 in 1834. The 16:1 ratio was in effect in 1900.

McCleary mentioned that in 1806, Thomas Jefferson ordered the discontinuance of silver coinage. The reason, silver coins were being purchased and shipped out of the country. Between 1805 and 1835, not a single "silver dollar piece was coined in the United States." McCleary mentioned that Jefferson, Madison, and Monroe were the presidents, all Democrats, during this absence of silver coin. All this seems peculiar since McCleary also stated that from 1792 to 1834, silver was the standard of value. Three hundred seventy-one plus grains in the silver dollar was established first; "by it the value of everything, *including gold*, was measured." Gold was "at a premium" measured against silver." After 1834, gold would become the standard of value. "Silver coins were at a premium as measured in gold."

McCleary reiterated that "gold was the actual standard even during the Civil War." Also, "that 'coin' bonds have always been gold bonds." Referring to the gold standard bill, McCleary said, "The bill gives to silver, either as coin or as silver certificates, the entire work of pocket money. It is believed that in this way all the tremendous amount of silver which the Government has bought can be safely used and that none need be sold." Since 1878, silver was purchased and coined "on Government account." It was McCleary's contention that "the Government has a right to buy silver for just one purpose, to meet the demands of business for silver coin." He compared the government business demands of silver coin, in "principal" to the buying of "oats for its cavalry horses." McCleary and the Republican side of the House held no esteem for silver as part of the nation's money.

As of July 1897, Lyman Gage, in his Treasury report, listed $696 million in gold "stock" in the country and 635 million in silver. The abundance of the silver was in Treasury depositories where it would remain. Silver certificates would continue to circulate into the twentieth century; they would represent a stilled silver stock.

> As I said before, this bill does not look to the retirement of the Greenbacks. It looks only to rendering their existence as little dangerous as possible; and there is little likelihood that in the immediate future the question of their disposition will have serious consideration . . . Personally, after considerable study of the subject, I am firmly of the opinion that we should move away from a political currency toward a business currency: away from an inelastic and unresponsive currency toward one which is elastic and which responds to the needs of business; away from the expensive currency which necessitates high interest rates to the currency which will give us, as a people, the best interest rates in the world.

McCleary didn't like the greenbacks. When finished, McCleary received "loud applause on the Republican side."

McCleary's comment, "It looks only to rendering their existence as little dangerous as possible," is amusing. Were the greenbacks "dangerous" because they were not interest bearing? Congressman McCleary mentioned getting "away from a political currency." Hasn't the currency always been political? The First Congress approved Hamilton's bank and currency scheme. The country's money—whether gold, silver, or paper currency—was political from the start. The currency is the exchange in the political economy. When looking up "economy" in the dictionary, reference is made to "political economy"; when looking up "political economy," reference is made to "economy." From this viewpoint, there is no other legal U.S. currency but a political currency as controlled by the government's Treasury and its retailer, the Federal Reserve System.

When looking at the function of capitalization in the money creation scheme, were the banking interests correct in the year 1900? A more elastic currency appeared the right way to go. Before the Civil War, the first and second central banks and the private and state banks printed and issued paper currencies that were elastic? After the Civil War, with government printing the paper currency, there was less elasticity, too many "fixed" currencies, according to Secretary Carlisle. But the many expansions and extreme contractions of currency, the money panics occurred during both periods. The one consistent variable constant—preceding the recessions, and depressions, with resultant business and property loss, since Alexander Hamilton's First Bank, during the entire time—was the banishment of specie, primarily gold. The owners of gold "held a veto on the action of money" the entire time, the apparent trick and accumulation of wealth by few always in place.

Congressman Coffeen did not want the banks to control the volume of currency.

> Their profits on circulation arise wholly upon the practice of increasing the circulation above the reserve, and the *more they are permitted to owe the people* on their circulation

the greater their profits. *They draw interest on what they owe*, which encourages them to put out larger quantities of their promissory notes.

It is a remarkable trick!

The statement by Congressman Coffeen emulated Thomas Jefferson's analysis, "drawing interest on what they owe." By the law of the First Congress, the First Bank was allowed to increase the volume of the paper currency well above the reserve at little cost, and the bank realized great profit when discounting that paper currency. The allowed increase in volume of the currency over and above the reserve was, and is to this day, currency the bank owes the people (as articulated by Thomas Jefferson more than two hundred years ago).

The 1792 money creation scheme, or capitalization in the form of paper currency, at great profit to money interests resulted because of the smarts of Alexander Hamilton. A later proposed application in 1895 was the Carlisle bill. Carlisle wanted the banks to deposit the legal tender greenbacks and Treasury notes in the Treasury as security reserve instead of bonds. This reserve proposal would represent 30% of a prospective National Bank Note issue. (In effect, U.S. legal tender currency would be taken out of active circulation.) A Carlisle-proposed expansion of bank notes allowed would be 3.33 times a reserve of almost 500 million in greenbacks and Treasury notes or a circulation of "$1,600,000,000." Coffeen remarked that the banks wanted to contract the government "legal tender currency" while at the same time inflating the paper currency of the banks. Congressman Coffeen expounded on the premise that the "fiat" of the government was "better" than any "fiat" of the banks.

Why did Secretary Carlisle pick a 30% reserve figure? From this perspective, this proposed scheme by Secretary Carlisle was a similar scheme as before. It was the security thing that in reality was a basis for a planned amount of paper currency circulation. The emphasis was, as always, put on the security of the currency. The Carlisle scheme would allow a quantity of bank fiat currency by the private banks to replace and inflate to past multiples, say, ten times or more than the fixed greenback/Treasury note reserves. A bank fiat currency would take preference in the circulation. This scheme would eliminate the people's interest-free currency.

The nation's currency was like a conglomeration. The banks couldn't capitalize on the greenbacks. The banks wanted to pyramid paper money on top of paper money, couldn't be done with a "fixed" greenback; that was a stalemate. The national currency was insufficient in supply, also somewhat fixed, because the Treasury printed the notes and the banks "bought" the bonds with the same notes; Secretary Carlisle didn't harp on that part of the deal. McCulloch wanted to fund the greenbacks out of existence. Apparently, a compromise was made; it was the Bland Act. The Treasury tied up 100 million in gold for a long time. The gold was kept in the Treasury. This saved the greenbacks. But it was gold; the banks collected interest in gold for more than thirty years. The gold reserve, held for greenbacks, apparently was there for the banks; the banks discounted the notes and collected gold on the bonds. The Treasury held the greenbacks, used the greenbacks for redemption of uniform currency of failing national banks.

There was a discussion in the Senate on May 7, 1890. The debate preceded the passage of the "Sherman Silver Purchase Act" of 1890. Senator Sherman and Senator Aldrich of Rhode Island answered questions about the mandatory $100 million gold reserve in the Treasury, also the greenback reserves. About the 100 million in gold and the 4 million in interest paid to banks each year, Senator Reagan said that we are keeping "that money idle in the Treasury, and we are doing it when there is such a dearth of circulation in the country as that men can not pay their debts; when especially in the rural parts of the country, they can scarcely pay their taxes; when all business operations are cramped . . . We ought to turn it loose." Senator Plumb earlier said, "Greenback notes are not presented for redemption here." He stated further, "I think the maximum of Greenback notes redeemed in any one year does not come to $6,000,000, and that includes defaced notes." Senator Reagan in reference to the greenbacks, said, "At all times since the resumption of specie payments, these notes have been preferred among business men to coin of either gold or silver. Nobody has asked for their redemption." (That is, not until the Sherman Silver Purchase Act of 1890.) Mr. Plumb felt that a reserve of "$10,000,000" in gold reserve "was ample." Senator Aldrich, in answer, mentioned that the Treasury held "$309,000,000" in silver coin, which was the reserve for $309,000,000 circulating silver certificates. Aldrich maintained that a reserve of 100 million in gold was not excessive for $346,000,000 in circulating greenbacks. Senator Sherman remarked that "no prudent man, no man familiar with the exigencies of the occasion, would like to see the Treasury of the United States in such a position, that it would only have $10,000,000 to meet the current demands, which account to about thirty to thirty-four million dollars a month." The 65 million in greenback reserve was a different matter. Sherman stated that national banks were "retiring by failure or the like . . . $50,000,000 a year." Sherman felt the 100 million in gold was necessary. In any event, gold and greenbacks were kept in the Treasury; it was currency not in active circulation. After 1878, the Treasury started purchasing silver bullion and coining silver dollars. Parity with gold and an increased circulation was the objective. Silver certificates were issued to replace silver dollars as part of the circulation. Silver certificates were legal tender, good for all public and private use and as a reserve for the banks. This was part of a predominate maze of ongoing active and inactive circulation in the latter part of the nineteenth century. When secretaries Carlisle and Gage presented their Treasury reports, the currency was listed "in" and "outside" of the Treasury. Currency outside the Treasury was money in active circulation.

A new type of organization was forming in the United States in the nineteenth century; it was the trust. The owners of the big industries were buying up the smaller competitors. This practice ultimately eliminated competition. "They eliminated most of the remaining competition by cutting prices to force smaller firms out of business. The Trusts then limited production and raised prices." The "Sherman Antitrust Act of 1890" was passed by the Congress to thwart the abuses. The law was supposed to "outlaw any contract, combination, or conspiracy in restraint of trade." Apparently, the law did not have full effect at the time. The law was "sponsored by Republican Senator John Sherman of Ohio; the law was deliberately vague about what in fact constituted a 'trust' or 'restraint.'" This was the "interpretation of the Supreme Court in 1895." President Benjamin Harrison signed the Sherman Act into law.

During the Civil War, Salmon Chase estimated the country's wealth at $16 billion. In 1895, the wealth was estimated at $66 billion, an indication of the industrial and commercial growth in the United States in thirty years. In 1865, the currency circulation, among the people, per capita, was approximately $40 to $50, depending on how one does the numbers. In 1895, during the money panic, the circulating per capita figure was approximately $20. The great industrial expansion and resultant wealth didn't reflect an increase in dollars among the people, irrespective of a proportionate increase in dollars among the people, during the period. Great wealth ballooned; it was owned by few, as the country grew rapidly, approaching the twentieth century, but the dollars in circulation per capita went in the reverse direction.

In 1900, the Gold Standard Act was passed: "That the dollar consisting of twenty-five and eight-tenths grains of gold nine tenths fine . . . shall be the standard unit of value." United States Notes (the greenbacks) and the Treasury notes issued since 1890 would be "redeemed in coin" of the standard unit of value of this act. One hundred fifty million in gold, for the purpose of that redemption, had to be maintained in the Treasury. "Currency Reform" was the continued purpose in the latter part of the nineteenth century, and the gold act was not a culmination. Section 3 of the act stated that the "legal tender quality" of the silver dollar was not affected by the act. But all money had to meet the standard of gold established by the act. Silver was still in the picture, but, as always, the country was going the way of gold. The Treasury notes issued under the act of 1890, redeemable in gold and silver, would, after 1900, be redeemed in gold. Gold certificates were issued for gold deposited in the Treasury. Gold certificates became eligible as bank reserves. There was new bond refunding and national currency issued to banks at 100% of the full value of the bonds, a big plus for national banking associations. Notes held by national banks, previously issued at 90% of bond value, would receive the additional notes. The new circulation would be taxed semiannually at one-fourth of 1% on the average of notes in circulation.

In 1900, the population had swelled to seventy-seven million people. Since the 1870s, almost a half million people had immigrated to the United States each year, mostly from Europe.

After 1900, the national banking associations would receive an increased currency to 100% of the secured bonds; but the multiple array of specie and paper money currencies, the maintenance of a Treasury gold reserve, and the bond security for currency issue would continue. The government/banking connection remained in place, and the beat would go on. The beat went on because the Panic of 1907 greeted the nation. Dewey wrote, "In October, 1907, business was brought to a standstill by a panic and depression, in some ways the most spectacular the country has ever witnessed . . . New York was the center of the crisis."

The trend continued. The beat went on into 1913. In 1913, a new beginning of the credit circulation, the permanent ultimate money scheme, became law; but the "crisis" wasn't over until 1915. Currency reform would begin anew; the Federal Reserve Act, the multiple rediscount system, would supposedly end the impasse. It was the cure-all, and it would be take-off time. In the uniform money scheme, in its new form thus far, the Treasury by way of the Bureau of Engraving and Printing, in the future, would print and issue the paper currency, borrow the same currency, and fund the national debt. The United States would have its Federal Reserve System, consisting of a Federal Reserve Board overseeing twelve regional reserve banks. Did opponents realize the country was getting its third central bank? The Federal Reserve Board and its chairman are the central bank. After 1913 and World War I, the national debt would soar and never look back. The Civil War debt, the nineteenth-century public debt, was a pittance compared to what took place after 1913. Alexander Hamilton's federal expenses as being permanently unlimited, "even in imagination," would begin to approach reality. Perpetuity was in place. Gold would be considered the standard, but paper currency was paramount; it always was. The Federal Reserve Note would become the predominant currency. The credit circulation would begin to take final form. Silver, for the most part, would stay in the vaults until 1918. The Pittman Act would start moving silver to the Far East.

Thomas Jefferson wanted the government to print, issue, and control the nation's currency, the paper currency "to which it belongs," according to the Constitution. Part of a Jefferson demand did begin during the Civil War. After 1913, part of his idea was continued; it was the printing and issue of a new currency by the Bureau of Engraving and Printing. But also established was the borrowing of the new paper currency, the Federal Reserve Note, the government's obligation. It was a tandem thing, the Federal Reserve and the Treasury. Early on, the Federal Reserve System and, principally, the secretary of the Treasury and the Federal Reserve Bank of New York, according to the record, would take the lead. Hamilton's first central bank in 1791 was authorized to print non-legal tender paper currency with which the bank purchased specie or gold. In 1913, a third central bank was authorized to redeem or purchase gold with a non-legal tender paper currency, the Federal Reserve Note. The Alexander Hamilton principle of central banking would continue. And so it was after 122 years; it was back to "square one." A third central bank would do as its two predecessors intended and did: accumulate gold with paper currency.

In 1863, a bill was passed to create a national banking system and a uniform currency in the United States. A tax on state bank currency issues was levied to eliminate state bank currency issues. It was hoped that the state banks would come into the national banking system. In 1900, there were 3,371 national banking "associations." The total number of banks was 9,322. "National Banks, organized under the 1863 Federal law were supervised by the Comptroller of the Currency, and State banks, by officials of the respective States." A controlling central uniform banking system was slow starting in the United States; apparently, many banks were reluctant in joining the system.

The government and the United States had grown; the country's infrastructure was starting to dent the expanse. Business as usual was an enormous undertaking. There was coastal and geodetic survey, the interior resources, mining, the army, the navy, manufacture, agriculture, world trade and commerce, industry, communication systems, conservation, expansion of the railroads, all transportation systems, canals, Atlantic cables, etc. There was still six hundred million acres of public lands. Forty thousand people ran the postal service. Although the government spent millions of dollars every year on services, the fate of the Indian nations was a continuing unsolved problem. Of great significance was the pension system. By the turn of the century, the pension system was costing $200 million each year. The United States government was rewarding its people for the sacrifices for their country. Pensioners included "soldiers and sailors of all wars; widows and relatives of deceased soldiers; army nurses in the war of the rebellion; survivors of the Indian wars and widows of such soldiers."

Before the Gold Standard Act, before the turn of the century, the United States declared war on Spain. It was in April 1898. The war lasted five months; it was over in August. According to the record, there was a depression in Cuba in 1895. There were depressed economic conditions everywhere in the United States, Europe, the Caribbean, etc. The depression in Cuba led to "insurrection," against Spanish rule. The United States "intervened." One of the "causes" of the war was the explosion and sinking of the battleship *Maine* in Havana Harbor on February 15, 1898. The *Maine* was sent to Cuba to protect American interests. More than two hundred American sailors lost their lives. The root cause, and blame, of the sinking of the *Maine* has never been resolved. The war involved the American Army and Navy from Cuba in the Caribbean to the Philippine Islands in the Pacific. The United States Navy had more than fifty combat vessels, including four capital ships; more battleships were under construction. The Spanish were overwhelmed. An act was passed on June 13, 1898, Chapter 448, "To provide ways and means to meet war expenditures, and other purposes." Taxes were levied on banks, tobacco, beer, porter, etc. Ten-year 3% bonds were also sold to pay for the war. The war was not totally popular in the United States. Expansionism, "colonialism," was taking place. The United States acquired the Philippine Islands and Guam in the Pacific and Puerto Rico in the Caribbean, all in less than a year. Cuba was granted independence from Spain. A treaty was signed in December of 1898. The Senate, by "one vote," ratified the treaty on February 6, 1899. The United States agreed to pay Spain $20 million "within three months after the exchange of the ratifications of the present Treaty." Money specifics were not detailed in this treaty of record. Although Spain quickly relinquished the Philippines, island rebels fought the American occupation. It took three years and thousands of casualties before peace was maintained. The United States ruled the islands until 1946. The islands were temporarily lost to the Japanese and regained during World War II (1942-1945). Independence was granted the Philippines on July 4, 1946. Guam and Puerto Rico remain United States possessions.

CHAPTER EIGHT
The Federal Reserve System

It was the beginning of the twentieth century. There were now forty-five states, eleven added since the Civil War. The population was almost 80 million. In 1916, it would be 100 million. Industrialization since the Civil War was dramatic. A quarter million miles of railroads were instrumental in the commercial and industrial expansion. The famous banker J. P. Morgan is credited with the financial expansion of the railroads. The railroads, telegraph, the telephone, electricity, gas, oil, steel, vast ore and mineral resources, and with the automobile—the United States was changing rapidly. The country was the land of inventions; the country had become an industrial force. In the beginning, the United States was predominately agrarian. The people now flocked to the industrial centers, to the cities, seeking factory and commercial employment. Utilities were there, jobs were there, the people were there. During the First World War, half the population lived in the metropolitan areas. Immigration continued in big numbers. America was the New World, the land of opportunity, a country of firsts. In 1902, an act was passed allocating $50 million to acquire the right-of-way to build the Panama Canal; work would begin in 1904. In 1903, the Wright brothers flew the first airplane at Kitty Hawk. In 1903, Henry Ford started the Ford Motor Company; the Model T was built in 1908.

William McKinley was elected to a second term as president of the United States. He would give his last annual message to the Congress on December 3, 1900. The country was on the upswing. For the first time in six years, there was a surplus in the Treasury; more than $50 million were applied "to the sinking fund." Three hundred sixty-nine new banks were added to the national banking system. Another important feature of the 1900 Gold Standard Act was the refunding of 3%, 4%, and 5% bonds, maturity in 1904, 1907, and 1908, over $800 million. New thirty-year bonds at 2% annual interest in gold (maturity in 1930) meant an annual savings in interest of $6 million. The tax the national banks paid on their currency was reduced (to 0.5 of 1%), probably an incentive for the banks to buy the thirty-year bonds. Foreign trade was on the increase, but 90% of the country's exports and imports were handled by foreign shipping. "Foreign ships should carry the least, not the greatest, part of American trade." The big ships and the ocean liners such as the future *Titanic* and the *Olympic* were built in the British Isles and Europe. McKinley "favored the policy of aid to our merchant marine which will broaden our commerce and markets and up-build our sea-carrying capacity . . . which, with the increase of our Navy, mean more work and wages to our countrymen."

About the currency, McKinley said, "The Party in power is committed to such legislation as will better make the currency responsive to the varying needs of business at all seasons and all sections."

War with Spain was over, but the war in the Philippines was not; insurgency continued. McKinley returned a commission to the islands "to aid the existing authorities." William Howard Taft, a future president, was one of the commissioners. It would be two more years before the insurgency was ended. McKinley stressed the need for "cable communication between the United States and Hawaii, with extension to Manila . . . Surveys have shown the entire feasibility of a chain of cables, which at each stopping place shall touch an American Territory." Cuba at the time was under United States military rule, which ended in 1902. Cuba then became an "independent Republic." McKinley mentioned, "The civil Government of Puerto Rico provided for by the Act of Congress approved April 12, 1900, is in successful operation."

The Boxer Rebellion had erupted in China. The Boxers rebelled against the presence of Western nations. Many lives were lost, foreign and Chinese. All the industrialized nations, including the United States, were in China. A military force "made up of Japanese, Russian, British and American troops" ended the conflict. A settlement was reached on September 1, 1901. McKinley lauded Japan as instrumental in bringing about the negotiations and settlement.

Why was the United States considered an isolationist nation? The United States was involved politically and economically with England, France, Spain, and the Dutch [Amsterdam] since the beginning. The Barbary States of North Africa raided U.S. shipping between 1795 and 1815. The hands off the Americas was dictated by the Monroe Doctrine; it was directed toward the Europeans. The war with Mexico followed; the entire Southwest Territory was obtained from Mexico. Half the country's continental territory was obtained from France and Mexico. Atlantic and Alaskan Ocean cables were in the scheme of things in the nineteenth century. The United States expanded its territory into the Caribbean and the Pacific in the war with Spain. Cables would span the Pacific in the twentieth century. Alaska was purchased from Russia. There was nineteenth-century trade and presence in Japan, China, South America, and Africa. The beginning of the twentieth century saw an escalation of foreign involvement. Prior to construction in Central America, the Panama Canal involved negotiations with France and Panama. President Theodore Roosevelt flexed the country's muscles, sending a formidable United States naval fleet around the world. Most importantly, European banking and gold controlled United States money since the beginning. It led to the banking events of 1913, and then the United States went to war in Europe, the First World War. From the time of the Constitution into the twentieth century, the United States continued as a debtor nation to England and Europe. In terms of money and indebtedness, the United States was never in isolation; it was a part of the Occident. An oil embargo would precipitate a war with Japan. The Monroe Doctrine did dictate a position of isolation of the Americas; America was behind in world trade. The London exchange controlled America and the world money markets and foreign investment.

McKinley hoped the import-export conditions with Brazil would improve. Meat inspections with Germany may get better with the recent telegraph hookup with that country. "Our friendly relations with Great Britain continue." A revolution in Nicaragua had rebels forcing import duties from American merchants. The matter was settled; a "British Consul returned" the duties to the merchants.

The "Trans-Isthmanian ship-canal projects" (the Panama Canal) were to be considered by the Congress. "In my last annual message to the

Congress, I called attention to the necessity for early action to remedy such evils as might be found to exist in connection with combinations of capital organized into Trusts, and again invite attention to my discussion of the subject at that time." The huge trusts had been formed in the United States by large corporations, the railroads, banking, the oil industry, steel, etc. Later, the antitrust laws were invoked to combat the trusts during the Roosevelt administration. J. P. Morgan, Rockefeller, Jay Gould, etc., were instrumental in the formation of the huge trusts. These most powerful people, among approximately "100" in number, "exercised dominating control over property amounting to $ 22,000,000,000, an unthinkable sum, practically a third of the national wealth, excluding the land of the country." Senator Owen in 1913 said, "A handful of men exercised practically commercial and financial supremacy over the people of the United States;"

McKinley emphasized better trade relations with all nations. "This Government desires to preserve the most just and amicable commercial relations with all foreign countries, unmoved by the industrial rivalries necessarily developed in the expansion of international trade." He mentioned the "exposition of the resources and products of the Western Hemisphere to be held at Buffalo next year." President McKinley gave an address at that exposition on September 5, 1901. The next day, September 6, in a receiving line, a lone gunman fired two close-range pistol shots at the president. McKinley was mortally wounded. President McKinley died on September 14, 1901. Theodore Roosevelt, the vice president, was sworn into office on the same day.

Millions of our countrymen remember the panic of 1907. It occurred in a year and at a time when this country was far more prosperous than it had been for years before. Farm, Industrial, and legitimate commercial business transactions were far in excess of the previous year. It came while all of our people were busily engaged in agricultural, commercial, and industrial enterprises, and without thought or warning of impending danger. It came like a flash of lightning or a thunderbolt out of a clear sky.

Michael E. Burke, congressman from Wisconsin, was speaking in the House on September 17, 1913. The debate was counting down on the Federal Reserve bill. Burke mentioned that things were quiet on "the 27th of October." The next day, "there had been an explosion in the financial centers of New York." Burke said that prices dropped "in 24 hours at least one third."

Things were happening before that. On the 22 of October 1907, the *Wall Street Journal* editorial stated, "The Clearing House and The Government." There was a "grave situation" that the clearinghouse took care of "in dealing with the Heinze and Morse Banks . . . Now this is the best kind of business government, a government of business by business men without interference by the political authorities." But the next day, the *Journal* confirmed, "Secretary of the Treasury Deposits $10,000,000." The article said, "It can be stated positively that Secretary Cortelyou is putting money in New York banks." Cortelyou was the secretary of the Treasury of the United States. The interfering "political authority" was beginning to bail out New York banks. Robert S. Minot stated in the *Journal* (October 22), "Wall Street is 'the longest Street on Earth.' Yet it is one of the shortest. It only takes five minutes to walk from one end of it to the other. Just now also it is short in other respects. It is short in credit and short in public confidence." Also, on Wednesday, October 23, a *Journal* headline printed, "A Trust Company was in Trouble." It was the Knickerbocker Trust Company. "Clearing House refuses to loan to Trust Company, Bank of Commerce stops clearing for it." The *New York Times* on the same day the headline read, "KNICKERBOCKER WILL NOT OPEN . . . The Conference of Bankers Deems it Unwise To Aid The Trust Company Today." Depositors had withdrawn "Eight Million Dollars." There was a "suspension"; the doors were closed and a "panicky day in Wall Street."

Unfortunately, suddenly, banks across the country didn't have any money, a circulating currency, that is; and why was that? Congressman Burke said, "This was a tantalizing situation. The banks were rich and overloaded with wealth. Yet they had no money. They were unable to sell or rediscount their commercial papers and other securities because every bank was in a like embarrassing position."

How could that be, all that wealth and riches and the banks had no money? The banks were wealthy; they owned indebtedness. The banks owned wealth, commercial paper, couldn't sell it and couldn't collect a dime on it either. Why did the banks across the country have no currency, and why did all the panics seem to trigger in New York? "And this at a time when there was more money in the country than ever before."

The people went to the bank for money, and the doors were closed. Where did the money go? It's as if, periodically, a hurricane, a twister, or maybe a flood came by and whisked the money away, everything. "No redundancy" again, the money was gone, but it must be there somewhere. Congressman Adolph Sabath of Illinois, on May 29, 1908, compared the circulation per capita to previous years. "In 1879, $15.32; in 1889, $22.52; in 1893, $ 24.56; in 1897, $ 22.87. and at the present time, [or in October 1907, just before the panic] $34.71 per capita. Does this not show we have more money than ever before? Absolutely so! The only trouble is, that it is not where it should be and is where it should not be."

The problem was New York. Banks across the country had deposited $300 million in New York banks. New York banks had borrowed 500 million from foreigners; the money was gone. The money went to New York again, and as before, it disappeared. During the year 1907, from January into November, the interest rates rose to heights of 25%, 45%, 75%, and 125%. A Senate report showed that "90-day time loans . . . were running as high as 12 to 16 per cent."

As before, the game would continue. From the record, the U.S. Treasury responded. The public's money was pumped into the system; about $47,000,000 went to the banks. The banking and currency laws had to be changed, improved again, and as before, it was back to the Congress. From the Treasury report, the *Congressional Record*, it was Treasury Secretary Cortelyou who had deposited $47,000,000 in New York banks.

The bank act of 1863, and as amended several times in the latter part of the nineteenth century, set up a reserve and redemption process whereby all the "associations" were allowed to deposit a percentage of their "lawful money reserve in cash deposits in the city of New York" (Section 32 of the bank act). When reading the statutes, the banking laws are difficult to understand. Maybe the banking practitioner may recognize any intended nuances. Thomas Jefferson knew the banking laws were never understood completely before the fact. It was after the fact, after trekking through the debris, after the resultant profit and loss, then maybe the law or the practices within the limits of the law were understood.

The bank act of 1863 and subsequent amendments set things up something like this: there were "Country Banks, Reserve City Banks, Central Reserve City Banks," and also the central reserve city banks in New York City. The minimum reserve in the country bank was "$15 on every $ 100 of their deposits." The minimum reserve in the reserve city and the central reserve city banks was "$ 25 on every $100 of their deposits." Speaking in the House on September 18, 1913, Congressman Dan Stephens of Nebraska said,

> The joker in this law is the right granted country banks to keep $ 9 of the $15 with a reserve City Bank; and a Reserve City bank can keep half of its $25 reserve in a Central Reserve City Bank. The result of this law was soon realized by the big bankers, who conceived it, when they began to pay the country banks 2 per cent on their reserves, the law permitted them to keep with reserve agents.

The result was "the reserves of the country were pyramided" in New York.

Congressman Burke said the banks went beyond the allowable cash reserve. "Secret agreements" were made. The New York banks paid substantial interest for additional cash deposits. Banks are in business to make money. Reserves were idle; apparently, reserves were sent out. The money went to "precarious investments" on Wall Street. The cash reserves were not in the country banks where the reserves belonged. The cash reserves, the currency, or cash wound up in New York banks; the reserves were lost. It was "the call-loan movement in New York, a market whose principal business is that of carrying speculative transactions largely on the New York Stock Exchange." The loans when called in abundance showed no liquidity, and there went the money. Congressman Burke conceded that a "decentralization" of the country's money was required; the concentrations of the money had to be removed from the "great financial centers, especially New York City." Congressman Burke—after lamenting about the agricultural and industrial losses suffered in the depressions of 1873, 1893, and 1907—said, "An almost unanimous demand has existed during the past five or six years throughout the length and breadth of this country for a change in our system of banking and currency."

There would be enacted a Federal Reserve System with twelve regional Federal Reserve banks located in strategic cities across the country and one located in New York City. But New York City would remain the "principal center for the use of surplus funds, and for the adjustment of banking reserves." Wall Street, New York, was the business and financial center in the beginning in the latter eighteenth century and throughout the nineteenth century. It would remain so after 1913 throughout the twentieth century, and it is so today. There are two economies in the United States; one of them is Wall Street.

In May 1908, there was legislative response to the currency problem. Congress passed the Aldrich-Vreeland Act, a two-part plan. The act authorized "National Currency Associations" and a "National Monetary Commission." The act was called an act to amend the national banking laws. The currency associations was an interim "emergency" plan to alleviate the effect of the 1907 panic. The commission was authorized to study the banking and currency problem. It was never ending; the Congress appeared jerked around by the banking and currency problems. Senator Aldrich of Rhode Island was most active during this period; he headed up the monetary commission. Eighteen members of Congress comprised the commission, nine senators and an equal number from the House of Representatives. The commission after three years of "the most extensive and far-reaching investigation" submitted a bill to the Senate in 1912. This bill, known as the Aldrich bill, was submitted in 1912 and again on April 13, 1913. The Aldrich bill recommended a "Central Bank, privately controlled." The bill couldn't possibly fly; it didn't fly. Congressman Stephens said, "This bill proposed a great central bank, privately controlled, in effect, which was the essential objection to the old United States Bank. This bill never stood the slightest chance of ever becoming law . . . the people will not stand for it." So the Aldrich bill was changed, rewritten. But the skeletal form of the Aldrich bill would form a revised bill, a Federal Reserve plan.

Senator Owen of Oklahoma and Congressman Carter Glass of Virginia, from the record, prepared the "Glass-Owen Currency Bill" (House Bill H.R. 7837). This bill was a banking and currency bill, which eventually became the Federal Reserve Act of December 23, 1913. Senator Owen was chairman of the Senate Finance Committee, and Carter Glass was chairman of Ways and Means in the House. During the Federal Reserve debate, Congressman Fess of Ohio compared copies of the Aldrich bill and the Glass-Owen bill. "What does this comparison show? The bill now before us is in many, features a copy of the Aldrich plan. The chief difference is in control of the system. The Aldrich plan was weak in this feature." The Aldrich plan was placing the banking "business in the hands of private interests."

In 1908, there was Democratic opposition to the Aldrich-Vreeland Act. The act was changing the currency issue. Senator Aldrich, the Republicans, and the money interests were conjuring up private control. United States government bonds would no longer be purchased as security for currency. The absent circulating currency had been gobbled up in the 1907 panic, and here was a new way to get needed currency back into the economy. The government would still print or create the added currency, but a new kind of indebtedness was needed to create the money. The landscape showed Wall Street had eliminated all credit issues. The new "Currency Associations" were going to provide new credit with their own commercial paper. The associations would get the added currency from the Treasury based on commercial paper, not government bonds. Commercial paper would be based on "sound business conditions," municipal bonds, state bonds, etc.; all this business required the approval of the secretary of the Treasury. The law stated that a minimum of ten national banks may form one association. Only one association may form in any one city. The aggregate capital of the ten banks had to be a minimum of $5 million. This bill was a "seventh edition" bill, and the Republican majority pushed it through the House on a "three hour gag debate" as commented by Congressman Charles A. Lindbergh of Minnesota in the House on May 14, 1908.

The Democrats were against the Aldrich-Vreeland plan. Wilson Hill of Mississippi, in the House on May 14, 1908, said this "emergency currency" would be "based on collateral of banks belonging to a certain Association approved by a Committee of that Association of Banks." He said the currency would be "asset currency, pure and simple; indeed it is asset currency run wild." Hill said, "The asset currency—is only a makeshift and is not sufficient, for this Commission is to examine into the currency question." Dewey wrote, "The plan for the establishment of 'National Currency Associations' as agencies for an emergency circulation was not, however, regarded as a satisfactory solution of existing defects."

Wilson Hill was right. The new banking and currency bill that became the Federal Reserve bill was going in that direction, a currency based on short-term commercial paper generated by the banks, which was the private side of the impending new system. The opposition question was, how good was the commercial paper? The Panic of 1907 brought on the Aldrich-Vreeland emergency currency plan. The National Monetary Commission then produced the Aldrich bill. The Aldrich bill became the Glass-Owen currency bill. This collective framework produced the eventual climactic legislation, the Federal Reserve Act.

Congressmen Adolph Sabath of Illinois and John Williams of Mississippi presented an editorial entitled "The Currency Crime" from the Republican *Philadelphia North American* newspaper. The article was dated May 29, 1908. The article was presented by the congressmen, in the House, in support of their denunciation of the emergency currency bill. The editorial was a scathing critique of the emergency bill, the period and the Panic of 1907. New York, Wall Street, the money interests, the administration, and the Congress were the evildoers, the bad guys, the unaware, and the do-nothings. This classic editorial included the following satirical blast; this was just great stuff:

- The bill was called a "mongrel, hybrid, cheating, swindling thing."

- The Congress was "the servant of the public enemies."
- The House was a bunch of "crouched cowards." They were "under the lash of the vulgar tyrant in the speaker's chair." The Speaker was going to deprive them "from their slices of 'pork barrel'" if they didn't do his bidding.
- The bill "will be whipped through the Senate in like fashion." The Democrats were "playing the donkey's role."
- President Roosevelt will sign the bill. The president "will do this sin because of lack of understanding . . . in the grasp of financial matters, he is an infant." Roosevelt trusted the Secretary of the Treasury "Cortelyou."

When it comes to the money thing, the people, all of us, are "infants."

- Roosevelt didn't have "enough friends there to save him from himself."
- The "original Aldrich bill was better than this iniquity." Senator Aldrich earlier had denounced the speculative "Municipal and Railroad bonds" as a poor purchase. That was before the senator "had new orders from 26 Broadway and the National City Bank." Senator Aldrich was "J. P. Morgan's office boy in Washington." The speculative bonds would be used as commercial paper in the emergency currency bill after all. The editorial called the bonds "illegal bond issues." These bonds would be in addition to "$ 250,000,000 deposits of the people's money."
- Before the 1907 panic, "New York owed outside banks $410,000,000." There was a payback of "$ 20,000,000"; and this was during a concurrent deposit of $47,000,000 in "New York Banks" by "Cortelyou," the secretary of the Treasury.
- The "Treasury" would be turned "over to the gamblers of the New York Stock Exchange for a period of six years." The emergency plan was slated to run from 1908 to 1914.

The emergency currency plan became law, and the Treasury would continue its role. The Treasury would continue to print new currency and issue the new paper currency to the banks based on new currency association commercial paper. More new money was needed to spark the economy. The circulating currency, abundant before the panic, had apparently vanished. The banks who had departed with the vanished currency were apparently the same banks that would form the new associations. These associations would receive 90% in new notes based on the value of municipal commercial paper and 75% in new notes based on the value of railroad commercial paper. There was no mention or major effort or consideration in gold during this legislation; it was strictly paper currency, another glitch, another contradiction in the scheme of things. The commercial paper had to be approved by the secretary of the Treasury (whatever was necessary in the scheme of things).

The "good times" and the "bad times" and the "bulls" and the "bears" will churn to the "pleasures of Rogers and Rockefeller in the National City bank and J.P. Morgan in the National Bank of Commerce."

"We wish merely to warn one and all . . . pay day will come. And the price will be a bitter one."

Concerning the expiration of the emergency currency plan in 1914, Dewey wrote, "Owing to the commercial disturbances in that year, it was temporarily continued and for several months did good service in affording credits in a period of emergency, while the new Federal Reserve System was being established."

In the Senate

On November 22, 1913, Senator Howe and the Finance Committee submitted to the Senate the latest report on the banking and currency bill with amendments. It was one month prior to the enactment of the banking and currency bill. Just before enactment, the name of the bill would be changed. Briefly, the conference report included the following:

- There were the causes of the 1907 panic, the implementation of the emergency currency bill, the monetary commission, and the Aldrich bill.
- The Aldrich bill was opposed because it ignored the independence of many districts in the country. Banking concentration was extreme; private individuals would control

the credit system. There would be no supervision by the government; private corporations would control the issue of the country's currency.
- The Pujo investigation showed that a vast concentration of power over the country's credit system was in the hands of a few men.

In presenting the report, Senator Howe said,

> I shall not pretend to believe for one moment that the panic of 1907 was an accident. It is a long story . . . I profoundly believe that the result in October, 1907, was part of a concerted plan by which a few men did two things; first, enriched themselves on the one hand at the expense of the nation, and administered what they considered a rebuke to the Administration then in power.

Senator Howe did mention the administration but not a "rebuke" for what? Was it Theodore Roosevelt? Who else? President Roosevelt's administration "used the Sherman Act in order to break up the Standard Oil Company, the American Tobacco Company, and several other large firms that had abused their economic power." The Sherman Antitrust law was strengthened in 1914 by the passage of the "Clayton Anti-Trust Act." President Wilson eventually signed the Clayton bill into law.

President Roosevelt's detractors blamed his policy for the 1907 crash.

> No man will stand more strongly than I will in the defense of property, so long as it is honestly acquired and used . . . I will protect every way in my power honest property . . . And in no way can I ultimately protect the honest man of wealth so effectively as by doing everything in my power to bring to justice his dishonest brother of wealth.

Roosevelt didn't "change policy" because the money interests had swallowed up the money. Roosevelt had opposed the "asset currency" scheme by the American Bankers Association. The scheme was first "introduced in Congress in 1906." James Sinclair, later speaking on "Money and Credit" in June 1921, said, "In my opinion, the panic of 1907 was brought on by the same selfish interests in order to discredit his administration and put over the Aldrich asset currency bill." It was Theodore Roosevelt America versus laissez-faire America.

- The Glass investigation was partial. It showed that financial matters had been thoroughly investigated; it was vigorously contested by those opposing the banking and currency bill.
- The Senate investigation outlined adequate mobile reserves, and a new elastic currency was needed. The new elastic currency would be the Federal Reserve Note. The reserve note would be a government obligation. The new system should be a regional system, not a central bank. The government should control the system, put an end to banks pyramiding the country's money reserves, and gamble those reserves on the stock exchange.
- Eight regional banks were planned; it was changed to twelve. A Federal Reserve Board of seven members, including the secretary of the Treasury would command the twelve regional banks. The chairman of the Reserve Board was appointed by the president. The board's location is Washington, D.C. An open market committee would do business in New York City.
- There were twenty-five thousand banks in the country; seven thousand were the national banks. There were eighteen thousand state banks, trust companies, and savings banks. The seven thousand national banks were expected to become member Federal Reserve banks. The Open Market Committee would deal directly with the nonmember banks.
- It was hoped a reserve of $672,000,000 would be paid into the system, which included the reserves of the national banks. This figure included a deposit by the U.S. Treasury of $150,000,000. If the state banks and trust companies came in, the reserve paid would amount to $972,000,000. The report estimated the total capital stock in the country to be $3.6 billion.
- Stockholder dividends would be a maximum 6%. The government would receive earnings above any surplus over 20%.

- There would be Open market operations and bankers' acceptances.
- Government deposits in the reserve banks.
- The bonds securing the national bank currency would be refunded. Federal Reserve Notes would eventually replace the national bank currency.

According to the 1912-1913 Treasury financial statements, the total "kinds of money" in the country included gold and silver coin, gold certificates, silver certificates, the national uniform currency or the national bank currency, the greenbacks, and 1890 Treasury notes. The "asset currency" of 1908-1913 was not shown. Based on the $3.3 billion figure listed outside the Treasury, the per capita circulation was about $34. It is remarkable that the dearth of money and reserves, which existed after 1907, suddenly surfaced in 1914 to support the start of the Federal Reserve. The system exploded into an abundance of currency and credits after 1914. It would appear the country's wealth was always there, the currency, and the potential for the creation of more credit and currency as well.

In 1914, the Federal Reserve Notes came into play with all the other currencies still out there. These new notes would be generated against the new banker's bills, commercial paper of member banks, and the transfer of the asset currency, etc. While discussing the report, Senator Howe assured the Senate that inflation would be controlled. "There would be a temporary expansion of currency against these commercial bills; but the important feature . . . it is measured and absolutely controlled by the volume of the commercial demand. The commercial demand must exist." On that note, Senator Williams directed a question to Senator Howe. Williams mentioned the greenbacks; if a bank would "bring in $100,000 of Greenbacks" instead of the asset currency or commercial paper, then "$100,000 of Greenbacks should be destroyed." There was assurance that the greenbacks would not be destroyed; the answer was "no." Also, if another "man, came in and wanted to borrow another $100,000; let us say, on more commercial bills of some other bank, then as I understand, the $100,000 in Greenbacks could be put out against the $100,000 of commercial bills instead of $ 100,000 of commercial-asset circulation?" Senator Howe replied "yes," and he continued that another "important control provided in the bill . . . the Federal Reserve Board can raise the rate of interest if they find abuse is extending to the use of these Federal Reserve notes . . . to prevent inflation."

The greenback was lawful money of the United States; and in 1913, after the Federal Reserve Act, the greenback dollars were still in circulation, 347 million of them, no more and no less. But there would be no capitalization of the greenbacks; the greenback was a "fixed" non-interest-bearing circulation, 347 million before and 347 million after.

Senator Howe mentioned earlier, "These elastic Federal Reserve notes are the best-secured notes that have been devised in any banking system in the world." Howe gave additional answers to Senator Williams; he was promoting the currency bill still further. Howe said,

> There are several checks: First, the demand of citizens for cash; second, the demand of a member bank for cash—actual cash; third, the demand of the Reserve bank; fourth, the putting up of commercial bills of the qualified class; the minimum gold reserve of 33%; sixth, the interest rate imposed by the Federal Reserve Bank; seventh, the interest rate that can be raised by the Federal Reserve Board.

People know cash; they recognize cash. The demand "for cash" by the people in the modern political economic society has always been there, consistently and constantly, and more importantly during the depressions and the panics. In 1913, currency reform again was right around the corner. But with all the assurances and all the checks, was the Federal Reserve System going to satisfy the continuing consistent and constant demand "for cash"? Would the demand "for cash" and/ or credit be satisfied through this new banking system? Elements that persisted before would continue to persist. The First World War came along, money abounded, the debt soared, and the beat went on. Year 1920-1921 rolled around. Inflation then deflation and the farmer, manufacturer, and laborer would be treated to the first hit by the new Federal Reserve System.

Chairman Carter Glass on December 22, 1913, in the House asked
for "immediate consideration" on the report of the bill. It was at this
time the bill was officially titled the Federal Reserve Act. Managers
of the Senate and the House conference, under the leadership of
Owen and Glass, had come together on the final report of the bill.
It was late in the day. The Senate was waiting on final action by the
House. Congressman Glass wanted to move things along. A debate
was agreed on to last no longer than two hours and twenty minutes,
one hour and ten minutes each side. The Speaker monitored the time.
Congressman Moore said "a 58 page document" had come back from
the Senate, and "the House is to accept after two hours discussion in
order that the President and the members may go off on their holiday
vacations." Lindbergh called the bill a Christmas gift to the money trust.
The extension of the Aldrich-Vreeland emergency plan was added to
the Federal Reserve Act.

Treasury Secretary Franklin MacVeagh expounded on the
Aldrich-Vreeland Act in his December 1, 1913, report to the Congress.
Earlier in the year, April through July, there had been periods
of "pessimism" and "nervousness" in the financial community;
"credits were being restricted, and that it was increasingly difficult
to secure funds for the normal needs of legitimate business." It was
"characteristic of our imperfect and unsatisfactory banking system."
To quell the anxiety, the secretary had announced that $500,000,000
was available in the Treasury. All the banks had to do was exercise
Aldrich-Vreeland, come forth with their commercial paper, and pick
up the currency. The announcement alone settled the unrest. In
the West, the banks were unable "to meet the seasonal demand
for the large amounts of money required to move a bounteous
harvest." This problem was alleviated because the secretary promised
a deposit in Western banks of up to "50 millions of dollars" for
"high-class commercial paper." This had never been done before;
"commercial paper had never before been accepted as security for
Government deposits." Congressman Wilson Hill said it was "asset
currency, pure and simple." The new Federal Reserve System was
headed in this direction—"asset currency." The Congress extended
the Aldrich-Vreeland emergency plan into 1914 as the new Federal
Reserve System was coming into effect.

If all this currency was being generated by commercial paper, how would the gold factor enter the equation? Why was there a need for gold? Gold was there; it would be considered the reserve, the banker's hole card, as part of the scheme of things.

Congressman Charles Lindbergh of Minnesota opposed the Federal Reserve. In a 1912 speech, Lindbergh predicted "that the Money Trust would cause a money stringency in order to force its bill through Congress." Sure enough, Secretary MacVeagh reported in December 1913 that "credits were being restricted." Nothing could be done; Congress was going to pass the bill. Lindbergh called the Congress a humbug because the Congress was passing the bill. "We expect Wall Street to cheat. Wall Streeters have not taken an oath to serve the people, but Senators and Representatives have. Wall Streeters could not cheat us if Senators and Representatives did not make a humbug of Congress." The Congress was a humbug because of the "party control of Congress. The division of Congress into political parties is a crime . . . There are now no conflicting interests except those fostered by a division of the people into political parties." Lindbergh felt the fault lay with the "party bosses" and the "caucus." The "bosses fence the people into various political pastures to oppose each other." Apparently, this was the problem with the bill according to Lindbergh.

> This bill is the Aldrich bill in disguise, the difference being that by this bill, the Government issues the money, whereas by the Aldrich bill the issue was to be controlled by the banks. No one should be deceived by that change, however, for by this bill, the Government can let no one but the banks have the money. Wall Street will control the money as easily through this bill as they have heretofore . . . The bill simply gives the bankers the privilege of extending credits to charge the people interest on, while the Government is to support it.

Congressman Platt, a Republican from New York, "congratulated" his "Democratic friends" for making the currency bill "a good measure." But there was a problem; "on the end of it you are extending a Republican measure which you have condemned in most unmeasured terms . . . There is nothing you have condemned more roundly and vehemently than the Vreeland-Aldrich law." Carter Glass told Platt that Aldrich-Vreeland had been amended. "We reduced the tax, so the people may get the currency should they need it . . . As a Republican measure, it was inoperative; as a Democratic measure, it may be operative." Glass received "applause on the Democratic side." Platt charged, "Well, I hope it will not be needed, but there is a good deal in this bill based on the Vreeland-Aldrich bill besides, and that is one trouble with it [laughter]." The banks would still get the currency at low interest and charge the people at high interest, which was Platt's objection. Platt called the low interest a special privilege extended to the banks. Platt contended that the farmers should get the currency at low interest, the same as the banks. "The banks are to keep the reserves and can redeem them, but for some reason unknown, or perhaps not entirely unknown, you have characterized these notes as Government notes when really they are practically bank notes and." Carter Glass interrupted Platt, "I will ask the gentleman if, under the National Bank Act, a distinctly Republican measure, you have not been loaning currency to the banks for 50 years on their collateral, while not loaning to farmers? Applause on the Democratic side." Platt responded, "No; we have not. We have been depositing money and taking security for it. You can call that a loan if you want to, but it is a deposit." Just as his time was running out, Platt, satisfied that the currency would be "secured sufficiently," said, "You have got to explain from now on, what business they have to read as Government notes, when they ought to be bank notes standing on the security of good banking and a sufficient reserve [applause]." There was no response from Carter Glass.

The exchange between Platt and Glass represented two different interpretations of old and new banking and currency reform. Platt was trying to illustrate the high interest rates afforded the people, which is the initial excessive cost of money to the people. Actually, the preponderance of the excessive initial cost of the money, the uniform currency, to the people, started during the Civil War; it was the National Bank Act of 1863. In the days of state sovereignty, when the states had their own currency, the initial discount or cost of money to the people was simpler and direct. Now it's the government/banking combined. Since 1913, excluding income tax, social security, compensations, etc., there are multiple discounts before the wage earner receives a Federal Reserve Note. From the Treasury to the Federal Reserve to the reserve banks to member banks to commerce to the people, results in excessive initial cost of money to the people.

Congressman Morgan of Oklahoma "concluded that I shall not vote for this bill." Mr. Morgan said the bill "contains no provision for the protection of the depositors in the National Banks." Federal Deposit Insurance wasn't provided until 1934, during the Great Depression. Morgan offered an amendment in September 1913 to protect depositors. It was voted down. Mr. Platt voted against the amendment. His reason was,

> It seems to me there is a great deal of misapprehension over the question of bank deposits. A bank deposit is not something that is put into a bank, but it is something taken out of a bank, and ought not to guarantee them without guaranteeing what is owing to the bank that created them." For instance, I never put a thousand dollars into a bank in my life in currency, but I had $ 10,000 in the bank. How did I do it? I went to the bank and borrowed it. You have got to guarantee the men that owe the money to the banks. That is what bank guaranty is.

Before, Mr. Glass said the currency was a loan to the banks; Mr. Platt said it was a deposit. According to Mr. Platt, borrowed money becomes the deposit, which means Mr. Glass was also correct? In any case, it was the beginning of the multiple discount system initiated by the government in 1863. The banks lend money; the banks lend deposits. The Treasury "hands" the money to the Federal Reserve.

There was going to be profit in the new system. The twelve regional banks, the member banks, the stockholders, and the government were going to earn a profit issuing the nation's money. Mr. Morgan asked Carter Glass, how much profit was in it for the government? The answer was "from five and a half to seven millions of dollars—per annum." Or about "five million dollars for 20 years would make $100,000,000" was Morgan's response. After Federal Reserve implementation in 1914 and by 1921, the government probably made, say, $40 million profit?

The national debt in the same period graduated from $1 billion to more than $25 billion (chapter 9). The government or the Treasury would gain 40 million, and the people would gain an increase in debt of more than $25 billion, beautiful; it was just the beginning. There could be rightful compensation if all the people may own all that public indebtedness. The public creditor was back; he wasn't back.

Congressman Morgan offered an amendment, which would allow the individual to invest in the regional reserve bank stock, the same as the member banks; the amendment was rejected. He offered an amendment providing "better credit, cheaper interest, and larger capital with which to develop the agriculture of the United States . . . It is said that the farmers of the United States owe something like $ 5,000,000,000 and pay something like $500,000,000 annually in interest . . . Nearly one-half of all the wealth produced in the United States every year is produced by the farmer." Morgan said that "better rural credit in this country" was needed. Was commercial paper in the East worth more than commercial paper in the West or the other way around? This amendment didn't make it either. If Morgan's numbers were correct, the farmers were paying at least 10% interest on their loans.

Congressman Underwood "congratulated the members of the Banking and Currency Committee of this House and the Senate." There were changes that made the bill much better. "The great banking system of England is often referred to as a banker's control system." In England, "our relatives across the water were wise enough . . . that the discount banker, or the man who lends money, shall not control the issue of that money or the extension of that money [applause]." A big change was in the makeup of the Federal Reserve Board. The Republicans wanted the bankers to control the board; the Democrats wanted the people as pointed out by Underwood. There was more applause. The board would now include the secretary of the Treasury, the comptroller, and the president would appoint the chairman. There would be government representation on the board. "This Board will carefully and safely manage this system not only in the interest of the American people and low interest rates, but also will have the wisdom to see that the great banking interests of the country are properly safeguarded and protected."

In the new Federal Reserve System, the Treasury, the central bank, the twelve regional reserve banks, the member banks, and the shareholders were going to profit on the issue of the new government obligation.

Woodrow Wilson, a Democrat, was elected president on November 5, 1912. The Democrats gained control of the House and the Senate. The Federal Reserve bill became President Wilson's bill, the Democrat's bill. The Democrats claimed a victory with the successful changes to the banking and currency bill, the Federal Reserve Act.

On that theme, Republican Congressman Mann of Illinois brought the House down with his remarks. "Mr. Speaker, I know how distasteful it is to the other side of the House to have the truth told at this time. [There was laughter on the Democratic side.] We have now had Democratic control in the country for a little more than nine months. That control has already cast its malign influence over two great countries, Mexico—[There was laughter on the Democratic side]." At this point, the Speaker had to break in, "The House will be in order." Mr. Mann continued, "Mexico lies prostrate and bleeding, and the only response which it receives is laughter on the Democratic side of the House." Mann went on to say that conditions in the United States were just as bad, and the only thing the new currency bill was going to do was inflate the currency. "There never has been a time in the history of the country when hard times struck the country that you people did not propose an inflation of the currency." Mann also mentioned the tariff bill. "You, now, in mad haste to inflate the currency, admit the bad results which come from your tariff bill, and the only man in the House who has not heard of the conditions in the country is the distinguished Speaker of the House [There was laughter on the Republican side]."

Carter Glass followed Mr. Mann; he took the last three minutes before the yeas and nays. Glass answered the inflation charge.

> When this bill was under consideration in another branch of Congress, the same charge was brought by a distinguished Republican Senator, and the amount of inflation that he figured out was $1,800,000,000. Two days thereafter he had

to admit that he made a miscalculation of $500,000,000 in that simple sum! [There was applause on the Democratic side.]

A Republican Congress had previously passed the Aldrich-Vreeland Act. "The Republican Party was committed to the Aldrich scheme of currency revision, but intelligent, practical bankers exposed the fact that it embraced possibilities of inflation amounting to $ 6,000,000,000! [There was applause on the Democratic side]." The Republican opposition had harped on the "exclusion of the Republican conferees" and the "caucus rule" during this latest legislation. They were

> forgetting the fact when the Vreeland-Aldrich bill was passed by a Republican Congress the Democratic conferees were excluded. I remember that fact distinctly because I was one of them. I was not admitted to the room until Senator Aldrich on the one side and Representative Vreeland on the other had completed the draft of the bill. Then I was asked in and had it handed over to me.

There was laughter on the Democratic side.

The discussion had ended; Carter Glass "asked for the yeas and Nays." The report of the committee of conference was passed; there were 298 yeas and 60 nays. The approved report went back to the Senate. The next day, there was a final discussion by the Senate and "the Report of the Committee of Conference was agreed to." The Federal Reserve Act became law on December 23, 1913. Eighty-five thousand copies of the Federal Reserve Act were printed for use by the House and the Senate.

Briefly, the Federal Reserve act was as follows:

- There would be established districts equally divided within the United States.
- There would exist Twelve Federal Reserve banks, minimum commencement stock reserve—$4 million each reserve bank. Member banks to pay in an amount equal to 6% of its stock in

one-sixth installments. The member banks have to place a 6% reserve in its district regional reserve bank. The Federal Reserve banks would discount Federal Reserve Notes when lending to member banks. The central bank resembled a retailer.

- Gold reserve—not less than 35% of deposits in each member bank, not less than 40% of the Federal Reserve Notes in circulation. The gold reserve and deposit factors were in place. Currency would be secured by a supposed gold reserve, but paper currency was not created based on a gold reserve. Currency is first created; then the specie factors with gold accumulated apparently allows credits many times the currency creation, either expanding or contracting. The voluminous expanse of credits increase ten to twenty times or more the actual currency circulation. Interest charges may reflect the ten to twenty times the actual currency. Since the Bank of England, since Hamilton, the primary scheme from the record had been the creation of paper currency; capitalization was the intent and the result. How could the escalation of capitalization be done with gold? Money market operations and the creation of currency through commercial paper belie a sum of gold. The 1913 paper currency creation scheme was called "asset" currency in the Congress. Gold was "managed," explained by Dr. Commons (chapter 11), a necessary contrivance to control the quantity of circulation and the accumulation of gold by the Federal Reserve System. The circulation of currency either up or down appeared coincident with the movements of gold, expanding and contracting and the extinguishing of currency. The creation of a non-legal tender redeemable paper currency allowed the central bank to accumulate gold, which was the real objective in 1913. The intended gold accumulation, the real purpose as stated in the first annual report of the Federal Reserve Bank of New York in 1915 appears in chapter 12. From the record, as to gold, it was, whatever was necessary, in the banker's scheme of things!
- Member banks were established within the reserve bank districts. There would be a Federal Reserve Board, seven members in Washington, D.C. The board is the heart of the system; but this board lacked the intended power in the beginning.

- Earnings of stockholders—6% annual cumulative dividend on paid capital stock after expenses. There would be earnings to the Treasury after stockholder earnings.
- Twelve reserve banks would be exempt from federal, state, and local taxation. The twelve banks would control reserves.
- National banks would become member banks.
- State banks and trust companies may become member banks.
- Open market operations—the money market.
- A Federal Advisory Council would be established
- Reserve banks would hold Government deposits
- The currency—Federal Reserve Notes in $5, $10, $20, $50, and $100 denominations.
- Reserve banks may open branch banks in foreign countries.
- Two new credits were inaugurated, the government *obligation* and the *acceptance* as explained by W. Randolph Burgess in his book *The Reserve Banks and the Money Market* published in 1927. The two new credits would produce the Federal Reserve Note.

The government obligation meant just that. The Treasury had to pay for the currency the Bureau of Engraving and Printing printed. The federal income tax law on individuals was passed September 8, 1916. A second income tax law was passed in October 1917. Revenue was needed to pay for the government obligation and World War I. This printed currency, which was issued or "handed" to the Federal Reserve bank, was interest bearing. Secretary Chase articulated a credit circulation in 1861. This newly created currency was the credit circulation; in 1913, it was a non-legal tender Federal Reserve Note, which was payable in gold. The Federal Reserve was given the power to set the rates of interest. The Bureau printed the currency; the Federal Reserve would control the printing of the currency. Today, people simply say, "the Fed is printing money."

The second new money instrument was the "acceptance." The acceptance was a bill primarily of short duration. Federal Reserve Notes would be printed or created against the acceptances; these notes were non-legal tender notes payable in gold. Senator Owen in the Senate said, "Federal Reserve Notes are the best-secured notes that have ever been devised in any banking system in the world." Maturity of these notes was "90 days." This was what the bankers had always wanted, *an elastic currency of short duration payable in gold.*

The acceptance draft, discounted in the banking system, is based on produced goods bought and sold, shipped, etc., primarily imports and exports. The acceptance, the ninety-day transaction, the second part of the new plan, according to Senator Owen, would assure a "safe" elastic currency. The acceptance had been in use in European banking for years; the acceptance became part of the permanent American banking scheme in 1913.

Senator Owen said, "One of the most important features of this bill is the establishment of what is called an open market for bills of exchange and bankers' acceptances such as has long prevailed in Europe, but which has not existed to any great extent in the United States."

When the 1907 panic hit, the circulation vanished. Where did it go? The currency was not circulating! The non-circulating paper currency was, at least in part, the silver certificates, the lawful money legal tender greenbacks, and the national currency. A viable circulation had to be restored to the economy, and it wasn't going to be the aforementioned. The aforementioned currency was apparently locked up somewhere; it was static. A Federal Reserve System would move it, unlock it. But in the meantime, a new and temporary currency had to be created; a new scheme was needed. How was that to be? The vanished currency wasn't in the Treasury. The emphasis, again, was reforming banking and currency in the United States; it was back to the Congress. Cash is what people needed, liquidity, so how can the people get cash again? Aldrich-Vreeland dictated that commercial paper produced by banks, with approval and initial discount by the Treasury, would temporarily solve a new currency issue until 1914. For a while, at least, based on new schemes, there would be no new purchases of long-term government bonds for currency.

During the winding down of the emergency period, the Federal Reserve Act was enacted. In the reserve system, a reserve bank governor or agent orders the printing and issue of the new currency.

The issue would be at the "discretion" of the Federal Reserve Board as stated in Section 16 of the act. The Federal Reserve Act doesn't describe ensuing government debt. In the Federal Reserve statute, the creation of new elastic currency, literally, does not appear as part of the description. The words "elastic currency" appear once in the title of the act.

In "REVIEW AND OUTLOOK" in the *Wall Street Journal* on December 23, 1913,

> However light-heartedly the new banking bill may have been put in final shape, it is in the nature of an experiment graver and broader in its character than that which established the National Banking System in 1863 . . . The names of the men who are to serve on the Federal Reserve Board will be awaited by the business community with more anxiety probably than were the names of the men in the Presidents cabinet.

It was up to "President Wilson to choose men of the most conservative views and the most intimate knowledge of the banking history of the world, in selecting the Federal Reserve Board." The board was the central bank; the board, supposedly, would call the shots.

There is a paragraph in Section 14 of the Federal Reserve Act in reference to the security of the Federal Reserve Notes.

> Every Federal Reserve Bank shall have power: [a] To deal in gold coin and bullion at home or abroad, to make loans thereon, exchange Federal Reserve notes for gold, gold coin or bullion, giving therefore, when necessary, acceptable security, including the hypothecation of United States bonds or other securities which Federal Reserve banks are authorized to hold.

The "hypothecation" is the pledge, the mortgage, the government security, the obligation; it secures the elastic currency, the Federal Reserve Note. The government, the Treasury, the people guarantee the currency with its revenue, customs, and the federal income tax, etc.

The credit circulation was taking shape in 1913. The Treasury by way of the Bureau of Engraving and Printing, would print the paper currency, issue the paper currency to the central bank, borrow the same paper currency, and spend the same paper currency. The government couldn't pay its debt to the new banking system with this paper currency in 1913, courtesy of the Congress. The new elastic currency was printed for the banking system, by order of the central bank; it was not legal tender.

The Federal Reserve System credits the fiat currency security within the system; it's part of the inner workings. This business goes all the way back to the Pennsylvania creditors. In their famous letter to the First Congress, the creditors mentioned the "transfer" of the debt principal without affecting the public credit. The Federal Reserve credits the security within the banking system; it is transferable by law. When the security is transferred, credit is satisfied within the system. Member banks may pay their debts to the reserve bank this way. This "transfer" may take currency out of circulation. Contraction may take place; when severe, credit is removed. Then money is not available; recession may occur.

The Federal Reserve Note of 1913 was similar in purpose to Alexander Hamilton's paper money of the First Bank. Both currencies were not legal tender. The currencies were not legal tender because the paper money was private banking currency. In 1791, the First Bank printed the paper money; the Congress gave the First Bank the power to do so. The Congress in 1791 gave the First Bank, by way of redemption, the power to buy gold with their paper currency. If one may redeem with the note, one may buy with the note. In 1913, the Treasury printed the new elastic currency. It was not legal tender; it was a currency for the banking system. In 1913, the Congress gave the power to the Federal Reserve to redeem or buy gold with the new currency, the Federal Reserve Note. Hamilton's First Bank bought and accumulated gold with its paper currency. The Federal Reserve System, by law, would perform the same function, the acquisition and accumulation of gold; the United States Treasury would complement the transfer.

The 1913 Federal Reserve Act was a continuation of the 1863 bank act; the banking system would continue to accumulate gold. But gold could be acquired quickly. The twenty-year bond was eliminated; it was now the ninety-day transaction.

"The Underlying Motive" was part 2 of the book *The Federal Reserve Act* by C. W. Barron. The book was published in 1914. The "motif" or motive of "this legislation" according to Barron was "to cheapen money." Barron wrote, "The whole primary discussion of this bank act was to make money easier, to cheapen it to farmer and producer and manufacturer and merchant." Barron stated, "The Balkan War scare in 1913 locked up at least 300 millions of gold in European strong boxes and stockings." The First World War was one year away; and gold, the supposed "real money," was already beginning to vanish.

Barron quoted, "'An elastic currency' could have been had by an enactment of 20 lines. The means of re-discounting commercial paper are already at hand." C. W. Barron was a journalist of the *Wall Street Journal* and *Barron's Weekly*.

If the means were "already at hand," why a Federal Reserve? The currency was there before, but it had been called. It had been expended, taken; it was locked up. Apparently, another round of financial mechanisms and new instruments were needed to release the locked-up currency and create new currency. Did Alexander Hamilton initially "cheapen the money" in 1791 when he prescribed a discounting and pyramiding scheme of paper money of the First Bank? The movements of gold, the vanishing currencies, it was 1913 and back to the Congress; and a new phase of "cheapened money" was taking place.

What was Barron's meaning, "to cheapen money" to farmer, etc.? Barron went on that a system was needed "that would give us an average rate approaching that of the Bank of France where interest over a series of years averages between 3% and 4%." Apparently, Barron's explanation of "to cheapen money" was a low interest rate. Why not another description of maybe less or no derision, that is, allowing the initial cost of money to be less expensive? Maybe after the interest on securities and the multiple discounts, the Treasury to the Federal Reserve Board to the twelve regional banks, to the member banks, to commerce, and then to the farmer, the farmer may get the money at less than a 4% interest of what is left of the multiple rediscounted note? How can it be possible?

Wasn't a sovereign state banking discount of currency within its domain before 1863 simpler initially to the farmer and the people than what came later, the multiple currencies and a twentieth-century Federal Reserve System? It appeared Salmon Chase's "credit circulation" was here to stay.

Barron disagreed that Wall Street was responsible for the "centralization" of the currency.

> The banks of the country and the National Bank Act were responsible. The New York banks never originated the system, but, of course, made money out of it . . . . The profit came to the financial powers in New York who knew the ebb and flow of currency, Spring and Fall, and changed their investments as betwixt money, bonds or stock, according to the money currents.

It appeared a natural connection from the start, government and the banking interests. Within a year from the start of Hamilton's bank in 1792, the money center commenced. Trading opened for business in New York in 1793, also in Philadelphia. Barron stated that New York and Wall Street was not responsible for the "centralization" of the currency. Yet, since the beginning, New York was where the surplus money of the country were drawn, centralized; it's confirmed in the *Congressional Record*.

The reserve board, the central bank, would be set up in Washington, D.C.

C. W. Barron wrote that the central bank should be in New York

> as New York city represents about one-quarter of the financial and banking power of the country, including foreign bankers, private bankers, State banks, and National banks . . . constitute about 40% of the banking capital in the regional reserve banks, this city should be the financial

center, for its regional reserve bank cannot be otherwise than the real Central Bank.

C. W. Barron was stating a future plan. There would be twelve regional Federal Reserve banks throughout the country. The plan was to curtail the "centralization" of the currency.

> The entire safety of the situation under this Bank Act is in maintaining "reserve rates" of discount, refusing the popular clamor for easier money or lower rates, and, if discounts must be made, the accumulation of discount reserves in foreign markets where they can be commanded without home disturbance.

Barron continued, "If the new Reserve Board is of the desired quality and character it will be the most unpopular board that ever sat in Washington. It will turn deaf ears to all political and sectional considerations. The greater the clamor for cheap money the tighter it will hold the reserves within or without the country." The C. W. Barron authority was telling it like it was/is.

Pure capitalism in America wasn't designed for all the players. Didn't Alexander Hamilton call the mass of people the great beast? The currency residual as seen, so far in this writing, hasn't included easier money, lower rates, or cheap money. "Cheap money" would require continuous money that was needed to maintain continuous viability, maybe for all, but it would be called expansion then later, inflation. "The accumulation of discount reserves in foreign markets where they can be commanded without home disturbance." From all appearances, this statement was about the movements of gold. The movements of gold during two centuries caused quite a "disturbance." All the gold mined in the United States in the nineteenth century wound up in England and Europe. Since her beginnings, the United States had been a debtor to Europe, primarily England and France. In 1914, Europe owned "10 billions in American securities." Those securities were payable in gold. The purpose, according to the proponents of the new Federal Reserve System, was to reclaim that indebtedness.

Barron wrote in 1914:

England is the creditor of all nations. She has a currency in her bankers' pocket books that gives her a greater per capita circulation at home and abroad than any other country in the world. She has $2,500,000,000 of bankers' bills due daily or within months, which all read 'sterling' or gold. With these, she holds the financial keys of empires. The world is her debtor. London's supreme confidence in her own creditor position is well illustrated in the declaration that the Bank of England has only to raise the discount rate and it can call gold from the moon.

C. W. Barron stated that England had a "greater per capita circulation at home and abroad than any other country in the world." It was the way things were. England's per capita circulation was more than adequate because England was awash in gold. The gold movements did not affect England's per capita paper currency. The gold movements meant payment in gold or its equivalent. In the debtor countries, it meant the disappearance of money or less per capita circulation or a panic or a depression. Remember the Mississippi Scheme? The vultures, the proponents of gold, descended upon France for payment in her specie; and the money disappeared. France's economy took the hit. The United States was enormous in the natural riches and potential growth, but the United States was always a debtor to England. The main reason was gold; the United States was short on gold. The Civil War compounded the problem. American banks shipped government bonds to England. It was payment for private debt; the payment was gold. The condition stayed that way until World War I.

The proponents of gold typified the schemes of the Bank of England and Alexander Hamilton's bank. Was it convertibility or accumulation of the gold? Benjamin Franklin knew the game. He stayed away from banking; he called it "stripping the bank." Thomas Jefferson wanted to deal in specie. Hamilton wanted to deal in specie but through the First Bank's paper currency. The First Bank through capitalization sent $10 million in gold to Europe. The proponents claimed the system was based on a reserve in gold. Thomas Jefferson called it fiction. But the scheme wasn't fiction; the pretense accumulated gold, the real deal.

The currency, the Federal Reserve Note, is created on an impending market, subsequent growth, resulting equity, and the creation of debt. Currency is created out of debt. The paper currency was never created on the basis of gold. The proponents placed gold above all values; it always lurked in the background for redemption to qualify the insidious scheme, the promise to pay. Why the promise to pay twice for the exchange? Gold in comparison to a vast proliferating paper currency and resultant capitalization within a domain was relatively a very small "fixed" quantity. Gold was the international exchange, small in quantity and big in clout; it was the way it was. Gold was the fictional "reserve"; gold was the banker's hole card by which the paper currency of others could be extinguished.

CHAPTER NINE

World War I, Aldrich-Vreeland,
the Federal Reserve

Woodrow Wilson was elected to a second term on November 7, 1916. Wilson was elected because he kept the United States out of the war in Europe. The year before, in his message to Congress, Wilson said, "We have stood apart, studiously neutral. It was our manifest duty to do so." The war in Europe was a year and a half old. "Austria-Hungary," backed by Germany, had declared war on Serbia in July of 1914. The warmongers believed Serbia killed the Archduke Ferdinand of Austria. Britain, France, and Russia, backing Serbia, declared war on Germany. It appears that nations, countries, and their continuous warring with each other is in parallel with and as intractable as the currency continuum. *World Book* states that "the war had its origins in the developments of the 1800's. The chief causes of World War I were [1] the rise of nationalism, [2] a build-up of military might, [3] competition for colonies, and [4] a system of military alliances."

Since 2003, there has been emphasis on the flag of the United States. It seems natural. It's patriotism; it's nationalism, a love of country in any country. The global economy complicates national ideals; it also neutralizes and compromises the fictitious ideals of war.

World Book states that a rise in nationalism was a cause of World War I in 1914. With the advent of the Federal Reserve, it appears a global political banking economy was fermenting almost a hundred years ago. There isn't any difference in principle between a state's sovereignty and a nation's nationalism; both expound in patriotism and independence. A global banking geopolitical economy is adverse to those principles. The word "national" is not in vogue; the emphasis is on domestic. There was once a national product; the United States now has a domestic product amid a global economy. When was the product redefined (later in chapter 18)? Nationalism is out; a global economy is in. Outsourcing of jobs in all directions to and by all countries is adverse to national patriotic flag waving in any country. International money will see to it. From this viewpoint, people will live, grow, and accustom to where they work; it is the nature of things. Immigration to the United States for those seeking money, a better life is constant, and American citizens are leaving the United States to maintain their employment elsewhere, peculiar happenings in the global economy.

The Americas "should keep the processes of peace alive, if only to prevent collective ruin and the breakdown throughout the world of the industries by which the populations are fed and sustained." But there was revolution in Mexico, ongoing since 1910. Wilson said, "We have been put to the test in the case of Mexico, and we have stood the test . . . we have at least proved that we will not take advantage of her in her distress and undertake to impose upon her an order and Government of our own choosing."

But from the record, Wilson had intervened earlier in 1914; he "sided with Carranza's revolutionaries" against "Huerta's dictatorship" in the Mexican Revolution.

Congressman William Bennet of New York in January 1917, before the second session, Sixty-fourth Congress, presented an address by Simeon D. Fess of Ohio.

> The real American problem in Mexico will come when the war in Europe closes. England owns near $500,000,000 worth of property in that country, much of which has been destroyed. So likewise in the case of Germany and France. These foreign investments were made upon invitation from official Mexico. These countries had recognized Huearta as the responsible head and protector of Mexican and foreign citizens and interests . . . these countries at the close of the war will give us the alternative to either pay up or allow them to collect.

Allowing them to collect in Fess's words: "We thereby surrender the Monroe Doctrine." Congressman Fess's address was entitled "Our Outlook after Thirty Months of War."

"After 30 months of the War" in Europe, there were "18,000,000" casualties of which "five million" were dead. The "bonded indebtedness" of the fifteen countries involved would escalate to "$75,000,000,000." England's indebtedness alone had increased almost 20 billion since the start of the war at "$28,500,000" per day. Congressman Fess had repeated these "Appalling Totals" in his address. "Whatever Europe is fighting for she will win but four things—graves, cripples, debts, and taxes." The United States had yet to enter the war. Fess also addressed Russia as the world's future serious threat.

In 1916, President Wilson sent General Pershing into Mexico after the revolutionary Francisco "Pancho" Villa. Villa had crossed the border, killing Americans in New Mexico. Pershing was recalled; Villa was never caught. As part of his neutrality stance, Wilson said "that the states of America are not hostile rivals but cooperating friends." As for Mexico, Wilson hoped for "the rebirth of the troubled Republic."

Although neutral, there had to be an "adequate national defense." President Wilson asked for a buildup of the army and the navy "within five years." The navy would be increased to ten battleships, six battle cruisers, ten scout cruisers, fifty destroyers, etc. The army buildup was an increase to 143,000 men-at-arms. The approximate total cost was estimated at about $100 million. "We cannot handle our own commerce on the seas. Our independence is provincial, and is only on land and within our own borders." The war in Europe had neutralized "independence" on the seas. McKinley had asked for a merchant marine in 1901; it was almost 1916. The United States was still using other carriers to transport its cargo overseas. "We must use their ships and use them as they determine. We have not ships of our own." Wilson stressed that "the United States should be its own carrier on the seas and enjoy the economic independence which only an adequate Merchant Marine can give it." The government had to take the initiative; "proposals will be made to the present Congress for the purchase or construction of ships to be owned and directed by the Government similar to those made to the last Congress."

Wilson said the government "should take the first steps, and should take them at once." Wilson continued, "When the risk has passed and private capital begins to find its way in sufficient abundance into these new channels, the Government may withdraw." This was the deal; it was government before, and as before, it would be government again. It would be government impetus that would change the balance.

"After Thirty Months of War" in Europe, the United States was still at peace, but how was the United States going to satisfy "the inevitable bitterness our policy as a neutral would produce among both belligerents"? Both belligerents were England and Germany. Germany became "incensed . . . not so much because American munitions were sold to the allies as because Germany could not deliver similar purchases." England was the naval, the maritime power, and controlled the seas and the "worlds markets." Germany was the "military power." It was England at sea and Germany on the land.

England established a blockade, and Germany waged unrestricted submarine warfare. Congressman Fess said, "Great Britain can shut us out of the markets of Scandinavia and Denmark and Holland." England was dictating "commerce" at sea. The United States had notified England that the blockade was "'illegal, ineffective, and indefensible.'" Fess pointed out in his address that England admitted that the blockade was "not effectual when she refuses us to sell to neutrals, on the ground that the goods reach Germany." Fess produced "for the RECORD tables of vessels, specifying the goods reaching neutral coasts, that have been seized by Great Britain . . . She does not only say what we may ship, but where we may ship and what route we must take, and at the greatest cost."

There was an agreement. "Contraband is both absolute and conditional." Absolute contraband may be guns and bullets and the like. Great Britain would seize absolute contraband. Conditional contraband such as "foodstuffs, clothing, drugs, automobiles, if going to a neutral port, can not be seized." But Great Britain seized everything. In August of 1915, Great Britain "placed cotton on the contraband list." This affected the markets in the Southern United States.

The "Test Case" was the "'WILHELMENA.'" Great Britain had seized the "Wilhelmena, loaded with foodstuffs and consigned to a Mr. Green, an American citizen." The ship was headed to Germany. Great Britain held "no respect for our rights" at sea. Congressman Fess would vote no more "munitions of war" to Great Britain. Why was it "right to sell her weapons of death and wrong to sell the noncombatants of Germany bread for life"? But Germany had infringed on United States' "rights upon the sea" with her unrestricted submarine warfare. Congressman Fess said,

> I would not stop munitions to aid Germany. Farthest from it, for I fear the militaristic spirit of that great country. And while I fear the spirit of militaristic Germany, I also fear the navalism of Great Britain as I feel it now on the sea. I would not vote for any embargo against any belligerent, but we may be driven to do it to compel respect for us upon the seas.

Congressman Fess touched on the movements of gold since the beginning of the war. Because of war demands from Europe, there was "a balance of trade in our favor of over $4,000,000,000." This was in early 1917. "We have in store the largest stock in gold ever collected by any Government." England and Europe needed munitions and goods, and the United States was shipping it as long as Germany wasn't sinking it. Because of international payments in specie, America was collecting the gold. Fess mentioned that the drain of gold from Europe would "threaten the entire financial fabric by an inevitable paper basis." To counter that, the European countries "mobilized the American securities by offering a premium in their exchange for British Consols." Fess said, "The present problem of Europe is to avoid more gold leaving Europe, and her immediate future problem will be to secure a return of the necessary redemption fund."

What was going to happen after the war as to the United States? Goods will be coming back; there would be an impending immigration problem after the war. Fess mentioned these things, plus the protection of American capital and labor. "The next serious result will be the turning of the balances against us and the inevitable flow of gold to Europe, which if not impeded beyond a certain volume, will endanger our entire money system as now built, with gold as a basis of redemption," this according to Fess. That was the way it was; the redemption thing, the promise to pay, the hole card was very much in place.

On April 2, 1917, President Wilson asked the Congress "for a declaration of war against Germany." Neutrality was at an end; American public sentiment turned against Germany. Earlier, a German submarine, off the coast of Ireland, sank the British liner *Lusitania*; it was May 1915. One thousand two hundred people, including 120 Americans, died. Germany claimed the ship was carrying munitions to Great Britain. Because of the outcry, Germany stopped submarine warfare for a time but later picked it up again. Many more sinkings followed. President Wilson said, "The present German submarine warfare against commerce is a war against mankind." Also, an anti-American plot was discovered by "British Intelligence." The plot was an "alliance" between Germany and Mexico. The plot was if the United States entered World War I, Germany would financially support Mexico's effort to seize the land lost to the United States in the war of 1848, a most ridiculous scenario. It wasn't the plot but the deliberate intent; it was the final blow? War was declared against Germany on April 6, 1917. The United States, again, would venture beyond the Americas.

> The outbreak of the European war precipitated many grave problems. International credits and exchanges were completely disorganized, ocean transportation was for a time partially paralyzed, the entire business and economic structure in this country was shaken to its foundations, and a catastrophe of calamitous proportions was narrowly averted.

This was Secretary McAdoo's opening statement in his annual report to the Congress on December 7, 1914.

The money mechanism, which would carry the country into the middle of 1915, was the extended temporary Aldrich-Vreeland Act. Earlier in July 1914, Secretary McAdoo reminded the "public" that "Aldrich-Vreeland" was ready

> to meet any emergency . . . It must be remembered
> that there is in the Treasury, printed and ready for issue,
> $500,000,000 of currency, which the banks can get upon
> application under the law. The 1863 Banking Act was still
> in place, that is, the Country Banks, the Reserve City Banks
> and the Central Reserve City Banks. Secretary McAdoo met
> with the leaders of the Central Reserve City Banks from New
> York, Chicago and St. Louis.

The topic was "the European crisis . . . it was the consensus that only by liberal and immediate issues of emergency currency could the situation be controlled."

The currency was shipped to the sub-treasuries around the country. The banks were organized into "National Currency Associations . . . The entire country has been divided into 44 National Currency Districts." Emergency currency was placed in these associations that possessed "an aggregate capital and surplus on October 31, 1914, of $1,197,771,001," almost $2 billion. A Federal Reserve Board report stated that over 3 billion was the capital figure. There was, by law, the redemption requirement; it was always the redemption thing, the clinker. Each association was required to place a 5% deposit in gold in the Treasury. McAdoo stated that 5% in "Lawful Money" could be substituted. The monies, and they were out there, took many forms; but the "lawful money" of the United States was the greenback. The greenback was still around, and it was as good as gold. Dewey stated that Aldrich-Vreeland did "good service" until 1915.

Secretary McAdoo was most busy and effective during the period. He organized the Conference for the Emergency Currency, the Conference for Foreign Exchange and Shipping, the Cotton Conference, the Emergency Currency on Cotton Secured Notes, the Cotton Loan Fund, the Gold Fund, as listed by the secretary in the 1914 annual Treasury Report, pages 4 through 17, etc.

"Congestion" was the situation at all the ports; exports had stopped. The railroads placed an "embargo" on all "shipments of grain to Baltimore, New Orleans and Galveston." There were "three pressing" needs: "[1] the restoration of the market for foreign bills of exchange,

[2] the provision of means for transporting grain, cotton and other merchandise abroad, and [3] war risk insurance." The conferences brought together the bankers, industry, businessmen, steamship and railroad companies, state governments, members of Congress, the cabinet, and the president of the United States.

It was "resolved" that the government of the United States would stabilize the currencies and foreign bills of exchange; merchant ships would be purchased and "operated under American registry, in foreign trade on equal competitive terms with all other maritime nations." Temporary "war-risk insurance" would be assumed by the United States government for the duration of the war. It was government initiative in times of emergency, first to last.

The Cotton Conference was called on August 14, 1914. In the words of Secretary McAdoo, "what is really wanted is a restored market for cotton at a profitable price . . . The value of cotton has been injured this year by the European war." The emergency currency would be distributed at 75% of the value of "warehouse receipts." The currency would be distributed by the Treasury to the sub-treasuries, to the national currency associations, to the national banks, to the farmers with rediscounting down the line. The "warehouse receipts" became "commodity paper" when the Federal Reserve System got started. It was in keeping with the new money market bankers' bills scheme. New money would be created out of commodity paper, which was another form of commercial paper. It was asset currency!

Initially, the Treasury would place the emergency currency in the sub-treasuries. The currency was then placed in the national currency associations after a 25% commodity value reduction. The Treasury made 2% interest on the currency issue. The currency associations discounted the currency to the member banks at 4% who, in turn, discounted to the farmer, merchants, and manufacturers at 6% interest or more. When the Federal Reserve System started, McAdoo removed the 2% interest charge to ease things during the cotton crisis; the Treasury and the central bank by law were going to make a profit issuing the nation's currency. In any case, this was Treasury currency; there was the initial cost of the currency to the farmer to commerce, to manufacture, to trade to the people. This was done because of the law passed by the Congress, the people. Thomas Jefferson would call this created currency, by virtue of the constitution, money owed or belonging to the people. The public debt was a "blessing. And to fill up the measure of blessing, instead of paying, they receive an interest on what they owe, from those to whom they owe." And so it went, and so it goes!

McAdoo urged cooperation between "the bankers, merchants, cotton manufacturers and the farmers." Unfortunately, there were banks that didn't cooperate; these banks hoarded money and charged excessive interest rates. McAdoo blamed it on old banking practices, the need to survive. McAdoo mentioned that the Federal Reserve System would alter things, correct those practices. In the meantime, these banks would not receive additional emergency currency by directive of Secretary McAdoo.

This was an interesting, complex period; it was described in Secretary McAdoo's Treasury reports. The emergency Aldrich-Vreeland Act was in place. The national currency associations were formed in all the cities, and a minimum ten national banks comprised each association; this action went on well into 1915. But the Federal Reserve Board was being formed during this time, August 10, 1914. Earlier, hearings were held, and a "Reserve Bank Organization Committee" decided on the twelve reserve bank cities in April of 1914. The Federal Reserve System was forming. The country banks, the reserve city banks, and the central reserve city banks were still in place; McAdoo met with these people in July of 1914. These banks had to be the national banking associations? There were the state banks and trust companies. During the emergency period, the multitude of banks had a surplus capital and reserve of $3.4 billion, but they had no currency? Congressman Sabath, concerning the absence of currency, said, "The only trouble is, that it is not where it should be and is where it should not be."

Five hundred million dollars of emergency currency would be made available to them. In addition to this emergency currency, the Treasury and the banks held national uniform currency, the greenbacks, silver certificates, gold certificates, Treasury notes of 1890, and gold coin. Silver coin was in the sub-treasury vaults. Silver was going to be melted down for later shipment out of the country, to Asia? Aldrich-Vreeland was also amended in 1914; $1 million of the emergency currency would be available if required by the secretary. Also, new plates were being prepared; the Bureau of Engraving and Printing made ready $250,000,000 of Federal Reserve Notes. The Federal Reserve would be "opened for business on the 16th of November" 1914. Considering the complexity of the money matters, McAdoo had to be one of the busiest Treasury secretaries since Alexander Hamilton.

McAdoo reported the London foreign exchange; $450 million of debt owed London by American Banks was due in January of 1915. And a holdup of primarily cotton exportations, which would account for the debt, all contributed to the cotton problem. A "Gold Fund" of $100 million collected from American banks was entrusted to New York banks. The "Gold Fund" to be "administered by a committee of bankers in New York, would restore confidence and afford relief." Secretary McAdoo exhibited the "Gold Fund Plan" to the Congress.

Income tax collection in its first year was slow. There were 357,598 returns out of a population of 100 million. "It is clear that there were thousands of persons who failed altogether to make a return as required by law." McAdoo mentioned that the internal revenue agency was in its first year; many changes were forthcoming. A revenue act in 1918 would alter things. The public debt in 1914 was just under a billion dollars, about $10 per person. McAdoo estimated the stock of gold in the United States in December 1914 at $1.9 billion, 1.2 billion of that was in the Treasury. Because of World War I, the "Fortunes of War," the gold stock grew to 4 billion in the United States by January 1917.

The Congress passed money bills on April 24, 1917; September 24, 1917; April 4, 1918; and July 9, 1918. The Treasury expended plenty in 1917-1918. The war had to be financed. The Treasury was authorized by the Congress to continue a practice adopted during the Civil War; that was the employ of certificates of indebtedness. Interest-bearing certificates at 3.5% to 4.5% were printed and payable in twelve months. The Treasury paid expenditures with the certificates. A revenue act was passed. Four "long term" Liberty Loans were authorized; the Treasury borrowed from the people by subscriptions through the banking system. Long-term bonds could be purchased with the certificates. The Liberty Loans also helped pay for the certificates plus interest, interest on short-term securities, interest on Liberty Bonds, etc. McAdoo was gratified at the favorable response of all the people. The thirty-year Liberty Bonds were payable in gold in principal and interest. Interest in gold at 3.5% was payable in six-month installments. The acts did not state what kind of money purchased a Liberty Bond. The money stock consisted of the following. The predominant circulating currency was the national currency and the Federal Reserve Note. Paper purchased paper, which was payable in gold:

- Gold coin
- Gold certificates—redeemable in gold
- Lawful money, the greenbacks—redeemable in gold
- The 1863 national currency—redeemable in lawful money
- Silver certificates—redeemable in silver
- 1890 Treasury notes—redeemable in gold
- The new Federal Reserve Notes—redeemed in gold

The Treasury purchased obligations from the European countries. The Allies sold securities, borrowing from the United States, to finance their war effort. Great Britain, France, Italy, Belgium, Serbia, Greece, Liberia, Romania, Russia, and Cuba—all borrowed from the United States. World War I had devastated Europe; the United States was transformed into a creditor nation because of it. World War I did come to an end; an "armistice was signed on November 11, 1918." The United States was involved for approximately nineteen months. Almost two million American soldiers and military equipment were sent to Europe. The United States suffered "300,000" casualties, "including 53,000 killed in action and 63,000 dead from war-related disease or accident." The war between the United States and Germany ended officially on July 21, 1921. President Harding interrupted a golf game to sign the document, according to the Complete Book of U.S. Presidents. A delayed Harding informal "ceremony" took place because a Republican-controlled Congress "rejected Wilson's Treaty of Versailles." The official end of the war was concluded by Harding and not by Wilson. The cost of the war was, using Congressman Fess's words, "appalling." Congressman James Sinclair in 1921 produced more "recent statistics" more staggering than Fess's figures of 1917.

Sinclair stated that almost ten million men died in the war. "The money lost was $337,946,179,657."

World War I ended, but war didn't end. The 1917 revolution in Russia, aided by Germany, had deposed the Czar Nicholas II. The czar and his family were interned and later murdered. Early prominent Russian revolutionary figures were Trotsky and Lenin; Stalin followed. The Russian Revolution gobbled up Eastern Europe; millions more would perish. The Communist purge continued into the 1920s. Stalin's personal purge carried into the 1930s. Russia added satellite countries, becoming the Union of Soviet Socialist Republics, the Soviet Union. Was this supposed to be something similar to a United States of America? The United States was maintaining a republic out of a collective United States of America. The reign of Communism had begun.

The Communist spread was rapid. The "Bolshevik" surfaced in the United States, becoming prominent in politics and the American labor movement. Republican Congressman Fess, in a January 1920 address, mentioned the "radical agitator, the revolutionist . . . We passed an Act forcibly deporting all alien enemies interned during the war. The arrests were made; the subjects were corralled at Ellis Island, New York, but no deportations were made; and some of them were soon out at large again." Fess claimed the deportations never took place because of "Bolshevik sympathy of the authorities." Fess associated President Wilson with Socialistic tendencies. "The President's fondness for Socialism is seen in the most motly group of self-advertisers collected about the Administration ever before given prominence." Fess claimed the "Department of Labor" was "overloaded" with "Socialists, if not of Bolshevik beliefs . . . In a brief space of time the most substantial of all Governments has become a topic of concern, in which Russian Sovietism is favored by high authority." Weren't there Soviet sympathizers and Communist membership in the United States for decades before and after the First World War?

Capitalism in the United States, in its purest form, with the addition of the Federal Reserve System and an assist from World War I, transformed the country into an international monetary power. The United States was an extension of the political economic creditor ethic. The United States' infrastructure was growing; the country took off in 1920, but almost immediately, the depression of 1921 hit. Then somehow, the money system would spawn the 1929 crash and the Great Depression, which lasted for a decade, the 1930s. A lot of loot was swept away again; no-redundancy time reared its ugly head. Capitalism, in its purest form, seemed adverse to continuous financial stability. Was Hamilton's capitalism and thereafter in parallel or in tune with the welfare principle of the Constitution? The banking system produced just as it was designed. The banking system, with government help, produced its own welfare system. The American banking collective couldn't, didn't, and wouldn't, in the nineteenth and early twentieth century, accommodate adequately more than 70% of the population.

CHAPTER TEN

"Readjustment"

In November 1919, Carter Glass was the secretary of the Treasury.

> In this period of readjustment from war to peace, reconstruction of regions swept bare by the havoc of the greatest war of all time, of political and economic change, and of world-wide unrest and anxiety, America stands strong economically, financially, and politically among the nations of the earth . . . our credit and financial structure is sound and secure, our gold reserves are the greatest in the world; prosperity flourishes in every branch of industry and in every part of the Nation, and the people of the country are fully employed.

In the period before the United States entered World War I, with business as usual, the Treasury had been spending about $1 billion every year. World War I changed everything. Another big war was over; Carter Glass presented the war period expenditure before the Senate Finance Committee and the Ways and Means Committee in the House. The Treasury spent or borrowed "$32,347,000,000" during the nineteen-month World War I period. It was a new ball game.

Secretary Glass said that "tax receipts, and other revenues" paid 9 billion of the expenditure, but the final total debt after the war was $25.5 billion. Included in the war debt was almost $10 billion owed by the Allies. The Congress had authorized the "secretary of the Treasury on behalf of the United States, with approval of the President, to establish credits in favor of foreign Governments engaged in war against enemies of the United States . . . A total of 10 billion dollars was provided for this purpose." In addition, the War Revenue

Act prescribed an income tax, a profits tax, etc., of $8,000,000,000 per year; the four Liberty loans authorized a total subscription of $20,000,000,000, and $8,000,000,000 in certificates of indebtedness was authorized. President Wilson, after the war in December 1918, asked for a reduction in the income tax. Carter Glass, in November 1919, was asking for a fifth Liberty Loan; "further borrowing must be done." The borrowing would be done with the issue of certificates of indebtedness "from time to time." These certificates would be funded "by the use of short-term notes, in moderate amounts, at convenient intervals, when market conditions are favorable, and upon terms advantageous to the Government." Secretary Carter Glass wanted a "continuance of ample revenues from taxation" and a "sober economy."

The secretary lauded the "patriotism of the American people . . . The loyal and efficient work of the organization in the Treasury, the Federal Reserve banks and the Liberty loan committees, great and effective as it was, would have amounted to naught had it not sounded the note of patriotic appeal."

"The telegraph and telephone lines will of course be returned to their owners so soon as the re-transfer can be effected without administration confusion . . . The Railroads will be handed over to their owners at the end of the calendar year." President Wilson stated this in his message to the Congress in May 1919. In December 1918, he said, "It was necessary that the administration of the railways should be taken over by the Government so long as the war lasted. It would have been impossible otherwise to establish and carry through under a single direction the necessary priorities of shipment."

Wilson had recently returned from Paris; he spent a great deal of time in Europe after the war, presenting his famous "Fourteen Point" peace initiative. Earlier in 1915, Wilson told the Congress, "The transportation problem is an exceedingly serious and pressing one in this country. There has from time to time of late been reason to fear that our Railroads would not much longer be able to cope with it successfully, as at present equipped and coordinated." Because of interstate commerce legislation, the railroads became a safer place to work and a much-improved way to travel. The eight-hour workday was established for railroad labor. In 1893, the Congress had passed the Railroad Safety Appliance Act. The act "required air brakes and automatic couplers on all trains." Excessive high rates were common on the railroads. Later legislation in 1920 would allow the Interstate Commerce Commission "control over railroad rates;" it was "the Transportation Act." Railroad rates became more favorable.

President Wilson said that the "railroads were taken over by the Government." Wilson didn't mention the cost. The government may have controlled the railroads during World War I, but it was more of a rental of the railroads to the tune of "$ 300,000,000" per year.

In 1919, the Federal Reserve had been in existence for five years. Secretary Glass brought up "Currency and Credit Expansion." Was there existing an inflation of the currency? "The Chairman of the Senate Committee on Banking and Currency requested the views of the Federal Reserve Board on the subject." Congress was asking whether legislation was necessary "for the gradual reduction of the currency in circulation." If there was inflation, was it the "cause contributing to high prices"? According to Secretary Glass, under the present system, the currency expansion was a result of market demand. "Currency expansion, therefore, is an effect and not a cause of advancing prices." Glass said, "The primary cause of high prices was the demand for commodities by the European belligerents before our entry into the war and by the United States and the belligerents combined after our entry into the war."

Governor W. P. G. Harding of the Reserve Board responded with a letter to Congress: "Currency regulation at this time is unnecessary and undesirable." Harding concluded the following in his letter:

- As to gold and silver coin, gold and silver certificates, and 1890 Treasury Notes, no legislation was required.
- There "remained" $347 million in greenbacks. They were not "a disturbing factor." To take them out of circulation would require funding. There was in reserve in the Treasury "45%" of the greenback circulation in gold. If the greenbacks were retired, they would have to be replaced with "another form of currency."

- There still remained $658 million in national currency in circulation. Sixty million had been retired since the Federal Reserve Act, Two percent bonds secure this currency. This currency would gradually be retired by funding.
- Three hundred fifty-seven million dollars in Federal Reserve Notes had been issued by April 1, 1917. The notes were "secured by United States obligations." Some of the Reserve notes "replaced national bank notes," and "standard silver dollars melted or broken up and sold as bullion under authority of the Act of April 23, 1918, known as the Pittman Act."
- More than $2.5 billion in Federal Reserve Notes had been issued by August 1, 1919. The increased reserve issue was more than half the total circulation outside the Treasury. The total circulation outside the Treasury was $4.8 billion. The total in deposits was $26.8 billion. The total in gold increased to $3.1 billion because of "heavy purchases of supplies" by the European belligerents.
- "It appears therefore that those who see in the larger volume of circulation in the United States the prime cause of increased costs of living and who seek a remedy by a forced contraction of the currency must have in mind the Federal Reserve note and Section 16 of the Federal reserve Act as amended June 21, 1917; which provides for its issue and redemption."
- The amended act required all reserves of all member banks shall be placed in the twelve reserve banks. Also, the "amendment authorized the Reserve banks to exchange Federal Reserve notes for gold." This legislation required all the banks to transfer their gold to the reserve banks.
- The reserve notes were not legal tender, but they were redeemable in gold. They could "not be forced into circulation in payment of the expenses of the Government, or for any other purpose, as they can be issued only in exchange for gold or against a deposit of negotiable paper growing out of a legitimate commercial transaction." They didn't "count as reserve money for member banks." If they became "redundant in any locality they are returned to the Treasury at Washington, or to a Federal Reserve Bank for redemption."
- There should be no currency legislation at this time. The country should save, not be extravagant, work toward the

"liquidation of the debt"; "while the bills have been settled by loans to the Government, these obligations, so far as they are carried by the banks, must be absorbed before the war chapter of the financial history of the country can be closed."

All the monies, all the currencies were still there—the greenbacks, the national currency, the gold and silver coin, the gold and silver certificates for coin, the Treasury notes of 1890, and the new Federal Reserve Notes. The Aldrich-Vreeland temporary currency was not mentioned. Harding wrote that the greenbacks were not a "disturbing factor"; he added that the greenbacks were circulating in $1, $2, and $5 denominations.

The greenbacks were held, and they circulated; the greenbacks were the "lawful money." The Treasury held them; they paid in gold. The Federal Reserve Notes could be redeemed for the "lawful money," the same as gold. The redemption requirement kept the greenbacks tied up in the redemption fund. The greenbacks couldn't have been and, no doubt, weren't a "disturbing factor" considering the proliferation of $2.5 billion in Federal Reserve Notes in five years. The creation of the new Federal Reserve Notes was the extension of the new printing/issue/funding/credit circulation. Governor Harding stated in his letter that those seeking a contraction had "in mind the Federal Reserve note . . . the Federal Reserve Act as amended . . . which provides for its issue and redemption." It appears Harding had intimated gold was on the mind of those wanting contraction and redemption? In other words, contract the Federal Reserve Notes and retire them for the gold. Gold was shipped to the United States from abroad during the war, in abundance, for war expenditures and safety; the United States, apparently, was also a repository.

Section 16 of the Federal Reserve Act states,

> Federal Reserve notes, to be issued at the discretion of the Federal Reserve Board for the purpose of making advances to Federal Reserve banks through the Federal Reserve agents as hereinafter set forth and for no other purpose, are hereby authorized. The said notes shall be obligations of the United States and shall be receivable by all national and member banks and Federal Reserve banks and for all taxes,

customs, and other public dues. They shall be redeemed in gold on demand at the Treasury Department of the United States, in the city of Washington, District of Columbia, or in gold or lawful money at any Federal Bank.

Federal Reserve Notes were printed in "denominations of $5, $10, $ 20, $50, $100, as may be required to supply the Federal Reserve banks."

The Federal Reserve Act was lengthy; it became more so by 1920. The act had been amended six times. The new Federal Reserve Note was a bank note; Congressman Lindbergh said that in 1912. The notes would be "handed" to the banks at their "discretion and "for no other purpose." The non-legal tender notes were issued to the banks and "retired" for gold. Alexander Hamilton did the same thing in 1791. After 122 years, the banking interests were achieving the same result with the third central bank, the accumulation of gold.

Governor Harding presented a table in his letter. The table showed almost $4.8 billion total in circulation, which included all the currencies, as of August 1, 1919. The circulating per capita figure was $45. The $45 per capita figure was about the same as during the Civil War period. The figure would reach $57 per capita in 1920. As with all the war periods, plenty of money abounded, plenty of material, plenty of goods, plenty of demand, and prices soared. The government debt generated in nineteen months was $26 billion; bank deposits totaled about 26 billion, this with a $5-billion circulation. It was the "pyramiding bank credit upon bank deposits, which consist largely of the very notes or obligations given for the security of bank credit" (E. F. Ladd of North Dakota in the Congress in December 1921). The 2.5 billion in Federal Reserve Notes issued during the World War I period, representing more than 50% of the circulation, probably purchased in considerable amount the Liberty bonds. The United States was running up the public and private debt with the credit circulation. The Treasury paid in gold on retired elastic currency. What could be the result of all this?

C. W. Barron wrote, "The Federal Reserve banks may become within a reasonable number of years the holders of substantially all the gold in the country."

In 1920, the Sixty-fifth Congress was in its third session. Business as usual included the illegal aliens, the Bolsheviks, the release and legislation of the railroads, an amended tariff to offset foreign "dumping," revision of the pension bills, repair of the naval fleet, maintaining an army, the war deserters (and there were thousands of them), the Indian nations, the postal service, the diplomatic service, rivers and harbors, the transfer of the national budget responsibility to the Congress, making gold certificates legal tender, etc., and a growing peacetime Federal budget of "$4,000,000,000 per year."

In February of 1920, Congressman Fess issued a "warning." European countries wanted more financial aid. Those same countries hadn't paid back any of the $10 billion borrowed during the war. At the same time, the League of Nations wasn't doing the United States any favors. The league wanted to "internationalize the war debt . . . the United States must be compelled to pay its share." According to the foreign press, for the United States "to make the world safe for democracy, its duty is not performed until it has shared the cost of the war." Reading into those words, it would appear the United States didn't suffer enough indebtedness, like ten million dead. In other words, the United States should forgive the debt; the United States was "wealthy." But, apparently, the profiteers were for it; the "financial leaders" in the country were "anxious to help finance Europe's needs." The owners of World War I indebtedness wanted more. Congressman Fess said, "For myself, I am through voting further Government extension of credit." The 10 billion was owed to the Treasury and the people of the United States. The United States Senate "rejected the Treaty of Versailles." The United States rejected the League of Nations; the country did not become a member. Today, the United States appears compromised because of its membership in and the existence of the United Nations as part of the global economy.

Year 1920 was a turbulent year; there was great "expansion" of credit. Federal Reserve Note circulation had reached more than $3 billion. In early 1920, the reserve banks raised the discount rate "to control the undue credit expansion; it persisted." On top of that, "Record Crops" had to be harvested. "The beginning of the crop-moving season found the banks with credits still largely extended." In addition, "Europe's demand for food and raw materials lessened." D. F. Houston was the new secretary of the Treasury; he said the banks recognized their obligations, which may have been questionable. "Federal Reserve banks in the industrial sections re-discounted in large volumes for those in crop-moving sections." There was "considerable expansion of credits. But still, for reasons beyond the control of the banking establishments, or the Government, prices of farm products fell, and fell suddenly; and those who were distressed began to look in other directions for relief."

Houston said, "The blame must rest largely on the public . . . Producers whose products could not be satisfactorily marketed and whose prices had fallen demanded that the Treasury intervene, they asked either that it deposit money in certain sections or that the activities of the War Finance Corporation be resumed." Secretary Houston mentioned that neither the Treasury nor the finance corporation had any money; the two would have to borrow at 6% interest. "But this system is obviated by reason of the existence and practices of the Federal Reserve system." The finance corporation was set up "to help win the war." It was an agency supposedly being phased out; it was restored later.

The Treasury would have to borrow at 6% interest? What happened to the desired 3% or 4% interest rate that C. W. Barron stated the new reserve system would bring to the country? Whatever works in the scheme of things! This was evident in the new system, the credit circulation. The Federal Reserve had increased the discount rate to curb inflation. The cost of money increases while the economy is moving forward. Inflation may be checked, but the banking system and the Treasury increase profits in the process. To afford the cost of the increased discount rate, the people pay additional, over and above, for the initial cost of their money because the economy is good. It's an apparent "blessing" afforded the people.

In March 1920, V. F. Newell, a "banking expert from Chicago," sent a report to the Congress explaining the "money conditions of the country . . . the leading 12 banks of Chicago." These banks showed 1.2 billion in deposits and 1.1 billion in loans; these banks had "loaned out most of their deposits" then borrowed over $160 million. The report was presented by Congressman Edward J. King of Illinois. The report stated that "inflation has become a menace when 12 Banks in a money center carry only 3 per cent of $1,200,000,000 deposits in cash on hand." Conditions were not much better than

> in the panic of 1907 . . . The big banks are responsible for the present unnatural conditions and the high cost of most values. The high cost of living is the result of their reckless policies and profiteering in interest rates . . . . Reserve Banks should not be run for profit any more than the Office of the Comptroller of the Currency, or the United States Treasury at Washington.

But the Treasury or the government was making a profit in the system. Senator Howe said that before the Federal Reserve Act was passed, inflation would not be a problem with the new system in place. Mr. Newell wrote,

> The result has been to undermine social conditions, rob the consumer, and add many billions of dollars to the national debt through unfair prices . . . . A higher power than banks or a Reserve Board must fix the volume of money in use. The amount must be continuous and uniform to insure stable conditions and prevent exploitation of the public.

Year 1920 was the beginning of the famous decade, the "Roaring Twenties," but it wouldn't begin until 1922-1923. The Nineteenth Amendment was ratified in 1920, "Woman Suffrage." Women finally had the right to vote. Also, the self-righteous turned the trick; the period of "Prohibition" began. It was the Eighteenth Amendment. The manufacture and sale of alcoholic beverage was declared illegal in the United States; it was boom time for Canada. The 1920s was a period of great expansion—airplanes, automobiles, radio, motion pictures, refrigerators, washing machines, illegal booze, contraband from Canada, the "speakeasies," the installment plan, and the incomparable stock market. Unfortunately, Prohibition, a big mistake, among other things, helped launch the so-called American gangster; the supposed crime family became an American institution.

Secretary Houston reported that there was plenty of money in circulation, easy credit, and available loans. Debts were "largely extended." Why did the bottom fall out of the agricultural market price? It was the new twentieth century thing called deflation. But there was also expansion or the new term "inflation" of the currency. Congressman Fess, at the time, said the dollar was worth about 63¢. According to Secretary Houston, it was not the fault of the banks or the government. Whose fault was it? Who pulled the string? Secretary Houston blamed the "public"; it was the fault of the people.

The Federal Reserve was seven years old; and the farmer, manufacturer, and laborer of the United States were taking the initial hit from the new Federal Reserve System. There was a huge contraction of Federal Reserve Notes. Secretary Houston said the Treasury had been "obviated" because of the existence of the Federal Reserve System. The government made the Federal Reserve its "agent," and apparently, there was no going back. The Federal Reserve resembled a retailer handling the country's currency. But "what the Government does by another, it does by itself." If an action or inaction by the Federal Reserve was cause that dumped on the farmers, agriculture, and the country in 1921, then the United States government, maybe more accurately the Treasury, gave cause to dump on them.

Congressman Edward King of Illinois, in June 1921, in the midst of the Depression, in the House, called the aftermath of two laws an apple of Sodom. In 1916, the Congress passed the "Webb bill." In 1919, the Congress passed the "Edge bill." King said the two laws did everything opposite to what was promised. Because of the Edge law, the price of cotton had "reached its present depths of degradation . . . Suffering had not been alleviated but increased among the farmers, manufacturers and laborers. International exchange has been 'stabilized' into bewilderment and order has surrendered to confusion, with chaos still reigning over all." An incensed and rhetorical King said the laws were supposed to

> boom the price of cotton, wheat and cattle; and cause to flow benefits to every working man in the country, accelerate the millennium, and nullify the "flu." Yet we are today confronted by diabolical deflation of the price of the

farmer's products, instituted last summer and followed by
stagnation of business and unemployment.

The "Webb" and "Edge" bills were enacted as amendments to the
Federal Reserve Act. The two laws expanded Section 25 of the Federal
Reserve Act. Section 25, originally, would allow reserve member
associations or banks with a capital and surplus of $1,000,000
(later expanded to $2,000,000) to establish branch banks in foreign
countries. The laws were enacted to expand United States trade in
foreign countries. Emphasis was outside the country; exit the Federal
Reserve Note.

Senator E. F. Ladd of North Dakota gave a speech before the "Monetary
Conference, held in Washington on December 15, 1921." The speech,
which covered "general agricultural conditions," was entitled "Why I
introduced Senate Bill 2342." The Federal Reserve System was seven
years in existence. Senator Ladd wanted the government to take
back the sole possession and issue or distribution of the nation's
currency "to give to all the people on equal terms access to the
productive facilities that all have created." The country's "buying
power" was "concentrated in the hands of a few"; the farm belt was
in a $38-billion debt crisis, and almost seven million people were out
of work. Agriculture affects the whole country. Ladd stated that his
bill, in "principle," had been endorsed by the "American Farm Bureau
Federation." The Farm Bureau had a membership of 1.5 million of
the "most progressive farmers in the country." The bureau wanted
a "proper system of financing which shall be truly national in its
character" and a system "not with a view of private gain." There were
several resolutions by the bureau, which would be presented to the
Congress. One resolution would give "proper credit for farmers on
12 to 24 months' paper instead of short-term credit now available."
Another resolution was "personal rural credits secured by proper
insurance features and the creating of machinery that will allow
cooperative societies to get money direct." Ladd wanted to establish
a loan bureau under the sovereignty of the government. Ladd wanted
"Lawful Money Only Loaned."

What was the lawful money? The lawful money was the greenback
or its equivalent. Actually, before the greenback, before the Civil

War, there existed "cooperative societies" within each domain. The societies were within the sovereign states. The farmers, the people were afforded the local or state bank from which to get their initial issue of money "directly." Wasn't it simpler? The people got their money directly! There hadn't existed an expensive array of currency rediscounting machination as in the Federal Reserve agent to the comptroller to any one of twelve reserve regional banks to the member banks to commerce to the people. It was the third try, and a central banking system was a done deal.

A uniform currency and collection system made sense, but the nation's currency issue should not function for excessive private gain. The initial cost of issue should be consistent with the expense of issue only. It was President Jackson's premise; the central bank becomes most powerful in conception and design. In 1912, Congressman Lindbergh said the system "simply gives the bankers the privilege of extending credits to charge the people interest on, while the Government supports it." The interest-bearing currency feeds those near the "seat of Government" before the people have access to the currency, truly a "blessing."

Senator Ladd didn't want the banks to

> lend on a basis of bank deposits, except in so far as those deposits consist of lawful money of the United States, issued by the proposed Loan Bureau under the provision of this bill. Thus the entire evil of pyramiding bank credit upon bank deposits, which consist largely of the very notes or obligations given for the security of bank credit will be done away with.

Ladd wanted "to adjust the volume of credit expressed in lawful money at all times to the volume of production."

The Federal Reserve System discounts deposits, which is money already borrowed, over and over again, the original discount by the board being predicated on future production. It was pointed out earlier by Congressman Platt, in banking parlance, a deposit is money borrowed, not merely just money deposited. An example, speaking in the House on November 1, 1919, Mr. Platt said J. P. Morgan's National

City Bank of New York had "a combined capital" of "$87,000,000; and deposits of about three quarters of a billion dollars." The deposits were about nine times the bank's total capital, or the money borrowed was nine times the bank's total capital. It followed the basic 1:10 ratio of circulating money to product. On the surface, gold did not appear any part of that equation. Consider lending the same $100 a minimum eight to ten times at 6% interest.

"The total resources of all banks of the United States on June 30, 1920, amounted to $53,000,000,000, not including Federal Reserve Banks." These resources, assets, credits, deposits, whatever, accumulated with a reported United States Treasury report circulation of about $5 billion, an example of the velocity of money, projected wealth, or owned indebtedness, whatever.

Senator Ladd wanted to end "the evils of the present system, the taking of enormous profits when prices are going upwards and the capitalizing of those profits against production when prices are going downward . . . . the periodical deflation of prices."

Ladd said there were "6,500,000 farms, and on these farms are employed 18,000,000 men." It was "the greatest Industry" in the United States, but it was hurting. There was deflation in the farm belt. The farmer was getting no price for his wheat and cattle, and yet "most of us cannot buy what we need." Deflation was "bankrupting the farmers by the millions." There was supposedly a glut of farm products, more than was needed, but the consumer couldn't buy the products anyway; the consumer couldn't afford the prices. There was deflation and inflation at the same time. The farms,

> a lifetime was swept away in a few months by unnecessary rapid deflation brought on, according to John Skelton Williams, former Comptroller of the Currency, deliberately and in cold blood by the Federal Reserve system officials, the officers of which have no interest or sympathy for the American farmer, nor do they understand his problems, because they reap their profits from the commercial and speculative interests of the country, and in the fleecing of the farmers by prearranged panics, apparently successfully

timed, brought on and managed by the great financial and banking interests who now control the worlds greatest monopoly, the lifeblood of the Nation—its currency and credit.

Before any of this business, before the Federal Reserve Act, Senator Owen said, "These elastic Federal Reserve notes are the best-secured notes that ever have been devised in any banking system in the world." Then in 1921, these elastic notes were still elastic. Unfortunately for the people, they were contracting; they were not expanding.

There was a problem with Ladd's plan. His plan would be based on the lawful money, which was the fixed greenback circulation. There were already $3 billion in Federal Reserve Notes put in circulation and counting. There was no going back. But the "and counting" figure peaked in December 1920. By July of 1921, it was a different story. In the *Wall Street Journal*, Friday morning, July 1, 1921, in the column entitled "Reserve Report Shows Volume of Credit Retired," the following "Federal Reserve notes in circulation throughout the country have declined from the high point of December 23, 1920 . . . 22%" A later *Journal* article showed the credit retirement from $3 billion to 1.2 billion, a 60% drop or contraction of the reserve money supply. A great influx of gold into the country coincided the contraction.

The Federal Reserve System had removed more than $1,800 million or 1.8 billion in Federal Reserve Notes from circulation in six months. The circulation had been reduced in amount to about 1.2 billion from the approximate previous high of 3.0 billion. This had to be a crippling contraction of the money supply. This was the beginning of many periodic currency manipulations or contractions that occurred throughout the twentieth century. Did the removal or retired notes result in a possible transfer in gold to the Federal Reserve banking system? The *Wall Street* article stated "credit retired." From this viewpoint, the system was not designed, principally, to have a reserve in gold but a means by which gold may be acquired by the Federal Reserve System. *Wall Street Journal* articles of July 6 and 7, 1921, confirmed the gold or "cash" sitting in the vaults of the Federal Reserve. Senator Smith in the Senate "charged that banks are being compelled by the Board to call loans and liquidate their holdings." C.

W. Barron, in a different fashion, confirmed the bank's collection of gold in his writing. Federal Reserve Notes were elastic; the system, apparently, retired the Federal Reserve Notes quickly and built up a stash in gold quickly. The gold was obtained apparently from all sources. A "reserve fund" had to be maintained in the Treasury for that purpose. In any event, the contracted circulation probably contributed to the depression of 1921. Many businesses failed; one of them was the Lincoln Motor Company. Henry Ford bought Lincoln. The Lincoln automobile became the Ford luxury product; it remains to this day. But Henry Ford was also in dire straights in 1921. Plants were closed; he owed "$55,000,000 in taxes." Instead of being forced to borrow $75 million from the banks, he forced his seventeen thousand dealerships to borrow against the cars. Ford "shifted the burden" to the dealers. The dealers who refused were "removed." Ford's move, a "Sound Economic Theory Proved Successful," was unprecedented. Henry Ford may have been ruthless in his will to survive; he had no love for the bankers. Ford blamed the banks, the Federal Reserve, for the 1921 depression. Davis Rich Dewey mentioned the depression of 1921, in passing, in his *Financial History of the United States*.

Governor W. P. G. Harding gave an address the day before the Senator Ladd speech on December 14, 1921, before the Washington Chamber of Commerce. The address was entitled "The Federal Reserve System as related to American Business." Apparently, there were misconceptions about the Federal Reserve System; Harding would present the system in a "fair and proper light." In his speech early on, Harding said, "The Federal Reserve Act did not establish a Central Bank. On the contrary, it made possible the establishment of as many as 12 Federal Reserve Banks." Harding acknowledged that the Federal Reserve Board "supervised" the twelve regional banks. But Harding said there was no central bank. After seven years, in 1921, there was no admittance of a central bank by a governor of the Federal Reserve, probably because of and to quell 130 years of central banking paranoia. But C. W. Barron called it for what it was in his 1914 writings. Barron declared that New York City should be the location of the "real Central Bank," not Washington, D.C.

Was Governor Harding's presentation of the Federal Reserve System in a "fair and proper light" correct? In those first years, apparently, the twelve reserve banks acted independently. The twelve banks were competing with each other in the purchase and sale of government securities. Where profit motive was incessant, twelve reserve banks, apparently, acted in their own interests and not in the interest of the public.

In November 1919, the First World War had been over one year. European countries were supposedly broke and picking up the pieces; they were short on "gold and goods." According to the latest estimate, the total cost of the war was "$200,000,000,000."

Apparently, European banks owned all that indebtedness except "$16,000,000,000" that was owed the United States Treasury and private U.S. entities. The aftermath of all wars is death and destruction; the profiteers, the owners of the indebtedness, always pick up the pieces. The Versailles Treaty, at first, dictated a reparation debt burden of almost $30 billion to be paid by Germany. The money figure didn't include the loss of "Alsace-Lorraine, Eupen, St. Vith, Malmedy, Moresnet, Danzig, and the Rhineland for 15 years," her colonies in East Africa, and also the Marshall and Gilbert islands in the Pacific. "Financially, the interest charge Germany must pay to our allies will amount to $1,250,000,000 annually. In other words, she must pay in gold or merchandise." Congressman McFadden was speaking in the House on November 3, 1919. The Versailles Treaty, from the start and from the record, almost assuredly dictated the start of another war twenty years hence, World War II.

The Civil War had altered the United States political economy. World War I financially impacted the Occident; the United States had emerged. The United States was transformed from debtor nation to creditor nation. It was the beginning of a new era. Before the war, England primarily, then Germany, France, the Europeans were the leaders of world trade. They were the leaders because of shipping, foreign investment, foreign banks, railway systems built in the foreign countries, an intricate network of foreign credit between London, Berlin, Paris, to Africa, South America, to the Orient and back again. To that extent, the United States, except for the National City Bank of New York (J. P. Morgan), was not in the picture. Morgan's "subsidiary" had "more than 70 Branches all over the world, many of them in Central and South America." It was understandable, considering Morgan's connection, from the beginning, with Great Britain and European banking.

During the war in 1916, the Federal Trade Commission reported the world trade situation to the Congress.

> If Americans are to enter the markets of the world on equal terms with their organized competitors and their organized customers; if they are to expand the foreign trade of the United States as they should, and if our small producers and manufacturers are to obtain their rightful share of foreign business on profitable terms; they must be free to unite their efforts.

The war was over; European countries were broke. Now was the time to move. Congress made the moves. The Edge and Webb bills and Section 25 and amendments thereto of the Federal Reserve Act were enacted to promote American export of foreign trade. The placement of Federal Reserve System branch banks in foreign countries was necessary to achieve that end.

In the first year after the war, American exports exceeded imports by about $4.1 billion. It was because of World War I; the war caused the favorable imbalance of trade. Conditions in Europe were dire; help was needed. Goods were shipped, but there was no payment. And currency exchange rates were down. World War I claimed $200 billion of European indebtedness except for 16 billion. The European countries apparently had money, a depreciating paper money; specie was in suspension. European countries, supposedly, would not be able to pay the United States for years. How were European countries going to pay the United States? According to Congressman King, they would pay by way of American debentures.

"Everybody who glances at the financial columns of the Newspapers knows of the unprecedented decline in foreign exchange, due to the fact that Europe owes to the United States vast sums of money and has not the gold or the goods to pay immediately or in the near future." The pound sterling had fallen from "a par" of $4.9 to $4.2.

The $4.2 was the exchange in New York. It was because England owed the United States more than $4 billion. On the London exchange, the "French exchange was 8.83 and Italian 10.82." The bottom was falling out of the German mark; by late summer, the exchange for the pound sterling was 90 deutsche marks. Congressman Platt was speaking in the House. It was November 1, 1919; he was promoting Senate Bill 2472, the "Edge Bill." Senator Edge had introduced the bill. The bill was eventually passed as an amendment and extension of Section 25 of the Federal Reserve Act. The promotion and the sustaining of export trade was the legislative initiative as an extension of the "Webb bill." The Webb bill became law on September 7, 1916. With the foreign exchange rates falling, imports were increasing. Platt said,

> Already, there has been a considerable decrease in exports and a considerable increase in imports, but we do not want our exports to Europe slump disastrously to ourselves and to our customers if we can devise a good means for payment. They have good assets and securities, and under the system proposed, we are to take their securities, under approval of the Federal Reserve Board, as collateral for payment.

And this was the crux of a new scheme; the "good means for payment" was the "collateral for payment."

England, the world power, controlled the world's exchange rates; she had for a long time. All currencies were based on the pound sterling. In the *Wall Street Journal* of July 1, 1921: "They have been, and are, the world's premier trading nation and in the face of the most stupendous task ever faced by a nation, they have kept sterling in the front rank as the currency in which the world transacts its business."

In 1919, as before, the United States would take the hit in an exchange. On November 3, 1919, Congressman Steagall elaborated. The 4.9 in England and the 4.2 in America meant $49,000 in gold in England and 42,000 in gold in the United States.

> This makes a difference of $7000. This sum represents about 40 bales of cotton at present prices. If we had in operation the banking system which the present bill seeks to establish;

the same firm could go to the American branch bank or Agency in Liverpool or London and negotiate a loan by putting up securities there which would be handled in this country without this vast loss in exchange. The difference would enable the English Firm to pay six cents a pound more for American cotton than under existing conditions.

Prior, American traders, according to the experts, had to go through foreign banks in negotiating credits.

Senate Bill 2472, which was another amendment to Section 25 of the Federal Reserve Act, created two kinds of American foreign banks. "Two classes of Corporations can be incorporated under this Act." On November 3, 1919, Mr. Nelson of Wisconsin was promoting the bill before the House. One bank would "engage principally in foreign banking business." The other class would "engage principally in investment banking, taking long-time paper, mortgages, and bonds, and issuing against such securities their own debentures, promissory notes or bonds, under such limitations as the Federal Reserve Board may prescribe." Nelson assured the House; there were plenty of "safeguards" in the bill. All business by these American foreign banks was to be foreign business, nothing stateside "except such as in the judgment of the Federal Reserve Board shall be incidental to its international or foreign business."

Congressman Edward J. King of Illinois was the bill's harshest critic. The bill became law on December 24, 1919. King and a small minority were opposed. The "collateral for payment" was the "incidental" part of its "international or foreign business." The bill stated these banks would do no business in the United States except what was incidental to their foreign business. Before the bill became law, Congressman King, speaking in the House on November 7, 1919, said,

> The purpose of this bill is to create an institution that will be the instrumentality through which we will receive foreign securities as pay for the goods we export . . . the fact is that the urgent thing intended to be done is this thing of marketing foreign securities here in America . . . . this new International foreign bank would take these securities,

and against them as a basis, issue debentures which the American public would buy, thus securing the money with which to pay for goods bought in this country.

King said that ex-secretary Redfield "explained" this to the "American Manufacturers Export Association . . . . the Secretary's words were, 'Thus we would pay ourselves for the goods we export, and so the good work would go on.'" Redfield had been the secretary of Commerce.

American investment money would purchase debentures offered by American foreign banks. The debentures were bonds or drafts against foreign securities, the securities being purchased by the American foreign banks. The device for payment of American exports to foreign countries was American currency for American goods.

Was there "no redundancy" in Europe, especially in Germany? The mark was falling out of sight. There was a protective American tariff in 1921. On May 20, 1921, an "anti-dumping clause" was added to "prevent the dumping of foreign merchandise in the United States to the injury of the home market." At the same time, the Edge law was being "perfected." Proposed amendments to the Edge law "would increase the importation into this country of foreign manufactures . . . While the right hand is erecting the barrier, the left hand is tearing it down." In June, Mr. King, in the House, was debating the proposed Edge law amendment. Earlier in January 1921, Congressman John Garner said the following about the protective tariff: "You can not sell in foreign markets and not buy in return. They have nothing with which to pay for your goods except an exchange of their goods or products." King remarked, "The truth of that statement is immovable. We therefore find ourselves at the start in this conflict between the protectionists and the International banker, at whose insistence all so-called foreign-trade legislation has been passed, in this anomalous position."

The European countries, according to the *Congressional Record*, were short on cash. Apparently, they weren't going to borrow from the European banker? Who would buy their securities? Mr. King said, "The exact method of stuffing the purse of the moneyless man abroad was never carefully explained." Maybe it went like something like this: American foreign banks set up in Europe; these banks purchased the European nations' securities. The American foreign banks created debentures against those securities and sold the debentures to the American investor. The American debenture money paid the foreign securities, paid the American exports, paid the debt to the European banker, paid the American foreign banker and the reserve system, paid the American manufacturer and farmer, etc. Everybody would get paid? Secretary Redfield said, "And so the good work would go on." It was another clever scheme. Congressman King did say, "Regardless of all other claims for the Edge Law, the fact is that it was built for no other purpose than that of marketing foreign securities here in America." American currency, the Federal Reserve Note was probably going to Europe.

King was convinced; the American people didn't need the Edge bill and its proposed amendments. World War I "is over." The Webb/Edge/Section 25 combined would not survive

> except by the contributions of our citizens . . . Our foreign-trade experiences of the war, when our Government was advancing money and credit facilities to enable foreign peoples to pay for our goods, can not be taken as a criterion for action at this time. Foreign trade is merely a barter; a swapping or exchange of goods. Periodic settlements of balances between the countries are made in gold, not coined in the mints, but in gold bars which are weighed and settlement made on that basis. This gold is used to settle international balances only when the balance is relatively small.

Year 1921 was a banner year for gold shipments to the United States, mostly from England, France, and Sweden, more than $671 million worth. The *Wall Street* headline of January 2, 1922, read, "GOLD IMPORTS IN 1921 ESTABLISH NEW RECORD . . . Original Sources chiefly are South Africa, Russia and India." The article considered "the gold movement . . . . as part of the primary gold flow, which began early in 1915, when Europe began to pay us for war materials and food supplies."

In 1921, Europe was in suspension; depreciating paper money was apparently the circulation. From the *Journal*, the shipments from Europe continued. The gold reserves of the "Principal Nations" was still intact, actually greater than before the war.

> Europe has little use for more gold until trade balances turn in her favor, as it would either flow out again or be used as immovable reserves. So whether we wish it or not, gold will probably keep coming to the United States, although in smaller quantities, but few bankers will register even a guess as to the probable duration of the flow.

Apparently, the gold movements didn't put a dent in the total debt owed the United States. The gold was not moving to pay the United States government. The *Wall Street Journal* of January 2, 1922, mentioned British government payments to J. P. Morgan and gold shipments from London to Kuhn, Loeb & Co. since March of 1920. American banks purchased African gold on the London market "as the purchase gives our bankers a use for exchange balances abroad and Europe, with its depreciated currencies, has to pay too large a premium to bid against us."

The "Central Reserves" of the "Principal Nations" was apparently intact. Gold shipments were coming to the United States, and the money circulation of those principal European countries had to be a depreciating paper currency. And so as before, as in the United States in the nineteenth century, an apparent similar condition was in place in 1921 Europe. A disastrous World War I occurred with resultant destruction, huge expenditures, subsequent indebtedness, death, and suspension of specie. Gold was being shipped to the United States, and European gold reserves remained intact? Apparently, there was no promise to pay in Europe? Senator Ladd in December 1921 said, "As a matter of fact, the gold basis is now pure fiction. There is not a country in the world that is on a gold basis. The gold that is now accumulating in this country is a serious embarrassment to our international finances." The *Wall Street Journal* stated that American bankers will not "register even a guess as to the probable duration of the flow." The non-legal tender Federal Reserve Note going to Europe was good for gold.

The debentures were long-term "pieces of paper," call them bonds. Europe still owed the United States government $16 billion plus 500 million in annual interest, which was not being paid. Apparently, gold shipped to the United States was going to private banks; it wasn't paying the public debt.

"The more Debentures we buy, the more Europe owes us . . . in other words, we are to loan our money to Nations and individuals in Europe and take our chances in getting it back when due." Congressman King was eloquent, articulate, and funny. He called the Edge bank a machine. The machine was

> prepared by inventors already expert in extracting money from the pocketbooks of the people without danger of arrest. This machine can extract the last coin from the deepest pockets, and at the same time transfuse to exhaustion the healthy blood of the United States farmer, laborer, and business man into the veins of anemic Europe.

It appeared Mr. King, with his humorous rhetoric, didn't like rescuing Europe at the expense of the American people. Congressman King said, "If we will do this, it will be highly pleasing to the International bankers in Europe and to their cousins in America, as the European to whom we will loan the money will use it to pay up what he owes to his International creditor."

Mr. King continued with the international money connection; it was "the eighth annual convention of the National Foreign Trade Council, a propaganda organization engaged in a campaign to teach Americans to forget America and 'think internationally.'" The convention was held in Cleveland, Ohio, in May 1921. An imbalance of trade in the Europeans' favor was desired, "and all this by and through the operations of Edge Corporations whose immediate and extensive creation the National Foreign Trade Council so joyfully urges." In 1919, Congressman King, before the Edge bill was passed, said, "The passage of this bill means the destruction of many American Industries." King compared the formation of the Webb/Edge/foreign banking combined as being similar to the huge trusts of the nineteenth century, which then prompted the Sherman Antitrust Act. He mentioned the "Unlimited

Bank of Nations of New York," an Edge bank as a forming leader of the combined.

> Institutions under this act will be the means of financing corporations in foreign countries, then we should call a halt before it is too late. Why should the American Congress legislate to tear down industry in the United States and build it up in foreign countries? . . . The money-making contingent are rapidly getting in line. They are forward-looking men . . . The Washington Post of October 29, 1919, says that Arthur J. Belding of McGraw-Hill Publishing will move his plant to Germany . . . Henry Ford will construct a factory in Cork.

American industry would begin the move to foreign countries financed by "American money" with "cheap foreign labor." King articulated the "exploitation" of American industry, labor, and the home market. It would be "nothing but the fun of chasing the fantasy of foreign trade." American industry, manufacture, and labor, outsourcing in foreign countries, sounds like the twenty-first century in America and beyond. This was 1919!

Congressman McFadden of Pennsylvania disagreed with King.

> The Gentleman from Illinois expresses the fear that this is going to be a combination in restraint of trade. I think the Gentleman is in error in that respect, because I think it is going to help trade in the United States. The Gentleman suggests that it will drive out of trade the small concerns in this country, and that they will be forced to do business with these large combinations of trade and that that will work a great hardship.

In 1914, the Clayton Antitrust Act was passed. The Clayton Act amended the Sherman Antitrust Act. The Clayton Act was amended when the Webb bill first amended the Federal Reserve System Section 25 in 1916. Congressman King objected because these foreign banks would be exempt from the antitrust laws. Directors of member reserve banks could also be directors of the foreign banks. McFadden added,

> When we passed the amendments to the Clayton Anti-Trust
> Law, under the Webb-Pomerene Act, permitting concerns
> to combine to do international trade or business, one of the
> very purposes of the bill is to finance business originating
> by authority of this Webb-Pomerene Act. Many of these
> small concerns have not the credit facilities, and great risks
> are involved should they assume the risks incident to the
> financing of the foreign business.

The Webb bill or the amendments to Section 25 of the Federal Reserve
Act rescinded the requirements (Section 8) of the antitrust laws as
pertaining to the foreign banks.

It was time to expand; the country possessed "the greatest
prosperity . . . industrial expansion . . . in natural resources we are
superabundant." McFadden mentioned the country's gold, food,
minerals, ores, metals, railroads, anywhere from 20% to 80% of the
world's production and supply. Closing, McFadden said,

> Now, we all realize, of course, in the financing of this
> great volume of business which is knocking at our doors,
> that some instrument must be created to take care of the
> payments that those countries in Europe have to give us.
> This instrument is nothing more than a hopper into which
> will pour long-time credits which may be in the form of
> notes, which may be in the form of bonds of Municipalities,
> or bonds or stocks issued by companies in France, England,
> or other parts of the world, which may be guaranteed; or
> secured by the Governments or Municipalities. Into this
> hopper they will flow, and out of this hopper will flow
> obligations of this company in a suitable form, a desirable
> form, for our people to invest in. That is about the sum and
> substance of what is contemplated under this act.

Mr. McFadden received applause from the House.

Later, King quoted McFadden's words and enhanced them with some
of his own. After the words "out of this hopper will flow obligations,"
King added "unguaranteed, repudiable, and subject to Sovietization";

and after the words "our people to invest their savings in," King added, "slaughter of the innocents."

The Federal Reserve Act inaugurated the short-term "acceptance" effective for the ninety-day short duration transaction. The proposed amendments to Section 25 would add to that; there would now be long-term acceptances for Edge banks. An exporter gets his money up front from a bank through an acceptance transaction. The new long-term acceptance "allows the Edge Bank 'to refund itself.'" In Section 25, "The Edge Law Banks, have been given the special privilege of issuing acceptances up to a year in tenure." Refunding itself

> in plain English, means that the Edge Bank can sell these 'acceptances' to a member bank of the Federal Reserve System, which can in turn rediscount them at a Federal Reserve Bank and which, through the joint operation of the Federal Reserve agents at such banks, the United States Treasury, the Federal Reserve Board, and the bureau of Engraving and Printing are transmitted from mere 'acceptances' into Federal Reserve Notes, which today constitute the principal paper money found in the pockets of the people.

Was the credit circulation, the Federal Reserve Notes, going to assist and revive the European countries and pay off the foreign creditors? Apparently, that was the intended course of action as intimated by Congressman King. The Federal Reserve Note had to be the currency of value; the Federal Reserve Note was created to buy gold. What was the depreciating European paper money buying?

In January 1921, the "activities" of the War Finance Corporation by Senate Resolution 212 were "revived to take certain action for the relief of the present depression in the agricultural sections of the country and other purposes." Later, on August 24, 1921, the War Finance Corporation act was amended. In this act, the corporation would be allowed "to purchase, sell, or otherwise deal in acceptances, adequately secured, issued by banking corporations organized under Section 25 [a] of the Federal Reserve Act." In this case, it was for agricultural purposes. The "tenure" of this acceptance was for no less than three years. The acceptance was a clever instrument and a most significant new addition to the United States credit circulation.

In 1991, President George Bush proclaimed "the New World Order." A new world order had been launched many years before. European banking expertise was introduced in the Federal Reserve System, namely, the government obligation and the acceptance. The acceptance was primarily of European origin. The United States had gotten its third central bank; it was the beginning of an eventual explosion in money, credit, growth and accumulation of gold, and a perpetrated debt never to be paid.

It appeared the American and European banking connections were becoming more connected. In 1914, 1916 and 1917, two major American enterprises and a major catastrophe began, the Federal Reserve System, the federal income tax, and World War I in Europe.

At that time, the United States comprised forty-eight "contiguous" states. Oklahoma was admitted in 1907. New Mexico and Arizona were added in 1912. After 1913, United States senators would no longer be appointed by state legislatures; this was no doubt incredible. Senators would now be elected by the people of their respective states "proclaimed" by the Seventeenth Amendment.

CHAPTER ELEVEN
The 1920s

From practically all angles, 1922 can be recorded as the renaissance of prosperity. Its statistics portray steady recovery from the deep depression of 1921. Then we were in the slough of deflation, doing penance for after-war boom excesses of 1919 and 1920—reducing prices, restoring credits, redressing inventories and costs, and meanwhile making, buying and selling less.

This was from the *Wall Street Journal* of January 1, 1923.

On March 4, 1921, Andrew Mellon was appointed secretary of the Treasury; he remained secretary of the Treasury throughout the decade. He served three Republican presidents: Harding, Coolidge, and Hoover. In November 1922, Mellon said, "The twelve months which have passed since the last Annual Report have been marked by further liquidation and recovery from depression, and, more recently, by a substantial revival of business." The year before, Mellon said, "In the past year we have suffered an industrial and business depression that has affected every class of our people and reached into every part of the country." In November 1923, Mellon said,

> The crisis of 1921 was one of the most severe this country has ever experienced, due to the fact the conditions were world wide . . . This state of affairs was the natural outcome of the great war and the social disturbances and international controversies which ensued . . . The conditions were unprecedented and, therefore, the uncertainties were many and contributed to a state of alarm and demoralization.

But things were turning around; it was a time for "recovery." Mellon reported to the Congress in 1923 that the "recovery" was more substantial. "The traffic handled by the railroads has surpassed all records." Employment was up because of the automotive industry and the building and highway construction. It was an "industrial revival."

Political economy and war appears the never-ending human experience; the human experience appears in parallel with the nature of things, creation, destruction, and restoration. The experience is a continuing human insanity. Where are we today in 2010? After 9/11, we are mired in wars in Iraq and Afghanistan, more death, destruction, and continuing indebtedness. Conventional warfare doesn't eliminate terrorism.

In 1923, the population was 111 million; the country's standard of living boomed. Economically and socially, the United States took off between 1923 and 1929. The United States prospered. It was the "Jazz age" with automobiles; it was the advent of airplane travel. It was a time for music, vaudeville, Hollywood, Broadway, Irving Berlin. Al Jolson made the first talking motion picture. Baseball was the sport; it had Babe Ruth. British actors and comedians had come to America; money was flowing. Charles Lindbergh, an American, was the first to fly the Atlantic solo in 1927. An example of the industrial expansion was the production of motor vehicles. In the *Wall Street Journal*, Monday morning January 8, 1924: "Motor Industry Smashes Record." The industry produced "4,014,000" cars and trucks in 1923. "Registration at the end of 1923 is estimated at 14,500,000, indicating 85% of the 17,000,000 motor vehicles in the world are in the United States." The trend continued through the decade until 1929. The country was saturated in illegal booze, the installment plan, and an avalanche of crime figures perpetrated by Prohibition. If it was happening anywhere, it was happening in America.

A different trend had "aroused" England; it was the "dole." There were, as of April 1925, "1,279,000 people drawing the Dole." The government, the employers, and the workers were paying for it. Since the end of World War I, more than $5 billion had been "given away." It was the dole in England. The "slackers" prevailed; the slackers were the Socialists' political "lever . . . Full maintenance" was their motto. "One dole-taker was discovered recently in London who was drawing $40 a week from eight different funds." Apparently, it was an "incurable" condition. It was a "wholesale demoralization of young men between 18 and 25." It all started with "the weekly pensions that are paid to the unemployed"; it was "unemployment insurance." See the *Wall Street Journal* of Tuesday morning, April 7, 1925.

President Harding took office in January 1921. Harding didn't finish his term; he died of an apparent stroke in August of 1923. He was fifty-seven. His first messages to the Congress were budgetary in nature. It apparently was his orientation; it accounts for his "establishing the Bureau of the Budget." The Congress would have to be more accountable for "federal expenditures." Harding was responsible for bringing the world's naval powers together to agree on a limited tonnage in warships. It was the "Arms Agreement" in November 1921. Countries were arming again as before the First World War. The principal nations were the United States, Great Britain, France, Japan, and Italy. Things were heating up in the Far East, especially Japan's "aggression" toward China. Harding's ranking among presidents is poor; he wasn't in office long enough, and his administration was marred by scandal. The most damaging incident was the "Teapot Dome" affair. Harding's Interior secretary accepted bribes when leasing oil-rich government property to oil companies. Vice President Calvin Coolidge succeeded Harding as president.

On Monday morning, April 3, 1922, the *Wall Street Journal* reported, "Five Banks Hold 67% OF Worlds Monetary Gold." The five banks listed were the Federal Reserve, the Bank of England, Bank of France, Bank of Japan, and the Bank of Germany. The Journal showed that Germany had lost "$95,000,000" in gold since 1914. The total figure held was 5.5 billion in gold. Of the five banks, the *Journal* called it "their success in mobilizing the world's gold . . . The Federal Reserve system alone has more of the yellow metal than the combined holdings of the other four banks." The Federal Reserve System held 3 billion in gold. C. W. Barron was right; the Federal Reserve System was well on its way in gobbling up the gold in such a short time. There was an additional 740 million in gold in the United States outside the Federal Reserve; much of it was in the Treasury "for the account of the Federal Reserve Board." It was the "Gold Fund, Federal Reserve Board." This was gold deposited by agents of the reserve system; it was the "security against outstanding Federal Reserve notes." It was there for the "account" of the reserve system. In December 1920, $3 billion in Federal Reserve Notes were in circulation. By April of 1922, approximately 1.2 billion were in circulation. During the same period, the Federal Reserve banks accumulated approximately $2 billion in gold.

On February 9, 1922, the Congress created the "World War Foreign Debt Commission." The commission was composed of five members; Secretary Mellon was the chairman. The president appointed the other four members, the secretaries of state and commerce and two congressmen. The commission was "authorized to refund or convert, and to extend the time of payment of the principal or the interest" of foreign debt held by the United States. Sixteen countries owed money to the United States. There would be no communication with three of the countries: "Armenia, Greece, and Russia; In none of these countries is there a Government recognized by the United States." Mellon's report didn't elaborate further. The secretary had the "authority to deal with the Austrian debt." Cuba was paying its debt, and Nicaragua's debt was "already in funded form." The commission would begin negotiating with the following countries: "Belgium, Czechoslovakia, Finland, France, Great Britain, Hungary, Poland, Romania, and Serbia."

It was a slow process; Mellon stated in his 1925 report: "Gratifying progress has been made during the year in funding the foreign obligations . . . agreements have been reached with Belgium, Czechoslovakia, Latvia, Estonia, and Italy since my previous Report." The amount of 7.4 billion had been refunded. Almost 5 billion remained "unfunded, principal and interest . . . the greater part of which are French obligations." The French had asked in 1922 for an extension of time; the French blamed it on the lack of "reparation receipts from Germany." It was the industrial Ruhr stalemate in Germany, an economic disaster; the Ruhr was finally settled in 1925 after French and Belgian occupations left the area. But the refunding with France wasn't settled. The payments of refunding for the settled nations were "spread over a period of 62 years." Imagine, the Second World War would start in fourteen years in 1939. The United States was most forgiving in spreading the debt over sixty-two years. Secretary Mellon said that the debt commission was "mindful of the havoc wrought in European Countries by the war."

Why was France making no payments to the United States government? The April 1922 *Journal* gold article showed that France possessed twice the gold of England; Great Britain was making interest payments on the debt. France made no payments of any kind. France was in a bind according to the *Wall Street Journal* of April 3, 1925: "French Budget Is Still In Doubt." The paper reported the French could not settle its internal debt because needed increased taxation was voted down. "German reparation payments" would not be "enough to enable France to reduce taxation."

There was foreign debt owed the United States government and foreign debt owed to private banks in the United States. "Recently there was made at the White House a short statement concerning this Government's attitude toward private American loans to foreign Governments." The *Wall Street Journal* reported that "many quarters" felt the statement was "specifically objecting to loans to France." When he was in the White House, President Harding held a secret meeting with "prominent American banking interests." The meeting was never made public. Regarding private loans, the *Journal* reported, "President Harding expressed the belief that there should be Government approval before the loans were made and the bankers, it is understood, came to this view, if they did not already hold it."

In the early 1920s, Germany was racked by huge inflation; cartoonists depicted people wheelbarrowing their paper money. This glut of paper money in Germany was the "emergency" paper money circulated during specie suspension? Was this emergency currency a belated effort in Germany similar to an Aldrich-Vreeland thing? Not really, there wasn't that much gold in Germany; it had been there but apparently gone? Anyway, the condition, supposedly, came to an abrupt halt "on News Years Day, 1924." It was like flicking a switch. Germany's currency and financial picture was going to change. So the story goes, "Hjalmar Schacht, the new Reich Commissioner for National Currency," had an audience with "Montague Norman, Governor of the Bank of England." Schacht went to England for a loan; it was time to get "Germany industry going again." The industrial Ruhr area would have to be settled first. Schacht wanted to start "a second credit bank in addition to the Reichsbank, a bank based entirely on gold." The bank would be called the Golddiskontbank. Schacht assured

Norman that foreign currency was in Germany, a currency that would constitute half the capital needed for the bank. "The remaining half I should like to borrow from the Bank of England." This "new second Bank would issue bank notes based on its gold capital of two hundred million marks." Schacht would issue the new "notes in Pound Sterling." Schacht convinced Norman of the

> prospects such a measure would afford for economic collaboration between Great Britain's World Empire and Germany. If we desire to establish European peace we must free ourselves from the limitations imposed by mere conference resolutions and declarations of Congress. Economically, the European countries must be more closely linked.

Montague Norman approved the loan. What foreign currency in Germany was capitalizing Mr. Schacht's bank? Gaging from the story, the money interests of the two principal opposing World War I belligerents were aligning financially with the help of outside money? German industry would begin to produce again, and not too long after that, Adolph Hitler would begin rearming Germany. The audience between Schacht and Norman, above, appears in John Toland's book *Adolf Hitler*, volume 1, page 194. The audience between Schacht and Norman also appears in the *Confessions of "the Old Wizard,"* pages 181-183. Hjalmar Horace Greeley Schacht was known as the Old Wizard.

Did this outside money include debenture currency from American foreign banks as part of the Webb/Edge/foreign banking combined? There was a Dawes Plan. A Dawes Plan would help Germany pay World War 1 reparations. The Dawes Plan was named after General Charles Gates Dawes, a banker from Chicago. Schacht's loan would include credits from J.P. Morgan and the Bank of England.

Whether it was J. P. Morgan's bank or other American foreign banks, it appears German reparations would be paid with American currency, which was apparently the Federal Reserve Note. The foreign money in Germany was American currency confirmed later by Secretary Mellon. Was all this business part of the Federal Reserve System's Webb/

Edge/foreign banking scheme courtesy of the American congressional legislation?

In his autobiography *Confessions of "the Old Wizard,"* Dr. Schacht met first with Montague Norman on New Year's Day. The next day, a three-year loan at 5% interest was presented by Norman. Schacht agreed. Montague Norman told Schacht, "A group of London bankers is prepared to accept bills to the value of several hundred million Marks, provided they are endorsed by the Golddiskontbank, so that you may count altogether on half a billion working capital for your bank." Norman added that there was "the possibility of discounting your bills in the London Market." The Golddiskontbank was a gold discount bank; the bank "was established on March 13, 1924." This bank stayed operative until the end of World War II in Europe 1945. Schacht met the "Dawes Committee" in Paris on January 23. There were representatives from America, England, Belgium, France, and Italy, etc. According to Schacht, the first deal with Montague Norman had given him some leverage when confronted by the Dawes Committee. German currency was already on the road to "stabilization," and he wasn't going to pay the French the overwhelming "billions" they demanded. Many foreign loans were made to Germany; many were never paid. About 10% of the reparations "were actually paid during the years 1924 to 1932. And they were not paid out of surplus exports as they should have been." Germany didn't "achieve any surplus exports." According to Schacht, "every year the agent for reparations claimed his two billion in gold marks in foreign currency from the Reichsbank. The money which had come into the country in the form of foreign loans went out of the country to meet the payments under the Dawes Plan." Schacht's description gave the appearance of simply a money exchange, borrowed credits in and money out. "This debt had to be paid in foreign currency and this foreign currency could only be obtained by surplus exports." According to Schacht, Germany could never build up sufficient surplus exports to achieve the foreign currency. The Fordney-McCumber Tariff of 1922 didn't help; it was a Republican protectionist tariff. "Duties on coal-tar products were avowedly in the interest of protection to ward off imports from Germany which stood preeminent in the chemical arts." Reparations were "written off" by the "Lausanne Conference" in 1932. Schacht said, "The Allied Governments pocketed the ten to twelve billions reparations, but foreign private investors lost their money on the loans made to Germany."

Gold was moving; it was going to Europe. It began in December 1924. Secretary Mellon stated in his November 1925 report: "The return of England and many other countries to the gold standard and the further progress made in the stabilization of exchanges, during the year, reflect substantial improvements in the world's affairs." But the foreign debt payment was apparently planned to go slow? In 1925, seven years after the war, the foreign debt owed the United States was still $12 billion, not including interest, and 5 billion of the debt was not yet refunded.

"ENGLAND RETURNS TO GOLD STANDARD . . . Chancellor Churchill, with his presentation of the 1925-26 budget, announced that provision had been made for what is practically an immediate return to the gold standard in England"; as reported by the *Wall Street Journal*, Wednesday morning, April 29, 1925. The embargo on gold export would not be lifted until "December 31," that is, gold exporting from England. As to the banking community, "it was stated that return to a free gold market in England ranked with acceptance of the Dawes Plan as a stabilizing factor for European and world finance in general." The article stated that the reserve banks would "place $200,000,000 gold at the disposal of the Bank of England, if desired. J.P. Morgan & Co. announced that the British Government had arranged a credit of $100,000,000 with them." Gold was moving; most of it was going to Germany. It started "in December 1924 . . . Either directly or indirectly, the monetary and fiscal reforms abroad in connection with the restoration of the gold standard are largely responsible for the movement of gold from the United States during the past year." Secretary Mellon mentioned that "Germany has been the source of the largest demand for gold." The gold was moving; Germany, apparently, was acquiring the gold as part of the big loan. Secretary Mellon in his November 1925 report: "A large part of the funds used by Germany to obtain gold was derived from the proceeds of the 800,000,000 Mark international loan floated a year ago." Mellon reported a "loan floated a year ago." A "loan floated a year ago" closely coincides with the Schacht/Norman meeting of News Year's Day 1924. Mellon reported that *United States currency was in Germany, which "created gold credits abroad."* The Federal Reserve Act, by Act of Congress, authorized the creation of the Federal Reserve Note, the new currency, which was good for gold. Mellon reported United States currency had "returned to the United States." Mellon said the Reichsbank was formed in the summer of 1924; and Germany's purchase of gold "more than doubled" its reserves to "$235,000,000." Mellon's report didn't mention from whom the gold was purchased, but gold was shipped from the United States. Germany's gold reserve had been depleted during and after the war. "During the War, gold was withdrawn from circulation in both belligerent and neutral European countries and concentrated in central reserves and Treasuries." The central reserves and treasuries were not named. Another guess says Switzerland was one of the central reserves or a depository; the United States may have been another. With the exception of Russia, Austria-Hungary, and Germany, withdrawn gold was "retained" by the warring countries after the war. Apparently, things were getting back to normal except, according to Secretary Mellon, Austria-Hungary and Russia; they "lost practically their entire gold holdings." Revolutions and wars cost more money than war. The revolution, apparently, cost Russia dearly in gold. At the time of Germany's 1924 loan, gold was in suspension; it wouldn't be for long. Germany needed her gold back. It was the way things were in the financial world; gold was apparently necessary to restore Germany's credit and to allow the creation of her new currency, the Rentenmark. There was the big loan, pound sterling, Federal Reserve Notes, and gold; Germany had apparently created more debt with the Bank of England and the American banking system, J. P. Morgan and Company et al.

Schacht recounted how his new Rentenmark had been attacked "as early as February 1924." It was the "foreign exchange hoarders." The Rentenmark was falling already at a discount of "fifteen percent." Time! Schacht blamed it on the Dawes Committee; negotiation was taking too much time. The "speculators" were more interested in their holdings of "stable securities" than the "purchase of imports." The Rentenmark had to be stabilized. Schacht shut down the Reichsbank; there would be no more "holding in foreign bills." It was unprecedented according to Schacht; the bank stopped extending credit. Schacht called the period "a painfull recovery." It took a while. Schacht took the hits from the press. He said the "innocent" would be hurt; some industry failed, but he neutralized the speculators. The country didn't need another round of inflation. The deed was done by July before "the decisions of the Dawes Committee came into operation."

The "Allied Governments" owed Great Britain £2.1 billion, which "included accrued interest" as of January 1, 1925; 2.1 billion pounds calculated to about $10 billion. This indebtedness was "on account of the war and post-war situation." It is because of this owned indebtedness, most likely, that Great Britain maintained her pound sterling supremacy during the period. Of the twelve Allied indebted countries, Russia owed Britain the most, more than $3 billion. None of the money, as reported to and by the *Wall Street Journal*, had yet been paid to Britain. The same countries, including Britain, owed the United States government a bundle. It seemed that everybody owed everybody almost; that is, the twelve lesser countries owed the two dominant countries. But literally, the "buck" didn't stop there. All the countries, including the two dominant ones, owed or would begin to owe the money interests who, because of gold, owned the ultimate indebtedness. Alexander Hamilton early on made the point: "The exigencies of the union could be susceptible of no limits, even in imagination." Hamilton's "union," apparently, was any central banking system or central government. Hamilton, more than likely, based his premise on the accelerating exigencies of the expanding eighteenth-century British Empire. Hamilton's "susceptible of no limits" was a harsh escalating reality in England, Europe, and in the United States in 1925, the aftermath of World War I. This harsh reality, after two and a half centuries, would bring England to her financial knees in 1946, the aftermath of World War II.

The 1923-1929 period exhibited a positive in government expenditures in the United States; there were no annual "deficits." Revenues exceeded spending. The Treasury was spending around $4 to $5 billion a year. The expenditures included the sinking fund, an extensive paying down of the public debt principal. By the end of the decade, Secretary Mellon reduced the public debt to $16 billion, a reduction of 9 billion, a superb effort. Dewey wrote, "By some, however, it was argued that the debt was being paid off at a too rapid rate, placing a too heavy burden upon a single generation; according to this argument, taxes should be lowered and redemption of debt be stretched over a longer period of years." Refunding by Mellon eliminated the immediate payment of several billion of World War I debt coming due, which included the Liberty Loans and the Victory Liberty Loans. Mellon offered Treasury certificates of indebtedness and Treasury notes. It was the continuing process of exchanging one kind of debt for another kind of debt, paying interest payments, lowering the interest rates, extending the ultimate debt, etc.

> The program of public economy and public debt payments which has been rigidly adhered to during the past five years, has been a direct contributing factor to the improvement in the credit and security markets. The return of over half a billion dollars annually to investors and financial institutions has not only reduced the public debt-burden and greatly improved the public credit, but it has released funds for investment in other securities.

The period reflected budget conscience spending by the Congress and the Treasury; could it be attributed to President Harding? Spending showed a surplus; revenue exceeded expenditures. There would be some changes; government revenue should be reduced. Secretary Mellon did recommend a reduction in taxes. It was the Republican platform for election in 1920; the country needed "relief from burdensome taxes." But congressional debates showed tax reduction was not a simple matter; who was not going to pay? Would tax reduction come in personal income, the surtax, the excess profits tax, luxury taxes, transportation taxes, corporate taxes, excise taxes, gift taxes, estate taxes; and how much from which tax or from any tax or from all taxes, etc.? A tax reduction was necessary, but yearly expenditures were running high. "The interest on the new public debt approximated a billion dollars, nearly as much as the entire cost of the Government before the war."

"High surtaxes drive capital from productive business to tax-exempt securities or other lawful methods of avoiding a taxable profit equally destructive of business advancement. The farmer is now complaining, and rightly, of the high freight rates and the high cost to him of that which he has to buy." In November 1923, Secretary Mellon said the railroads needed a "billion dollars a year" to maintain good service.

"The cost of capital is, therefore, one of the largest items of expense in the conduct of the railroads. Nothing has so contributed to this additional cost of capital as the high surtaxes, which have driven the large investors from railroad to tax exempt securities . . . The escape from taxation" amounted to "$ 11,000,000,000." Then there are the municipal bonds. An amendment was introduced in Congress to remove the "tax-exempt features of Municipal Bonds," another escape hatch for taxes. The amendment was set aside. The Congress had the power to reduce the surtax that would "divert capital to productive investment, such as railroad securities, which tend to the reduction of costs, thus giving relief to the farmer and consumers generally."

Secretary Mellon said, "The cost of capital was high." Mellon blamed it on high taxes and tax-exempt securities. Taxation is most important; it's the revenue sustaining the pyramid. Like all money pyramid schemes, without a continuous inflow of currency, the scheme collapses. Taxation is the backup revenue guaranteeing the government expenditure and its pyramidal obligation. The cost of capital is also high because of the system. The creation of the Federal Reserve System guaranteed its own profit before initial issue of money. The member banks pay the reserve banks; commerce pays the member banks thence to the people. The Federal Reserve owns the obligation. Thomas Jefferson said this is the credit the bank owes the people. The cost of currency before issue is high because the Federal Reserve bank is a retailer. The cost of the currency issue involves the Treasury, the central bank, the twelve reserve banks, their agents, dealers, speculators, national banks, commercial banks, etc.

The *Wall Street Journal* reported the "Federal Reserve Earns $425,000,000." This profit, by law, appears to have been instrument profit; the bank is an instrument. This profit announcement covered the period 1914 to 1923. It was reported in 1922 that the Federal Reserve had accumulated 3 billion in gold. Wasn't this also the real profit the reserve bank acquired during the period? How about the shareholders and their profit on the obligation? The government's profit was $131 million, which was in the form of a tax. If the central bank was an arm of the Treasury, the 3 billion in gold would belong to the rightful owner, the Treasury. Andrew Jackson would say the central bank was gaining considerable power in its accumulation of gold. Taxes are oppressive. Isn't it because "the cost of capital is high"? The private central bank and shareholders get independently rich and most formidable with currency "handed" to them by the United States Bureau of Engraving and Printing. That's why taxation, perpetual taxation, pays those "close to and within reach of the seat of Government."

Over a period of seven years, taxation was restructured, reduced. Secretary Mellon was at the head of four revenue acts in 1921, 1924, 1926, and 1928. The excess profits tax was repealed; this tax had targeted the huge World War I profits. The tax was gone. The surtax, after much bickering in the Congress, was reduced from "65%" to "50%" to "20 %" on incomes over $200,000. "Individuals" and "corporations remained the chief fiscal support of the Government." Dewey reported that "in 1922 there were nearly 7,000,000 returns made, and of these, 16,000 persons who reported incomes of $50,000 or more, paid one-half of the total income tax." As the tax reductions were made, revenues still exceeded expenditures; it was the period. Annual estimates were difficult to determine. "It was the miscellaneous sources, such as collection of back taxes, refunds from railroads, and payments by foreign Nations in settlement of debt obligations." The personal tax exemption was increased; the gift tax and many excise taxes from the war period were repealed.

Secretary Mellon's 1929 Treasury report included almost a thousand pages of the country's public and private financial picture. In 1929, there were "25,330 banks, which included 7,536 national banks and 17, 794 banks other than national." The national banks were part of the Federal Reserve System. The majority of the banks (17,794) were state banks and trust companies within the state jurisdictions. Approximately "1500" of these state banks were in the Federal Reserve System. In the 1920s, state banking was still "independent" and a major influence. The state banks had to stop printing their paper money long ago; the federal government taxed it out of existence by 1879. But the varied money maze hadn't changed; the total money still contained gold and silver bullion, gold and silver coin, gold certificates, silver certificates, the national bank currency, the Federal Reserve Notes, Federal Reserve bank notes, and the Treasury notes of 1890. Last but not least, our never ending greenbacks were still circulating;

the "repudiated" legal tender lawful money of the United States, all $347 million worth, were still fixed and still circulating. And they were good for gold. To be exact, the greenbacks totaled $346,681,016. All the above monies from the "Circulation Statement of United States Money" in and outside of the Treasury, according to Secretary Mellon's report, totaled $8.5 billion. The population was just under 120 million, and the circulation per capita was about $40. Gold certificates and Federal Reserve Notes made up $22 of the $40 total. A "Gross National Product" was a phrase not yet in vogue? It wasn't in Mellon's reports. As we go along, we will touch on the many monies and/or the currency and the distribution thereof.

Secretary Mellon totaled $4.3 billion in gold coin and bullion in the United States in 1929. The Federal Reserve System and the Treasury held about 90% of the total.

Secretary Mellon showed a net export of 1.1 billion in gold between 1915 and 1929. England and Europe were reclaiming gold, especially since 1924 and the return of England to the gold standard. The *Wall Street Journal* of February 6, 1926, mentioned

> the reversal of the gold movement from an import movement in 1924 to an export movement in 1925 . . . The largest amount of exported gold went to Germany, representing part of the proceeds of the $110,000,000 German loan provided for in the Dawes Plan . . . This gold was transferred to the vaults of the Reichsbank to serve as reserve for the reestablished currency of Germany.

The foreign debt owed the United States government was about $11 billion. The United States public debt in 1929 was $16.9 billion.

With Great Britain back on the gold standard, movements of gold would again be "normal." According to the *Wall Street Journal*, when pound sterling passed "$4.90" on the exchange, gold would be shipped or "attracted" to London; when it went the other way, say, "$4.82," gold was shipped to New York, all this at the "discretion" of the Bank of England.

Banking laws were continually changing in the United States except for the national banking associations. The pressure was on since 1923 for consolidation of the national banks' centralization; more federal control was looming, and it was back to the Congress. There was opposition. There were banking people in the United States who felt the country's strength was in its independent banking; many competing banks were better than many banks monopolized by the few, but change was imminent. Banking differed in Great Britain and Canada. In those two countries, a few powerful banks controlled all the banks; a few powerful banks had thousands of branch banks. It was more centralized control. With the need and the help of the Congress, the United States would move in that direction. Again, it was the Wall Street banks and the Federal Reserve, the money power assisted by their friends in government and the Congress who favored and wanted federal control and/or change; this was the opposition's contention. But the national banking associations, as members of the reserve system, were in need of help. It was an "emergency"; they were supposedly restricted in their operations compared to the state banks and state branch banks. This was the contention for change. All this pressing necessary change and the Treasury and the Federal Reserve tandem and banks, although less in number, controlled the nation's credit.

The McFadden bill (H.R. 2) became law on February 25, 1927. It was "an Act To further amend the national banking laws and the Federal Reserve Act, and for other purposes." The new law amended the act approved on November 7, 1918 "for the consolidation of national banking associations." Congressman McFadden was chairman of the House Banking and Currency Committee. He introduced the bill in January 1925; the bill was passed in the House and died in the Senate because of branch banking restrictions by the Federal Reserve. McFadden came back with the bill in December of 1925. Secretary Mellon initially pushed for branch banking in 1924. In 1926 and 1927, the Sixty-ninth Congress sessions 1 and 2 would bring the bill to a close.

It was a law to strengthen the national banking associations amid the existing state banks and trust companies and their branch banks. Some states allowed their chartered banks to have branch banking; some states did not allow branch banking. The Federal Reserve, originally, didn't allow branch banking to their member national banking associations. But national banks had branches as a result of state banks coming into the national system in 1865. Banking just like the currency, in the United States, continued varied and complex in the 1920s. The Federal Reserve had branch banks in foreign countries; it was whatever was necessary in the scheme of things. In the beginning of this legislation, the Federal Reserve was not for branch banking, but the Federal Reserve really was for branch banking.

State banks could join the federal system; but there was a problem. State bank supervisors and Federal Reserve policy didn't jive; state branch banks, the location, population limits, etc., were conflicting, apparently in the way. The McFadden bill would get in the way of that. Another example, state banks engaged in the "insurance business." The Federal Reserve disallowed this practice to its member banks. This made sense; "there was the Insurance business and there was the Banking business." State bank supervisors disputed Federal Reserve power; state banks would not relinquish their banking practices as members of the reserve system. The McFadden bill featured branch banking along with seventeen other features of the bill, but the branch banking feature was the bill; it was the debate. Chartered state banks and trust companies were an integral part of the country's commerce and industry at the time; there were at least seventeen thousand of them. The individual states were very much alive, still flexing their financial sovereignty in the 1920s. Maybe the many varied currencies contributed. They were the distribution; they kept the pot boiling. The Federal Reserve Note wasn't the only currency in and then out of action. Along with the maze of currencies, there was a concurrent maze of banking institutions when totaling the Federal Reserve banks and their national bank members, the state banks and their branches, and the trust companies and their branches, etc., all 25,353 of them.

Congressman McFadden, in January 1926, said, "The general purpose of the bill is to adjust the National Banking laws to modern banking conditions along the lines of conservative banking and without any deviation from the high standard which has been set by the

National Banking system." The national banks were disadvantaged because their charter life was limited; the Federal Reserve Act was a twenty-year charter (that was going to change). State banks did not have a "charter limitation"; the result, national banks became state banks. Some were leaving the Federal Reserve System along with state banks. The national banks were restricted in their lending practices pertaining to real estate as in length of term and amount of the loan. State banks within the same districts were not so restricted. McFadden emphasized the need for change for national bank survival.

> Changes in the banking laws have not kept pace with the revolutionary changes which have taken place within recent years in production, transportation, and communication. Many of the State Legislatures have recently enacted new banking codes in order that the State commercial banks and Trust companies may be equipped to meet those needs . . . It is necessary now to put the National Banks on their feet.

McFadden received applause when finished.

McFadden named the many organizations that favored the bill; a few were the national banking associations, state banking associations of the approving states, the Treasury Department, the comptroller, the Federal Reserve System, and the Federal Reserve Board, which "approved the bill as a whole except as to branch banking."

Congressman Nelson of Wisconsin was for independent banking; he didn't like the bill in 1925, and he didn't like the bill in 1926. The United States was going the way of Great Britain and Canada; Nelson called it the Continental system of branch banking in this country. Nelson called the bill the "branch bank hook." Nelson claimed that many of the principals who spoke of the "evils" of branch banking originally were actually always clamoring for it. "This measure means, if it passes, inevitably the end of our independent banking system." The principals, according to Nelson, were J. P. Morgan, the Chemical Bank of New York, the National City Bank of New York, Kuhn, Loeb & Co. of New York, the Federal Reserve Board, the comptroller of the Treasury, etc.

"We have a condition before us that has to be met . . . millions and millions of dollars in the past year . . . have been lost to the Federal Reserve System." National banks had left the reserve system; state banks had become "denationalized . . . placing their branches everywhere." Congressman Stevenson of South Carolina was a member of the banking committee. An exchange between Stevenson and Mr. Fulmer revealed that the Federal Reserve Board was against branch banking and also for branch banking? Fulmer asked why the board "allowed a State bank to come in with a chain of branch banks some time ago." Stevenson said, "Some of that Federal Reserve Board are in favor of the Canadian System of abolishing all except about one bank and putting branches all over the United States."

The proponents of the McFadden bill contended that the Federal Reserve System was in trouble. The national banking associations had to be propped up; too many of them were leaving, becoming state banks, and branching out so to speak. That is why Congressman Steagall said, "Let no member of the House be deceived by the claim that this bill is intended to limit branch banking. Its purpose is to extend the practice to National banks."

Mr. Steagall countered the proponents of the bill; the Federal Reserve System was alive and very well. Steagall mentioned some impressive numbers: almost a billion dollars in loans in one month, deposits and investments were all rising, investments were up 3 billion more than the previous year. Steagall took his figures from the "Federal Reserve Bulletin of January this year." He mentioned the Federal Reserve Act. "Under that law we financed the greatest war of all history and emerged from that conflict the creditor nation of the world and financial center of the universe . . . it is today the outstanding stabilizing force in the affairs of the world."

From an international standpoint, Congressman Steagall was correct. The United States was now the creditor nation; it happened because of the Federal Reserve Act and the First World War. The United States government, its Treasury, and a couple of powerful private American banks were owners of foreign indebtedness. The international scene appeared in hand. The year 1925 showed 4.5 billion in gold was in the United States. The Treasury and the Federal Reserve System controlled the country's gold; the result of the 1917 amendments to the Federal Reserve Act, in effect, "impounded the gold in the Federal Reserve Banks." Gold may now be shipped out of the country, supposedly, without apparent distress. England and Europe no longer held a hammer over the United States, and why was that? In the nineteenth century, when England sent gold abroad, it was for investment, for purchase, or England was lending to somebody, like the United States. When the United States shipped the gold abroad, many times to England, it was for payment; the United States was in debt in the nineteenth century. England could afford to ship gold abroad; the United States could not. It was always panic time. Now in 1926, a present focus was on the home front, the national banking associations. The Federal Reserve System controlled the country's credit and yet made up only one-third of the total banks in the United States. Apparently, that had to change; it was the national banking scene that had to change. The U.S. Treasury, the Federal Reserve System, and most of the national banking association members were federal. The independent banks and their branches were the state banks and trust companies under sovereign state banking jurisdictions. The present Federal Reserve Act, supposedly, didn't allow the national banking associations to have branches, but they did have branches. Aside from the national scene, the Federal Reserve, under Section 25, established branch banks in foreign countries. According to Congressman Steagall, members in the House didn't understand what was going on, or they would vote against the bill. It is no wonder the branch banking issue was complex. The McFadden bill debate, from its introduction till its final approval, consumed three years in the Congress.

The McFadden bill went to the committee of conference in 1926; it was near approval, but the bill disintegrated. It was the Hull amendment, one of the main reasons why the bill was held up. There were forty-eight states in the United States; twenty-six of them didn't allow branch banking. The Hull amendment would not allow the national banking associations to establish branch banks within those twenty-six states if in the future those twenty-six states changed their stance and allowed branch banking to their state banks. The House originally and overwhelmingly passed the bill with the Hull amendment. The Senate rebuffed. The amendment was discriminating; the House eventually acquiesced. The Hull amendment was stricken from the bill. The door was opened for the spread of national association branch banking throughout the country; eventually, all the states allowed branch banking. This was the "Branch Bank Hook"; although supposedly declining early on, the Federal Reserve wanted branch banking since the beginning. Those in favor of independent banking in the country were losing the battle.

"Branch banking is contrary to public policy, violates the basic principles of our Government, and concentrates the credit of the Nation and the power of money in the hands of the few" (no kidding). This was from the American Bankers Association in 1922 as presented by Congressman Steagall. By 1927, their policy had changed.

The chair recognized Mr. Kurtz of Pennsylvania. The theme was the small independent banks in the outlying communities. He mentioned the people who ran the small banks. "They become the school directors, the justices, the notaries, the men of affairs in the region where they live . . . Destroy the small bank and you destroy one of the most potent influences for good in every small community today."

Congressman Celler presented a different view. Mr. Celler of New York was for branch banking, and he was opposed to the bill. Mr. Celler presented a list of 610 failed banks within the past two years. Sixty-five percent of the failed banks were banks possessing a capital of $25,000 or less. "I am informed by responsible officials of the Federal Reserve Board that it is the small unit banks that are the common source of trouble to the clearing houses and bank examiners and that they are the ones who go down and fail during the money panics." Celler contended that a small branch bank of a larger city bank would not fail.

Celler mentioned the "teller windows" of New York. It was the comptroller of the Treasury; he was at fault. Celler said the "Public National Bank" in New York had twenty-four branches called teller windows. Celler presented a table listing New York national banks and their fifty-one branches. In New York, they called them teller windows, but they were separate buildings, branch banks. People worked there; "they receive deposits, pay out deposits and lend money, discount, and do an actual banking business." The comptroller allowed it; it was illegal. The Federal Reserve Act did not allow that practice, but the comptroller allowed it anyway. Celler contended that national banks would be shown preference; there was nothing in the McFadden bill to protect state banks and their branch banks from such federal action. Mr. Stevenson answered Celler: do like President Roosevelt did, when the ruling couldn't be changed: "Change the Comptroller." The eventual enacted bill did rule out teller windows.

Mr. Celler wanted equality in the bill; he wanted an amendment stating that the Federal Reserve could not "impair the charter or statutory rights . . . or impose any conditions or restrictions other than those under which National Banks shall operate." Celler wanted equality because there were more independent banks than federal banks. Just by the number of banks, there was more total independent bank wealth than national bank wealth. Celler's figures showed $33 billion to 22 billion or "50 per cent more" in total wealth. Why should the state bank supervisors kowtow to the federal system? Mr. Celler didn't like Chairman McFadden's statement that state bank "propaganda" urged the Congress to vote against the bill. The $55 billion represented demand deposits in the banking system. The demand deposits, in reality, were the extensions of credit by virtue of loans. The approximate currency in circulation outside of the Treasury was about $5 billion. The $55 billion deposit figure, about eleven times the currency, was an example of the system's expansion multiple, which existed as part of the velocity of money principle. The system didn't lend money; it lent deposits or credit.

The country was going the way of branch banking. Congressman Black of Texas mentioned that "in the last two years 25 National banks with a capital of $136,000,000 have surrendered their charters and gone into the State banking system in order that they might establish branches throughout the State of California if they desired."

In the *Wall Street Journal*, on the morning of January 29, 1926, an article about G. T. Thomas illustrated the success of branch banking in Mississippi. Mr. Thomas was "president of the Grenada Bank of Mississippi." The farmers needed help in the form of "better credit." The "small cotton growers were exploited by the 'supply merchants.'" The small "unit" bank, by law, in the outlying community couldn't help the farmer, couldn't lend beyond 25% of its capital, which may be just "$2500 or $3500 at most; whereas, a branch bank located in the town could lend, say "$25,000 or more, depending upon the amount of capital and surplus of the parent bank." Thomas established a dozen branch banks as part of the Grenada banking system. Thomas's "plan helped to make the local community prosperous and caused a Macedonian call from neighboring localities for the same service." According to the article, Thomas's banks survived the 1907 crash; "the twelve branch banks paid every check drawn against it in cash, regardless of amount, something not another bank in the State did." Thomas's banks survived the 1907 panic because surplus funds, apparently, didn't go to New York. Thomas's banks probably survived for no other reason, within the domain, in Mississippi.

When the Federal Reserve Act was passed in 1913, Section 4 of the act stated, "To have succession for a period of twenty years from its organization unless it is sooner dissolved by an Act of Congress, or unless its franchise becomes forfeited by some violation of law." The 1913 Federal Reserve System had a life span, "a succession," of twenty years. The act did not literally specify a twenty-year charter. One of the objections to the McFadden bill was the apparent need to extend the length of "succession" six years before its designed expiration in 1933. In Section 18, the McFadden bill stated, "To have succession after the approval of this Act until dissolved by Act of Congress or until forfeiture of franchise for violation of law." The Senate added the limitless succession as a "rider"; it came in on the "tale end of the bill." The Federal Reserve System as of February 25, 1927, would continue its function forever. The bill's primary intention was to strengthen the national banking associations, broaden branch banking in the federal system while limiting the expansion of state branch banking when entering the federal system, and to make the Federal Reserve System permanent among other things. It was a bill "to place the National Banks on a plane of equality with the State banks." At the time the McFadden bill was becoming law, President Coolidge was vetoing the McNary-Haugen Bill. McNary-Haugen was a price support program for the farmer. Coolidge said to the Senate: "The difficulty with this particular measure is that it is not framed to aid farmers as a whole, and it is, furthermore, calculated to injure rather than promote the general public welfare." Agricultural surplus remained unsolved.

On February 24, 1927, the *Wall Street Journal* reported, "CHANGES IMPENDING IN RESERVE SYSTEM." Governor Harding declared in 1921 that the Federal Reserve System was not a central bank. The twelve reserve banks did go their independent merry way, flooding the country with Federal Reserve Notes. The Federal Reserve Board, apparently, didn't have full control of reserve bank operations in the beginning. The article pointed out the "clash between the board chairmen of the Reserve Banks and the Governors for the position of authority." The Federal Reserve Board picked the Chairmen of the Reserve Banks, but the Reserve Banks picked their own Governors. "The governors, selected by the banks, are under no real authority from the Federal Reserve Board, and they are frequently in a position to disregard the chairmen as other than Reserve agents to whom they must apply when they want currency." The McFadden bill was going to "clear the way for the Federal Reserve Board to carry out its new policy of gathering itself the reins of control over the activities of the different institutions of the System." Apparently, the Federal Reserve Bank of New York was the "leader of the pack." The article mentioned Benjamin Strong; he as "governor of the New York Bank, overshadowed the rest of the system as a national figure, and hence exercised an influence which made the Federal Reserve Bank of New York looked upon internationally as the representative of the entire system."

Senator Heflin of Alabama was against the branch banking bill; it was extending more power to the Federal Reserve. Heflin mentioned Governor W. P. G. Harding; Heflin referred to him as William "Poison Gas" Harding. In 1920, the Federal Reserve was being amended again. "Harding appeared at the Capital." Harding was pushing for a "progressive interest rate" that supposedly would stop surplus money from going to New York. "There is no harm in it. What we are trying to do is to keep the bulk of money from going to New York, so that we can send it to the South and the West to aid them at crop-moving time." The amendment was added to paragraph (d) of the infamous Section 14, which governs the discount rate. Heflin said, at the time, that only two senators in the Congress recognized its destructive power: Mr. Smith from South Carolina and Mr. Owen of Oklahoma. "Senator Smith of South Carolina said to Governor Harding 'If that amendment is adopted, it will precipitate the worst financial panic that ever came upon the country.'" Apparently, the South and the West were not helped. High interest rates followed; there was the contraction of $2 billion in Federal Reserve Notes to 1.2 billion in eighteen months. The voluminous Federal Reserve credit disappeared.

There was another Mr. Harding; W. L. Harding was a former governor of Iowa. Governor W. L. Harding spoke before the North Dakota State Legislature in February 1927. This Harding disliked the Federal Reserve System. He deviated from his main topic to give his description of Federal Reserve credit. Harding said that people didn't borrow money; they borrowed credit. "It was a system of bookkeeping. The debts were created, but the money did not go into circulation." Harding said the credits extended "were ten times" the circulation. When the Federal Reserve stopped the extension of credit or decided to contract the currency or call the loans, it was no-redundancy time. The Federal Reserve System did their trick, contracted or "held the money, and they owned the debts." People couldn't borrow; people had to "sell their property" at "deflated" prices to pay their debts. This happened in 1921; the ones hurt the most was "the farming class."

The "mystifying" Federal Reserve System—it was the way it was; it is the way it had been. The people know little of the Federal Reserve System today; the Sixty-ninth Congress of 1927 didn't know much about it either. Dr. John R. Commons of the University of Wisconsin appeared before the House Banking and Currency Committee in February 1927. He appeared as a witness for twelve days from February 4 to 15. While explaining the system's function, Dr. Commons covered the depression of 1921 and the expansions and contractions of the currency during the twenties. There were the transactions between the twelve reserve banks and their agents and the member banks, the open market, willfully intended inflation and deflation of prices by the reserve board, and the gold thing. In the middle of the discussions, Congressman Stevenson said, "Well, I don't understand, Professor, the difference between the Federal Reserve buying Government securities and buying in the open markets. I don't understand."

He wasn't the only one.

In the early twentieth century, when gold was still the thing, the basic money creation scheme hadn't changed since Hamilton. The principle remained the same; the paper money was going to obtain the gold. In 1792, Hamilton's bank printed the paper money; in 1927, the Bureau of Engraving and Printing printed the Federal Reserve Note. The governor of a reserve bank is also the agent; when the agent wanted currency or Federal Reserve Notes, he ordered currency to be printed. A security was "purchased"; the security was purchased with the printed currency. The Federal Reserve System had its currency for issue. The Federal Reserve Note was bank currency. The currency was interest bearing and a government obligation. The Federal Reserve Note in 1927 was a bank note; it was not legal tender, but it was good for gold. The security is government debt.

In the Federal Reserve System, the Federal Reserve Note, by Act of Congress, was made redeemable in gold, the promise to pay. Hamilton's paper currency was redeemable in gold. The reserve system was also authorized to issue Federal Reserve Notes against a short-term acceptance of ninety-day duration. An elastic Federal Reserve Note was created for the short term then redeemed for gold. C. W. Barron said the Federal Reserve System was going to accumulate the gold, and it did, with the help of the Congress and the Treasury of the United States. The government was printing the currency, borrowing the currency, and issuing the same currency, funding and/or creating its debt at the same time, the credit circulation. In 1913, the Treasury could run up the debt with Federal Reserve Notes, but the Treasury could not pay its debt with the Federal Reserve Notes.

The security, the government obligation in the Federal Reserve System, is the mounting debt of the credit circulation. The Congress taxed the people during the Civil War to secure the greenbacks. Customs, land sales, was the government's security. The security belonged to the people. It was non-interest-bearing currency. As a result, the Treasury hoped to lessen the cost of issue of paper currency during the Civil War. Later, Congressman Coffeen emphasized the preference; a fiat of the government was better than a fiat of the banks. The banks simply wanted that security back; the banks wanted to control the bond. It was the scheme to control the money. The private bank got the security back in 1863 and secured it in 1913.

Secretary Mellon's 1927 annual report of the Treasury showed the Federal Reserve banks and agents still held $2.8 billion in gold, which included coin, bullion, and certificates. This was gold accumulated by the Federal Reserve System since its beginnings. When the Federal Reserve System started, the twelve reserve banks in 1914 held $0.2 billion in gold.

The power of money in the past centuries had achieved the position of financial authority, with government assistance, first in England, France, Germany, and then the United States. After World War I, $200 billion of added indebtedness was tacked on and owed to this financial authority by all the industrialized countries, including the United States, the cost of the First World War. James Madison said it right in opposing the First Bank when he said, "The plan was unequal to the public creditors—it gave an undue preference to the holders of a particular denomination of the public debt, and to those at and within reach of the seat of Government." The basis of the plan guarantees control by few; it would be equitable if a representative of all the people should be within financial reach of the seat of government.

American political economic history has shown the similarity between Hamilton's beginnings and the beginnings of the Federal Reserve. Congressional legislation authorized both banks to acquire gold, but there was reversal of fortune. In 1792, financially, the United States was poor in terms of gold. Hamilton's bank acquired gold, but the United States was a debtor nation; gold was sent to England, to Europe. In the early twentieth century, the United States became an industrial force, a much stronger nation but still short on the gold thing. The First World War and foreign indebtedness sent the gold back. The United States had become the creditor. In addition, the Federal Reserve System was enabled to acquire the country's gold. Since Hamilton and into the early twentieth century, paper currency begot gold.

"Our present business is not conducted on gold. The gold is impounded and has no influence whatever. The reserves are no longer gold reserves, they are credit reserves at the Federal Reserve banks. The money that is used is no longer gold, but it is those demand deposits." During testimony, Dr. Commons mentioned that the "business man himself is creating the money." He illustrated the "present" and the "future" in the credit scheme. "The banker is buying future expectations, promise of business men payable in 90 days, and he is selling a present credit, which is the present worth of that future promise." Since the beginning, it was always the promise to pay.

There wasn't a "free" gold system anymore; the Federal Reserve System "managed" the gold. Before the Federal Reserve System, all the banks had some gold in their vaults; that condition was no longer the case. The reserve banks and their agents and the Treasury maintained and now controlled the gold. The Federal Reserve Act changed the rules; all national banking association reserves had to be placed in the twelve reserve banks. Dr. Commons discussed the 40% reserve in gold, the percentage determining the circulation, either expanding or contracting. But most importantly, why the key figure of 40%? It wasn't explained. A 40% reserve in gold and the 35% against deposits in gold was determined as part of the Federal Reserve Act. An explanation of the percentage factors, their origin, wasn't found in the record.

Professionals who practice many pursuits because of experience know the ends; determining the means is part of the practice. Probably, the bankers, through a predetermined amount of circulation desired and a subsequent expansion of credits based on an approximate supply of gold and known bank reserve requirements at the time, may determine the above 40 % and 35% rates. The factors, possibly, were determined working from a known or desired result; it's a common practice. An example of the calculation using the 40/35 percentages, which accounts for a known reserve requirement of the member banks that determines the expansion of credits, was presented by Senator Nye in the Senate on February 15, 1927. Senator Nye was from North Dakota. The credit expansion is calculated to a total in demand deposits or loans, which accumulates many times the currency circulation.

A newspaper, the *Commercial and Financial Chronicle*, a critic of the reserve system, called the system too much power. Senator Wheeler, in the Senate, on February 16, 1927, presented a piece from the *Chronicle*. The paper had urged the Congress to vote down the

McFadden bill. The amendments of 1917, which the paper considered "War Measures" should be removed. Primary was the power given by which the Federal Reserve consumed the country's gold. Secretary Mellon's 1927 report showed 4.5 billion in gold in the country. The *Chronicle* illustrated that "$11,250,000,000 of Federal Reserve notes could be ultimately issued and put in circulation if the Federal Reserve officials saw fit." This number becomes a possibility because of the 40% gold in reserve factor. That meant, by law, for every dollar of gold, there could be $2.5 in Federal Reserve Notes; do the arithmetic. "This is too vast a power to confer upon any body of men, even if they were endowed with wisdom from on high."

It was the Federal Reserve System and its gold accumulation.

The McFadden bill covered the Federal Reserve System, the national banking association members, The independent state banks and trust companies, all 25,330 of them; the bill did not cover or include the operations of the Federal Land Banks. On July 17, 1916, the "Federal Farm Loan Act" was signed into law. The law was enacted to promote "agricultural development . . . investments based on farm mortgages . . . to equalize interest rates . . . to establish a market for United States bonds . . . create Government Depositories and Financial Agents, etc."

It was a federal government—sponsored system. The act outlined a system, in structure only, similar to the Federal Reserve System. A farm loan board of five members was set up, one person of which, and in charge, was the secretary of the Treasury. A bureau within the Treasury Department was under the direction of the board. The Farm Loan Board was set up in Washington, D.C.; twelve separate agricultural districts were established within the continental United States. A Federal Land Bank with branches was set up in each of the twelve districts. For each farm land bank, "the capital stock . . . was divided into shares of $5 each, and may be subscribed for and held by any individual, firm, or corporation, or by the Government of any State, or of the United States." The minimum starting capitalization of each land bank by subscription was $750,000. The Treasury supplied the balance if the minimum capital was not achieved "within thirty days after opening."

The act provided for the incorporation of joint stock land banks and farm loan associations. The joint stock land banks were private banks organized for private profit; these banks made loans at 6% interest. The farm loan associations were the "subsidiary organizations," the farmers, the borrowers, and the stockholders in the Federal Land Banks. The farm banks made loans at 5 1/2% interest. The twelve Federal Land Banks "opened in the spring of 1917 with an aggregate capital of $9,000,000; of which $8,892,130 was subscribed by the Government and $107,870 by individuals." By design, increased association subscriptions gradually reduced government stock over time. The government started the land bank program; the goal was eventual farm loan association ownership. The starting aggregate capital of all the banks was about $18 million; by October 1919, the farmers had borrowed $303 million from the system's banks. From the record, there wasn't a specie reserve consideration in the design of this system. In 1927, there were more than 5,600 farm loan associations.

In June of 1920, the Federal Land Bank system virtually stopped for almost a year; the "constitutionality of the Federal Farm Loan Act" was challenged "in the United States district court in the western district in Missouri." The suit charged that the Congress didn't have the constitutional authority to create the land banks and that the banks could not sell bonds as legal securities create exemption from state and federal taxation, and that all the powers given under the act didn't justify their creation, etc. The case was taken to the Supreme Court; the Court upheld the act on February 28, 1921. Notables on the Court were Chief Justice Edward White, Oliver Wendell Holmes, and Louis Brandeis. The land bank system resumed operations in the early summer 1921.

The Federal Land Banks made the long-term mortgage loan variety; the Federal Reserve System credit was of the short-term ninety-day acceptance variety. Apparently, intermediate financial help was lacking. In order to assist the farmer in farming and livestock, the Congress amended the Federal Farm Loan Act in 1923. Twelve federal intermediate credit banks were added to the system; they were located in the twelve Federal Land Bank districts under the direction of the land banks. The credit banks sold debentures to provide credit for loans of six months to three years; the debenture maturity was for "not more than five years." The interest rate to the farmer could not be more than 1% above the debenture interest rate. The secretary of the Treasury subscribed the funds to the credit banks by selling debentures; the debentures were purchased "at par by 25 of the leading Banks of the country." More than $20 million in debentures were purchased "at 41/2 per cent, with a maturity of six months" during the period of inauguration of the credit banks. These credit banks took the place of the War Finance Corporation, which was phased out in 1925. There were now in the government-sponsored program Federal Land Banks, joint stock land banks, and the intermediate credit banks. In between all this business were the seed-grain loans.

President Coolidge in 1924 asked the Congress and the business community to assist the "wheat growing sections of the Northwest." The result was the organization of the "Agricultural Credit Corporation." Ten million dollars of private capital was to be raised with the cooperation of the Departments of the Treasury, Commerce, and Agriculture; the Farm Board, the Federal Reserve Board, the banks, the farm loan associations, etc. Coolidge called on the many businesses "whose welfare is immediately connected with the welfare of the farmer." A conference was held "in Washington on February 4, 1924, 'to consider the pressing agricultural needs of the Northwest.'" The corporation was organized and the capital raised by the "bankers and business interests" who attended the conference. Secretary Mellon, in his 1924 report, stated, "The Corporation had assisted 230 banks, having deposits totaling $54,000,000, by making loans aggregating $5,142,000 either directly to them or through their directors or stockholders." The credit corporation also assisted in tax relief and the "seed wheat" program. From the *Wall Street Journal* of February 11, 1924: "J.P. Morgan & Co. is subscribing $500,000 to the $10,000,000 Corporation being organized to render assistance in the agricultural sections of the Northwest."

In promoting the program, President Coolidge said, "The Government can not supply banking capital, nor can it organize loan companies." The statement is puzzling. What did President Coolidge think the Congress, Secretary Mellon and the Treasury was doing when the Federal Farm Loan Act was passed and almost $9 million was subscribed by the Treasury to initially augment the twelve land banks? Treasury generated capital inaugurated the twelve credit banks. Calvin Coolidge wasn't around in 1917 when the Federal Land Bank system was started? The country's major banks were there later when money was to be made with the joint stock banks and the debenture credit banks.

The federal government, by way of the Treasury, supplied the impetus to assist the American farmer during the distressed periods of the 1920s. By June 1929, the Federal Land Banks had made 494,000 mortgage loans to farmers since its beginnings in 1917. "The net amount of mortgage loans outstanding as of June 30, 1929, was $1,204,915,569.79." The farm loan associations were down; they numbered 4,664, but their combined "capital stock" was $65 million out of a total of 66 million in the system. The complexity of the nation's banking system, along with the currency, had become more complex.

Secretary Andrew Mellon's annual Treasury reports, in conjunction with the treasurer and the comptroller, through the decade, were comprehensive. The total money in the country, which included all the currencies from gold bullion to the lawful money greenbacks, remained the same from 1927 through 1929, about $8.5 billion. This was money in and outside of the Treasury. The total money reached a peak in 1924 when there was an $8.7-billion total; that was before the gold started going back to Europe. The population in 1924 was 112 million; the currency per capita was $42.2. In June 1929, the per capita figure for 120 million people was $39.6. The per capita figure reached $54 in 1920 when more than $3 billion in Federal Reserve Notes were circulating. The per capita currency was gradually reducing as the country approached 1929. Population increased; currency circulation remained fixed.

In June 1929, the types of money remained the same; it included gold bullion, gold and silver coin, gold and silver certificates, the national banking association currency, the "circulating notes" of the bank act of 1863, the new Federal Reserve Notes, the new Federal Reserve Bank Notes, the "repudiated" currency or the lawful money or the legal tenders or the greenbacks, the Treasury notes of 1890, and "subsidiary silver." This was the currency maze, the money makeup in the United States in 1929.

The circulating notes, the Federal Reserve Notes, and the Federal Reserve Bank Notes were not legal tenders. The Treasury printed these notes, principally, for the Federal Reserve banks and the national banking associations. There was $2.2 billion of these notes in circulation in 1929.

On April 23, 1918, the Pittman Act, Senate Bill 4202, became law. The bill was passed "to conserve the gold supply of the United States, etc." The bill would allow the settlement of trade imbalances in silver bullion with foreign countries, particularly the Far East. Silver dollars were melted down, taken out of circulation, thus the birth of the Federal Reserve Bank Notes. These Federal Reserve Bank Notes took the place of deposed silver dollars. These notes reached a high of 201 million in 1920. In 1921, the new "Peace" silver dollar was coined; as the Peace Dollars were coined, the Federal Reserve Bank Notes were retired. In 1929, there was $3.6 million in Federal Reserve Bank Notes left in circulation.

Gold certificates, as part of the circulation, represented gold in the Treasury. A $1 gold certificate equaled $1 in gold. But the 40% gold reserve as per the Federal Reserve Act could generate $2.5 in Federal Reserve Notes at any time, an apparent plus for the reserve system. It was advantageous for the Federal Reserve to accumulate gold certificates; this was illustrated in the *Chronicle* newspaper, the potential power of the Federal Reserve as part of Senator Wheeler's presentation. Gold certificates were made legal tender, payment for all dues, public and private, on December 24, 1919; it was Senate Bill 3458. Gold certificates were made legal tender because of the demand for "high-value Greenbacks," and there were so few of the greenbacks; the greenbacks were good for gold, and the banks needed more notes good for gold. There were $1.4 billion in gold certificates outside the Treasury in 1929, 900 million were in circulation. The Federal Reserve held the rest, about 500 million.

Four hundred seventy million dollars in silver certificates stayed constant in circulation throughout the decade. The silver certificates represented "dollar for dollar," the silver coin held in the many Treasury depositories. The secretary listed $304 million of "subsidiary silver." The subsidiary silver was the half-dollars, quarters, dimes, and nickels in circulation. These coins were called fractional currency in the early nineteenth century. Mellon would call them fractional currency in his next report.

The treasurer listed them as "National Bank Notes." These notes were the "Circulating Notes," the currency established for the national banking associations in 1863. Seven hundred four million dollars of these notes were in circulation in 1929. These notes, authorized by the bank act of 1863, were still secured by long-term United States bonds, the continuing debt in principal and interest against the Treasury and the people of the United States. The steep cost of these notes, to the people, was the discount or interest for the note plus the cost of the bonds in principal and the interest in gold, the security for the notes.

The greenbacks were listed as United States Notes; they were also the legal tenders and the "lawful money" of the United States. The total "fixed" circulation remained $346,681,016. The cost of the greenback note was negligible compared to the cost of the 1863 National Bank Note, and the greenback was useful; it was redeemable for gold. The Treasury held 2 million in greenbacks; the Federal Reserve held 82 million. The rest were in circulation. The Treasury notes of 1890 totaled $1,288,450, all in circulation.

The treasurer showed denominations of four currencies issued, redeemed, and outstanding for the years 1926 through 1929. The four currencies were the gold and silver certificates, the greenbacks, and the Treasury notes. Federal Reserve Notes and the 1863 national currency notes were not shown. Gold certificates were issued in $10 to $10,000 denominations, silver certificates from $1 to $10,000. The greenbacks from $1 to $10,000 and the Treasury notes from $1 to $1,000.

On June 3, 1929, a "new small size currency" was issued. "The new issue consisted of $1 silver certificate, $2 United States note, and $5 and $10 dollar Federal Reserve note." The larger paper issues were gradually phased out of circulation.

From Mellon's annual report: "1929 was, for the most part, a good year. Production and, incomes, was on the up side in automobiles, railroads, trade, business, industrial construction and agriculture. Residential housing construction was down; interest rates were high." Automobile production showed "an increase of approximately 53 per cent." There was an increase in "steel ingots" for automobile manufacture, but other industries were down; as a result, total manufacture increase was "22 per cent . . . Freight-car loadings increased 4.3 per cent during the year . . . The foreign trade of the United States approached $10,000,000,000 . . . This was an increase of 10.2 per cent in exports and 3.5 per cent in imports over the preceding year." Based on 1927-1928 projections, business profits indicated a probable increase of "11 per cent." The "gross income of agriculture" was up but not by very much. There was a surplus in the Treasury of $185 million, $124 million of it went toward the public debt. The public debt was reduced to $16.9 billion. The 1929 overall economy showed growth in the nation as in the year before and the year before that and the year before that, and then there was Wall Street. Secretary Mellon called it "an active and rising stock market." Mellon reported, "The number of shares of stock sold on the New York Stock Exchange alone increased from 720,000,000 during the fiscal year 1928 to 1,042,000,000 in 1929, an increase of 44.6 per cent." The value of the capital stock more than doubled from $2 billion to 5 billion.

The comptroller reported that twenty-four banks in New York cleared $457 billion in transactions in 1929. The twelve Federal Reserve banks cleared $598 billion. "The total clearings of the 244 cities reporting to the New York Clearing House Association in the current year aggregated $714 billion dollars"; the total was $100 billion more than the previous year, 1928. The comptroller included a table of call loans, sixty-day time loans, for the "range of rates for money in New York annually" for the period 1920 through 1929. The call loans reached their highest rates of interest during the years 1920 and 1929. The rates of 25 and 20% doubled the rates during the years 1921-1928.

Do the above figures show an absurdity or what the figures really represent the velocity of money and the product of the country? All of the above on a reported $5 billion in circulation! Credits, deposits, debts, the real inflation total more than the physical money.

Prohibition continued to foster the crime family and millions of dollars of government expense in what now appears to have been a senseless pursuit of illegal booze. The Bureau of Prohibition reported sixty-seven thousand arrests in 1929. Boat and automobile seizures were valued at more than $3 million; fines totaled more than $7 million. Nineteen thousand people were sentenced to more than seven thousand years in jail. The average sentence was a $350 fine and six months in jail. Narcotics violations were considerably less in number.

Prohibition was a big issue in the 1928 presidential election. Herbert Hoover was for Prohibition; he was the third successive Republican president of the decade. Hoover felt Prohibition was a "noble" effort. Hoover defeated the Democrat Alfred E. Smith by a substantial margin, getting 58% of the popular vote; the electoral margin was 444-87. It was a landslide victory. It is most interesting that maybe a commanding majority of the American people voted against, not for, in 1928. The country wasn't ready for Al Smith who was Roman Catholic; the result was religion, another major issue. Andrew Mellon remained the secretary of the Treasury during the Hoover administration.

As of October 30, 1929, the gold reserve in the Federal Reserve System was $3.2 billion.

> At the request of the Federal Reserve Board, another change was instituted on August 1, 1929, when the keeping of the Federal Reserve agent's gold redemption fund account was discontinued . . . On August 1, 1929, the balance in the agent's gold redemption fund was transferred to the gold fund with the Federal Reserve Board.

Tuesday, October 29, 1929, was the fateful day; maybe that dark day was like the curtain coming down on a remarkable decade of the American experience. It was the day of the "crash," the collapse on Wall Street.

CHAPTER TWELVE
The Crash: Imminent Depression

There was a collapse on Wall Street in October of 1929. There appeared no indication when first reading Secretary Mellon's annual Treasury report for the year 1930; it was business as usual. "The finances of the Federal Government for the fiscal year 1930 continued the favorable record of recent years." On February 21, 1930, the *New York Times* reported "4,012,210 passenger cars" were sold in the United States. It was "an increase of 8.7 per cent for the United States during the year." In November 1930, Secretary Mellon's Treasury report showed the total money was down a bit from $8.5 to $8.3 billion. The per capita figure had been falling since 1920, from $54 to $43 in 1923 to $37 in 1930. The population was up; the currency was down. It was the new decade, and the economy would begin its descent. In the middle of 1930, four million people were unemployed; in 1933, fifteen million were out of work. The total money was there, but somehow, another raid; the stagecoach was robbed again. Banks would eventually take a holiday. It was the credits; the credits vanished. The Wall Street crash did a number on credits and the country. The country's vaunted Federal Reserve currency, the Federal Reserve Note apparently would not exhibit its elasticity.

There was $3.2 billion in gold in the Federal Reserve System. One gets perplexed reading the Treasury reports. Gold was in the reserve system; gold was in the Treasury. The gold was in the Treasury; gold was in the reserve system. It was a combine, a tandem thing, a bit complex; but Mellon's reports were most informative. Based on that gold reserve, the Federal Reserve System by the reserve act, theoretically, by way of the comptroller, could print $8 billion in Federal Reserve Notes? A minimum of $80 billion in credits and deposits, theoretically, could be generated? The Federal Reserve System controlled the country's credit. Did the Federal Reserve System sit on the gold and the credits?

Apparently, there would be no credit as before; too few controlled it. The Federal Reserve System and its banks totaled less than half of the nation's banks, and yet the Federal Reserve System controlled the country's gold and credit courtesy of the United States Congress. In November 1930, there were $1.4 billion in Federal Reserve Notes in circulation. Ten years earlier, there were more than 3.0 billion of these notes in circulation. There was supposed growth in the United States in the 1920s. The population increased by fifteen million people. The amount of circulating money should increase; the money should reflect the country's growth along with its population? Growth, subsequent equity, debt formation, money creation, capitalization—it's all part of the equation? There was Federal Reserve expansion and contraction in the 1920s. The money was there; it was not there. The physical money, the circulation into 1929 hadn't accumulated, but the wealth did; it was the wealth of indebtedness. More than half of an impending $200 billion debt had to be paid in gold, $100 billion, think of it, on a 5-billion circulation! A pause here, the real form of inflation; this apparently is what really happens! It was credits and deposits then the crash; it was no-redundancy time again, probable classic manipulation by the money interests. Crash or no crash, ballooned debts had to be paid. Values plummet, but debts stay put; that's pure capitalism. The explosion and the annihilation of credits had to be and were part of the Wall Street operation and the collapse. Who pulled the plug? Who was responsible? The money was a national thing; it was an international thing. The Treasury Federal Reserve combine did a ten-year number on America.

Many changes were made in the '30s; but as before, to affect those changes, it was back to the Congress. Franklin Roosevelt was elected the thirty-second president in 1932. There was a half-truth about the Great Depression; "there was nothing to buy and no money to buy it with." The half-truth was there was no money for 25% to 30% of the people; this was the heart of the Depression, the people who were out of work, out of the system. Somebody said, "Give the country back to the Indians." The capitalistic state in 1933, the Republican Hamilton ethic, did not account for these people. Pure capitalism was not all people friendly! President Roosevelt would start his work programs, get these people back to work, but he needed money to do it; he needed credit in order to get the money. The crash had demolished the credits; there wasn't acceptable commercial paper for rediscounting, and apparently, the private side of the Federal Reserve System wasn't going to generate that credit. The people, by way of government, would have to generate it. Currency would be created based on a new "collateral" security with some effect. Currency deflation in a land of plenty escalated a currency devaluation process. Federal Reserve Bank Notes would be generated based on a silver maneuver; then Roosevelt devalued the dollar. The Federal Reserve had the gold; the Treasury had the gold. It didn't matter. Roosevelt first hauled in the gold then reduced the value of the dollar against gold. A gold ratio was there; why wasn't it used? An Andrew Jackson objection was in place. The "formidable" central bank, created by the United States government, was sitting back, apparently in domestic neutral, dictating. Is this how a country may financially devour itself, manipulated by its own hand, in the creation of its "private" central bank? About the First Bank, James Madison said, "It gave an undue preference to the holders of a particular denomination of the public debt, and to those at and within reach of the seat of Government." Devaluation of the dollar allowed President Roosevelt to obtain some credit. The president had some money; just like that, the currency became somewhat elastic again? Not really! The Treasury printed, issued, borrowed, and spent the same currency by way of the Federal Reserve, the credit circulation. More securities would perpetrate the public debt, and the people would pay for the securities to pay for the money to get back to work. This is the same as being hit while you're already down; the working class would not own the securities, but would forever pay for them. "And we are to be responsible after all, that is all there is of it." President Roosevelt began his "New Deal; Roosevelt created the Public Works Administration." But we are way ahead of the story; other things happened first. Herbert Hoover and the Republicans were still in power!

On January 20, 1930, three months after the Wall Street collapse, a convention was held at The Hague in the Netherlands. The convention, which involved banking principals of the industrialized countries, established a bank for their central banks. It was the Bank for International Settlements (BIS). This bank would be established in Basel, Switzerland. The *Wall Street Journal* covered the story on January 22. This bank was being "formed to arrange transfer of the reparations functions from the Dawes Organization to the new institution." A new Owen Young Plan as part of the BIS would pick up where the Dawes Plan left off. The Owen Young Plan was a fifty-nine-year payment plan combining German reparations and war debts. Owen Young was an American businessman; he had been "chairman of the Board of the General Electric Company." The paper reported, "The American Banking group which is acting for the United States in lieu of the Federal Reserve includes J.P. Morgan & Co., First National Bank of Chicago and First National Bank of New York." The article stated that a "prominent American with connections with the Federal Reserve is in view for the presidency" of the BIS bank.

On February 26, 1930, Chairman McFadden of the House Banking and Currency Committee submitted two resolutions in the House. "On several occasions during the past year I have invited the attention of the country to the possible danger of mixing our Federal Reserve system and its policies with international policies and the International Bank." McFadden submitted information to the House about principal members of the Federal Reserve Bank of New York and principal bankers of New York and their involvement with foreign central banks in the formation of the Bank for International Settlements. McFadden was "calling on the State Department and the Secretary of the Treasury, respectfully, for full information in this matter." Mr. Wingo chided McFadden. Congressman Wingo said the State Department had to already know about the situation; also, "the Federal Reserve Bank of New York does what it wants to do; it goes contrary to the policy of the Federal Reserve Board."

McFadden began his address quoting from George Washington's Farewell Address.

> The great rule of conduct for us, in regard to foreign nations, is, in extending our commercial relations, to have with them as little political connection as possible. So far as we have already formed engagements, let them be fulfilled with perfect good faith. Here let us stop.

All that must have sounded good then; but doesn't owed money to foreigners, internationals, apparently change everything?

The principals of the Federal Reserve Bank of New York were Gates W. McGarrah and G. L. Harrison. Mr. McGarrah, chairman and agent, reportedly "was to become chairman of the Board of Directors of the Bank for International Settlements." Governor Harrison was sailing to Europe to discuss "the foreign-exchange markets and the international gold situation." The *New York Times* of February 22, 1930, had covered the story as reported by McFadden. The newspaper reported that the BIS would open in April. Governors would meet in Rome to select American representation. The article stated that governors of central banks were visiting each other on a regular basis. Montague Norman had visited the United States twice in 1929. McFadden said,

> It will be recalled that on the first visit of Governor Norman a definite change in Federal Reserve policy took place—a policy of inflation to a policy of deflation. On his second visit, further restrictive measures were agreed upon and put into operation both by the Federal Reserve system and the Bank of England, and shortly thereafter the financial debacle of last October occurred.

McFadden pulled no punches; he linked the central banks with the Wall Street collapse. McFadden mentioned a "secretive" meeting in the Treasury Department in 1926. Montague Norman, Hjalmar Schacht of Germany, the head banker from France, and reparations agent Parker Gilbert attended. A note pledging German railways was planned. The note was

> to be underwritten in France, Germany, and the United States, and which, I understand, was agreed to by our Treasury authorities, but was headed off by President Coolidge . . . If this plan had not been blocked by President Coolidge, we would have witnessed a commercialization of the German War Debt and a transference from the Allied countries, to whom Germany owed these debts, to the private investors of these countries and the United States, principally the United States.

Nothing had changed; according to McFadden, all this business was planned in the Versailles Treaty. The "German war debt should be commercialized and unloaded upon the United States. So the framers of the Dawes and Young Plans and the reparations agents and the international bankers have not changed—they never do; they still intend to do this in some way. They know not defeat." A plan did take place, a Dawes Plan under President Hoover; large loans granted Germany against railroads, industry, etc.

McFadden mentioned the "conferences" of the Federal Reserve Bank of New York with "foreign bankers" as covered in the newspapers. Were these conferences "contrary" to government policy? McFadden referred to State Department policy of May 1929. The Federal Reserve System was not to get involved with the BIS. The State Department "would not permit any officials of the Federal Reserve system either to themselves serve or to select American representatives as members of the proposed international bank." McFadden named "J.P. Morgan & Co." McFadden intimated that the Federal Reserve was involved with the BIS through J. P. Morgan and Company. McFadden made it clear that the Congress should make such involvement "forbidden."

McFadden presented the government's position:

> As to "American Policy" . . . step after step consistently, the United States has insisted that the war debts to it were not to be conditioned upon German reparation payments. This was sound policy. We wanted to stay clear of European entanglements and to treat with those to whom we loaned money, not with strangers. In this there was also logic because our debts represented war costs, and under the Armistice terms and the Treaty of Versailles, Germany was not required to pay war costs of the Allies.

Before the First World War, England was the power; London, England, the pound sterling was the exchange. England owned or controlled 70% of the world's gold mines. England was supreme; C. W. Barron stated as much. World War I changed all that. McFadden mentioned, "Monetary conditions were in a state of chaos. Exchanges were completely demoralized." There was a monetary "reconstruction scheme" set up within the League of Nations. This required cooperation of all the central banks. "The Bank of England made an advance to the Austrian National Banks for stabilization purposes." This didn't happen before the war. One time previously in the nineteenth century, England and France cooperated during the "Barings crisis." After World War I, with debts incurred and indebtedness all around and in crisis and America with gold, it would appear, from this viewpoint, that England, that is, its central bank, had to act. The banks, primarily of the belligerent nations Austria, Hungary, Germany, were in disarray; their currencies had to be "stabilized." As to Russia, she was not in this part of the record? Russia had been stripped of its gold? Russia was not mentioned in this business. Russia was now the Soviet Union and was not part of the diplomatic accord with all nations?

McFadden mentioned the Federal Reserve System; the system became involved through the efforts of Montague Norman. Norman and Benjamin Strong were friends; Strong was the governor of the Federal Reserve Bank of New York. Through this "friendship . . . the United States was induced to cooperate financially, if not politically, in European affairs." Norman, the "moving spirit" behind this business, worked "behind the scenes." An alliance was set up of the leading institutions, the central banks. Japanese banks and Egyptian banks were included. There were two important objectives. The first was monetary stabilization and the prevention of a scramble for gold by central banks, and the second was the cooperation between the central banks to affect reparations transfers. The objective was that Germany must pay.

McFadden, when introducing his resolutions, mentioned the following: "I append here an article in today's New York Journal of Commerce headed 'Broad Powers for Reparations Bank.'" The article contained remarks by "Jackson E. Reynolds, President of the First National Bank of New York." His remarks included future functions of the Bank of International Settlements. Mr. Reynolds helped frame the "details" of the BIS:

- The bank may become depository of the world's gold.
- The bank may borrow from and lend to central banks.
- The bank will coordinate all the central banks.

- The bank will buy and sell gold.
- Gold will be deposited by owners of the gold.
- The bank will grow like the Federal Reserve System through the borrowing and lending between districts in the United States.
- The bank would not issue currency.
- Transfer rates will be less of Reichsmarks transferred into the currency of creditors.
- The bank will deposit in central banks and receive deposits from central banks.
- The BIS and the central banks will act as agents for each other.

Montague Norman was for the Bank for International Settlements. Montague Norman was apparently gathering the world's central banks and their accumulation of national gold and setting up shop in a bastion of international gold. This bank, which was probably the first world bank, was to locate in Basel, Switzerland. Is this why world wars are not fought in Switzerland, where the money is? Most people don't know of the BIS. Where is Basel anyway! Did the BIS idea also spring from Schacht? Hjalmar Schacht was in agreement with the idea. In his *Confessions*, Schacht revealed a conversation he had with Owen Young. According to Schacht, Germany, after the war, was still an industrial force. The large loans after the war should have gone to the "backward countries," not Germany. These underdeveloped countries could exploit their natural resources and production with machines and mechanical tools built in and purchased in Germany. According to Schacht, Germany, trying to compete in world markets as before the war, was not the thing to do; making big loans to Germany in this respect was wrong. Germany could better pay reparations distributed through a bank like the BIS. Reparations payments would be made by Germany by way of an international bank, the BIS. The central bankers wanted the bank in Belgium; Switzerland was Schacht's preference for such a bank.

The *Congressional Record* indicates that over a period of several years, the Federal Reserve Bank of New York, J. P. Morgan, Owen Young, Montague Norman, and others were instrumental in planning the BIS with foreign central banks.

The debtor nations owed the creditor nations, and the creditor nations owed their central banks. The international wealth of indebtedness had to be sustained; it could only be sustained by maintaining financial stability of the debtor nations. The BIS, apparently, was going to be a world banker's central bank. In 1927, Dr. Commons testified, "We have created a managed gold system, because we impounded the gold in the Federal Reserve Banks, and the member banks can not get it out . . . Furthermore, the Reserve System has made agreements with nine countries—" Dr. Commons didn't finish his remark; the record shows he was interrupted. Since the Federal Reserve, Commons said, "There are no gold reserves anymore." In the meantime, Wall Street had collapsed; the economy in the United States would begin its downward spiral. America appeared secondary. The Bank for International Settlements, according to Chairman McFadden and the events unfolding, appeared paramount. There were foreign loans and debts to be made and paid. And that is the way it was, and apparently, that is the way it was going to be.

The details of the Owen Young Plan were presented the year before in Europe. The important people of all the countries were there, the central bankers from France, Italy, Great Britain, the United States, Belgium, and Germany. Hjalmar Schacht reluctantly signed the Owen Young Plan on June 7, 1929. In Schacht's *Confessions*, he revealed his wife's sentiments; she didn't want him to sign.

McFadden presented his synopsis of the proposed Owen Young Plan; the United States was going to pay for the plan. The new BIS was going to issue reparations bonds. "Accredited authorities estimate, that the United States is to absorb within the next five or six years between five and six billion dollars' worth of these German reparations bonds." The bonds would be sold through J. P. Morgan and Company. Congressman Briggs questioned McFadden, "The effect of that would be to transfer from European Nations to the United States the relationship of creditor to Germany with respect to reparations?" McFadden answered in the affirmative.

McFadden presented an issue of the London *Economist* of February 15, 1930; the "article headed: The Reichstag and the Young Plan." The bill, pending in Germany, was referred to as the bill for the enslavement of the German people. The Reichstag, the German parliament, did not want a payment plan beyond ten years. This would be in conflict with long-term reparation bonds, the "validity of the Bonds" held by American investors. How good was a fifty-nine-year plan when Germany wasn't going to pay past "the decade"? But the Allied governments approved the plan in March of 1930; apparently, the Germans would pay past the decade? Later, President Hoover declared a "moratorium" for one year to start July 1931; the approved joint resolution (147) became official December 23, 1931. Sixteen European countries, including Great Britain and Germany, were absolved of debt payments to the United States for one year; this action, supposedly, would keep Germany from going bankrupt. Schacht wrote that Germany paid about 10% of the war reparations, "between ten and twelve billions," between 1924 and 1932. "And they were not paid out of surplus exports as they should have been." During the period, private "foreign loans were made to Germany, amounting to a clear twenty billions." This debt was never paid. According to Schacht, "Foreign private investors lost their money on the loans made to Germany." Schacht revealed in his *Confessions* that the Allied countries got the "12 billions" in reparations.

> The ultimate victims of this procedure were the foreign lenders. They loaned money to German firms, public companies, corporations, municipalities and towns. The Reichsbank exchanged these foreign remittances [bills of exchange] for German money; the bills of exchange however constituted the funds from which reparations were transmitted. In this way the foreign politicians obtained the money which foreign private capitalists had supplied to Germany in the form of loans and credits.

It would appear that American debenture money (probably Federal Reserve Notes) was a part of the losses of the "foreign lenders." According to Schacht, Germany's economy escalated, but the expense was the country's loss of "property" and "German Colonies" and the cost of reparations and the "interest payments on the foreign loans," which would never be paid. The collapse on Wall Street and the beginning of a deteriorating world economy, apparently, couldn't facilitate any payment plan?

The planning by the principals of the Federal Reserve Bank of New York for more than two years apparently went for naught. Chairman McFadden probably was part of the congressional action that would eventually deny Federal Reserve membership in the Bank for International Settlements?

Foreign banks were established; the Webb/Edge banks were formed and loans made to Germany. The loans, which took the form of debentures, were sold to American investors. In effect, Germany borrowed American money, purchased gold, and paid reparations to the Allied central banks; and a system inaugurated and authorized by the Congress and created by the bankers apparently paid heavily on American banks and the investor? First, it was the debentures as part of the Dawes Plan? With the Young Plan, it would change to the reparations bonds as issued through the Bank for International Settlements? McFadden's belief was that it was an effort by the Dawes and Young people "that the German war debt be commercialized and unloaded upon the United States." A Young Plan may also recoup losses suffered under the Dawes. It would appear the American investor, in addition, paid heavily when Wall Street collapsed?

In the House, McFadden presented a *New York Times* article of February 22. The article referred to a "change in Federal Reserve policy." Currencies in the foreign exchange market especially the pound sterling and the franc had gone "to levels little above those at which gold might be expected to flow here from abroad." Apparently, Governor Harrison was going to Europe to discuss these matters with the "Bank of England and the Bank of France." U.S. banking authorities, according to the article, supposedly, were against a "movement" of gold coming to the United States from Europe. Why shouldn't Governor Harrison discuss this matter at home to "avert" this movement of gold? The New York Federal Reserve Bank and the world central banks were interested in the formation of the BIS. Why the apparent meeting in Europe? This was McFadden's contention. The article stated that the Federal Reserve Bank of New York was going to buy "bills in the London Market"; the "purchase," supposedly, would stop "such a gold flow."

McFadden had many questions about credit, the volume of credit since the crash. "It seems to me that it is about time that we had a clarification of our views regarding the purpose and significance of our banking policy and its effect on the money market and upon general business." About the gold reserve: "The reserve is now beyond our needs and far above the legal-reserve ratio." McFadden referred to the "changed policy" of the Federal Reserve after the 1920-1921 inflation/deflation debacle. "We should remember, however, that the maintenance of the gold reserve ratio has never been the basis for the establishment of Federal Reserve policy, and during the past two years the two factors to which I have already referred were paramount in the formation and carrying out that policy." McFadden mentioned 1927. The discount rate was reduced in the United States after Europe restored the gold standard; $500,000,000 in gold was shipped to Europe "and the release of excessive amount of credit here." Secondly, "the attempt to prevent the diversion of the Federal Reserve credit into the market" in 1929.

What was McFadden saying? If the gold reserve was absolute to the supply of currency, how is it that a half-billion dollars in gold is shipped out of the country and then easy credit is established? But Europe was going back on the gold standard. Then, when credit may have been needed in the stock market, it was denied? As to the movement of gold, it becomes a little less cloudy about the banking schemes when reading Adam Smith? "And as it can find no advantageous market at home, it must, notwithstanding any prohibition, be sent abroad." For the central banks, the Federal Reserve, to an international "advantageous market," the gold reserve, the supply of, the gold ratio, credits, the discount rate; it was whatever was necessary for the banks, in the scheme of things.

John Kenneth Galbraith examined the period; he mentioned the Churchill thing, England returning to the gold standard. "Britain returned to the Gold standard at the old or pre-World War I relationship between gold, dollars, and the pound." According to Galbraith, Churchill was thinking the prewar "$4.86 pound." England suspended specie had been on paper currency. There was inflation; a lot more paper was needed to pay the bills. Galbraith mentioned that Churchill didn't understand the "subtle consequences of over valuation." It was as before; in the nineteenth century in the United States, first the suspensions then the paper period, a subsequent return to specie and then it was crunch time. "Customers of Britain had now to use these costly pounds to buy goods at prices that still reflected war-time inflation."

Galbraith called them "the three August pilgrims"—Norman, Schacht, and the Frenchman Charles Rist. They "came to the United States to urge an easy money policy." They met with Andrew Mellon and the Federal Reserve. The result of all this was the reserve reduced the discount rate from 4% to 3.5%, and the Federal Reserve "bought" several hundred million dollars in government securities; this released a ton of money (billions in credits). This was the period of easy credit. The currency, no doubt, was Federal Reserve Notes. "The funds that the Federal Reserve made available were either invested in common stocks or [and more importantly] they became available to help finance the purchase of common stocks by others. So provided with funds, people rushed into the market." Galbraith's information came from testimony by Lionel Robbins before a senate committee in 1934. Robbins was professor of the London School of Economics. Robbins's conclusion (after 1927) was "from that date, according to the evidence, the situation got completely out of control." Galbraith commented,

> This view that the action of the Federal Reserve authorities in 1927 was responsible for the speculation and collapse which followed has never been seriously shaken . . . The danger of being guided by foreigners is well known, and Norman and Schacht had some special reputation for sinister moves.

Secretary Mellon, in his November 1927 Treasury report, listed $2.7 billion in government securities owned by the national and member banks. Member banks may purchase securities from the reserve banks to satisfy reserve debt payment, and resultant contraction may take place. Apparently, this action by the banks is a correction of indebtedness within the banking system. The effect takes money out of circulation, out of the economy, and things may come to a stop.

The "stabilization" of European currencies—what was the meaning? Did it mean the moving, transferring, lending, the borrowing, of gold among the central banks? Chairman McFadden's presentation from his standpoint was indicating that the Federal Reserve, more importantly the Federal Reserve Bank of New York, was most active in this mobilization process. The chairman mentioned that Governor Harrison was going to Europe to discuss "the foreign exchange markets and the international gold situation." At the time, there were huge debts all around, especially to be paid by Germany; apparently, those foreign debts could not be paid with unsound currencies. While this international money scene was taking place, McFadden was asking what was the national money policy going to be at home, in the United States, after the Wall Street collapse.

McFadden claimed the Federal Reserve's intent was to place "important deposits of gold" in the Bank for International Settlements. McFadden produced letters, and newspaper articles, in support of his presentation. In the *Financial Chronicle* of February 22, 1930: "It remains only to add, as emphasizing the need of getting implicit assurance, that the gold holdings of the Reserve Banks are not, in large part or in small part, in the shape of deposits or otherwise, to be part of the command of the Bank for International Settlements."

England had reigned supreme, that is, the Bank of England, for a long time; England commanded the exchanges, the gold, but paper money was the heart of the matter, the capitalization process. Alexander Hamilton repeated the principle. The principle was repeated in 1913. The record indicates that the third bank used the non-legal tender paper money, the new Federal Reserve Note, to acquire gold, to mobilize gold. The third central bank was a successful extension of the Hamilton bank, and the BIS was apparently trying to utilize United States' gold, national gold, with other central banks on the international scene?

During the Federal Reserve legislative process (1910-1913), emphasis was placed on the creation of an elastic currency based, supposedly, on a gold reserve. The new elastic currency was created on the basis of short-term acceptances and government securities. The currency would turn over quickly. The bankers didn't want currency based on long-term bonds. This was the direction when the Congress debated the creation of the new Federal Reserve System. The Federal Reserve Bank of New York compiled its first annual report in 1915. It was in that report that the New York bank stated its purpose of gold accumulation on page 19. "What the Reserve Bank does in accumulating gold behind its Federal Reserve notes is to establish with the holder of each note a credit which may be availed of whenever the occasion requires." Apparently, the holders of the Federal Reserve Notes at retirement were primarily the agents of the reserve banks. As of 1922, the Federal Reserve System had amassed more gold than held totally by the Bank of England, the Bank of France, the Bank of Italy, etc. It was a remarkable achievement courtesy of the U.S. Treasury by Act of Congress. The Federal Reserve System had become most formidable in a very short period of time. An elastic currency that turned over quickly achieved a stash of gold quickly. Remarkable!

During the Civil War, the Treasury introduced a short-term security; it was called the certificate of indebtedness. The certificates helped finance the Civil War; the certificates continuously paid interest within twelve months. The certificates had been used extensively for short-term borrowing ever since, especially during World War I. The short-term Treasury bill as it is known today was introduced in June 1929. Mellon reported, "This new instrument of financing is now established as a valuable supplement to certificates of indebtedness in the conduct of short-term borrowing operations." The "sum" of such Treasury bills at any one time could not exceed $10 billion. Treasury bill maturity was for two and three months; certificates of indebtedness maturity was for twelve months.

In November 1930, Secretary Mellon stated,

> The credit conditions in the United States went through a complete readjustment. Money rates, which at the beginning of the period were at a higher level than at any time since 1920, began to decline rapidly about the middle of November, 1929, and by the summer of 1930 were at the lowest levels of postwar years.

There was a "firm" money policy from 1927 to 1929; there were also Federal Reserve stock market "warnings" during the period. In November 1929, the discount rate was 6%; by November 1930, the discount rate in New York had fallen to 2.5%. The call rate had reached

20% during the period. Mellon mentioned the high rates trading on Wall Street, between 1926 and 1929, "to record proportions." The high rates attracted money to Wall Street "from all parts of the United States and from abroad." Mellon said, "This led to an inward movement of gold, which added about $270,000,000 to the country's gold stock of monetary gold between January and October" of 1929. Apparently, there was money to be made, one way or the other. In addition to member banks, "corporations and non-banking lenders" made loans to brokers. Mellon said that reported brokers' loans in New York City had reached $8.5 billion by October of 1929. Things changed late in 1929; Mellon reported "a conspicuous failure in the British market and by withdrawals of foreign funds from this country." Late in the year, there were declines in "security prices" and "stock prices," which resulted in the "liquidation of loans on an unprecedented scale." Corporations and other entities withdrew funds from the market. Secretary Mellon stated that although member banks in New York City picked up the slack, liquidation by "lenders other than member banks" reduced the total liquidation to $4.0 billion by the end of December.

According to Mellon, the Federal Reserve reversed its tight policy of the past "two years"; this was done after the "withdrawal of funds from the market by non-bank lenders and out of town banks." After the liquidation, from November of 1929 into 1930, the reserve banks purchased about $500 million in government securities, which allowed "easier money conditions." Brokers then borrowed from member banks.

In May 1930, President Hoover spoke to the United States Chamber of Commerce. Hoover applauded the Federal Reserve for "promoting the supply of capital after the collapse." But he questioned the high discount rate of 6% and the tight money policy of the member banks prior to the collapse. Hoover said the reserve policy, "by their efforts, they segregated the use of capital for speculation." During the period, the call rate went as high as 20%. The president said that this "attracted capital from productive enterprise, and this was one of the secondary factors in producing the crash itself." Later, when he felt things were getting better, the president mentioned the capital was leaving New York and finding its way back to "productive enterprise." This would be the other economy.

During the summer of 1929, the stock market was beginning to fragment. "BLAME RESERVE FOR HIGH MONEY . . . . Speakers at Bankers Convention Find Fault with Credit Policy." This was the headline of a two-column article in the *Wall Street Journal* on Tuesday morning, June 18, 1929. The latest results were in; the New York Bankers Association held their annual convention in Toronto, Canada. The Federal Reserve Board was "censured . . . for the way it tackled the stock market problem." The speakers were "M.C. Cahill, president of the Association and former Governor E.C. Stokes of New Jersey." In brief, the two speakers accentuated the following:

- Public warnings were ill advised; it created panic among the people.
- The Federal Reserve Board did not seek the cooperation of the New York banks.
- There was too much government control in our banking.
- The New York Federal Reserve Bank didn't confer with the New York Bankers Association; an orderly liquidation process could have been implemented. This action was needed in the future.
- The Federal Reserve Act needed to be amended. The twelve reserve banks apparently made most of the profits. Net earnings should be more equitable between member banks and government.
- Collateral loans, in addition to the commercial thing, should be available for rediscount in the reserve system.
- The reserve board's restrictive credit policy against broker's loans raised the country's interest rates, hurting business, the farmers, and government borrowing.
- There was no sympathy for a banking system that didn't have humanitarianism as its objective; the reference was to government banks and the ownership of our banking system by the government.
- The "Group Eight" didn't help at all.
- The government didn't provide proper credit, which forced the people to cease buying securities.

The Federal Reserve was "censured" by the association. It was the government control of the system. According to the association, the Federal Reserve System was a government system. The association speakers called the problem a government problem. The association in concluding stated, "The Federal Reserve system is Government restriction and it is not cooperating with community self-help in credit but is restricting it." The system wasn't ethical? Who was the Group Eight? Was the Group Eight New York's big banks, that is, J. P. Morgan, Kuhn, Loeb & Co., Guarantee Trust Company of New York, etc.? The article didn't mention that the Federal Reserve System held the country's gold courtesy of the U.S. Treasury.

An apparent nemesis is the profit in the system. The association speakers made reference to excessive Federal Reserve profit. Since Alexander Hamilton, the originators, the creators must have realized the enormity of centralized profit and control. The cream in the bottle of milk was always at the top. The Pennsylvania creditors prompted George Washington early on; let's get on with it! The New York Bankers Association was effectively stating that the government and its agent was dumping on the people.

John Kenneth Galbraith wrote,

> The New York Banks stepped into the gaping hole that was left by these summer financiers, and during that first week of crisis they increased their loans by about a billion. This was a bold step. Had the New York banks succumbed to the general fright, a money panic would have added to the other woes. Stocks would have been dumped because their owners could not have borrowed money at any price to carry them. To prevent this was a considerable achievement, for which all who owned stocks should have been thankful. But the banks received no credit. People remembered only that they had bravely undertaken to stem the price collapse and had failed.

And the finger-pointing would begin. "Such was the fate of the bankers. For the next decade they were fair game for congressional committees, courts, the press, and the comedians."

It is remarkable when reading of the expansion of credits and deposits. The total physical money in the country, according to the United

States Treasury, was $8.3 billion, which included gold bullion. Actual circulation in the United States outside the Treasury and the reserve banks, according to Mellon, was $4.6 billion. Who knows the actual stockbroker exchange money involved by October 1929 in New York City? It was probably around a billion dollars or so, but it was the compilation of credits and/or deposits upon deposits that totaled the loans up to $8.5 billion before liquidation began. The banks in New York, in that "first week," didn't prevent the collapse of prices because their infusion of dollars was probably not enough. Galbraith mentioned a "billion" in loans. Maybe the billion in loans was likely credits and deposits; actual money was probably one-tenth or less? If one does the numbers, the brokers' loans (8.5 billion) indicate that surplus money or maybe 25% of the nation's circulating credit was tied up on Wall Street before the crash? Bank deposits and credits in the country were between $40 and 50 billion.

After an entire decade with a population increase of fifteen to twenty million people, the money in circulation was less. How could that be? Assets and resources were growing in the United States, that is, owned indebtedness, the wealth. In 1920, banking resources were more than $53 billion. In 1930, debts well exceeded $200 hundred billion, and the circulation per capita went from $54 in 1920 to $37 during the same period. The total circulation of money declined; it was less. The perpetual debt payment gap was widening, taking off. In 1930, the public debt was around $200 per citizen, which was more than half an annual family-of-four income; today it's near $50,000 per citizen, which is three times an annual family of four income. Does the wealth per citizen today make up the difference? The President Bush annual deficit of $400 billion, which was projected as nil, just 4% of GDP, appears a smoke screen. Bush's deficit spending was pumping money into the economy, multiplying credits ten to twenty times over. The answer to today's senior problem is the reverse mortgage, a liquidation of his or her equity.

Crash recoil started in Washington. On Thursday, October 31, 1929, Senator Nye of North Dakota introduced Senate Resolution 144. Was it possible that $16 billion "of intrinsic value in stocks and bonds" could be lost "in a single day"? Was it because of the "speculative operations on the stock exchanges of the Nation"? Would such operations "threaten . . . the commercial and industrial life of the country"? It was "resolved" that a committee of five senators would suggest the necessary hearings to investigate the Wall Street collapse. "The Supreme Court of the United States has confirmed the power of Congress to elicit information as the basis of necessary legislation."

The accusations began; it was just the beginning! Senator Robinson of Arkansas, the minority leader, had released the following statement to the press: "THE STOCK EXCHANGE DEBACLE." It was

> bankruptcy and ruin . . . a collapse greeted by foreign experts as a great relief to their business institutions . . . Everywhere the surface of the financial sea reveals broken masts and fallen spars. Along the beach are stranded shattered hulks and wasted cargoes. Will the scavengers of the financial sea feast and fatten upon the garbage and the refuse?

It was a Republican decade from start to finish, all presidents and one secretary of the Treasury, and this was Senator Robinson's political orientation. "It may be well to trace the beginning of this calamity." Robinson called Coolidge, Secretary Mellon, and President Hoover the prophets and high priests of American prosperity. It was their "unduly and repeated optimistic statements to the creation of enthusiastic if not frenzied ventures in stocks . . . for that partisan political advantage." It was Robinson's contention that the principals of the Republican Party should have done more to "prevent the collapse."

The next day, November 1, from the other side of the aisle, his namesake, Senator Robinson of Indiana, said, "Herbert Hoover is no more responsible for the situation in the stock market than the man in the moon." Senator Robinson pointed to an article "last night in the Washington Star." The headline: "EUROPEAN TRADERS BLAMED FOR CRASH." The article stated "that European traders caught their American brethren off their guard . . . large selling came from London . . . the time had come to unload."

It was John J. Raskob's fault, the leader of the Democratic Party. The minority leader took a jab at President Hoover, so the Republican senator from Indiana took a jab at Mr. Raskob. John Raskob had been a $7.5-a-week stenographer, became a millionaire playing the stock market, among other things, an American success story; this related by Mr. Robinson. The Republican senator referred to a newspaper article of the year before, the "New York Times of May 7, 1929." The headline read, "RASKOB WILL HELP WORKERS TO INVEST." And in the article:

> John J. Raskob, who fathered the installment plan, for the sale of automobiles before he left the chairmanship of the Finance committee of the General Motors Corporation to manage Alfred E. Smith's presidential campaign; revealed here yesterday, that he was preparing to launch the installment plan on a large scale in the field of stock investment.

The article stated Raskob would start an investment company; his plan would allow the small investor, the working man, to invest in Wall Street via the installment plan. "He denied that Calvin Coolidge . . . and . . . Alfred E. Smith" were involved in any of his plans. John Raskob stated in the article that he had made a lot of money, and he wanted "other people make some." Republican Senator Robinson of Indiana referred to what people were saying about the Democratic leader; they were calling "'Mr. Raskob, the financial genius.'" "So I say there is a question of psychology."

This exchange in the Senate came about because the Senators Robinson, each referred to the radio address given the night before by the assistant secretary of Commerce, Julius Klein. It was an address of positive note, upholding administration policy and reiterating President Hoover's words of October 26, "The fundamental business of the country—that is, production and distribution of commodities—is on a sound and prosperous basis." In his address, Klein referred to the stock market,

> We have been under the influence as regards stock prices, of a boom psychology. Many persons have bought stocks with little knowledge of their present or probable future dividend paying capacity. Many, moreover, have borrowed money in order to make these stock purchases. A reaction was bound to occur.

Klein went on to emphasize the "definite upward trend" in wages in all sectors across the country, and it was not due to any "boom psychology nor to temporary or fleeting causes."

The Democratic minority leader, Senator Robinson, called Klein's statement ironic. Robinson mentioned periods of

> alarming depression . . . There has been substantial diminution in the purchasing power of consumers, due not alone to the losses and bankruptcies which have occurred through stock transactions but due in part to the natural and logical reactions which always follow periods marked by unusual speculation; reactions which bring contractions and slowing-down processes in various spheres.

It appears the minority leader was referring to the periods of tight money and subsequent recessions. John Kenneth Galbraith recalled the time, "Money, by the ordinary tests, was tight in the late twenties."

Did Julius Klein's boom psychology fit the leader of the Democratic Party? Republican Senator Robinson's inference caught some flak from Senator Harrison of Mississippi. "What has Raskob to do with this controversy?" Mr. Harrison emphasized that nobody in the Congress knew the cause of the calamity, only the "effect." Mr. Harrison mentioned that newspaper articles supported the needed efforts "to restore actual values in the economic life of the nation." Mr. Harrison was all for that.

Senator Barkley of Kentucky referred to Republican Robinson's remarks as fulminations. Barkley didn't want "to waste any time" with the previous exchange, "brilliant though it is, that the stock crash during the last week or 10 days is attributable to John J. Raskob and King George." Again, nobody in the Congress had an inkling of why the crash. Barkley, a Democrat, gave credit to President Hoover; Hoover's words of October 26 stating "sound business conditions" were made to calm "hysteria and panic." Barkley presented into the record an editorial from the "Washington Post, Saturday, October 26, 1929." Although "not unfriendly to the Administration," the *Post* editorial was favorable.

President Hoover has taken timely and wholesome action
by informing the people that the fundamental business
conditions of the country are sound . . . The President
finds that high interest rates induced by stock speculation
have to some extent affected the construction and building
industries.

The president was critical of any "senatorial investigation." Senator
Barkley was not as kind to former President Coolidge and Secretary
Mellon. Since 1924, the Wall Street thing had been referred to as the
Coolidge bull market. On November 1, 1929, the "New York World
editorial called it 'That Coolidge-Mellon Market.'" The editorial
affirmed the minority leader's charge. Between 1927 and 1928,
Coolidge and Mellon always came to the rescue when the market
sagged; their statements and interviews to the contrary and "the bull
movement was soon under full headway again." It was their "careful
fostering of conditions which made the break inevitable." Thank
goodness the Republicans were in power; otherwise, the Democrats
would have been crucified; this from Senator Barkley of Kentucky.

President Hoover had been pressing the Senate to pass the contested
Smoot-Hawley Tariff bill. Hoover was blaming the Democrats and the
"insurgents" for the bill's delay. Who were the insurgents? President
Hoover had pushed for the passage of the bill the day after the
crash. The Senate had been dragging its feet for six months. The
new tariff was a Republican bill from start to finish. The bill was
"sponsored by Republican Senator Reed Smoot of Utah and Republican
Representative Willis C. Hawley of Oregon." It was a protective tariff
to protect the farmer "from foreign competition." The Baltimore Sun
reported in a November 1, 1929, editorial, "And it is known, it has
been demonstrated over and over again, that the Smoot-Hawley bill
gives additional tariff subsidies to concerns that have been breaking
all records in profits." The new tariff became law on June 17, 1930.
But the tariff did nothing but thwart trade in both directions; it was
eventually overturned in 1934. Senator Tydings, Democrat from
Maryland, presented the Sun's editorial for the record.

In November 1931, Secretary Mellon presented his last annual report.
The government was spending more with less revenue. Revenue was

down because of the "decline in business activity." Mellon reported a deficit of $903 million. The public debt increased for the first time in ten years; the debt was $16.9 billion. The Treasury had spent more money in "agricultural aid and relief for additional benefits to war veterans, and for accelerated governmental construction activities." Mellon, by way of the Treasurer, showed a listing and historical description of the currencies; all the forms of money were still there, including the greenbacks. The total "stock" of money in the United States had increased in 1931; the total was $9.1 billion. The Federal Reserve Note was eighteen years old, and it remained non-legal tender currency; it was bank currency and a government obligation. In 1933, the total stock of money in the country had increased to $10.1 billion, and it was "the worst year of the depression."

The problem wasn't the stock of money; it was the credit system. Senator Trammell presented the following on December 15, 1931: "Credit is far more powerful than money," this from Judge John W. Dodge in an editorial of the Deland Florida News, December 15, 1931, [This article was placed in the Senate record of the 71st Congress, Session 3; it can be found in the Congressional Record, in the Micor-Film Reading Room, in the Jefferson Building, Library of Congress, Volume 190, page 540. The editorial was called "Money-Credit-A Blessing-A Curse"]. Money wasn't readily available. From the newspapers and the Congress, the record indicated available money was being "hoarded." The credit system was lacking; the country's "credit circulation," the vaunted elastic currency excluded those outside the system. The Federal Reserve controlled the non-issuance of credit.

"Confidence" was the title of an article in the *Wall Street Journal*, Friday morning, September 18, 1931, "CASH UP, BANK CREDIT OFF." The article quoted a "memorandum" on economics; the economics part is not included here. The bottom line was the article's referral to that "intangible element that we call confidence." The article mentioned the "'bonus' legislation." This legislation pumped "$800,000,000" into the money supply since the first of the year. "Yet at the same time, member-bank 'credit' has shrunk some $700,000,000!" The article covered investing, the buying of securities or obligations. Apparently, there was no confidence? The Treasury made money available for lending but the lenders were not lending. And people who had surplus funds preferred to save it or invest it. Eight hundred million dollars would amount to eight billion in credits and deposits; it didn't happen. The buying of commodities, consumer goods moves the economy, but the money was not made available to the people. What did happen was a 0.7 billion dollar deficit handed to the taxpayer during a time of no jobs. The article didn't name names, but the banking system was the lender. The article mentioned hoarding. Was banking in-house book-keeping going on? Previously, the New York Bankers Association had blamed the Government; the Government's banking system was profit oriented; it was a government banking system. America, 70 odd years later, in the year 2009, and the same business is going on? Hoarding? No confidence? Actually, by the 1930s, pure capitalism had done the job; about 70% to 75% of the people were managing. The article ended saying, "And so long as this condition lasts, the mere addition of cash to the money supply will not help much. It is the 'metaphysical' element rather than the 'physical' that needs to be changed." That explains it? This was touched on before. The central banking thing was secretive; and its inner soul, apparently, wasn't going to change.

In December 1931, the Seventy-second Congress, in the midst of impending depression, was wrangling over Hoover's moratorium. Why did the president want to stop foreign debt payments to the U.S. Treasury for one year? Hoover also asked to renew the War Debt Commission, for what reason, to eventually cancel all the debts? The U.S. Treasury loans to Allied foreign countries during the war came by way of the Liberty Loans courtesy of the American taxpayer. These war loans and subsequent debts owed the United States government were separate; they were not connected to Germany's war reparations. There was one small exception, the United States Army of occupation. The Versailles Treaty dictated reparation payments by Germany; the United States had separated itself from that treaty. Indebtedness included the foreign private debts; J. P. Morgan and Company had, "for the past several years, been engaged in the flotation of foreign securities in the United States." These are some of the loans that placed Federal Reserve Notes in Europe?

There was a problem; money was flowing out of Germany, payments to private interests, this after the start of the moratorium. According to Senator Shipstead, the moratorium was supposed to save Germany from collapse; it had the opposite effect. That's when the money really started leaving, to and by private interests, almost a billion dollars in six months. This was the problem? The private banks were after the money; governments were after the money. Was it going to be private debts paid or public debts paid? Senator Reed mentioned the foreign debtor nations; could they pay both public and private debts after the war? The bankers made their loans "with eyes wide open." And "now to ask that the private claims of some American citizens should be given priority over the inter-government claims, which are the claims of all American citizens, seems to me to be a piece of outrageous effrontery."

"The enthusiasm of Europe over the moratorium was based upon the idea that this was the opening wedge for the cancellation of the debts to the United States." Senator Johnson mentioned Ramsay MacDonald, prime minister of England. "The moratorium, thank God, ended all foreign debts, and never again will our people, those of the English nation, or those of any other country in Europe, be troubled with the payment of the debts that have been asserted to be due from those countries into the United States of America." The Senate wasn't buying it. It would be an additional burden to the American taxpayer. If the foreign public debt was added to the national public debt, the real total public debt would be almost $30 billion, not $17 billion. The United States was the creditor nation; all the countries, including Great Britain, owed the United States. But Great Britain was a creditor and a debtor; all the Allied countries owed Great Britain, and Britain owed the United States. Senator Reed recalled, "I have been told by British people, who said there never could be any real friendship between us and them so long as we were extorting payment on the British debt." Reed reminded that "the British treasury is not suffering . . . not one penny of British taxation comes to the United States." Great Britain collects from her debtors; she then may pay the United States, but when and for how long?

Things would not go well for England. Maybe this foreign debt payment business was fiction. International indebtedness could be complex and nasty, especially with President Hoover's moratorium. Foreigners would not pay the debt to the United States, but the United

States would pay the foreigners in gold. Foreign countries owed the United States $15 billion in public and private debts, and this was the deal. These events were covered in a *Saturday Evening Post* article in December of 1931. Senator Copeland presented the article in the Senate; it was for the record. The article emphasized the raiding of gold by France and the European countries, England suspending gold again; it was the beginning of England's demise, and America was learning to be a creditor nation. The article was not read, debated, or commented on; it was entered for the record.

From the *Saturday Evening Post*, all the countries owed all the countries; and all the countries, in addition to the debts owed, had deposits and investment credits in each other's country. Most of the European countries were desperate for gold; the exception was France. The United States had the most gold, about 5 billion at the time. And France had half that much; but France, according to the article, was richer in gold because of comparative population. France had surpassed England in gold. The total gold in the world was estimated at $11 billion. The power, apparently, was always with the gold. But all this business appears ludicrous, 5 billion in gold, 2.5 billion in gold, when all the indebtedness of the countries were in the many hundreds of billions of dollars, payable in gold, all perpetrated by the velocity of paper currency. Ludicrous but real!

The Hoover moratorium created the gold raid. England suspended the payment of gold on September 20, 1931. Britain's debtor countries began raiding her gold, and it was France who led the charge. Britain borrowed "gold credit" from New York banks; it wasn't enough to stem the tide. The *Post* stated Great Britain's credit decline was like a humiliation. The crux was the promise to pay. It was 1931, and England was back on gold; the United States was also paying in gold. When the creditor agrees to pay in gold, it pays in gold "or confess itself insolvent." The *Post* article presented England and the United States as being in a predicament; "their credits were frozen in Germany," and the Europeans paid only in paper. According to the *Post*, the Europeans had the "keys" to the payers of gold, England and the United States.

France had large credits on deposits in England and demanded payment in gold. Holland followed suit; "the Dutch, too, began calling on England to pay them in gold." All the European countries followed. England suspended, and after the debacle, France "looked westward" to the United States. France owed the United States $3.8 billion. She also had $600 million in credits in the United States; for that, France would ask for payment in gold. The French, the Europeans were "protected by our moratorium."

France's credits in the United States banks were short-term credits; she demanded the interest rate in New York be raised, or she would remove her credits and ask for the payment in gold. Part of the credits was the money Germany borrowed from American investors to pay German reparations to France. "The Germans transferred it to France on the books of American banks, and the French left it here at interest." The credits had been accumulating interest on a deposit payable in gold. The article stated, "If she insists, we shall have to give her the gold." France could do this because of the moratorium. The one-year moratorium was supposed to save Germany from financial collapse.

France put the pressure on America; would the United States have to suspend as did England? "Wall Street stands firm." The New York banks said, "If France wants her credit balances, let her take them. If she demands them in gold, the gold will be ready."

There wasn't going to be any change in the interest rate. And in this case, according to the article, it was the New York banks dictating. France was the first to pull money out of Germany, making a dire situation worse, "the financial breakdown in Germany." France wanted more than gold. She didn't want to pay the United States any of the 3.8 billion; she wanted more reparations from Germany, which included reviving the Young Plan, etc. The gold situation somewhat stabilized. Premier Laval of France visited President Hoover. The gold flow was abated although 42 million in gold went to France when Laval exited the United States. The *New York Times*, of October 26, described the Hoover-Laval conference and the coincident exit of gold from New York to France as strange, the demands of a debtor nation upon a creditor nation. There were "no immediate concrete benefits from the Franco-American exchanges." The Europeans extracted $1.5 billion in gold (730 million in six weeks) from the United States during the summer of 1931. If France had demanded 600 million more in gold, would the United States have suspended, gone off the gold standard? The *Wall Street Journal* on January 1, 1932, "weekly reports of the Federal Reserve Bank show that the total turnover in the yellow metal amounted to $ 1,751,520,100."

The *Post* called the whole business a "One Way Grace . . . We had relieved our debtors. We had eased them of their obligations to us without limiting in any way our obligations to them." The United States, or rather Wall Street, held firm. "If we refused the gold in any case, that instant we were off the gold standard." At the same time, foreigners owed the United States a ton while selling everything in America to get America's gold. There was gold to spare, but the United States was "not prepared for a raid." France didn't need the gold; France would "hoard it." The *Post* described the gold's hiding place, a "chamber," a vault two hundred feet deep underneath a man-made forty-foot-deep lake as part of a "dammed subterranean river that flows beneath Paris." Man's endeavor to secure gold, the hole card, was unequaled. The *Post* article continued that the French raid on America's gold started the "rumors" flying in Europe. There was

> imminent financial collapse in the United States . . . French papers kept saying with one sound that the franc was the sound gold money of the world . . . foreign liquidation in New York . . . The United States had entered the path to inflation . . . This was the beginning of the end of the gold dollar . . . The franc was the good gold money of the world . . . The dollar declines In Europe . . . The Polish people . . . sold 1,000,000 American dollars to the Bank of Warsaw at 99 cents.

Of course, the British newspapers picked up the beat. "Bring Your Money Back To Britain . . . Sell Dollar And Franc Securities . . . Don't be trapped. When the break on Wall Street comes, the reaction may be far reaching." Another British headline read, "Who Will Go Off The Gold Standard Next." A reminder to the flag-wavers as to our Allies, there was apparent glee in England and Europe; the United States, or rather the American banking system, may fold financially. Maybe there was glee among the central banks. Stabilization was in progress; gold was moving back to Europe, but England was in trouble. It was her declining credit; she was in suspension. And in the United States, there was imminent depression.

The *Post* continued, "A familiar Figure Missing." No longer would the British pound be "worth $4.86 in gold anywhere in the world." England, in 1931, devalued the pound sterling by 40%. Before, the value of dollars and francs and all the other currencies were expressed in the pound sterling; the condition was now reversed. Would the pound and other currencies be expressed now in dollars or French francs? Would the United States be the place of exchange, or making the banking profits with the exchanges, or would it be the French?

Before, in the nineteenth century, the United States was always sucking up to Britain and France because of the lack of gold. But war, death, destruction, and indebtedness changes things. During this latest crisis, Britain borrowed "gold credits" from New York banks; it wasn't enough to stem the tide. England was forced to suspend specie. It was the same familiar game, but the shoe was now on the other foot. If there were any winners in all this business, it would probably be the central banks and the Bank for International Settlements; the BIS shows no political boundaries. The *Post* continued about the gold,

> Once, the quantity of it was important merely as money. That is no longer true. The actual quantity existing is very small. Yet if the mechanism of credit and exchange were perfect and all people could be trusted by themselves and by one another to keep the convention, 1 ton of it—1 ounce of it, in fact—would serve the purpose.

It was the "Convention of Gold."

What did the "Convention of Gold" mean? The dictionary would simply say it would be the "agreement" of it. That's all very nice, and in the real world, it didn't play out; we are all corrupted by it. In 1931, France and Europe suddenly had leverage. It was the moratorium; the foreign countries took the advantage. They went after the gold. It was the promise to pay. England went under; the contradiction held, but the United States banks paid the gold. The *Post* article, as to the United States, intimated a bluff by France. But since the inception of the Bank of England, with gold and the bill of exchange, suspensions abounded. With the manipulation of gold, the money interests could always maintain "a veto on the action of money." Maybe the raid was planned as part of the financial stabilization process among the central banks. The *Post* article concluded with an analysis of an apparent apprenticeship of the United States as a creditor nation. The United States became too wealthy too fast, and with that wealth the "delusion that American credit was inexhaustible," that is, more debt and the creation of more credit.

> We had come new to the business of world creditorship, with no experience in it, no philosophy of it that was our own. Europe read us endless lectures on the obligations of a world creditor, always with emphasis upon its obligation to keep its credit at the call of debtor nations. For otherwise how should the debtors keep going or ever be able to repay what they had already borrowed? We did not forget the law that the first responsibility of a creditor Nation is to itself; and that if it fails in this it fails the world. We had never learned it. If now we comprehend it, the frightful cost of educating American credit abroad has not been wholly wasted.

Secretary of the Treasury Ogden Mills mentioned the 1931 movements of gold in his 1932 annual report but not to the degree covered by the *Saturday Evening Post* article.

CHAPTER THIRTEEN
Depression

The unparalleled world-wide economic depression has continued through the year . . . . The banking and financial system is presumed to serve in furnishing the essential lubricant to the wheels of industry, agriculture, and commerce, that is, credit. Its diversion from proper use, its improper use, or its insufficiency instantly brings hardship and dislocation in economic life.

The time was December 6, 1932; President Herbert Hoover delivered his final message to the Seventy-second Congress, second session. The president asked for "the complete reorganization at once of our banking system. The shocks to our economic life have undoubtedly been multiplied by the weakness of this system, and until they are remedied, recovery will be greatly hampered." The president mentioned the failure of "4,665 Banks" in the past year. "We have witnessed hoarding of currency to an enormous sum, rising during the height of the crisis to over $1,600,000,000." Hoover mentioned the shocks in Great Britain although "worse than our own, there has not been a single bank failure during the depression." It was the same in Canada. "In all the history of Canadian Banking, the total volume of losses to depositors of failed Banks was $13,500,000." American depositors lost $2.5 billion in "the last two years," 1930-1932; this from the comptroller of the currency. Many of the failed small banks were the so-called one-crop banks.

What was unique about the American system whereby approximately 25% of the American banking system was wiped out under, supposedly, less severe conditions? What were the conditions in Great Britain? What were the conditions here, there, everywhere, nationally and internationally? It was bank runs, liquidation, hoarding, and no extension of credit in the United States. The twelve Federal Reserve banks and their branches controlled the reserves and the gold; the twelve reserve banks were OK, according to the record, courtesy of the U.S. Treasury and the member banks. This appeared to be the setup in 1932; approximately 25% of the population would begin to take the hits.

The original purpose of the Federal Reserve System was to deter member bank liquidation. But the member banks, the state banks, the smaller banks were the failing banks. The Federal Reserve failed America; its credit system appeared a catalyst to the gaming house, to Wall Street; profits were swept away, locked up. The crash was more than two years old. The Federal Reserve banks were not accepting "paper for rediscount"; liquidation continued. Maybe it was capitalism's finest hour; the controlling few didn't "take any prisoners." It was the "fear" period; there was no "confidence" in the system. President Hoover had his view; it was the credit system, "its diversion from proper use, its improper use." Government and the Treasury had to be right there and part of it; the Federal Reserve System was its profit-making agent.

President Hoover was for cutting back, balancing the budget; he would recommend to the new Congress a government appropriations reduction of "$830,000,000." Hoover recommended an extension of the 8.5% reduction in government salaries "under the furlough system"; the furlough system was already in place. At the time, government salaries averaged $1,400 a year. He recommended consolidation of government agencies, reduction in military armaments, reduction in veterans benefits, equitable taxation of the industries, etc. The economy was way down; resultant government revenue was down, almost 50%. While President Hoover was emphasizing budgetary restraint, his Reconstruction Finance Corporation was borrowing $2.5 billion trying to revive the country's paralyzed credit system. Unfortunately, and as always, the workers and the non-workers wouldn't own the securities that financed the finance corporation. An outgoing president was for a reduction in government spending; this was in December 1932. In March 1933, an incoming president would also ask for government in-house cutbacks but also for eventual spending going in the other direction. When President Roosevelt did take over, his immediate executive order began with shutting down the banks.

Meanwhile, the Hoover administration and the Seventy-second Congress was busy with emergency banking, the Glass-Steagall Act, the Unemployment Relief Act, the Agricultural Adjustment Act, the Home Owners Relief Act, the amendments to the Federal Reserve Act, impending changes to the Smoot-Hawley Tariff, the Home Loan Bank bill, an amended Federal Land Bank Act, and a new revenue act of the Reconstruction Finance Corporation. Herbert Hoover said that we need "to furnish during the period of the depression credits otherwise unobtainable under existing circumstances in order to give confidence to agriculture, industry, and labor against further paralyzing influences." President Hoover said the "discount facilities" of the Federal Reserve were "inadequate"; he said the system "limits the liquidity of the banks and tends to increase the forces of deflation, cripples the smaller businesses, stifles new enterprise, and thus limits employment." Amen!

And so it went. It was a time of deflation, "stifled" enterprise, and resultant unemployment. There would be more money stock in the country in 1932 than in 1929; why didn't things turn around? The banks were hoarding money. There was the movements of gold, heavy investments in Germany. From Mellon's record, Federal Reserve Notes traveled to Europe, apparent international stabilization of foreign central banks and their monies and the new world bank, the Bank for International Settlements. The result was apparent insufficient credits in the United States. How to free up the money? Action was taken; it was government action. Locked up money wasn't freed; new money was created and resultant public debt. Remarkable work projects took place during the Depression. Today, they are called modern marvels, the Golden Gate Bridge, the Hoover Dam, the Grand Coulee Dam, the Tennessee Valley Authority, all public works projects, all built in the 1930s. Those projects are, to this day, part of the country's greatest achievements in its effort to put people back to work. It has been observed and documented; these massive energy-producing giants served the United States well in another war that was coming, World War II.

Most of the failing banks were the smaller banks in the small communities. The need for an expansion of branch banking was the emphasis in the Congress in May 1932. "Moreover the Comptroller of the currency points out that there are hundreds, if not thousands, of communities in the United States where banks have become so weakened by this frightful depression as to make it improbable that they can much longer stand alone," this from Senator Glass. "If we had branch banking authorization, the strong banks that have survived this catastrophe could open up their branches in those communities and afford them not sparse but ample credit facilities." Senator Glass said that a strong "Parent Bank" would secure the branch banks. The proponents of the Federal Reserve System, Senator Glass included, emphasized this point when pushing for the central bank in 1913. The central bank was the cure-all; the Federal Reserve central bank would control the reserves, not allow the failing of the facilities of national banks and member banks.

"The last three fiscal years have witnessed a world-wide depression of unprecedented severity and duration." These were the words of Ogden Mills, the new secretary of the Treasury. It was a repeat of the past; it was no-redundancy time again. This time it would be worse; the Depression was just starting. Another round of cards was over. As before, the profits were taken. The gambling house had cleaned the tables; players were expended. There would be another big game; a new round of play would begin, but to attract the players, it was back to the other houses, the Congress.

Industry, commerce, trade, and employment continued the downward trend. Tax receipts, accordingly, were less. This was the start of a borrowing, spending thing. The Treasury borrowed to finance the emergency measures; the yearly deficit, as reported by Secretary Mills, had grown to $2.9 billion. Five hundred million dollars was subscribed by the federal government to start the Reconstruction Finance Corporation. The government would spend $2.5 billion financing railroads, banks, insurance companies, building and loan associations, agriculture, public works, highways, naval vessels, hospitals, etc. It was government relief and subsequent debt in the wake of private economic failure. After a decade long Republican government climaxed by the crash, the people in November 1932 voted a change; Franklin

Roosevelt was elected president. A Democratic administration would face the coming depression. The population was 120 million.

In January 1932, the Democrats in the House wanted changes to Smoot-Hawley. According to Mr. McFadden, foreign dumping of cheap foreign products was killing the American economy; it was the reason for decreased domestic production and the increasing unemployment. The cheap foreign products made up the "69%" of the products on the Tariff "free list." In the consideration of House Bill H.R. 6662, Chairman McFadden introduced for the record the "Bankers Manifesto." The manifesto was a proposal reported in "Bulletin No.3 of the Free Trade League of New York City in November, 1926." The manifesto proposed "the reconstruction of Europe through the removal of the barriers of trade." The leading bankers of Europe, Great Britain, and the United States signed the manifesto. World War I changed the political economic landscape; trade barriers in all directions were the order of the day, and the bankers blamed the politicians. "There can be no recovery in Europe till politicians in all territories, old and new, realize that trade is not war but a process of exchange, that in time of peace, our neighbors are our customers . . . If we check their dealings, their power to pay diminishes and their power to purchase our goods is reduced."

American "banks, Insurance companies, and investors" invested heavily in Germany; loans were at high interest rates. These assets were at a standstill. International bankers had saturated American financial institutions with securities; these were the private debts. Greater debts were owed the United States government; and President Hoover's moratorium, apparently, opened "Pandora's Box." The manifesto was a move by the bankers to salvage their investments. This was McFadden's claim; he blamed the substantial concentration of money, credits, and investment outside the United States for the "unemployment" at home. It was the same array of people, J. P. Morgan et al, Gates McGarrah, the banking consortium. McFadden mentioned that McGarrah had become the head of the Bank for International Settlements. McGarrah had been the chairman of the Federal Reserve Bank of New York.

McFadden's "correspondent" provided the nasty details; the problem was "payroll robbery." The diversion of the American payroll "to foreign trade is an inhuman payroll pirate breaking the hold which human beings here have on life." The American financiers, apparently, were the "payroll pirates." The correspondent's communiqué reported an opinion by Calvin Coolidge from

> Calvin Coolidge Says . . . paragraphs in the Herald Tribune last year . . . "Yes; we Americans are given by the tariff laws the blessed privilege of shooting it out with the pay-roll pirates to see which will have our own pay roll." No; there is nothing mysterious about our business cycles . . . the merry-go-round of the pay-roll pirates.

The correspondent referred to "international trade gangsters like the Morgans et al . . . and the solid South." Raise the tariff; this was the issue, especially products on the free list. This would save American production and employment. With this action, the correspondent assured there would be a "'fight to the death'" between the payroll pirating "'cartels'" and the "'American producers.'" This was McFadden's presentation; there was a push by the Democrats to change the tariff but in conference with the Europeans to remove "unfair trade practices."

Republican congressmen Sparks and Horr responded. The Democrats wanted to "enlist the wisdom of Europe in the solution of our domestic problems." The United States will solve its "problems confronting it without the aid and assistance of those who are antagonistic to its laws and regulations for the protection of its people." Washington State Congressman Horr said that bill H.R. 6662 was a political maneuver, a "tariff gesture" by the "Democratic majority." Any tariff changes at this time involved the "Tariff Commission, hearings, long investigations"; any result would result in a Herbert Hoover veto. One thing the Congress didn't need were more conferences, especially with the Europeans. "Have we not had enough of international conferences? Have we forgotten the failures of former International conferences? Do the Gentlemen have any remembrance of the recent disarmament conferences when we agreed to scrap good naval armament in exchange for blueprint destructions?" Horr quoted Will Rogers: "The good Democrat from Oklahoma . . . We are the only Nation that never lost a war and never won a conference." Both sides of the aisle wanted changes; it was when and how and what would be the priorities. Mr. Horr said his state of Washington never received any protection; its timber, pulp, and shingle industries were rendered nonexistent, dead, finished. Foreign currency devaluation and importation (Sweden) and Canadian imports did the damage. Horr indicted "General Motors, the rubber industry, and Henry Ford going into foreign countries to establish their factories and in some instances returning their product to the United States duty free." Horr said there were "Henry Fords in our State"; they had "invested their American-acquired dollars in Canadian timber."

Smoot-Hawley, apparently, was a monster tariff. The Democrats had called it infamous, but according to the Republicans, the Democrats did nothing to amend it before enactment. Republican protectionism created it. "Special privilege is responsible for this situation." Congressman Cochran of Missouri continued, "The great Corporations that have dominated the Republican Party's tariff policy for generations have gone too far in their demands." The result of this was the relocation of "American manufacturers" in foreign countries. Cochran said that "this present tariff law has destroyed our foreign trade." The politicians blamed the money interests; the money interests blamed the politicians.

Chairman Steagall of the House Banking and Currency Committee reported, "Since 1929 our foreign trade has fallen off $5,092,000,000, a decline of 50 per cent in the period of two years." The domestic industrial decline and world trade prompted the passage of H.R. 7360 on January 15; the Reconstruction Finance Corporation became law on January 22, 1932. The Treasury subscribed 500 million dollars to start the Corporation. The Treasury could augment that capital three times or have two billion in capital with the sale of bonds, debentures [obligations], etc. This Corporation would lend money to all the country's ailing industries mentioned previously, including the failing banks. The new Corporation directors, by the Act, included the Secretary of the Treasury and the Governor of the Federal Reserve Board.

"All redemptions, purchases, and sales by the Secretary of the Treasury of the obligations of the Corporation shall be treated as public-debt transactions of the United States, such obligations shall not be eligible for discount or purchase by any Federal Reserve Bank;" this from Chairman Steagall.

This new extension of credit was an extension of the public debt; it was corporate welfare. The public pays the increased public debt to get the opportunity to aid private industry to get back to work. The rediscount credit circulation system had broken down; President Hoover called it a diversion from proper use. The new finance corporation would furnish an assist, a jump start.

In the summer of 1929, the New York Bankers Association had "censured" the Federal Reserve for restrictive credit policy, this before the crash. The association called the reserve system a government system. On its face, the secretary of the Treasury, the Federal Reserve Board, the comptroller are integral to credit policy. Dr. Commons said the Federal Reserve maneuvered, dictated, and controlled market conditions. Chairman McFadden was critical of Secretary Mellon's dealings with European central bankers; McFadden cited the lessened interest rates to suit Norman and Schacht in 1926. People within this credit system, "censured" by the New York Bankers Association, would be directing the new finance corporation. Congressman Lambreth of North Carolina was disheartened when he realized Wall Street types would represent the finance corporation in his district; these people, "they make a fetish of liquidity." Lambreth hoped the finance corporation would help the small businessman, the farmer as well as the banks, the railroads, the insurance companies, etc.

Congressman La Guardia of New York hated the finance corporation bill. La Guardia wanted aid for the depositors before aid to the banks, railroads, and insurance companies. La Guardia said the House was "forever estopped from criticizing me again for urging unemployment insurance by calling it a dole. This is a millionaire's dole and you can not get away from it. It is a subsidy for broken bankers—a subvention for bankrupt railroads—a reward for speculative and unscrupulous bond pluggers." La Guardia said the proponents of the new finance bill were blaming the people; the depositors withdrew their money, causing the banks to close. The comptroller of the Treasury reported that only 3% of deposits had been withdrawn from closed banks. La Guardia cited "the damnable lies of some of our big bankers." Congressman Boylan asked La Guardia, "Would the Gentleman hang the bankers?" La Guardia responded, "What would you do? Give them a medal? [Laughter]. Yes; I would hang a banker who stole from the people."

Chairman Steagall reported a farm value loss of "$6,000,000,000 since 1929." The same day, January 11, 1932, Senator Blaine of Wisconsin, presented a "Joint Resolution of the Legislature of the State of Wisconsin." The Resolution was "referred to the Committee on Banking and Currency." The resolution claimed abuses by the Federal Land Bank system. The system was originally started and owned by the government in 1922. The federal government started the farm system to assist agriculture. By 1929, the farm loan associations owned 98% of the Federal Land Bank stock; this from Secretary Mellon's 1929 annual report. The farmers had borrowed from the Federal Land Banks when land values and prices were high. The Depression nullified all values, the farms, their products, and their prices. Farmers were broke; they couldn't pay the previously high valued mortgage (the debt remains, the value drops, and the vultures move in). The Federal Land Banks were foreclosing and selling the farms at depression value level to the new buyers. The farmers wanted the opportunity to refinance at the lowered value of their farms. It would appear the farm loan associations were dumping on the farmers. The Wisconsin State resolution was asking both houses of Congress "to eliminate all abuses now existing in the Federal Land Bank system and to extend to farmers sufficient time to meet their obligations." On January 23, 1932, the Federal Land Bank Act was amended. The secretary of the Treasury "was authorized to take out shares" in the system in the amount of $125,000,000. Public money was being put back into the system to help the farmer help himself, a scenario supposedly similar to the Reconstruction Finance Corporation. It created more public debt; Abraham Lincoln may have approved as long as "we owed the debt to ourselves," very true as long as everyone may collect. But the farmer, the working man wouldn't own the securities perpetrating the debt before issue. Madison said it goes to those "at and within reach of the seat of Government." It's the system; the Federal Reserve agents acquire the currency and collect interest before issue. It was the Hamilton continuation; the Pennsylvania creditors couldn't wait. Jefferson and Jackson disagreed in principle. In principle, if there was more money to go around, there would be more money to go around.

An emergency banking bill H.R. 9203 became law on February 27, 1932. This law was another amendment to the Federal Reserve System. The law was to be effective for approximately one year until March 3, 1933. This act would make credit available to member banks, where money or credits was not obtainable, at the twelve reserve banks. The bill was entitled "To improve the facilities of the Federal Reserve System . . . to provide means for meeting the needs of member banks in exceptional circumstances, and for other purposes." The twelve reserve banks were not rediscounting member bank commercial paper; the member banks had assets, but assets the reserve wouldn't accept. Banks were also hoarding money. Congressman La Guardia of New York said the emergency bill and the finance corporation bill was inflationary. The working man would pay because wages were being reduced while commodity prices increased; the two bills were supposed to help the wage earner as well as the credit of the corporations.

The Federal Reserve Act of 1913 authorized the central bank, by way of the comptroller, to create money, the Federal Reserve Note,

- against the bankers bill, the acceptance, the ninety-day short-term contract and
- through the "purchase" of the government obligation, the government security.

The new emergency bill authorized the central bank, by way of the comptroller, to create more money, the Federal Reserve Note, a new "advanced currency"

The new advanced currency would be created against the government obligation, the government security as "collateral." But wasn't the Federal Reserve doing the obligation thing since the beginning but in a different fashion? All this business becomes confusing!

Federal Reserve Notes were generated both ways with acceptances and government securities, the obligations. The acquisition of government securities, or bonds, in theory, goes all the way back to the

Pennsylvania creditors, the ownership of the principal of government debt and the transfer of that debt between the principals, namely, the reserve banks, the shareholders, the member banks. James Madison would call these principals the people "at and within reach of the seat of Government"; there was profit to be made before issue in this process as in the additional "purchase" of 400 million in obligations in the late '20s. The probable profit after was the 400 million in Federal Reserve Notes, which translated into billions in credits released for speculation and run-up on Wall Street before the crash. Senator Glass said that "10 of the larger New York Banks alone in 1929, over a period of six months, borrowed a billion dollars in credits from the New York Federal Reserve Bank, with United States bonds as collateral security, chiefly for stock speculative purposes." Senator Glass said they had "no right to borrow a dollar for that purpose."

Congressman McFadden would say the same thing. Mr. McFadden said this emergency bill was changing the rules. McFadden said the bill would allow the creation of currency not by the elastic system, but currency or Federal Reserve Notes "secured by Government bonds" at the discretion of the Federal Reserve Board. Basically, McFadden intimated that this was like the old system, the 1863 bank act. "This is not releasing money and credit in response to the demand of trade and commerce. This money and credit is going to be placed at the beck and call of speculators, if they see fit to use it, just as it was used in 1927 and 1928." Mr. McFadden appeared correct; the 400 million, mentioned in the preceding paragraph, is a part of the record. And those $400 million in obligations translated into billions in credits. The 400 million were in addition to the several billion dollars in government obligations "purchased" by the Federal Reserve in the '20s. McFadden said the emergency bill was also releasing 750 million in gold for shipment out of the country. And gold, supposedly, was the necessary reserve for Federal Reserve Note circulation. As for the rules, it was, as Adam Smith would imply, "if there were no market at home, send it abroad."

Eugene Meyer, governor of the Federal Reserve Board, objected to the collateral thing. Meyer said the collateral issue "would be confusing and would create uncertainty as to its exact relation to the other currency obligations of the United States." Why this strategy?

Was it because the securities settled debts within the reserve system and it may upset their already usage of the purchase and/or sale of obligations for contraction and expansion of the currency?

The new emergency bill had limits; it would broaden the scheme temporarily. For a one-year period, there would be money creation by obligations, acceptances, and collateral. The obligation, since the beginning, was a creation of public debt indirectly; the collateral for currency would be the creation of more public debt directly. The credit circulation/debt-funding scheme was becoming more significant. The new "advanced currency" was going to cost more; the Federal Reserve was allowed to charge 1% above the discount rate. So what was the difference between the obligation thing and the collateral thing? The collateral thing was costly; the people were going to pay more for their currency. In the scheme of things, it was another scheme; it was just another way to create money, more currency!

When one reads the Federal Reserve Act, the word is "purchase"; the phrase used is the "purchase of Government Securities." The Federal Reserve, literally, didn't or doesn't buy the securities; there is no money exchange. The central bank "purchased United States Government Securities *with United States Government credit*," this quote by Mr. McFadden. Congressman Lindbergh remarked in 1912, that the Treasury will simply "hand" the currency to the central bank. Congressman McFadden put it another way; the central bank will get the currency *"with United States Government credit."* What is the meaning? Government credit is the Federal Reserve Note; the central bank simply "purchases" the security with the currency the comptroller prints, a pretty neat trick. The Treasury, by way of the comptroller and the Federal Reserve, is printing, borrowing, spending, funding, etc. The money people on Wall Street say that "the Fed or Chairman Greenspan is printing more money." The comptroller, by act of the Congress, prints the currency; at least, that is what the law states? Wall Street eliminates the formality, the Federal Reserve prints, and controls the currency; the shareholders wind up owning the government obligation.

Alexander Hamilton mentioned in the Federalist No. 34: "In framing a Government for posterity as well as ourselves, we ought in those provisions which are designed to be permanent, to calculate not on temporary, but on permanent causes of expense." This is the credit circulation, the permanent expanding debt; the government obligation is integral to the system. The collateral security appeared a downshifting to another powerful gear, creating currency at government expense, part of the "permanent causes of expense." President Bush reduces taxes, allows the printing of more currency, running up the debt. The people, in effect, finance President Bush's tax cuts when paying more future taxes. It looks like a Republican fast buck, a trick to gun the economy!

From the record, when the Federal Reserve Notes were "retired" in the 1920s, the central bank may receive gold from the Treasury. The notes were payable in gold. This practice was probably done over and over again to accumulate the gold. Congressman McFadden called it this rotary process. The central bank did what C. W. Barron said it was going to do—get the gold. The Bureau of Engraving and Printing printed the nation's money, and the annual cost of the debt was payment in gold to the central bank. Transactions included the participation of the secretary of the Treasury as a member of the Federal Reserve Board. The New York Bankers Association called the Federal Reserve a system run by the "government." It would appear naturally so. Secretary Mellon was there and the Treasury, the Reserve Board, and the twelve reserve banks. It was the country's clever money creation scheme, the central bank and its shareholders feeding off the people at very little cost. The one entity who never loses, always gains, never in debt in the credit circulation, is the central bank, the retailer. "And we are to be responsible after all; that is all there is of it."

The Acceptance, the short-term ninety-day contract, created elastic currency. The acceptance was more the private side and the other part of the money creation scheme. In 1933, the money system accommodated about 75% of the nation. During previous recessions and depressions in the United States, approximately 25% of the people took the hits, probably the pure capitalistic functional average. In the year 2008, the 25% figure includes the poverty-level people with low wage, no health insurance; more money abounds, but disparity widens.

From Ogden Mill's 1932 Treasury report, industrial production was down "33 per cent from the peak reached in 1929 . . . building contracts, a decrease of 42 per cent, factory employment, a decrease of 22 per cent." This was reflected in freight charges and retail sales, all down an average of 20%. What was the real condition in the country, financially, socially? There were winners, and there were the losers; the majority was doing with less, and for the wealthy, there was no depression. The country was moving along; good things were happening, incredibly, in a time of deflation. Hollywood and romance in America! Detroit was building cars; government financed roads, and bridge construction would ensue along with home building. The Empire State Building was completed in New York. There was air travel, Howard Hughes, the big German airships, air shows, communications, radio, and, of course, baseball with Babe Ruth, Lou Gehrig, and Hank Greenberg. On July 10, 1932, 41,500 fans in New York saw the Yankees win a double header against the Detroit Tigers. The concentration of money was primarily in the Northeast, Boston, New York, Chicago, and St. Louis. A new DeSoto convertible was going for $675. There was horse racing, Man o' War, later, War Admiral and Seabiscuit, the motion picture industry, dance with Fred Astaire, Shirley Temple, and Walt Disney. The movies and the stars were part of America's dreamworld of fantasy. There was vaudeville, Broadway, and household finance! The government was spending $750 million on the military. There was another plus; Prohibition was done away with finally, but the crime figures remained. American heroes were gangsters robbing banks, part of the culture. Agriculture remained down. This was the 1930s.

Pure capitalism wasn't doing it at home; was it doing it abroad? Gold shipments were continuous; gold shipments probably compromised the currency circulation. England was off the gold standard; the United States continued paying in gold. Securities and acceptances held by foreigners, especially France, and payable in gold as part of the Federal Reserve/Webb/Edge/BIS/foreign banking scheme probably created a currency contraction at home. France was instrumental in the 1931 gold raid. The gold reserve, the 40% ratio, 35% deposit thing, always present, always reared its lawful ugly head; it was the reserve amount, the amount held for circulation and the amount to be held for shipment out of the country. The Federal Reserve gold thing was a built-in "catch 22." Crunch time always activated the Congress;

the country needed a restoration of credits at home. The emergency
bill for one year would put currency in circulation by an extension of
the government collateral obligation. The early amendments to the
Federal Reserve Act had set up the foreign banks, and Americans lost
investments in Germany following World War I.

On May 11, 1932, in the Seventy-second Congress, first session,
there was a new bill in the Senate. The finance corporation and
the emergency bills had been enacted, but more legislation was
forthcoming. Senator Kean suggested that H. Parker Willis was the
real author of a new Glass banking bill, Senate Bill 4412. The bill did
not originate in the Senate Banking Committee. The bill, therefore,
was not "in the best interests of the United States," this from Senator
Kean. H. Parker Willis was an economist and author. He studied in
Europe and the United States; he was the secretary of the Federal
Reserve Board. Kean said that Willis was also "employed" by the
Senate Banking Committee. Willis had access to all Senate committee
and Reserve Board information. It was during the Senate hearings
investigating Wall Street speculation in New York; Eugene Meyer, a
member of the Federal Reserve Board, was called to testify. From the
public record, Senator Kean said that Willis sat behind Carter Glass
during the hearings; Willis directed the questions, not Carter Glass.
Parker Willis sent daily telegrams of the proceedings to a newspaper
in Paris; the French, apparently, were kept aware of the congressional
initiatives, the new finance corporation, possible inflation of the
currency, United States stock in gold, agreeable Federal Reserve gold
for shipment, etc. All this business was in concert with the emergency
bill and the release of 750 million in gold for shipment. Senator Kean
"sent to the desk Mr. Parker H. Willis's telegrams, taken from the
French paper." As of April 1932, 358 million more in gold was shipped
out of the country. This gold was in addition to the 1931 raid. Mr. Kean
said, "Nothing affects the credit of the country as does the shipment
of gold." Senator Kean illustrated a loss of credit in the United States
of almost $4 billion because of the loss of gold. Kean's assertion may
have made sense; all the nuances of banking couldn't be fully known
to all senators and congressmen. Senator Carter Glass was another
matter; he refuted Kean. Glass said the bill was solely the product
of the Committee of Banking and Currency. Senator Carter Glass
was staunch in his support of the banking system. Glass was one of

the architects of the Federal Reserve Act. Glass gave a speech in the Senate, defending the reserve banks after the 1921 debacle. Glass emphasized the elimination of the old rigid currency, the elimination of the "Panic Breeder" control in New York and their restrictions and control of the country's credits. Glass called the bank reserve system of the nineteenth century a vicious reserve system. In spite of what the detractors said, the "Reserve System Saved the Nation." Glass called the Federal Reserve the instrument of their salvation. According to Glass, the reserve system poured plenty of credits into agriculture. The farmers should "organize for a cooperative marketing of his product . . . for the cooperative purchase of his requirements."

A "cooperative" would be necessary to survive the banking system. Cooperatives, credit unions, and household finance surfaced in the United States. The cooperatives surfaced in the United States because the government's banking system dumped on the people. Cooperatives are nonprofit. Why is the Federal Reserve profit oriented? Thanks to the Congress!

Senator Glass defended "his child," but the arrogant abuses of the 1920s would have to be corrected; there would be no more Federal Reserve speculation with the country's money. Another big change was coming; the Glass-Steagall Act, the bank act of 1933, would alter the banking system again. The Federal Reserve Act had been amended thirty-two times since 1913. The Federal Reserve currency/gold thing appeared a game of tag; catch me if you can.

During the period in 1932, there was approximately $11 billion in gold in the world. The United States and France were handling about 70% of it, the United States, apparently, "managing" most of the 70%. Some of the gold in the United States was "earmarked"; it was gold owned by foreigners sent to the United States for "safekeeping." Foreign nations "had a right to withdraw it." Senator King of Utah had responded to Senator Kean's remarks.

In the nineteenth century, the predominance of gold existed in England and Europe. In the early twentieth century, the gold shifted to the United States; the routine suspensions of gold appeared to coincide with the shifts. It was truly the power of gold. Benjamin Franklin wanted no part. Gold was the hole card, controlling capital markets in countries by the money interests, eliminating credits, expanding credits, extinguishing paper currencies, neutralizing debtors.

During these movements of gold, the economies of the world were going into the tank. The sting of the Versailles Treaty would begin to rear its ugly head. Schacht had restored Germany's currency in 1924 with the help of Norman, Morgan, the Federal Reserve, Secretary Mellon, and others. But the 1929 crash had a crippling effect in Germany; people lost jobs by the millions. Another result was the emergence of Adolf Hitler and his Nazi Party. Winston Churchill called Hitler the corporal. Hitler was a corporal in the German Army during World War I; he may have been a corporal, but he rose to full power in Germany. How and why could that happen? In 1933, because of an ailing economy and an aging President Hindenburg, Adolph Hitler gained power, becoming Chancellor of Germany. Hitler promised the German people an improved economy. On the other side of the world, there was Japanese wartime presence in Manchuria, Korea, and China. Benito Mussolini of Italy relieved his country of the Communist predator and crime. Mussolini ventured to North Africa, conquering Ethiopia in 1935. These three countries—Germany, Japan, and Italy—formed an alliance and waged war against the rest of the industrialized world, World War II.

Why did Herbert Hoover set up the moratorium? According to the *New York Times*, there was a "financial crisis" in Germany in June 1931. The crash and the effect on credits caused the "runs on German banks." Herbert Hoover "proposed a moratorium of one year on all reparations and inter-government debt payments" to avert a "financial collapse in Germany." France objected but conceded. It meant no foreign payment to the United States government and the American taxpayer; the delinquent public debt of $11 billion dollars owed by foreigners was seemingly in limbo. One thing the moratorium did do, it prompted the gold raid. The door was opened; foreigners moved in. The United States was paying in gold. While France was raiding the gold, demanding higher interest rates on her American-owned short-term securities, France was not paying the almost $4 billion owed to the American taxpayer. Prior to the gold raid, there was 5 billion in gold in the United States.

What was more important during this period? The money had international implications? Securities, acceptances, Federal Reserve Notes, gold, the stalemated Dawes loans, the Young loans to Germany, the movement of foreign loans and payments in gold appeared more important? The new world bank for central banks was set up in Switzerland, the Bank for International Settlements. It was a direct result of World War I and the huge international debts incurred. According to the *Congressional Record*, the New York Federal Reserve Bank, under Benjamin Strong, the Federal Reserve central bank, J. P. Morgan, and others were an integral part of the formulation of the Bank for International Settlements.

Credits in Europe, according to Herbert Hoover, would take preference to credits in the United States. President Herbert Hoover, apparently aware of, and in the middle of the events, expressed the way it was, the way it was going to be.

> It is all part of one problem, the national debts due us, those debts owed by corporations and municipal subdivisions of those foreign nations to us must be worked out, in order that credit may be restored in Europe before it can be really restored here, because whether we like it or not; we are a part of a situation world wide in extent and beyond the power of any one nation to solve.

Those words, in part, appear applicable to the global economy in 2008, the new world order.

Franklin D. Roosevelt was inaugurated on March 4, 1933. The *Times of London* editorial of March 6, 1933, stated, "Mr. Roosevelt has made an admirable beginning . . . Mr. Roosevelt has addressed himself to his colossal task with candor, with courage, and with determination." The *Times* reported that the "suspension of banking facilities" by the state of New York "took place on the very morning of his inauguration."

"The only thing we have to fear is fear itself" were President Roosevelt's immortal words; these words are known to most people. The news media plays these words over and over! Roosevelt's other

more significant inaugural words are not played over and over; the
other words are just part of the record. Not since Thomas Jefferson,
Andrew Jackson, and Theodore Roosevelt had an American president
expressed more fury against the country's banking system.

> Practices of the unscrupulous money changers stand
> indicted in the court of public opinion, rejected by the hearts
> and minds of men . . . The money changers have fled from
> their high seats in the temple of our civilization . . . there
> must be an end to a conduct in banking and in business
> which too often has given to a sacred trust the likeness of
> callous and selfish wrongdoing . . . Our greatest primary
> task is to put people to work . . . . in our progress toward
> a resumption of work we require two safeguards against a
> return of the evils of the old order; there must be a strict
> supervision of all banking and credits and investments; there
> must be an end to speculation with other people's money,
> and there must be provision for an adequate but sound
> currency . . . I shall ask the Congress for the one remaining
> instrument to meet the crisis—broad Executive power to
> wage a war against the emergency, as great as the power
> that would be given to me if we were in fact invaded by a
> foreign foe.

The president's own government credit system was the enemy.
The government was part of the upside and the downside. "What
the Government does by another, it does by itself." The Congress,
prodded by the money interests, legislated the banking system,
which perpetrated periodic redundancy, the never-to-be-extinguished
"permanent causes of expense." Only through government, the
Constitution implied, the Congress and the money power could such
a pyramid scheme emerge. The Hamilton scheme was the embryo, a
"federally subsidized" scheme whereby those "at and within reach of
the seat of Government" feed the most off the principal. Ingenious
really! Why not? Those at the top feed the top first! Wasn't it designed
to do just that? In the 1930s in the United States, it was pure capitalism.
It was a country moving forward with resultant depression for those
out of the system, about a third of the population. America was the
casino! Pure capitalism, financial oppression, and depression cultivated

Communist activity in America. It was there in 1880, progressed in 1914, after the war, behind the scenes, in labor, in politics. In the 1930s, a social form of government surfaced, would take financial root, and would also feed off the American credit circulation. It was the Roosevelt administration; no doubt, the depression prompted it, whatever works for the multitude.

President Roosevelt's words were critical of the practiced creditor ethic. The president's "New Deal" policy was dubbed the welfare state; it was adverse to the pure capitalistic principle. From this perspective, Roosevelt was launching his vision of "Social Capital." Social Security would eventually result; the "ultraconservative who thinks alone in terms of acquisition," the Republican, he or she would disapprove. Say what you will, but almost forty million people in the United States would not be "retired" in the year 2008 if not for Social Security. Not too long after he took office, President Roosevelt recognized the Soviet Union, unfortunately, an unpopular move. Diplomatic relations with Russia had been severed since the Russian Revolution in 1917. Russia was now Soviet Communism, capitalism's enemy; this action by Roosevelt turned a lot of American people off. But pure capitalism in America in the 1930s, during an ugly depression, turned a lot of American people off.

Recent prior legislation, the finance corporation, the land bank bill, the emergency bill, among other bills, was almost a year old; what was the effect? A very real effect was the increasing public debt; it was $23 billion, up from 16.9 billion. The government was borrowing and spending. Entities, close to government borrowing, owned and collected interest on government securities, the security before issue of the new advanced currency. It was 1933, the year unemployment reached 15 million. People with savings supposedly compounded the problem; they were a small part of the hoarding, withdrawing money from banks across the country, but a crisis was at hand; the smaller banks were shut down. The big New York banks, the twelve Federal Reserve banks and branches, apparently, were in domestic neutral; there was no credit for the depressed at home. Was the potential for the creation of more money there for the unemployed? It was there, in the form of government borrowing, but was it doing any good? The 1932 annual Treasury report showed a total stock of money of $10.1

billion, a per capita of $46 dollars and a circulation of $5.7 billion, an average increase in money of more than 20% above 1929 figures. This increase in money, apparently, was a result of currency created by government borrowing based on the "collateral" obligations. The spending was government corrective measures by the Hoover administration. With all this additional money and three years after the crash, the country as a whole was not affected; it was the credits. Before the crash, when money was "cheap," when there were credits, when the borrowing, deposit, banking scheme was cranking, a dollar would turn over, not just ten times but maybe fifteen to twenty-five times. Those days were gone. There were insufficient credits; the Federal Reserve System, which was the credit system in the interest of the nation as a whole, was a domestic dud! An outgoing Herbert Hoover had voiced no credits in the United States; and sure enough, there were no credits in the United States.

The Lausanne Conference in Switzerland took place during July of 1932. The Hoover moratorium was to end in July 1932. The conference was a meeting of creditor nations, debtor nations, and Germany. The conference would achieve, hopefully, a final settlement of the World War I debts and reparations owed by Germany. Germany owed Great Britain and the European countries, and the European countries owed Great Britain. Great Britain and France and all those European countries owed the United States, and all the countries, including the United States, owed their central banks. The principals at the conference included Prime Minister MacDonald of Great Britain, Premiers Herriot of France and Renken of Belgium, and Chancellor Von Papen of Germany. The German contingent included five officials. Money was the important thing; the other serious ingredient was "War Guilt." Article 231 of the Versailles accord "set forth the German war guilt." The hard-liners, the right, in France, condemned Germany for the war. The *New York Times* of July 7 boldly reported, "ACCORD AT LAUSANNE BALKED BY PROPOSAL ERASING WAR GUILT. Chancellor Von Papen Pushes Hard for Liberation of Germany from Charge." The *Times* reported that Herriot would "drop" the charge, but not "retract it"; it was politics at home. The French and the Germans had been at each other's throats since the inception of the Versailles Treaty, the Ruhr impasse, etc.

The *Times* reviewed the payment plans proposed, prior to, and since the Versailles Treaty:

- Original reparation demand was an absurd $125 billion, which was "abandoned."
- The next figure was 64 billion, another figure that was dropped (1920).
- Under Versailles Treaty, a third still-unsettled amount due from Germany was 32 billion (1921).
- The "Dawes Plan set a scale of annuities but set no total of payments" (1924). This was the currency stabilization process period in Germany (a part of this 1924 German period appears in chapter 11). Loans poured in from the United States, Great Britain, Holland, and Switzerland, totaling $7.5 billion "between 1924 and 1930." It was foreign private investment money at 7% interest, a future hoped for foreign wealth of indebtedness based on a renewed future German economy. The *Times* mentioned that Germany was paying reparations with the borrowed money; the *Times* statement corroborates Schacht's description of what took place. Schacht, in his *Confessions*, stated that German surplus exports did not exist; thus, borrowed money had to pay the war debts. Germany didn't like the plan because no total of final payment was agreed upon; also, Germany was "irked by the foreign control to which she had to submit."
- In 1929, the Young Plan set the final figure at $8.8 billion. This plan, according to the *Times,* of Thursday, July 7, 1932, "was to be paid over a period of years until 1988, with 51/2 per cent interest, the total in the end would amount to about $26,500,000,000 . . . Under the Young Plan, 65 per cent of the amounts paid by Germany was to go to pay the Allied debts to the United States, the remaining 35 per cent paying for war damages, chiefly those suffered in France." McFadden, earlier, in the House, had said the war debts owed the United States were not to be part of the reparations; President Coolidge turned the bankers down, but the reparations were included anyway as part of the Young Plan as reported in the *Times*. The Young Plan went through after Coolidge in the Hoover administration; the details in Paris by J. P. Morgan,

Thomas Lamont, Owen Young, and the principal foreigners. The *Congressional Record* of February 1932 shows that government loans after World War I (beyond an approved $8 billion) were made to foreign countries by the executive and the Treasury without the approval of the Congress. The final foreign debt owed exceeded $11 billion.

- At Lausanne in July 1932, the French were asking Germany for a final adjusted figure of $952 million. Germany didn't want to pay any more than 619 million. Germany had asserted that 16 billion had already been paid; Schacht mentioned a figure of 12 billion had been paid; the French stated Germany had paid but 5 billion. Who knows what the final figures were? The Socialist Party in France were "willing to get nothing from Germany if nothing need be paid the United States" as reported by the *Times*. There was apparently an attitude in Europe about the United States. Apparently, they didn't like Germany and the United States. Money does things to people.

At the same time, disarmament talks between the major powers were setting up in Geneva. The United States, Great Britain, France, Japan, Italy, Germany, all had varying proposals—fewer ships, smaller ships, the scrapping of ships, the end of gas warfare, no bombing of civilians; an American proposal from Congress would eliminate conscription for "thirty years." The ultimate result of disarmament was tragic; Great Britain and the United States were totally unprepared for World War II.

On the home front, the *Times* reported the same day, July 7, that Congress passed an economy act. The act would shave $175,000,000 from the government payroll. Details were not specific, but essentially, a "thirty-day furlough is promised by the end of the week." Government workers would be required to take a one-month cut in pay. The paper reported "confusion" reigned as to application of the "Economy Plan." The army was affected by the act. "Army Has No Money, So Bills Go Unpaid." There was no money appropriation, and all promotions were canceled. President Hoover touched on government appropriations in his December 1932 message to the Congress.

On July 8, 1932, reparations were ended by the "Lausanne Accord." Premier Herriot and Von Papen agreed on a final payment by Germany of $714 million. Prime Minister MacDonald of England was instrumental in the conclusion of the agreement. Germany, that is, Von Papen agreed with fifteen nations. "World peace, especially European peace" preempted a hard money line. There was no agreement on war guilt; it was "avoided." Germany agreed to a later action on Article 231. Germany would issue $714 million in bonds through the BIS but not for three years. As was anticipated, the BIS was in place. The bonds would pay 5% interest, with a 1% sinking fund. The bonds would be exempt "of all German taxes, present and future . . . . The Bank for International Settlements shall hold the bonds as trustees." Herriot indicated France gave up considerably; 32 billion marks were lost. France was in deficit. Herriot would have to ask the French people to make up the difference in lost revenue. The 714 million was "scarcely sufficient to pay one year of Hoover-postponed annuity and one Young Plan annuity."

The Lausanne agreement was just that, an agreement in Lausanne. The times were ripe in Germany. Reichstag elections were forthcoming at the end of July; the elections didn't involve Von Papen who would be returning to Germany. Other things concerned the "electorate"; according to the New York Times, it was "Hitlerism versus democracy." The "Conservative and radical Nationalists camps," all the factions opposed the Lausanne agreement. "Herr Hitler's speakers are noisily proclaiming their rejection of Colonel Von Papen's bargain because he sold the Nation's birthright." There was a blast by Dr. Joseph Goebbels, Hitler's propagandist: "Germany could not and would not pay more. We have paid enough and demand foremost to be acquitted of the stain of war guilt, and if the world resists this demand we shall declare the Versailles Treaty null and void." It would appear that the Nazis didn't want to pay anybody anything. Adolf Hitler tried to defeat the Young Plan in 1929. About the proceedings in Lausanne, "Dr. Hjalmar Schacht expressed his opinion in one word in a telegram to Colonel Von Papen reading 'Bravo.'"

Lausanne was a step to settle debts owed in Europe by Europeans; debts owed the United States by Europeans was another matter. The Europeans hoped an American agreement would coincide. The New

York Times explained that although Germany was "freed" from her commitments to her "European" neighbors for three years, "she must still carry the heavy burden of interest and amortization of the Dawes Plan and the Young Plan loans . . . the American Army of Occupation . . . her private creditors, from whom she borrowed so freely in the past six years." Germany owed the United States $1.32 billion in "long term debt" as part of the Dawes and Young Plan annuities. The $1.32 billion was not part of the $11-billion public debt owed the United States. The *Times* reported that the reparations problem, "the major obstacles to world-wide recovery from the depression, has been removed, in the view of bankers here." Bonds were up "sharply" in the New York market.

What was American reaction and disposition? One answer was in the newspapers. On July 9, 1932, the *New York Times* published that the "War Debts to us Total $ 11,261,176, 719.57." The paper listed all fifteen countries and the amounts owed. Britain and France lead the pack with more than $4 billion dollars; Italy owed more than $2 billion. The total annual payment, if the moratorium were to end, for fiscal year 1933 was $270 million. European pressure was on the Congress "for a Revision of the Debts." It was so stated in London and Paris newspapers. President Hoover's latest "stand" was no cancellation of debts; the president "would consider capacity to pay."

Congressman Rainey of Illinois, in the House, said, "When the President of the United States, without Constitutional authority, granted the moratorium a year ago, he practically canceled the war debts owed to this country. Whether we do it openly or not, the European countries have canceled the debts." The *Times* published the divided and varied views of thirteen members of the United States Senate. Most said the Europeans should pay, or otherwise the American taxpayer pays. Senator Norbeck said, "You can't get blood out of a turnip." World War I had cost the European countries $200 billion.

There was the debt in the United States. Senator Barkley of Kentucky presented a debt figure of $154 billion on February 7, 1933. Congressman Patman, in the House, said the American indebtedness was $200 billion. The debtors were the "farmers, railroads, corporations, Government," small business, and private citizens. Local, state, and federal government debt was about "20%" of the total. Annual interest was "8.6 billion dollars." The American people owed this money; debts were way up, and circulation was way down. This was the American deflation scene in the 1930s. There was no depression for the wealthy. A 75% majority was managing, doing with a lot less; and the depressed 25% minority, about thirty million people, were out of the system.

World War I, the 1920s, and the crash accounted for the $200-billion tab. The annual Treasury reports showed an average circulation of $4.5 billions during the run-up. The velocity of money in 1929 was turning over rapidly. "In 1929, there was a velocity of currency and credit multiple of 25 to 1; that is, currency and credit turned over about every two weeks, or twenty-five times during the year," this from Congressman Patman on February 11, 1933. In 1932, circulation was 5.5 billion; the stock of money was up by 20%, but the velocity of money was way down. It wasn't turning over. It is most interesting; how was a circulation of 5.5 billion going to pay an annual interest of 8.6 billion? How does a 4.5-billion average circulation run up a tab of 200 billion? It was a deflation in money and an inflation in debts. The debt process is working when a market is there. The banking system is cranking with credits and deposits; the velocity of money is doing its thing. Congressman Patman wanted to increase the volume of currency, but the volume of money was already up; apparently, there was no effect. What was the answer? Was it the "volume" of currency or the credits or both? Congressman Patman was for increasing the circulation via his Veteran's Bonus bill; the bonus bill didn't go through. Had the excessive indebtedness compromised the world's economies?

> The fundamental difficulty is a lack of an adequate market for the goods we are able to produce. This market must come largely from increasing the real income of American consumers. This can be done by writing off capital losses and accepting lower profit margins; to accomplish this we must have lower prices or higher wages.

Dr. Arthur Adams was a "professor of economics at the University of Oklahoma." In a 1932 address, Professor Adams cited what he called fundamental forces that caused the Depression; he disagreed with President Hoover's "liberal" credit policies and presented recommended corrections among other things. The "forces" were the following:

- Between 1900 and 1929, the new technologies, inventions, improved mass production, was "more rapid than ever before," and World War I.
- It was the $11-billion foreign loans during the war. The private bankers' loans to Europe ("eight to ten billion") paid for American "overproduction" a favorable "32 billion dollar" export for the U.S. (This was apparently paid for with the debenture money).
- The Federal Reserve was adopted, "a strong Banking System," the increase "of our gold supply," "excessive amount of bank credit in speculation," the stock market "boom," and the crash.
- The installment plan. According to Adams, the American consumer "purchased large quantities of goods on installment purchases; they also bought many goods with paper profits made on stock exchange speculation." According to Adams, the favorable trade supported by the foreign loans, the installment sales, and the stock market paper profits were "highly artificial sources of purchasing power for goods."

Adams was against more loans to Germany; the economy should not depend on consumer installment purchases. Adams was for "balanced trade." Foreigners bought American goods with American money, borrowed money, the debentures; Adams called this practice artificial sources of purchasing power. Adams said the depression didn't "originate in any of the European countries." The loans from America stopped. The Europeans weren't and couldn't buy American goods; there was no American money, and the favorable balance of trade stopped. Adams was for higher wages, lower prices, and fewer labor hours for workers; Adams wanted "jobs for more workers." Adams said Hoover's Reconstruction Finance Corporation extended credit, but it would not "furnish a market for the goods of American industries or increase the money income of American consumers." The finance corporation bought the "frozen assets" of failing banks, extending government credit by way of the funding process, more public debt for the American taxpayer. President Hoover wanted the Federal Reserve to rediscount the "paper" of the finance corporation. Carter Glass disagreed; the Senate "refused to accept Mr. Hoover's recommendation 'to liberalize' the Federal Reserve System." Professor Adams agreed. "The measure would have greatly weakened the strength of the Federal Reserve Banks." Did the "frozen assets" or "paper" purchased by the finance corporation include those foreign debentures owned by American banks rendered non-payable? Congressman McFadden said the American people were choked, "loaded and clogged with worthless European paper."

It was a period of deflation; American workers had taken wage cuts across the board. Commodity prices were down. Congressman La Guardia of New York said the farmers "prices were deflated by the bankers a few years ago." There was apparent surplus of food, clothing, and products; but there was no work and fewer dollars. The American people had incurred their debts when there was work and many dollars; now the same debts had to be paid with no dollars or few dollars. It was the same as a "doubling" of the debts. The value of the dollar was way up; the cost of paying the debts would be way up. It was a pronounced devastating repeat of the past. Those huge "paper profits" (inflation) also translate into huge paper debts, excessive debt, which never deflates, during a period of increased deflation, and no credits stagnating a much-needed velocity of circulation. Where was that elastic currency? A lot of it was "abroad or lost." Former Senator Owen of Oklahoma estimated about "$500,000,000" was out of the country. Senator Owen and Carter Glass were the reported government architects of the Federal Reserve Act.

It was the same, always the same, after the periodic money panics. What were the causes? What were the remedies? How could things be fixed, made better? There were members of Congress, those who wanted to bring silver back into the mix, bimetallism again. There were no permanent fixes; constant and consistent money power and greed ruled the country. It was the repeated run-up, resultant-inflated debt, and liquidation. The Federal Reserve was the supposed cure-all, it wasn't; the forces that prevailed before, prevailed after.

In January 1933, Franklin Roosevelt was the president-elect. The absence of money was dramatic. Barter was in vogue. The second session of the Seventy-second Congress was debating the soon-to-be-enacted Glass-Steagall banking bill. Senator Thomas of Oklahoma didn't like the Glass bill. Thomas had the floor; he had one purpose: to illustrate there was no circulating money in the United States and the Federal Reserve was doing everything to make no money happen. The Glass bill wasn't going to help the situation either. The reserve did some in-house banking in the summer of 1932. The Federal Reserve was supposedly putting money into circulation; they weren't.

Thomas explained it this way:

> During the summer the Federal Reserve Board actually bought about eleven hundred million of Government Bonds, paying for those bonds with Federal Reserve Notes. The Board thereby placed in circulation $1,100,000,000 in money; but as soon as the banks which bought those Bonds received the money, they sent it back immediately to the Federal Reserve banks to pay off there indebtedness.

This was an in-house banking move; no money went into circulation. Senator Glass called it a bookkeeping operation. Glass didn't contest the accusation by Thomas of the Federal Reserve move; Glass did cite Thomas on a technicality. The board doesn't buy the bonds; the reserve banks do that. The reserve banks don't "buy" the bonds either; the bonds or securities are paid for with the printed Federal Reserve Notes.

Think about this for a moment. According to Senator Thomas, the central bank printed $1.1 billion and sent the money to the member banks; the member banks sent the money right back, paying off indebtedness to the central bank. The central bank retained the 1.1 billion in public debt. The member banks collect interest on the government security. No money goes into circulation.

Senator Thomas continued that a "nation-wide survey by the United Press discloses that bartering was part of community life in the United States."

- A farmer trades a bushel of potatoes for a haircut.
- Farm produce paid school tuition.
- Workmen trade labor for food and clothing.
- Wheat paid for the farmers' machinery.
- Farm produce paid for general merchandise.

There was a movement in "Utah and southern Idaho" called the Natural Development Association, embracing eight thousand farmers and workmen. [The Utah and Southern Idaho movement piece can be found in the Micro-Film Reading Room in the Jefferson Building congressional record, 72nd Congress, Session 2, Reel 199, Page 1735]. The workmen comprised every profession, "doctors, cleaners, merchants, dentists, mechanics, geologists, plumbers, craftsmen, and tradesmen of all kinds." There was plenty of necessities to sell and plenty of people who wanted to buy, but there was no money. The association issued scrip, placed it in circulation as money; the people "became economically self-sufficient and independent." Senator Thomas compared this with the Federal Reserve taking another $80 million out of circulation within the "past seven days."

The Federal Reserve money system supported by government was simply feeding the contingent that supported it. Bartering was the American people's alternative over the South and the western part of the country.

Thomas continued, "Los Angeles has a Cooperative exchange with more than 4,000 members." There was barter in Montana; Nebraska; Abilene, Corpus Christi, and Henderson, Texas; North and South Dakota; Kansas; New Hampshire; and on and on. Thomas presented an article in the *New Republic* of January 4, 1933; the headline read "Back To Barter." Another article: "During a modern world upheaval a system used by the ancients serves again":

- Range horses are traded for vegetables in the Northwest.
- Clergy in the Dakotas take wheat for performing marriages.

- Filling stations in Kansas accept umbrellas, lamps, vacuum cleaners, etc., for gasoline.
- A college coed on horseback drove "a herd of nine steers as requital for her fees."

"If the Board and the power that now controls the currency circulation of America refuse to give the people a medium of exchange, the people will provide their own medium of exchange." Senator Thomas contended the new bill would not create a circulation. Senator Glass was changing the Federal Reserve Board; the secretary of the Treasury would be removed. An open-market committee was planned; a liquidation corporation and $125 million from the Treasury would help eleven thousand failing banks. Security affiliates of banks would be eliminated; branch banking would be extended. Thomas wanted to know "how is the creation of that Liquidation Corporation to help 120,000,000 depressed people in the United States?" Glass countered that the corporation would "permit the victims of banks to get their money back."

Senator Long of Louisiana refuted Glass; the liquidation corporation would only help Federal Reserve member banks with "the money of the people." Long said the Reconstruction Finance Corporation [RFC] was already doing the same thing for all the banks and with "the money of the people." In other words, the taxpayer was funding the RFC.

Senator Thomas said the people "will provide their own medium of exchange." The bartering in communities on such a large scale was a necessary departure from the nonexistent elastic currency. In 1932, the people, in communities across the United States, possessed the goods and industry to sustain their commerce, their existence; but there was no elastic currency, no medium of exchange. Apparently, money was there; the hoarding by people and the banks was excessive. The newspapers and public officials reported as much. The result was that communities and people provided their own medium of exchange. It was barter or the creation of scrip, a form of money, a means of exchange. It would appear parts of the country were turning back one hundred years.

Before the bank act of 1863, the sovereign states in the nineteenth century were an existing financial departure from the federal government. The states had their own currencies; the sovereign states, through their state banking systems, provided the commercial exchange for the citizens within their domains. Central power took away that financial sovereignty, their currency, and now twentieth-century central power was keeping the distribution of "uniform currency" from them. Alexander Hamilton, from the record, was for American plutocracy; he started the all-purpose central money power.

On March 1, 1933, a *Wall Street Journal* editorial captioned, "BANK DEPOSITS ARE MONEY, TO BE KEPT IN CIRCULATION." There was $42 billion in deposits in the country's banks; it wasn't cash money, but it was money. "Bank deposits are money, the kind of money with which the great bulk of the country's transactions are carried on." The editorial stated that the banks had come under pressure because of the demand for cash, the demand by hoarders; the banks could not afford to revert to yesteryear, "the returning to a cash basis of trade." The editorial urged banking to continue business by "bank check, certified or otherwise" and to limit cash withdrawals. "Everyone Can use Checks, we don't need currency to do business with anything like as badly as we think we do, provided the banks keep checks in circulation among banks and direct their restrictive measures against hoarders." The editorial mentioned that $6 billion in currency was in circulation, which, based on the gold in the Federal Reserve System, could be expanded to 12 billion. Here again was the suspect gold reserve controlled by the Federal Reserve and probably a suspect United States Treasury. There was no guarantee how much of that additional currency would go into "hiding." The editorial urged business by checks; it would be a bookkeeping operation during the present emergency period.

Senator Thomas presented telegrams and letters from state legislatures, economists, and newspaper articles from across the country. Prices and the value of everything were falling, commodities, properties. Farms were almost worthless; one farm was auctioned for "$1.18." Foreclosures were common. Entities, with money, were making the fortunes, a practice that always happened during no-redundancy time. Great wealth, as part of the American way, was acquired this way. America in 1933 was suffering economically and socially. America appeared a one-way street. America, its financial setup, appeared to foster the wealthy. But there was the consistent cry; an "inflation of the currency" was needed "to restore commodity prices, incomes, and employment."

This was, apparently, part of the insidious plan and the contradiction; "terrible" inflation raised the price and the value of everything. The end result was the huge debts to be paid and the indebtedness owned by the wealthy. During the periods of run-up inflation, the Federal Reserve and the Treasury gained more profit in the raising of interest rates. The system is a double-edged sword.

Thomas claimed the $200-billion debt was in reality 400 billion. The debt was incurred when the dollar bought a dollar's worth of goods. In 1933, the dollar bought $2 worth and rising; commodity prices were falling, and there were no dollars. "So, when the dollar goes up, the buying power of the debt goes up. The debts have been doubled. So, when the people go to pay their debts, they find that they must have values doubled in order to liquidate the debts." Thomas said the real debt would be $400 billion. The estimated total wealth in the United States was $365 billion. Also, the interest on 200 billion wouldn't be 10 billion per year; it would be 20 billion per year. Thomas felt that under the current conditions, the debt would never be paid.

Thomas introduced for the record the "conclusions" of economist Reginald V. Hiscoe. Mr. Hiscoe's report was entitled "More Currency, or Cutting Gold Content of the Dollar, Called Best Way to Recovery." Mr. Hiscoe reported everything was "out of balance."

- Debts would never come down; they were mounting.
- Commodities, labor, earning power, salaries, and wages were in decline.
- Debts mount in an inverse ratio to the decline of commodities, labor, earning power, etc.
- Because of the inverse ratio, debts are doubled.
- The inverse ratio affects the wage earner, cities, railroads, corporations, all entities.

Mr. Hiscoe stated that the "debts cannot be paid off with the present prices of commodities, earning power, and labor . . . It is obvious that, unless a balance can be brought about by some means, bankruptcy or reorganization must result." There were "two ways out. A cheapening of the dollar, or bankruptcy." Hiscoe ruled out bankruptcy; it would be too "painful" for too many people. Herbert Hoover had recommended bankruptcy as an option. One of Hoover's last deeds was to sign the amended bankruptcy law, March 4, 1933. The law would allow "reorganization" to keep businesses going.

Mr. Hiscoe added that "the holder of the Government obligations, who so far has not suffered but has really gained, because the same income buys more commodities, will escape unscathed." Hiscoe's conclusion was to cheapen the dollar against gold. "We have only a certain amount of gold." Hiscoe was for devaluing the currency. "Now, if more dollars or currency are issued against our gold reserve, the value of the dollar declines, debts also decline, and the price of commodities advance." Hiscoe admitted "that most economists would disapprove of this policy." Would the dollar go the way of the German mark? Not really! The pound sterling had declined, "keeping our dollar at par tends to force foreign currencies lower?" These were Hiscoe's arguments and conclusions. President Roosevelt would devalue the dollar in 1934. The money game was like a poker game. Apparently, the dollar devaluation was necessary; it would be President Roosevelt's next move, his play, in the money game.

Reginald Hiscoe listed his positives in the devaluation of the dollar:

- It would reduce unemployment.
- Foreign debts could be paid.
- It would raise the price of commodities.
- There would be more revenue for the government.
- It would effectively be a tax on government securities; the entities who own them can afford the tax.
- Railroad receiverships would be averted as well as other receiverships.

In early 1933, eleven thousand banks were in jeopardy; seven thousand had already failed in the United States. Secretary of

State Stimson blamed the U.S. failures on "the failures of banks in countries all about us." Carter Glass said the claim by Stimson was a "shameless falsification of fact indulged in by a responsible public official." In a November 1932 radio address, Carter Glass put the record straight. "Since 1929, not a single Bank failed in England; only one Bank had failed in Canada since 1925; there were no failures in France and Italy." Carter Glass set the record straight, but the record of the American banking system was glaring, almost obscene; the American banking system appeared a game of craps. In spite of that, Carter Glass was staunch; he said the Federal Reserve System was a "Democratic measure that has saved this country from total wreck and that now, under wise Administration, will make recovery possible." The Glass address was also political; he was touting the Democratic president-to-be—Franklin Roosevelt.

President Franklin Roosevelt began his administration in March 1933; he would serve as president until his death in April 1945. Roosevelt was elected four times; no one before and no one since has served more than two terms as president of the United States. Roosevelt's beginning was not auspicious, or was it? President Roosevelt came in, and the banks were taking a holiday. Roosevelt began closing the national and member banks of the Federal Reserve System and hauling in the gold. A new law was amending the Federal Reserve Act, giving the secretary of the Treasury more discretionary power. The citizenry, by the new law, could no longer own gold; it was Monday, March 6, 1933. Actually, banks had been shutting down before this executive order. Bank runs had continued.

The amended act of October 6, 1917, gave a president the authority to take this "National Emergency" action as part of the act of March 9, 1933. The title of the act was "To provide relief in the existing national emergency in banking, and other purposes." The banks would be closed; and all gold bullion, coin, and gold certificates held by individuals, corporations, associations, according to the statute, was to be turned into the Treasury. Well, no one was going to approach the Treasury. Gold coin, gold certificates, and bullion were turned into the Federal Reserve banks. Anyone not complying would be penalized twice the value of gold slated to be turned in. Payment for the gold by the Treasury would be in the equivalent value in currency. Any banking association not complying with closure would be fined $10,000. The president had the power to prohibit specie shipments, including earmarked gold. Official bank closures was to affect from March 6, 1933, to March 13, 1933, a period of approximately one week. Federal examination of the banks was required before resumption.

The act of October 6, 1917, was

> amended to read as follows: During time of war or during any period of National Emergency declared by the President, the President may, through any agency he may designate, or otherwise, *investigate, regulate, or prohibit*, under such rules and regulations as he may prescribe, by means of licenses or otherwise, any transactions in foreign exchange, transfers of credit between or payments by banking institutions as defined by the President, and export, hoarding, melting, or earmarking of gold or silver coin or bullion or currency, by any person within the United States or any place subject to the jurisdiction thereof.

The statute summed it up; apparently in 1933, it was time for another correction.

The *Wall Street Journal* of March 6, 1933, listed thirty major cities from Boston to Philadelphia to Tallahassee to Kansas City to New Orleans to Des Moines to San Francisco where banks were shutting down from one to five days from March 4 to March 8. The governors of the respective states ordered the closings, officially observing the holiday. The Federal Reserve Bank of New York was closed; the paper reported "many of the country's other Reserve Banks were closed." The holiday was most dramatic in the Midwest. "Governor William Langer declared an indefinite bank holiday in North Dakota." Both houses of the Dakota legislature "within two hours" authorized the "printing of State Scrip." The state banking holiday preceded the action of the "national holiday."

A *Wall Street Journal* editorial urged a quick response to the president's action. "President Roosevelt, after ample consultation with his Cabinet advisers, has acted quickly and skillfully to bring about early resumption of their normal functions by the banks," this from the *Wall Street Journal* editorial on March 7. It was imperative to get the banks "off the cash basis it has temporarily adopted and to restore at the earliest possible moment the circulation of bank deposit money." The *Journal* stated that the president's gold embargo was a "powerful condemnation of our own hoarders of gold and Federal Reserve notes." The editorial listed the "facts": the banks had ample cash; the need was getting the "check currency again current." The clearinghouses had to work with all the houses and the Federal Reserve System for the acceptance of "clearing house certificates." When the banks reopen, all the exchanges were urged to reopen.

In addition, on March 11, 1933, the president "in a special message called on the Congress for a grant of drastic powers to balance the budget, and Congress in turn prepared to grant to the President today, authority to slash the Government's outlay for veterans and payroll by $500,000,000." Compensations, pensions going back to the "Civil War" would be revised; the president asked that his name "head the list." Salaries would be reduced by "15% . . . Cost of living drop is basis." The *Journal* reported a congressional "Caucus to Speed House Vote and Senate also Hastens." The *Journal* reported that commercial banks were open in New York for "funds for food and payrolls, cashing small checks, for essentials."

In five days, $200 million in gold coin, certificates, and bullion had been turned into Federal Reserve banks across the country. The returnees, those officially classified in the newspaper as the hoarders, included the citizenry, individuals, and individuals of corporations; most of those returning gold were bankers. It was estimated earlier that individuals, the people, represented about 3% of those hoarding gold and currency.

The *Journal* of March 11 showed a picture of a long line of returnees; the caption read "A Few of the Thousands Who Redeposited Their gold or Gold Certificates Yesterday. Many Carried Boxes or Bags." Some people, individuals, were nervous. Some thought immediate penalties were in order; some brought nothing. Could they turn in their gold at "the post office" or their "private bank"? A receipt would help. How long could they keep the gold before penalty? There was no answer for that one. The *Journal* reported "a large individual hoard" of bullion was returned "held by a corporation, which had been brought in to escape the penalties imposed by the new banking law." Two hundred million in gold represented approximately 5% of the country's gold.

One *Journal* article stated that the return of the gold "rapidly relieves the strain upon the banking system because of the extent to which Bank deposits can be expanded on the basis of the gold." The paper used $3.5 in gold and $100 of member bank credit as an example; the example was based on the 35% of the deposit in gold thing. For every $100 in a member bank, $10 of reserve had to be placed by the member bank into the reserve bank. The reserve bank, by law, was required a reserve of $3.5 in gold for the $10 in its reserve (35% of 10 is 3.5 or 35% of the deposit in gold). The example was showing that for every $3.5 additional in gold reserve, the banking system could maintain $100 in member bank credit. This bank credit was deposit credits; the example was working from the deposit credit end of the multiple money system. The 200 million in gold turned into the Federal Reserve banks work out to approximately $6 billion in member bank deposit credits; the example represented deposit money, not cash money.

"Upon receipt of such coin, gold bullion, and gold certificates, the Secretary of the Treasury shall pay therefore an equivalent amount of any other form of coin, or currency coined or issued under the laws of the United States." What equivalent money was paid the returnees or the "hoarders" of the gold? Since most of the hoarders were bankers, according to the *Journal*, the payoff, or credit, could have been in any of the following currencies? Details, such specifics, were not in the papers; the varied currencies were the following:

- Silver dollars in coin
- Silver certificates
- National bank currency as per the National Bank Act of 1863
- The greenbacks (Yes, the greenbacks, the lawful money, were still with us.)
- The Treasury notes of 1890
- The Federal Reserve Notes
- The Federal Reserve Bank Notes
- Fractional currency

One dollar in gold coin was worth $2.5 in Federal Reserve Notes. Because of the Federal Reserve Act, the 40% gold reserve thing, $1 in gold would generate $2.5 in Federal Reserve Notes. The $1 gold certificate was worth $1 in gold; therefore, a $1 gold certificate would return $2.5 in Federal Reserve Notes. If the returnees were paid in Federal Reserve Notes, the payoff may have amounted to $500 million in Federal Reserve Notes or 2.5 times the 200 million in gold returned in currency. Most of the gold returned was gold coin and gold certificates. Before the return of gold, the *Journal* reported that the currency circulation, based on the present gold supply, could be doubled to $12 billion. Why the need for the return of the gold by the people? A payoff of 200 to 500 million in cash for the gold shows that currency, in cash, was there in the banks, in the Federal Reserve banks, in the Treasury? Because of the amendment to the Federal Reserve Act in 1917, the absolute hoard of gold, about 4 to 5 billion, was in the Federal Reserve banks and the United States Treasury, the tandem.

The gold held by the "hoarders" was small in comparison. What was the reason for the return of gold by the citizenry? Was this the prelude to the eventual? The *Wall Street Journal* expressed the need for the banking system to get off the cash basis. There was cash. Yet the North Dakota State legislature authorized the printing of scrip. From the record, the circulation wasn't getting to all parts of the country; the money was primarily in the east again as before since Alexander Hamilton. The surfacing of the hoarders and their gold sparked an outflow of cash?

Cash, apparently, was not a problem; it all depended on who one was and where one was. The *Wall Street Journal* of March 10 reported that "GM. Divisions and Hudson Motor Payrolls Met with Currency. DETROIT—Divisions of General Motors Corp. are meeting their current week's payrolls with currency. Hudson Motor Car Co. paid its employees 100% in cash." The amount of money was $250,000. The article said, "Production has been on the increase lately due to a marked gain in sales."

Based on the events, private citizens would no longer legally own gold; the Treasury and the Federal Reserve System would maintain and own the gold supply, the gold reserve, and/or a management of gold. Would the payment in gold remain? There would be no payment in gold as money, at least in the United States? What about a gold standard? If there is no payment in gold, there is no gold standard? The charade was almost over? Not quite; it would take, supposedly, another thirty-eight years.

The *Journal* reported that the banks would be reopening on Monday, March 13, 1933. Member banks would have to file applications through the reserve banks, state banks, and savings banks to their respective "State Banking Boards." The embargo remained. There would be no gold exchanges; there would be no "foreign exchange dealings." The reopening of Federal Reserve banks, the sound banks, state banks, "clearing-house groups," the exchanges, after examination, was, to say the least, a complex matter. In 1929, before the crash, there were 16,000 state banks and savings banks; there were 8,500 member banks in the Federal Reserve System. In 1933, there were 11,000 state banks; 7,000 member banks remained in the Federal Reserve System. The *Wall Street Journal* reported that "the Federal Reserve member banks have not suffered as have the non-member banks." In 1933, 11,000 banks were still not in the Federal Reserve System, and why was that?

President Roosevelt's Emergency Banking Act became law on March 6, 1933. Between March 6 and March 9, the president rushed through another bill; this one pertained to the reopening of the banks. This new bill was rushed through special sessions of the House and the Senate and passed in two days; the rush was on to reopen the banks on March 13. According to a message from President Roosevelt, the "legislation was absolutely necessary in order to reopen the banks in the nation and provide them with additional and adequate currency." The question was, in the Congress, which banks and how many?

America was a land of plenty, things made available for purchase, and there was no money, mostly for those out of the system. The Congress, for a considerable time, wanted to inflate the currency, raise commodity prices, more currency to buy those commodities, resultant-increased production, revitalized industry, more employment, more jobs.

Congressman McFadden was back with his usual blast. McFadden figured the return of the gold, "the impoundments of the gold," had the natural purpose to increase the circulation. With more gold, the Federal Reserve banks and the Treasury would allow the "issuance of Federal Reserve notes." McFadden questioned Chairman Steagall: "I am a little at a loss, in the hurried way I have had to read the bill, to understand just how this new money is to be handled." The new money was not going to be more Federal Reserve Notes; the "new money" was going to be Federal Reserve Bank Notes. This was the answer from Chairman Steagall. The new bill stated that the security behind the bank notes would be government obligations, drafts, bills of exchange, bank acceptances. "This law provides 5 percent back of Federal Reserve bank notes, just as is maintained in case of National bank notes." So additional money issued to the banks, upon reopening, would be a new issue of Federal Reserve Bank Notes, not the Federal Reserve Notes. Steagall said the present supply of the reserve bank notes was not "outstanding. This contemplates a substantial addition to it." The interest on the Federal Reserve Bank Notes, before issue, would be 1% above the discount rate (more cost before issue). The issue of this currency would extend for one year until March 3, 1934. The acceptances, obligations, etc., would be deposited with the Treasury.

Remember the Federal Reserve Bank Notes? They were introduced after the 1918 Pittman Act. Silver dollars were melted down; equivalent silver certificates were retired, taken out of circulation. The Federal Reserve Bank Notes replaced the silver certificates. A new Peace silver dollar came on the scene in 1921; the Peace Dollar replaced the Federal Reserve Bank Note, which was taken out of circulation, reduced to a couple million. The emergency action by Roosevelt in 1933 brought back another addition of Federal Reserve Bank Notes. Mr. Steagall said the new money would "respond to the demands of business and liability to their depositors." These new notes would be issued to 100% of the value of the government obligation and to 90% of the value of notes, drafts, acceptance, etc. These notes, drafts, and acceptances, which would be deposited in the Treasury, was paper from troubled banks. These notes, drafts, and acceptances, apparently, was the paper the Federal Reserve banks did not discount prior to this emergency bill. But President Hoover's Reconstruction Finance Corporation discounted or bought up a lot of these notes, drafts, and acceptances with the people's money, the taxpayer's money, $2.5 billion worth.. President Hoover ran up a deficit of $5 billion in his four years, trying to get things going. Unfortunately, according to the *Congressional Record*, the money went to cover the losses of the big banks, the railroads, insurance companies, etc. Congressman Rankin of Mississippi said the money was "poured into a sink hole." According to Congressman Patman, J. P. Morgan headed the "sink hole" list.

From the *Congressional Record*, predominant government welfare prior to Franklin Roosevelt was payment to the wealthy, to the big banks, to the insurance companies, to the railroads, etc. These entities headed the "sink hole list."

This emergency law stated that the new Federal Reserve Bank Note, when presented, would be redeemable at the Treasury in the lawful money of the United States. The lawful money was the greenback. The greenback was redeemable at the Treasury in gold coin. So the redemption thing was still there, but within the banking system?

The new currency, the Federal Reserve Bank Note, was emergency currency to subsist approximately one year. This currency, which was a switch, would be obligations of the Federal Reserve banks. According to the *Wall Street Journal*, this emergency currency "would be backed by the resources of the Federal Reserve System, which amount to more than $7,000,000,000." The *Journal* reported approximately $300,000,000 of "free" gold was included as part of these "resources." The 300 million in gold was not part of the Treasury and Federal Reserve gold as part of the 40% gold thing behind the Federal Reserve Notes. The new Federal Reserve Bank Notes were to be on a par with the National Bank Notes of 1863 (also redeemable in the lawful money); more than $700 million of these notes circulated as part of the country's varied circulation. It is not clear at this point why Roosevelt, the Treasury, was calling in the gold and not issuing more Federal Reserve Notes. Is any of this business understandable? Maybe things will become clearer as we go along and with the Treasury/Federal Reserve hoard of gold and the dollar devaluation in 1934?

The day was March 9 in the special session of the Seventy-third Congress; the banks, after examination by a conservator, were scheduled to reopen on Monday, the thirteenth. At the time, $15 billion in government obligations were outstanding in the United States owned by banks and individuals. These obligations, based on the "requirements of applying banks," would generate 100% face value of the new currency, the Federal Reserve Bank Notes. "My friends, if you ask me if this is going to cure the situation in the United States, I do not say it will cure all our ills." Chairman Steagall's words appeared solemn, melancholy. "This is simply one step." Steagall admitted the banking system was "prostrate and in ruins." It was going to take time to make things right. He uttered the following:

> Heaven is not reached at a single bound
> But we build the ladder by which we rise
> From the lowly earth to the vaulted skies
> And we mount to its summit round by round.

Congressman McFadden hoped the emergency bill "represents the ideas of the new Administration—the new deal." McFadden said that "if this bill has been proposed and written by the same influences that are responsible for this financial situation, I shall fight it and do everything that I can to defeat it." McFadden wanted to "audit" the Treasury. "We want to know the amount of gold in the United States Treasury, and we want to know the amount of gold in the Federal Reserve System. We want to know the total amount of outstanding Government obligations." McFadden was telling his Democratic friends to wake up, to know the "operations" of the Treasury and the Federal Reserve System. McFadden had been beating the drums for a long time; the plan of the money interests was to centralize the banking system in the United States. Later on, in the Seventy-third Congress in May, McFadden, a Republican, would vent further frustrations; McFadden would claim fraudulent and unlawful financial practices by the Republican administrations from 1921 through 1932.

Annual Treasury reports are presented by the secretary of the Treasury with the assistance of the treasurer and the comptroller. The reports are prepared annually and presented to the Congress and the president of the United States as required by constitutional law. The 1933 report showed $10.1 billion in total money in the country; in 1929, 8.5 billion was the total. The 1933 per capita figure was $46; the

1929 figure was $39. Circulation increased from $4.7 billion to $5.7 billion. There was more money, but no change in the economy. Year 1933 was the worst year for unemployment. Congressman Sabath, on May 29, in the House, said 16 million were out of work.

William Woodin, an "industrialist and personal friend of Franklin Roosevelt," served as secretary of the Treasury in1933. William Woodin was director of the Federal Reserve Bank of New York before taking the Treasury secretary post. Henry Morgenthau Jr. served as secretary of the Treasury from 1934 until 1945.

The work in the House was done; the bill went to the Senate and passed in a rush. "Mr. President, I am sorry for the vote I cast on Thursday night. I voted for the bill. I did not have an opportunity to read it at all, except while the clerk was reading it at the desk . . . . I am sorry for that vote." This was the lament from Senator Huey Long of Louisiana. It was March 11. According to Huey Long, the big banks would open on the thirteenth; most banks would remain closed. Senator Long called it the banking "execution." The same people were still calling the shots; they have "had their finger in the pie during the last 20 years."

There was a problem; the emergency legislation favored the big banks, the Federal Reserve banks and the member banks. State banks, eleven thousand of them, were disadvantaged if the banks opened March 13; that is, if they opened at all. "The Law Curbs State Banks." The *Wall Street Journal* reported that nonmember banks were already looking for membership in the reserve system; it was a question of survival. "State banks that are not members would be unable to obtain any of this currency under the bill as it stands." Governor Lehman of New York rushed a resolution to Washington asking for relief of state banks. The *New York Times*, March 11, 1933, covered the story. "LEGISLATURE ASKS AID FOR STATE BANKS." New York State banks could not "issue non assessable stock of any nature." The New York State resolution was asking for "changes in Titles 3 and 4 of the National legislation." A change in the law would allow state banks to sell "debentures or other form of securities" to the Reconstruction Finance Corporation. When this legislation was in the Senate, Senator Huey Long of Louisiana submitted an amendment asking for a similar change; the Senate rejected the amendment. The Senate reason for rejection was the pressure to pass the bill. An amendment to the bill would have required the standard conference between the two houses. The bill would have been delayed; the White House didn't want any delays. About his state banks, Governor Lehman said, "Banks that were in need of cash and were not members of the Federal Reserve System would be without relief."

"We want you to know that we know it, and we want you to have all the warning on earth. We are going to close. That is what you have already done. We will have to stay closed." Huey Long was speaking in the House, but he was talking to the "financial barons." It was Huey Long's contention that the big boys have "shut us down." Actually, the state banks closed down first before Roosevelt made his federal move; the state banks were out of business. Long mentioned that Senator Thomas "stood there, day after day, arguing with the Senator from Virginia [Mr. Glass], undertaking to convince him and the Senate that we had to inflate the currency." Prices of commodities kept falling and falling to the virtual bottom, but nothing was going to be done. Nothing was done until the state systems finally shut down. It was only then that this new federal currency plan came to the fore. The emergency plan to shut down and reopen the banks favored the reserve system; the state banks, a lot of banks not in the Federal Reserve System were not going to open.

> One banker from the State of Tennessee came to my room this morning and brought another Gentleman with him—I will not call his name—and here is what he said: "Everybody except Congress realizes that this thing is going to be destructive of everybody . . . I have a bank . . . when I undertake to open that bank, with every bank all around me closed, I will not only not be able to accommodate the community but there will be no way on earth for me to stop the panic and fright of those people; and unless I have in the bank every dollar that I have on deposit; I do not even dare to open; and if I do open, I will be nothing but a liquidating concern."

It was a federal government operation. The Federal Reserve was printing the new currency, issuing it to the twelve Federal Reserve banks, who, in turn, would begin the distribution through the member banks.

The *Wall Street Journal* of March 13, 1933 explained the new currency distribution, "HOW NEW NOTES ARE CIRCULATED." The Federal Reserve banks were in total control of the currency issue; the reserve banks were the "only institutions empowered to get the currency from the Treasurer of the United States, under whose authority it is printed." The reserve system controlled everything. The operations were the same, the control of the discount rate (it was higher), the required reserves at the reserve bank against the deposits at the member banks. The currency was different; it was the new Federal Reserve Bank Note. The *Journal* called the securities for discount "collateral," the drafts, notes, bills of exchange and acceptances, etc. "Since the Reserve Banks have $1,000,000,000 of Government securities not now in use for Federal Reserve note collateral, the Banks can obtain large amounts of the new currency without delay." The only institutions that could deal directly with the Treasury were the twelve Federal Reserve banks and their agents. According to the *Journal*, all state institutions,

> not members of the Reserve System will be able to obtain new currency from the Reserve Banks by discounting their United States Government obligations at the Central Institutions. Even if they could not do so, they would be able to discount at member banks. Consequently, there seems little question that all banks will have access to the new currency.

The central institutions were the twelve reserve banks. President Roosevelt, in a radio address, on Sunday, March 12, assured the country that the nonmember banks "can and will receive assistance from member banks and from the Reconstruction Finance Corporation." Secretary of the Treasury Woodin "pointed out that Federal Reserve Banks are authorized to make advances to individuals, partnerships and Corporations on their promissory notes, for periods, not exceeding 90 days, secured by direct Obligations of the United States, and non-member banks may avail themselves of this privilege."

This new currency was temporary, to be phased out; the currency would be "retired" when things returned to "normal." A 1% tax was imposed on the reserve banks; the tax was passed on to the member banks and state institutions, etc. The tax was imposed to encourage removing the currency from circulation; it was going to cost more than other currencies. How was the currency retired? The statute stated these Federal Reserve Bank Notes were redeemable in the lawful money at the Treasury. The lawful money was the greenback; the greenback was redeemable in gold. When currencies are retired, the redeemer buys back the value against which the currency was issued. As this currency transacted and found its way back, a Federal Reserve bank may redeem the currency for its value at the Treasury. The 100% value, in the principal case, was the government obligation. Government obligations were supposedly payable in gold, principal and interest. But gold was being turned in; did the Treasury return the obligation to the reserve bank? Was a payment in a gold certificate made to the reserve bank? Only "those at and within reach of the seat of Government" would know. The law stated redemption in the lawful money. There was a limited amount of the lawful money; it was the greenback circulation. There was no more payback or redemption in gold to member banks, state banks, corporations, and individuals. Only the Treasury and/or the twelve reserve banks had access to the gold or gold certificates as of March 1933. The *Journal* reported an extension of five days, before penalty, for the return to the reserve banks of all the gold. The *Journal* also reported a total of $570 million, in gold, had been withdrawn, mostly by bankers and corporations, during the hoarding period. According to this latest figure, the hoarders held about 12% of the gold supply.

President Roosevelt asked the Congress to give the president the authority to reduce the federal budget by $500,000,000, cutting wages, pensions, etc. The Congress wasn't given much time to mull this one over either. It was another rush job, a gag order. In the House, the bill was under special order, all points of order "waived"; the debate would last two hours, "equally divided," no amendments, etc. It would be a similar thing in the Senate. The bankers had gotten theirs, and now unfortunately, government workers and the veterans would get theirs. The bill was run through Congress in quick order; those opposing vented their frustrations against the money interests.

"Why the haste on this bill. Is this an emergency matter? We were not permitted to see this bill until an hour ago." Congressman Patman claimed J. P. Morgan "will be protected by this bill. Before the World War, Mr. J. Pierpont Morgan was financial agent for France and England, just as he is today." Patman said France and England had borrowed $400 million from Morgan before the war; the borrowed money was "unsecured." Morgan wanted America in the war, and Morgan wanted his $400 million. The United States got into the war, and Morgan got his money; the first $400 million of the Liberty Loan money "went to pay off Mr. Morgan for the money he had furnished to England and France that was unsecured." It was Morgan's idea that Congress create the Reconstruction Finance Corporation; Morgan "got the first money that was paid out." President Hoover's moratorium stopped for a year, the payment of foreign money owed the American people about "a quarter billion dollars, so Wall Street bankers could collect their debts in full. I tell you my friends, Mr. Morgan, Mr. Mellon, Mr. Meyers, Mr. Mills, and Mr. Mitchell are the Gentlemen who are profiting by such legislation as this." Congressman Patman referred to the "banking racketeers"; the government interest payment to them was $700 million annually. "We are willing to cut off everybody else in order that such banking racketeers of this country may continue to get their bonus." And the beat went on, and it would continue to go on.

"We have the spectacle now of seeing the rich swarming to Florida with their pockets lined with gold; with satchels and trunks filled with gold, filling the liners of the ocean in their ignoble exit to other countries." Congressman Lundeen of Minnesota placed into the record, the *Washington Times* of March 10, 1933. The newspaper reported that a total of $438 million of "earmarked Gold" was held "for foreign account on Friday, March 3, 1933, immediately preceding Roosevelt's inaugural." The paper stated the "bulk of this earmarked Gold was for the account of rich Americans." The *Times* called them "PANIC STRICKEN PATRIOTEERS. Panic stricken by their guilty knowledge that continuance of the Senate stock investigation must reveal scores and maybe hundreds of Mitchells and Bakers." It was time to skedaddle. Huge selling of dollars in foreign markets "actually was the sale of dollars by American Patrioteers intent on building up for themselves foreign currency balances in the capitals where they expected it might shortly be necessary to find domicile . . . DEPOSITS RAPIDLY DRAINED." The *Times* reported in the week before the inaugural "both demand and time deposits fell to new lows for recent years," almost a billion dollars. "Today they are seeking to escape the very thing they themselves have brought upon this country."

Congressman Lundeen referenced George Washington: "Trade with the world and be friends with the world, but don't mix with their quarrels." How does a country do that when foreign money fueled the country from the start?

Things were going well in France; there was no unemployment. Why was France so well-off? Conditions were just the opposite in Germany. France had the biggest army in the world, "650,000 men," costing "$500,000,000 in cash for upkeep per year. France has the second largest gold reserve in the world; the largest military and naval aircraft reserve in the world; and is the second largest empire in the world." Congressman Lundeen asked the Congress why France had been excused from paying her $4-billion debt to the United States. Actually, the entire foreign debt of $12-billion had been "canceled, the debtor nations agreeing to help us out in paying interest on the money we had borrowed to loan to them." The American people were paying 500 million in interest alone on the $12 billion; the foreigners would pay about half that interest amount per year for sixty-two years.

> AMERICAN GOLD LOST IN THE BRITISH ISLES—We have kissed good-by to $4,715,000,000—a gift to the British Empire, the greatest Empire in the history of the world . . . they have more undeveloped resources than any other Nation that ever existed, more gold mines, more diamond mines . . . their navy is the greatest in the world. And we are too poor to pay our Federal employees . . . . our postal men . . . and our soldiers . . . We have money enough for the British King and the British Empire.

All this business appears ludicrous but real; those debts were very real and inexhaustible. Congressman Sirovich of New York mentioned in the House on March 10 "that the great Napoleonic Wars in which all of Europe was involved 117 years ago have not all been paid for to this day." This was the reality; this was Alexander Hamilton's reality. This was the same as federal expenses being permanently unlimited, "even in imagination." It becomes a manipulative planned blight upon people unless all people are recipients of the reality. The $12-billion foreign debt was a debt payable in gold. How was this debt to be paid except over time, which is the crux of the burdensome money scheme, the payment of indebtedness heaped on the American taxpayers? The American obligation guarantees payment forever to the owners of the indebtedness.

There was approximately $11 billion of total gold in the world in 1933. There it was, fifteen years after World War I, and the public foreign debt owed the United States was still $12 billion. Members of Congress during this period wanted the debt paid; why couldn't this debt be paid? Later, in May of 1933, Congressman McFadden would charge the members of the Federal Reserve Board, agents of the Federal Reserve banks, and the secretaries of the Treasury of conspiring with foreign central banks. McFadden would charge them of defrauding the Treasury and the people of the United States in the loss of gold and billions of dollars in Federal Reserve Notes during the period 1923 to 1933.

During this period, the central bankers, Montague Norman apparently in the lead, had been busy in the stabilization process, in the distribution of the gold by way of credit among the central banks. With the gold that had been accumulated from the respective countries, the central banks set up the world's central bank, the Bank for International Settlements in Basel, Switzerland. Wasn't this done to maintain international control? World War I created huge debts; those debts had to be paid to the banks. The $12-billion foreign debt, from this viewpoint, was not allowed to be and was not going to be paid to the people of the United States. This condition was assured by the distribution of gold among the central banks. The world's indebtedness was in the hundreds of billions of dollars, a paper scheme all payable in gold. Congressman Busby of Mississippi called the gold thing a farce, impossible of performance, but it was a farce that was deftly performing; the gold thing was the banker's hole card, payment over time and forever. It was the accumulation of gold amid devaluing currencies whereby monies are extinguished, a stranglehold on humanity. Montague Norman reportedly made it imperative that no one country, bank, or entity shall hoard the gold. Did Great Britain, in the eighteenth and nineteenth centuries, want to distribute the gold when Great Britain ruled the world with most of the gold and controlled the exchanges? From the record, the United States and France gained a dominant amount of gold. Distribution then, apparently, was the Montague Norman imperative thing? Distribution did take place after World War I in the twentieth century.

President Roosevelt and this Democratic Congress apparently concentrated on the $5-billion deficit run-up during the Hoover administration. Roosevelt sent a message to the House emphasizing the "unimpaired credit of the United States Government"; it had to be preserved. "National recovery depends on it."

This whole business was about credit; ever since the crash, there was no credit as before. Wasn't a potential United States government credit always there? In looking back, the $12-billion foreign debt owed the United States was a debt equivalent in gold; it was a wealth of indebtedness belonging to the taxpaying people of the United States. Using the suspect premise of the money interests, that is, a reserve of gold, a potential scheme was there, a security for money? The people of the United States possessed that security; there was no dearth of credit. Foreigners owed the United States Treasury plenty of credit; it was the $12-billion debt, a debt payable in gold. World central banks could not allow this payment to be made, if it could be made? Theoretically, a United States currency could be created based on 12 billion in equivalent gold owed the United States. The security for the currency would be owned by or payable to all the people of the United States to whom it belongs, not primarily the private banking and money interests, Federal Reserve shareholders.

A central bank with no profit motive, an Andrew Jackson model, as an arm of the Treasury, could issue a United States currency; there would be no private profit in the initial issue of the nation's currency. All this business is the writer's hypothetical; none of this, apparently, could ever happen.

Later, after 1934, the United States would obtain three-quarters of the world's gold. A sizable portion of this gold was slated for international distribution.

Apparently, a "powerful minority," assisted by an agreeable Congress, controls the money process and the country? In 1933 and thereafter, the $12-billion foreign debt was not going to be paid to the people of the United States. What was the world's total in gold? Maybe $11 billion in gold in the entire world, supposedly supporting $500 billion of indebtedness! The scheme was somehow workable in the distribution of gold by the world's central banks.

The latest legislation was called maintenance of the credit of the United States government. The *New York Times* reported President Roosevelt signing the budget bill on March 21, 1933. "ROOSEVELT STARTS $500,000,000 CUTS," "Veterans' Slashes to Become Effective July 1 and Federal Employees' April 1." The Democrats had fulfilled the "platform pledge to reduce the cost of Government by not less than 25 per cent." The actual figure was $508,652,000. "It is regrettable that in all great, similar crises the great masses of the people and those least fitted to bear the burden, are called upon to make the sacrifices for the errors and shortcomings of an unscrupulous but powerful minority." More than $300 million in veteran's allowances and pensions would be eliminated in addition to $125 million in government salary deductions. Well, the government was beginning to inflate the currency; the Treasury/Reserve was hoarding the gold, and more people would be taking more hits. Money would be taken away from veterans and government workers. One can't be in the wrong place at the wrong time.

The *Wall Street Journal* editorial said the banks reopening and the government budget cutting of $500 million "will open the door to a successful appeal direct to investors to finance their Government—something they have not been doing the past three years." Apparently, there was no dearth of money; money was there for the right price. American banking and currency was like the gaming house; when a new attractive game was arranged or coerced, new chips were placed on the table, a new currency, the right credit, the right interest rate, "shuffle up and deal." Play would begin again. It appeared the *Journal* editorial, in a different fashion, was telling it like it was.

Mr. Busby of Mississippi, in the House on March 13, said, "The United States is where Germany was in 1931. Germany had borrowed some $300,000,000 on short-term paper." The bankers were not going to accommodate Germany unless the United States Treasury canceled its foreign debt. "So they said to Germany, 'We will not renew the short-term debts; we will throw all Europe into a financial collapse if we do not get consideration about the debts that are being collected by the United States Government from European debtors.'" It was at this time that President Hoover declared the one-year moratorium; Mr. Busby said that "they importuned the President." So the taxpayers of America didn't get paid; the bankers got paid. At this same time, the bankers weren't going to buy United States Treasury short-term paper unless the Treasury raised the interest rate considerably. "We have surrendered to Wall Street." They "demand" the control of our country's credit and "expenses." This was Mr. Busby's contention.

Congressman Busby verified his statements; he presented "from a leading publication published in July 1931" the following events that took place in Germany:

- The stock exchanges were shut down.
- All the banks throughout the country were shut down on July 13 and 14.
- There were no withdrawals from credit institutions.
- Severe credit rationing was directed by the Reichsbank.
- There was the establishment of foreign control; all nationals had to declare foreign holdings. Such holdings had to be sold to the Reichsbank.

"That is what happened in this country," Mr. Busby asserted that the people in the United States have just been compelled to do the same thing. "We are off the gold standard. Why we have passed a law declaring that a man may be sent to jail if he keeps his own gold and does not turn it into the Treasury." Mr. Busby asked the question, "Are we in any better shape than Germany was when she made the settlement with the international bankers of the world?"

Busby asserted, "My dear friends, we are not." Mr. Busby said that "international bankers" were dictating "on their terms" how we will finance our immediate maturing bonds.

Congressman Patman continued the barrage. Patman introduced "Resolution # 31 to investigate the Treasury of the United States, and the monetary, financial, banking, and currency laws of the United States. An investigation will disclose that our President had sufficient reasons to say that the money-changers should be driven from the temple." Earlier, on January 6, 1932, in the House, Patman charged Andrew Mellon with complicity, "carrying on the business of trade and commerce" while having personal ownership of stock in "300 Corporations" and serving as secretary of the Treasury.

Apparently, public service and private enterprise didn't complicit in those days? Apparently, Andrew Mellon didn't have too many friends on the Democratic side. Before becoming the secretary of the Treasury, he was one of the wealthiest men in America. As secretary of the Treasury, he paid down the World War I debt by almost $10 billion; he donated his entire art collection of $25 million to the government. He was ambassador to Great Britain in 1932-1933. Mr. Patman claimed that Mellon "fled under fire to England in order to get away from this country when his unlawful activities and criminal acts were being exposed."

Patman wanted changes; most of the banks weren't in the Federal Reserve System. "Something has to be done in order to aid and assist two thirds of the banks of the nation that cannot get assistance from the Federal Reserve System." Patman went on to tell how the central bank gets currency against securities that a bank purchases. But the bank doesn't purchase the securities with the bank's money. The Treasury's printed currency pays for the securities, which is the government's credit. Patman called the practice idiotic! Didn't the people in the Congress know or understand these things?

Congressman Patman called it an idiotic practice; whatever the practice, it was a pretty neat trick. Whether it was on the public side or the private side, the Bureau of Engraving and Printing printed the currency and handed it to the Federal Reserve agent, the agent or governor of a Federal Reserve bank. The printed currency pays for the security, which the people pay for forever. The bankers were most clever in engaging the Congress. Legislation handed the central bank control of the country's money.

The Federal Reserve bank is the government's agent. In twenty years, the central bank had accumulated considerable wealth, utilizing government credit. It was an Andrew Jackson objection in place; a central bank does become most formidable. According to the *Congressional Record*, Federal Reserve wealth and power had afforded itself to foreign central banks and the Bank for International Settlements. The United States became the creditor power among nations. But more changes by the government, the Congress, were forthcoming in 1933, 1934, and 1935.

Meanwhile the countdown to 1939 was beginning. The same day Roosevelt signed the budget bill, March 21, the *New York Times* front page read "REICHSTAG MEETING TODAY IS PREPARED TO GIVE HITLER FULL CONTROL AS DICTATOR." It was the beginning of what would eventually be another venture and fateful ending in German history. Fifteen years of Adolph Hitler's anti-Semitic preoccupation was showing its ugly face. The *New York Times* was full of headline events:

> Einstein's Home is Raided; Nazis to put Bavarian Foes in Concentration Camp; Jews Here Demand Washington Action; Nazis Hunt Arms In Einstein Home; Jewish Judges and Doctors are ousted; Physicians Are Removed From Hospitals and Judges From the Criminal Courts . . . The American Jewish Committee and the B'nai B'rith have for months past addressed themselves actively to these serious problems which have now reached a crisis.

Leaders Cyrus Adler and Alfred M. Cohen "have requested the American Government to make proper representations to the Government of Germany and we pledge ourselves to continued and unremitting efforts in behalf of the Jews in Germany."

Hjalmar Schacht visited President Roosevelt during this period. Schacht mentioned the trip to the United States in his *Confessions*.

Schacht told Roosevelt that "in a very short time Germany would be compelled to cease payment of the interest on the American loans." Roosevelt was apparently amused at first: "Serves the Wall Street bankers right." A private Roosevelt note to Schacht later told a different reaction. Schacht didn't reveal what the note said. David Sarnoff of Radio Corporation of America [RCA] was a friend of Hjalmar Schacht; at a dinner party, Schacht spoke to a group of David Sarnoff's "friends about the anti-Semitic attitude of the National Socialists." The audience was primarily Jewish; Owen Young and Alfred Smith were there. Schacht said he spoke "as decently and tactfully, but also as honestly as possible." Schacht admitted his talk made no impression because no "discussion followed." At the time, Schacht had been named for the second time as president of the Reichsbank; later in July 1934, Hitler wanted Schacht as "minister of Economic Affairs." Schacht said he questioned Hitler, "Before I take office I should like to know how you wish me to deal with the Jewish question?" Hitler responded, "In economic matters the Jews can carry on exactly as they have done up to now." Schacht wrote, "As long as I remained head of the Ministry of Economic Affairs, I protected every Jew against illegal economic injury at the hands of the party." Schacht "was opposed to inflation as a means for paying foreign indebtedness and for restoring international trade." The German economy turned around in 1934; the German industry and war machine escalated from that point on.

In the Far East, Japan expanded the war with China. The Japanese delegation to the League of Nations was over. The same day American banks were to reopen, Monday, March 13, 1933, "JAPAN QUITS LEAGUE." The *Wall Street Journal* reported from Tokyo:

> While the victorious advance guard of the Japanese army occupied a key portal of the Great Wall of China, the Japanese cabinet on March 11, approved the decision to resign from the League of Nations. Japan's memorandum of resignation includes the statement of her determination to keep the mandated islands, former German possessions in the Pacific.

The islands were the Marshall and Gilbert islands; these islands were taken from Germany after World War I by order of the Versailles Treaty. The Japanese blamed Chinese aggression as responsible for Japanese military action, but Japan was in China. Depression-afflicted Japan lacked natural resources; Japan's economy was dependent upon the importation of raw materials, which were, unfortunately, owned by Western powers; this was the Occidental-mandated presence and control in Asia, which angered and precipitated Japanese aggression in the Pacific. An eventual U.S. raw material and oil embargo prompted the Japanese to attack the United States at Pearl Harbor.

The *Wall Street Journal* of March 17, 1933, reported, "Europe again is an armed camp . . . . As before the World War, Europe is splitting into two factions—France and her allies against Germany and her allies. Britain is desperately anxious to remain neutral, but fears she cannot." Depression and apathy reigned in the United States and Great Britain. France's vaunted military and naval power would prove to be a farce. A destructive Versailles Treaty, a decade of incessant economic subservience heaped on Germany, and the dictates of Adolf Hitler destined a Second World War in Europe.

Twenty years had passed since the Federal Reserve Act; international banking, the Bank for International Settlements was in place amid a worldwide depression. A financial rape of the United States had taken place. Apparently, the BIS was more important than ending depression in America. To the dismay and counter to the pure capitalist, President Roosevelt would eventually introduce his form of "Social Capital," the Social Security System. The new administration escalated more banking reform, appropriations for more government borrowing of almost $10 billion; congressional hearings involved former government officials, those from the Federal Reserve, financial scholars, and a host of bankers, including J. P. Morgan. The gold thing and dollar devaluation would also dominate the scene. Silver would surface again.

Meanwhile, the banks were reopening. The *Wall Street Journal* of March 15, 1933, listed 545 banks opening in seven Federal Reserve districts. There were no figures reporting the remaining five districts. Fifty-two banks out of sixty-one had opened in New York City. In November, Secretary William Woodin covered the reopening status of the banks in his 1933 report. "By March 15, the third day of the scheduled reopening, 5,077 member banks were licensed to resume operations on an unrestricted basis." The report showed approximately twelve thousand of the approximate seventeen thousand total banks licensed to operate as of "April 12," 1933. These banks held about $30 billion in deposits. The total deposits in all the banks had been estimated earlier at about $45 billion.

Woodin documented the "Emergency Banking And Monetary Measures" of 1933, which included Roosevelt's bank closures and the hauling in of the gold. Foreign indebtedness could be paid in silver up to $200 million for a period of six months, this by the Agricultural Adjustment Act of May 12, 1933. This act also allowed the "secretary of the Treasury to enter into agreements with the Federal Reserve banks and the Federal Reserve Board for the purchase of additional United States obligations in an aggregate sum of $3,000,000,000." The result of this purchase was "the issuance of United States Notes—not in excess of $3,000,000,000 to be outstanding at any one time." The United States Notes were the greenbacks, the lawful money of the United States. Since 1900, $347 million in greenbacks was the fixed amount as part of the circulation, no more and no less. The greenbacks were the lawful money of the United States, and in 1933, 3 billion were to be issued to pay off government obligations (chapter 14).

Woodin stated that the act was amended in June; all "currencies of the United States including Federal Reserve Notes were "hereafter . . . legal tender." Things were changing; the gold thing was changing. The people couldn't have gold anymore; there was no redemption in gold for the citizen. In effect, the country was off the gold standard, and now the Federal Reserve Note was legal tender. The Federal Reserve Note was now "legal tender for all debts, public and private, public charges, taxes, duties, and dues, etc." Before, as per the Federal Reserve Act, the Federal Reserve Note was not legal tender; it wasn't a government note. The Bureau of Engraving and Printing [BEP] printed the note; it was a bankers' note for the bankers' purpose and "for no other purpose" created by the Congress. Things were changing, but the credit circulation thing wasn't changing.

"The Pro And Con Of A Gold Market," this was from the *Wall Street Journal* of June 9, 1933. "It is pertinent that the British suspension of the gold standard did not involve a prohibition of gold exports but merely relieved the Bank of England from redeeming its notes in gold."

The United States Treasury wasn't redeeming Federal Reserve Notes in gold either to the citizen. The article stated that England was still the "world's largest free market." The "situation" in the United States was "different"; gold was now "contraband." It was illegal to have it. "Those who are still hoarding gold in defiance of the Presidential order would be able to dispose of the metal at a substantial premium." The price per ounce of gold in the United States was $20.67; in England, it was $25.40. "The metal is now sent to London where it is disposed of in the open market and the exchange premium obtained . . . the metal will be shipped abroad and the dollars bought in the exchange market, rather than by direct sale of the gold to the Federal Reserve as *was done formerly*." Wasn't the article stating that Federal Reserve Notes were good for gold over there and not in the United States? Hopefully, we may understand some of this business as we go along.

The Congress passed the famous Glass-Steagall Act on June 13. Two main features were the creation of the Federal Deposit Insurance Corporation (FDIC), and security affiliates of banks were out. It would be forbidden for banks "making loans on the security of stocks, bonds and other investment securities to brokers or dealers in stocks, bonds, and other investment securities." The FDIC was created as a private corporation owned by the banks as shareholders. The Treasury subscribed $150 million to the new insurance corporation; many in Congress objected to this action, another of the many public funds, initially augmenting private venture.

The National Industrial Recovery Act of June 16 created the Public Works Administration. The role of the Treasury Department was being reduced; it was subjugated to the new Public Works administrator, Secretary of the Interior Harold Ickes. The big Public Works projects were built in the '30s: the Tennessee Valley Authority and the modern marvels, the great dams in the West. The CCC was formed in 1933; it was the Civilian Conservation Corps to aid young men from poor families. The Roosevelt administration created the National Recovery Administration. "The NRA suspended" antitrust, supposedly to aid business. Instead, it became the big evil. There was price gouging; the system apparently belied supply and demand. The big fish continued to eat the little fish; it lasted two short years. The system backfired amid the protests from small business; the NRA would be declared unconstitutional in 1935. Farm land banks were aided by the "Emergency Farm Mortgage Act of 1933," This act was approved May 12, 1933. Two billion dollars would be made available, through a special bond issue. The government was exercising its power under Section 8 of Article I of the Constitution.

The Roosevelt administration was making the big effort trying to move the country, expanding the currency, borrowing, and spending. More corrections and a big change in banking, currency, and gold was forthcoming. Another big addition was the Twenty-first Amendment in 1933. Prohibition was repealed. Prohibition was a mistake; America's loss was Canada's gain. Canada brewed the booze; people never stopped drinking. Besides, federal revenue was lost; it would now be restored. This latest amendment was a necessary correction; it didn't eliminate or reduce but more than likely altered the initiative and the direction of crime bosses and racketeers in the United States.

CHAPTER FOURTEEN
Depression Part Two

From 1933 into1934, the Roosevelt administration was in full swing; it was the "New Deal." Roosevelt's New Deal was establishing the "modern welfare state." Money interests, national and international, had fleeced the country; credits were diminished. Between 10 and 15 million people were unemployed; that's a lot of people in a population of 124 million. Debts in the United States and Europe had ballooned. From the recorded events, a gold reserve appeared a deception; gold accumulation was always the goal. Vast capitalization wasn't achieved with gold. From the *Congressional Record*, the first official specie dollar of the United States was the silver dollar, not gold; gold was based on silver. Gold, when money and not money, was/is the power and manipulation by those who possessed or possess it. Paper currency bought gold, and gold extinguished the same paper currency. Payment in gold was all consuming and perpetual. Gold is statutory; gold is a commodity. After 1929, it was no-redundancy time again. What was to be done to correct the latest infamous hit, another repeat, the biggest ever in the political economy? In the United States, the people's only belated choice and counter to the debacle was a new administration. The Republicans were out; the Democrats were in.

What happened to the circulation of elastic currency? The currency disappeared. In 1913, Senator Owen said this elastic currency was the best thing that ever happened to the country. Who was responsible for the money? The money was apparently in the United States Treasury; the Federal Reserve Bank of New York, the other Federal Reserve banks, J. P. Morgan's bank, Kuhn, Loeb & Co., Montague Norman's bank, and, apparently, entities benefiting from the collapse. There were the foreign central banks. The money wasn't in the people's pockets. There are always the winners, the minority at the top in this business. Money disappeared because credits disappeared. The Federal Reserve controlled the credits and the creation of money. The control of money, adequate money or the lack of, after more than a decade, a Republican era, brought the American people to their financial knees as of 1929, 1933, 1937. The 1913-1933 Federal Reserve Note was a banker's note for the banker's purpose and "for no other purpose," which was not legal tender, which was good for gold, which, apparently, zoomed to Europe in a credit of billions. A result was the accumulation by the Federal Reserve of all the country's gold. Another result was the reacquisition of lost gold by Germany whereby an acceptable German currency was reestablished. The Versailles Treaty, apparently, took this gold from Germany, and Germany had to buy it back. Another result was the Bank for International Settlements, by the world's central banks, was created. This was like a first world bank. The BIS is the global bank for central banks and is seventy-nine years old. International financial stabilization and a guarantee of future payments to central banks appeared the goal; financial globalization was a realization. The record indicated insufficient credits at home; 1930 national monies were planned for deposit in the Bank for International Settlements. The economy of the United States, supposedly for all the people and in other nations as well, on the whole, went into the tank. National economies appeared to be in a resultant state of neutral, not a priority after 1929.

President Roosevelt's counter to the financial shocks and the unemployment was his "New Deal." There had to be a change, a New Deal. What was the New Deal? It was Roosevelt's annex to the pure capitalistic state. At the time, it was called recovery. It appeared the inner workings of the banking system continued to demand "recovery." The New Deal was government initiative, government programs, corporate and social welfare, public works, government borrowing and more spending, putting people to work, more public debt; some of the monumental work projects were mentioned in chapter 13. The New Deal was going to cost a lot of money, public money. President Roosevelt needed more credits as the New Deal progressed. The emergency legislation in March, May, and June of 1933 gave President Roosevelt broad executive power; and he exercised that power.

John Maynard Keynes was a British economist. President Roosevelt used Keynes's ideas in his "New Deal program," this from *World Book*. Keynes's book *"The General Theory of Employment, Interest, and Money*, revolutionized economic thinking." Keynes believed nations should "spend their way back to prosperity." President Roosevelt surely did that! In 1919, John Maynard Keynes wrote another book; it was *The Economic Consequences of the Peace*. In this work, Keynes was critical of the Versailles Treaty. Keynes was critical of the reparation payments, and its crippling financial effect heaped upon Germany after World War I. Germany, as stipulated previously, was also stripped of prewar land and colonial possessions. Germany would begin to reclaim some of those possessions one by one, plus the addition of Austria, the Sudetenland, and Czechoslovakia in 1938-1939. Germany was striking back using political deception, economic smarts, military rearmament, deployment, and intimidation assisted by British and French appeasement. Ultimately, Hitler invaded Poland in 1939, starting World War II.

President Roosevelt and "acting Secretary of the Treasury Acheson" had met previously with Governor Black of the Federal Reserve Board; the meeting covered "credit and financial matters." This meeting took place on July 7, 1933, as reported by the *Wall Street Journal*. "CUT IN DOLLAR'S GOLD SEEN NEXT" was the *Journal*'s caption. Black said that the board and the president were in "complete harmony on credit policies and in planning for the future." About the meeting, the *Journal* stated that Governor Black "refused to comment," but Black did say that the reserve had been "purchasing" $25 million in securities each week "for the past five weeks." The comptroller, no doubt, was printing $25 million in new currency each week. A governor, who is also the agent of a reserve bank, demands currency from the comptroller, the Bureau of Engraving and Printing. The reserve bank doesn't pay out any money for new currency. What does the remark mean "purchasing 25 million dollars in securities each week"? There isn't payment up front for securities with its own existing "funds" or money! Why would the reserve bank pay currency for currency when the bank wants or needs currency? Congressman Lindbergh in 1912 said the Treasury would simply "hand" the currency to the reserve bank, and apparently, that is what happens. If there is a purchase, the securities are "purchased" with the newly printed currency. This goes all the way back to after 1865 when the Treasury and the banks initially swapped currencies and the banks owned the bonds. The reserve banks first and then shareholders and banks in the "transfer" will have the bonds or securities, collect interest forever as part of the government debt, the cost of the printed paper currency.

The Treasury borrows and spends the same money through its agent, the Federal Reserve System; it's the government's credit circulation. The government couldn't pay its debt to the bank with this currency from 1913 to 1934. The government had to pay its debt to the bank in gold. Would the "purchases" continue? Chairman Black said the "purchases" depended on the future, "or whether other forms of inflation would be adopted by the Government in its goal to raise commodity prices to the average of 1924-25-26."

The Federal Reserve may lessen the circulation when a security transfer occurred or extended no credit, which may stop the economy. This action may force the government, President Roosevelt, to print fiat currency, putting money in circulation; then Chairman Black calls it inflation. The central bank is the political creation, a creation that subtly rules the political and guarantees infinite non-payable debt.

As part of the "Emergency Farm Mortgage Act of 1933" under Title III, "Financing and Exercising Power Conferred by Section 8 of Article I of the Constitution: To Coin Money and to Resolve the Value Thereof," President Roosevelt expanded the currency; Roosevelt devalued the dollar, and gold coin was melted down into gold bars.

Three billion in currency was to be issued as part of the act of May 1933; Secretary Woodin documented the planned purchase of $3 billion in government obligations by the Federal Reserve in his 1933 report. Three billion in new Civil War "greenbacks" would be issued "for the purpose of meeting maturing Federal obligations" primarily. Senator Byrnes of South Carolina put it this way: "It offers nothing but the substitution of a non-interest-bearing demand obligation for an interest-bearing time obligation of the Government." From Senator Byrnes's viewpoint, it was a swap! The government had to pay for new obligations to have the new greenbacks printed; Roosevelt would relieve payment of old obligations for new, but the new lawful money would go to the reserve banks as substitute reserve. This was the continuing operation! The so-called repudiated currency would supposedly be back in abundance. The "lawful" non-interest-bearing money, the greenbacks, would play another important role. If Secretary Woodin didn't get the cooperation of the Federal Reserve, then the president had the power to authorize the devaluation of the dollar, and that's what he did. Roosevelt reduced the weight of gold in the gold dollar in order to get more dollars, more paper currency; it was done also according to the record "to stabilize domestic prices or to protect the foreign commerce against the adverse effect of depreciated foreign currencies, etc."

Hjalmar Schacht had his view on Roosevelt's devaluation; "there was no reason for it." America had the most gold and the "most stable currency in the world." Maybe the currency was too stable; it wasn't moving, no velocity. It wasn't moving at home. Great Britain had devalued its currency in 1931; the move enhanced her exports immediately. It was Schacht's contention that Roosevelt wanted "to reap the same commercial advantage that Great Britain had done from her devaluation . . . to counter this artificially created preference in favor of Britain."

Roosevelt signed the Gold Reserve Act on January 30, 1934. Roosevelt issued, from the White House, "Proclamation [2072]; Fixing the Weight of the Gold Dollar." The Gold Standard Act of 1900 established the "former weight of 25.8 grains, nine-tenths fine." Roosevelt reduced the weight to 15.25 grains, nine-tenths fine. The new weight was 59% of the former weight, a reduction of 41%. Reducing the weight of gold in the gold dollar devalued the dollar. In other words, there could exist more paper dollars against the amount of gold. In the United States, the price of gold was fixed at $20.7 per ounce; Roosevelt's action increased the price of gold to $35.0 per ounce. There was no calculation in the proclamation, but if we use the equation:

$$\frac{\text{Old Price}}{0.59} = \frac{\text{New Price}}{0.59 + 0.41} \qquad \text{New Price} = \$35.00$$

Fifty-nine percent of the new price would equal the old price: 0.59 x $35.00 = $20.7

The secretary of the Treasury was authorized to "buy through the Federal Reserve Bank of New York as fiscal agent, for the account of the United States, any and all gold delivered to any United States Mints or the Assay Offices in New York or Seattle, at the rate of $35.00 per fine troy ounce."

The proclamation stated that

> the entire stock of monetary gold in the United States . . . heretofore held by the Federal Reserve banks and the claim upon gold in the Treasury represented by gold certificates is vested in the United States Government, and the "profit" from the reduction of the gold content of the dollar, made effective by today's Proclamation, accrues to the United States Treasury.

The amount of the profit was "two billion dollars."

How was the $2-billion profit determined? The proclamation did not explain. There was approximately 5 billion in gold in the United States at the time. The weight reduction was 41%, meaning 41% more dollars could be realized against gold. Using round numbers, say, 0.4 x $5 billion, the profit would equal $2 billion at the start (chapters 15 and 16 indicate how this money was probably spent). The proclamation stated that "the two billion dollars under the terms of the Gold Reserve Act and of today's Proclamation, constitute a stabilization fund under the direction of the Secretary of the Treasury. The balance will be converted into the general fund of the Treasury." President Roosevelt had more credit. Roosevelt had $2 billion dollars to spend, just like that, at the start. The secretary of the Treasury would have the authority to maintain "parity" between future currencies issued and the new standard weight of gold. The *Wall Street Journal* had stated earlier that a government gold weight reduction move versus the dollar would deal a "big profit for the U.S." Great Britain, and the United States were devaluing, and why? Was it the gold thing, no credits? Prices were down, economies were down, debts were way up; what translates into a viable economy more than an ample currency that is allowed to move? Hopefully, it would translate to more purchasing power, more production, employment of labor, more agriculture and manufactures, an enhancement of foreign trade.

All this past gold business; it was the way it was, the many entities and countries moving their gold, getting their price. England wasn't paying in gold; the United States wasn't paying in gold at home, but the world currency values, the market values, resulting availability of credits, were still being manipulated based on gold. England was off the gold standard and according to many, so was the United States. But according to the *Wall Street Journal*, London, England, was the world's free market, and that is where the gold was going. "LONDON GAINS 62,459,389 IN GOLD" (The 62 million was in pounds). The *Journal* of June 12, 1933, stated the "Europeans" were sending their gold to London "for safe keeping." Because of this, a "large stock of gold" in London was private; it wasn't part of the "official stocks." According to the *Journal*, Europeans feared a "similar" U.S. "restriction" in their own countries. The French were "hoarding," buying on the London market, driving up the price; the French were not buying "from their own Central Banks." There was no market in the United States; the gold market was in London and at a premium. The *Journal* stated, "Our Loss, London's Gain." Countries normally shipping their gold to the United States were now sending it to London. "Canada, China and the Latin American States" were getting the premium price for gold in London, then buying "dollars in the exchange market."

Was gold coin to continue as money? Not in the United States, gold coin was to be melted down, turned into bars; gold was now a commodity. But gold, apparently, would still be the tool in the money interests' international manipulation of currency values and exchanges, that is, gold bullion.

President Roosevelt's Proclamation 2072 stated,

> "Settlement for the gold coin, bullion and certificates taken over from the Federal Reserve Banks on Tuesday upon the approval of the Act was made in the form of credits set up on the Treasury's books. This credit due the Federal Reserve Banks is to be paid in the new form of gold certificates now in course of production by the Bureau of Engraving and

Printing. These certificates bear on their face the wording:
'This is to certify that there is on deposit in the Treasury of
the United States of America_____ dollars in gold, payable
to bearer on demand as authorized by law.'" The certificates
were legal tender, good for "payment of all debts and dues,
public and private."

The gold had been transferred to the Treasury, but the gold could
be claimed by the Federal Reserve banks when the need arose. The
reserve banks didn't literally possess the gold, but the reserve banks
had been paid the certificates, which were payable in the gold. By
virtue of the gold certificate, the Federal Reserve owned the gold. The
new gold certificates were set apart from other currency; although
the same size, the certificates were printed yellow on the back. The
gold certificates came "in denominations of $100,000." The Federal
Reserve would also possess the new greenbacks, the lawful money,
which were legal tender and good for gold. The Federal Reserve didn't
hold the gold anymore, but they would possess the gold certificates
and the lawful money as the reserve for deposits and Federal Reserve
Notes. These two currencies, the gold certificates and the greenbacks,
took the place of a supposed gold reserve thing in the reserve banks.
These two currencies would constitute the 35% to 40% ratio behind
the Federal Reserve Note circulation and deposits. This action was
taken care of in the Gold Reserve Act, which amended Section 14
of the Federal Reserve Act. In the Book of Statutes, Seventy-third
Congress, session 2, page 338:

> [3] The first sentence of the third paragraph is amended to
> read as follows: "Every Federal Reserve Bank shall maintain
> reserves in gold certificates or lawful money of not less
> than 35 per centum against its deposits and reserves in
> gold certificates of not less than 40 per centum against its
> Federal Reserve notes in actual circulation."

The Gold Reserve Act also made all the currencies legal tender,
including the Federal Reserve Note. And what were and where
were the currencies? They were all still there: the new and the
old greenbacks, the Federal Reserve Notes, the National Bank
Notes, the gold certificates, the silver certificates, the Federal

Reserve Bank Notes, the Treasury notes of 1890, all of them now legal tender.

The law would allow President Roosevelt to devalue the dollar further "if in the interests of the United States," but further reduction in weight could not exceed 50% of the 1900 standard weight of the gold dollar. The upper limit of the weight of the gold dollar was fixed at 60% and the lower limit at 50%.The emergency enactment of 1934 was to last two years; the president could extend the period one year if the emergency warranted. The weight of the silver dollar was also fixed "in relation to the gold dollar." The proclamation was to "remain in force and effect until and unless repealed or modified by Act of Congress or by subsequent Proclamation" (by the president).

The biggest change of all was gold; payment in gold had reached its end. Payment in gold was over? It was over for the citizen! President Roosevelt "appended" an explanation immediately following his proclamation whereby he reasoned the actions of the Congress and his administration since March of 1933. The Congress had debated the gold thing the entire month of May in 1933. It was during this debate that Congressman Busby called the gold thing a farce, impossible of performance. It was the banker's ingenious "farce." Congressman Goldsborough remarked, "The gold standard has been the cross of the world for hundreds of years." There was over $200 billion in total debt in the United States. Goldsborough mentioned the existence of "91 billion dollars" of debt in the United States, inflationary debt, all payable in gold. The government, the railroads, the states and municipalities, the corporations, all owed these debts in gold with but 5 billion of total gold in the country.

President Roosevelt noted that this Congress passed a joint resolution on June 5, 1933. Roosevelt said, "The provisions for payment of money obligations in gold coin or in gold—were declared invalid by the Congress." Gold was the insidious plan. Was all this coming to light? The payment in gold was against the "public interest." The president declared, "This was another measure designed to prevent unfair profits from accruing to a very small group of creditors and the placing of unfair burdens not only on the corresponding debtors, but on the general tax-paying public as a whole. It assured payment of the dollar amount of the obligation rather than of a purely fictitious gold value." Roosevelt said the Congress would dictate "control of our monetary system and of the metallic reserves of gold and silver as its base; and to make clear that it belongs where the Constitution says it does, in the Congress rather than in the hands of the bankers and the speculators." There would be no payment in "gold except as directed by the Secretary of the Treasury with the approval of the President, and then only in gold bullion." Gold coin was out; it was melted down. The gold feature was out? Alexander Hamilton's creation of non-legal tender paper currency to be paid in gold had come to an end? Hamilton had followed the creation of the Bank of England, its genius in creating gold out of nothing.

President Roosevelt made the Federal Reserve Note good for all debts, public and private, and for public dues and customs. The note was now good for the public debt; in 1913, it wasn't. In 1913, the Federal Reserve Note was a bank note and not legal tender and good for gold. In 1933, the Federal Reserve Note was made legal tender but not good for gold. What was the deal in 1913? The government had to pay its debts in gold; that was the deal! It seems there is a time, a place, a mentality, a design, and acceptance by the sovereign, the Congress, the money interests for a specific money scheme for a United States currency, a Federal Reserve Note. The note in 1933, after twenty years, was legal tender, not good for gold (for the citizen) but good for the public debt. There was hypocrisy in all this business; it's whatever works in the scheme of things. Except for all the currencies still around, the credit circulation was nearing its intended role. The Treasury would be printing, issuing, borrowing, and spending the Federal Reserve Note at the direction of the Federal Reserve and funding the national debt with that currency.

The president noted, "This was an emergency measure, but it was also the first of the steps in transferring to the Federal Government the more effective control and regulation of the monetary system." On the surface, it looked pretty good. Thomas Jefferson may have approved. The Gold Reserve Act was debated aggressively in the Congress. Silver, bimetallism were again an issue. Why not bulk up the gold reserve with a silver reserve? The Silver Purchase Act became reality; the silver stock would be increased to at least one-fourth that of the gold stock. The secretary of the Treasury had the authority to purchase silver and maintain that ratio. This was bimetallism, gold and silver as a currency reserve. This silver move followed the silver agreement of countries at the World Economic Conference in London. Was this peculiar? Didn't England hate silver? Roosevelt's monetary changes were dramatic, but how effective? The *Wall Street Journal* called it the inflationary movement that has been sponsored by the administration here. There it was, the "catch 22." As 1935 approached, the total money in the country had increased from $8.5 to $13.6 billion since 1929. As 1936 approached, the total money increased to $15.1 billion. Money was being generated by government spending. The money was there, unemployment lessened; depression eased for forty million people. The velocity of money was there; money was moving? It was/is the system whereby credits and the velocity of money, by those controlling, are more important than just the money.

The *Journal* article of July 7, 1933, spelled out Roosevelt's "current" doings and what he planned to do six months later. There were the "natural" forces and "deliberate obstacles" against such plans. The *Journal* mentioned "three successive phases." They were Roosevelt's current expansion of money in an effort to "raise commodity prices" then the devaluation of the dollar and then the management of currency; these two things signed into law in 1934. The Roosevelt administration called the last "phase" a stabilization fund; the *Wall Street Journal* called it a "management of money." How could "stable prices" be achieved with a managed currency, and the period of time was so short? Roosevelt's opponents favored the "adjustments of credit in relation to both its supply and velocity," but where were those credits? The article stated that Roosevelt's management of money wouldn't work; "management will stop with somewhat more intensive use of such known devices as the discount rate and open market operations; in other words, that while prices may be influenced, their close control through currency management will be found impossible." But again, where were those credits? The article concluded the profits to be made by the government when devaluation of the dollar would take place.

> In the past it has been the practice of the sovereign power
> to claim ownership of this increment on the grounds that

it arose from the acts of the sovereign. There would, of
course, be constitutional questions in connection with this
process, but good opinion here is that the courts would take
the side of the Government.

But the Treasury, the Federal Reserve, the money thing, they appeared
as bedfellows.

In a favorable economy, it is the movement of "credit in relation to
both money supply and velocity." It would appear an elastic currency,
for all the country, in the United States, was in limbo in the 1930s. A
good description of how bad things were can be found in *World Book*;
living conditions were the worst in the South and in the Midwest in
the towns and on the farms. *World Book* described it; it was "human
suffering." But pure capitalism produced a viable market for those in
the system as in "$50,000,000,000 in tax-exempt securities"; the few,
mostly, claimed this bounty. Where jobs held families together, one
family in five may have owned an automobile. There was a vast number
of people without jobs and the "poor suckers who had nothing to
eat." On the same day, July 7, 1933, the *Journal*'s "By the Bye in Wall
Street" was about Andrew Carnegie "and the conditions of today. They
produce millionaires." Russia didn't produce any millionaires; England
didn't produce any millionaires. Only in America are millionaires
made. Here it was, 1933, the worst period of the Depression, and the
millionaires were being made. America, before and since the crash,
must have resembled a gaming house, a casino; the house produced
a few big winners, and there were millions of losers. What came first,
the chicken or the egg? Or was it the casino or the central bank? The
central bank and the casino appear to have similar functions; roll out
the money for play and then haul it in! Banks were the losers too;
the smaller banks, the member banks of the Federal Reserve System,
state banks, more than seven thousand banks failed. No banks failed
in England, France, and Canada. Times were harsh; times were good,
America was the dream. In the '30s, America was money and no
money; America produced the millionaires.

In the midst of President Roosevelt's initial emergency moves at
home, the World Economic Conference was taking place in London.
The conference took place in June and July of 1933; sixty-six nations

attended. While Roosevelt was working to rectify a national economy in the United States, the World Economic Conference was doing its thing in London. The *Journal* called the conference an atmosphere of unreality. The reason was the ongoing war debts, and "the dollar-sterling ratio" were excluded from the talks. According to the *Journal*, unless those two things were resolved, the conference was awash; this was the conclusion from the experts. The London Conference, according to the *Journal*, was apparently zeroing in on national economies. The conference "hoped that they can check further growth of economic nationalism." It would take most of the twentieth century; America's national product would grow each year, and President George Bush in 1991 declared a "new-world order." The big result was America would lose its national product; it would become a "domestic" one.

France was losing its gold. "FRANCE STUDIES ITS GOLD LOSS." This was the headline of the *Journal* of March 1, 1934; the gold was leaving France for London for pound sterling and dollars. Britain and the United States had devalued, were off the gold standard, and apparently, there were more dollars and pound sterling obtainable for the gold. Were the gold boys from France after the dollars and the sterling? France was wavering but still on the gold standard. Congressman Hoeppel of California had pushed for silver. Silver and gold together would increase our currency value at home; the gold boys didn't like silver. Hoeppel didn't like the dollar devaluation to an eventual 50%. "The devaluation of gold at the ratio of $41.34 per ounce will actually reduce the war and private debts owing the United States by the European nations exactly 50 percent." The statutory devaluation of the dollar, much later, reached 50% of gold. "Unless the nations of Europe join us in devaluing gold at a stabilizing figure, the debts which our citizens owe to Europe, payable in gold, will be actually doubled." Hoeppel mentioned England's advantage in the dollar devaluation; "England produces 70 percent of the gold of the world." Hoeppel mentioned England's Rand mine; "the Rand mine in South Africa—produces, alone, one half of the gold production of the world." Hoeppel mentioned the recent visits to the White House by Montague Norman and J. P. Morgan. The "Internationalists" favored devaluation. The devaluation will "wipe out the war debts owed to the United States." It was the gold thing; the "farce" was doing the job! Hoeppel said, "The Federal

Reserve system should be abolished," and all the gold; it should be "sunk in the Atlantic . . . . The ideal monetary system would be paper money issued by the Government based entirely upon wealth."

The new administration was described as a rescue party in a *Wall Street Journal* article of May 15, 1934.

> The roughly $10,000,000,000 of extraordinary expenditures, scheduled by the federal Government; represents loans to banks, railroads, mortgage companies, farmers, home owners, and for PWA undertakings, etc., some of which are not good enough for private capital; but which the Government is making as a rescue party, and some of which are Government loans which private capital would like to make.

This statement was made by Hugh Knowlton, a partner of Kuhn, Loeb & Co. banking while speaking to CPAs in New York City. Mr. Knowlton said that private capital was there for capital improvements to the tune of $1,200,000,000. Mr. Knowlton blamed government legislation. "The remedy for this, according to Mr. Knowlton, is to supply capital through adequate amendment of the Securities Act and a tempering of the Stock Exchange Bill." Apparently, the price wasn't right for idle or locked up private money.

Knowlton's use of Roosevelt's 10 billion of public money and 1.2 billion of probable private money appeared a most significant set of numbers for Mr. Knowlton's presentation? Senator Byrnes of South Carolina said, "The Public Works Administration, with its loans for the construction of public-works projects in order to provide jobs for the unemployed, is a willful waste of public funds. It is a waste only if the money is not to be repaid." Byrnes admitted that public funds, for construction in his state, were never repaid; when this happens, the taxpayer pays the bill. Were the loans to the banks, the railroads, insurance companies, etc., headed to the sinkhole? Or would these public funds turn over and over as in privately loaned money? The private funds would exhibit velocity? Mr. Knowlton's 1.2 billion of private available money would transform into $10 billion of the banker's credits, loans, and deposits, the banker's money scheme, deposit money. Giveaways don't work; locked-up money doesn't work either, and pure capitalism was taking no prisoners. It was still no-redundancy time. At the time, it was active public money versus inactive private money. If and when private money gets active, the new money initially issued is public money. In any case, the perpetual debt was going up.

Reforms were needed; the money interests had wiped the slate clean. Government legislation plowed ahead, providing relief. "The Farm Mortgage Foreclosure Act" of June 11, 1934, provided loans to farmers; the farmers were able to reclaim property "owned by them prior to foreclosure." The "Homesteaders Relief Act" allowed people to leave the "homestead" unattended "to seek employment . . . to obtain the necessities of life" during the years 1932, 1933, and 1934. There was an "Air Mail Act" in June 1934; improvements were made related to interstate commerce. The "Collateral Security Act" got that one-year extension, and Roosevelt could extend it two more years if needed. This was the act whereby the Federal Reserve could use government securities as collateral for their "notes and credits," more ways to put money in circulation by way of public debt. The FDIC was amended in June 1934; deposit insurance was raised from $2,500 to $5,000. The Reconstruction Finance Corporation (RFC) was extended two more years, and directed "to purchase the obligations of the FDIC, on the request of the latter, to the extent of $250,000,000." It was more initial public funding for the benefit of the private banking corporations. It was a period of corporate and social welfare all around—RFC money to banks, insurance companies, railroads, industry, farmers, the unemployed, etc. The RFC was set up during the Hoover administration to spike the economy. This federal agency purchased or discounted obligations, debentures, stocks, and commercial paper held by banks, railroads, and insurance companies. These obligations, debentures, etc., apparently, was commercial paper the Federal Reserve System didn't accept for rediscount after 1929. The debentures were probably the foreign bonds purchased in the 1920s, which sent many a Federal Reserve Note to Europe. As of March 1934, the RFC had "advanced" a total of $5.7 billion. According to the *Journal* of June 11, 1934, the "Government Owns Shares in One-Third of U.S. Banks." According to the latest figures, there were 15,406 operating banks. Eight thousand six hundred nineteen banks were still not members of the Federal Reserve System, and why was that? The *Journal* reported that "5,190 banks have sold stock, capital notes or debentures to the Government."

In addition to the relief acts, there were municipal and corporate bankruptcy acts; the FCC, the Federal Communications Commission, was created. "Six Federal Crime Control Acts" were approved in May 1934; the acts provided punishment for offenses against "federal officers," extortion using wire services, kidnapping, fleeing across state lines avoiding prosecution, prison mutiny, and offenses against the Federal Reserve System. There were labor, liquor, insurance acts, and the "Kick Back Racket Act." Labor got a boost during the Roosevelt administration. The Wagner Act of 1935 established the National Labor Relations Board. Collective bargaining was allowed; there would now be bargaining between management and union representatives. Roosevelt wanted to enlarge the Supreme Court, "stack" it in his favor; he was defeated in that maneuver.

The Roosevelt administration created a multitude of bureaus, commissions, and organizations from the AAA to the FHA to the PWA to the WPA, thirty-seven new government agencies. Roosevelt's welfare blitz was government counter to the inaction of the encompassing pure capitalistic state. In 1913, the country's money stock was $3.7 billion. In1934, the money stock was $13.6 billion, an increase of 368% since 1913. The circulation of money in 1934 was $5.4 billion. The comparative circulation of money per capita change during the same period showed an increase of 23% ($35 to $43). The population increase over the period was 31% (97 million to 127 million people). The total stock of money outpaced a necessary circulation. A dearth of money among the population existed; 30% of the people didn't have any money. Why the lack of circulation? The money stock apparently grew, where it always would, in the East, in the big New York banks in tandem with government, in the Treasury, and the twelve Federal Reserve banks. The money disparity continued; the twelve Federal Reserve banks and the Treasury were supposed to distribute credits, foster security, and eliminate default. It didn't happen; otherwise, why the need of scrip and barter throughout the land? The per capita figure was/is arbitrary. The remaining 70% of the people supposedly had money; this translates to a per capita figure of $61. But less than

5% of the people owned, controlled, or held probably 90% of the circulation. Seventy percent of the people, or 89 million, had money; and 5% or 4.5 million owned 90% of the $5.4-billion circulation or $4.9 billion. Five percent or the wealthy possessed most of the money, a per capita figure of $1,089, say, $1,100 ($4.9 billion divided by 4.5 million people). The remaining 65% or 84.5 million people possessed a per capita of $6.0. At that time, a working man with a family of four made about $25 a week. Isn't it probable, considering the lack of unequal currency distribution, deflation, sinkhole money, idle or locked up money, and American currency in Europe, a realistic per capita number in America may have been the following? The above figures are based on U.S. annual Treasury report money.

- Thirty percent of the people had zero money.
- Sixty-five percent of the people had $6 per capita, and
- Five percent of the people had $1,100 per capita.

The early twentieth century saw the physical money grow five times, four times more than the population. Yet an economic depression occurred in the United States in the 1930s. Along with unequal distribution, pure capitalism exhibited its grand international performance. Too few controlled the country's credits; domestic credits were diminished, and too many credits were shipped out of the country. From the debates in the Congress and the testimonies, the Federal Reserve and international central banks with their accumulated gold had set up shop and apparently were in control of the world economies. The above money amounts, population and circulation figures were taken from page 368 of the 1934 annual Treasury report in the Madison Building, Room 201, the Law Library Reading Room, Library of Congress. Henry Morgenthau Jr. was the secretary of the Treasury.

The gold was going to London; the gold was coming back to the United States. As of June 5, 1934, an increase of $760 million in gold was imported during the year, mostly to New York. Based on $35 an ounce, the latest gold stock in the United States was worth $7.8 billion. The previous worth was 4.6 billion based on the price of $20.7 an ounce; this was reported in the *Journal*. The previous year, the United States exported more gold, the stocks going to "France, Sweden, Norway,

Switzerland, Italy and Czechoslovakia." The next day, June 6, 1934, Neville Chamberlain, prime minister of England, notified, as reported in the *Journal*, that the latest debt payment to the United States could not be made; France and Italy would follow suit. The debt burden of the World War I remained; all the European countries owed their central banks. All the countries were debtors. England was a debtor to the United States; France was a debtor to Great Britain and the United States. Great Britain and the United States were creditors but also owed their central banks. Germany owed everybody.

From the *New York Times* bureau in Berlin: "British Debt Note Pleases Germany." From the German

> Rheiniscche—Westfaelische Zeitung, organ of heavy industry, writes: For England to resume payments to America, she would naturally have to demand payments from her own debtors. The British debtors would turn again to their own debtors, and at the end of the chain hangs Germany, which was supposed to meet the debts of the entire world. Every American knows today that this is impossible.

There had been a recent "debt conference." In Germany, one official remarked, "All we have to do is substitute 'Germany' for 'Great Britain' in the British note and our case is perfect." The paper exclaimed, "Dr Hjalmar Schacht has also opened a drive for a re-adjustment of payments on the Reich loans, including the Dawes and Young loans." The *New York Times* reported, "The whole press supports with approval the arguments presented in the British note that a reopening of the pre-moratorium system of collecting from Peter to pay Paul would be utterly disastrous at this time, when recovery seems just around the corner."

What were the debts in 1934? United States federal debt had grown to about 28 billion; with foreign debt owed, the total was $40 billion. European debt exceeded $200 billion. It was the continuing international scene since World War I, since all wars, unending debt. World depression dried up the money, compounding the problem; big debts had to be paid with diminished credits! Was devaluation the way to go? Currency, the money, the exchange was needed to get things going. Credits, first the credits, credits were needed; how to get the credits? *Devalue gold!* England devalued first. Devaluation was a key part of Roosevelt's recovery program.

The "note" from the prime minister appeared to stir things up. The *New York Times* (June 6, 1934) listed editorials from fourteen leading newspapers from across the country, from New York to Hartford, Connecticut; to Dallas, Texas; to Los Angeles, California. In New York: *The Herald Tribune*, "The British End the Farce"; *The News,* "The Note Seems Reasonable"; *The Sun,* "John Bull Defaults." In Philadelphia, PA.: *The Inquirer*; "Britain Disperses War-Debt Fog." In Washington D. C. *The Star*, "Challenge to All Governments." In Portland, Ore. *The Oregonian*,

> We Have Tied Debts to Trade . . . . We have ourselves more definitely than ever before tied foreign debts payments and foreign trade together and can have neither in full measure. Reciprocal tariff legislation cannot be broadly effective unless some change is now initiated by ourselves in the debt situation.

President Roosevelt had a special day during this period. Franklin Roosevelt was a navy man; he had been the assistant secretary of the navy, under President Wilson, from 1913 to 1920. The United States Navy sailed eighty-one warships from the West Coast, arriving in New York Harbor on June 1, 1934. Battleships, cruisers, destroyers, and aircraft carriers sailed the "6300 miles." The *New York Times* covered the event; the headline called it the great naval pageant. The *Times* coverage included several pages of articles and pictures of the "magnificent ships." New York City welcomed thirty-five thousand sailors for an extended period; the navy was expected to stay "18 days." President Roosevelt "reviewed" the fleet aboard the cruiser *Indianapolis*. Naval officers from the major foreign countries, including officers from Japan and Germany, were there. Most of these ships, especially the battleships, were at Pearl Harbor on December 7, 1941.

What was the "Securities Exchange Act of 1934"? The *Wall Street Journal* called it a "Stock Measure." On June 7, 1934, the headline read, "President Signs Stock Measure." It was an act to regulate the stock market. This was the legislation Mr. Knowlton of Kuhn, Loeb & Co. mentioned. In 1929, a seat on the exchange cost "$650,000." A Wall Street insider said that it was the "largest gambling house in the world . . . owned and controlled by its broker members." The players were called boobs. The boobs didn't know anything; they were manipulated by the brokers. Congress, again, would control the money game; Wall Street would be transformed from one of absolute speculation to one of ethical investment. In the Congress, it was the Fletcher-Rayburn bill. Senator Fletcher was chairman of the Senate Banking and Currency Committee; Rayburn was chairman of the House Interstate Commerce Commission. In New York, "Curb Exchange Cooperation Pledged," this from "E. Burd Grubb, president of the New York Curb Exchange . . . . With the signature of President Roosevelt, the Securities Exchange Act of 1934 becomes effective." The Securities and Exchange Commission (SEC) followed "to protect the public from investing in unsafe securities and to regulate stock market practices."

The federal trade commissioner, James M. Landis, speaking in Chicago, was "hopeful." The *Wall Street Journal* described his remarks as "orderly, efficient and honest market operating on an investment, rather than a speculative basis, and full and continued disclosure of the character of offerings made; he said, however, that these hoped for results will not be overnight products, but the result of years of sustained and equitable administration." Mr. Landis said,

> It seems to me that the prospect of selling securities under appropriate regulation, with the least possible interference to honest business, is a bright one . . . . The prescribed margin requirements are conservative and only slightly in excess of those now demanded under the regulations of the New York stock exchange itself.

The *New York Times* headline read, "Margin Provisions Of Exchange Bill Seen As Moderate." The bill wasn't going into effect until October first. "Traders will take advantage of the clause permitting brokers to lend up to 100 per cent of the lowest price since July 1, 1933, provided the loan is not more than 75 per cent more than the prevailing market price." Year 1934 proved an improvement over the 1933 act. The *Times* reported,

> While it would have been preferable to have met 100 per cent the valid criticisms of the original act, and to have freed directors and bankers entirely from unjust liability, nevertheless, what has been accomplished by the amendments is of the very greatest importance and should result in an immediate stimulus to financing aid to recovery and re-employment.

Under the heading, "TOPICS IN WALL STREET, 'The Affiliates Go,'" the article covered the Guaranty Trust Company, the Chase National Bank, and the National City Bank. All three affiliates of these banks were "dissolving." The Guaranty Trust Company was the last to go.

> The Chase National Bank and The National City Bank, [J. P. Morgan] had already announced plans for the winding up of their security companies. None of the three names which bulked so large in the heavy financing days of the Twenties is to be perpetuated . . . It will seem a little strange to find on the offering notices of the future none of the big names that dominated the scene a few years ago,

this coverage from the *New York Times*, June 7, 1934. The Glass-Steagall Act of 1933 dissolved the affiliates.

The Senate Banking and Currency Committee held hearings during the period. The big banks were summoned: Kuhn, Loeb & Co., Dillon, Read and Company, J. P. Morgan, etc. Morgan admitted not paying taxes during the years 1930, 1931, and 1932; "our capital losses [deductible under the law, just as previously the profits had been added] were such as more than to wipe out all our income, and leave nothing taxable." The record showed that Morgan, since 1917, had paid $51 million in federal income tax.

"BIDS OF 7 BILLIONS ON TREASURY ISSUES." A *New York Times* front-page article covered the bids of government offerings of long-term bonds. The Treasury was probably paying off short-term debt by borrowing long; this is done all the time. The lead article said the offerings were "Subscribed More Than Eight Times." These were "cash subscriptions." It was June 7, 1934. It was the amount of the cash offering; it was the "Huge Reserves" of the banks that made the news. Morgenthau, in his 1934 report, listed a total of $13.6 billion, including gold bullion, total money in the country. Of the total money stock, $7.5 billion was outside the Treasury; of that amount, $5.4 billion was in circulation. Yet 7 billion in cash was subscribed for the bonds; the long-term interest rate was 3%. The good reception of bids was not expected on the government bonds "because of the large borrowings expected to obtain funds to carry forward the recovery program." What were the totals in cash money in the country? No doubt, hordes of existing cash existed in the big banks, and Roosevelt was printing new money for his recovery programs. How much money was outside the Treasury? Who knows? The main thing, credits, money would remain unavailable; the country's economy was only partially viable in the east. The Depression continued elsewhere. A devastating Midwest drought didn't help; wheat, cattle, about 125,000 families were affected. It was the time of the famous "dust bowl." Although famine was ruled out, Roosevelt asked for a $500-million appropriation to aid the stricken areas.

The credit circulation was beginning to take a future form; it wouldn't be complete for awhile, but it was getting there. "TREASURY TO ISSUE NEW PAPER MONEY . . . . A Billion Pieces Will Be Replaced With Face Value of $4,800,000,000 Within Five Years." It was June 7, 1934, this from the *New York Times*. The "replaced" paper money would consist of four currencies, the Federal Reserve Note, the gold certificate, the silver certificate, and the United States Note. The 1913-1933 Federal Reserve Note was a banker's note; on its face contained the words "Redeemable in gold on demand at the United States Treasury or at any Federal Reserve Bank." The "replaced" Federal Reserve Note would contain the words, "This note is legal tender for all debts, public and private, and is redeemable in the lawful money at the United States Treasury or at any Federal Reserve Bank." Gold was out of the picture for the Federal Reserve Note; it was not redeemable in gold anymore to the citizen. The article said this: "The gold clause will be eliminated; that is, there will be no statement of the promise to redeem paper in gold." The new "silver certificate will be issued in denominations $1,

$5 and $10, backed by the new policy of the purchase of all newly mined silver by the Treasury. Officials emphasized that there would be no change in the intrinsic value or purchasing power of paper money." The possession of gold certificates was illegal; this was the only reference to gold certificates other than that gold certificates were legal tender. The United States notes would be legal tender, not good for customs and not good for interest on the public debt. The United States Note was the lawful money, the "greenback." And so within five years, the four paper currencies above would make up the paper currency. The article did not include that gold certificates were issued to the Federal Reserve banks in $100,000 denominations as substitutes for gold. All four currencies would be legal tender. The circulation was given as "$5,370,000,000."

The $100,000 gold certificates were part of the transfer of gold from the Federal Reserve banks to the Treasury, the certificates going to the reserve banks as a reserve for gold. These gold certificates were "payable to bearer on demand as authorized by law." The reserve banks would also receive the new lawful money. These two currencies were substitute "reserves" for gold by the Gold Reserve Act of January 30, 1934.

According to the latest amendment to the Federal Reserve Act, the gold certificates and the lawful money greenbacks were replacement "reserves" for the currency circulation as part of the Gold Reserve Act of 1934. Actual future circulating currency would be primarily the new legal tender Federal Reserve Notes and the silver certificates. The big change—there would be no more redemption of paper money for gold. The whirlwind period appeared over. The Federal Reserve Note had done the job C. W. Barron said it was going to do; the non-legal tender Federal Reserve Note had accumulated the gold. The gold was owned by the Federal Reserve banks. In 1934, President Roosevelt hauled in the gold and transferred the gold to the Treasury. After approximately 142 years since Alexander Hamilton, the accumulation of gold with paper money was over? Not really!

Before devaluation, what was the total value of gold in the world? The value in dollars had to be changing. The United States gold stock had increased from $4.6 to $7.8 billion because of devaluation.

Great Britain had devalued. Later in Chapter 16, we get an idea of the value.

Conditions were different in France. There was no unemployment in France compared to the United States, Great Britain, and Germany. There were "enormous financial reserves" in France, but the reserves didn't belong to the government. There were massive debts; that apparently was the problem. More than half the government payroll was wages and pensions and pensions for "orphans" of war veterans. More than six million people were on the "Government of National Union" payroll. Borrowing from the Bank of France had to be stopped; therefore, a deflation policy was favored. Wages, pensions would all be cut back. Three French factions were against this policy, the Socialists, the Communists, and the General Federation of Labor. These three groups would make no impact collectively because they "hated" each other. "Mr. Roosevelt has shown that devaluation may be tried as a remedy. But apart from a few economists and industrialists, devaluation has no appeal here." France was going the way of deflation; "France had been through inflation and devaluation. She is now completing her experience by deflation. It is not a pleasant one." The above was taken from the *Wall Street Journal* of June 6, 1934. France, according to the article, favored the "Old Deal." The old deal was gold. According to the latest world figures, in June 1934, the United States and France held two-thirds of the world's gold.

Germany didn't want devaluation; that is, Dr. Hjalmar Schacht did not favor devaluation. According to the *Wall Street Journal*, "advocates of devaluation are mainly exporting interests while opponents are headed by Dr. Hjalmar Schacht, President of the Reichsbank." Schacht had succeeded in obtaining Adolf Hitler's approval, but "for how long . . . . The issue will depend upon the development of German foreign trade and Germany's ability to secure imports of raw materials which are necessary for the development of industrial activity within the country, which is the principal aim of Government authorities." In his *Confessions*, Schacht had complained of Germany's lack of exports; according to Schacht, reparation payments couldn't be maintained by Germany because of an imbalance of payments. Germany had constantly borrowed to make reparation payments. America borrows in 2007-2010 to accommodate the imbalance of payments

Things were happening that first week in June 1934. There was the big naval splash in New York; the Securities Act was passed, and the Treasury announced a future streamlining of the currency with new paper issues. The security affiliates of the big banks had "dissolved," and there was lots of government borrowing.

A *Wall Street Journal* article was critical of the Treasury's course, that it was inflationary. It was "U.S. Securities and U.S. Credit." It was "Taking Both Capital and Credit." So what was happening? Actually, the Treasury had control of the market, and why was that? The answer could be found in the article; "it is interesting to observe that the dearth of new private security flotations has given the National Government a virtual monopoly on the capital supply." This article was a perfect example of the period. The private side was doing zilch; apparently, not enough profit was there, or nothing was there for 30% of the people. The Roosevelt administration had taken the initiative; it was a time of "recovery." Recovery was the government projects; the private sector wasn't part of any recovery program or didn't or wouldn't initiate a recovery program. The Treasury was borrowing both ways by fiat credit and capital credit. Apparently, Mr. Bernard Kilgore who wrote the article had a problem? He didn't approve of the happenings. His problem, apparently, was private capital wasn't moving; private capital wasn't getting its interest rate. The title of his article was "Treasury Orthodoxy More Apparent Than Real—Borrowing Fiat Bank Credit as Well as Capital."

What is fiat credit? Fiat credit is when the Treasury is borrowing newly printed money. Previously, Chairman Black said he was in agreement with Roosevelt's credit policy. The central bank was "purchasing" government securities; Chairman Black was printing new currency for Roosevelt's spending programs. The government was borrowing money; this was fiat credit. This fiat credit is part of the debt process; the new currency is interest bearing, the government's obligation. The fiat credit security goes directly to the Federal Reserve coffer. The Federal Reserve System winds up owning the security, principal, and interest as a part of government public debt; it is part of the currency creation scheme. Capital credit is also Treasury-borrowing government debt, but the people are lending, purchasing the security.

Capital credit is the other form of borrowing; the Treasury borrows currency already in circulation.

Why did the fiat thing continue as a money interest lament? There was the problem? The capital interests didn't like the fiat process; it was Roosevelt's spending thing. Roosevelt was putting currency in circulation by way of fiat credit. Mr. Kilgore's inactive private capital credit was not this fiat credit. There was a dearth of Mr. Kilgore's money. Yesterday's $5 billion may become today's $10 billion. But 10 billion in money didn't reproduce itself. Five billion new dollars has to be printed. Money is printed, created; currency is created against wealth, equity, because of an increase in production. In 1934, it was Roosevelt's spending programs. Society grows; money is produced and augments that growth. Deposits and credits may multiply the money ten to twenty times; that's the resultant activity, the product. It is part of the capitalization process. But currency has to be printed; the money has to be created initially. That's what Alexander Hamilton did in 1791; he started the first central bank to print money, to generate money. By law, he had the first central bank print its bank paper currency. In Hamilton's time, it was the banker's fiat approved by the First United States Congress. In 1934, it resembled a U.S. Treasury's fiat, but it was still bank currency. What was Mr. Kilgore's problem? Apparently, in 1934, the Treasury had a "monopoly" on fiat credit and capital credit. In June 1934, the price, apparently, wasn't good enough on the private side; there was a "dearth of new private security flotations."

Roosevelt was moving along. The president delivered a message to the Congress on June 9, 1934. The housing bill was a big issue. The mortgage debt in 1934 totaled $43 billion; half of which was home ownership. Foreclosures were running 20,000 to 25,000 a month. Roosevelt had "three great objectives—security of the home, the security of livelihood, and the security of social insurance." President Roosevelt was pushing the housing bill, but he was also laying the groundwork for future Social Security. "Fear and worry based on unknown danger contribute to social unrest and economic demoralization. If, as our Constitution tells us, our federal Government was established among other things, 'to promote the general welfare,' it is our plain duty to provide for that security upon which welfare depends." The

Social Security Act became law in 1935. In 1934, the "housing bill" was passed; it was the National Housing Act. This act created the "Federal Savings and Loan Insurance Corporation, the Federal Housing Authority, and the Federal National Mortgage Association." It was government initiative, first with public money together with private capital to put life back in the housing market in the United States. Since the beginning and before the 1930s, the "general welfare" in the United States had exhibited a predominance of wealth controlled and owned by few. President Roosevelt apparently believed the "general welfare" in the United States, by the Constitution, should exhibit a social side, maybe an obtainable share in the wealth for more people. Anything with a social connection is adverse to capitalism.

The emergency legislation of 1933 was another correction. The emergency was for two years, but the legislation enacted in 1933 and 1934 was continually extended. With each new session of Congress, the emergency legislation was extended another two years. The devaluation of the dollar was extended into the 1940s; it remained at $35 an ounce of gold. As part of the extension of emergency powers, Roosevelt devalued silver by 13¢ an ounce. This move was "the administration's policy of stabilization in monetary affairs." The Treasury's profit was almost $8 million. The *Times* of January 1, 1938, reported "Silver Bloc Defied." The collateral for Federal Reserve Notes was extended into the 1940s; the direct obligations of the United States was the collateral for the printing of the currency, a pyramid on top of a pyramid. The Federal Reserve Act was constantly being amended; a most important change was added. In addition to the issue of the country's currency, the twelve reserve banks could now make loans. The administration of the Reconstruction Finance Corporation was extended into the 1940s. Every year, there was an amended revenue act; the tax rolls were constantly being changed in the search for more revenue. Actually, the emergency legislation of 1933 remained in place as President Roosevelt and his administration approached the 1940s.

Franklin Roosevelt was elected to a second term in 1936; his opponent was Alf M. Landon, a Kansas Republican. The election was never close. Roosevelt received 61% of the popular vote; the electoral count was 523-8. It was a "landslide victory." The pure capitalists didn't like

Roosevelt, but, apparently, the election showed the people did. The times were looking better in the year 1936. Roosevelt had put people to work in the Works Progress Administration (WPA). What was the effect? Unfortunately, better times didn't last long. Everything, apparently, came to a screeching halt in 1937; there was a recession. It was no-redundancy time on top of no-redundancy time.

Congressman Wilburn Cartwright of Oklahoma received a letter from retired ex-senator Robert Owen from Oklahoma. The time was January 6, 1938. It was the Seventy-fifth Congress, Session 3. Senator Owen was responding to a request from Congressman Cartwright. Remember Senator Owen? It was Robert Owen and Carter Glass who put the Federal Reserve Act together in 1913. Cartwright felt if anyone could explain the financial problems confronting the country, it was Senator Owen. Cartwright presented Owen's letter in the House: "His letter should be read by every member of the Congress."

"All depressions are caused by the contraction of the money supply." These opening words summarized Senator Owen's opinion. Parts of his letter tell the story:

- The Federal Reserve Board, the reserve banks, and the Republican Party planned the contraction of the money supply in 1920. Inflation of the currency was presented as a problem.
- This action was part of the Republican platform of the 1920 election; it was to be a courageous and intelligent contraction of credit and currency. Senator Harding, the Republican nominee, presented the plan at the convention in his acceptance speech.
- The Federal Reserve Board and directors of the reserve banks secretly decided on the contraction of the currency; the amount of the contraction was not made public at the time of the convention.
- Five billion dollars in currency and credit was the amount of the contraction. The eventual result was the 1921 depression.
- The reason for the contraction? It was done to lower the cost of living.

- The depression of 1921 increased the purchasing power of money in terms of commodities and labor 80% within twelve months.
- The American people lost $15 billion in national income.
- The value of farms dropped more than $20 billion.

Lowering the cost of living meant reducing the cost of everything. Apparently, the abundance of commodities remained; only the money disappeared. Those who contract the currency allow their possession of money to purchase the commodities and lost properties at the low deflationary price. Dr. Commons, in 1927, before the Senate Banking and Currency Committee, confirmed the intent and action of the Federal Reserve Board in 1919 and 1920. Two anonymous Federal Reserve Board members were the confirmation.

The Federal Reserve banking system was supposed to be a public servant; it had become a dangerous public enemy. Senator Owen said, "I forecast this depression on May 18, 1920, on the floor of the Senate."

On May 18, 1920, during the Sixty-sixth Congress, Session 2, in the Senate, Senator Owen said,

> The Federal Reserve Board is taking its advice from those who think there ought to be a deflation of credit in this country. Certainly I am not in favor of inflation; I am not in favor of speculation; but I want to say to the Senate that if this policy is pursued of broadly deflating the credits of this country there can be only one result, that of depression and ruin to many.

Was it coincidence that more than $2 billion in Federal Reserve Notes were removed from circulation, and the Federal Reserve accumulated gold during this period of deflation? Owen said,

> There are two ways open for lowering prices. The best way is to increase commodities by stimulating both production and saving and letting credits for such purposes. That is the best way; that is the true way—to work and to save and to

give men credit who need to have credit for the purpose of working, for the purpose of creating value.

Then there was 1929 reactionaries who controlled the Federal Reserve Board and the reserve banks; they contracted credit to the businessmen of the country on the theory of controlling speculation by raising the interest rates to a prohibitive point and permitting fantastic rates on call money in the security exchanges.

Congressmen McFadden and Patman were most critical of the Federal Reserve System. These two frustrated congressmen didn't call them reactionaries; they called the members of the Federal Reserve System and the Treasury other names. McFadden wanted to impeach them.

- Herbert Hoover was warned of this action in May 1929.
- The most violent contraction of credit took place in 1929-1932.
- Twenty billion in loans, deposits, and money supply was contracted. The farmers were ruined again; 100 billion of the market price of stocks were lost.
- Check money was reduced two-thirds.
- Hoarding resulted; bank deposits remained in the banks.
- Scrip money and barter exchange surfaced.
- Fifteen million people were unemployed.

The Depression was in full swing in 1933; the crash of 1929 cleaned house, but the destruction of the credits (1929-1932) by the banking system solidified the Great Depression. The money wasn't there, but potential money was there! Again, there would be no credits. It was deflation time in spades; Farms and estates were purchased at a fraction of their original worth. Redundancy time affected about 25% of the population. A majority managed with less, and the few owned the wealth; incredibly, lots of things were happening. As 1936 emerged, Hollywood was beginning its peak. There was Walt Disney and Mickey Mouse; people listened to the radio shows, the news broadcasts. It was a time for music; the recording industry was growing. It was a time of romance, the movies and this with little money. It was the big band era; swing was the thing. New model cars rolled off the Detroit assembly line every year; professional baseball was the national pastime. The baseball teams in those days existed where the money and the people of wealth were predominant, in New York, in the Northeast, to Chicago and St. Louis. There were no baseball teams in the South, in the Southwest, in the Northwest; there was no real money there. But college football swept the country, and there was the sport of kings, horse racing, and golf with Bobby Jones. All this was happening, but it was tough finding a job. During this time, there was the other society within the society; it was Black America, somewhat silent, in the background, segregated, taking the hits. Black America was struggling but doing many of the same things, and doing them quite well. The large part of this society made up a large part of the 25% exclusion.

Owen's letter continued; it covered 1937:

- A recession was coming; this was prophesied by the Roosevelt opposition.
- The idea was to sell stocks that were going to fall in value.
- Cash would be needed; purchasing power would increase again during the deflationary period.
- President Roosevelt mentioned that liquid capital was not working. Roosevelt mentioned Andrew Jackson in his most recent address; it was the constant battle between government public policy and the money interests.
- Most unfortunately, Secretary Morgenthau and Chairman Eccles of the Federal Reserve Board warned the country against inflation and thereby justified the prophecy, which resulted in the sale of securities and the hoarding of demand bank deposits.
- Two billion physical dollars was contracted by the banking system.

The $2-billion currency contraction translated to a nonexistence of 20 billion in bank deposits and credits; the deposit money is discounted ten times over when credits are there. According to the experts, this money turns over many times in a year, the velocity of money. To make matters worse, because the period was called inflationary, the Reserve Board may raise interest rates in the process. Secretary Owen called it most unfortunate. C. W. Barron said the Federal Reserve would do things the people wouldn't like, and the Federal Reserve System was doing things people didn't like. It would appear, in looking back, the Federal Reserve System was like a Frankenstein; the government had created the monster, and the government couldn't or didn't want to deal with the monster.

- The money power has defeated the people in the public control of money over and over again. They defeated Bryan in 1896, in 1900, and in 1908 by the threat of a panic; and some of them are hoping for the defeat of democracy now by the Depression of 1937.
- The Roosevelt administration was being blamed for the panic, which the money speculators themselves had caused.
- Roosevelt's advisers were partly to blame.

With a prayer to the Congress and the president, Senator Owen closed his letter:

> After 5 years of this administration, which was going to drive the money changers out of the temple; we find that our Uncle Sam still prints the Federal Reserve notes, and gives them to the money changers through the Federal Reserve Banking System for seven-tenths of 1 cent per bill, the cost of printing.

Congressman William Lemke, in the House, served up his lament on January 6, 1938. Lemke said the cost of printing was the same whether a $1 bill or a $1,000 bill.

President Roosevelt made a lot of changes. He pumped a lot of currency (liquid capital) into the system; he put a lot of people to work in government projects. What was the total money he printed, about $10 billion? From *The Complete Book of U.S. Presidents*, "WPA employees constructed 125,000 public buildings, 650,000 miles of roads, 75,000 bridges, and numerous other public facilities." But the country had returned in 1937 to the economic quandary of 1933. Maybe President Roosevelt didn't or couldn't make enough changes; the monster was in control and still at large.

Marriner S. Eccles, chairman of the Federal Reserve Board, gave an address on December 14, 1937; the address "Factors in the Present Slump" was before the American Farm Bureau Federation. His address was extensive and comprehensive. Eccles agreed; there was recovery.

> From 1934 up to the last quarter of 1936, we had an orderly recovery movement . . . . The basic causes of the present situation are not to be found either in the capital-gains tax, the undistributed-profits tax, or in monetary policy; but as I have indicated, in the rapid price and cost advances of last winter and spring.

Chairman Eccles mentioned

> heavy Government expenditures giving a sharp additional impetus to consumer buying. The organizing campaign of labor, together with the drive for higher wages and shorter hours, added to expectations of higher prices. The rearmament program in various countries [prelude to World War II] contributed to the inflationary sentiment . . . We must recognize the fact that competition has declined and monopoly elements have increased over large sectors of our country. For example, it could only have been the absence of competition that permitted building costs to soar on the low volume of building that took place last spring . . . How are we to achieve and maintain full employment if private groups and organizations raise prices and costs whenever increased demand appears, although there is still an abundance of idle and unused manpower, plant facilities, and raw materials? Does this necessitate steady increases in consumer buying power through deficit spending? How long can we pursue such a course? Are we to attempt to return to a truly laissez faire economy?

What were the "alternatives"? Mr. Eccles refuted the claim

> that monetary policy has been primarily responsible for the present recession. They think that sterilization of incoming gold by the Treasury and the actions of the Board of

Governors of the Federal Reserve System in increasing the reserve requirements of member banks caused a reversal of the upward movement.

Did the "sterilization of gold" mean the useless storage of gold? "Increasing the reserve requirements of the member banks" was apparently Chairman Eccles's description of the Federal Reserve in-house banking thing, that is, transferring securities, taking the money out of circulation?

Credit is more important than money; people rarely saw the money they borrowed. It's that way today, and it was that way in the 1920s as set up by the Federal Reserve System. The following was a congressional record of how the Federal Reserve contracted the money supply:

> If you went to the bank to borrow, your loan was placed to your credit at the bank and you drew your checks against it. You saw very little of the money that your debt was supposed to represent. It was a system of bookkeeping. The debts were created, but the money did not go into circulation. When the Federal Reserve System was ready to contract, it simply stopped the issuance of bank credit, and you could not borrow from your bank any more. They [the Federal Reserve] had no bank credit to loan. It had been stopped by the system. There was about ten times as large an amount in debts due through the Federal Reserve System as there was money in circulation. It was only a matter of a short time after these debts were called for payment until all the money in the country was drawn into the Federal Reserve Banks, and still the larger proportion of the debts remained unpaid. Then the only way the people could get money with which to pay the debts or to purchase the necessities of life was to sell their products or their property. They [the Federal Reserve] held the money, and they owned the debts.

The money would disappear; there were no credits. Contraction, the diminishing of money and credits affects an economy; recession/

depressions occur. Collection time completes the redundancy. Money is lost; the casino clears the tables, and a new round of play begins.

By June 1939, the total stock of money in the United States was $23.8 billion. Sixteen billion of the total money was gold; the stock of gold in the United States had more than doubled since 1934 (more about this in Chapter Sixteen). The percentage of gold to the total money was 68%. What did this mean? The stock of gold was way over the required 40% reserve by 70%. Although, supposedly, there was no more payment in gold, the 40% gold thing was still in place. Couldn't the circulation have been increased by 70% and the credits and deposits ten times that? The total stock of money (23.8 billion) had almost doubled since 1934. The population, 131 million people, had increased just 2%. For what it's worth, the arbitrary per capita figure was $54. There were eleven million people out of work; these people didn't have $54 per person. There was a lot of money, and where was it? Where was it going, savings, more securities? Unemployment didn't continue because of a lack of potential money in the country. Other than public works, there was no apparent substantial market to support more credits in 1939. More autos and more housing could have been built in 1939; there were no credits. Credits abounded for war when more death and destruction was in the offing when World War II started.

Secretary Harold Ickes, secretary of the Interior, delivered a radio address on January 8, 1938. The address was delivered in Nashville, Tennessee, in honor of Andrew Jackson. The time, apparently, was right, the conditions in the country ripe to bring to light Jackson's famous struggle with Nicholas Biddle and the Second Bank of the United States. Jackson said no to a twenty-year recharter of the Second Bank. Andrew Jackson won the eventual political fight although big business, the money interests, the Congress, and Nicholas Biddle opposed him. Biddle and the bank were the economic political power over the government, the state banks, and the people; this was Jackson's view. "Henry Clay moved in the United States Senate a resolution of 'censure' of Jackson for violating the Constitution and the laws." Harold Ickes addressed Biddle's action; it was after Jackson had refused to grant a new bank charter.

Biddle was willing to wreck America. It was for him to precipitate a panic and this he proceeded to do. He reduced discounts, called in balances against State banks, limited bills of exchange to 60 days, raised exchange rates and rigged the financial sails so as to draw capital from the West and South to the East.

Who was running the country in 1832? Was it President Jackson and the government of the United States, or was it Nicholas Biddle and the Second Bank? President Jackson nixed the bank recharter; he paid off the public debt. And, ironically, Jackson did that primarily with paper currency, then there was the Specie Circular; the Treasury accepted only gold and silver thereafter. This was in 1836. But there was so little specie in the country. Biddle's handiwork did the rest. Biddle fractured the economy. Biddle took the paper currency out of circulation; gold left the country. There was no abundance of credits in the United States after 1837. It started the famous "Panic of 1837"; this was the country's gift to President Van Buren as he took office, a recession that lasted seven years. One hundred years later, a third central banking system was doing a similar thing, fostering a depression then a recession; there was no overabundance of credits in the United States in 1937. Before all this business, before 1837, in the early nineteenth century, the country was moving ahead. From the record, the primary exchange appeared to be the paper circulation by state banks and Biddle's banking system. Paper currency was moving the country, not gold and silver; the contradiction was there, holding. Gold and silver, mostly silver bullion, what there was of it, was in the vaults where it stayed. Daniel Webster said that; he also said there was virtually no gold in the country. If there was any gold, it was being shipped to England, to Europe.

There were many Jackson speeches heralding "Old Hickory" to the irritation of the pure capitalists. Andrew Jackson was right about the power of the Second Bank, but was Jackson right about specie or the lack thereof and its effect on the economy?

In 1937, was the country going back to the depths of 1933? "On November 20 [1937], the Christian Science Monitor published replies from 996 economists to four questions. The first question was: 'Is the 1929-32 depression likely to repeat itself at this juncture?'" The answer from eight hundred economists was "no." This was presented in an address by Msgr. John A. Ryan, DD., professor of social ethics at the Catholic University of America at Hartford, Connecticut. "What can be done to check and reverse the downward trend . . . tax relief, balancing the Federal Budget, restoration of confidence, and encouragement of capital investment"; these were the answers to the dilemma reported by the newspapers. Msgr. Ryan called them "ballyhoo remedies and I would condemn them all as futile, if not worse." Most of the economists agreed that taxation wasn't an issue; the confidence thing was "enormously overworked during the Hoover administration . . . confidence is at best a negative device." John Maynard Keynes referred to the "confidence" thing as rubbish. The last remedy was investment. "Investment in what?" Ryan said we didn't need "more factories, railroads or more banks. We are unable to sell all the products of those we have." So what were the reasons for the "slump"?

"First, the completion of the spending of the soldiers' bonus; second, the greatly reduced payments by the Government to WPA workers and a considerable reduction in other forms of Government spending." Government spending "helped to keep industry going." There was the case of "installment Buying." It was an "artificial stimulus"; it didn't last. "Another cause of the recession is the considerable rise which has taken place since 1936 in the prices of commodities." Ryan estimated "75 percent of the price increases have been unnecessary and unjustified." It was nothing more than "the deadly sin of greed." Last but not least, Msgr. Ryan said the recession "was bound to come sooner or later." Msgr. Ryan said, "The present decline is the accumulated effect of the unbalanced distribution of income and purchasing power."

The gap between capital and labor was huge in America. Too few had most of the income. What was this writing's previous approximate per capita estimate? It was $1,100 to $6 to no dollars. The published per capita figures always appear to be bogus. The big bucks of the few went to savings, to securities, etc. The big bucks didn't buy enough commodities; the "upper classes" didn't consume. This was part of Ryan's address. Labor, facing low wages and unemployment, apparently, wasn't going to make up the difference. President Roosevelt tried putting a dent in the pure capitalistic ethic; it wasn't working. Its money agent, apparently, was drying up the money supply again; the contraction gimmick was a built-in device. According to the numbers, that is, the number of people and the total money, there was a ton of money. But "we must bring about a better distribution of purchasing power and a better distribution of the national income as between capital and labor."

This was 1937; the United States and capitalism had done its thing. The beat went on; 146 years after Hamilton and the basic principle continued, whereby credits, money, and wealth was controlled by a central power, by few, the original intent, the principle of the Pennsylvania creditors. Roosevelt's Works Project Administration (WPA) put people to work, but it didn't end the unemployment problem. The pure capitalists, the opponents of the WPA, prevailed in 1942; the WPA was dissolved. The unemployment problem straightened out temporarily. The biggest market ever solved the problem; it was World War II. Unemployment in the United States during World War II was 1%.

In January 1938, the Japanese were advancing their war in China; Japan wanted to remove from Asia the mandated presence of the British, the Dutch, the French, and the Americans. The United States deployed the cruiser *Augusta* in Shanghai; the British maintained naval vessels in Chinese waters. Japanese aircraft attacked and sank the American gunboat *Panay* on December 12, 1937; the incident occurred on the Yangtze River. It was more provocation; it was another attack by Japan against the hated foreign presence in Asia. Adolph Hitler was beginning his taking back and overrun of Europe, putting the pressure on Great Britain and France. It had been twenty years since World War I. Another war was coming. People in the United States knew it; they sensed another involvement in a foreign war. There was a resolution introduced in the House by Louis Ludlow of Indiana; it was called the Ludlow Amendment. There was a movement in the House to amend the Constitution; should the people decide whether the country goes to war? It was a democracy; the people should have say in the matter? In a democracy, the people decide; it was a futile gesture. The United States was a republic, or is it a democracy? Is there a difference? In any event, the elected representatives decide such things. On December 21 in the *New York Times*, "President Roosevelt made it clear today that he was not for a policy of peace at any price. The American People want peace, he said, but 'ultimate security' cannot be assured by a blind policy of isolation." The newspaper reported that Alf M. Landon and Frank Knox, Republican opponents in the '36 election, had supported Roosevelt in "the diplomatic crisis with Japan." There was an "article in the New York Times of January 9, 1938, containing a statement issued by 14 church leaders in support of the Ludlow war referendum resolution." President Roosevelt and his administration were against the Ludlow resolution. The resolution came to a vote on January 10, 1938; the resolution was defeated.

The industrialized countries were rearming, gearing up in spite of the costs. "Britain Leads Race To Rebuild Navies"; the race was on. A *New York Times* article on December 21, 1937, produced excerpts from the "year book of the world's navies, 'Jane's Fighting Ships.'" Great Britain led the pack; "Japan, Italy, France, Germany quicken the pace in completing large fleets, review says." The United States "Lags in Construction." The thirty-five-thousand-ton fast battleship was supreme; this ship type was being built by all the naval powers. Cruisers, aircraft carriers, destroyers followed; these new ships were bigger, faster, and with more firepower than their predecessors. The Japanese, in secret, were building the two largest battleships ever constructed: sixty-thousand-ton monsters with eighteen-inch guns. Japan, at one time threatened by Admiral Perry, had learned her lessons well; Japan had become the formidable naval power in the Far East. It was insanity again but in greater proportions. The United States was building up the navy, but the country was way behind the others. It seemed the American people were interested in other things like, trying to get a job, getting on and off relief, dancing to swing music, listening to the radio shows Jack Benny, Fred Allen, *Amos 'n' Andy*, *The Shadow*, and *Gang Busters*. People went to the movies for 10¢; great films were made during this period. Year 1938 was the year Lou Gehrig became ill and had to leave the Yankees. It was the year of the great match race; Seabiscuit beat War Admiral at Pimlico. The exhibit of the future, the New York "Worlds Fair" of 1939-1940, was in the offing.

The naval fleets and the world's perpetual indebtedness was growing; what of Germany's indebtedness? Germany was rearming with what money? Germany's foreign creditors, including American banks, weren't getting paid? In 1933, the Dawes Plan was transferred to the Young Plan. Only interest on the Young Plan would be paid; the Young Plan payments and "other loans was to be postponed." This from Hjalmar Schacht's *Confessions*. Later in 1934, Schacht would tell Roosevelt that the interest on the Young Plan loans wouldn't be paid. Germany at that time, apparently, wasn't paying anybody anything? "The stopping of interest payments meant, of course, that the foreign creditors suffered considerable loss." Schacht stated that he wanted to do something about it. German debtors would not get off the hook; they would have to pay their debts, but high tariffs had eliminated 90% of German exports. To counter the problem, Hjalmar Schacht created the "Conversion Fund and the 'Mefo Bills.'" There was idle money, "unused capital lying fallow in business concerns." The conversion fund involved the German debtors, foreign creditors, the Reichsbank, and the Golddiskontbank (the gold discount bank). German debtors paid their foreign debts to the Reichsbank in marks; the foreign creditor received their credit in marks only. The Golddiskontbank, by permission of the Reichsbank, bought the credits at half their value. Schacht said,

> Dealings in these vouchers for mark credits, known as Scrips, soon became very lively. The profit accruing from the fifty per cent saving went to the promotion of export. Germany's use of the Scrips to pay for additional exports gave the creditor countries an interest in buying as many goods as possible from Germany in order to preserve or increase Germany's ability to transfer payments.

Is this why Schacht refused to discontinue supposed payment in gold within Germany? The purchase of the foreign credits by the gold discount bank made the scrip and/or vouchers more attractive? What was the purpose? There was the claim that "the German motive was to gain political control of foreign countries by making them economically dependent on Berlin." The foreign creditor could "only make purchases in goods in the debtor country," which was Germany. Secretary Morgenthau was critical of Schacht's schemes when commenting before the Senate Banking and Currency Committee in June of 1945. It was the "economic warfare period of the 1930's."

According to Schacht, the Mefo bills got German industry going. The Mefo bills were short-term securities. From Schacht's "Confessions, the name Mefo derives from Metal-Forschungs A.G. [Metal Research Company Limited], a limited company founded, at the instigation of the Government, by the four big firms Siemens, Gutehoffnungsshutte, Krupp and Rheinstahl." The state's credit was behind the Mefo bills. "The Reichsbank declared its willingness to exchange these bills at any time for ready cash over the counter." The "money lying idle in the safes and cashboxes of business firms" surfaced; the idle money was attracted by the 4% interest-bearing short-term securities, which, after a couple years, "had risen to twelve billion marks." According to Schacht, the securities took the place of cash, turning over and over again. The Mefo bills financed German industry and rearmament from 1934 into World War II. Germany was also building the new superhighway, the autobahn. Schacht, apparently, was working to improve the economic conditions in Germany. At the same time, Hitler was coming down hard on German Jews; concentration camps were filling up with persecuted Jews.

Conditions in the United States appeared in stalling mode. The latest census showed between 7.8 and 10.8 million people still unemployed in America. This was reported in the New York Times on January 2, 1938. A big issue in the early 1939 Congress was the debate over additional money appropriations for relief of destitute families. President Roosevelt, in his latest message to the Congress, asked "for $790,000,000 for a five-month relief plan." Congressman Alexander of Minnesota would eliminate the WPA work relief programs "by eliminating the foreign imports coming into this country." Alexander gave an example whereby the "10,000,000 people on relief" could be put to honest employment by eliminating imports, no doubt a hard sell. In addition to Roosevelt's five-month job relief plan, there was Social Security.

Along with Social Security, unemployment insurance became law. This was the headline as reported in the New York Times: "36,000,000

On Roll Of Social Security." Twenty-one million people were "eligible for unemployment insurance." The list included 1.6 million aged, 514,000 children, and the blind numbered 44,000. The *Times* reported "140,000" people in New York City were seeking help.

> The division of placement and unemployment insurance of the State Labor Department got its first concrete indication of the extent of joblessness in the metropolitan area yesterday when 140,000 filled-out applications for unemployment insurance benefits cascaded into the division's offices at 342 Madison Avenue.

As reported in the *New York Times*, it was a time of "Labor's Fight For Equity." The Supreme Court had "validated the Federal Labor Relations Act and the Social Security Act and also State unemployment compensation and minimum wage laws." It was January 3, 1938.

War had begun in Europe. It was the Spanish Civil War; it started in July of 1936. As described in *World Book*, rebellion initiated in Morocco; Spain was to be a monarchy or a republican form of government? The "Communists, socialists, trade unions and the liberals" made up the Republican side and were in power when war started; this Republican group was called the loyalists. The "army leaders, the monarchists, and Catholic groups" favored a monarchy. In the Spanish Civil War, the loyalists fought the "rebel" army of General Francisco Franco. It was Communism and Socialism against the monarchy. Germany and Italy supported Franco; Communistic Russia "sent aid" to the "loyalists," and "loyalist sympathizers from the United States and many other countries" fought in Spain for the loyalists. The war lasted three years. Franco won the war and assumed a dictatorship until 1975. The war was costly; "several hundred thousand died." Destruction was widespread. The Spanish Civil War ended in April 1939. World War II followed. Franco remained neutral during World War II; Franco was sympathetic to German interests early but changed over to the Allies late in the war. Spain in 1939 was equivalent to third world status; Spain was no longer the nation of world dominance that existed in the fifteenth and sixteenth centuries. *World Book* described Spain at the time as a poor country.

Meanwhile in the Senate, Senator Harry Flood Byrd had objected to Roosevelt's latest intended spending spree. There were letters of exchange between Senator Byrd and Chairman Marriner Eccles. "The way to get money into operation is for the Government to spend more than they collect. If you spend more than you collect, you create that budgetary deficit that puts money into operation." Eccles made this statement before the Senate Banking and Finance Committee in December 1937. The government had stopped spending; this is what caused the 1937 recession, according to Chairman Eccles of the Federal Reserve Board. Senator Byrd quoted Will Rogers: "We ought not to spend money that we haven't got for things we don't need."

In January 1939, there was a new "fiscal program" advocated by Eccles; the program was "adopted by the President of the United States." The new program was spend, spend; the goal was to achieve an $80-billion income from which additional taxation would be achieved. "The Budget will automatically balance from increased yields from taxation."

That was the deal; Roosevelt, if he listened to Eccles, would be deficit spending. Roosevelt would run up the debt; Byrd objected. The projected debt into 1940 was $50 billion. Senator Byrd wanted restraint, a balanced budget; Byrd wanted to eliminate the thirty newly created government corporations that didn't "operate through the Budget." The money borrowed by these corporations were government obligations but were not reported as part of the public debt. Chairman Eccles claimed that Byrd was "attacking the Government." Senator Byrd refuted Eccles in his response: "If I attacked the Government . . . I did not know it . . . I did not even suspect that you and the Government were one and the same."

Byrd mentioned John Maynard Keynes; he called Keynes erratic. Keynes was out in England, his native country, and in, in the United States? Not really, but "England, rejecting his fantastic fallacies of spending, borrowing, and lending, adopted a rigid policy of retrenchment and economy, reduced her capita tax, balanced her budget, and revived prosperity."

There it was, the "spending, borrowing, and lending" thing sounds familiar, as in a credit circulation. After more than two centuries, about 240 years, the Bank of England had done the job. Cracks were showing in the empire. The British Empire growth rate was straining; while debts were spiraling upward, the empire was nearing neutral. The Empire's grip on the Far East was starting to slip. England wasn't paying in gold anymore. With credit waning, how could there be more spending, borrowing, and lending? World War II expenditures, more loans, and more debts would be the final blow. Wasn't borrowing from the United States during World War II a lend-lease thing at a cost of tens of billions? It would appear British retrenchment was its only recourse? Great Britain would borrow billions of dollars from the United States after the war.

The things that bankrupted England during World War II could bankrupt the United States in the warring twenty-first century.

Retired Senator Owen sent a letter to Senator Logan of Kentucky; the letter was in response to the Byrd-Eccles exchange.

> It seems apparent that Senator Byrd relies upon private business restoring employment and national production and income by restoration of business confidence . . . Until you correctly diagnose the cause of depression you have no adequate basis for discovering the remedy. The cause of the depression of 1929-1932 was a contraction of $21,000,000,000 in loans to business people by the banks and a corresponding decrease in 1932 of the volume of money in the form of potential and actual demand bank deposits of $21,000,000,000.

Roosevelt had interrupted the contraction "through Government borrowing" into 1936. "Corporate and individual profits" ate up the new demand deposits; they wound up hoarded and "concentrated in our great financial centers." Owen said the hoarded money reduced the velocity of money by 50%.

> The President has been mislead by the advice he has received from Mr. Eccles. It is not necessary to impugn Mr. Eccles' integrity of mind. His subconscious thoughts as a banker control his conclusions because his premise is false.

He thinks that the banker should create the money of the country by loans and contract it by contracting loans.

The central bank was creating the money then.

President Reagan spent more than he collected in the 1980s. Reagan began the big increase in the debt while reducing taxation. Reagan, before the 1986 tax law, was spending for defense while running up the debt. Congressman Robert Dornan of California, on September 9, 1985, called it the deficit dilemma. Dornan said that Reagan

> put pressure on the Federal Reserve for monetary expansion. Economist James Solloway of Argus Research Corp. has recently shown that the Fed has again started to monetize more of the debt than it should. Mr. Solloway sees the huge increases in the national debt each year—caused by continued large budget deficits—obscuring a sharp acceleration on the rate of growth of the monetary base, and, in turn, the money supply.

> Embarrassment in the economics profession is understandably widespread. Despite their warnings that continued large deficits would "crowd out" private borrowing and drive interest rates higher, interest rates have fallen to their lowest level in years, with the likelihood of further reductions in the coming weeks,

this from Congressman Dornan. Later in December 1985, Chairman Paul Volcker of the Federal Reserve told a senate committee he was going to raise interest rates (probably in 1986) for fear of inflation. Apparently, it was whatever worked in the scheme of things.

During the Reagan presidency, the national debt increased to nearly $5 trillion. The second George Bush spent more than he collected; Bush reduced taxation and ran the debt to 11 trillion before he left office, a repeat of the Reagan past, the deficit dilemma. President Bush had the war in Iraq in his favor; he was an incumbent president running for reelection during a time of war. He couldn't lose! Fiat credit is helping to finance the war. Chairman Eccles said it a long time ago: "If you spend more than you collect, you create that budgetary deficit that puts money in operation." Chairman Eccles appeared a proponent of government spending; he said it was "for the purpose of promoting prosperity by spending borrowed money." The cost is a vast debt escalation. The wealth of indebtedness bypasses the majority of the people who pay the wealth; no big deal. It was the Hamilton plan.

It would appear, looking at globalization and continued foreign money buying up the United States, the American homeowner is that last bastion of national wealth in the United States. In the 1980s, when American corporate equity was exhausted, the real wealth in the United States was the American homeowner. That wealth was tapped; new currency was created, hail the American homeowner. The equity loan was created in 1986; it would increase the creation of money by way of the second mortgage. The new law was an equity loan at 7.5% interest, and it was tax deductible. Before 1986, a second mortgage cost 16% interest. After 1986, installment loan interest was no longer deductible. The new equity loan tapped the American homeowner; it lessened one tax burden while the renter took the hit. New money could be generated, putting currency in circulation. To beat that, the 1987 crash occurred! The "domestic" product in the year 2006 was about $13 trillion. The yearly deficit was about $400 billion, which is less than 4% of the product. In 1939, Chairman Eccles told Senator Byrd, the cost of the deficit was about 1% of the projected yearly income. We don't worry about perpetual national debts when put in this perspective?

How does a Bush $70 billion tax reduction and a $400 billion deficit equate? The 70 billion may translate to 700 billion in credits and deposits, the trade-off, more spending, more debt; it's the debt process moving the economy. Chairman Eccles mentioned these things. The Pennsylvania creditors said a long time ago, there was a "national benefit" to a "funded debt"; let's get on with it. There was a "new kind of money to be made." The eighteenth-century creditors were interested primarily in investments at public expense, the guaranteed payment of interest. The scheme guaranteed infinite payment. Additional money was invested money and a printed currency continually funding a perpetrated United States debt. The twenty-first-century creditors, the owners of the indebtedness, many of whom are foreigners, after 217 years, are doing the same thing. The principal does not appear a big deal. The principal will never be paid; the principals don't want the principal to be paid! A demand on the payment of the principal would exhaust income and the currency.

Principals in the state of Maryland took the queue a long time ago. In a local newspaper in Baltimore, Maryland, on Friday, February 9, 2007, a headline read, "Bill Barring New Ground Rents Backed." Finally, some officials wanted to protect homeowners from the state of Maryland's "archaic rent system." The paper called the system "predatory and evil." The system is predatory and evil because people couldn't buy the land their new home rested upon; the home buyer had to pay rent for the land, at least for the life of the mortgage.

The capitalistic ethic is predominant in America; disparity widens. This business is not new; America is primarily money and profits. The experts continue to preach more education, as if education was/is the only answer. There is a tremendous gap in income between the working person and the CEO, management, entertainers and athletes. The wage disparity escalated some time ago with the decline of the unions. This condition has been referred to as the "sea change." But the real gap is between the Wall Street economy and America, the other economy. There is the basic inequality that was set up more than two hundred years ago. Unfortunately, the inequality may remain.

The lack of full employment, proper wages, benefits, retirement, and health care is the inequality. In the year 2007, the middle class struggled to keep up. Financial America, by design, fosters the dream but also furthers the "Bernanke inequality." The disparity of wealth will continue. More of the public is benefiting; more money, credits, and investments appear available to the public. The public markets have apparently made this possible. The government's answer for the senior is the "Reverse Mortgage." The senior will sacrifice equity while trying to keep up.

All this business appears academic. The currency itself, the Treasury's currency obligation, the money supply, is a primary part of the public debt. Do the people own this part of the debt? On this subject, Congressman Patman of Texas, when speaking in the House on November 6, 1963, said, "The amount of Federal Reserve currency in circulation is about equal to the value of the Treasury obligations it holds." It would appear, by virtue of the bond or the security, the Federal Reserve shareholders own these government obligations, which is the money supply, the credit circulation. If the government paid its obligations, the currency would extinguish, disappear? Can an obligation be paid with an obligation?

"And we are to be responsible after all; that is all there is of it."

CHAPTER FIFTEEN

World War II,

Bretton Woods Agreement Act

"We have all been suffering under the tortures that the Versailles Treaty has been inflicting upon us. The Treaty of Versailles is, for us Germans, and has been, for us Germans, not a law." This statement by Adolf Hitler was reported in the *New York Times*. Adolf Hitler made the broadcast after his German army and air forces had invaded Poland. The immediate military objective was Warsaw and the port of Danzig. World War II had started; it was September 1, 1939. At the same time, Germany tricked Russia into a non-aggression pact; Poland was neutralized when Russia attacked Poland on its eastern border. Later, Germany would attack Russia.

First England, then France, in defense of Poland, declared war on Germany. Although France had the largest army and the Maginot Line, France was entrenched, outflanked, offered little resistance; France surrendered early. Ultimately, England, the United States, and the Soviet Union formed the "Allies." The Allies fought the "Axis" powers: Germany, Italy, and Japan. Japan had formed an "alliance" with Germany and Italy in 1940.

The United States entered the war on December 7, 1941. A Japanese naval task force sailed several thousand miles and, without warning, attacked the U.S. naval base at Pearl Harbor in the Hawaiian Islands. World War II covered the globe. The war lasted six years. Italy first, then Germany surrendered unconditionally. United States B-29 bombers dropped two atomic bombs on two Japanese cities, ending the war. In 1945, Japan wasn't going to surrender. Japan was Bushido, suicidal; the militarists in Japan were going to fight to the death. Japanese suicide attacks had inflicted horrific losses on American naval and marine forces in the Pacific. The fighting across the Pacific claimed a two to one death ratio of Japanese to American lives.

An invasion of the Japanese home islands would have cost one million American lives; two million Japanese military were waiting for them. This was the American estimate revealed to the public after the war was over. The atomic bomb was a horrible thing, but it ended the war in August 1945; the Japanese surrendered unconditionally. For the Japanese, the atomic bomb was the wake-up call; more than 150 thousand Japanese people were killed in a flash, but at a probable minimum, two million Japanese and one million American military lives were not jeopardized. It would appear, from this viewpoint, although pragmatic, more lives were saved because the atomic bombs were dropped.

"World War II killed more people, destroyed more property, disrupted more lives, and probably had more far-reaching consequences than any other war in history," this from *World Book*. Tragically, it was not the war to end all wars. The emergence of atomic energy and the spread of Soviet Communism assured a "cold war" that would last forty years. Periodic hot wars continued; it's the human insanity since antiquity.

After World War II, it was estimated that fifty-six million people, military and civilian, had been killed or wounded. World War II was fought on land, at sea, and in the air in north Africa, across the islands of the Pacific, in the Atlantic, the Philippines, Burma, China, and through the villages and towns of Europe. Cities in England, Germany, Russia, and Japan were bombed. Most of the people killed were civilian men, women, and children. *World Book* documented a military death toll of seventeen million. The Allied countries suffered more dead than did Germany, Italy, and Japan—ten million to seven million—and twice the number of casualties. Russia suffered the most.

There it was again, death and destruction, as after World War I, only this time World War II was five times worse. The Nuremberg trials revealed the "Holocaust"; Adolf Hitler had directed the elimination of innocent people, an estimated "six million European Jews," an unbelievable tragedy. According to *World Book*, "the Nazis systematically killed millions of other people whom Hitler regarded as racially inferior or politically dangerous."

World War I cost the United States more than $26 billion; European war cost was more than $200 billion. Most of these monetary debts hadn't been paid when World War II started. The cost of World War II was estimated at $1.3 trillion; property damage was estimated at 239 billion. The United States public debt in 1940 was about $43 billion; in 1946, the debt was 270 billion. The war costs of the Allied countries was more than $600 billion; the Axis spent almost 300 billion. All of it was spent borrowed money, borrowed money that wasn't there before, all of it, money created out of nothing.

In April 1944, Henry Morgenthau Jr., secretary of the Treasury, on behalf of President Roosevelt, sent a message to John Gilbert Winant. Winant was the American ambassador in the United Kingdom. "Please call upon the Chancellor of the Exchequer and inform him of the following personal message from me. I should also appreciate it if you would supplement the message with an oral explanation of the urgent necessity for an immediate reply." The British chancellor was Sir John Anderson. The date was April 5, 1944. This was two months before the Normandy invasion of France.

Roosevelt's message contained several points. A monetary conference was planned; "an International Monetary Fund and a Bank for Reconstruction and Development" would be established. Roosevelt wanted the "UK. technical experts" to examine a preliminary draft before a public statement was made to the other participating countries. The United States and Great Britain would agree before anything further was done. Roosevelt wanted a reply within five days. Things didn't happen that quickly; debate and agreeable response from Great Britain would take some time. It would take even more time confronting the Congress. After a public statement, Morgenthau would be appearing before Congressional committees about the details. The planned conference was the "Bretton Woods Conference" of July 1944.

The war was still in progress; the continuing devastation and death was enormous. The worst was yet to come! Restoration after and the indebtedness thing were paramount. What about the cost? Huge debts were piling up again; how was the cost to be paid for and paid for by whom and to whom and controlled by whom? Apparently, it was the compounding international wealth of indebtedness thing all over again.

After World War I, the creditor moved swiftly. Montague Norman and others sought the stabilization of international currencies, the movements of gold. Debtors had to be restored, maintained. Apparently, England had many debtors; England, the creditor, was also a debtor to its central bank and to the United States. If the debtor countries couldn't pay, creditors couldn't collect; new schemes prompted debtors to borrow to pay creditors. The Bank for International Settlements was formed, the gold intake and distributor. The American economy went into the tank in 1929-1932 amid a descending world economy. The Bretton Woods Conference, apparently, would be a broader undertaking to correct the disaster of the '30s. It would involve the United States internationally. The Bretton Woods Conference would initiate the "stabilization" process of international currencies after World War II.

Early communiqués involved the principal countries: the United States, the United Kingdom, the Union of Soviet Socialist Republics, and China. Initially, there was opposition to the plan, principally from the "directors of the Bank of England." Ambassador Winant sent the following: "This opposition argue that if the plan is adopted financial control will leave London and dollar exchange will take the place of sterling exchange." Times had changed; England was supposedly broke, no longer the dominant world power. As of 1944, the United States had possessed the predominant portion of the world's gold. A 1944 Treasury report by Secretary Morgenthau listed a gold stock of more than $20 billion in the United States.

Secretary Morgenthau gave an address before the "Foreign Policy Association" in Minneapolis, Minnesota, on March 12, 1945. A monetary fund would deal in exchange rates; a reconstruction bank would lend the money, "loans of 20 to 30 years or even longer." The

Bretton Woods Agreement, hopefully, would correct the international economic "disorder after the last war." Morgenthau mentioned that countries had returned "to gold—some with the help of stabilization loans. But the first serious pressure was too much for them. The wolf pack of exchange speculators was on the prowl, seeking out week currencies to destroy." Morgenthau said it "was an era of economic warfare . . . The aim of each country was to save itself at the expense of others." According to Morgenthau, Germany used the "bilateral agreement" at the expense of the Balkan countries in her

> preparation for war . . . Germany agreed, for example, with some Balkan countries, to buy most of their wheat and raw materials at good prices in Marks. But the Balkan merchant did not get marks. These were paid into the Reichsbank. The Balkan countries then had to purchase in goods in Germany to get the value of those marks. The Balkan importer paid into his Central Bank the price of the German goods, and only then could the seller of the Wheat or other raw material get his money.

According to Morgenthau, Germany shortchanged the Balkans in the exchange of goods; Germany also used the raw materials from the Balkans to build her "war machine." It was mentioned earlier foreign countries had to purchase in goods in Germany to balance credits; this was Germany's political control of foreign countries?

Who were the good guys and the bad guys in all this business: the European governments and their banks; the governments of England, France, the United States; Montague Norman and the Bank of England; J. P. Morgan; Kuhn, Loeb & Co.; Hjalmar Schacht; the Federal Reserve Bank of New York; the U.S. Treasury? Then there was Krueger and Toll. It appeared Germany got screwed at Versailles coupled with protectionist foreign trade and loans from the West. Perhaps, Germany went East and screwed the Balkans.

> The Bretton Woods agreements were conceived in the very practical spirit of cooperation . . . The legislation to carry out the Bretton Woods program is now before Congress. Its approval will show that the United States is thoroughly

in earnest about joining with other nations to achieve international security.

Morgenthau applauded all the participating nations, especially the Soviet Union; the Soviet's first subscription to the fund was $900 million. The Soviets changed the figure to $1.2 billion. Morgenthau said the Soviet Union did this "not because there could be any direct advantage to the Soviet Union but in order to create a stronger bank with a larger capital—able to contribute that much more to the rebuilding of the world."

The cold war would prove otherwise!

Congressman J. Edgar Chenoweth, on February 2, 1945, in the House, presented a speech by Congressman Smith of Ohio. The speech was delivered before the "Colorado State Mining Association in Denver on January 27, 1945." Smith called the "Bretton Woods Agreement" a "Keynes-Morgenthau Scheme." Keynes was now Lord John Maynard Keynes; Keynes was "advisor to the British Exchequer and Governor of the Bank of England." Keynes introduced his "International Monetary" plan in early April 1943. There was another scheme by "Mr. Harry D. White, Assistant to the Secretary of the Treasury."

Chenoweth claimed the two schemes in final became the Keynes plan. Chenoweth was critical of Keynes; England was for England, to restore the pound sterling, and retain London as the place of international exchange. Chenoweth called Keynes the "spearhead of the scheme." Chenoweth mentioned Keynes' statement before the House of Lords: "So far from an international plan endangering the long tradition, by which most empire countries, and many other countries, too, have centered their financial systems in London, the plan is, in my judgment, an indispensable means of maintaining this tradition."

In England, before the House of Lords, would Keynes have said things differently?

The Monetary Fund would comprise a membership of forty-five countries, each country subscribing a "quota" in money. The Monetary Fund "would largely serve as a lending agency. The participating countries would be divided into two groups, lenders and borrowers. The United States would become the principal, if not almost the sole lender. Most of the other nations would become the borrowers." The beginning capitalization figure for the fund was $8.8 billion. The United States subscription was almost $3 billion in gold and paper currency. Twenty of the countries joining the fund were already in "default" on loans owed the United States prior to World War II. According to Congressman Smith, the fund appeared to be most lenient toward these, the "poorer countries."

The United States would subscribe almost $3 billion to the Monetary Fund and $3 billion to the bank for a total of $6 billion. The total monies to be subscribed by all the nations to both entities would amount to about $18 billion in gold and currency. The United States was contributing a third of the subscribing capital.

For some time, as Dr. Commons had pointed out that since 1927, the function of gold in the world had changed; gold was "managed." Congressman Chenoweth was for a return to a free gold market; Congressman Smith referred to Chairman Eccles's statements before the House Banking and Currency Committee. The subject was the gold reserve. When questioned, Chairman Eccles said, "I do not deny that the amount of the gold reserve, the gold requirements have anything to do with the price level, which means it has nothing to do with the value of the currency." Eccles had admitted that "there is no relation whatever between the gold in this country and our currency."

In 1945, the credit circulation showed about $25 billion dollars in Federal Reserve Notes. The gold reserve was more than 20 billion; the gold showed an 80% reserve against this currency. By law, the circulation could be increased to $50 billion considering the 40% reserve clause? It would appear Chairman Eccles's statement jived with the numbers; there appeared no connection between the gold and the currency.

The Federal Reserve Act was amended in June 1945. The reserve in gold was reduced to 25% against the currency; there could now exist four times in currency against gold or $80 billion in Federal Reserve Notes. "The Federal Reserve Act was amended to require the maintenance by each Federal Reserve Bank of minimum reserve gold certificates equal to 25 percent of its Federal Reserve Notes in circulation and of its deposit liabilities." This is from the annual Treasury report of 1945, page 96. The circulation is the base; deposits and credits is ten to fifteen times the circulation, the velocity of money many times that. The 1945 Treasury report showed a "gross national product" of $210 billion during the period. The report showed that government spending, because of the war, was almost half the national product and with that, an unemployment rate of 1% in the country. It's part of the record; during World War II in the capitalistic system, government spending guaranteed almost total employment. It is also interesting to note in the Treasury reports of World War II that there for the first time, the income, product, borrowing, spending thing in the country was described as a "gross national product."

Also, in 1945, "the use of direct obligations of the United States as permissible collateral security for Federal Reserve Notes was extended indefinitely." This would be forever, the credit circulation; this was the fiat credit thing, when the currency is printed and borrowed. On Wall Street in the year 2005, the money people would say that Mr. Greenspan is printing more money. The governor of a reserve bank, who is also the agent of a reserve bank, orders the printing of new currency. It's not stated literally in the statute, our banking law, but the Federal Reserve runs the show.

Professor Edwin Kemmerer of Princeton University was well-known; he was "professor emeritus of international finance." Professor Kemmerer, in an address, said, "There was a popular proverb: 'We have gold because we cannot trust governments.'" Kemmerer was against Bretton Woods; the "plan threatens to debase the American dollar and, therefore should be rejected." Professor Kemmerer emphasized the period prior to 1914; he mentioned Keynes, "who is today the world's most vigorous critic of the gold standard, who said in 1923, referring to England's '88 years' experience ending in 1914, the remarkable feature of this long period was the relative stability of the price level."

For England, the price level was always stable since England owned or controlled most of the world's gold; England controlled the exchange rates. England called all the shots; the world was her debtor. C. W. Barron said as much. That was the period, apparently, according to Professor Kemmerer, of the real gold standard. All the countries, including the United States, were on gold during that time, and they all kowtowed to the British pound sterling.

Professor Kemmerer mentioned countries going off gold because of the World War and the return to gold by all the countries in the twenties, but he said, "It was a very different kind of gold standard than the one prevailing before the war." It apparently was different; Dr. Commons called it the "managed" period. Professor Kemmerer wanted "an International Gold Standard Plan." Kemmerer wanted the United States to "rehabilitate its own gold standard after the war, and in due time call an international conference of all other countries desiring to return to a gold basis."

Professor Kemmerer was for the free gold standard; his address related most positively to the gold standard period prior to 1914. Professor Kemmerer didn't mention the emergency periods, the gold suspensions, the extinguished currencies, the resultant recessions or depressions, and the assurances of "no redundancy," which occurred many times during the same period; it was apparently Great Britain and her gold dictating. And this was what Professor Kemmerer, apparently, wanted to return to. Anyway, the IMF scheme, as we shall see, was an apparent gold contrivance in the making.

There was another conference held; it was the Dumbarton Oaks. It was held in "August-October" of 1944. Dumbarton Oaks was "an estate in Washington D.C." The conference was the seedling for the eventual creation of the United Nations. Delegates from the United States, Great Britain, the Soviet Union, and China attended.

What was the "Bankers' Strategy? . . . In the first place, the American Bankers Association, as a body, has never passed upon the Bretton Woods proposals." Recommendations and proposals were before Congress from the association and the big New York City banks; it was early 1945. Southern and western bankers approved "the program in its entirety." This is from Congressman George Outland of California. Should the fund be incorporated in the bank, or the other way around? "The Strategy of the international bankers who are trying to hamstring the program is an obvious and familiar one, to amend and make reservations, to stall, to kill by indirection." Outland said, "The big bankers know their way around Washington, and are clever."

Congressman Outland appeared to be questioning their clout before Congress. How could the Congress accept what the big bankers recommended? The bankers' "international financial operations of the Twenties which went sour, were revealed to the public in the Senate Banking Committee investigations."

Congressman Frank Sundstrom of New Jersey presented a report by the American Bankers Association. The Monetary Fund should not be approved; it was "too big, too elaborate, too complicated, too difficult for the public to understand." The Congress

> should approve, with modifications, the proposed International Bank for Reconstruction and Development. The bankers recommend also an expansion of the American Government's Export-Import Bank, the repeal of the Johnson Act [the Tariff], the removal of hampering barriers to international trade, and the firm stabilization of the United States dollar in relation to gold.

> The whole idea of the Conference came from John Maynard Keynes, the worlds most celebrated advocate of inflation . . . Keynes has been trying to get his inflationary schemes adopted for years, but never made any progress in England, altho' he made quite an impression on Mr. Roosevelt . . . There was advance agreement by Roosevelt with Keynes before a meeting was called. To guard against any slip-up, the delegates to the conference had to be who would not upset the apple cart. None of the Nation's celebrated experts went to Bretton Woods.

This from the *Chicago Daily Tribune* of Wednesday, February 14, 1945, as presented by Congressman Noah Mason in the House on February 20, 1945. "The *New York Times* was moved to say that the list of delegates, 'in all candor is not encouraging.'"

The "celebrated experts" referred to, apparently, were bankers from the American Bankers Association and the big bankers of New York, the Group Eight? The Bretton Woods Agreement, apparently, was an all-world government thing; all-private banking experts were excluded? Secretary Morgenthau was there; the undersecretary Harry D. White was there, and Cordell Hull, secretary of state, was there. "One leading banker after another told of his grave alarm about the Bretton Woods proposals." The *Tribune* reported that the Bankers Association would "approve the creation of a bank to make loans to foreign governments, but under an arrangement far different from that planned at Bretton Woods. The schemes the President calls upon Congress to approve have no support in any informed quarter."

Congressman Daniel Reed of New York had questions about the lending, borrowing, and the financing of the fund and the bank. Reed questioned Morgenthau's remarks about the fund. "Now let me make this clear—the Fund is not a scheme for lending money to debtor nations—and those who see it in that light are missing its entire meaning." But private bankers "ought to know a lending institution when they see one . . . 'it introduces a method of lending which is novel and contrary to accepted credit principles. Under the system of quotas in the Fund, a member country would be virtually entitled to borrow in certain specified amounts.'"

How was the $6 billion to be raised? The American taxpayers would pay for the $6 billion plus interest. Congressman Reed was a member of the Ways and Means Committee.

> I find that, in the anxiety to get the Bretton Woods program enacted with a minimum of questioning in Congress; they have worked out a method of financing the Bretton Woods program that will bypass not only the Ways and Means Committee; but also the Appropriations Committees of both House and Senate. Evidently, we're not supposed to be inquisitive about this program. It will be financed partly by inflation—using profits of the 1934 devaluation—and principally, by increasing the public debt.

Later in this chapter, we will see what Reed was talking about; that is, the "method of financing . . . by increasing the public debt." President Roosevelt got a $2 billion credit devaluing the dollar, and the gold reserve was being reduced to 25% of circulation. Was this more devaluation? In addition, collateral credit for government obligations would now be infinite; this was the fiat credit thing, the borrowing of money when printing more currency. Was Congressman Reed thinking these things when he mentioned the public debt? President Roosevelt was going to start the Bretton Woods thing with fiat credit? Congressman Robert Grant of Indiana asked a similar question. Where are we going to get the money? Grant illustrated the Congress raising of the "debt limit" many times since the New Deal; the war had everything to do with it. When was it going to stop? The latest debt limit in 1945 was $300 billion. If need be, the debt limit would be raised again.

Congressman Hugh De Lacy of Washington was positive about Bretton Woods; "5,000,000 Jobs" would be created. Bretton Woods would further international "prosperity," help to eliminate the economic chaos that brought on World War II, and "raise the standard of living in backward countries." Who was against Bretton Woods?

> Since the agreement was signed a small group of big bankers in this country and in England has decided to oppose Bretton Woods . . . The real reason behind this minority opposition is a hankering for the 'good old days' of uncontrolled currency manipulation, uncontrolled lending, and speculative profits for the few. The big banks didn't lose anything when countries such as Germany defaulted on loans. That loss was taken by the suckers who bought German bonds from the banks.

The "suckers" referred to by Congressman De Lacy, according to the record, were apparently the insurance companies, the railroads, the small banks, and the member banks, which bought the bonds or debentures from the big banks. After 1929, weren't these the same corporations who couldn't discount the bonds or debentures through the Federal Reserve System? President Hoover started the Reconstruction Finance Corporation with public money; the RFC bought these debentures from the insurance companies, the railroads, the smaller banks to help cover their losses—a lot of corporate welfare. Also, the big banks were paid by the RFC, according to the *Congressional Record*. Congressmen Rankin and Patman mentioned these things in the Seventy-third Congress, session 1. Rankin said the money was "poured into a sinkhole." See chapter 13.

What is the "sinkhole?" The sinkhole, apparently, is the pocket. The money or currency is paid out and goes into somebody's pocket; it doesn't become elastic currency.

American bankers were against Bretton Woods. "They say we might lose our money." American bankers didn't like $2.8 billion put into a "stabilization fund." The cost to maintain the peace, the Second World War, was almost $300 billion. The Monetary Fund was only going to cost "1%" of the cost the war. "The next peace will be the most expensive property the American people will ever have bought."

Samuel Grafton didn't think it was "an extravagant suggestion that we put an amount equal to less than 1 percent of the purchase price into a maintenance fund to keep the property in good condition." Grafton made these points in a *Philadelphia Record* article of February 27, 1945. The American investor lost a lot more than $3 billion in worthless bonds and debentures the big bankers sold them in the twenties. "It is a matter of simple historical fact that these bonds were sold to Americans by the same interests which today declare that a world stabilization fund involves a wild risk." Congressman Francis Myers of Pennsylvania presented Mr. Grafton's article in the House on March 12, 1945.

At this point, let's step back again; it was the gold thing. The United States possessed a predominant amount of the world's gold in 1945; the United States possessed three-quarters of the world's gold. How did this happen? According to former Congressman Charles Binderup,

> For 12 long years we wondered why we bought, until we had three-fourths of the gold of the world at $35 an ounce from foreign lands and put it in the Kentucky hole, when

we didn't use the gold, didn't want the gold, as we were
off the gold standard, and never wanted to go back, but
Bretton Woods explains.

Binderup summarized the fund's creation in his critical but amusing
letter in the House. Binderup was opposed to Bretton Woods, Wall
Street, and the international bankers. Briefly, some of Binderup's
quips follow:

- Bretton Woods was a "conspiracy."
- Congress had to destroy Bretton Woods, or the conspiracy
  would destroy us.
- Our corrupt money and banking system could never be
  reformed by going into partnership with Morgenthau and the
  international bankers; it was the same as a partnership with
  the devil and his imps.
- Bretton Woods was the illegitimate offspring of that
  immoral spot, Wall Street, the cancer at the heart of our
  government.
- The Bretton Woods offspring was really foreign, a bastard
  child, and the foster father was Henry Morgenthau out of the
  president's Cabinet.
- The bastard child was this miserable brat; it really came
  from England. It was first guarded from the public by
  Morgenthau.

Actually, there were two "brats."

- When it became known the baby had been born, everybody
  pointed to Keynes.
- But Keynes came to Bretton Woods with his own brat right
  from Downing Street. the kid wasn't welcomed; the kid lacked
  gold corpuscles in its bloodstream. The conference drowned
  the baby; they tied gold around its neck!

Who was the real father? There was total denial.

- When the swaddling clothes had been removed and the
  bastard lay bare, the scheme had been revealed. It is the

skeleton of the gold-standard witch all padded up with its face lifted, the same old son of a witch we buried in 1934, resurrected by the international bankers, fostered by Morgenthau, and prompted by President Roosevelt in the same voice that sang the swan song at the funeral directed to the London Monetary Conference: "We are not interested in stabilizing the English pound or the French Franc. We are only interested in stabilizing the American dollar so it will have the same debt paying and purchasing power, now and generations hence," and the refrain, "We will drive the money changers out of the Temple and move the capital out of Wall Street back to Washington."

- And do you remember we shouted back, "Amen, amen; thank God for a leader who is for America first, who will lead us in the terrible unequal fight against Wall Street and international bankers, the Nations most ruthless dictator." And with profound faith, we waited for action to give force to his magnificent words, but the words died away, drowned by the noise of the coin in the cash register of the international bankers.

In too few words, President Roosevelt spoke those fighting words, but he didn't fulfill his promise to the people; the money changers were still in the temple. Charles Binderup said as much.

- There was no mistake; Bretton Woods was putting us back on the old corrupt gold standard that we repudiated long since.
- After twelve long years, we finally realized what had happened. Roosevelt took the gold, made it $35 an ounce. Morgenthau bought up all the gold; the gold still belonged to the bankers in the form of gold certificates redeemable in the gold.

[Binderup's evaluation is covered again in Chapter 16,]

- The devaluation was a gift to the bankers' currency amounting to 60% more than the face value of the gold certificates. Then the gold reserve was reduced from 40% to 25%.
- Morgenthau, without the knowledge of Congress, would buy the worthless IOUs of foreign nations. Now we know, the forty

nations destitute for gold could qualify at the Bretton Woods Conference and go on the gold standard with 25% gold back of their currencies. About the 40% to the 25% thing, it was another donation from the people to the bankers amounting to $4,800,000,000 including the 60% bankers privilege.

Chairman Eccles admitted there was no connection between the gold and the currency. The Federal Reserve Act supposedly stated otherwise. Morgenthau's Treasury report showed the existing gold stock dwarfed the required reserve amount against which the existing currency circulation exists. Charles Binderup said, "Now we know!" Based on the huge gold stock and the reduction to 25% reserve requirement, and Bretton Woods right around the corner, it would appear huge credits were at the ready; the United States Treasury would become the "company store" for the world.

Apparently, a whole lot of paper currency was going to be rolling off the assembly line; the paper currency was the legal tender Federal Reserve note. It would be the credit circulation in full swing. Silver certificates were still circulating; these certificates would be discontinued in the future. The American taxpayer would pay for all of this business. With the Bretton Woods Agreement, the American dollar, the Federal Reserve note, would represent a gold dollar.

- Bretton Woods was a vicious so-called agreement. Charles Binderup ended his letter asking the Congress to defeat Bretton Woods.

Congressman William Lemke of North Dakota presented Binderup's letter in the House on March 20, 1945. When in Congress, Binderup, a Democrat, spoke many times "on both the national and international monetary situation." Lemke lauded Binderup, called him a "student, an authority. He was not a partisan. He voted for the best interests of the people regardless of partisan politics." Binderup's satire was better than that.

"Why are the bankers opposed? The answer is that the bankers are not opposed, in the sense of being what Bretton Woods stood for." This is from a May 1945 report by the National City Bank of New York, as presented in the House by Congressman Daniel Reed of New York. In brief, some of the City Bank report's arguments follow:

- The Bretton Woods people were guaranteeing currency stability and freedom from exchange controls. No plan could do this.
- There was prejudice against the international bankers of Wall Street. These people did not want to make profits out of unstable exchanges. The bankers did not want to drag an unwilling world back prematurely to the gold standard and rigid exchanges.
- The bankers wanted stable exchanges; unstable exchanges are risky and speculative, with ultimate losses.
- Bankers make their money in foreign trade where stable markets exist.
- The Bankers Association was in agreement with the International Bank for Reconstruction, but the Monetary Fund should be merged with the bank, concerned only with short-term credits required; the fund as planned would make credit too easy and automatic.
- There would be bad loans, too much borrowing, etc.
- The merger of the fund and the bank should be set up as soon as possible.
- The United States, in the case of the bank, would have a veto power over loans floated in dollars, just as other countries would have such power in respect to loans in their currencies. Changes should be made to the present agreement.

The Treasury was opposed to any Bankers Association changes; "the agreement has been adopted by 44 countries." The Treasury asserted the following disagreement:

- Another conference would have to be held.
- There were adequate safeguards. Each country was assigned a quota; a member's net borrowing could not exceed 100% of its quota, with no more than 25% in any one year.
- A merging of the fund and the bank would "wreck the entire program."
- Assistant Secretary of State Dean Acheson said, "The heart of the Bretton Woods proposal is that there must be some

action to get the nations to agree to abandon methods of economic warfare—such methods as competitive exchange depreciation, multiple currencies, and exchange controls. If you can't get countries to abandon these practices, it does no good to make stabilization loans."
- Will Other Countries Accept Changes?
- The delegations of each country had agreed at Bretton Woods, but the governments of the respective countries remained uncommitted, so there was no agreement yet.
- The British Chancellor of the Exchequer had characterized it as "a difficult document, inevitably long and technical."

The following from the *London Times*:

- Would other parties in England share the view of Lord Keynes and the Chancellor of the Exchequer?
- What about economic slumps?
- Suppose a depression would occur in the United States such as that that occurred in 1929 and again in 1937, this would lead to the exhaustion of Britain's credit in the fund.
- It was unclear about British and Americans on postwar currency policies.
- Britain wanted more currency flexibility and firmer commitments.
- In England, the plan was spoken of as being associated with the gold standard, but Lord Keynes said it was "the opposite of the gold standard."

World War II cost $1.3 trillion, this on top of hundreds of billions of World War I indebtedness. There was a total of $27 billion of gold in the world in 1945; the United States held $22 billion of that gold. The U.S. public debt was nearing 300 billion; the total public and private debt was nearing a trillion dollars. A trillion dollars of debt was accomplished with $25 billion of Federal Reserve Notes, the primary currency circulation in the United States in 1945. (The real inflation thing tells the story; gold storage was way up, and the wealth of indebtedness also.) The credit circulation turned into deposits and credits coupled with the velocity of money, and we have this colossal debt with, in comparison, a small circulation. This couldn't be done with physics and mathematics.

The closing of World War II required restoration and reconstruction in Europe, Asia, and the Middle East. Credits, a ton of more credits, was needed; the United States government would take the lead and the initiative to supply those credits by way of the IMF. Alexander Hamilton was right; Federal expenses or worldly expenses were truly to be unlimited, "even in imagination."

In March of 1945, Henry Morgenthau appeared before the House banking committee; he stressed the importance of Bretton Woods, especially in connection with Dumbarton Oaks. "Dumbarton Oaks is for international organization on a political basis; Bretton Woods, on an economic basis. They go hand in hand as interdependent as the blades of a pair of scissors." The Dumbarton Oaks plan would be taking place in San Francisco in April; the failure of Bretton Woods in the Congress "would have a dampening effect."

"Bretton Woods should be honestly considered by itself, and not be falsely tied to Peace Conferences." On Friday, June 1, 1945, Congressman Howard Buffett of Nebraska said, "Some promoters of Bretton Woods lack either the integrity or the intelligence to present this scheme straightforwardly." Buffett presented an article by the *New York Herald Tribune* of March 4. The article stated that "hooking up Bretton Woods with peace conferences was deceitful and dishonest." The article was negative about the administration and the Democrats; the peace conference was a smoke screen "to drive through Congress without alteration, the so-called Bretton Woods program, on which hearings are scheduled to begin this week before the House Ways and Means Committee."

"Mr. Speaker, the American people have been assured that Bretton Woods means the end of economic warfare." Again, it was Congressman Howard Buffett of Nebraska; he told the House that the Bretton Woods claim was a myth: "This assertion is largely created out of thin air." Buffett produced an article from C. W. Barron's *National Financial Weekly*. The article, written by Paul Wohl, exploded this notion in a realistic discussion of British trade plans: "Their trade plans go contrary to the freer trade claims of Bretton Woods." Great Britain, in reality, was in financial straights.

"The British, like it or not, have to take a page from the book of Hitler's former economic adviser, Dr. Schacht." Briefly, some of the article's conclusions follow:

- Britain's threefold master plan was
  1. retooling—American credits were needed;
  2. revamping export/import activity; and
  3. creating the sterling bloc, gathering up all the countries by agreement, which would establish three-quarters of the world's imports and two-thirds of its exports.
- Britain's policy after the war would be the same as Germany's policy before the war.
- Germany borrowed capital from America to rebuild its industries and then its war machine.
- Five years of war took its toll. Britain had to rebuild its industry; there would be direct loans from America or loans through Bretton Woods. The only difference is that Britain wouldn't be building a war machine.
- Britain had supported Germany's barter and clearing scheme. They might help to cement the sterling bloc.
- Schacht had created the mark bloc. According to Schacht, Germany's creditor was supposedly satisfied by making the exchange in goods and services in the debtor country, Germany.
- There were blocked sterling balances in London totaling £2,000,000,000—
- claims by the British Commonwealth and many other countries.
- Britain would have to pay her debts mainly in goods and services unless she could obtain large dollar balances through American loans.
- Britain held sway in the Middle East; it was the sterling bloc there.
- Britain's subtle political influence in many countries around the world was widespread; there would be little room left for an expansion of American commercial exports.
- The only way for the United States to bolster its exports would then be to finance them by supplying prospective buyers with the funds for which to pay for American goods or services—not exactly a commercial operation.

The "not exactly a commercial operation" sounded like the debenture fiasco of the twenties.

Germany dominated creditor countries with Schacht's economic schemes. According to Paul Wohl and Barron's *Financial Weekly*, Great Britain was out to do the same thing after World War II. According to Schacht's *Confessions*, the Allies from the West, the Versailles Treaty, and the removal of Germany's land and colonies dumped on Germany after World War I. As a result, Dr. Schacht, the "Old Wizard," using his economic "tricks," countered by dumping on creditor countries from the East and the West. Barron's *Weekly* was saying that England, by using Dr. Schacht's economic tactics, that is, by borrowing American dollars, was ready to resume its world trade dominance. Based on this C. W. Barron authoritative analysis, economic warfare was apt to stay alive and well!

Henry Hazlitt was another against Bretton Woods. Editor Henry Hazlitt wrote an article in the *American Scholar* in 1944-1945. Henry Hazlitt was another for the gold standard.

> Freedom of trade, in the eyes of Adam Smith and his Nineteenth Century successors in the liberal tradition, meant freedom from government interference. All that the "classical economists" asked of governments in the field of international trade was that they should permit it to occur. They wanted a removal of prohibitions and of nearly all tariffs. But they did not ask for positive "encouragement or artificial stimulants."

Congressman Daniel Reed of New York presented Hazlitt's article in the House.

Did this "freedom from government interference, encouragement or artificial stimulants" also include the creation of currency, the money thing that has something to do with trade and international economics? A banker of international and European origin came to the United States and encouraged the United States Congress to create the non-legal tender Federal Reserve note. This non-legal tender note was a new U.S. government obligation, which was good for gold, which was "handed" to the Federal Reserve bank. The income tax law was passed to pay for this new obligation forever. This Federal Reserve note was created to accumulate gold, and it did just that; it gobbled up the gold, and the note became international in trade. The note went to Europe for worthless debentures, which helped Germany build for the Second World War.

Before that, hundreds of millions of the notes were released by the Federal Reserve in 1927, which, according to the *Congressional Record*, helped fuel the crash. The "classical economists"—all they ask of government is that "they permit it to occur." Henry Hazlitt said that the Bretton Woods fund was a bad deal; constant devaluation destroys money. "Governments should stay out of international trade." Government officials "rarely understand."

It is rare if any of us know or understand the origin of the money schemes. The money interests have needed government since the beginning, since the Bank of England. The record shows that controlling money interests have achieved; they have achieved because of "government interference."

While these discussions and the House Banking and Currency Committee hearings were going on, in the spring of 1945, President Roosevelt died; the date was April 12, 1945, in Warm Springs, Georgia. The president had gone there for a rest. "Roosevelt had been suffering from high blood pressure and arteriosclerosis." President Roosevelt wanted to be there at the end, but he wasn't there at the end. The following month, the war in Europe was finally over; Germany surrendered on May 7, 1945.

The House of Representatives passed bill H.R. 3314 on June 7, 1945: "An Act to provide for the participation of the United States in the International Monetary Fund and the International Bank for Reconstruction and Development." It was officially called the Bretton Woods Agreement Act. With the passage in the House, the bill would go to the Senate. But first, hearings were held before the Senate Banking and Currency Committee beginning on June 12, 1945. Senator Wagner, the chairman, and eleven senators comprised the Senate Banking and Currency Committee.

> As you know, during the 1930's a number of countries began to use their currency systems for the purpose of securing unfair advantages in international trade. Germany in particular developed numerous devices for exploiting her creditors and competitors. The use of these tricks by Germany forced other countries to adopt similar measures in self-defense. The result was an era of currency warfare that virtually destroyed international trade and investment and prepared the way for total war.

This was part of Henry Morgenthau's opening statement to the committee. According to Morgenthau, American companies were victims of Germany's "tricks," the same as the exploited Balkan countries. German marks were blocked; payment was in goods only. "The American commercial attaché in Berlin reported that one company had to take 8,000,000 mouth organs in payment for petroleum; another 200,000 canaries for a large press for making automobile bodies; and a movie company was bamboozled into taking a live hippopotamus for its films." Morgenthau said when

> Nazism is destroyed, its strong-arm currency practices will be destroyed, too . . . Many countries had to adopt similar measures in self-defense. They still have them . . . If we do nothing to help establish orderly exchanges, to help these countries get foreign capital for reconstruction, they will feel compelled to revert to barter deals, clearing agreements, competitive exchange depreciation, and multiple currencies.

Senator Taft had questions: "I should like to know what other American money will come into the picture."

The war in Europe was over; but the lend-lease program was still in progress, with the British, the Dutch, the French, the Belgian plan, and Russia. The Committee wanted to know; what amount of more money was involved in addition to Bretton Woods? What happens when the war ends, VE Day, and VJ Day? Will the lend-lease dollars stop flowing? VE Day was victory in Europe, and VJ Day was victory in Japan.

The Senate didn't know the commitments or the exacting numbers; there was the Lend-Lease Administration. Senator Taft said information from them was "in the nature of propaganda." There were no definitive answers to these money questions from Morgenthau and Secretary of State Dean Acheson except that lend-lease would extend in the form of loans to the end of 1945. The committee had the lend-lease statement as of March 31, 1945. Twenty-four billion dollars in lend-lease was owed the United States government. Senator Taft in speaking to Morgenthau and Dean Acheson, said, "These lend-lease debts, like the debts of the last war, will probably never be paid."

Six billion dollars was the initial United States Treasury outlay for the "fund" and the "bank"; this figure was in the House bill. The House bill also stated that the Federal Reserve bank would act as a depository and agent; the country's gold and the Federal Reserve note was to be the main ingredient, and the "board of governors of the Federal Reserve System shall supervise" courtesy of the United States Congress.

Germany and Japan were not part of the Bretton Woods Agreement. Secretary Morgenthau wanted Germany to be "deindustrialized" after the war, "eliminating her as an exporter and importer." Secretary Morgenthau answered "no" when asked if Japan and Germany had "a very large volume of trade before the war?" Morgenthau wanted German trade confined within the limits of Europe: "all of the studies which we have made show that her former position in world trade, in the export and import fields, could so readily be absorbed by just continental Europe, not including England, that it never will be missed."

Hjalmar Schacht stated in his *Confessions* that because of the lack of exports, Germany was unable to pay reparations; Germany was forced to make loans at excessive interest rates to pay reparations. Based on Secretary Morgenthau's statements, it would appear that postwar economic warfare was possible; it would remain alive and well. In looking back, Secretary Morgenthau's suggested limitations concerning Germany's future economy was not a correct prognostication.

Dean Acheson gave the committee a history lesson. Acheson mentioned the "Moslem conquests" of the seventh and eighth centuries; the known world was "split in two." The ultimate result: Europe was "cut off from the rest of the world, it took Europe a thousand years to get back to where it had come from before." Acheson said this same thing could happen again. When Hitler marched into Poland in 1939, Europe was cut off from the rest of the world; all the world's imports to European countries ceased. Acheson mentioned a figure of "$180,000,000" of imported goods was the ongoing trade to Europe every year. World War II interrupted this trade; it stopped. The European economic infrastructure had been destroyed.

In 1945, "except for France, the European countries are practically without foreign exchange or foreign funds of any sort. They would have to indulge in every kind of a restrictive practice to force their exports on other people and to get such imports as they vitally need." Acheson stressed that Bretton Woods would help to restore what had been destroyed.

Senator Murdock mentioned the gold thing; the country held 75% of the world's gold, and a reduction in the gold reserve requirement had been implemented from 40% to 25%. Murdock wanted to know "if the entire gold monetary holdings of the world are sufficient to adequately base this international monetary system that is contemplated by the fund . . . to maintain it at 25 percent?" Acheson said there was no "percentage basis" in the fund. "If currency is defined in terms of gold then you know what it is in relation to the other currencies. That is the importance of the fund." Acheson said that gold would be the "common denominator." Senator Tobey mentioned silver; "if there is not sufficient gold there is plenty of silver to augment it." Senator Taft mentioned that as far as Lord Keynes was concerned, it was going to be "a managed paper-money currency that was contemplated by the fund." Chairman Wagner said another witness would deal with "gold and silver." That was fine with Acheson.

What did the amendment to the Federal Reserve Act have to do with the Monetary Fund? A ton of new currency was going to be printed; the U.S. Treasury and Federal Reserve were going to be instrumental in the fund and the bank's beginning and function. Maybe that was the reason for the reserve reduction from 40% to 25%.

The Federal Reserve Act was amended in 1945; each reserve bank would be required to maintain its gold certificates reserve at 25% of its notes in circulation and of its deposits. The gold certificate in the Federal Reserve was the reciprocal of the gold in the "Kentucky Hole." The Congress called Fort Knox the Kentucky Hole. Why did Senator Murdock connect the "entire gold monetary holdings of the world" to this change in the Federal Reserve Act? Dean Acheson mentioned the British.

> The British like to say that this is a departure from the gold standard. We like to say that this resembles the gold standard. Neither one of us has any differences as to what the plan provides. We differ in the words we like to use about it . . . the first thing the Fund asks its members to do is to define their currencies in terms of gold.

Apparently, this was the deal, whatever was necessary by the money interests, in terms of money, in terms of gold, in the scheme of things. The original 1913 non-legal tender Federal Reserve note had a destiny. The note acquired gold; the note went to Europe after World War I. The 1945 legal tender Federal Reserve note was a Bretton Woods paper currency at $35 an ounce of gold destined for international finance after World War II. The U.S. obligation was to be a global currency; its fiat security, principal, and interest would be at American taxpayer expense. It appeared to be a new global economy in the offing, a lot of it paid for by the American people.

The Senate Banking and Currency hearings went into July 1945; many important people testified. Secretary Morgenthau appeared briefly at the beginning; he was followed by Secretary Dean Acheson, Assistant Secretary of the Treasury Dexter White, members of the Federal Reserve System, the Bankers Association, bankers from across the country, and many economists. Many points were made—quotas, percentage of quota to be borrowed in one year, interest rates, currency devaluations, nations in default, a British loan of $3-$4 billion, England's world trade sterling bloc, currency restrictions, impending trade dumping by Russia, the gold thing, the geopolitical scene, rogue nations, other blocked currencies, etc.; there were those for the agreements and those against.

One of the early considerations in the 1944 Bretton Woods proceedings was the recommendation to eliminate the Bank for International Settlements. Bretton Woods was setting up a new world bank. The BIS appeared the first world bank for all the central banks located in Basel, Switzerland. The BIS was never brought up or discussed during the Senate Banking and Currency hearings. Apparently, the order went out. The BIS exists today as one of the world's big money unknowns. Most people never heard of the BIS; Do we really have two world banks?

No one testifying made clear any details the specific money operations of the "fund" and the "bank" until Gertrude Coogan testified. Gertrude Coogan cut through the routine questioning. Gertrude Coogan, an economist from Chicago, and her assistants explained the intended money operations of and future effects of the Monetary Fund and the bank. "I think it qualifies me to interpret what actually is meant by the wording of the Bretton Woods Agreements, which may appear to be very obscure to people who really never delved into banking literature and the operations of metropolitan banks and the operations of foreign exchange markets." Apparently, the "obscurity" thing was relevant in the House of Representatives; the House passed H.R. 3314, the Bretton Woods Agreement. Gertrude Coogan testified that the Monetary Fund was going to create currency; this was the heart of the scheme. The fund was going to be a money machine; a lot of new money had to be created, and the Monetary Fund was designed to do just that.

At this point in the Bretton Woods research, things immediately became clearer for this writer; understanding of the scheme was at hand. The Bretton Woods fund was going to be a money creator. From the dictionary, a fund "is a supply that can be drawn from, a stock." As in all banks, funds or entities, which will lend money, need capital; a starting capital is required. The quotas in money to be placed by the United States and the forty-five countries was the original stock. Gertrude Coogan explained to the committee how currency would be created after the quotas or stock would be paid in, just like currency is created all the time by the Federal Reserve and the Bureau of Engraving and Printing. Gertrude Coogan reminded the committee that the subscription quotas would stay in the fund; quota money was not money to be lent or borrowed, and Secretary White admitted this earlier in the hearings. Coogan said that Secretary White's testimony, his example about the money lending process, that is, what money, and from where that money came from, was nonexistent in Secretary White's testimony.

The committee didn't believe or understand when Gertrude Coogan revealed the money operations of the fund and the bank. A remark by Senator Taft was "No, no!"

"I shall prove that the United States Government commitments are not limited to approximately $6,000,000,000, but could be up to $17,770,000,000 without any further appropriations from Congress." Members of the committee had read the statute but apparently didn't understand its meaning. This writer, when reading the hearings, didn't understand the borrowings and the extent of the quotas, the money placed by all the countries, the operations. Quota money eventually would exhaust itself? Those testifying, who were close to and part of the Bretton Woods Agreement, did not mention the heart of the scheme, the money creation process, not until Gertrude Coogan appeared. But this was the case; new money was going to be created after the subscription quota. The agreed subscription quota of the United States was $6 billion.

Gertrude Coogan told the committee that she and two assistants "searched all the money and banking statutes of the United States from the colonial period to 1943. This research included how the statutes were written, interpreted, and applied and the effects upon the whole American financial and economic system."

The people never understand the money statutes at the time of inception; aftershocks are the revelations. Thomas Jefferson had mentioned a long time ago how difficult it was for the "gulls" to understand the money schemes. Many in Congress never understood them either. The layperson, including this writer, may read the Banking and Currency statutes over and over and not understand them. The House had passed this bill; how much did they know or did not know.

Senator Taft read from the statute referred to by Coogan: "For the purpose of keeping to a minimum the cost to the United States of participation in the fund and the bank, after paying the subscription is authorized and directed to issue notes of the United States from time to time at par and to deliver such notes to the fund and the bank in exchange for dollars to the extent permitted by the respective articles of agreement."

Gertrude Coogan would show the committee that the U.S. Treasury would have two functions, a "participation" and a "subscription."

The committee's understanding was that the U.S. commitment to the fund and the bank was going to be $6 billion. Senator Taft said, "But this fund hasn't any right to accept deposits, as far as I know." There was to be no "duplication and I don't think it is." Senator Taft said Dexter White denied it certainly.

Gertrude Coogan explained,

> The words "in exchange" used in all banking statutes means that the person giving up a bond or note gets a deposit. If you go through the National Banking Act, and all the banking statutes, all the way through, the Federal Reserve Act, section 13 and section 24; the National Banking Act, section 5136 and section 5202 you will see that language every time and it means that the bank takes in the notes from the Treasury and gives a deposit offsetting it. It doesn't mean that the fund or the bank hands to the Treasury previously existing currencies or previously existing bank deposits.

The committee didn't accept the fact that more deposit money was forthcoming, that more money would be added to the quota subscription, a duplication of money. Ms. Coogan said, "Well, you are doing it in your legislation." Senator Taft said, "It is not intended to be a duplication and I don't think it is." Coogan stated, "It is, I would be glad to prove that if you want me to take the time . . . I would be glad to come over here with all the statutes and show them to you."

Apparently, congressmen didn't understand how the money scheme worked!

> Gentlemen, under this fund we are entering into deficit financing on an international scale; in other words, allowing foreign governments and our own Government, to put their notes into the fund and have new moneys created. We are going one step further out into the deep by allowing international deficit financing on top of domestic financing. Instead of the United States Treasury putting United States Treasury notes into domestic banks and receiving a "deposit," H.R. 3314 authorizes the Secretary to put United States special notes into the International Fund and receive a "deposit."

On the domestic scene, in the Federal Reserve System, the security represents the exchange for dollars. The Bretton Woods statute did not use the word "security"; the word "note" was used. Coogan used the words "United States Treasury Notes"; House Bill 3314 called them "notes." It was the same kind of transaction; the international fund would receive these "notes," which was similar to the Federal Reserve getting a security through its agent. The "notes" represented currency, and currency would be placed in the fund. Hopefully, this business becomes clearer as we go along. Money is created against a value, a credit; in these particular cases, it was a security, a bond, or a "note."

Gertrude Coogan submitted existing statutes and translated the wording of the Bretton Woods H.R. 3314 for the committee; briefly, her points follow:

- House Bill H.R. 3314 dictated two separate and distinct commitments of the United States government.
  1. There would be a subscription quota; after the subscription quota was paid in.
  2. There would be a participation transaction.
- The quota subscription would come from the 1934 Stabilization Fund and sale of savings bonds to the public (credits existed in the Stabilization Fund).

- The Congress would have to raise the public debt limit.
- Total U.S. quota subscription money to the fund and the bank—$6 billion.
- After the quota was paid in, the participation function would take place. This function was of the secretary of the Treasury.
- H.R.3314 would allow the secretary of the Treasury to issue "special notes" to the fund and the bank in "exchange for dollars." The "exchange for dollars" meant just that; the fund, on a demand to the Treasury, would receive new currency or Federal Reserve Notes for the participation "special notes."

Coogan explained that the fund and the bank did not give up any part of the quota, that is, the currency and gold paid in initially. "Where else could the Fund or the Bank get the dollars for the United States participation in the Fund or the Bank?" Currency had to be created. The fund and the bank got the spending money after the Treasury issued the special notes. It wasn't clear when first reading the recorded hearings. Each nation would be allowed to borrow 25% of its quota in one year; after four years, the quota was exhausted? This was one of the questions raised by the committee; there didn't appear a definitive answer to the question until Coogan appeared. There was to be no exhaustion of the quota! The subscription quota was stock, the reserve.

Based on the statute wording, the U.S. participation would be 100% of the quota.

The special notes issued should not exceed the subscription amount paid in; that meant equivalent to or equal to the quota amount paid in. The fund and the bank would receive a "deposit" of dollars for the special notes given up by the Treasury. This new currency did not exist before the U.S. Treasury participation transaction. The 100% participation would double the amount of money in the fund and or the bank.

In the past, amendments to the National Bank Act increased a deposit in dollars to 200% of deposits paid into a bank. A similar scheme was made part of the Bretton Woods plan. Coogan reminded the committee that this money creation business had been going on since the "Congress, under the National Bank Act and amendments, the Federal Reserve Act and amendments, the Liberty Bond Act and amendments . . . conveyed to the domestic banks identical power to create new and additional dollars [deposits]." H.R. 3314 extended these powers to the Bretton Woods Agreement.

The National Bank Act started the credit circulation thing in 1863; Secretary Chase planted the seed in 1861. The credit circulation was broadened in 1913 when the non-legal tender Federal Reserve note, the U.S. government obligation, was introduced when fiat money was borrowed, that is, new money was created. In the Federal Reserve System, the new currency created is interest bearing; we, the people, are paying interest on the currency and the security upon issue forever.

The subscription quota to the fund and the bank was $6 billion. The participation notes called for another $6 billion. Two billion of the quota money came from Roosevelt's 1934 Stabilization Fund. Twelve billion dollars would be added to the public debt. The total U.S. commitment, now doubled, would be $12 billion; we are not quite finished.

Coogan added that if the U.S. Treasury were to redeem the $6 billion in participation notes as stipulated in H.R. 3314, then according to the statute, the $6 billion would be an additional commitment to the fund and the bank. The total U.S. commitment to the fund and the bank could amount to $18 billion. Coogan's actual figure was $17.77 billion. The redemption would be by way of the Federal Reserve process. Countries in the Monetary Fund in the future could use these participation dollars to claim gold from the Treasury/Federal Reserve System.

Gertrude Coogan illustrated a maximum payout. She said the total "could be" up to $18 billion. The "notes" represented debt, the security for participation currency paid in. If the Treasury redeemed the "notes," it would be the same as paying off the debt. It didn't appear the Treasury was going to pay any of this debt, up to $6 billion more. A new IMF debt scheme was just the beginning, a debt scheme to create money.

The new participation currency would go on the books of the Federal Reserve bank. Most of the subscription quota came from the Stabilization Fund, already credited. The participation currency was more deficit spending. This was the fiat credit, the printing of paper currency against a security. In the Bretton Woods case, it was the participation currency against the "notes."

The participation notes, the "special notes," or "Treasury Notes" were similar to U.S. government "obligations," the same as a security for circulation. What else could the notes be? Coogan didn't go that one step further and say; the Treasury notes were similar to the security for the currency? There was a difference; these notes, although payable, would be non-interest bearing. On the national scene, the security is interest bearing.

On the national/domestic scene, the security for the credit circulation is part of the ongoing public debt; the government continues paying the interest but never pays off the principal or the security. It's the endless fiat credit debacle, interest-bearing currency, the credit circulation. The government did pay some principal when it swapped greenbacks for security obligations; this supposedly happened in the gold swap, the gold to the Treasury, the greenbacks and gold certificates to the reserve bank.

Foreign countries eventually claimed gold instead of dollars through the Monetary Fund between 1945 and 1970, causing a drain on United States gold. All this, apparently, was a designed redistribution of gold to the world's central banks.

The testimony by Coogan explained the subscription and participation commitments of the United States. The Bretton Woods Agreement, approved in House Bill H.R. 3314, covered all forty-five countries. All the countries, apparently, would perform similar functions, that is, to subscribe and participate? Foreign currencies would be created as well by their central banks, convertible into dollars? This Bretton Woods

Agreement was to be a remarkable creation of international money. The predominant currency would be United States dollars.

Gertrude Coogan went through the statutes and amendments thereto, covering the period 1863 to 1945, explaining the creation of dollars (deposits) in the United States government's creation of the private banking system.

> Thus for the first time the monetary reserves in the United States will not be confined as now to United States lawful money and United States Government obligations now issued under direct acts of the United States Congress, but will consist of foreign currencies and foreign government I O U 's and foreign central bank I O U 's [all countries]. The powers of the International Fund and the powers of the International Bank to create new and additional deposits [dollars] is identical with the powers to create new and additional dollars [deposits] conveyed by the United States Congress to the domestic commercial banks under the National Bank Act of 1863 and amended by the Federal Reserve Act of 1913 and its amendments . . . deficit financing would be carried on internationally.

The money creators have shown a remarkable record in the continuing search for more money.

As part of the money spiral in the Bretton Woods scheme, Coogan continued,

> Thus in addition to creating new and additional deposits [dollars] to take in United States special notes up to "a sum not to exceed in the aggregate the amount of United States subscriptions actually paid to the fund." [sec. 8(c) H.R. 3314] The fund could create new and additional deposits [dollars] to buy foreign currencies or to lend dollars to foreign countries up to a sum equivalent to 200 per cent of the subscription quota of each purchasing or borrowing country.

It was now a 200% figure. Again, the "United States special notes" was the security, and along with the security came the dollars. Apparently, down the road, when the U.S. Treasury paid in the participation dollars, foreign countries were asking for payment, not in dollars but in gold.

Gertrude Coogan said a probable total commitment by the United States to the "International Bank" was to be $9.5 billion: "The International Bank had the same power of money creation as the Fund." According to the Gertrude Coogan's testimony, without further Congressional approval, the cost of the fund and the bank to the United States at its inception could amount to almost $18 billion—$8.3 billion to the fund and $9.5 billion to the bank. (Again, Coogan was adding the $6 billion redemption figure; quota and participation monies would total $12 billion.)

> I shall be glad, if requested by this Committee, to submit amendments to this bill [H.R. 3314], which I think would serve to keep control of United States money and bank reserves in Congress and to limit the obligation of the United States under the Bretton Woods bill to the $6,000,000,000 which the American people have been told is to be their burden under the agreement. As it is, it is not too extreme to say that the Bretton Woods agreement is a swindle against the American people.

Senator Taft said, "I think if you would submit those amendments we would be glad to see them."

The Senate Banking and Currency Committee concluded its hearings on June 25, 1945, after which the committee went into executive session. The executive session was not open to the public. After the executive session, the House Bill H.R. 3314 went to the Senate with four amendments recommended. There was little noticeable change to the bill in the Senate. According to the debates and testimonies in the *Congressional Record*, the administration and the Treasury wanted no changes to the wording of the agreement. On July 19, the Senate passed H.R. 3314 by a vote of 61-16. "The Bretton Woods Agreement Act" became law on July 31, 1945.

The Bretton Woods Agreement would restore, rebuild, get world trade moving again. The Bretton Woods fund and the bank would not pay for the World War II debts incurred or debts incurred prior. The $1.3 trillion World War II debt was one thing; the future world restoration cost was another. Alexander Hamilton's federal expenses were permanently unlimited, "even in imagination"; expenses were moving into a higher gear.

Republican Senator Taft of Ohio, the bill's sharpest critic, wanted to postpone the agreement for two years. Why the need for Bretton Woods when there is the existence of the Export-Import Bank? The House was approving "an Export/Import bill providing $3,000,000,000 dollars in foreign loans"; these loans, apparently, were destined for Europe. Also, in addition to Bretton Woods, Great Britain was getting a $3,750,000,000 dollar loan. By joint resolution, this took place on July 15, 1946: "Whereas in further implementation of the purposes of the Bretton Woods Agreements, the Governments of the United States and the United Kingdom have negotiated an agreement dated December 6, 1945" (Public Law 509, the Book of Statutes, 1946, Vol. 1, Page 535). There was the continuing yearly lend-lease of $4 billion going to Great Britain. An amount of $1 billion in loans was slated for Russia in addition to Bretton Woods. Why the need for Bretton Woods?

What was the difference between the new fund and the Bank for Reconstruction and the Export-Import Bank? The new International Monetary Fund and Bank would be lending currency to member countries of the fund. The Export-Import Bank would lend to "American exporters, by financing exports, and also in direct loans to Governments." Senator Taft presented this comparison.

Senator Taft also disagreed with Article XIV of the agreement. Because of the war, Article XIV would allow exchange restrictions. World War II was still going on. The war had placed the industrialized world into social and economic chaos; there had to be outright despair in some countries. The United Kingdom, standing alone early on, had borrowed heavily; she owed billions worldwide. Senator Barkley said, "Britain was all that stood between the rest of the world and Hitler." The sterling bloc existed where Great Britain had borrowed. Article

XIV would allow countries such as Great Britain to maintain currency restrictions for a minimum period of three years to get their house in order. Great Britain maintained $15 billion of blocked sterling around the world.

Senator Taft mentioned the testimony of Secretary White and Mr. Williams of the Federal Reserve. They both "suggested that if we were going to solve the British problem, if we were going to get the British to remove any of the exchange restrictions which are supposed to be removed under the fund we would have to lend them or give them $3,000,000,000 in order to help them solve their whole world problem of $15,000,000,000 of blocked sterling which would have to be funded, and a lot of other things."

Great Britain needed financial assistance; the present administration, the planners of Bretton Woods, according to the testimony, were granting that assistance to the United Kingdom. According to Sidney Campbell, financial editor of Reuters, Britain didn't want a "commercial" loan with interest; "A grant-in-aid would, of course, be accepted . . . In return for such aid, Britain would be only too glad to make what Americans would regard as concessions in regard to freeing sterling and mitigating the exclusivity of the sterling area." This is "what Lord Keynes wanted and what the English wanted . . . a grant-in-aid."

The Monetary Fund was planned to fix the values of the world's currencies in terms of the United States dollar, to allow the purchase of a member's currency by another member's currency, to allow the borrowing of dollars based on a quota of a member's currency subscribed to the fund. No member could borrow, in one year, more than 25% of its quota paid in, this with no restrictions pending. An initial 10% currency devaluation would be allowed. Why, in the first place, were currency restrictions a part of the Bretton Woods Agreement? Restrictions were adverse to the planned stabilization of the world's currencies. Apparently, it was the input of Lord John Maynard Keynes. Senator Taft wanted Article XIV changed. A currency bloc of sterling would impair United States trade. Taft presented an amendment whereby no member "shall be entitled to buy currency of another member from the Fund in exchange for its own currency until it shall have removed all restrictions referred to in Article VIII, sections 2, 3, and 4 which have not been approved by the Fund." Senator Taft's amendment was rejected.

Chairman Wagner of the Banking and Currency Committee said, "The question before us is whether by default we will allow the world to repeat the tragic blunders of the 1920's and 1930's." Wagner mentioned the decline in world trade during the period, the economic warfare.

> Between 1929 and 1932 the dollar value of world trade fell nearly 70 percent. Even after substantial industrial recovery had taken place in many countries, the value of world trade in the 1930's remained 40 percent below the level of the 1920's . . . Japan and Germany—employing every unfair economic weapon that could be devised—were among the small group of countries that gained relatively at our expense . . . Would a large gift or loan solve Britain's balance of payments problem? . . . Britain can do this only if world trade is stabilized at a relatively high level. Britain's basic problem, therefore, is to obtain a fair share of an enlarged world trade.

Wagner mentioned the 1934 Stabilization Fund; he said,

> The United States set up an exchange stabilization fund with the object of helping to stabilize the exchanges between ourselves and other countries . . . In 1936, a modest beginning was made toward multilateral action, through the tripartite declaration, which at first covered only the United States, Great Britain, and France. Subsequently, Belgium, the Netherlands, and Switzerland were added.

"The Fund will help countries maintain these fair-exchange practices by helping them at a time when there is pressure on the exchanges. The Fund will have resources of $8,800,000,000 in gold and currencies to be used specifically for this purpose." This from Chairman Wagner.

An amount of $8.8 billion was the total subscription to the fund by all the forty-five countries while $9.1 billion was the subscription total by all to the bank, a total of $18 billion of quota. The United States total subscription quota to the fund and the bank was $6,000,000,000. The above figures were quota, "reserve," not to be touched, according to Gertrude Coogan. These figures were the planned numbers before the bill went to the Congress. The act became law, and the Articles of Agreement of the International Monetary Fund was signed on December 27, 1945; the above monies remained a part of the approved act and the agreement.

The $8.8 billion and $9.1 billion quotas were monies to be subscribed by the respective forty-five governments through their central banks; the monies, apparently, were public monies. The subscription quota was a reserve or stock.. Secretary Dexter White testified that the quota money or stock was not to be used, but a lot of money was going to be used, to be exchanged and borrowed. Secretary White, in his public testimony, did not disclose the source of currency to be used, to be borrowed and/or exchanged.

Gertrude Coogan's testimony primarily concerned one section of the Bretton Woods Act. It was Section 8(c). This section became Section 7(c), but the wording remained the same. This section specified the "participation in the Fund and the Bank" after the subscription quota was paid in. Wagner's committee did not alter or change the wording in this section.

Section 8(c) was not included in the Senate debate; Senator Wagner, chairman of the banking committee, and the Democratic majority didn't bring it up. Republican Senator Taft, who spearheaded the opposition, didn't mention Section 8(c). Apparently, the Senate "dummied up." Section 8(c) was not to be touched; it was the crux of the scheme. This section was not going to be changed. Section 8(c) described how the fund and the bank would "create new and additional deposits [dollars]," the currency needed to conduct business.

The amount of $6,000,000,000 was the figure publicized to businesses, church organizations, and farm associations; the American people were told that $6,000,000,000 was the American commitment to the Bretton Woods Agreement, and this was the legislated amount. Congress approved the agreement, a scheme, which revealed a $6,000,000,000 "subscription" commitment. A probable $12,000,000,000 expenditure, a total quota and participation would not be foreseen, which was a United States commitment to the fund and the bank as described by Gertrude Coogan.

The *New York Times*, on July 19, 1945, on the front page reported, "The bill provides for ultimate contributions by this country of close to $6,000,000,000 to a $8,800,000,000 International Monetary Fund to stabilize currencies and outlaw restrictive currency practices, and a $10,000,000,000 Bank for Reconstruction and Development."

The Congress removed Section 6 and stated, "When the United States is requested by the Fund to communicate the par value of the United States dollar, such par value shall not be communicated as other than 15 and 5/21 grains of gold nine-tenths fine." Why was Section 6 removed? According to Roosevelt's 1934 Gold Act, the dollar could be devalued again from its then present 60% value in gold to 50% of its 1900 value in gold. Apparently, the possibility existed of a further dollar devaluation?

The Bretton Woods Act Public Law 171 is in the Book of Statutes, 1945, volume 1, pages 512 to 517 in the Madison Building, room 201, the Library of Congress. The Articles of Agreement of the International Monetary Fund and the bank are documented as part of the Treaties And International Agreements Other Than Treaties. The Articles of Agreement were signed December 27, 1945, as seen in pages 1, 401 to 1,482.

From "REVIEW and OUTLOOK, Without a Foundation" in the *Wall Street Journal*, July 20, 1945, the following is stated, "Bretton Woods by itself will not revive American export trade—except possibly for a brief period followed by a most disastrous slump. Bretton Woods by itself will not stabilize any exchanges. The energy to operate it is lacking under the present conditions." The editorial mentioned the

> restrictions and discriminations in foreign trade which the Nazis developed to the highest degree will by no means disappear with the Nazis . . . If Great Britain, for instance, attempts to protect her internal economy with

a series of exchange quota agreements and bilateral trade arrangements, other nations will take retaliatory measures. The result will be a world of state barter. It would be like a small primitive community where a man wanting a pair of shoes first had to find someone who would accept so many pecks of potatoes or so many hours work in payment.

In America, the money is in New York; on Wall Street, the word "barter," naturally, doesn't bode well. The C. W. Barron paper was predicting an eventuality. Great Britain, apparently, was going to do that same terrible thing Germany did before World War II; Great Britain was going to barter. Great Britain and the Bank of England had created a money scheme that propels us today. In 1946, after 250 years, England could not pay in gold and or the equivalent in currency; England wanted to pay her 15 billion in debts with the equivalent in goods. Great Britain, the creator of this money creation business, was going to barter?

A *New York Times* editorial stated, "It is important that every effort be made to make this plan work." Bretton Woods was called "a symbol of internationalism." The opponents were "dubbed nationalists."

While this business was going on, Great Britain was making bilateral agreements with Belgium, Sweden, and France. "Federal Reserve Bank Sees Danger In Europe's Financial Agreements." This was an article in the *Journal* on August 1, 1945, after Bretton Woods became law. The Reserve Bank of New York was concerned about Britain's agreements with these countries. But the Federal Reserve was an integral part of the Bretton Woods Agreement. The article stated that "there is a possibility, it notes, that if Britain's balance of payments difficulties are not adequately resolved, the agreements may be extended beyond the transition period for which they were designed."

Senate hearings continued; the agenda was the "ANGLO-AMERICAN FINANCIAL AGREEMENT." Extensive Senate debate followed. In 1946, the $3.75 billion loan went to Great Britain, and where was England headed? It was now Prime Minister Attlee and the "Labor movement." The great warrior and leader Winston Churchill was voted out of office in 1945 in the midst of the remaining war with Japan; this event seemed unbelievable in the United States, a real shocker. The political and economic climate had changed in England, but its attitude toward the United States was the same when it came to money. The climate in the Congress was reciprocal.

Was England "stone cold broke"? Loans were in the works; Great Britain was lending Greece "$44,800,000" and Czechoslovakia "25,000,000 gold pounds." Mr. Celler of New York, in December 1945, was speaking in the House; England would be lending our money to these countries. About the British loan, the American people would pay more, a "4%" interest to raise the money to lend to England; it didn't matter. About the payments and the "1.62% interest; "The London *Economist* is quoted as saying that the terms are cruel . . . Britain's plight is due to the fact that she fought the war the earliest, the longest, and the hardest, and for that it charges we are to pay $140,000,000 annually for the rest of the twentieth century."

There were members of Congress who felt that this loan and the 24 billions in lend-lease would never be paid. The World War I debts were never paid. Senator Brooks, on December 17, 1945, said that some of this loan would be spent in the United States. Payments to the United States would be spent in England? Apparently, agreements were made between the two governments that were beyond the scope of Congress and the newspapers.

The empire of Great Britain was waning; after 250 years and two world wars, perpetual indebtedness, apparently, had exceeded the growth rate. Socialism was in the offing; the British government had taken over the Bank of England? Great Britain needed money to get back on track; financial aid was there from the United States government. In the "Loan Agreement the United Kingdom agreed that after July 15, 1946, it would not apply exchange controls in such a manner as to restrict payments or transfers in respect of the products which it imported from the United States, or the use of sterling balances which United States residents had acquired as a result of current transactions." There were the exceptions as to "the settlement of its accumulated sterling balances." There were "certain countries with which the United Kingdom Government had not yet negotiated agreements."

There was another matter, the UNRRA agreement; this was the United Nations Relief and Rehabilitation Administration to the tune of $1.35 billion. What was "the money to be used for and what countries will receive it"? this from Senator Taft. There were "six million homeless people in the devastated areas of the Byelo-Russian and the Ukraine Republics of the Soviet Union." Money went for housing and the restoration of industry for these people. The American people responded. UNRRA was responsible for the "sorting, baling, and shipment of approximately 160 million pounds of new and used clothing contributed by the people of the United States for relief overseas." This was just part of the need, but at the same time, the Soviet Union was swiftly dominating in its

Communist influence and takeover in Eastern European occupation. Winston Churchill called it an "Iron Curtain" toward world domination.

The San Francisco Conference, which was the extension of Dumbarton Oaks, established a charter in June of 1945. In 1945, members of fifty nations signed the charter; this was the beginning of the United Nations. These nations met for the first time in London in October of 1946. The United Nations assembly was later transferred to New York, its present location. Many world changes were to come. India was critical of the 1945 Charter: "The great powers had shown no inclination at San Francisco to give up colonial possessions and special privileges enjoyed at the expense of dependent peoples." It was the "old mandate system of the league of nations . . . independence" was out of the question. The "evidence" was there; "that the Imperialist powers still are functioning in their old imperialist way and intend to retain and exploit their possessions."

In 1946, twelve million American military men and women began the transition to civilian life. There were that many people out of work before World War II. The war interrupted and ended an abyss in America. In 1941, the United States was behind, unprepared for war. Its dramatic massive wartime military and naval buildup in four war years was awesome; the effort will never be equaled. The United States supplied itself, Great Britain, France, and the Soviet Union. Germany and Japan were eventually overwhelmed. Historians called it brute force.

America came together in war. There was full employment; the people had jobs in defense plants to complement those who fought in the war. The defense plants changed the American demographic, swelling metropolitan areas. In the coming peace, existing underlying social and economic ills resurfaced. Segregation, racial hatreds, secular injustice, the lack of credits and money in all places, and more wars occupied the national existence, this while America became an international economic custodian and benefactor. President Truman put a dent in some of the domestic ills; President Truman ended segregation in the military and the navy. Truman improved Social Security. Labor got a lift, and the minimum wage was increased.

John Snyder was the new secretary of the Treasury; in 1947, the International Monetary Fund began "active operations." The International Bank for Reconstruction and Development "opened for business" in 1946. The secretary, in his 1947 report, said that U.S. "subscription" money was paid into the Monetary Fund; about $700 million in gold, almost $300 million in cash, and $1,800,000,000 came from the 1934 Stabilization Fund, almost $3 billion in gold and currency as stipulated by the agreement. The secretary stated that $1.78 billion in non-interest-bearing notes were paid in; there it was! "These notes are payable on demand in dollars when needed by the Fund in its operations." The secretary didn't call them participation notes in his report. The initial participation would be the 1.78 billion in non-interest-bearing notes; this was the United States Treasury "participation" to the Monetary Fund. This was the beginning of the operational money to be paid in by the Treasury to the fund; the fund could then conduct business.

When needed for "operations," the fund would "demand" 1.78 billion in new deposits (dollars) or currency to be paid into the fund by the United States Treasury. This was Gertrude Coogan's description of deficit spending, which is currency ordered to be printed by the Treasury courtesy of the American taxpayer "paid in." At the start, the money paid in to the fund by the U.S. Treasury would be $2.8 billion subscription quota plus $1.78 billion participation, which equals $4.58 billion.

There was the bank. Approximately 20% of subscription money, by all members, was to be paid into the bank by May 26, 1947; the United

States total was "$635,000,000." Foreign members' total figures were not shown. "The remainder of the United States subscription to the capital stock of the Bank will not be called unless funds are needed to make payments to investors to meet obligations of the Bank." Apparently, bank operation differed. But like all banks, this bank, no doubt, was going to make a profit. The statement "payments to investors" illustrated the reality; the bank was just opening for business, and a return to investors was its first course of action. The Treasury kept the total initial outlay less than the six billion publicized dollars: 4.58 (fund) + 0.64 (bank) = $5.22 billion.

The 1947 report stated,

> Soon after the Bank opened for business on June 25, 1946, the United States Executive Director consulted the Council as to whether Article IV, section 2 [a] and [b] of the articles of agreement required the Bank to obtain United States approval in order to lend or invest dollars derived from the 2 per cent payable in gold or dollars by all members on their capital subscription [no approval was required]. The Council also advised the United States Executive Director that it saw no objection to the investment of these funds in short-term obligations of the United States, if the Bank found that it had adequate authority under the articles of agreement to invest these funds in such securities. Subsequently the Bank invested $127, 500,000 in short-term United States Government securities.

Apparently, before anything else, the bank invested public currency in United States public securities.

According to the 1947 report, the money totaled $127,500,000. The secretary and the council called it an investment. These transactions would go on the books of the Federal Reserve System? Who were the investors? The investors were apparently the member nations, including the United States. The securities were sold on the open market. There was no mention of the Treasury and related "participation notes" paid into the bank, only subscription money; but participation notes had been paid into the fund.

The International Bank's inaugural action, according to Secretary Snyder's 1947 report, showed in-house profit motive with public subscription stock paid in. This apparently was a second leg of the deficit spending, an initial creation of fiat currency for investment; it would be nice if the taxes paid in by the working people for this fiat currency was a monetary investment for the people. There appears no discernible return.

The money market or commercial banks probably buy these securities, an apparent extension of the Pennsylvania creditors' declaration. Federal Reserve member banks would buy the International Bank securities. Initial public funds profits this business. From the record, American fiat currency was there for the bank in its national and international operations.

"March 1, 1947, was the date established by the Fund for the beginning of exchange transactions." Secretary Snyder said that "almost all of the member countries had completed payment of their subscriptions . . . In the course of the fiscal year . . . Applications for loans totaling more than $2 billion were received by the Bank." France had borrowed "$250 million." Apparently, quota and participation money necessary for these loans was $2 billion.

Bretton Woods was under the direction of the "National Advisory Council on International and Monetary Financial Problems." The council directors were the following:

- Secretary of the Treasury (Chairman) John Snyder
- Secretary of State George C. Marshall
- Secretary of Commerce W. Averell Harriman
- Chairman of the Federal Reserve Marriner S. Eccles
- Chairman of the Export-Import Bank William Martin Jr. (The council approved $325 million in loans by the bank in 1947.)

The council was responsible for the "settlement of lend lease and other wartime obligations" with fourteen countries, including Great Britain. As early as 1947, the Soviet Union had no intention of participation in the Monetary Fund. Lend-lease and other debts owed by Russia were apparently never paid. Wasn't the intent of the Soviet Union from the beginning the demise of capitalism? All of Russia's hoopla in the beginning of the IMF was just that, a bunch of crap!

"It is true that Russia has so far declined to join the Fund, although the Soviets were one of the originators of the plan; but all of the red satellite nations of Europe are waiting in line for the cashiers wicket to open. This takes a load off Russia's back, in effect giving Russia a loan without requiring her to guarantee payment." Congressman Frederick C. Smith of Ohio presented this *California Mining Journal* article in the House on March 7, 1947.

The Communist cloud was forming. From the record, Great Britain, for more than two centuries, had colonized and dominated the modern financial world in trade, gold, and the money exchange. Congressman Fess in the 1920s said the new world threat was going to be Russia. Enter the Soviet Union in 1947, its political takeover of Eastern Europe, and the beginning of the cold war.

It was the beginning of the Eurodollar thing. The United States, within its domain, was always considered national; financial entities, like banks, identified with the national prefix. International would eventually dictate domestic to the United States; it's the dictates of money. With the vast manipulation and control of money appears the world's contradiction. How can international exist if national does not exist? The International Monetary Fund was a money creation scheme. The predominant currency was the United States Federal Reserve Note created by the U.S. Treasury and paid into the International Fund.

Foreign countries created their paper currencies, which were paid into the fund, "and it may be merely a coincidence that the amount of gold payable by foreign nations is just about the same as that the New Deal has shipped abroad in the last 3 years," this from the *California Mining Journal* of March 1947. Many of the foreign paper currencies, according to the record, weren't worth zilch, but the Monetary Fund gave them value. The foreign currencies were valued against the U.S. dollar and used to obtain the U.S. Federal Reserve Note. The note found its way into a separate European money market, the Eurodollar market.

The International Monetary Fund was a plan of distribution and stabilization of currencies among nations on the international scene, a plan to help restore a basis of money in Europe, Asia, the Middle East, South America, etc. Huge sums of money, grants, and loans to foreigners was continuous; there was the Economic Assistance Program. "There were serious shortages of food in many countries. Foreign countries thus required more in goods and services from the United States to supply their immediate needs and to provide capital for reconstruction than they could obtain by the sale of goods and services to the United States."

Fortunes in a world at intervals of war were constantly changing; the United States was now the creditor, and the creditor doesn't sustain without a paying debtor. With all the grants and unpaid loans, the United States was doing the bulk of the paying. The "Gold Declaration of February 2, 1944" was being enforced; "looted gold" by Germany was being returned to the rightful countries. It has been said, there are no winners in war, but to the victors go the spoils; the United States and the Soviet Union looted Germany of its top scientists, engineers, and advanced technology and weaponry after World War II. The two countries were gearing up for the impending cold war.

In 1796, George Washington, when leaving the presidency, told a very young United States not to get involved with foreigners, their policy and affairs. International money changes everything; a poor United States began as a debtor and became a creditor. The transition took 130 years; the United States had become rich, powerful. The involvement in two world wars was instrumental; the United States had accumulated most of the world's gold. With the international monetary setup, the U.S. Treasury would be buying and selling currencies and gold. Foreign governments and their central banks would be buying dollars and gold from the fund with their currencies and the other way around.

The currency exchange rates were set during the war, in 1944. The Monetary Fund did allow a devaluation process as part of the agreement; it wasn't used at first. The rates did change after a period of five years. Great Britain was the first; an imbalance in trade in England's favor was what she wanted. "The devaluation of the pound sterling in September 1949 by 30.5 percent was followed by the devaluations of many other countries." The pound was reduced from $4.30 to $2.80. Great Britain slashed U.S. imports by 25%.

The Treasury in 1950 reported that the original rates "had become increasingly less satisfactory." A "balance of payments" wasn't working, especially with the U.S. economy. There had been a lull in trade, which, according to the Treasury, picked up again after currency adjustments to the dollar. The buying of United States gold with foreign dollars picked up in 1950; it was the beginning of a continuous credit movement of more gold from the United States to the foreign country. The reason: the trade imbalance had shifted and foreign dumping of manufactured products became a problem. For the first time since the war, the United States was importing more than exporting; the redistribution of gold had begun.

The National Advisory Council reported in March 1950 that currency block restrictions persisted. Great Britain was having problems as early as 1947. Its payments in dollars and gold had been going fast; there were still fourteen countries where United Kingdom agreements had not been made. The International Bank had been making loans; its loans up to 1950, according to the Treasury, "were financed in large part from the United States subscription." As stated in earlier reports and the 1950 report, this bank had "floated its securities on the United States market." The International Bank was lending money obtained from securities sold in the open market; these securities were more than likely purchased by the bank with money paid in by the Treasury and other governments?

As of 1950, the bank had invested $434 million in government obligations. The record was vague; there was no specific account of participation notes sent to the bank as reported by the Treasury. The International Bank had loaned a total of $738 million. Aside from the Monetary Fund and the bank, Treasury loans and grants to foreign countries by 1950 totaled $23.3 billion; this was in addition to World War II Lend-Lease and the $12 billion World War I foreign debt, which remained unpaid. "The United States Economic Assistance Programs" was responsible for the "European Recovery Program" (the Marshall

Plan), which included billions of dollars in aid to all the countries including the Soviet satellites.

World War I ended, but war didn't end; World War II ended, but war didn't end. Soviet Communism spread quickly to Poland, Yugoslavia, Hungary, Bulgaria, and Romania.

Russia controlled the political economies of Eastern Europe. The peace process sliced Germany into two parts, East and West. The Russians occupied East Germany; the United States, Britain, and France occupied West Germany. Military occupation was the norm. Berlin's location guaranteed confrontation; Berlin was in East Germany. Secretary John Snyder reported that the United States wanted a uniform currency for Berlin. The Russians refused the legal tender deutsche mark currency, which circulated in West Berlin; the Russians printed a Soviet mark, which was allowed to circulate in West Germany. This was another concession to appease the tyrant.

In 1948, the Russians shut down all access in and out of Berlin. All roads and railway routes were closed; West Berlin was shut off from West Germany and the outside world. It was a commercial shutdown. The Russians wanted to chase the Americans, British, and French out of Berlin, this from Secretary Snyder's 1952 annual report. Starting in 1948, the United States airlifted thousands of tons of supplies to west Berlin. Allied airplanes flew in and out of west Berlin daily until May 1949. The people of west Berlin survived; the "Berlin Airlift" succeeded, a remarkable achievement. Either this or outright war. The Soviets called off the blockade.

Communism reared its disruptive influence everywhere. World War II started because Poland was invaded. The invader was finally beaten back, defeated, and what was the result? Poland did not regain its independence, its nationality; Poland was now under Soviet Communist domination. The Korean War started in 1950; Communist North Korea invaded South Korea. In 1956, there was a revolution against Communist rule in Hungary; Russian tanks put that insurrection down. The Chinese Communist leader Mao Tse-tung and his army chased Chiang Kai-shek and his nationalists out of China. China was now Communist China; and the United States had been sending tens of millions of dollars in aid to China. Chiang fled to the island of Formosa; the island's name was changed to Taiwan.

In 1950, in the middle of the twentieth century, more than a quarter of the world's population was under Communist domination. World War II traded one tyrant for another, and the beat would go on. The cost was $1.3 trillion more of indebtedness and almost sixty million lives. The cost of the cold war would up the ante. Secretary John Snyder, in his 1952 summary, indicated the "disturbing elements" to the international economy because of the outbreak of the Korean War. It was not just a case of economic "recovery," but of a recovery of "defense." The International Monetary Fund and the bank had to move forward; necessary "adjustments" had to be made. Eight years after Bretton Woods, Secretary Snyder mentioned that the "Board of Governors have recently voted Jordan, Germany, and Japan to membership" in the fund and the bank.. Czechoslovakia was the only Communist country remaining in the membership.

The International Bank had lent $1.3 billion to foreign countries as of 1952. The bank's earnings in six years was $55 million. The bank members' "outstanding capital" was $8.5 billion. Secretary Snyder said the bank's money comprised three distinctive parts of this capital. Part (a) was 2% paid in, "in gold and currency." Part (b) was an 18% subscription quota in the "form of non-interest bearing demand notes, or in the form of cash." John Snyder explained, "The Bank may loan 18 per cent capital funds only with the consent of the member concerned." The remaining part (c) was 80%; "this capital subscription is subject to call only to meet obligations of the Bank."

Secretary Snyder stated, "The Bank has been able to finance its operations out of paid-in portions of capital subscriptions and by the sale of securities, principally in the United States market."

In an earlier Treasury report, Snyder said the bank was allowed to use "capital subscriptions" paid-in to buy government securities as an investment. This was done right away; this was done in 1947. What securities did the bank sell in the open market? Snyder said, "The bulk of the United States subscription to the paid-in capital originally consisted of non-interest bearing demand notes in accordance with" the agreement and the statute. Snyder showed a table listing the paid-in monies. The 18% U.S. amount for lending was $571.5 million as of 1952. The 18% foreign amount for lending was $950 million.

According to Secretary Snyder, the International Bank used its funds to invest in United States Securities, to lend to foreign countries, to sell securities in the United States open market; the open market was banks and syndicates, both domestic and foreign. U.S. banks underwrote the securities sold by the International Bank. The bank's profit in six years was $55 million.

In trying to understand this business, Secretary Snyder said the bank had to "secure the bulk of its funds from the sale of its securities to private investors"; this was the secretary's report. Snyder didn't use the words "participation" and "exchange for dollars." Snyder used other words; he said "converted into cash" when describing the Treasury function with the International Bank. Secretary Snyder used the words in the "form of non-interest bearing demand notes, or in the form of cash."

The "converted into cash" was the outlay of currency handed to the bank by the secretary of the Treasury for operations before investing and lending? Snyder seemed to lump subscription money paid in with the non-interest-bearing "notes" paid in. The notes paid in, according to the statute, was the participation process for operating capital?. In any case, subscription quota money was supposedly reserve capital not to be used?

It would appear from Section 7(c) of the statute that before the bank's investments in U.S. government securities and the sale of securities to private investors, the bank needed the "exchange for dollars?" It was confusing reading Secretary Snyder's report; he never used the words "exchange for dollars" or "participation" money paid in. The exchange for dollars is the participation—the deficit spending fiat currency printed—needed by the Treasury to hand to the International Bank for operating capital? Secretary Snyder used the words in the "form of non-interest bearing demand notes, or in the form of cash."

CHAPTER SIXTEEN
Bretton Woods Altered

On August 16, 1971, President Richard Nixon ended it; the gold thing was over. Some would say the "farce" was finally at an end. The next day, President Nixon's picture was on the front page; the headlines in the *New York Times* were big and bold: "NIXON . . . SEVERS LINK BETWEEN DOLLAR AND GOLD." The *Wall Street Journal* coverage was not big and bold; a column stated, "Altering the Course, Nixon Devalues Dollar."

"Mr. Nixon said he was not devaluing the dollar. But he said, 'If you want to buy a foreign car, or take a trip abroad, market conditions may cause your dollar to buy slightly less.'" From that point on, the "United States would cease to convert foreign dollars into gold—unilaterally changing the 25-year old international monetary system." President Nixon said, "The time has come for exchange rates to be set straight and for the major nations to compete as equals." The gold drain was over!

Maybe the foreign nations were no longer stepchildren; they were getting well real fast. For too long, they'd been gobbling up too many dollars and too much gold. After World War II, the United States helped rebuild Europe at enormous cost. "In the period from July 1, 1945, to December 31, 1947, approximately $18 billion of aid in the form of grants or loans was made available by United States Government agencies," this from the 1948 annual Treasury report.

In the year 2006, foreign countries were still gobbling up the dollars; the trade imbalance was rumbling along. We are international now; the difference in the trade exchange is called the account balance. Since 1985, the United States was a debtor again; the United States appears to be the world's marketable dumping ground. The imbalance in trade is sending hundreds of billion dollars to the foreign country. The United States is borrowing back those same billions of dollars. The Chinese and the Japanese are probably funding American real estate. The account difference in 2006, from the *Wall Street Journal*, is minus a trillion dollars favoring the foreigner. Toyota Motor has built eleven factories in the United States.

The United States today appears primarily as a buyer of goods, as a producer, trader, and seller of goods taking second place. If the United States may someday falter, as Great Britain once did, the world's future money market will probably swing to China, Japan, Russia, the Middle East? America will be one country of many countries. Global economy, international money has become paramount; the wealth of indebtedness takes no prisoners and knows no boundaries.

In 1950, there was $24 billion in gold in the United States; in 1972, there was $11 billion in gold. This is from the 1972 annual report of the United States Treasury; George P. Schultz was the secretary of the Treasury.

The *Times* reported, "A period of turmoil in the foreign exchange markets is all but certain, which means uncertainty for American tourists, exporters, and importers." The dollar was going to "float" against other currencies. "The President said he was taking the action to stop 'the attacks of international money speculators' against the dollar. He did not raise the official price of gold, which has been $35 dollars an ounce since 1934." It was the end of the gold exchange? There would be a dollar devaluation to $38 in 1972; Secretary Schultz stated this in his 1972 report: "Reform" was expected in the International Monetary Fund and the International Bank, which would still continue to function. Gold was not a monetary exchange; it was a commodity again? People would eventually own gold again but as a commodity, not as money. The BIS was still there, the other world bank in Basel, Switzerland, the other bank people know nothing about.

It wasn't the best of times in August of 1971. President Nixon was winding down United States involvement in the Vietnam War. Richard Nixon was elected president in 1968.

Since the end of World War II and the start of Bretton Woods, the nuclear threat was constant. The American people built air-raid shelters in their homes. Russian pressure in Eastern Europe forced the United States and fifteen countries in Western Europe to form NATO, the North Atlantic Treaty Organization. NATO was formed to prevent the Soviet takeover by force of more European countries. West Germany and Italy were part of NATO. The United States—Soviet confrontation was very real; this was in 1949. President Dwight Eisenhower followed Truman in 1952; the Korean War was in progress. At home, Communism was in bloom, this from Senator Joseph McCarthy. Senator McCarthy became destructive; he did himself in, but Alger Hiss and many others were caught in the expose.

Eisenhower launched the Interstate Highway System; in the United States, it was to be the automobile and the truck, commerce on wheels. The railroads took a back seat; there wouldn't be any railroad passenger service in the United States if not for the Amtrack and state-subsidized commuter services. Eisenhower ended the Korean War. Enter Elvis Presley. The Russians launched Sputnik in 1957; the space race began, and the cold war escalated. Who would build more bombers, atomic bombs, and antiballistic missiles, the Russians or the United States? Eisenhower had his confrontation with the Russians; there was the Russia flyover incident in 1960 by a United States U-2 spy plane. In looking back, maybe the cold war was a colossal myth, an inducement for both countries to spend more money than either country had.

President John F. Kennedy in 1960, the first Catholic president, followed Eisenhower during a beaten-down economy. Kennedy started the Peace Corps; the Russians countered with the Berlin Wall. American presence in Vietnam became acute when Kennedy increased the number of military advisers in Vietnam. The Bay of Pigs was a disaster in Cuba, but Kennedy bested Soviet Premier Nikita Khrushchev during the Cuban missile crisis. Kennedy was for low-key in Vietnam, no major military force. Kennedy served just two years in office; he was assassinated in 1963. Enter the Beatles and the love generation. Lyndon B. Johnson of Texas became the thirty-sixth president. Johnson's first term in office went well; the economy was up, but Johnson escalated the Vietnam War. He sent five hundred thousand troops there. The draft stirred things up; this action by President Johnson escalated social disruption in the United States. America's young people rebelled; there were two wars, in Vietnam and civil strife at home. Notables like boxing champion Ali and American Olympic athletes in Mexico City denounced American policy. Civil rights legislation passed through the efforts of President Johnson, but there was no civil rights yet. The African Americans continued the fight for acceptance. Desegregation was unpopular, especially in the South; Governor George Wallace of Alabama led the segregation charge; he was later gunned down in Maryland. Civil rights demonstrations and the Ku Klux Klan preceded murder in Mississippi, riots and burning in city streets. Draft card burning, antiwar demonstrations, and drugs followed; it was the order of the day.

Reverend Martin Luther King led the black civil rights movement; for that, King was murdered in 1968. Robert Kennedy, former attorney general under President Kennedy, was murdered in Los Angeles, California, in 1968. Robert Kennedy was John F. Kennedy's brother; he had been campaigning for the Democratic nomination for president of the United States. President Lyndon Johnson was tired; he wanted no part of a second term. The war and more than fifty thousand American dead, apparently, did him in. It was a banner time in America!

The newspapers and television captured all the events; the media coverage permeated the American scene. Antiwar demonstrations and brutal attacks by police marked the 1968 Democratic National Convention in Chicago. The killing of demonstrating college students by National Guard units came later at Kent State University in Ohio. There was the plus side; American astronauts landed on the moon in 1969. After twelve years, America took the lead in the space race. The cold war persisted. The Soviet Union and Communist China, two former allies, kept the United States busy on the international scene amid a cultural revolution in America. Premier Khrushchev blustered, "We will bury you." Apparently, this was the Soviet's plan; capitalistic America, hopefully, would spend itself into oblivion confronting Communism and unrest around the world. Was this international money dictating? The industrial world had turned 180 degrees since World War II; Germany and Japan, two former enemies, were now America's friends.

President Richard Nixon was elected to a second term in 1972; his landslide victory carried every state but one. Nixon practically eliminated draft card burning. He instituted the draft lottery; the move interrupted the draft-dodging invasion into Canada. Nixon ended the fighting in Vietnam in August 1973; things were looking up. President Nixon coupled the ending of the war with renewed relations with Russia and China. President Nixon was on a roll, but Nixon's popularity faded fast. He was forced to resign in 1974 because of a political cover-up. Nixon was implicated in the Watergate scandal. The Watergate incident was the break-in of the Democratic National headquarters at the Watergate Hotel in Washington, D.C., by agents employed by the "Committee To Re-elect The President," the president being Richard Nixon. President Nixon's chief of staff, Bob Haldeman, Attorney General John Mitchell, and others were involved. Nixon, apparently, had spun a web of dirty politics and illegal search, which involved the FBI and the CIA. The FBI and the CIA don't get along; like army and navy, they should play an annual football game.

While this was going on, Nixon's point man, Vice President Spiro Agnew, in speeches around the country, was denouncing the liberals, the draft card burners, the antiwar demonstrations, exits into Canada, and the burning in the cities. Agnew ran into trouble; opponents went after him. He had been accepting kickbacks from people in his home state of Maryland. Spiro Agnew, the vice president of the United States, became another casualty; he was forced to resign. Spiro Agnew accepted gratuities; he felt he was innocent. Was there anything new here? President Nixon and the Republicans replaced the Democrats because of domestic chaos and Vietnam. Later in 1976, Jimmy Carter and the Democrats replaced the Republicans because of the Watergate stench.

Before Carter, Vice President Gerald Ford replaced Nixon as the thirty-eighth president. President Ford's legacy was his unending effort in trying to mend the country's differences. It was a no-win, considering the Watergate hangover; there were too many suspect administrators and politicians, and the economy was starting to sour. America the beautiful had shown an ugly side; returning Vietnam veterans, needing acceptance, were scorned. Ford's pardon of Nixon appeared as his right thing to do, but the pardon wasn't popular.

When it rains it pours. President Ford, the bystander in all this ugly business, took some nasty hits; he eluded two assassination attempts. The assassination attempts were unprecedented; the two attempted assassins were young women.

Ford's predecessors created the dark cloud; the cloud defeated Ford in the presidential election of 1976 by the Democrat Jimmy Carter, former governor of Georgia. Jimmy Carter became president when the economy was doing another downturn. The cyclical hits were doing their thing; inflation was to blame. Another problem was the usual unemployment; the consistent percentage of unemployed people appeared a capitalistic mainstay.

The first recession of impact after World War II occurred in 1959-1962. It was tight money and higher interest rates. This writer experienced the period; the economic drop-off was severe enough. Layoffs continued for more than a year; in some places, more than 15% of a workforce was reduced. There's never a problem if one has a job. In 1951, President Truman and Chairman Eccles had differences. Truman wanted interest rates to remain fixed; they had remained fixed since World War II. Truman replaced Eccles. But the Federal Reserve had its way because Eisenhower wasn't Truman. Interest rates would continue to rise; in 1959, short-term rates on securities were three times higher than the year before. Rates were higher; money was tight. What else? The government needed to pay its short-term debt. There was the fight about the ceiling on long-term interest rates. Eisenhower and the Federal Reserve Board were apparently in agreement; the Federal Reserve wanted a "free hand in dealing with credit."

The squeeze was on; as of September 1959, the government had to "borrow a sum greater than the whole year's budget—a whopping 85 billion." This is from the *Wall Street Journal* of September 10, 1959, as presented by Senator Byrd of Virginia. The *Journal* reported a "grim outlook for the money market . . . a wholesale loss of confidence in the U.S. Government's ability to meet its financial obligations without inflation." The discount rate was going up. Member banks had to pay the twelve Federal Reserve banks more money, so the banks would sock it to industry, commerce, and the people, all this to the apparent delight of Federal Reserve shareholders.

In the middle of business as usual in August of 1959, during the Eighty-sixth Congress, session 1, Hawaii became the fiftieth state of the United States.

The United States was induced to mend the world's money problems, but the United States was spending too much? By the early 1960s, the deficit was growing; the imbalance of payments was growing. The foreigners owned $16 billion of government securities; in the exchange, gold was credited to the foreigner. It was apparently a great plan by international money interests approved by the Congress. The American people with their taxpaying dollars, while spending too much, were apparently bankrolling the foreigners with currency and gold.

The Monetary Fund and the International Bank received an infusion of $4.5 billion in 1959; no doubt this money was the resultant "exchange for dollars" currency. At the same time, there was less confidence in the U.S. dollar because of the imbalance of payments and a mounting United States deficit. What was all this business about anyway? Spread the money around! The United States Treasury was printing currency for the foreigners, and the foreign members of the World Bank were investing in U.S. securities, and U.S. banks were investing in the International Bank, and the United States couldn't pay its debts.

Some said it was "panic time" in the United States. Eisenhower would call a special session of Congress. It was always back to the Congress, but the House shot the bill down; the 4.5% interest rate ceiling on long-term loans would remain, and so would tight money. Senator Proxmire presented an article by Sylvia Porter of the *Washington Star*: "Tight Money Coming Again." Interest rates had been raised "150 percent since a year ago"; they had been increased from 1.5% to 3.9%. "The likelihood that the Federal Reserve System soon will turn the credit screws again, act deliberately to cut down the supply of money in the banks available for loans." When the discount rate goes up, the people, the businesses, the schools, industry, everybody pays more.

A new administration in 1960 would continue spending. It was the needs of the people, the cauldron, the cold war, the fear of

Communism, the Monetary Fund and the International Bank, the plight of the foreigners, the grants in aid why spending would continue. Spending would continue; it had to. The question was, how much would the new money cost and who would get it? Was it pressure by the Federal Reserve Board to raise interest rates, not because of inflation, but to increase its income? It was the continuous game. Was there really panic time or the pressure by the capital markets and the move for higher interest rates? There was government spending in the past and the present; and in the future, government spending would continue. It was the continuous game; no capital credit, then fiat credit and securities, then the inflation thing, then higher interest rates.

In 1961, John Kennedy initiated government programs to reverse the Eisenhower drop-off. John Kennedy gave American young men and women a choice, something other than the draft and military service; Kennedy started the Peace Corps. Another Kennedy escalation was the space program; the space program was a race to the moon and back. John Kennedy was doing the Roosevelt thing, jump-starting a sagging economy. More government borrowing required the fiat credit thing, deficit spending. There was the continued grumbling by the Republicans, debunking the Kennedy programs. Kennedy's administration took up some slack; Keynesian spending would get things going again. Kennedy increased the physical circulation to $3 billion in two years, this from the 1963 Treasury report.

The Johnson administration continued the deficit spending to support the Vietnam War. In 1963, the debt ceiling was raised to $315 billion. By 1963, the import/export exchange had changed for good; it was favoring the foreigner. The imbalance of payments was a calling for the exit of gold; the United States supply was down to $16 billion, down $7 to $8 billion since 1946. Henry Hazlitt, in a May 1959 *Newsweek* issue that was presented in Congress, said, "It is also contended that this loss of gold is actually healthy because it makes for a sounder distribution of gold reserves and strengthens the currencies of other countries." Hazlitt mentioned compensating factors; in 1945, the Congress had reduced the currency/deposit requirements against gold from 40% to 25%. The gold supply against currency was still considerably above the 25% of currency in circulation.

The currency/deposit thing had been reduced to 25% because billions and billions of dollars of new currency was going to be created after World War II. The result was more credits, borrowings, and deposits by all the countries, apparently for world distribution. Actually, the percentage was approaching zero all along. President Nixon completed the zero thing in 1971 when the "farce" became a reality.

On August 21, 1963, in the House, Congressman William S. Moorehead of Pennsylvania presented the following about the "Euro-Dollar Market": The euro market's total value had reached $5 billion; 85% of this figure was in "U.S. dollars." These numbers were compiled by Oscar Altman of the International Monetary Fund. Congressman Moorehead placed in the record a study of the "Euro-dollar market which appeared in a recent issue of the Economist." The market was composed of Eurodollars, "Euro-sterling, Euro-Swiss [francs], indeed Euro-every significant currency in world trade." The study stated the euro market was causing "concern" among the "monetary authorities"; it was "outside the range of controls and regulations on financing in the usual way." The euro currency market was a "lending and borrowing" of "deposits" (currencies) in a bank in one European country to a bank in another European country or "to a faceless international speculator."

The normal regulated exchange process "comprises simply a straight purchase or sale of foreign currencies, for spot or forward delivery." The euro currency market was a lending/borrowing currency process; the dealings might take place in one center, but the process "originated in another center." The study stated, "Thus the whole market is based on a great pyramiding operation, and for this reason there can be no very meaningful estimate of its size." Great Britain controlled euro-sterling and Europe-controlled Eurodollars. According to the study, as reported by the *Economist*, this euro currency market was "inherently anomalous" or irregular, outside the norm; it was because, according to the study, the world currency markets were not "free." Did that mean the money markets were too regulated? But the *Economist* reported that

> at least two-thirds of the funds in European markets are estimated to have emanated from Central Banks and

monetary authorities, either directly by placings of their own or by channeling dollars and other currencies to commercial banks that are provided with an exchange back [a "swap"] into their own currency, so that the Central Bank remains the beneficial owner of the foreign exchange. (presented by Congressman Moorehead, August 21, 1963).

Why had the government adopted the central banking system? The central bank orders the printing of United States money, the issue of the money, the control of the money, interest rates, credits, everything. The currency is, by the Federal Reserve Act, a government obligation. But is the obligation the government's money? The Federal Reserve Note is a central bank note; the note apparently belongs to the bank. Why was there "concern" among the "monetary authorities" about the currency operations of the euro market? Most of the money in the market, according to the *Economist*, came from the monetary authorities and the central banks. Maybe the "faceless speculator" was any central bank?

The *Economist* said the euro currency market was a restoration of "a truly international money market, previously disrupted by official restrictions which these 'Euro' dealings calculatedly bypass." Was this partly the crux of the scheme, the apparent elimination or continuation of currency restrictions? The International Monetary Fund was a manufacture of money by the United States and all the member countries, a paper currency creation scheme with gold added. It was to "provide financial assistance" to all the countries, "to promote exchange stability and orderly exchange arrangements, and payments," between nations; to promote growth, trade, and full employment in and among all nations, etc.

Gertrude Coogan called the creation of the new currencies when referring to the banking statutes, the banking scheme, the "exchange for dollars." It was deficit spending, "international deficit spending on top of domestic deficit spending." The Eurodollar market seemed to grow after the International Monetary Fund began operation.

There was almost full employment in the United States during World War II. John Kenneth Galbraith called it "minimal unemployment."

Secretary Snyder, in his 1952 Treasury report, stated, "The Government's obligations represented 60 percent of all outstanding debt, public and private" in the United States. It was the "World War II defense and war finance program." It was the biggest capitalistic market in United States history; unfortunately, it was wartime. All the American people were living and working at home, fighting and dying away from home. The government's debt soared to $270 billion. The total debt was $450 billion in 1946. Snyder reported that the commercial banks and the twelve Federal Reserve banks held 108 billion of the debt, "representing 71 percent of their earning assets." By the end of 1952, government debt had been reduced to 40% of all debt, public and private.

The 1960s decade was the brief period of John Kennedy and then the presidency of Lyndon B. Johnson. It was the period of "liberal legislation . . . Civil Rights, Head Start, the Youth Corps, the War on Poverty." It was Lyndon Johnson's "Great Society." But the Vietnam War escalated and so would government spending, public expenditures for the people's needs and the war. Government spending meant government borrowing, much of it the fiat credit thing. The government was doing a Keynesian policy, more deficit spending. By 1967, the Federal Reserve had responded with tighter money and higher interest rates. Critical short-term interest rates had reached their highest level ever; the rate was 4.81%, this from the Treasury Department as presented by Congressman Patman.

Congressman Patman of Texas was the chairman of the House Banking and Currency Committee; Patman's apparent vigil was the constant disposition of the Federal Reserve System. Patman's not-so-favorite person was William McChesney Martin; Martin was chairman of the Federal Reserve Board. "I remember well Mr. Martin's appearance before the Joint Economic Committee on February 26, 1965. He said at that time: 'The Federal Reserve Board has the authority to act independently of the President, even despite the President.'" Patman claimed the problems began with Eisenhower; the Federal Reserve was private, and there would be no interference from the U.S. government. Patman said that Martin had spread this "false propaganda . . . the public has no right to participate."

There was a steady climb in interest rates since "Martin and the Republicans took office in the 1950's." The discount rate had increased from "1.59 percent to 4.50 percent . . . the highest in 40 years." Patman said the member banks made record earnings in spite of the discount rate charged by the Federal Reserve banks. Wasn't this another form of inflation while the Federal Reserve was raising interest rates to curb inflation? The reserve was creating its own inflation, and that was more wealth.

A January 1967 *Washington Post* editorial recommended Chairman Martin's retirement from the Federal Reserve Board. Congressman Patman wanted Martin removed; it didn't happen. President Johnson reappointed Martin for another term in March 1967. Chairman Martin's tenure extended into the Nixon presidency.

"PROFESSOR GALBRAITH HITS FEDERAL RESERVE'S RELIANCE ON TIGHT MONEY." Congressman Patman presented an interview with Professor Galbraith; the interview in January 1967 covered monetary policy in the United States. Galbraith's thoughts in brief follow:

- Monetary policy is an ally of the rich and big businesses.
- There was no balance between public and private policy.
- Poverty and urbanization was a continuing problem; it was a problem of the public sector. At least, it had become more recognizable.
- Public services were not a menace to liberty.
- The unemployment problem occurs and then public expenditures.
- Minimal unemployment during World War II. There were wage and price controls.
- Increase the labor force through education and training, and this is done through the public sector.
- The Vietnam expenditure would override, thus the starvation of the public sector; civilian needs take the hits.
- With tax cuts, some unemployment would be eliminated.
- Conservatives found out that Keynes could be had by tax cuts; they would embrace the faith with too much fervor (sounds like the Reagan and Bush administrations, tax cuts, and deficit spending).

- Interest rates should be set at a moderate level; this would reduce the power of the Federal Reserve.
- "Ultimately, the Federal Reserve will be a minor instrumentality of the State concerned with accounting and administration matters, standing in importance somewhere between the Bureau of Printing and Engraving and the Interstate Commerce Commission. The sooner this day comes, the better it will be for all of us." [2008-2009 has shown otherwise]
- High interest rates are very good for people who have money to lend.
- During active monetary policy, interest rates are wonderfully high.
- Monetary policy doesn't affect big corporations; they have internal financing. Small business does not fare as well.
- The monetary policy favors the rich and big business.

President Johnson's Vietnam War and the "Great Society" required increased government spending; with that spending, the Federal Reserve was pushing for higher interest rates. John Kenneth Galbraith was an economist who understood a monetary system in apparent fallacy. Galbraith's words inferred that the Federal Reserve System was operationally unbalanced in wealth distribution.

Alexander Hamilton's bank was in cognizance of the Pennsylvania creditors, the distribution of wealth by way of the central bank.

Congressman Patman said the system "ignored the Constitution of the United States." John Kenneth Galbraith was the "Paul M. Warburg Professor of Economics at Harvard University." Yet Galbraith, in his assessment, was critical of the Federal Reserve System and its policy and advocated its eventual demise. Paul Warburg was instrumental in the creation of the Federal Reserve.

Congressman Patman presented the following: The General Accounting Office (GAO) of the United States audits the books of all government agencies; the GAO doesn't audit the books of the Federal Reserve. Open Market Committee meetings were secret, not to be revealed for five years; the "Open Market Committee should be abolished." The president of the United States was not privy to committee meetings. Patman went so far as to compare Open Market Committee meetings to the politburo in the Soviet Union. The politburo had eleven members; the Open Market Committee had twelve members. The politburo was secretive; the Federal Reserve was secretive. The politburo "ignores the Soviet Constitution"; the Federal Reserve "ignores the Constitution." The Soviets seized power (not elected); the Federal Reserve seized power (not elected). "The Communist Party takes care of its friends in Russia, and in the United States, the Federal Reserve takes care of its banker friends."

The Federal Reserve was a government agency; it was not a government agency. During the Depression years at a convention in Canada, the New York Bankers Association claimed the Federal Reserve was a government agency. The convention concluded that because too much profit was made within the government's banking creation, the system didn't have the public interest in mind. From the record, the United States government banking creation appeared a dump on the American people.

Later in September 1979, changes were imminent to Federal Open Market Committee minutes; a bill was before the House. The FOMC didn't start keeping minutes until 1936. After 1964, "the minutes were released for all meetings before 1959; and the policy of publishing them with a 5-year time lag was adopted. Then in May 1976, the FOMC voted to stop keeping minutes." Hearings were held. Milton Friedman, John Kenneth Galbraith, and other experts objected; they "favored reinstatement." The bill was passed; minutes were reinstated. There would be a lag time period of three to four years before the release of the minutes; their release depended on the date of the committee meetings.

The "extra cost" of this business would be borne by the U.S. Treasury. There were exceptions. "The Board may delete from such minutes any information regarding any foreign country, central bank of a foreign country, or any international institution which has a majority of members who are foreign countries or central banks of foreign countries." There was stipulated a fifteen-year and a thirty-year consideration after such committee meetings regarding the possible release of the original deletions.

Congressman Patman introduced legislation to curb increasing government debt. In 1967, the public debt limit was to be raised to $315 billion. Forty-five billion dollars in collateral securities was included as part of the debt; the securities were held by the Federal Reserve Bank of New York. The Treasury was paying $1.9 billion in yearly interest on these securities. Congressman Wright Patman, in his H.R. 9156 bill, wanted the $45 billion of "collateral" securities removed from the public debt. The collateral securities were held against the Federal Reserve Note currency in circulation. Patman said the securities had been paid for once; the securities shouldn't be paid for a second time. On October 5, 1967, Patman testified before the Ways and Means Committee in the House. Patman explained to the chairman of the committee, "How does the Federal Reserve buy anything? They don't have any money to buy it with. They create the money . . . They have a right to create or manufacture money . . . . So the Federal Reserve Banks create the money on the books of the banks, to buy, say a million dollar bond."

Congressman Lindbergh, in 1912, expressed it his way; Lindberg said the Treasury, by way of Engraving and Printing, was going to print the currency and "hand" the currency to the banks to spend. What is puzzling is the original conception of the currency, the "elastic currency." The Congress made the new currency an obligation of the United States; the new currency was based on the credit and security of the United States. The Democrats wanted the new currency to be a "function of the Government . . . They are not to be the notes of the banks in any sense, but the notes—the obligations—of the Government"; this was the Democratic stance when the act was up for approval.

The Democrats wanted a public system, yet the Congress made the new currency, the Federal Reserve Note, a non-legal tender note. In the Federal Reserve Act, it is stated that the new currency was for the "bankers purpose, and for no other purpose." Wasn't this a contradiction? It became a banker's currency but a government obligation; the people would pay for it forever. How could it ever be a public system when the people would not own their own currency in this so-called democracy.

We know why the 1913 note was not legal tender, but the new elastic note was redeemable in gold. At that time, a legal tender United States currency did exist; it was the "lawful money" of the United States, the greenback. The greenback still circulated; however, the greenback circulation was fixed, non-pyramidal. The Federal Reserve Note was "elastic." Anything that is elastic can expand or contract. A $1 Federal Reserve Note could become seven Federal Reserve Notes in credits and deposits or up to fifteen Federal Reserve Notes in credits and deposits.

Those credits and deposits may also disappear, which is another function of the banking system. The government could not pay its debt with the 1913 non-legal tender Federal Reserve Note; the government had to pay its debt in gold. The government paid in gold to the Federal Reserve System when the Federal Reserve Note was redeemed. A remarkable scheme achieved the gold. The Federal Reserve System owns U.S. gold courtesy of the Congress.

The collateral thing started in the 1930s; it was an extension of the government obligation, a never-ending payment of interest on the circulating currency. Congressman Patman wanted to end this continuous interest payment on the security, this obligation, which had already been paid for once. Patman was saying, it was not the people's money; it was the reserve's money.

"And we are to be responsible after all; that is all there is of it."

> We are practically the only country in the world that requires collateral. So, if you want to, why not cut off the collateral, the Government bonds back of the money and go ahead as almost every other country in the world does. It is a serious waste of money and an entirely unnecessary one . . . Why have gold or collateral, Government bonds back of your currency? This is the currency of the United States Government, and they are the backers of that money. Why have any collateral back of that? (U.S. Congressional Senate Committee on Banking and Currency Hearings on S. 510; Seventy-ninth Congress, first session; February 20, 28 and March 7, 1945; page 29) This from Congressman Wright Patman of Texas.

In 1942, during World War II, the Congress amended Section 14(b) of the Federal Reserve Act. The new amendment allowed the Federal Reserve to buy Treasury securities "directly" from the Treasury of no more than $5 billion printed at any one time and deposited in a reserve bank. It was an emergency thing for the Treasury in need of funds to spend at specific times like "at tax time." This authority has been extended many times since 1942. It was extended in 1966; House Resolution 1113 renewed the amended Section 14(b) in 1968, and on and on it would go. In 1970, there was another extension. One congressman sounded "gimmickry," "printing press money." The Treasury, needing money to spend, was placing printed currency in the central bank.

The Federal Reserve had been purchasing securities and printing currency during the twenties. In the Senate in 1932, Carter Glass said,

> [Ten] of the larger New York banks alone in 1929, over a period of six months, borrowed a billion dollars from the New York Federal Reserve Bank, with United States bonds as collateral security, chiefly for stock speculative purposes—not all at once; I said over a period of six months—when they had no right to borrow a dollar for that purpose from the Federal Reserve Banks; it was contrary to the express provision and the real intent of the law.

This was before the crash. From the words of Carter Glass, we can assume that the governor, the agent of the Federal Reserve Bank of New York, ordered to be printed $1 billion of Federal Reserve Notes; and those notes were lent to the big banks of New York! That billion dollars of Federal Reserve Notes printed by the United States Treasury apparently disappeared on Wall Street. With that disappearance of cash went the disappearance of credits.

Before the direct purchase law and after, a governor or agent of a Federal Reserve bank maintained the continuous flow of money when purchasing securities with the printed currency. According to Carter Glass in the 1929 case, it was the Federal Reserve Bank of New York. Congressman Patman mentioned other actions by the New

York Bank. Early on, "using the credit of the nation," the bank bought New York municipal bonds with Federal Reserve Notes. The Federal Reserve banks had easy access to printed currency from the Treasury by their governors or agents, and this was the banking practice with the nation's money. There was another practice; a lot of Federal Reserve Notes went to Europe and Germany between the world wars. Secretary Mellon verified this action in his Treasury reports. In 1929, the Federal Reserve Bank of New York, from the record, was the mainstay, the predominate bank of the Federal Reserve System.

"During World War II, the Federal Open Market Committee increased their purchases of Government securities to about 25 billion, and from there it has gone up until now it is 45 billion." In 1967, that 45 billion in securities represented the circulation. The Federal Reserve holds these securities, which are passed on to shareholders. Shareholders collect the unending interest on the circulating interest-bearing Federal Reserve currency. This is the Chase credit circulation, a perpetual funding. Vallandigham never wanted it; it is the extension of Alexander Hamilton and the Pennsylvania creditors.

Back in 1884, the national banks held maturing bonds payable in gold; the bonds represented the interest-bearing national currency in circulation. The price tag was $135 million in gold; the gold wasn't paid. It couldn't be paid; otherwise, the country's circulating money would have disappeared. The debtors, which are the people, can't do without the creditor. Panic was abated; the banks got a better deal. The tax on the currency was removed. The banks got 100% in currency based on the market price of the bonds; the government 10% discount was removed. The bonds, however, were still payable in gold; that was the deal in the nineteenth and into the twentieth century.

The banker's scheme escalated in the twentieth century. In 1967, the shareholders of the Federal Reserve System still held the securities representing the currency of the United States. Patman said, "The national debt can never be retired, without depriving the public of circulating currency." Nothing, apparently, ever became of Patman's bill; the security for money would remain in the control of the Central Bank.

In 1970, David M. Kennedy was the secretary of the Treasury. Inflation was always the continuing threat; a whole lot of spending had been going on. Richard Nixon was the president. Defense spending was winding down; it had fallen during the year by "$3 billion." Kennedy called the previous period an overheated inflationary environment, but the decrease in military expenditure cost "400,000" jobs, this from the 1970 annual Treasury report. Interest rates were steadily climbing; 3-month short-term Treasury rates fluctuated between 6.5% and 8%. Long-term rates were somewhere between 7% and 9%. By 1980, interest rates would be out of sight—the discount rate, the prime rate, installment loan interest, mortgages, second mortgages, etc.

The Treasury in 1970 was spending $206 billion; the expenditure and the deficit, by today's standards, was not excessive. The deficit was $2.7 billion, about 1% of the public expenditure. The circulation was increasing about 5% per year, approximately $3 billion in Federal Reserve Notes. In 1970, the paper currency totaled $58.8 billion; $50.4 billion were circulating Federal Reserve Notes. The growth rate in 1970 was set at 3.7%. The public debt had climbed to $283 billion. Kennedy said the "quasi-Federal Agency" debt, which was not included in the public debt, was an additional $11 billion.

In 1970, in addition to the Federal Reserve Note, the other paper currencies were still part of the circulation:

- There were the "gold certificates prior to Series of 1934."
- The silver certificates were being phased out starting in 1965.
- The Treasury notes of 1890 still existed.
- Federal Reserve Bank Notes were being retired; this currency originally replaced the silver dollar in the 1920s.

The National Bank Notes represented the beginning of the uniform currency; this currency of the national banks was the national currency started in 1863. These notes were slowly being retired. This national currency was also represented by interest-bearing bonds. The cost of this currency to the people was the interest paid on the bonds and the discount in interest payment on the borrowed currency since 1863. These are the same notes of 1884 at a cost of 135 million in gold.

The banks bought the bonds with the national currency, which was handed to the banks by the Treasury. This currency upon retirement in the twentieth century was redeemable in the "lawful money" of the United States.

Last but not least was the "lawful money" of the United States, the greenbacks. An amount of $323 million in greenbacks were still on the books. Greenbacks were held in the Treasury for the redemption of the national currency. It appears the national and central banking systems since 1863 have cost the people of the United States a ton of money. The cost occurred because of the required premise and security of a gold reserve. All this cost and resultant profit was the cream in the top of the bottle, to those close to the government's banking system.

In June 1968, Congress passed the "Special Drawings Rights Act." Secretary Kennedy said there was a new development within the International Monetary Fund. A new "facility" was added; it was the "Special Drawing Rights facility." The facility began operations on "January 1, 1970"; Kennedy said the "first year's allocation was $3.4 billion in SDR."

What were "Special Drawing Rights?"

The executive directors of the International Monetary Fund had amended the Bretton Woods Articles of Agreement. Approval by the Congress would authorize the president of the United States "to accept the amendment proposed," the amendment to allow nations to produce special drawing rights. In 1968, there were 107 countries in the International Monetary Fund.

President Johnson said, "The rapid growth in world trade and in the flow of capital is outpacing the growth of monetary reserves. The world must take action to provide sufficient reserves for this growth." In the House of Representatives, Congressman Patman said, "The need for a new international reserve asset, to meet the requirements of a growing world economy in which the supply of gold and dollars would not be adequate, was seen a number of years ago by the Congress and the Administration."

A new international reserve asset was needed to supplement a dwindling U.S. gold reserve. The new international reserve asset was going to be "Special Drawing Rights,"

If we could ever understand this business.

A "two-tier" gold system had arrived; the statutory price of gold between Governments and the international market price of gold for the speculators. The monetary reserve of gold had become considerably less because of hoarding and speculation. Gold was being mined and, apparently, being hoarded by those mining the gold. And the farce, apparently, was still playing the game, a major roll with currency valuation, especially the dollar.

Twenty-three years had passed since World War II. There was $31 billion in Europe; United States gold was down to $11 plus billion and counting. Yes, something had to be done. United States gold and dollars was the international reserve, but it was dwindling. A trade imbalance and a United States deficit at home didn't help things. Congressmen did ask, was this U.S. initiative or foreign initiative, or both? From the record, the planning of SDR was five years in the making by supposedly all concerned. Bill H.R. 16911 was before the House; Congressman Berry from Louisiana remarked, "Mr. Speaker, this would be a great day for Lord John Maynard Keynes had fate permitted him to live and witness congressional action today."

Since Hamilton, proponents hammered it home: reserves, reserves. Above all else, the monetary system required the gold reserve. Since 1945, the foreign countries were doing just that, acquiring their gold reserve. What foreign countries apparently did was accumulate the gold they once held? In the scheme of things, wasn't this bound to take place? Was the Fund designed for this to happen? Paper currency, in dollars, in the IMF scheme, was redeemable in gold; the paper currency was apparently redeemable in gold within the international central banking scheme. Paper currency had continued its primary function, the accumulation of gold. The 1968 accumulative stash, the $31 billion in Europe, was apparently a potential claim against more United States gold.

Congressman Berry continued,

> Lord Keynes, the great architect of socialism in the 20th
> Century, envisioned a program of special drawing rights,
> or "paper gold," if you prefer, and tried to establish the
> theory at Bretton Woods in 1944. At that time, however, the
> International Monetary Fund was established, and, largely
> at the insistence of the United States, who had then not yet
> spent itself into inflationary bankruptcy, decided to retain
> the traditional predominance of gold as the international
> medium of exchange.

According to Congressman Berry, Chairman McChesney Martin of
the Federal Reserve called the SDR scheme, "financial gimmickry."
Chairman Martin made this assertion before the "Detroit Economists
Club."

In the United States, Special Drawing Rights was to become a "part of
the Exchange Stabilization Fund established by Section 10 of the Gold
Reserve Act of 1934." The 1934 act gave the secretary of the Treasury
expenditure power in obligations of the United States. Remember, in
1934, the United States gained a $2 billion credit when the dollar was
devalued against gold. It appeared a similar kind of deal was taking
place in 1968. "Special Drawing Rights Certificates" would evolve and
take their place alongside of the "Gold Certificates." It is spelled out
in the new Special Drawing Rights Act, which amended the Federal
Reserve Act.

In 1934, the Federal Reserve was given gold certificates when the gold
was transferred to the Treasury and then to Fort Knox. Fort Knox was
referred to in the Congress as the Kentucky Hole. The gold certificates
in 1934 issued to the Federal Reserve were good for the gold. Special
drawing rights, according to the SDR Act, would be "held to the credit
of the Exchange Stabilization Fund."

The statute stated, "The Secretary of the Treasury is authorized to issue
to the Federal Reserve banks, and such banks shall purchase, Special
Drawing rights certificates in such form and in such denominations
as he may determine, against any Special Drawing Rights held to the

credit of the Exchange Stabilization Fund." These new SDR certificates were the new "asset," the replacement for gold, or as referred to by Congressman Berry, the paper gold. The SDR statute stated in Section 4(b) that the Federal Reserve "owned" these new certificates. Why did the Federal Reserve "own" these certificates? There apparently was no transfer of money; the Federal Reserve didn't spend its money for these certificates? The statute isn't definitive; obscurity, again, appears relevant here.

In 1934, the U.S. government received a credit of $2 billion when the dollar was devalued. The Treasury was getting another credit in 1968. These new special drawing rights was another credit alongside a gold reserve, as part of the Exchange Stabilization Fund. This was a government fiat credit happening. Apparently, it's similar to the Federal Reserve "purchasing" securities for new fiat currency. What remarkable schemes in this business!

The statute stated that the Federal Reserve could redeem these certificates "from the resources of the Exchange Stabilization Fund." This business appeared an extension of the 1934 act. The Federal Reserve held the gold certificates, which were redeemable in the gold in the "Kentucky Hole." The Federal Reserve now held the Special Drawing Rights certificates. The United States Treasury would have new credit in the Stabilization Fund, the same fund created in 1934. The secretary of the Treasury could tap this fund, expend money for all purposes; in this case, the secretary would spend for special drawing rights within the Monetary Fund. In any case, it was fiat credit debt, and the Federal Reserve held the obligations.

Apparently, central banks in other countries would be doing a similar thing? This would be more a Gertrude Coogan "International deficit financing" thing? The Monetary Fund had been a worldwide gold/currency stabilization exchange experiment. In 1968, there were countries running surpluses; there were countries running deficits or imbalances of payments. Countries in deficit would use the special drawing rights. Unfortunately, the United States was running a deficit, a trade imbalance of payments. The United States, if necessary, might use the special drawing rights to "cover losses in existing reserves." Countries running surpluses would be "requested to accept Special

Drawing Rights." There were limitations in the use of the SDR over a five-year period. The United States might recover losses, but the United States people would be incurring more debt in the process?

The world was growing, expanding in trade, resources, industry, commerce, advanced technologies in mostly the advanced industrialized nations. The United States initiated and accepted about 17% of the exports and imports of the entire world. There were still the backward countries. An example was the continent of Africa, where impoverished populations were exploding. England and the Dutch owned the gold mines in Africa. Gold mines existed in Russia. From the record, the international monetary system was short on gold, and gold was being sold outside the monetary system. The record showed that newly mined gold was not supplanting the monetary gold. The world was growing, and apparently the international monetary system didn't keep pace; United States gold/dollar reserves didn't keep pace. In reality, on the international scene, gold continued its manipulative ways. It was short in supply. Gold continued the expansion and the replacement of currencies; the same currencies accumulated the gold.

Congressmen Brock and McClory had problems with this new "two-tier" gold system. It was a "device for the creation of a Fund, by fiat, if you will, of money—money in the international sense—money that can be used only between Government central banks to reduce the impact of short-term fluctuations in balance of payments situations." Also, the international bankers at the Stockholm Conference had admonished the United States for not getting its economic house in order. What would this new system do to the price of gold at $35 an ounce?

Before Stockholm, the IMF member countries met at Rio de Janeiro in September of 1967. Senator Proxmire, for the record, presented an article by Hobart Rowen; the article appeared in the *Washington Post*. The SDR plan was apparently firmed up at the Rio Conference. The SDR plan "was a step away from, in Rowen's words, 'a blind dependence on gold.'" The article began, "Any way you measure it, the 107 nations who comprise the International Monetary Fund turned in a great accomplishment at Rio de Janeiro last week. The plan they adopted for Special Drawing Rights [SDR]—paper gold—is a step toward deliberate creation of international monetary reserves, and away from a blind dependence on gold."

The secretary of the Treasury wanted "no change in the monetary value of gold and the dollar relative to each other." McClory didn't see how this was possible, considering a two-tier system. Where were the other nations, and what were they doing? They hadn't considered legislated approval yet. "France has refused to support the system and agreement for which the Committee urges approval today."

Congressman Widnall of New Jersey answered Mr. McClory, "President de Gaulle wants to continue to exert pressure upon the dollar. He wants to return to a pure gold standard. A pure gold standard would only reward France, South Africa, and the Soviet Union." According to Congressman Gross, the French "hold a big chunk of the world's gold, why are they not in this papering the world with printing press money?" Mr. Widnall said, "France is not into this because this would reduce pressure on gold and they do not want to reduce pressure. They want to increase pressure."

In the scheme of things, on a national scale, what was the impact of the Monetary Fund on the United States economy? The U.S. quota to the International Monetary Fund had been increased several times since 1945; the subscription quota would be increased again to $6.7 billion, this from the 1970 Treasury report. This 6.7 billion compared to 50 billion in circulation in the United States. The figure did not include what was going to the World Bank. The actual original subscription fund quota was $2.8 billion in currency and gold. In 1970, the United States was spending over $200 billion; the national product, public and private, was around $600 billion. The national circulation was 50 billion in Federal Reserve Notes. United States gold on the national scene was disappearing fast. American gold appeared to play its role on the international scene where money numbers were significantly lower. The "farce" wasn't being played out on the national scene; it was becoming a reality on the international scene? Chairman Eccles of the Federal Reserve stated in years gone by that the gold reserve in the United States had nothing to do with the currency circulation.

At home, America was spending, running up the debts; there was a deficit, an imbalance of trade payments, and the gold credit was leaving the country. Was this the scenario since Bretton Woods began? About the gold, Adam Smith said, "And as it can find no advantageous market at home, it must, notwithstanding any prohibition, be sent abroad." The Fund had to be working; worldwide gold distribution was working. The gold was going to the forward, industrialized countries. France alone had taken $2.3 billion of American gold since 1962. France still hadn't paid its World War I debt of $5 billion; at the time this debt was initiated, the debt was payable in gold. The monetary system seemed to continue in mysterious ways.

What was the effect of SDR, this paper gold? SDR would create "liquidity." Congressman McClory said, "There is popular belief that the special Drawing rights will increase international liquidity and thus improve international trade and expand our exports. This is probably a myth." According to McClory, there would be no impact. An "increase in liquidity—if any—would be small indeed." McClory said he was "informed by the economists that most imports are financed by the local economy through local internal reserves and not through the international reserves used for settling balance of payments accounts."

Apparently, the liquidity attained was to be international liquidity, not national or domestic liquidity?

"Mr. Chairman, the system now laughingly called the International Monetary system quite closely resembles the oldest established continuous floating crap game of that musical comedy a number of years ago." It was Congressman Reuss's turn. Reuss had "two questions . . . . who needs these special rights? . . . and how do they work?" According to Reuss, the monetary system became "fragile" because the mined gold in Africa and the Soviet Union was kept out of the market. There were the "hoarders and speculators in gold."

Weren't the countries mining gold in Africa in the Monetary Fund? Were they the hoarders? Reuss said there was a "plus side, what happens to be the balance of payments of the United States and the United Kingdom." On the negative side were the "167 nations scattered all over the world which decide to take gold from the United States."

The foreigners had gobbled up the gold; an apparent reaction was the planning of SDR. It was a debit-credit thing; nations in balance of payments deficit would borrow currency from nations with surpluses in payments. A 1.5% interest was charged on the borrowed currency, payable to the nation in surplus. No nation could borrow more than 70% of its paid in quota. Reuss explained there was no convertibility into gold in these transactions, where dollars were not involved. Nations would be granted special drawing rights based on their percentage of subscription quota paid in. Nations would be debited or credited special drawing rights based on the lending and/or a borrowing practice.

The *Congressional Record* stated that 65 of the 107 member nations was required for approval of the SDR plan.

The House debate on SDR was "not to exceed two hours." The chairman of the Banking and Currency Committee (Mr. Patman) directed the proceedings, which was under the "five minute rule." There would be no objection to Section 3(b) of the bill; it had been "waived." No amendments would be considered. Section 3(b) covered the credits in the Exchange Stabilization Fund. Apparently, House Bill 16911 was a done deal; SDR would be approved. The SDR bill was passed by a count of 236-15; the record showed those not voting—182.

There would be no objection to Section 3(b) because new currency had to be created. "Special Drawing Rights" (SDR) was the device whereby currency could be created. From this new "Drawing" device, "certificates" were printed first. The certificates, as part of the SDR, was exchangeable for currency. These new certificates were called Special Drawing Rights certificates. The Treasury's Bureau of Engraving and Printing (BEP) would manufacture these new certificates, and the Treasury would issue the certificates to the Federal Reserve. The Treasury, by the new amendment to the Federal Reserve Act, was given new credit or additional currency to draw from. The law stated that the Federal Reserve would purchase and "own" these certificates; again, it was the purchase thing.

These new SDR certificates took their place alongside the gold certificates in the Exchange Stabilization Fund. The new certificates equaled "the value of the Special Drawing Rights" in future IMF transactions. In 1934, the $100,000 gold certificates issued to the Federal Reserve represented the real gold. The real gold was moved to Fort Knox in Kentucky. In 1970, SDR was called paper gold. SDR was another way in which more currency was created against a particular value, in this case, a paper gold value. It was the creation of fiat currency credit, more currency and more deficit spending.

Apparently, all the central banks in all the countries would be doing a similar thing? Gertrude Coogan said the IMF creation would be "international deficit financing on top of domestic deficit financing." Coogan called it "going one step further out into the deep." Could it be the Alexander Hamilton prophecy, the unlimited permanent expenses and beyond, "even in imagination"? The money schemes were just that—schemes to create money out of something.

Congressman Rarick voted, but he didn't vote for the bill; he didn't understand it. How many really did? IMF "members have a veto which could deprive the United States of any favored position in membership or stability." Rarick didn't like the "international share-the-wealth program." Rarick didn't like the international bankers; they are responsible for all the "chaos." Mr. Kyl simply wanted the United States out of the program. Congressman Gross of Iowa was another opponent; since the last 25% of the gold "cover" had been removed, he considered the currency "printing press money."

Whether it was printing press or not, Congressman Gross and the rest of us were going to pay for it forever.

The Senate bill was passed, and SDR became law; SDR was activated in 1970. Secretary Kennedy said the first year's allocation of SDRs would be 3.4 billion. The United States held 20% of the world's subscription quota; the United States would then be allowed $680 million of special drawing rights, however that was to play out.

The year 1971 rolled around, and "International Affairs" weren't better; the "outflow" of money was worse for the United States.

Treasury Secretary Schultz spelled it out. "The U.S. payments picture darkened at an accelerating pace in the first half of the calendar year 1971." There were "heavy outflows of short term capital." The imbalance of payments was "$12 billion at mid-August." A lot of the "outrush of dollars" was going to Japan.

It was just the beginning of a ballooning imbalance of payments favoring Japan. Japan did learn her lessons well. Japan became foremost in industry, shipping, trade, airpower, weaponry, warfare, and colonialism; that was before and during World War II. After that war, United States aid put Japan back on its feet; apparently, it was necessary to keep the Russians out of the Pacific. Japan would no longer build weaponry; Japan became formidable in electronics, automobiles, robots, tools, machinery of every type, and especially in banking and awareness of the Western monetary scheme.

Japan is three islands and no inner resources. Japan imported the raw materials, produced, exported, and sold her wares to the United States and others and imported the cash. For Japan to try and compete with the West on an equal export/import basis meant suicide, third world status; it wasn't going to happen. Japanese markets were closed to outsiders. Japan would export but not import manufactured goods. The plan and the practice seemed simple enough; Japan became an industrial and economic giant. It would appear Japan wasn't going to fall into the trap; Japan wasn't going to run up huge deficits owed to foreigners, which seemed programmed for the United States. Japan's national debt today is owed to itself? The United States national debt, whoops! Domestic debt is not entirely owed to itself. United States monetary propaganda seemed to always tell a muddled story about the Japanese economy.

The imbalance of payments continued; Nixon ended the gold thing in August 1971. Convertibility into real gold was over. Foreigners wanted "convertibility to continue," but it was a done deal. Secretary Schultz reported the meetings of the "Group of Ten nations in London and then in Washington in December 1971." The result was a devaluation of the dollar. The secretary reported "a change in the parity of the U.S. dollar by 8.57 percent, resulting in a new official monetary price of gold of $38 per ounce."

The 1972 Treasury report showed surplus currencies in Dutch gilders, Belgian francs, German marks, British pounds, French francs, Japanese yen, and Italian lire. These currency-producing countries were the major industrialized nations. The United States purchased $1.1 billion ("drawings") of these currencies, "reflecting the serious deterioration in the balance of payments position of the United States," this as reported by Secretary Schultz in 1972.

In July 1978, the "Federal Banking Agency Act" became law. The Federal Reserve System and its banks could now be audited, but exceptions and the veil of secrecy persisted; the audits would not include

- transactions with foreign central banks, foreign governments, and non-private international financing organizations;
- deliberations, decisions, and actions on monetary policy matters, including discount window operations, reserves of member banks, securities credit, interest on deposits, and open market operations;
- transactions made under the direction of the Federal Open Market Committee including transactions of the Federal Reserve System Open Market Account, etc.

Apparently, the president of the United States and the Congress were not privy to the inner workings of the central bank and the Federal Open Market Committee.

In 1968, President Johnson said, "The rapid growth in world trade and in the flow of capital is outpacing the growth of monetary reserves." The dwindling monetary reserves was the gold. A substitute was needed; a new reserve was needed, a new device to supplement the reserve. Enter the special drawing rights, "the paper gold"; there would be another financial wonder in the scheme of things. The drawing right was created from which a certificate was created. The certificate went into the Federal Reserve bank; the certificate, apparently, had a dollar sign on it. The certificate with the dollar sign on it was the credit device; this credit went into the Exchange Stabilization Fund. The secretary of the Treasury could get more dollars against this new certificate. The Federal Reserve would print the currency, and the secretary had his currency for special drawing rights. The borrowed currency was apparently interest bearing.

What value did special drawing rights have? The Drawing Rights was apparently, like a statement, a document, a device to produce money, another clever means in the continuing search for more money. The Drawing Rights was a scheme to try and eliminate the imbalances, the surpluses. The emerging industrial countries had surplus currencies; apparently, the Drawing Right was valued against the surplus currencies. A country in deficit would have a drawing right against a country in surplus; surplus currencies were purchased by a country in deficit. The United States, in deficit, purchased surplus currencies. Before all this business, countries in surplus were getting gold; these countries would now get dollars or "paper gold" and other deficit currencies. Apparently, the United States went into more deficit in the process? Interest-bearing fiat currency purchased foreign currency at 1.5% interest. The interest payments were going to the foreign countries in surplus? In the year 2009, huge surpluses remain and are rising; America's deficit account approaches a trillion dollars.

Congressman Binderup had said, "Now we know." Binderup had referred to the purchase of gold after 1934. President Roosevelt obtained a $2 billion credit against gold when he devalued the dollar. This credit in dollars went into the "Exchange Stabilization Fund." The Treasury of the United States obtained a special line of credit dollars when the Exchange Stabilization Fund (ESF) was established, and the secretary of the Treasury had the power to use it. Binderup said, "For 12 long years we wondered why this gold collected was given to the bankers in gold certificates, a mortgage on the gold that can only be redeemed by taxation, and we add to the gold gift; we give to the bankers currency amounting to 60 percent more than the face value of the gold certificates, but Bretton Woods explains it all."

In other words, the government of the United States awarded the Federal Reserve the gold by way of gold certificates; the 40% reserve factor was reduced to 25%, which was a 60% increase in the amount of credit dollars against gold. Binderup's contention: the country had been "off the gold standard and never wanted to go back, but Bretton Woods explains it all." Bretton Woods would operate based on gold;

the reduction in the reserve factor would allow more currency to be printed, to be borrowed. The government had more credit and money to spend, more obligations and the creation of more debt.

This fund, apparently, became a revolving Exchange Stabilization Fund. Secretary Morgenthau had the authority to use or spend this fund. According to Binderup, Morgenthau bought gold with these credit dollars. In 1934, the United States held approximately 5 billion in gold. By 1945, the United States held more than $22 billion in gold, about 75% of the world's total. Congressman Binderup wasn't specific; he simply stated, "Now we know" when the International Monetary Fund was being pushed by the Roosevelt administration. All the gold obtained by the secretary, apparently, became a working property of the banking system plus currency for discounting.

This gold heist by Roosevelt and Morgenthau had to be another unprecedented event; the United States was supreme and most formidable after World War II. This tremendous stash in gold had to propel the Roosevelt administration in their implementation of the IMF. In 1947, the new International Monetary Fund got $1.8 billion from this Credit Stabilization Fund. Where did all these credit dollars come from? President Roosevelt and Secretary Morgenthau started with $2 billion in 1934, and there was at least $1.8 billion in the fund after more than $15 billion in gold had been purchased. Apparently, as gold was purchased and the gold storage increased in the "Kentucky Hole," the credit in dollars had to increase. A guess says this is how it worked?

The increase in credit would allow new currency to be printed, to be spent buying gold. Fantastic! Imagine, fiat paper dollars buying all that gold. The scheme continued, and the money interests will deride the "fiat" dollar; it's called the "greenback" again, the repudiated currency. The derided fiat dollar is the Federal Reserve Note, the obligation, where the real power exists behind the money scheme. Apparently, the Federal Reserve Notes were good for gold within the international banking scheme. The centuries-old practice of accumulating gold with paper money continued; it manifested again in Secretary Morgenthau's colossal acquisition of gold. The United

States had a lot of gold, and the sellers of gold, no doubt, apparently possessed a lot of Federal Reserve Notes.

In the nineteenth century, was California gold purchased with redeemable bank paper money? California gold was shipped from San Francisco to the big banks in New York.. The United States was a debtor nation in those days. Apparently, when debts were paid to foreign countries, gold went to England and Europe. All the gold mined in the United States over a period of time had been shipped out of the country.

In the twentieth century, as of August 1971, after twenty-five years of the IMF money creation machine and redistribution, United States gold was more than half gone, divvied up to foreign central banks. In the process, the IMF operation was apparently accumulating its gold along the way. The United States in 1971 still possessed more than twice the gold of any one foreign country. But collectively, the future European Union would have more gold than the United States. President Nixon probably stopped the gold transfer at the right time; distribution to the international was complete.

Because of the gold draw down, the IMF gold dollar scheme had to be changed; enter the "paper gold" scheme, "Special Drawing Rights," and more credit stabilization dollars. These new dollars could be added to Gertrude Coogan's description of "further out into the deep" international deficit financing dollars. Chairman McChesney Martin described this business as "financial gimmickry." Congressman McClory called it "gimmickry." Was it "gimmickry"? Is all of this money business gimmickry? This latest "paper gold" thing was clever; another remarkable scheme in the continuing monetary search for more money.

CHAPTER SEVENTEEN
"The New World Order"

The years 1973 to 1979 had to be the Vietnam/Watergate hangover period; the '70s decade was not a banner episode nationally or internationally for the United States. In 1973, Saudi Arabia cut off its oil supply to America and other countries. It was the infamous "Oil Embargo." For more than a year, long gas lines was the regimen for motorists in most cities, primarily in the Eastern United States. *World Book* stated that King Faisal of Saudi Arabia used the embargo "as an economic weapon against nations supporting Israel." Continuing Israeli-Egyptian warfare since 1967 was a problem; Israel had occupied Arab land, and Egypt was trying to take it back, without success. The embargo magnified America's dependence on foreign oil, a dependence that persists to the present day. The American people have friends in the Middle East? It would appear the oil embargo perpetrated a spike in the price of oil, and the price of oil has continued its steady climb.

A depression followed in 1974 and 1975; the American economy took another hit. Unemployment increased to 9.2%. The young and the minorities took the brunt of it; it was the period of "high rates of unemployment and high rates of inflation," this from the 1975 annual Treasury report. In 1975, the United States diplomatic exit from Saigon in Vietnam was a nightmare, a total embarrassment. There were pluses. In 1974, the Congress passed ERISA, the Employee Retirement Income Security Act. The American employee, hopefully, would benefit. Full disclosure was required by the employer to the employee of pension plans, their finances, the effects of income taxes, the involvement of the fiduciary, etc.

The "Oil Embargo" threw a wrench into the international scheme of things. According to Secretary Simon, inflation had caused a depressed economy, and inflation was caused by the "oil embargo and resulting price rise." There was an energy problem, but what was the energy problem? President Carter asked the country to conserve energy, and the working people would try to conserve energy while there was an energy glut in the world. The American people are a consumption breed. At the same time, the environmental issues were beginning to occupy the United States economy. Wasn't there a need to expand existing rich inner resources of the United States for energy? And why not? But there would be no offshore oil drilling. There would be no nuclear plants; there would be no oil refineries, just an apparent national economic cripple effect. Apparently, the United States was going to go elsewhere for energy; it appeared the international way of things? And the United States had always been the isolationist?

Suddenly, the high cost of petroleum and inflation was worldwide; enter more workings of the IMF. There would be more quotas and more participation monies and more quota monies for SDR. Congress would have to legislate the increases in the printing of American fiat tax dollars to fill new quota and participation requirements of the United States in the International Monetary Fund and "the World Bank Group." According to the Treasury report, developing countries were hit the hardest because of petroleum prices. A new $2 billion trust fund within the IMF was formed "to help meet the balance of payments needs of the poorest countries." Contributions from the oil-producing countries and member countries plus "the sale of a portion of the IMF's gold reserves" were planned to fund the trust.

There was another development; the oil-producing countries were investing their oil-producing glut of dollars in the United States. Was there a problem with this? The Treasury report stated that the United States was an "open" economy; it would stay that way, but the "impact of foreign investment" would be monitored "by Executive Order 11858."

In 1975, approximately $73 billion was the Federal Reserve Note circulation; these figures included "fractional currency" (coin). The United States Notes, the civil war greenbacks, were still there, considered as circulation, almost $323 million; this from the 1975 annual Treasury report. The gross national product was a trillion dollars. Approximately $300 billion was the national debt. Since the beginning of the United States, invaluable information had been documented by the secretaries of the Treasury. Things, apparently, were about to change! The comprehensive annual Treasury reports weren't there anymore as America entered the 1980s. As a result, this writer lost track of the lawful money greenbacks.

Jimmy Carter was elected president in 1976. President Carter brought Israel and Egypt to the bargaining table at Camp David in Maryland. The occasion was the "Camp David Peace Accords" in 1978. The principals were the prime ministers Menachem Begin of Israel and Anwar Sadat of Egypt. Anwar Sadat had made the initial peace offering. War was officially declared over between the two countries in 1979. This agreement was a real plus for the Carter administration, but the Middle East was submerged in oil and continuous sectarian hostility. Anwar Sadat was assassinated in his native country, apparently his reward for peace with Israel. Prior to this, King Faisal had been assassinated within his own family.

The Middle East nation of Iran had been an ally of the United States, but the friendly shah had been deposed. The exiled Ayatollah Khomeini returned as religious leader of Iran. Khomeini's stance was the United States was and had been the "Great Satan." Before long, the American embassy in Tehran was taken over by Iranian militants in 1979; more than fifty Americans were held hostage. The Carter administration made a military attempt to free the hostages; the attempt failed. Failing diplomacy kept the hostages captive for "444 days." The hostages were released in 1981 after Ronald Reagan became president. It appeared as a knock against President Carter and his administration. The hostage crisis was followed by the Iraq-Iran war, which lasted eight years from 1980 to 1988; border disputes were part of the problem. The United States supported Iraq in that one.

By February 1979, the Congress had raised the national debt limit to $798 billion; deficits and high interest rates was the norm in the United States during the Carter administration. GNP had passed $2.1 trillion. Ronald Reagan, in a speech on September 24, 1981, emphasized "tax cuts . . . and an end to continuing deficits and high inflation." Apparently, what President Reagan said and what he did were two different things. Reagan said the debt didn't mean anything as long as we owe it to ourselves, but we don't owe all the public debt to ourselves. Reagan's debt limits were raised to the hundreds of billions of dollars in each of the first five years. Naturally, expenditures exceeded revenues; borrowing was necessary to fill the void. It was more debt, and the Federal Reserve was increasing the money supply. It was deficit spending time!

On September 9, 1985, Congressman Dornan of California said, "Given America's precarious foreign trade imbalance, rapidly expanding money supply, and still high real interest rates, it is imperative for continued economic growth that we enact serious spending reductions in fiscal year 1986, and we keep reducing spending in the out years."

The Reagan spending policy created the "deficit dilemma." President Reagan, according to discussions in the Congress, stopped the Democrats from spending by running up the debt, a pretty neat trick. This was a Reagan-David Stockman plan? David Stockman was President Reagan's short-lived "supply side economics" budget director. Reagan raised the debt limit every year. Between 1981 and 1985, the public debt limit was raised to $2.1 trillion. This was not the total debt; there was also government agency debt.

The Federal Financial Bank (FFB) was started in 1973; government agencies borrow from this bank. This bank was started "to assure that such borrowings are financed in a manner least disrupted of private financial markets and institutions." The bank borrows/lends/pays back between the Treasury Department and "U.S. marketable Treasury securities." In 1975, according to the Treasury report, the bank loaned "$15.8 billion to Federal Agencies and federally guaranteed borrowers." The report stated that an "obligations" issue to private lenders proved to be more costly. The FFB lends the money to the government at a higher interest rate than the marketable treasuries.

The Soviet "evil empire" still loomed; the Russians shot down a South Korean commercial jetliner in 1983, killing everyone, hundreds of unsuspecting people. It was the period, since the Carter administration, of double-digit interest rates and, in the Reagan years, of insurgency and death in El Salvador, Nicaragua and the Sandinistas, the invasion of Grenada, repeated acts of terrorism against American installations worldwide, drugs in America, offshore money laundering, South African apartheid, the corporate raider, the Chrysler loan, deregulation, and the 1986 tax law. The Reagan administration planned the "Strategic Defense Initiative" (SDI), a military venture into space. President Reagan's detractors called SDI, Star Wars, an apparent knock by the liberal media. Reagan fired eleven thousand government air traffic controllers; the controllers had gone on strike. Government workers don't go on strike; the controllers were fired.

President Reagan talked of a balanced budget, but Reagan's practice was deficit spending. The economy had been down; the economy was up. There was nothing new there. According to the record, millions of new jobs were ultimately created during the Reagan years. The employment surge was coincident with mounting public debt, hostile takeovers supported by junk bonds, and a severe crash on Wall Street; that was 1987. Two years before, in 1985, it was official; the United States was again a debtor nation. Unbelievable! Not really! Japan held "35% ownership of our Treasury." About the mounting debt, Senator Proxmire said, "The corporate debt equity ratio was rapidly approaching an all time high." But the debt thing runs with accelerating economies and decelerating economies. The wealth of indebtedness continued; it was worldwide, in the hundreds of billions of dollars.

Ronald Reagan, in a later trip to Berlin, voiced a "tear down this wall." The "Berlin Wall" did finally come down after Reagan left office. George Bush had succeeded Ronald Reagan as president of the United States; it was November 1989. The Berlin Wall separated the people of Berlin for twenty-eight years. East Germany and West Germany were reunited. Chancellor Helmut Kohl faced a gigantic financial task in the restoring of East Germany, this after forty-four years of Soviet occupation. Money from the West would pay the freight, not the Communist Bloc. Who wanted rubles?

Communism, amid apparent financial collapse, had run its course in Europe. The Soviet Union gradually dissolved as the confederated "Republics" declared their independence from Soviet domination. It would be as before, before World War I, after seventy-two years of Communist domination in Eastern Europe, a one remaining formidable republic was vast imperial Russia. But Russia couldn't maintain a crumbling economy in a country possessing 75% of the world's resources? The cold war would end as the United States and Russia agreed to a reduction and a pullback in arms on the European continent. The principals involved were President George Bush of the United States and the Russian leaders Premier Gorbachev and President Boris Yeltsin.

"Mr. Speaker, this coming weekend, finance ministers, central bankers, and commercial bankers will be meeting in Washington under the auspices of the International Monetary Fund and the World Bank," this from Congressman John LaFalce of New York. Mr. LaFalce spoke of the conditions in Eastern Europe; it was May 1990. The United States would be asked to cough up more monies for the IMF and the World Bank. Apparently, more monies would be the initial fiat dollars for the quotas and the participations to the fund and the bank issued by the secretary of the United States Treasury and more debt on the books of the Federal Reserve. "Since 1953, the IMF has entered into 708 arrangements amounting to over 92 billion standard drawing rights [SDRS] which at present are worth somewhat more than a dollar," this from Senator Roth of Delaware.

The United States had upped the ante in "1959, 1965, 1970, 1978, 1980, and 1983." Senator Roth, in 1989, wanted to know "what portion of IMF funds are finding their way to commercial banks? What will be the IMF's role in Eastern Europe? How will the IMF respond to the Soviet Union's desire to become a member? How are the IMF's short term, high interest rate resources helpful to developing countries, whose economies need to build for the long run?"

Congressman LaFalce presented the words of Michael Camdessus, managing director of the IMF. Mr. Camdessus had discussed the success or failure of "Eastern European Reform—Best of Both Worlds." He said, "These domestic elements of reform will work best if the system is simultaneously reformed to open the economy to foreign competition and the benefits of fuller participation in the world trading system."

The countries of Eastern Europe, "Poland, Czechoslovakia, Hungary, East Germany and Yugoslavia" were destitute. Mr. LaFalce said, "The United States is in the process of trying to help these countries make the unprecedented transition from Communist rule to Democracy and free markets. It will be a long and difficult struggle—particularly on the economic front—and the financial resources of the United States are embarrassingly short at this time." There was opposition in the Congress for more economic aid to the Fund and the Bank.

Unemployment was up again; yearly deficits were running around $300 billion, a carryover from the Reagan years. President Bush's administration faced the Savings and Loan collapse in 1989. Deregulation and junk bonds contributed; new laws allowed the S&Ls to make loans. "Greed, fraud, mismanagement, and speculation were the precepts for S&L default and failure . . . windfall profits went to . . . S & L executives," this from Congressman Bruce Vento of Minnesota. "Who Pays?" There was a backlash in Congress because S&L failures occurred primarily in "13 States." Who would pay for this one? Estimates were in the $160 billion range. Apparently, all the states would pay; there were the "inequities of the bailout, most people agree that the Government has no choice but to honor its commitment to reimburse depositors in failed thrifts." An economist, James Smith, said, "We have deposit insurance to spread the risk and we spread it."

The Continental Illinois bank collapsed in 1984; $6 billion of taxpayers' money by the Federal Reserve was the transfusion. Residential properties took a dive in the 1990s, another recession period. Real estate values in sections of the country fell 30% to 40% between 1990 and 1996. Meanwhile in 1990, taxation and the revenue bill was business as usual in the Congress, the continuing debate; Republicans were for a reduction in the capital gains tax, the Democrats against. President George Bush went against his campaign promise of "no new taxes"; the Bush administration found loopholes and shelters for the wealthy and increased taxes across the board, which mainly affected the working class.

Some will remember, around this time, the latter 1980s into 1990, Japan supposedly had all the cash; America was broke. The United

States was on plastic. Japan was investing in America. Then the "wall" came down; Helmut Kohl needed a ton of money restoring East Germany. Fish and Wildlife sued the Corps of Engineers over the wetland issue. It was 1987 in America; this business had crushing results. Land development hit a brick wall. The American industrial complex was moving out of the country. Real estate collapsed until 1995. Japan's economy went into the tank; Japan's cash was no longer the issue. What happened?

Conditions continued tense in the Middle East. The year 1990 produced "Operation Desert Shield." American troops were sent to Saudi Arabia. In January 1991, the United States and allied countries waged war against Iraq; Saddam Hussein had invaded and plundered neighboring Kuwait. The United States and the allies rescued Kuwait by driving Hussein's army back to Baghdad in forty-one days. It was the period of stealth and smart bombs, American advanced military hardware and technology. Baghdad was bombed, and Hussein's army suffered tremendous losses in soldiers and material. American soldiers also died, and many returned home sick. The devastation in Kuwait was complete. "Operation Desert Storm" put Saddam down. More war, death, and resultant restoration and reconstruction would continue to feed the international wealth of indebtedness.

In April 1991, Secretary of the Treasury Nicholas Brady sent a letter to Dan Quayle, president of the Senate. Brady was asking the Congress to beef up the IMF again. "To amend the Bretton Woods Agreement Act . . . for an increase in the United States quota . . . The IMF is currently providing timely and effective assistance to countries adversely affected by the Gulf crisis." Another letter of urgency went to Senator Bob Dole in July. In October, regarding international development, Brady wrote, "Passage of this legislation is crucial to U.S. efforts to maintain the open, growing international economy on which our prosperity increasingly depends." Secretary Brady called it a "time of historic global change, the IMF is playing a pivotal role in the movement toward free markets and democracy . . . in support of the U.S.-led international debt strategy." Brady stressed the need for "economic reform in the Baltic States, as well as the Soviet Union and the republics."

IMF amendments would deal with arrears (unpaid monies) amounting to $5 billion from nine countries; changes included a reserve fund pledge in ounces of gold. The American people were being asked to pay more quota monies into the International Monetary Fund. The Congress had a problem with sending money to the former Soviets; the money was for the creation of a free market system and not for the probable payment of debts.

American money would continue the parade to Europe. In 1992, the Russian ruble was somehow worthless. Financially, Eastern Europe resembled post World War II; another currency stabilization process was in order. In the Senate, the purpose was to legislate the creation of more dollars for the former Soviet Union "to establish stable currencies and promote free enterprise in the CIS countries." The CIS countries was the Commonwealth of Independent States.

Sorry, this stuff does get old; it's the "stabilization" thing since way back. United States money interests were spreading the money around, moving the global economy.

A "Freedom Support Act" featured two parts, the already existing IMF fund and an exchange stabilization fund, a possible two-part payment plan. The cost of a separate stabilization fund was another United States participation of up to $6 billion. Apparently, this stabilization fund was separate from the 1934 fund? This stabilization fund would set up "Currency Boards," as recommended, and not central banking systems within the CIS countries, the currency boards acting independently of government bureaucracies. The Senate was informed by economists of the successful histories of currency boards. Senator Symms of Idaho explained the currency board system: "Unlike a central bank, a currency board simply issues notes and coins, convertibles into a foreign reserve currency at a fixed rate on demand." A Symms analysis included these:

- The foreign currency has to be a "sound" currency (probably dollars).
- A fixed rate on demand was important.
- There was no risk of loss of money. (We've heard that song before.)

- The interest rate is the same as in the reserve country.
- Past currency boards existed in seventy countries and were successful.
- Currently, Hong Kong and Singapore use currency boards.

The 1992-1994 government "Financial Highlights" showed "Special Drawing Rights Allocated by the IMF; Borrowings from the Public."

1991 - $6.7 billion
1992 - $7.2 billion
1993 - $6.9 billion
1994 - $7.2 billion

From 1980 to 1991, U.S. loans to the IMF averaged $4.1 billion; these are the SDRS dollars per year. Quotas are listed, but that's all. Descriptions of the participation issues; the "exchange for dollars"; the inner workings, the "special notes"; the creation of fiat currency, taxpayers money; and investments and sales of government securities are omitted. These descriptions were covered by Secretary Snyder in past Treasury reports. Senator Roth wanted to know "what portion of IMF funds are finding their way to commercial banks." Senator Roth, apparently, was asking questions because IMF and World Bank specifics were apparently not part of the government financial statements anymore. Comprehensive "Annual Treasury Reports" by the secretary of the Treasury were discontinued after 1984. Again, this writing has lost track of the lawful money greenbacks.

"Government Financial Highlights" were the featured reports of the 1990s. Twenty-first century "Consolidated Financial Reports of the U. S. Government" was a later designation. Now they are called "Financial Reports of the United States Government" audited by the GAO. These reports appear terse; they do not compare with the comprehensive Treasury reports of the past.

Federal Reserve System activities are not audited; Henry Gonzales of Texas wanted changes. Gonzales introduced a Federal Reserve Accountability Act in 1993 (H.R. 28). "Today, the Fed can decide the fate of an administration through still having domestic control of such things as interest rates . . . In HR 28, What we say is: We want you to tell us an accounting of your actions. What were the reasons? What do your deliberations show that led you to this decision?" Previously, Gonzales introduced a Federal Reserve Reform bill. Congressman Gonzales was critical of Federal Reserve interest rates; secret FOMC meetings and the "trilateral facility"; Federal Reserve loans to foreign countries, the Exchange Stabilization/$30 billion swap fund, unappropriated billions of dollars to Mexico; the NAFTA agreement, the big banks, and foreign subsidiaries, among other things. Gonzales had succeeded former Congressman Patman as chairman of the House banking committee.

Gonzales said that decisions by the Federal Reserve Board and the FOMC were privy to the Federal Reserve System and apparently not the business of government or the Congress. The Congress gave this power to the central bank, and that power, apparently, is not the business of the Congress. Maybe Congress is no longer a powerful body; the wealth of indebtedness apparently neutralizes the Congress. Gonzales also wanted a Federal Reserve Reform Act. A Government Management Reform Act did pass in October 1994. Government agencies had to submit audited financial statements to the director of Management and Budget, but Federal Reserve activities were excluded; there would be no thorough auditing of the Federal Reserve System.

Chairman Alan Greenspan appeared before the House banking committee on many occasions. In October 1993, he told the committee, "From time to time, I have briefed members of various Administrations about the outcomes of FOMC meetings, because that knowledge could assist them in the formulation of government policies for which they have responsibility. This qualification has not, however, been a relevant one over the past year or so, as the Federal Reserve has not altered its instrument settings."

Gonzales wanted his banking committee to know more about the "newfangled financial instruments called derivatives." Gonzales called them newfangled, but derivatives were not new! Derivatives were high-risk investments, and the derivatives were unregulated; the banks were involved. This, apparently, was another problem. Hedge funds heavily financed by the banks were the "purchasers of the derivative products," this from Gonzales. The derivative, from the calculus, is "a rate of change, as in a value changing with respect to another value reaching a limit of value"; the derivative is that limit of value. In the calculus, the limit may be a positive or a negative. There is the math derivative and the market derivative. What happens in mathematics and the market are apparently two different things, but the principle has to be similar? There is the rate of change, a plus or minus. An apparent negative difference is that the financial derivative may deal in the marketplace, the unpredictable.

Hedge funds bet for or against the positive or the negative. Mathematics finds derivatives of absolute functions, a true science; the financial derivative deals in the economic marketplace where there are no absolutes, no guarantees—the human factor, another matter. Derivatives in the future's markets are identified in notional amounts. From the dictionary, "notional" means "imaginary." The notional amounts traded are stated in the hundreds of trillions of dollars. The derivative markets appear as a separate marketplace in themselves, another separate economy supported by the investment banking system. But apparently, real money is created against the derivative. And that real money can be lost? Is all this business mythical figments, explosions in money terms? Maybe, the notional amounts could be abstract extensions of Alexander Hamilton's "beyond imagination."

Chairman Gonzales, in 1993, spoke of the size of hedge funds compared to the New York Stock Exchange. Bank loans to a fund "management" are as much as twenty times a fund management dollar, and these are extensive credit dollars. The hedge fund "daily volume" in currency transactions dwarfs the New York stock exchange; it's in the "$1 trillion range" compared to the stock market "$10 billion" range, this from Gonzales. In 2010, transactions and manipulations dwarf these figures.

The total physical United States credit circulation today, in 2010, the money in people's hands, money outside the Treasury, is about $1.5 trillion? This circulation plus foreign money generates a United States GDP of about $15 trillion. The derivative market, which is global, apparently dwarfs the GDPs. Then when a 2007 U.S. subprime housing loss of $200 billion hit the market, with hedge funds leading the charge, the result was enough to shake up the credit markets in the United States and Europe. Credits, deposits, assets, today's colossal pyramid, apparently teeters on the edge in real money? The liquid central banks are the only entities without any debt; these are the government creations, the central banks who create and own the cash. What is the total liquid cash amount compared to the global credit in tens of trillions?

The European Central Bank doled out the equivalent of 131 billion liquid dollars to help stem the subprime crisis. Central bank bailouts are there for the biggies, at a price, and payback is in a short amount of time. The Wall Street big boys may claim trillions in assets, and then a $5 or $10 billion subprime loss supposedly rocks their cradle; the extensions in credits today are apparently enormous. As with all past recessions and depressions, the banks had tremendous assets, and yet the banks and the money houses had no money. More accurately, the same banking system, in the past, with the central bank at the head, simply eliminated credits.

In 1993, more United States currency was going to the other international, the World Bank. Nine billion dollars was slated to go to Russia and the former Communist republics. Bill Clinton was president, but this money, according to the record, was apparently arranged and authorized by the Congress when George Bush was president. The principals of the World Bank had come back to the Congress for more money. Why more money to the bank at this time? This from Congressman Kasich of Ohio. The bank had a "37.5 percent failure rate," and bank practice was costly. Highly paid bank officials pay no income tax on an average salary of $123,000; Kasich presented a critical *USA Today* editorial by a former bank employee. The World Bank was called "hypocritical . . . with continued internal malaise and financial extravagance." A differing view by Congressman Obey explained the bank's role. The United States commitment to the World Bank was 19% of total public-funded monies by all countries. "The World Bank is the way we leverage other countries to provide assistance to countries like Russia rather than having to do it all ourselves."

When President Bush made the agreements with the Russians in 1991 and the cold war appeared over, the president declared "the new world order." Along with this new world order, the gross national product of the United States was redefined; the product was domesticated. The product was now a GDP, not a GNP. Why was the description of the economic product changed? The GNP had been a gross economic output of production made in America by American companies; it was a national product. The world's economic environment was changing; Treasury Secretary Brady called it "historic global change." American investments and companies are over there, and foreign investments and companies are in America.

In the open market scheme, outsourcing is the thing. American labor is taking the hits, and labor appears everywhere and by all nationalities. If an American has a telephone or Internet problem, a technician in India will resolve the communication problem? Many of the products and parts of those products made in America are made by foreign companies; it's a mix of American and foreign companies making products, interchangeable in and out of the United States. The American aircraft company Boeing is having problems today because of outsourcing. Parts for U.S. military hardware are produced outside the United States? If so, that's a good one? American seaports are run by rich foreigners. The global market apparently necessitated a descriptive change.

A country's gross product was somehow more of a domestic product because of foreign economic infusion; the product wasn't national anymore. With the advent of the new world order, all the countries within the international economic framework were also domesticated. Economic production figures reported for all the countries are shown as gross domestic products (GDP). The industrialized world had become a domestic economic mix in the international community, this only in the money scheme. Russia and China are new major players in the supposed free market system, not cold war enemies, which is an apparent positive thing. But Communism, "rogue" nations, continuing warfare, probable takeover of American foreign interests, anti-Americanism in the Middle East and in Europe, and terrorism's 9/11 persist. The control of resources, resultant economic leverage, the Iraq war, and nuclear threats remain.

In the United States, there are literally tens of thousands of national societies, associations, companies, professional and college sports teams and associations, and banks. Many of these entities are named with the national prefix; it has been that way a long time. The word "national" does denote patriotism within the domain, within the sovereign nation. The word "national" is an extension of the word "nation." But sovereignty in the global economy appears kaput! No doubt, national banks in America deal in foreign currencies. Maybe all the banks and associations, insurance companies, etc., should denote the domestic prefix, like maybe the "Domestic Banks of America" or the "Domestic Football League," the DFL.

Domestic means "home, not foreign." But the international global economy, which is a foreign mix in America, has domesticated all the products. From the *Congressional Record*, approximately a third of the member banks in the "New York Federal Reserve district" are owned by foreign banks. How many banks in the United States are subsidiaries of foreign banks? The Federal Reserve System initiated a banking infusion into Europe after World War I. From the *Congressional Record*, 1985 accelerated the tremendous influx of money by foreign countries; Japan, Great Britain, Germany, Middle East countries, etc., buying up the United States. The United States had become officially, domestically, a debtor nation.

The global thing has been in the making for many years. During June and July of 1933, a World Economic Conference was held in London, England. The *Wall Street Journal* called the conference "an atmosphere of unreality." The London Conference, according to the *Journal*, was apparently zeroing in on national economies. The conference "hoped that they can check further growth of economic nationalism."

In the literal sense, if not international, it's national. But apparently, we are living in the real world. In the money scheme of things, if not international, it's declared domestic. Domesticating the products of all nations appears as the continuing act of subjugation by the money interests. In 1991, President George Bush called it "the new world order." As of 1991, domestic was in, national was out!

CHAPTER EIGHTEEN
Prophecy

Alexander Hamilton referred to federal expenses as being permanently unlimited, "susceptible of no limits, even in imagination." In the twenty-first century, United States federal expenses are susceptible of no limits. This is what Alexander Hamilton wanted and predicted; this is what the American people got. Section 8 of Article I of the Constitution gave the Congress "the power to coin money and regulate the value thereof." The implication and interpretation was that the government, the Treasury shall create and control the nation's money, interest rates, credit—a Jackson model. This interpretation of Section 8 of Article I was the choice of Thomas Jefferson, James Madison, and Attorney General Randolph; those three lost the Constitutional debate.

Alexander Hamilton, George Washington, the Pennsylvania creditors, and a majority in Congress decided that a private bank would create, control, and regulate the nation's money. The U.S. Treasury wasn't destined to create money out of nothing; a private bank would be allowed to create money out of nothing with the help of the Congress. Apparently, the Constitution was considered upheld; Congressman Bingham reminded us: "What the Government does by another, it does by itself." Later, Senator Collamer said, "And we are to be responsible after all; that is all there is of it."

In 1933, President Roosevelt, using executive power, regulated the value of the nation's money when he devalued the dollar. President Roosevelt exercised the power of Section 8 of Article I of the Constitution of the United States. But the country's gold and the Federal Reserve Note, apparently, would remain in the control of the central bank.

The total accelerating government national or domestic debt was about $11 trillion when the Republican George Bush left the presidency on January 2009. Money interests will say it's no big deal; it's simply the cost of moving forward. The debt escalation since 1980, propelled by deficit spending, has been almost totally a Republican agenda! The debt will escalate, the built-in cost of the political economy. Absolute growth and continued oppressive taxation can only guarantee its redemption. Since the beginning of the Reagan presidency, GNP/GDP has increased from $2 trillion to $15 trillion, about 7.5 times or 750%. The national debt has increased from one trillion to 11 trillion dollars, about 11 times or 1100%. Debt progression exceeds economic production; this is propelled by the Republican "deficit dilemma." The debt progression is growing faster than real growth within the domain. The trade imbalance is on the negative side, now escalated to almost a trillion dollars per year and growing.

According to the 2007 account imbalance in the world investment economy, the United States appeared to invest less than it surrendered to foreign countries and bought a whole lot more than it sold. The sale of American equity, with approval of the Bush White House, appeared the order of the day, from corporations to small businesses to the homeowner. The American large and small businessperson sells to the foreign entity. Americans have no cash? The latest gimmick is the reverse mortgage. The American borrowing/spending GDP is 2.5 times larger than the closest competitor Japan, but Japan leads in the balance of payments; that means a plus in money. America has the big GDP, but is a big minus in money. America has the largest industrial output of any country; America is the second largest exporter, but is way behind in the balance of payments. The reality is, America plays to the debt money scheme, the big borrower and spender. American money out and less American money back in is apparently integral to the United States economy. Global is it! American business, commerce, manufacture, trade, investments, and, now traditionally, American sports teams are working and playing outside the United States. Americans are spending dollars borrowed from foreigners, and foreigners are buying up the United States with the same dollars. Fortunes reverse!

China, Japan, the Middle East, and Russia are doing a lot of the selling from toys, clothes, machines to oil; American corporate offshore business and outsourcing is a major part of it. The foreign countries, and the multinationals, are collecting United States dollars. During this period, the dollar was decreasing in value against foreign currencies. It's the trade imbalance; it's the expectation. America is way ahead of any one country in productive output, but borrowing and spending guns the GDP. The dollar fall was coincident with the eight-year Bush administration. This business will probably turn around; who knows what will happen next? The experts don't know or say. The money interests dictate the interest rates and the ascending/descending value of the currencies. If export/import reverses, the dollar will rise again; there will be a resurgence.

About the private debt, since the American civil war and the advent of big government, federal debt may be 20-25% of total United States debt. The exception was World War II; the government expenditure then was almost 50% of the national product, this from the 1945 Treasury report. Private debt in early 2008 before the meltdown was four times Federal debt or approximately $40 trillion. This would make the total federal and private debt $50 trillion. The credit circulation before the 2008 crash, was approximately $1.5 trillion; total debt to circulating money 33 to 1. In the 1920s, approaching 1929, it was about 40 to 1. Maybe all this is countered by United States household wealth, which is now down from 65 trillion to 58 trillion thanks to the crash.. This wealth is the nation's true equity base, the American household. Everything is for sale in the creation of more money, the credit circulation. What's the total wealth of the United States beyond the homeowner?

A big United States debt owed to itself was considered acceptable, this from President Abraham Lincoln. But gold was owed to England and Europe, then a monetary obligation was legislated, then a de-emphasis of monetary nationalism and a global economy was orchestrated. International dictated to national; then national became domestic. This business has secured a United States debt in perpetuity. The United States, while buying the world economy, owes escalating debt to the international, the new world order.

A 2008 projected federal budget of $3.1 trillion was issued by the Bush White House. The federal government has been spending 15% more each year since 1980. The GDP increase during the same period shows a 26% increase per year and a federal debt increase of 37% per year. Since 1990, the CPI tells us that inflation is running anywhere from approximately 2%-4% per year; no wonder working people are behind the eight ball. Wages increase based on the probable bogus CPI inflation figures. It should be clear where the real inflation exists and persists, the wealth scheme. The explosive global economy inflates growth, then debt, the wealth of indebtedness; it's the Alexander Hamilton prophecy in global terms.

The federal debt increase through 2008, occurred primarily during the tax-reduction deficit-spending years promoted by the Republicans. Since1980, government spending has increased from $660 billion to $3.1 trillion, an increase of 470%. GDP has increased 750%, a plus; but the debt has increased 1100%, more than 2 times spending and 1.33 times more than GDP. These figures are before the 2008 meltdown. The cost of the economy is promotional excessive debt propelled by the tax cuts, the Reagan trick confirmed by Eccles and expanded by Bush.

Taxpayers are automatically behind in the future payment of escalating debt for future generations. The average household income in 1980 was about $28,000; 2008 income was estimated at approximately $60,000. Let's say income has doubled, a 100% increase. The United States boasts of the largest per capita GDP in the world, but the average American is not keeping pace and is not a principal part of the GDP increase of 750%. This may also qualify as a part of the Hamilton prophecy. The money interests keep harping on the government deficit as small as compared to GDP; isn't this a smoke screen, more like baloney?

This recalls the per capita figure. The Treasury or the Federal Reserve or the government may publish a per capita figure based on the currency circulation and 300 million people in the United States. The *Wall Street Journal* stated in October 2007 that "1% of the people have access to 21.2% of the country's income." That 1% or 3 million people would calculate to $105,000 per capita wealth in the United States. Although a considerable income, American wealth could never pay the national debt, much less the private debt. What is America's cash equity? Is it about 3% or 5% of the total public and private debt? This is the money system. The middle 74% of the people have access to approximately 66% of the income or $4,500 per person. Fifty percent of the bottom half may possess 12.8% of the circulation, according to the article; the bottom half may have access to about $2,550 per person. The approximate numbers show the natural accumulating disparity in the United States. The American people are doing better. In the 1930s, 25% of the people, or the bottom half, had zero money. Back then, state scrip and barter was in vogue.

Oil futures recently hit $142 dollars a barrel, and the latest word was a possible recession in the United States in 2009; the economy is taking a nosedive. The United States consumes 25% of the world's oil. Prices are escalating; gas reached $4 a gallon. Then gas fell to $1.55 per gallon. Does any of this make any sense? Before this, President Bush, with apparent no leverage, after spending probably a trillion dollars in the Middle East, went to the Middle East, wanting more production and lower oil costs. Maybe it worked! By the way, where is the abundant Iraqi oil? Wouldn't this oil make a difference? The price has dropped! Maybe the fall election! Politics!

And George Washington had to be dreaming; his words to his countrymen suggested a lasting national existence, leaving the foreign country to its own devices. Alexander Hamilton had an agenda; he had to be thinking international. Isolation in money had to be a pipe dream. Debts were owed to foreign countries—more than $10 million plus interest, a lot of money then—and debts had to be paid. How could America ever have been considered in isolation?

Another reminder—Alexander Hamilton's first central bank had a principal purpose to create paper money for discounting, for lending, for profit. There was the public creditor, the shareholder and the public transfer. Hamilton's first central bank set the tone, the country's future course, the country's growth, and a destined wealth disparity, the financial way of things, today's reality.

In the 1990s, President Clinton's administration interrupted the Republican harvest; the tax cut floodgates appeared closed temporarily. There was a slight interruption; President George Bush Sr., against his promises and demise, increased taxes. President Clinton, during his eight years, stopped the rapid acceleration of the national debt. Clinton, each year, consistently reduced deficit spending, but his Treasury and the Federal Reserve, according to the *Congressional Record*, engineered the big Mexican bailout. Chairman Gonzales referred to the "big banks"; there was a Mexican "exposure of over $80 billion . . . boy, we get NAFTA pushed through, and, when it is in place, Mexico will be able to pay us $10 billion a year."

A financial crisis started in Mexico in 1994; the peso had dropped from 3.5 to 7 pesos against the dollar. Foreign money was leaving the country; Mexico was printing money, igniting a currency crisis. The currency speculator was at it again? President Clinton, with the Congress stalemated, pledged a $20 billion loan to Mexico in February 1995; his original figure was $40 billion. Clinton had the agreement of the Congressional leadership and the authority under "Title 31 of the United States code, Section 5302." The money would come from the Exchange Stabilization Fund. Clinton pledged the American taxpayer wouldn't be paying the tab. But the IMF pledged almost $19 billion; the BIS pledged another $10 billion. Based on the money scheme, all these dollars originate with the treasuries and the central banks. Aren't these interest-bearing tax dollars? This business is on the backs of the world's taxpaying public. By 1997, economic conditions were better; Mexico was beginning to pay the money back.

Although economic conditions were supposedly better, Mexicans seeking jobs have been sweeping across the American border by the millions ever since. NAFTA is working, and so is Mexican illegal immigration into the United States. It's a problem the Congress can't seem to solve. The present global economic mix is like a tidal wave, apparently beyond committed United States Congressional action on American health care, Social Security, the drug problem, the country's infrastructure, affordable education, good-paying jobs, and crime-ridden city streets. These conditions don't take priority. These conditions are overhead maintenance expenses; there's no money in it, and the problems get lost with the emphasis on international financial venture and profit.

By 1997, the yearly deficit had been reduced from a built-up Republican high of almost $300 billion a year to $22 billion. The

Clinton administration was reaching for a budget surplus, God forbid, a surplus? But the total debt by then had reached $6 trillion. The 1997 Consolidated Financial Report showed another interesting development. Based on the "London fixing," the statutory price of gold was listed at "$42.2222 per fine troy ounce." Why a London fixing? The 2006 gold holdings in the United Kingdom are minimal compared to the United States, or are they? Wasn't the dollar devaluation based on the 1934 United States statute? The dollar had reached the 50% value against gold in the United States as per the 1934 Roosevelt final limit of devaluation.

There is the statutory price of gold and the market price of gold. The statutory gold price apparently sets the exchange rate for world currencies. The euro was originally set at $1.17. The European countries, the European Union, collectively held approximately 1.17 times more gold than the United States? The statutory price of one euro then, set in 1993, was worth $1.17? The British pound was worth approximately $1.65.

The 1997 Financial Report listed the market price of gold, the commodity, at "$332.10 per fine troy ounce"; in 2007, the market price again reached $850. In early 2008, gold was over $900; some say gold will reach $2000. Who knows? The United States gold stock was listed at 11 billion statutory dollars; this was approximately the amount of statutory gold in the United States when President Nixon stopped the hemorrhaging in 1971.

While United States gold stock, from the *Report*, has apparently remained the same, IMF gold, an apparent reserve of member countries, has grown. IMF gold is now referred to as a "hoard." IMF gold, in millions of ounces, is reportedly about 40% of the United States gold stock, a considerable amount. Maybe the IMF sells gold at the market price, apparently, to strengthen its currency base, especially at an accelerating $1100 an ounce—a good deal and climbing? Apparently, gold, at the surging market price, serves as a reserve function within IMF international dealings when doing business with member countries, the United States, and the banks? Paper currency begot gold, and now gold begets currency—the continuum. The United States now is third in the world in mined gold behind South Africa and Australia, this from the Economist 2006 *Pocket World in Figures*. More about market gold later.

Gold has no credit circulation function in the United States; gold is the commodity for the speculators on the national/domestic/international scene. Statutory gold in the United States is less than 1% of the credit circulation, down from the 40% reserve factor to practically zero. Chairman Eccles said, long ago, there was no connection with the currency circulation against gold in the United States. When President Roosevelt gobbled up the gold, there was to be no more payment or exchange in gold (for the citizen). The circulation, then the Federal Reserve currency, by statute, was declared intrinsic. There is statutory gold and market gold, a two tier crazy system. Today, individuals, investors, speculators, sell commodity gold for currency in the open market.

Recently, in the *Wall Street Journal* of Wednesday, December 12, 2007, an article by Alan Greenspan stated,

> In theory, central banks can expand their balance sheets without limit. In practice, they are constrained by the potential inflationary impact of their actions. The ability of central banks and their governments to join with the International Monetary Fund in broad-based currency stabilization is arguably long since gone. More generally, global forces, combined with lower international trade barriers, have diminished the scope of national governments to affect the paths of their economies.

Chairman Greenspan explained the central bank money creation function in just a few words. In addition, his words explain and confirm. The chairman suggested an apparent impasse exists between IMF international dealings and "central banks and their governments." The "paths" of national or domestic economies have apparently been affected? Alan Greenspan mentioned the words "national governments," which is reassuring. But the money dictates domestic! There are the central banks and their BIS, the secret colossus in Basel, Switzerland. Central banks are secret; the BIS is secret, an apparent necessity. The central banks deposit money in the BIS. Isn't this domestic/national money deposited in the international bank?

The BIS sets agendas, interest rates, etc., for all the central banks, which affect all banks in the respective countries? The BIS, the IMF, the World Bank, the speculator, the superrich, the multinationals are powerful competing, yet integral internationals? And member domestic economies appear subject to them? Economists describe "national economies." At the same time, the new world order has determined their economies to be gross domestic products.

The world economy includes the separate nation, the member nation, the debtor nation, the creditor nation. The "national governments" and their "economies" appear relegated to the subjugated roll. All the countries and their national economies comprise the international; they also appear separated out, and included in, with limiting financial sovereignty? When looking at more than three centuries of political economic history, Great Britain had subjugated her colonies. All the states in the United States have been subjugated. The Socialist republics were subjugated in the Soviet Union. The nations in the new European Union have been subjugated. It's the centralizing of financial power, a consuming power.

In the twenty-first century, in the marching new world order, the nations of the world, including the United States, appear as supporting collectives. Are the respective governments puppets? The 2008 credit currency crisis exhibited central bank world subjugation. There is the other deal fermenting as part of the mix—the North American Union, a future "Amero" currency for Canada, the United States, and Mexico?

The industrialized countries are subjected to and fueled by the principal central banks and their BIS. Following are the investment banks, international markets, the IMF and the World Bank, and the currency speculator, etc. How many separate, integral, and competing economies are there in the global picture? The world economies apparently include the Federal Reserve System, world central banks and their BIS; investment banks, the stock exchanges, trusts, hedge funds, derivatives; the NYMEX, the CME, the British LIBOR; the currency speculator; all the domestic/national economies, including the fifty United States; the IMF and the World Bank.

The above entities comprise the global pyramid, and they are all fed by the currency-creating central banks. Currencies and all liquidity originate with the central banks. Pyramids collapse unless continuously fed. The 2007 subprime housing debacle was the latest hit; its absolute collapse surfaced because many millions of working people in the United States, a bottom-feeder, couldn't pay their mortgage payment. People were duped by the principal cog of the scheme, the adjustable rate mortgage. The ARM contrivance is another form of bait and switch. Accelerating the interest rate in the amortization process rockets the mortgage payment, apparently the core of the hedge fund investment and a bum deal for the mortgagee. According to the *Journal*, the principals, the CEOs of the mortgage lenders, received their big payment up front before mortgages were packaged into securities and sold to the losing investors.

Hedge fund management schemes gamble both ways, for success or failure. The hedge fund betting on the probable subprime collapse was rewarded. Do these types of practices support a forward economy? The practice appears separate, destructive—the casino in action! According to the reports, the players were people with suspect credit and also speculating people with good credit; they got caught in the escalation of the interest rate. The pyramid survives when bailed out at the going interest rate by the central bank. Taxpayers, by way of the Treasury, pay the central bank. Thousands of those taxpayers apparently couldn't make the mortgage payment. The big pyramid scheme works; the entity at the top runs off with the money. Hopefully, government initiative may limit the 2-3 million or more expected foreclosures. The real estate vulture is already on the attack.

The directional flow of American money hasn't changed; the fifty United States domestic economies apparently continue feeding surplus monies to Wall Street. The deal is more than two hundred years old. In 1920, Will Rogers said, "Let Wall Street have a nightmare, and the whole country has to help them get back in bed again." The system of bailout hasn't changed, only the source. Wall Street now needs outside additional help, a feed of cash from the international.

Wall Street needs Europe, the Middle East, and Asia to "help them get back in bed again." But it appears a two-way street.

Where would financial globalization be without the international currency speculator?

The world market in money and currency exchange rates are apparently targets of hedge fund speculators; the 1997 Asian currency crisis was an example. Mahathir Bin Mohamad, president of Malaysia, denounced the speculator in the *Wall Street Journal*. The date was September 23, 1997. Mahathir claimed, "With these self-serving systems the big players can wreak havoc in the stock market. And that is precisely what they did to the share markets of Southeast Asia." The speculator was apparently lauded by those who benefited financially; it's part of the free world market in money. But the effect was an "attack" on the Malaysian currency, the ringgit. Do governments take action, or do markets simply stabilize? Dr. Mahathir admitted "taking a big risk" when he attacked the "open societies" for allowing these practices to happen. Dr. Mahathir said the open societies were "not so open. In fact they are shady and shadowy. And when anyone criticizes them, like authoritarian rulers they punish with all means in their power."

Speculators deal in huge sums of money. The speculator, apparently, can destroy banks, a country's money! A country? How does the speculator evolve? Where does the speculator come from? Does the speculator carry the money around in a big satchel? Are the speculators acting agents of banks, of central banks? The *London Economist* referred to the "faceless international speculator" during the Eurodollar market. There were exchanges, the "swaps" between banks, and the result: "the Central Bank remains the beneficial owner of the foreign exchange," this from the *Economist* as presented in the House by Congressman Moorehead on August 21, 1963.

The twenty-first century came in without Y2K; the computer glitch didn't happen. The stock market appeared suspect. The price earnings ratio in 2000 was like two hundred times; how was that supposed to work? Dow Jones is the future's market. By 2002, the Dow Jones was down to 7,200 from a high of over 11,000 in 1999. Dot-com companies took the big hits; CEOs apparently ran off with the money.

The NASDAQ plummeted 80%. The Wall Street economy continues, prices escalate, a cyclical collapse may occur, there are the winners, bonuses continue, and there are the losers. Corporate America showed an ugly side; accounting firms, apparently, falsified the numbers or earnings. Enron Corporation, the big energy giant, collapsed. Eleven thousand people lost their jobs, pensions, everything; suits were filed, with Enron blaming numerous banks. America's energy grid, where apparent excessive profit occurred, dumped on the people, especially in the western United States. The Enron collapse escalated another back to Congress fix with Sarbanes-Oxley.

The second President George Bush, the son, was treated to the 9/11 tragedy, a terrorist attack, the destruction of the twin World Trade Center towers in New York City. The day was September 11, 2001. Almost three thousand people lost their lives. For Americans living sixty-seven years ago, this was an act of war. Sixty-seven years ago, the United States, declaring war, may have bombed the hell out of somebody. Now, it's the United Nations and international political economic conquest. It is now a time of "national security" in the domestic financial society—the continuing hypocrisy. It was freedom America with armed guards at airports. Unbelievable! And vengeance, there would be vengeance, but how do you fight terrorism with conventional warfare? This was to be America's direction pushed by the Bush administration.

A recessed economy picked up in 2003. President Bush resumed the tax cuts, and the deficits soared. Bush gives back 70 billion in taxes and runs a beginning deficit to almost a half a trillion dollars; this makes sense to the public investor. Chairman Eccles told us it was the way to get the economy rolling. An amount of $70 billion may translate or escalate to maybe $700 billion in a forward economy. The economy responds, the shareholders collect when the investors dip into the Treasury, the government spends, and the cost is more debt. Debt creates money, which will create the eventual demand for taxes on Bush's tax cuts; the demand for more taxes pays the interest, and the security on the money created, the cost of the obligation and the economy.

Both political parties tax or produce taxation. Future taxation results because of the Republicans; their scheme promotes the backdoor approach, but a forward debt-ridden economy. The Republicans are the good guys; they reduce taxes. The Democrats are the bad guys; they tax directly. The oppression is necessary; at least the Democrats appear to come in the front door. Funding a debt in the global economy gradually erodes. Apparently, it's not a big deal today; American posterity is not a consideration.

Bush placed a 150,000-man "lean" American army in Iraq and more sacrifice of America's young. Was it a lean army because the army wasn't handling its own logistics anymore? According to the *Wall Street Journal*, "180,000 contractors" were in Iraq. The U.S. Army in Iraq doesn't total that many. Think of it, a war zone, 180,000 contractors and probably 180,000 insurance policies. The latest cost estimate for this war was $1.6 trillion; that's public money. It really is a different time; the global economy is generating a ton of new money.

Hamilton was right; the amount of created money is "susceptible of no limits." Gertrude Coogan would call it "further out into the deep" domestic and international deficit spending money! The working people get the dribble down, a piece of it. In 2007, the Democrats wanted withdrawal from Iraq: "bring the troops home." At the same time, the Bush administration was pushing for an eventual stationary army in Iraq, a necessary occupation. An American army is in Germany and Korea; those wars ended sixty-five and sixty years ago. This military presence shows a very thin threshold of world peace and a ton of indebtedness. The Republican candidate for president mentioned a military presence of one hundred years in Iraq.

The Democrats appear frustrated, complaining about deficit spending. The Republican Bush administration continues spending on the war, performing the Reagan/Eccles trick; and the Democrats spending is reduced. What a deal, and it's all for the country! Besides, the rich are getting richer. The politicians never tell how the rich get richer. American wealth, foreign wealth, the international wealth of indebtedness, all feeding on United States public money.

It all appears just as a colossal trick! John Kenneth Galbraith called it. Galbraith said the "conservatives" favored this policy; "Keynes could be had by tax cuts."

CHAPTER NINETEEN

And the Beat Goes On

The year 2008 was an election year in the United States, and recession was imminent. A recession occurs because of a credit crunch. A credit crunch looms because hundreds of billions of liquid dollars disappeared. Money disappears, then credit disappears; it was the subprime thing. Big financial banks, apparently, overextended balance sheets. The Glass-Steagall Act of 1933 removed the investment practices of the big banking affiliates; those affiliates could no longer invest and gamble the people's money in stocks and bonds, a dereliction of the past. A 1999 Congressional action, signed by President Clinton, apparently restored the investment practice of banks. The rules were changed to the practices of the past. Maybe the emergence of the public markets sparked the legislation; banks would do their thing again. Weren't investment banks armed with an arsenal of derivative performance backed by hedge funds? On top of that came the credit default swaps.

The 2007 Wall Street rumblings resembled throes of the past. Things were supposedly going OK? Access to credit, an abundant money supply was there, low interest rates and electronic ease of purchase. But Wall Street greed and investment banks can screw things up. Money gravitates to New York. The financial experts may say it's not Wall Street. But the Federal Reserve was quick to extend more credit to those investment banks into January 2009. It's apparently the connection of the Federal Reserve, the Treasury, the Federal Reserve Bank of New York, and Wall Street. Financial markets had to be rescued, stabilized. Not all were rescued.

The housing market took a dive! Capitalism's ways can be devious, consistent ways; home values are plummeting while mortgages remain fixed, and the real estate raiders waste no time gathering recruits while gobbling up the foreclosures. America can be painful for the losers; people are left behind in the surge. Banks will be suing banks, jurisdictions suing banks, and people suing brokers, etc. America, the land of litigation, pursues the money. The credit crunch cranks the Congress. There will be more credit rules and then probably new financial innovation. There will never be enough rules! More rules, more gimmickry! Newton's law! The subprime matter had global implications; Great Britain's debt crisis was reportedly worse than the United States. Prime Minister Brown was already feeling the heat. This brings to light the Bank for International Settlements and the regulation of domestic banking systems by way of the central banks?

Some may downplay the subprime crisis; it's only Wall Street. How many mortgages were involved, 2 to 3 million? It may exceed 5 million; it's a small percentage. There are 130 million households in America. But the crisis was big enough to involve the Treasury, the Federal Reserve, central banks in England and Europe, big banks on Wall Street, the mortgage industry, Fannie Mae and Freddie Mac, the FHA, the Federal Home Loan Banks, the Middle East, the sovereign wealth systems, equity firms, and on and on. It apparently was a market crisis? Not a nation crisis?

But the shenanigans do shake the nation's economy. From the record, it always has and it always will; credit takes a tumble. The American and the global economy moved rapidly because of the expansion of the public markets; it's apparently Michael Milken's "Social Capital" and more control of the money outside the banking system. [From Michael Milken's Wall Street Journal article "Prosperity and Social Capital," June 23, 1999]. But the central banking system still creates the currency, sets interest rates. Public money will bleed some more, and the result is more national debt.

Mortgage wrapped securities appeared as the big problem. The small homeowner couldn't make the mortgage payment, and all of a sudden, the securities, apparently, were like ten-ton bricks. The pyramid collapsed! The government, the Treasury had come to the rescue, again; the Federal Home Loan Banks will get involved, hopefully to purchase the bricks? This agency was covered before; it was started in the 1930s. The government banking system was not people friendly then; the banking scheme isn't people friendly today. The private banking system created by government seems to dump on the people, as in 0.3% savings account interest and 20% interest on credit cards. Why else the nonprofit cooperatives? The market has been pummeled; it's regulation time.

Initially, the Congress worked on a possible $300 billion housing bill insured through the Federal Housing Administration. An important cog is which homeowner will qualify. An overhaul of Fannie Mae and Freddie Mac was being considered. The latest possible consideration was for America's mortgage-strapped industry. The American home owner is America's real wealth.

America's pulse is New York! New York is the place! If it happens anywhere, it happens in New York. Wall Street elements ran off with the money, and investors take the hits. How many hits, how many times? Shall we count them since 1837? Wall Street bonuses remain, numbering in the billions of dollars. The stagecoach is always held up somewhere between here and there. Carnegie said it, only in America, in the worst of times, millionaires are made in America. In the other economy, American people take the hits and lose jobs and their homes; the ripple effect hurt the auto industry, with big hits in early 2008. The price of oil prompted General Motors to squelch the gas-guzzlers—more hits to the autoworker.

People can lose faith in the system, but this is the system. It's the roll of the dice; every day is a new play in America, and now the international scene. The creation and movement of money in America compares to the deep-sea fisherman; bait is cast, the big play, the fish reeled in, and there is "no redundancy." The central bank answers the call, furnishing new bait, and a new round of play begins. And the beat goes on! The American capitalistic experience, "domestic" and global, continues the masterful game. There is no bailout for the players; the players made the play and lost. The casino delivers an infusion of cash, and play begins anew. The Fed has come to the rescue with more dollars—liquidity for Wall Street elements. Are these the same people who collected bonuses for their trouble? Wealth is supposedly not about money, but when there is a crisis, it is all about the money. There is great wealth, assets, yet where is the liquidity? The money has been taken; new money is created!

At the insistence of the Bush White House, the Congress passed a stimulus package; $152 billion was mailed to taxpayers. This money, in increments of $300 to $1200, would stimulate the economy; it could translate to a trillion dollars in the economy? Not really; this was like sinkhole money. Money is so easy to come by sometimes! The package is not a big deal, according to President Bush; he said the stimulus was only 1% of GDP. It is remarkable when a certain legislation demands no obstacles; the bill was passed and signed into law. There is no debate; it's rammed through the Congress. Each legislator has five minutes, and each five minutes of talk will not change the bill. This reminds of the supplemented bus trip promoting gambling at the casino. The "stimulus package" maintained the Bush deficit at $400 billion, which will be paid for in future taxes probably starting in the following year, so we must pay our taxes. Four hundred billion is more debt; the debt goes on the books of the Federal Reserve Central Bank. The government's obligation grows and grows. The deficit approached a trillion dollars as per the 2008 meltdown.

It was campaign time in the United States, and the political issues were illegal immigration, securing the Mexican border, Social Security, American jobs, American infrastructure, health care, the economy, and tempering the foreclosures. What happened to the war on drugs? And the war on cancer? President Bush occupied America with the war in Iraq! Bush was democratizing Iraq. What about Saudi Arabia, Kuwait, Egypt, Iran, etc.? What did the president say about Iraq? "Bring 'em on!" Great!

The Republicans apparently wanted the war in Iraq and more tax cuts; the Democrats wanted to end the war and restore taxation to revenue levels. The problem for many Americans is the global economy and a decent wage. Foreign plants in America have created thousands of jobs. But thousands of jobs have been lost; American manufacture and production moving outside the United States and the excessive corporate tax doesn't help. It's really a perfect deal, this global economy. The global economy fits the money scheme. American companies in foreign countries, foreign companies in the United States. National governments, now domestic, appear compromised trying to follow the money. Labor is cheap; duties are neutralized. Taxes aren't paid because trillions of dollars are apparently held in limbo by clever people outside the domestic domain. Oppressive taxation trying to harness America's currency obligation breeds the practice.

The Republican pitch is homeland security and fighting terrorism in Iraq and Afghanistan. The latest possible preponderance is a proposed superhighway planned through Texas to Canada. Apparently, big money is behind this, and the people of Texas can't do anything to prevent it? NAFTA is thriving, and illegal drugs and crime will continue up the highway. Illegal drugs is a lucrative industry, powerful, and worldwide! The Mexican migration across the border is an integral part of the low pay, big push in the global economy; it's an avalanche. Conservatives, apparently, want it, and the Congress can't deal with it. Shouldn't the Congress not allow the new world order to crowd and weaken America's financial responsibilities to its people? United States national issues are important to the American people. But the Bush Republicans apparently want international crowding, as in more profits, amnesty for illegal immigrants, and the selling to foreign interests of United States companies that run American seaports. And Americans are preoccupied with retirement, selling out for cash. The American small businessman sells his business to the foreigner who has cash.

The creation of currency since the Reagan years has been record setting; the credit circulation has increased 500%, almost 20% per year. The money created has paralleled the economy. It should! No money supply, no economy! It appears the Federal Reserve System has been busy creating money, this as it should be. It's not like the old days, the cyclical currency contractions of the past. How much currency has been created, expended for investment banking, for the derivative and hedge fund schemes? It was stated in the *Congressional Record* that banking money obtained, or loaned, may be twenty times the hedge fund management dollar. It's really more than that! GDP is 750% larger since 1980, and the population increased 30%. The explosion in money is seventeen times larger, and GDP is twenty-five times larger than the increase in population. Money has ballooned; wealth has ballooned, and financial disparity increases, the money of the people going in the opposite direction. The growth and retention of money remains primarily close to and at the controls; distribution remains unequal. It always will since Hamilton.

The rate of increase in debt in America appears to exceed everything else. The increase in debt since 1980 is 1,100%. There is the constant erosion of equity, especially in home ownership. A particular crank is the equity loan; it creates money, the credit circulation. This device has been used improperly, people paying credit card debt, sacrificing equity—a bum deal. And the vultures who want to buy a person's house right away for cash—this is another double bum deal! A mayor, a governor, a president will not jeopardize political standing by telling people this practice is a bum deal in the free market system in America! The rate of increase in American debt exceeded the rate of growth; a Republican deficit agenda fed the economy.

America has the best health system in the world; the problem is, health care, because of cost, is not available to all Americans. The best health care in America somehow parallels the best car, the best house. It's not available to all because of money; this is why America is thirty-seventh in the world in health care. Health care costs a bundle and is big, big profit in America. Until the huge profit motive is removed, which is the moral thing to do, respectable health care costs in America is a dead issue. And the politicians can't do anything about it! Health care in America will never take care of all Americans. Let there be profit in America's growth, but let there be no excessive profit in health care. Insurance companies are insurance companies; they are not health care providers.

The United States Congress, in the course of its history, created the central bank and the vast network of funds and agencies, which implemented and complemented the private economy. All the funds and agencies, including the central banking system, were started with assisted public money, Treasury money, taxpayer money. The wealth structure in the United States is the result.

The government of presidents Hoover and Roosevelt started agencies in the 1930s to buy frozen assets of businesses, insurance companies, railroads, farms, and banks ripped off by the credit collapse in 1932. These private entities at that time were not helped by the Federal Reserve System (chapters 13 and 14). The government started the Reconstruction Finance Corporation to assist failing businesses. Five hundred million dollars of public money, taxpayers' money, augmented the start of the Finance Corporation. Chairman Patman of the House banking committee stated that J. P. Morgan was the idea behind the Finance Corporation, and Morgan's bank was a recipient of the corporation's money—more corporate welfare. Freddie Mac, Fannie Mae, the Federal Home Loan Bank System, FDIC, all started with public monies, and many other agencies are all part of the United States wealth system today. The wealth system, sponsored by the government, has grown, evolving with private shareholders. But when there's a bailout, most times, the taxpayer pays the freight; public money comes to the rescue, and the working class remains the indebted player. It's a public start, private wealth, and a public bailout!

The Roosevelt administration implemented the International Monetary Fund and the World Bank, an international benefit for approximately fifty countries. All the monies paid into the fund and the bank were Treasury funds, from all the treasuries of all the countries, printed public currencies. According to the *Congressional Record*, printed currency from some of these countries was worthless; the IMF gave the currencies value. There was gold involved, and the gold was purchased with Treasury credit dollars—more public money. Fiat credit dollars, Federal Reserve Notes from the Stabilization Fund, paper money bought all the gold. The secretary of the Treasury bought the gold in the name of the United States government. Congressman Binderup said the IMF was bringing back the gold standard again, a standard the American people did not want.

The money paid into the IMF and the bank was subscription public money paid in. Those public funds paid in were supplemented with more public participation money "paid in" in accordance with public law legislated by the Congress. Member countries were immediately allowed to purchase United States securities with their public monies paid in for investment purposes, commercial banks participating.

This business is documented in the Library of Congress, in the Congressional records, in the Treasury reports. These transactions created by and with the use of public funds, the credit circulation, has helped produce two formidable international bureaucracies, the IMF and the World Bank. The bank was originally the Bank for Reconstruction and Development. Is it true that people who work for these institutions pay no income taxes? Isn't that like taking profits and not paying any dues?

In 1945, Gertrude Coogan said this was "one step further out into the deep by allowing international deficit financing on top of domestic deficit financing." All this business was done, apparently, to further international monetary interests. President Roosevelt and his Secretary Morgenthau fostered two huge institutions for the international community with public funds. The IMF and the World Bank and participating banks, augmented by public funds, represent great wealth today.

> For the purpose of keeping to a minimum the cost to the United States of participation in the fund and the bank, after paying the subscription—is authorized and directed to issue notes of the United States from time to time at par and to deliver such notes to the fund and the bank in exchange for dollars to the extent permitted by the articles of agreement.

The above statute is the crux of the IMF and World Bank schemes. The Treasury had two functions, first the subscription then the participation in the new scheme. Gertrude Coogan mentioned its similarity to the function of the banking monetary scheme, the creation of money, the continuous flow of monies paid in to supplant monies paid out. The bankers opposed the IMF and the World Bank in 1944-1945. The bankers called the IMF plan a banking plan. It was not a fund; the fund was a planned bank! The creation of money was the scheme; functions were similar. The bankers wanted the IMF and the World Bank combined; one international bureaucracy was enough.

The IMF scheme utilized "notes" to obtain participation currency from the secretary of the Treasury. The participation currency at

100% equals the subscription money paid in. Subscription money is reserve; participation money is operating capital. In the banking scheme, additional monies paid in was changed to 200%. In the Federal Reserve System, a "security" is apparently the exchange for dollars in the printing of money. In the IMF scheme, the "notes" are the exchange for dollars. The security in the Federal Reserve System is debt, an "IOU," and it is interest bearing, the government's obligation. In the IMF scheme, the notes are debt, an "IOU." The Fed securities are interest bearing; the IMF notes are not interest bearing. Securities and special notes are total debt and go on the books of the Federal Reserve System and, probably, will never be paid. The central bank, the IMF, the World Bank are money machines integral in the monetary search for more money.

Why not domestic or national deficit financing on top of domestic deficit financing, for a proper Social Security, in the United States? The Congress of the United States has seen fit to provide plenty of public funding for the internationals and participating banks. Developing countries are becoming rich now! Republicans wanted Social Security money invested privately, a feeding of Wall Street. This figures, the subprime debacle is an indication of where Social Security money would disappear. The money interests—the Republicans got tons of public money funded for their private interests—all going back to the 1930s.

Why not a Social Security Bank or fund similar to the IMF and the World Bank schemes but with private money, the people's private money! Social Security original funding goes one better than the original IMF funding. Social Security money paid in is privately earned money paid in by the American people, not public funds. The people's earned money, the banker's credit circulation, has already paid the multiple price! The people's earned money has paid a profit to the United States Treasury; an excessive discount profit to the Treasury's agent, the Federal Reserve Central Bank; an excessive discount profit to member banks, to commercial banks; an infinite interest on the obligation; and additional income taxes for federal and state. The people's earned income has been worked over plenty by the Treasury and the Congress's legislated private banking system and other agencies and capitalized for their profit, and debt is never to be paid up front.

In the scheme of things, the United States GDP may reach $30 to $40 trillion in ten or twenty years, based on the international economic surge of the past two decades. Social Security revenue presently exceeds expenditure; the paid-in private surplus funds can equate to or resemble a subscription reserve or quota. Now is the time to supplement paid-in, surplus-earned money by the people, the subscription money paid in at 1% of GDP. Each succeeding year, as GDP increases, the subscription would increase up to $300 to $400 billion annually. A participation or the exchange for dollars by the Treasury would also kick in, doubling the money. The money interests espousing 1% of GDP is no big deal; hence 400 billion down the road for Social Security would be no big deal.

Why not an exchange for dollars for Social Security invested in marketable securities, cooperatives, credit unions, and the people participating. When the money interests needed money, it was always back to the Congress, and they got their subscription and participation monies paid in by the United States Treasury. Plenty of money was printed, created for international interests, for private interests. An adjusted set of rules, a different set of values, are required in the money creation scheme. Maybe it's time the Congress went back to the Congress for the people, for Social Security, Medicare, health care, and the country's infrastructure. Can any of this business materialize? Where would the Congress be on this issue? But global warming is the deal, the next big colossus, and a ton of taxpayer money. It's the next big bogus market in the creation of more money, like a tidal wave smothering what's really needed.

In the global economy—with Wall Street's multiple financial complexities, greed, and incremental hits—the United States economy will continue the Hamilton prophecy. The United States, in the continuing violent world, has no option; military strength is imperative. But where is the United States military industrial complex? Some of it has apparently been farmed out? The United States leads industrially, but why this? Parts for the Air Force commercial and military hardware continue to be built outside the country. Boeing is outsourcing the building of its parts for its planes. America appears in transition, a center of outside operations, a stopover for those making the big buck. The latest conquest, the Russians, are buying Bethlehem Steel.

The pentagon accepts bids from foreigners on military contracts; who are these people anyway?

And the United States is not energy independent. The United States didn't bring World War II to an end because Germany and Japan supplied the war materials. The United States is defending the free world? How is that? United States defense systems are outsourced? Are these outsourced systems within the limits of the friendly free world? Can the United States defend itself when a potential adversary is supplying military parts? It's nuts! America's young people, defending their country, appear compromised.

A dependent international investment community—all countries willing, participating, working in partnership—should prevent wars, no borders, the mythical "Camelot." It's not working. Warfare continues; the threat of and the spending for impending warfare persists. It's a big market, and it consumes; it's the play in the search for more money, man's consummate end. The past Republican administration appeared to promote impending war with Iran and Syria, a lot of money making for the war profiteers, and the global wealth of indebtedness. Israel threatened Iran with an air attack. The cauldron stirs in the Middle East and in Afghanistan, south of the Caspian Sea, and the world's future oil supply. In the Far East, China is arming, building a navy and military war machine. Russia was broke not too long ago. Thanks to American money, the IMF, and the World Bank, Russia has renewed wealth and inner resources, is making a lot of noise and flexing military muscle again.

A significant Journal article on April 28, 2008, said that nations are spouting "nationalism." The title of the article was "GLOBAL TIES UNDER STRESS AS NATIONS GRAB POWER." These nations are apparently rich now; it's the rising power of "national governments." From this writer's viewpoint, these countries don't need the American-created IMF and the World Bank anymore. Maybe the IMF and World Bank should be dissolved, their riches returned to the American people. From this writing's view, the article appears to indicate a possible dent in global economic harmony when self-sufficient sovereignty regains and prevails. Nationalism, apparently, is making a comeback? The global economy was a strategy, the crossing of all borders, and that was the happening. The article mentioned many "obstacles" have taken place. One obstacle was uncontrolled immigration. Immigration was a big problem because of ease of "transportation," ease of access negatively affecting countries. Illegal immigration is the big problem in the United States. The article stated countries are closing borders physically and electronically. The article stressed a "Changed World." The article called it the "globalization backlash."

Sovereignty means "freedom from outside control"; it's the natural way of things. Where global financial power may control and corrupt, sovereignty is disrupted. Is this new national "backlash" economic sovereignty and its money adverse to the creation and control of more money in the international globalization money scheme? From the article, it appears countries are reestablishing their sovereignty; nationalism may be back in vogue? Do these reacquired "national governments" run or control their central banks? These countries or nations may be spouting a new nationalism, but how do they define their economies? Are their products still gross domestic products? What about the sovereign wealth thing? Where is this money going?

Foreign central banks have been piling up the dollars. Central banks are solvent, no debts. America and the global economy has been good to foreign central banks. Central Banks of the developing countries have been piling up trillions of dollars. These developing countries include the oil producers. Their central banks are solvent, no debts. Apparently, these are the countries that are getting rich; these countries are sending their dollars back, investing in the United States. Is this sovereign wealth money? The developing countries are getting well while the American consumer paid through the nose for gas. It's really like pure capitalism's finest hour versus capitalism. The dollar has fallen because of the continued imbalance of payments, deficit spending, and subsequent foreign wealth. The 2008 currency crisis will probably reverse the trend.

Third world countries were generally poor. Third world countries were poor because they had no inner resources. Third world countries were poor because they couldn't balance payments. Third world countries devalued their currencies paying for imports. So what has America been doing? America is borrowing money paying for imports.

America is devaluing its currency while paying for imports. In the trade imbalance, America imports goods and exports cash. Japan did the opposite, exported the goods and imported the cash. Japan has big debts but is a creditor nation. America has big debts owed to others, a debtor nation; America seems to buy mostly everything. Japan has big savings; America saves little. America appears directed toward the non-self-supporting role. America appears to be competing with the international collective, the rest of the world. America's deficit spending is supporting the global economy. America is the service, technology, and entertainment center; America leads industrially, but America trails the collective industrial countries in total GDP.

The one substantial equity is the American homeowner and consumer, and Wall Street and the mortgage industry took the big swipe at its continuing growth. And the American Treasury and the Federal Reserve are swiping at the senior homeowner in their creation of more money. Investment priority appears elsewhere; it's foreign investment, outsourcing, and cheap labor. It appears America has lessened its heavy industry and resources because environmental issues dominate and multinationals profit internationally. And here comes global warming. The great American experience is caught up in this business. America's oil, natural gas, refineries, steel mills, oil drilling, and atomic energy have taken a back seat? Their priority is in limbo. They are not profitable in the domain? America is supposed to survive as the serene electronic service center, the borrowing/buying overseas investor, invader, renter, and debtor.

Two hundred dollars a barrel for oil? Gold will be $2,000 an ounce? The election came along with the descending price of oil and gas. The gold farce in 2006 directed people to buy gold; then in 2008, people were asked to sell their gold trinkets for cash; currency was more valuable than gold. Gasoline in America was going to be $7 to $8 a gallon, the future predictions by the experts? These figures reflected a real inflation in the endless pursuit of more money? Gas is now down. The damage has been done; industries are declaring bankruptcies.

The 2008 credit crisis arrived. What happens now? The big shutdown! And there are so many needs within the domain. A global warming, now a climate control scheme shouldn't be one of the needs. Forty-five trillion dollars is the predicted price tag for global warming or "1.1% of world GDP"; apparently, this is no big deal. More than likely, America's portion would be 10-20% of the $45 trillion or at least $4.5 trillion. How about 1% of American GDP, a whole lot less, to save Social Security, and that would be no big deal. Would this be possible? Otherwise, American posterity is screwed! The next American president and a compromised Congress probably can't do anything about it, not with the global economic avalanche.

England built an empire. It was an encompassing world reign funded by its central bank. The empire lasted two and a half centuries. By 1945, debt reigned; Great Britain was broke. Too many wars! Great Britain's wealth was outside its domain; Great Britain's money system eroded the system; the empire couldn't be sustained. After two centuries, United States growth and wealth is evident. America's growth and wealth was primarily from within, funded in the twentieth century by the central bank. Domestic America is now part of the global economy, and while in the global search for more money, the credit circulation is eroding and exhausting America within the domain.

America has been ushered outside the United States. It's the spread of democracy? It's more the spread of capitalism in the new world order. George wanted a self-sustaining republic devoid of outside influence. Good-bye! The Republicans, the globals, the money interests lean toward unending low-pay immigration, outsourcing, the tax cut deficit spending trick, outside resources, and a lean army with costly logistics by private contractors. All this apparently leads to more riches and wealth for multinationals, internationals. It's all about the money! The global thing is vast, voluminous, a growing world economy, and nationalism and sovereignty take a back seat. As America becomes the renter, absorbs more deficit financing on the wrong things, the debt soars, equity declines and exhausts, no redundancy takes place, and fractures occur within the domain. Global wealth feeds in the process; countries decline, countries get rich! Money moves on; money is constantly moving. It's the big push in the continuing search for more money, and the big push is global.

Money knows no boundary, and it has no flag!

CHAPTER TWENTY

Abeyance

In his bank report to the Congress, Hamilton wrote,

> But the last and heaviest charge is still to be examined.
> This is, that Banks tend to banish the gold and silver of the
> country. The force of this objection rests upon there being
> an engine of paper credit, which by furnishing a substitute
> for the metals, is supposed to promote their exportation. It
> is an objection, which if it has foundation, lies not against
> Banks, peculiarly, but against every species of paper credit.
> The most common answer given to it is, that the thing
> supposed is of little, or no consequence; that it is immaterial
> what serves the purpose of money, whether paper or gold
> and silver; that the effect of both upon industry is the same;
> and that the intrinsic wealth of a nation is to be measured,
> not by the abundance of the precious metals, contained in
> it, but by the quantity of the productions of its labor and
> industry.

Alexander Hamilton articulated a country's principal value; it wasn't
gold. Hamilton placed labor before industry. Labor is the people;
without people, there is nothing. But in the scheme of things, the
people became secondary; gold was the lever. The gold keeper was
the wedge between the sovereign and the people.

Alexander Hamilton started a paper money machine in 1791.
Hamilton's first United States bank was a specie bank dealing in paper
money; the charter lasted twenty years. The Congress got rid of the
bank. The bank was like, or equivalent to, a foreign bank; England and
France owned most of the stock. That was 1811.

Another war with England and five years later, Congress started a second bank. A second twenty-year charter ended in 1836. Andrew Jackson was right about the tremendous power of the second bank. From the record, Nicholas Biddle dried up the money supply; gold left the country, and the economy went into the tank for seven years. That was 1837.

In 1861, a civil war started; the United States Treasury had no money. Money was needed, and a whole lot of money was created, just like that! It was the war; a big market loomed. The Congress woke up during the civil war, realized its power, created the greenbacks, and the fun began. The opponents, the bankers, would never agree, but there was plenty of credit backing the greenbacks. A financial war began within a civil war.

Paper currencies, good and bad, dominated the state economies during the first eighty-seven years. In 1862, the Congress decided the government wasn't to be cheated again with bank paper money; that was the plan. Greenbacks were created, and gold vanished, but gold didn't vanish. Gold played its important role; gold devalued the greenback. In 1863, the Congress legislated the bank act. The Congress acquiesced; the Congress dealt the banks the hole card, payment in gold. The U.S. Treasury, thanks to the Congress, ran up inflated debts with paper currency and had to pay those debts to the banks in gold; this business carried on until 1934. From the record, European 2%-4% interest rates were the norm, consistently lower than the 6%-7.3% interest rates in America. Why the disparity in America? Apparently, it promoted foreign investment in America. After 1863, banks got their gold loan back in relatively short time, considering 6% interest in gold annually on a war debt that escalated from $90 million to almost $2 billion in three years, 1865.

In 1913, the Federal Reserve Act became law; a new elastic currency was created. Senator Owen said it was the greatest thing happening to the country; it was for the central bank. The currency was for the bank's purpose "and for no other purpose." A big change was the security behind the currency, the government obligation, interest-bearing currency payable to the clever central bank and its shareholders forever. Also, maturity of the currency payable in gold was now ninety days, not twenty years; maturity was quick time. A quick turnover in gold had been achieved. The national debt went from 1 billion to 26 billion in less than two years. Remarkable! Paper money, created out of nothing, continued to beget gold. Paper currency was always capitalizing to inflate, then payment in gold, the scheme. The Federal Reserve, by 1922, had accumulated more gold than all the major world banks combined. The United States, through its Federal Reserve, became a creditor nation.

The income tax law, the first in 1916, then another in 1917, complemented the Federal Reserve Act. An oppressive permanent federal income tax was imperative, in order to pay for the obligation, to secure and redeem everlasting indebtedness. The 1917 act was supposedly a World War I measure. The crank for a future non-payable national debt was assured. As originally petitioned by the Pennsylvania creditors, the "powerful body of stockholders," a considerable minority, would remain as the recipients and claim the government's obligation, the nation's currency. This was a major consideration in the Hamilton scheme, the inclusion of the public creditor. Andrew Jackson objected to this powerful body of stockholders. If the recipients or holders of the obligation are the American people, then the American people are not burdened by their own currency. Actually, it's the bank's currency. It was the third try at a central bank; later, a possible termination of the bank charter after twenty years was eliminated. Rulers of developing countries—apparently realizing the riches, advantages, control—adopted central banking systems.

The Federal Reserve Note remained non-legal tender for twenty years. In 1934, President Roosevelt reigned in the gold; the Federal Reserve Note was made legal tender. The Federal Reserve Note was now legal tender but not good for gold, for the citizen. Gold and the lawful greenback would serve as supposed reserve for circulating currency; the Federal Reserve Note was declared intrinsic. The $100,000 gold certificates were printed and issued to the central bank. The gold certificate was redemption for gold. Roosevelt, in the name of the United States, hauled in the gold, but the central bank owned the gold, could claim the gold. The Federal Reserve Note eventually replaced all currencies; America had been provided a uniform currency, the credit circulation. After World War I and the 1929 Crash, global subjective money was in the offing. Economic nationalism was being de-emphasized at the 1933 London Conference. World central banks created the Bank for International Settlements, a bank in Switzerland for world central banks.

During the years starting in 1934, President Roosevelt and Secretary Morgenthau orchestrated the unparalleled gold stash, then formulated the IMF and the World Bank after World War II. America repeated the centuries-old scheme, the buying of gold with paper money. The currency, apparently, came from a revolving Credit Stabilization Fund; the Federal Reserve Bank of New York was the agent. Secretary Morgenthau acquired three-quarters of the world's gold with Federal Reserve Notes—20 billion in gold by 1940, a 400% increase in gold reserve. Remarkable! There was a depression in America when this gold was being stored in America and the "Kentucky Hole." America's currency increase of 140% was not consistent with the increase in gold during the same period—these figures are confirmed in the 1941 Treasury report. Did this vast storage of gold have an international purpose? Congressman Binderup stated that it did. Gertrude Coogan's description of "international deficit financing on top of domestic deficit financing" took off after World War II.

During the next twenty-five years and with the beginning of an imbalance in world trade, the United States credited more than half of the gold back to world central banks. President Nixon ended the gold exchange in 1971. The Bretton Woods standard of gold was over, but the IMF became a powerful entity, garnering considerable gold along the way. America, apparently, retained more than twice the gold of any one country. Enter special drawing rights, the paper substitute for gold. In world trade, America would give up paper dollars instead of gold in exchange for more debt. McChesney Martin called the drawing right paper exchange "financial gimmickry." Today, emerging developing countries and their central banks have a ton of surplus dollars; the United States does not appear to have surplus dollars! It appears every dollar America spends is borrowed, an apparent negative. The restoration of the belligerent nations, Europe, Japan, and other countries, by the United States, after World War II, had been accomplished. In 1993, the European Union established the euro currency at $ 1.17.

Chairman Eccles confirmed the connection between the gold reserve and the money supply; there wasn't any! Since the end of the farce, gold, apparently, is playing two roles; it is the two tier system. There is the important statutory role in establishing and maintaining the approximate exchange rates of the world's currencies. The market price of gold is another matter. The market price of gold, bidding the commodity up and selling it down, internationally, apparently plays the other role. Roosevelt's 1934 gold devaluation set the dollar at 60% of the gold price. Roosevelt's statutory price at $35 an ounce remained for an extended period. After President Nixon's 1971 move, the market price of gold accelerated in the 1970s to more than $800 an ounce. The final devaluation of the dollar to 55% then 50% of gold followed; the dollar was set at the final statutory price of $42.22 an ounce.

The statutory value of American gold, as listed in the 2006 United States Government Financial Statement, is $11 billion as of September 2006, the same amount as in 1971. This gold "was pledged as collateral for gold certificates issued and authorized to the FRBs [Federal Reserve] by the Secretary of the Treasury." This American gold is the gold stored at Fort Knox? The final 50% devaluation of the dollar was based on Roosevelt's 1934 proclamation. A considerable increase in dollars had to be realized based on the final devaluations and the increase of the statutory price. The Federal Reserve Bank of New York is a repository of foreign gold at no charge. The amount of this foreign gold is valued at "160 billion dollars," quite a bit more than the storage at Fort Knox.

So where is America today? The United States eclipsed Great Britain's 250-year reign in sixty-three years. By 1985, American creditor status was over. Again, too many wars! America's gain and loss, its debt progression, has been guaranteed by its credit circulation, the world wars, the spread of Communism, nuclear arsenals, the cold war, deficit spending, the IMF and the World Bank, international deficit spending, Korea, Vietnam, the Middle East wars, the infamous oil embargo, the Panama Canal giveaway, the new world order, the domestication of its national economy, the environmentalists, the global economy, terrorism, the Iraq war, Afghanistan, illegal immigration, illegal drugs, liquidation, twenty-first-century oil, and the deficit account. Maintaining world leadership is costly. The United States maintains its position in the Middle East, and the price is young American lives and the cost of more infamous oil. The next big choker will be the impending global warming scheme. Proper funding for American Social Security, Medicare, health care, and the country's infrastructure warrant investment by the people, but these necessities appear as nuisances and not top priority.

America has the big GDP, an accelerating $15 trillion product. Except for Japan, America's product dwarfs every other economy in the world. This apparently makes America the richest country, but at what cost? Everything and anything—from electronics, toys, food, communications, autos, machinery to money—is produced in and outside of America; people are working everywhere! America's product is a borrowing/spending binge dependent on growth. And where is America growth? America's inner resources appear dormant. America is buying over there, and foreigners are buying more than that over here. It's a global thing, and people keep waving the flag! In the search for more money, America's growth direction is outside the domain, supporting foreign economies, and the big sell-off is within the domain. Can't survive this way! This should help explain America's GDP. America is buying, supporting the global economy with its exhausting credit circulation.

Free trade, equal distribution of goods, a pullback to America and imperative restoration and production of inner resources, and a balance of payments should be America's direction. Apparently, it's not money's direction. Money and profit rules! This kind of direction is destructive to sovereignty. It's a no-win for the United States of America in the global economy. America, now, among nations, is a confirmed debtor country while supporting the world. Is it possible for the United States to redirect? There is only one strength, and that strength is from within.

The search for more money can be taxing. The global economy suits the money interests; it's perfect! The global economy appears in harmony with the offshore fix in investments, incomes, and the payment of no taxes; it's the safe haven thing. What else? Who wants to pay oppressive taxes? American industries in foreign countries either pay a double corporate tax or do the safe haven thing. American entities become less American; they don't pay their share of taxes? In the first place, why oppressive taxation? Federal taxation had been practically negligible from Hamilton till 1913. The public and national debt was not a monster until 1913. One only has to look at the tax tables after 1916-1917. The central bank, the public creditor, the shareholders were cashing in on public money. How else was the Treasury going to pay for the newfound, oppressive government obligation?

The American tax code has been called perverse; if that is so, the Federal Reserve Act is perverse. Carter Glass, when debating central bank issues in the Congress, told the opposition, "Start a Cooperative." Today, there are almost nine thousand cooperatives in America. Why is that? Why cooperatives act in the interests of the people. After 1914, the debt went from 1 billion to 26 billion in nineteen months. The government banking monster was profit motive from the start. The rest is history. Great Britain did the bit and went down!

The domestics, which includes the United States, can't seem to deal with hidden offshore money. The Republicans do the tax cut thing; wealth gets a break. The Republicans claim more revenue, and the national debt accelerates, the Republican gimmick. There is great wealth in America; that wealth is investing elsewhere, placing wealth offshore, avoiding oppressive taxation. Is America still rich as a nation? Surpluses (no deficits) were beginning to realize during the Clinton administration, but apparently, this was the wrong direction. Surpluses are, apparently, adverse to the deficit account. In the search for more money, President Bush renewed the tax cut scheme; the Reagan/Bush record validates the huge debt acceleration. The debt-ridden economic fix is in; the politicians can't deal with it. It's the cost of moving forward. The perpetration of debt propels the forward international economy and, unfortunately, more warfare. Anyway, the experts, the economists, tell us sovereign wealth goes to only one place, to the stock market.

Inflation! Inflation is the modern description and apparent deception. In the eighteenth and nineteenth centuries, the popular phrase was froth and bubble. Froth and bubble appears more explicable; the froth is taken during the trading frenzy, and the bursting bubble results in no redundancy time. Twentieth-century increases in interest rates were used to stem inflation. The result has to be the increase in the cost of money, all around. This business guarantees more profits to the banking system.

Inflation is the natural process in the political economy. Populations inflate, production and consumption inflate, money inflates. Values, prices, growth, equity, all accelerating and accommodating in the rapid search and creation of wealth, debt, and more money—the endless chain, the profits spiral at the top. Inflation is the American experience, like an exhilarating pyramidal insanity in motion. Trading today is the thing, the complete frenzy, driving up prices for profit. The NYMEX, reportedly, was driving up the price of oil, and there was no apparent connection with supply and demand. The price of oil dropped from $148 to $38 a barrel; huge profits were apparently gained. Oil is up again to $80 a barrel; reports say the cheap dollar is the cause. The auto industry, the people take the hits.

The past ten years have seen the rising costs of housing, assessments going through the roof. It's the driving up of values and the resultant creation of a ton of new money. The insanity has propelled the astounding bubble and the cost? It's the Hamilton continuum, "susceptible of no limits even in imagination!" Hopefully, not a speeding down the highway to financial oblivion. The creation of more money and credit today has been astounding. Prices and values were skyrocketing before a September 2008 crash. This appears as the real inflation, a deliberate inflation, the guarantee of big profits skimming off the top. The pyramid works for those at the top, and interest rates were low; there is no correlation. It's whatever works in the scheme of things.

A fixed low interest rate, with no profit in the creation and initial issue of currency, would benefit a working viable society, not the profit takers. After that, fixed low rates. Of course, this would be the real insanity! Fixed low rates! Greed wants the casino, the speculator, the hedge fund practice, the derivative economy. The power of exponential money is power rewarding itself since Hamilton. The outright planned and intended profit in the creation and issue and manipulation of money thereafter was promoted by "those close to and within reach of the seat of Government." The cream in the bottle of milk was always at the top.

As of July 14, 2008, the big bailout of Fannie Mae and Freddie Mac was in the works. The bailout would combine with a housing bill already before the Congress. It was important that Fannie Mae and Freddie Mac remain solvent; there would be no faltering of the two big institutions. As of July 27, 2008, the bill had passed the Congress; signing by the president was expected. The success of the bill, reducing foreclosures, will depend on the banks taking a loss on delinquent mortgages.

Foreign central banks are buyers of Fannie/Freddie securities. The U.S. government will guarantee the United States Treasury, the Federal Reserve, primarily the OK of the Congress and the president, the FHA, HUD, the foreign investor. The credit express continues; it's always back to the Congress. The perpetual complaint is too much government, yet the money interests go back to the Congress and the Treasury when they want more money. The Congress provided a free pass to the two big institutions, and apparent poor regulation, mismanagement, and private greed did the rest? The subprime meltdown contributed. It's the public start/private invest/public bailout continuum.

This new effort will entail a fiat credit and probable capital credit infusion. It's the casino in action, but more currency will be provided by the players, the taxpayers—more debt on the books of the Federal Reserve System. There is profit in these bailouts. The cost of creating currency results in profit to the Federal Reserve bank, to the shareholders, and tax profit to the Treasury. Propping up Fannie/Freddie sustains the pyramid. The bill, hopefully, will help first-time house buyers, assist the foreclosure problem, and provide tax breaks, etc. The bailout estimate will be anywhere from $25 to $300 billion, probably for starters. The bailout supposedly would keep the housing market from submerging, which is a big part of the economy to the tune of $11 trillion. These exercises mark the political economic history.

Twentieth-century corporate and banking welfare created by the United States Congress had vaulted the country; then a third of the country was crippled. Roosevelt's agencies was the backlash. Somewhere a welfare of all the people was a part of Jefferson's declaration? Newton's law again! But Fannie/Freddie created by government apparently evolved into two private monsters like Frankensteins on the loose. Growth is unquestioned, but foreign dollars feed the monsters, apparently, a common essential assist in the America economy. To assist the bailouts, the debt limit would have to be raised to $11.3 trillion. More fiat tax dollars created to feed the endless chain. It's official, from newspapers and television, as of September 8, 2008, the Treasury would bail out and take control of Fannie/Freddie. Two hundred billion dollars was the starting figure. The derided fiat dollar, the "greenback," will breathe life into the mortgage lifeline; it's the endless creation and movement of taxpayer currency and a big sigh on Wall Street.

In 1861, Secretary Chase said, "If a credit circulation in any form be desirable, it is most desirable in this." The financial subjugation of the states had begun. There were many congressmen objecting, but there was money to be made by the wealth of indebtedness.

A continuing condition of state subjugation is evidenced by the latest happening on Wall Street. Apparently the big banks short-changed the 48 contiguous states in the sale of auction rate securities. New York Attorney General Andrew Cuomo and state representatives reached a settlement with the big banks. The big banks will pay penalties for sales totaling more than 300 billion dollars. In this case, investor losses across America would be reduced? But this supposed action preceded the banking crash of September 18, 2008.

The juggernaut abounds! The Chase credit circulation developed into a non-payable obligation, a principal part of the public debt, a debt which now exceeds $5 trillion and counting; it just jumped a couple more notches. The latest bailout credit infusion guarantees the national debt exceeding $11 trillion before President Bush leaves office. What's the final number? Apparently, there isn't a definitive final number! The derivative economy appears as an exponential extension of Hamilton's prophecy.

The 2007 "Financial Report" of the Treasury shows a projected 2080 public debt at 600% of GDP. This kind of number doesn't work! This writing indicated a debt rate exceeding the growth rate; the 2007 financial report substantiates the eventuality, the untenable. The Treasury financial report called it unsustainable debt. The report stated, "At some point before the debt reaches such unprecedented levels, the world's financial markets would likely cease lending to the United States." Why the continuous borrowing from foreign markets? It's apparent! The American GDP, the colossal American market, appears suspect. It's not supported solely by an American market; it's the new world order. This is the present and looks like the future. Seventy years down the road, our great-grandchildren will have to carry the load. This is American posterity's problem? Not so! It shouldn't be so! The financial report states a demand for action that is needed now!

The big mistake, the government, the Treasury, the Congress, by way of the banking system, allowed and extended America's public debt to foreigners. The owning of the public debt to ourselves appears as a myth. Not a bright picture for American posterity! The public debt was supposedly owed to the "public," the Treasury states this. The public, in this case, was supposed to be the American people. This is what Abraham Lincoln wanted. This is what President Reagan thought was the case. But the American people do not, now and in the future, own all the untenable public debt. The original intent, apparently, has been scuttled; "what the Government does by another, it does by itself."

The creation of fiat currency is public debt. How can a nation survive when its currency may be owned by foreigners? The new world order jacks the economy, but subjugated countries lose their identity. Civil war public debt was shipped out in the nineteenth century; the big New York banks did that. The United States is not sustainable from within. America's GDP, dependent on foreign money, has come a long indebted way, from the Pennsylvania creditors to foreign central banks. A lack of national control by the American people results to wealth moving out. Wealth, money controls, is mobile; it's no big deal! Money knows no boundary, and it has no flag!

The Republican tax cut trick increases revenues, moves the economy, but the repugnant debt will someday go out of sight. Declining equity assures the eventual self-destruct; the condition becomes more transparent every day. America is dependent on foreign money. It's impossible to pay off America's obligation with the obligation; it was never the intent. This insidious business couples with the cyclical Wall Street hits and foreign oil. The result is the infinite cost of the credit circulation. General Motors, following others, reneged on health care, declared bankruptcy. Fiat bought Chrysler. The present path assures future American retirement dollars dependent on foreign dollars.

The 2007 financial report stated, "Avoiding the catastrophic consequences of this fiscal path will require action to bring program expenditures in line with available resources." Alexander Hamilton's "susceptible of no limits even in imagination" is real, foreign, and "unsustainable."

Meanwhile, in the global search and creation of more money, up and until the September crash, fortunes had reversed. The developing countries accumulated the surplus dollars. Trade talks in Geneva broke down, this from the *Wall Street Journal* of July 30, 2008. Apparently these countries want to protect their export/import dealings. These countries maybe want a balance in free trade? Wouldn't this make sense? Apparently, a balance in free trade doesn't make sense in America. Do countries really matter in the movement of money, in the international collection and disposition of money?

People, entities, countries, who are liquid, have surplus dollars; cash is available, over and above expenditures. The United States, in the search for more money, appears to be liquidating. Anheuser was the latest sale. The United States is busy going out, selling out, borrowing money, printing currency, creating currency, feeding investment bank and corporate delinquency, devaluing the dollar, creating more debt, paying for the big GDP, and the imbalance in payments.

The beat goes on; the recent hit was the Wall Street crash of September 18, 2008. The real inflation reared its ugly head. According to the published accounts, it was credit default swaps, derivatives, hedge fund schemes, and the mountainous bundling of securities. Apparently, it's a colossal pyramidal pyramid; it's the apparent ascending/descending Wall Street craze. The ongoing craze bundles huge sums in the pockets of the few while destroying the country's credit system. Wall Street elements also went down; the system takes no prisoners. America's credit system is the system. Wall Street investment gambling destroys the credit system. Wall Street will blame the housing market, the subprime thing. Wall Street elements, apparently, were set to make a bundle (entities apparently already had) when the ARM contrivance kicked in. The ARM contrivance (government, the mortgagor, the banking system) submerged the small home buyer. The house-buying speculator also went down; the schemes didn't work. The bottom-feeder collapsed like a Ponzi scheme. Then the credit default swap bailout, in one door and out the other?

Clever Wall Street practices are beyond the people and government understanding and regulation. Apparent financial play behind the scene transcends a lot more than the reported twenty to thirty times the physical dollar. The real impact is the currency created and lost behind the scene, the monies funding the credit default swaps. The Congress, the president, the people appear as examples of total ignorance. The collapse of subprime mortgages prompted the collapse of Wall Street mania.

The investment mutual fund lending-borrowing production chain starts to come apart. American credit goes into the tank. Our money experts never explain the result, like who's got the money? Where did the money go? Trillions in assets and no liquidity? The accent is on feeding the insidious game, this while entities holding the captured stash will probably be part of the recapitalization. The private bankers, with the secretary of the Treasury in the lead, run to Washington for more money. The hypocrisy abounds in "too much Government."

While markets tend to collapse, President Bush, the Congress, the 2008 presidential nominees, and the American people—while dogged by the system and invasion of privacy, etc.—appear as stooges separated out of and from the inner workings of the money system, the Treasury, the Federal Reserve Board, European central banks, the New York Federal Reserve Bank, the big investment banks, and Wall Street.

The reality—it's government initiative again, another repeat of the past! And the government is meddling again. Shouldn't the private financial system "stabilize" itself while the country goes down as it did seventy odd years ago? Ouch! This is what segments of the party of acquisition wanted to do, pick up the pieces! On the other hand, the government will absorb the losses; hopefully, there will be a payback to the American people in the future? Wall Street will continue their innovation in all this crazy business. Wall Street gets a reprieve; the casino suffers some losses, but the players lose everything.

A $700 billion Wall Street bailout strategy was rushed to Washington. The numbers were changing daily. Why so much money? Maybe the amount of money tells the story. This bailout figure is almost half the Federal Reserve liquid M1 currency circulation, the money in people's hands, demand deposits, etc. Other central bank monetary aggregates are M2 and M3. M2 includes M1 plus time deposits, savings, etc. M3, which included M1 and M2, wasn't published after 2005; this money included the money in the big institutions and money outside the country. M1, M2, and M3 have been the distinctions of the money stock provided by the Federal Reserve since 1971. Apparently, the total money isn't published anymore, the money from citizen to the big banks to the money outside the country. An Internet per capita statement dated 2001 showed almost $8 trillion in and outside the country. Whatever the total stock of money, paying off the national debt would extinguish the circulation. In the past, gold extinguished the currency.

Secretary Paulson appeared to be in a big hurry; President Bush was agreeable. What else? The secretary wanted the 700 billion right away, carte blanche; the central bank can then do its thing. And where was the additional money going? To whom? To the same people responsible for the credit crunch? The Treasury secretary presented a three-page document with a $700 billion price tag. The money was intended for the financial markets; incredibly, the money has to go to the banks, the credit system, the perpetrators. Congress objected!

The $700 billion, not counting $300 billion to Fannie/Freddie, reveals the enormity, almost a trillion dollars. Most of the country's credit may have been wiped out? But there was more to come. It doesn't seem possible, but the machinery was in place! Wall Street trumps the casino; money disappears, then the credits! All this business appears sinister; while the debate ensues, the central bank may be already printing the money.

This credit crunch primarily involves America, the United Kingdom, Europe, Japan, and Switzerland? The developing countries with all their surplus dollars and sovereign wealth are not affected by the credit crunch? The economy is global, which brings to mind the IMF and the World Bank. These two entities, all of a sudden surfaced. They are concerned about the poor countries. According to the IMF, the G-7 should continue concentrating their efforts on the undeveloped countries; this was specified during the IMF and World Bank October 2008 meeting in Washington. Does this mean more participation money paid into the fund and the bank by way of the Treasury and the Federal Reserve, this while a capital market bailout loomed?

During the week of September 29 till October 3, 2008, first the Senate and then the House approved the $700 billion bailout bill. The president signed the bill. This borrowed money will go on the books of the Federal Reserve System. George has already rolled over; now it's Jefferson's turn. Jefferson would say this is the people's money. But it's not the people's money; it belongs to the bank. The people have to pay for it. Hopefully, the people, by way of the Treasury, will lease some of it back. In the search for more money, the money guys made another trek back to Washington.

The Dow on Thursday, October 9, 2008, fell below nine thousand. The market was down 40% in one year. Republican factions blame the Democrats; the country is headed toward socialism, this while the private free market gambling investor group sent their leader, the Treasury secretary, to Washington for more money. The voice of acquisition screams against a nationalizing of the American banking system. Wasn't a Republican administration in power? Besides, the United Kingdom and Europe were doing the same thing. There appears an international nationalizing of all the banks? But the money systems are domestic! The market, approaching 2010 was up over 10,000.

Including the stimulus packages, in fall 2008, Congress legislated more than a trillion dollars of committed money to prop up private mismanagement and greed. These additional public funds must be added to President Bush's $3.1 trillion budget? The increasing deficit figure had to be approaching a trillion dollars. The tax cuts, the bailouts; less revenue; the colossal Republican Keynesian spending thing kept rolling right along to the tune of the exhausting credit circulation.

The latest—the Treasury secretary committed $290 billion of the legislated $700 billion. An amount of 250 billion was to be injected into the banking system. The purchase of bad loans, assets, shares, etc., are on hold? This latest scheme was revealed to the House Financial Services Committee on November 18, 2008. The country is in a credit crunch; money to the banks does make sense. The advancement of credits is the goal. Where else the inclusion of credits except by way of the banking system? Unfortunately, abuse rears its ugly head! In the banking scheme of things, $250 billion translates to trillions of dollars in credits and deposits. That's the goal and the price? More public debt, which keeps the economy going. Hopefully, the banks don't spend more of the taxpayers' money on other banks, bonuses, and dividends.

Forty billion more dollars was committed to AIG reportedly by the Federal Reserve Bank of New York. There was disagreement; the House committee wanted money directed toward foreclosures. The money will get there by way of the credit system through the bank lending process; this was the preference of the secretary. A remaining delay of $60 billion completed the secretary's $350 billion commitment, all this reported by the *Wall Street Journal*. The new Obama administration would have 410 billion bailout dollars to spend in 2009? All this business appeared to be changing daily. What of the auto industry? The Big Three in Detroit were in financial trouble. General Motors and Chrysler received $17 billion. GMAC will supposedly get a six billion dollar aid package. The treasury, reportedly, will get a dividend on the investment. GMAC will issue warrants to the Treasury for money. Warrants are apparently an exchange for dollars.

The 2008 public assistance was similar to Franklin Roosevelt's government public start-ups of the 1930s. The difference in 2008 and in 2009—the agencies, the banks, the private entities were already in place. Franklin Roosevelt, while searching for credit, was putting people to work while pure capitalism was serving up what appeared to be a dose of deflation to one of every four Americans. Contradictions abound in the political economy! The Roosevelt administration and the money system stored three-quarters of the world's gold in the "Kentucky Hole" while 25% of the American people had little or no money. But maniacs like Adolf Hitler and World War II came along, and the economy boomed.

Chairman Bernanke proposed another stimulus package. The chairman wanted to pump more money into the mutual funds industry, like a half trillion dollars. This was proposed in October 2008. Apparently, redemptions have depleted mutual funds; people were getting out. It surely is a different time; the Federal Reserve was buying commercial paper, restoring credits. This business didn't happen in the 1930s. Will the taxpayers get their money back? Probably not, not all of it! Interest-bearing currency is costly. Any equity payback by private interests will take years. The initial cost and interest on the bailout money may offset any profitable payback realized by the taxpayer. Bailout, assistance currency will probably be several trillion dollars.

Incredibly, the central bank was doubling the currency circulation? In the scheme of things, currency in circulation is approximately 10% to 20% of GDP. So what does all this new currency mean?

The central bank is replacing stolen money? Isn't the creation of all this money inflationary? But the dollar was jumping in value against the euro and the pound sterling? It's whatever works in the scheme of things! Foreign markets are smarting; investors are cashing in while the speculators are probably buying dollars? The Treasury, the Federal Reserve, the big banks are being fed. They have to be fed; it's the system. The pyramid on the backside of the dollar perseveres. Will Wall Street banking executives and workers get big bonuses with bailout money? This bonus money could be called private sinkhole money? Can Congress do anything to stop the bleeding? The casino is getting new cash; what about the players? Apparently, credits and the money are being spread around. FDIC coverage is increasing to $250 thousand; this will help the people with IRAs, bank deposits, etc. The $250 thousand represents a 250% increase in FDIC. The banks fund the FDIC, so doesn't new money have to go the banks? Social Security got the biggest increase ever, minus increased Medicare coverage!

The debt rate has been exceeding the growth rate in America, and this was before the present dilemma. The 2007 Government Financial Report showed a projected public debt at 600% of GDP in the year 2080. What will be the rate of growth? Presumably, based on the past thirty years, American GDP will approximate 50 trillion in 2080? The public debt will be $300 trillion? The public debt limit or its acceleration was never a concern of the public creditor; the only concern was the collection of the perpetual payment of interest. That collection of interest may someday dissipate, extinguish. Kaput!

Approximately 20% of American homeowner equity today could wipe out the present national debt. Will this condition exist in 2080? Will the public debt exceed homeowner equity? Present home equity is falling, now at 18% less than one year ago, and the debts remain fixed; and jurisdictions increase property assessments. The buying of debt, the money market, propels the economic scheme, growth, equity, money creation, debt, the debt spiral. It's an accelerating borrowing/ spending insanity, and debt is outpacing growth. The buying of debt may not exist in 2080. Homeowner equity may be $200 trillion, less than the public debt.

Inflationary disparity is the probable cause and reason for the money creation reverse mortgage scheme; this scheme will eat into homeowner equity. The buying of debt will no longer support a future GDP. America cannot support the world economy anymore, or is it the other way around? America's direction is liquidation. And now, emerging countries may not be emerging; the credit crisis is worldwide. The present debt at $50,000 for each American is not even a consideration. In the year 2080, considering the Treasury projection, the interest payment on the American mortgage will wipe out the credit circulation nullifying any GDP.

As to the present, a positive event for all people, Barack Obama was elected president of the United States on November 4, 2008. A new time, place, and social change in American history, the first African American president! A lot is in store for the new president. The Democrats have control of the House and the Senate. Once again, the Democrats are in; the Republicans are out, a possible repeat of the past? A Republican decade of the 1920s preceded the 1929 crash and imminent Depression. The eight-year Republican Bush administration preceded the 2008 crash. It's fraud and greed all over again. Imminent depression looms? Another repeat! No redundancy time approaches.

The American experience produced George Washington, Thomas Jefferson, Alexander Hamilton, James Madison, Andrew Jackson, Abraham Lincoln, Theodore and Franklin Roosevelt, Harry Truman, Lyndon Johnson. Since Hamilton, from the record, and it seems apparent, the creation and control of money is America's preoccupation. The Federal Reserve System, Wall Street, the Federal Reserve Bank of New York, the big New York investment banks, and the Treasury, while growing America and its debt, courtesy of the Congress, have determined the country's financial direction.

Continuing that direction in early 2008, rapid infusions by the central bank of tens of billions of dollars immediately went to faltering Wall Street investment banks. Later, the secretary of the Treasury dictated $700 billion for the financial markets; the Congress passed the $700 billion TARP bill (the Troubled Asset Relief Program). Also passed was a couple hundred billion dollars for Fannie/Freddie. Citigroup, although possessing 3 trillions in assets, is getting more money, an additional $20 billions of dollars. AIG is getting more than that—insurance for worldwide banks. Trillions of dollars are being committed. It's more than another ball game. If there is no money; there is no game. The Federal Reserve is doing what it's supposed to do.

And Social Security is a problem when the central bank can create this kind of money? A Social Security fund should be in order! Social Security national deficit financing on top of national financing should be considered. Why not a Social Security National Fund, a scheme similar to the IMF and the World Bank schemes, the other money machines. Apparently the Federal Reserve has raised the bar, so let's get on with it. The IMF and World Bank bureaucracies gain profit with public money for themselves and the international. A new Social Security fund would profit from Treasury participation funds duplicating the people's private surplus money paid in to the fund. The money interests start new schemes for their principal purpose, to create money. A new Social Security fund should be a money-creation machine like the IMF and the World Bank, only better because it's the people's private money paid in. Commercial banks, cooperatives, and the American people would participate in the investment. It's time for another money machine to take place. Why do the money interests call all the shots. It makes more sense than a global warming scheme, now the "Climate Change" thing, a tens of trillions of dollars scheme, a public money creation, which will be created by and for the oligarchy.

Continuing current money creation, the Federal Reserve will extend $600 billion to the mortgage markets—$200 billion more for the credit card, college loan, the car buying industry; the $800 billion reported as "committed" money. A question was asked on television, where is the money coming from? The currency will be created, printed. The Federal Reserve Bank, apparently, with Treasury and without Treasury, is printing tons of money. The central bank is lending money on a colossal scale. The central bank, apparently, is reasserting its power. Almost two centuries ago, Andrew Jackson dismantled a similar power, but the power has sustained.

Two, three trillion dollars is a ton of money. It's trivia when compared to the derivative world of "notional amounts." The derivative economy is called the "phantom" economy, but it is an economy with real implications? The American people, and this writer, having no conception of such an economy, may realize the implications when they no longer can borrow money. Is the derivative economy responsible for the fracture of the credit system? A probable credit collapse appeared as a worldwide collapse; the derivative economy is a worldwide economy. The derivative economy, apparently a gigantic pyramidal pyramid almost exponential in scope, reportedly generates hundreds of trillions of imaginary dollars. It's imaginary, but it's a market? All pyramid schemes fail when the bottom-feeder stops as in the ARM contrivance.

The derivative economy relates to an impending market from which great sums of money are probably created; money borrowed, money lost. Lost to whom? The credit crunch. Great! The colossal scheme has apparently imploded. The American and global credit markets are in jeopardy. Wall Street investment banks and the AIG, in their derivative indulgence, although having trillions in assets, ditched their reserves in the process? Imaginary figures for huge profits? Trillions of dollars are apparently replacing trillions lost to whom?

The Treasury secretary, in what appeared as panic mode, ran to Washington for public assistance—more money. Nothing like too much government! The TARP plan will feed the banks, and the report is, they are hoarding the bailout money. How do banks make money when the banks are hoarding money? The legislated banking system is indebted to the banking system. If hoarding is going on, that means that banking in-house bookkeeping is probably going on, taking care of in-house indebtedness, and making money on public debt. This was stated in the Congress, long ago, during the Great Depression. C.W. Barron said the central bank would do things people wouldn't like. Who knows what the central bank and its member banks are doing? Does the president of the United States know? The Congress legislated the monster, and does the Congress know? The basis of central bank operation is secret and never audited. The American taxpayer, by way of the Treasury, will support the banks during the period of no redundancy.

It's apparently a continuing cyclical story when markets collapse; hoarding and deflation take place; debts stay put, and values decline, and predators do their thing. The money has been taken from circulation; the credit system shuts down. Recessions, depressions, apparently, are no big deal. It is the deal! Only that certain percentage of people are affected—the people out of the system, losing jobs while pure capitalism is stabilizing. It's capitalistic history repeating itself; the difference in 2008 and 2009 was the central bank making the big effort in its financial rescue.

The year 1929 collapsed the credits, and the central bank did little to restore national credits for the people. The full impact of the Great Depression didn't hit until 1932-1933. The vaunted Federal Reserve Note had gone to Europe and back again; the BIS was established.

Gold had gone to Europe, to Germany. The period was one of pure capitalism's finest hours. Capitalism appeared adverse to the "general welfare." America had been fleeced by the casino; there was no bread, and new millionaires were being born. This was twentieth-century America. The Roosevelt administration was trying to pick up the pieces, and the big war was coming. Roosevelt devalued the dollar. Gold was removed from circulation; then the devalued dollar purchased most of the world's gold.

While this was going on, approximately 25% of the people had no money; barter and scrip was the exchange. International financial order was paramount; there was insufficient credits within the domain, and the world central banks were doing their thing. President Roosevelt, taking the initiative, spent public money trying to move the country and the national debt accelerated—the "catch 22."

The 2008 crash produced another thud, the beginning of economic descent amid a demolishing of credits. This time, the banking system is the driving force pushing the Congress when necessary. The central bank and the Treasury secretary, with Congressional approval, is printing money, spending, buying, lending, investing via fiat credit and capital credit. Wall Street and the banking system is bolstering its reserves with public money—money the investment banking system, apparently, was instrumental in losing. Will the infusion of trillions of dollars free up the credit markets? Bailout money is in the form of loans, investments; the money will be paid back?

America is relegated to deficit financial degeneration; business goes offshore, driven by oppressive taxation in the search for more profits. It's growth outside with no taxes, consumption inside; it's the new world order. America's growth has been big; the debt will get bigger than that. Infamous foreign oil, Wall Street fraud and greed, and global money are dictating. The credit circulation, in combination with the pyramidal pyramid, is gradually eroding America's equity. Growth looms outside, disorder inside. Uncontrolled demographic infusion can diffuse America. Debtor status is negative leverage status, but the creditor needs the debtor. There is the lopsided exchange. The global market is working. For whom?

Warfare and huge debts persist; it's a disruption of America's sovereignty and nationalism. The wealth of indebtedness is the winner. America has been ushered outside the United States. Montesquieu said the money power "was always at war with its own boundaries, always restless with its own limitations." This, apparently, is where America is today. It's the way of things, and the international economy is taking place within. Maybe a bit of irony—an impending depression may be tempered because of foreign credits. American shareholders vote for foreign takeover if it means more profits for themselves. Baffling! Not really! It is all about the money. Hypocrisy abounds! The American people keep waving the flag—flags on helmets, uniforms, flags everywhere!

The G-20 summit met in Washington, D.C, recently in October 2008. The G-20 is an extension of the G7. Leaders of the industrialized world, presidents, premieres, prime ministers, etc., were meeting to seek a financial rescue of the new world order. In the new world order, America is a political domestic, America is a subsidiary. America is another country but also the leader in the global scheme of things. Where will America and the dollar's future be in all this business?

Barack Obama is president of the United States—a new cabinet, a new administration, and a new secretary of the Treasury. Changes are in order. A monstrous $825-$900 billion stimulus package was the latest bill, reduced to less than $800 billion. Trillions of new fiat dollars will be created, an apparent bombardment of the interest-bearing credit circulation. It may be a no-win because all the money is not slated for the credit system, which caused the crisis. No doubt, ballooned deficit figures will accompany the economy. The massive interest costs of the accelerated debt will probably negate a sufficient pay back..

The Congress, the Treasury, and the banking system will cooperate more closely. What does that mean? Transparency is the new administration's theme; the nation needs more transparency in the money business. This would include central bank operation? And the big fear with the banks is nationalization of America's banks; a similar dilemma persists in the United Kingdom. The new world order saw fit to domesticate G7 gross national products, and now suddenly, national is back in vogue. Nationalizing the banks is nationalizing the credit system and the economy? Will the Congress and the

Treasury nationalize America's domesticated product as part of the international scheme of things?

Ever since President Reagan's tax cuts, hell-bent deregulation, deficit spending, and foreign money, a jacked-up economy is coincident with and fed by the rapid acceleration of the public debt. President Bush repeated the act. The deficit account is suspect. It's America's direction; it's western financial mania. A jacked-up economy needs the crippling debt process. China and Japan respond to a point. Capitalism's outward advance is America's inward demise; it's the pyramidal return in the political economy. Whether a Democratic or Republican agenda, the agenda is borrow and spend. The borrowing spending binge is really no big deal; it is the deal. It's whatever the creators of the imaginative limits of the money system intend it to be. Inflation and the excessive profits to be made and a subsequent debt system are designed never to be paid. It's the twenty-first century, and cyclical crashes exacerbate the debt. Needless to say, something is amiss. Hail the public creditor, foreign and domestic; hopefully, the ship doesn't slip beneath the waves.

Mutual funds, IRAs, pension funds, savings, etc., are reportedly in trouble. The money isn't there? No cash? Why isn't the money there? The American financial chain is borrow to expand, borrow to pay taxes, borrow to meet payroll, etc. Suddenly the credit system gets clobbered. The banks aren't lending; the banks are gobbling taxpayer money. The corporate structure, small business, the people can't borrow, and the system shuts down. Once again, the pyramidal pyramid has produced the froth, and the froth has been skimmed by the wealth of indebtedness. But this nasty business, apparently, adversely affects only those out of the system, if the system gets real bad from 6% to 25% depending on events.

After the 1929 crash, Senator Robinson of Arkansas said, "Everywhere the surface of the financial sea reveals broken masts and fallen spars. Along the beach are stranded shattered hulks and wasted cargoes. Will the scavengers of the financial sea feast and fatten upon the garbage and the refuse?"—a relishing again during no-redundancy time! But the casino stays operational. The tables are cleared for the credit circulation; new currency is created for another round of play.

The March 2009 G-20 summit in London is over, and the conclusions: the United States was responsible for the worldwide credit collapse. France, Germany, China no longer consider America the world's financial leader. The big news: the IMF is back in business; 500 billion to a trillion dollars, depending on the source, will be pumped into the international fund by the member countries. This will curb inflation. And what about the World Bank? The trillion dollars will probably be public money? Is this trillion-dollar infusion added to the subscription quota? Will a trillion-dollar participation follow? It's taxpayer money, and how will the member countries and the banking system invest this money? What will be the benefit to the developing countries? All this business will expand the IMF bureaucracy. The America taxpayer will contribute the American share, probably $200 billion and probably more. This is more debt on the books of the Federal Reserve System.

Money and the utility conduct society. The money system is the ingenious scheme, the contrivance; the utility is not. The utility by the municipality distributes for all; the money system does not. Because of cyclical events, society suffers losses in money and the utility. The losses in the utility are mainly from natural causes. The record shows that crippling losses in the money system occur because of abuse of power, manipulation, fraud, and greed.

Hamilton ventured a future America with "no limits, even in imagination." There's been a change since then; it's not the exigencies of Hamilton's union, but exigencies of the new world order in the international scheme of things. Hamilton's 1791 exigencies were "permanent causes of expense." America's 2009 permanent causes of expense are the engulfing public/national debt and crippling taxation paid to foreigners. Thomas Jefferson said that "public debt was the biggest danger to be feared." The public creditor behind the system could be staring at a dying debtor. The ascending interest payment on America's mortgage will eventually negate the credit circulation. No credit circulation, no GDP/GNP.

In the meantime, Wall Street cyclically corrupts the financial system. A hundred years ago, senators and congressmen didn't want the country's money concentrated in New York; otherwise, there's the power of the legislated few and unequal distribution. Those members of Congress were in the minority. Too much government? The *Congressional Record* shows that the Congress put the money power and control right there, controlling government. C. W. Barron said the money belonged in New York, and that's where the money was placed and has stayed; it's been there since Hamilton.

America is democratic or capitalistic? America is capitalistic within the democracy? Apparently, America is a capitalistic democracy? America is a republic within the democracy? Didn't the framers describe America as a republic? "And to the Republic for which it stands." The politicians call America a democracy.

John Quincy Adams said,

> Remember, democracy never lasts long, it soon wastes, exhausts, murders itself. There never was a democracy yet that did not commit suicide. It is in vain to say that democracy is less vain, less proud, less foolish, less ambitious or less avaricious than aristocracy or monarchy. It is true in fact, and nowhere appears in history. Those passions are the same in all men, under all forms of simple government, and when unchecked, produce the same effects of fraud, violence, and cruelty.

Once upon a time, nationally, within the domain, America appeared supreme! But apparently, America was for sale. In the scheme of things, the American Congress made a deal with the bank. The deal was the bank would buy America. In the deal, America gave the bank the money with which the bank bought America. The bank charged America interest on the money America gave the bank while the bank bought America. When American equity exhausts, America's leased money will extinguish. The bank statute calls it "hypothecation," but the bank apparently controls the mortgage. The bank owns the money, courtesy of the Congress.

"And we are to be responsible after all; that is all there is of it."

SUMMARY

It appears America's manufacturing base is steadily going to zilch. The Treasury—Federal Reserve combine and the foreign entity is buying General Motors, Chrysler, others. These manufacturing giants helped building the great war machine during World War II. All great things end sometime. The United States supposedly leads the world industrially, apparently, not for long. From this viewpoint, America's manufacturing base appears in the process of dissemination. With the latest crash, the big New York investment houses and banks, AIG and the European connection have been propped up. Asset packed Wall Street suddenly had no money, plenty of wealth and no money. These entities are principals in the global scheme of things; their rescue, apparently was priority. The center of money creation performed the rescue; it was the combine, the tandem. The Congress had to say OK. What else?

The Treasury via the Federal Reserve is borrowing, buying, lending tons of money, running up huge deficits. It's nationalization? How can a domestic product be nationalized? Trillions more dollars are being created, the credit circulation. The money supply is critical to economic viability, but this latest infusion of currency appears beyond the normal function, out of site. It's more corporate welfare at a steep price. More sinkhole money? Government will own everything? Not really! With insurmountable deficits, the Government will owe ownership to the bank. Abysmal floating finance, all this to the delight of America's creditor.

President Roosevelt did a similar thing. It was the backlash of the 1930s; more than thirty new agencies were created. Social welfare was in the works, slicing into the corporate pie. Looking back, apparently, there was room to work, then; a bigger debt was just beginning. The 1913 act had been ignition time, a time of new growth and a time of new debt. The public creditor, again, and oppressive taxation was off and running.

Hoover's Reconstruction Finance Corporation bought debentures owned by banks, railroads, insurance companies; the action reportedly saved investments. The Federal Home Loan Banks and the FDIC were created. More corporate welfare was in the works. The public debt took off again. It was government public action because the private Federal Reserve had debunked the debentures and the public interest. The deal was the same: the government buying private shares, the purchases made with borrowed money. Whatever the sortie, the Federal Reserve collects. What's this private sector crap anyway? It's been a Treasury / Banking / public / private combine since the beginning.

President Roosevelt's political business was an attempt to clean up the wreckage strewn by repetitive capitalistic frenzy, fraud, and greed.

What's different today? Keynesian spending then; Keynesian spending now. Keynesian spending, apparently, is the thing! The country has experienced the 2008 crash. Great sums of money have been taken and held somewhere. The people know nothing of where the money went or is. In any event, new money was required to replace the void, public money to keep the economy going. Enter the "money creators."

The banking system received the cash, the country's credit system. Part of the stimulus, with interest, has been paid back; hopefully all the money, both fiat credit and capital credit will be paid back.

Chairman Bernanke did the right thing, restoring credits. It has been said; credits are more important than money. Money and credits flowed or otherwise a repeat of the1930s debacle. The arch-conservative wanted the political economy to "stabilize." Stabilizing the economy is the equivalent of no redundancy time. Crashes mostly hurt the working class, lost homes and jobs; the vultures descend upon them. It appears at least, one place to be in America is at, with, or close to Government, federal and state. James Madison knew the game; Madison was president and close to Government more than two hundred years ago.

The legislated Treasury—Federal Reserve combine is more aggressive, pushing the Congress and the Treasury. It's the controlling new world order in domesticated America.

Forgetting global complexities, the drug problem, and rampant daily holdups on city streets, the twenty-first century appears as a joyride with amazing technology. Remarkable, it's a separate economy. And the right to privacy is nowhere! The people talk endlessly to others, tracking, hacking, texting, sending notes and pictures everywhere, around the world with a hand held wireless gadget; it's done in seconds. Credits move the same way. But credits disappear the same old way; nothing has changed in the money scheme. The stagecoach periodically gets robbed. Government "interference" is the response; the public play, again, lessens the pain.

The great American experience continues; where else to live but in America, working, playing, trading, investing, gambling. But the economy is not all people friendly now. Not long ago, America talked a four day work week and early retirement. Now it looks like 3 and 4 day work weeks and no retirement. The games persist—stay put debts, diminishing values, vanishing credits, and rising costs. The new world order is global growth absorbing national equity negating national growth. American posterity appears in jeopardy. Infrastructure, making poor educational standards better and health care are priorities and the battle rages, public money or private money. Americans do prefer private health care but the costs are excessive. The word is socialized medicine produces inadequate medical services in foreign countries. Perhaps too few doctors, nurses and facilities dictates the problem.

America does move; America buys everything. G7, G20 countries don't; their exports exceed imports. America is the reverse; imports exceed exports, the mounting deficit account. Global new world order economics appears suspect, unequal distribution. This condition will correct only when all countries buy as well as sell, if that could ever be possible. There appears a dilemma; capitalism's rapid expansion shows colossal growth; it can be erosive, destructive. This to the delight of opposing countries and their terrorism. During the interim, the dollar will remain strong? America is in "common" with imports and exports from all countries. Commodities flood to America. The dollar remains the world's reserve currency, for now?

It's twenty first century cyberspace mania, blogs and imaginary money. Money creation, by design, appears top heavy. What amount of money creation is behind the notional amounts, money probably lost in the "phantom economy?"

The amounts of available money flowing today generates fierce debate in the Congress. There is so much money to be had, and deflation is mentioned along with inflation? The Federal Reserve has placed the discount rate at practically zero. Factions in the Congress say there is no inflation; this is really unbelievable. This means no colas for Social Security. This while prices are rising in oil, gasoline; banks, others are raising fees and interest rates on credit cards, making up for losses. People will have to drive their cars; states are cutting back commuter train Service. This while trillions of dollars are being printed by the Federal Reserve, and there is no inflation.

Republicans and Democrats will borrow and spend on climate control, playing to the tune of the environmental fiddler and the new world order. The colossus is forming, the new venture and more ballooning money creation. Being green in the global economy; the Oligarchs will see to it, the emerging market while submerging the taxpayer. The foreign segment of the G8 appears cautious; other things seem more important. Will the climate control market create jobs for people wiped out; replacing lost jobs? The American dream, the worked for retirement income is fleeting, in the private sector.

Republicans spend money and run up the debt when cutting taxes. The Democrats spend money and run up the debt when raising taxes. Crazy business! The record shows a ballooning economy since president Reagan. The record shows a whopping increase in deficits and national debt since Reagan and Bush, the Democrats now picking up the pieces. The latest estimates predict a deficit reaching 1.8 trillion dollars. The Treasury / Federal Reserve / public creditor combine may eventually sink the ship.

It's after Republican time and the Democrats will raise taxes. The Democrats want revenue to pay for deficits; the Republicans want to cut taxes to move the economy. The conservatives realized "Keynes could be had by tax cuts," this from John Kenneth Galbraith. Chairman Eccles told us this business was a means of putting money in circulation. Now its Keynesian spending and the Democrats are in. Chairman Greenspan constantly emphasized the need for growth. How else the buying of debt? In America, now, utility costs accelerate; health care and climate control looms, and debt is overtaking growth. The senior is asked to sacrifice equity for spending money.

At the time of the impending 2008 crash, the Treasury secretary, formerly of Wall Street, demanded more money from Washington. Apparently, there was no reserve on Wall Street and the European connection. There were plenty of assets, but no money. The Congress had to up the ante, again. At the same time, the chairman warns the Congress about the budget; the Congress must reduce borrowing and spending, running up the deficit, or there won't be any recovery.

Most presidents don't stay popular very long. How does any American president and party control the financial abyss? With president Reagan, the deficit was 200-300 plus billion; later with the second president George Bush, the deficit was 400 plus billion during his first term. The deficit approached a trillion dollars before George Bush left office. Reports say the deficit will reach 1.8 trillion dollars in 2010; this is Washington's financial gift to the Obama presidency. Debt progression appears to be surpassing growth.

President Reagan wanted tax money returned to the States; this made sense. From the record, revenue was taken from the States in the beginning when the Constitution was ratified. Alexander Hamilton wanted central power. The next big hit occurred in 1863. The States would begin to lose their financial sovereignty forever. Once upon a time, there were the colonies, then the States, and then the country; all this business revolving around the power and control of money. Since 1913, world wars, communism, terrorism, the global economy, and with everything else in between; the States find themselves in financial trouble. Like, no money! The States are cutting back in education, health care, commuter train service, coupled with increased property assessments, fees and taxation. Counties increase assessments although home values have decreased 20%. Not long ago, a State governor, when trying to curb spending, said, in so many words, the federal Government had it made. The federal government simply prints more money.

The economy is rebounding, but slow, and the experts say unemployment will continue to increase. Hopefully, this is not the trend. Wireless technology and on line ease of payment and purchase, will dominate, and like a lean army, the people will be facing a lean economy. How does this work when America faces increasing population and immigration? Corporations, banks, businesses are profitable again; but reports say they are downsizing. What is the future of the American worker?

Before, Detroit and its automobile was second to none. Then something happened; Detroit became careless, sloppy, arrogant! The Foreign infusion of fuel efficient dependable automobiles changed everything. The present General Motors and Chrysler dynamic is the result. Restoration is in order. A massive wholesale rebuilding of America, its auto industry, infrastructure, small business, health care and Social Security should be the first call. But the global economy, world wide strife, and never ending warfare dictates.

Since 1930, from the record, the Central Banks and the BIS have been at the forefront. In London, in 1933, emphasis was placed on checking further growth of economic nationalism. Global control of political economies was in the works eighty years ago. After World War II, two additional money machines joined the fray, the IMF and the World Bank. These banking or funding entities, initiated by government, are bankrolled with public money. Is another money creation scheme about to start? A global climate control money machine? These schemes generate the continuation of created national monies made domestic for international purpose. Climate control has to be an enormous undertaking. It is a new market which will create money and hopefully jobs, The banks are at the ready.

At the time of this writing, the G20 were meeting again in Pittsburgh, more meetings to follow. The war in Afghanistan is about to escalate. American occupation and suicide bombs is the story in Iraq. Iran and the Palestinians keep stirring the cauldron; Israel responds. The cost of world conflict continues. The international wealth of indebtedness sits back and collects.

The global scene is mobile; money is more mobile than that. Thomas Jefferson would say the people are swept up in it. In the scheme of things America has been ushered outside the United States. It's Capitalism's outward advance; the never ending advance guns the market place. Opposition reigns, What else? When growing up, one stayed out of the wrong neighborhood. America's capitalism shows international growth within the domain dependent on growth outside the domain. American multinational profits stay outside the domain. How American is that? It is all about the money. Sovereignty and nationalism is compromised, de-emphasized.

It's the currency trade bloc amid the world economy. Great Britain ruled for two and a half centuries. The pound sterling was the exchange, this while America was emerging. Germany countered with a bloc before the World War II. There was a transfer of power after World War II. American and Soviet Union power joined the pack. The dollar exchange won out in 1989. Pound sterling remains the expensive currency. The Middle East, Asia, the European Union, third world countries, and terrorism have arrived. It's the new world order. In 2010, the dollar is waning, What will be the future formidable currency exchange? A future Asian trade bloc, China included, is in the news, this as a result of the 2007 Wall Street caper. It's on-going! Money knows no boundaries and it has no flag.

Into 2010, the stock market is up over 10,000. The crisis is over! The credit system continues feeding the credit system. This while 25% of home buyers are having trouble making the mortgage payment. Sections of America report 15% unemployment. Young people borrow $200,000; graduate from college and can not get a job. The money system works; it's top heavy; it was designed that way.

Meanwhile, wealth aside, America, the great experience, is becoming a renter among renters in today's global economy. America as part of the mix of indebted countries, appears subjugated, domesticated. America started as a debtor, became a creditor. America became a debtor again while geared to global growth and global strife. When the debt process eventually extinguishes American equity, what then in the international scheme of things? Alexander Hamilton started it. The third central bank with Treasury, Wall Street, and the global contingent will finish it.

BIBLIOGRAPHY

CHAPTER ONE *The Civil War*

Pages 9 and 10, Lincoln's messages to Congress—37th Congress, 1st and 3rd Sessions; July 4, 1861, and December 1, 1862; from the Congressional Record, micro-film reading room, Reels 19 and 20, Library of Congress, Jefferson Building, Globe Printing Company; messages appearing on Page 3 of the record.

Page 10, "Bank Note List" [Paper Currency, % discounts] from the Saturday Evening Post, June 15, 1861. Newspaper Room, Madison Bldg, Library of Congress

Page 10, Indirect taxation, Direct taxation, from the Federalist Papers, No. 21, by Alexander Hamilton. Bantam Classic Edition, 1982; Publications, New York.

Pages 11, 12 and 13; Chase's message to Congress, as above [Reel No. 19] pages 4, 5, 6

Page 13, Vallandigham, as above, [Reel No. 19] pages 56, 57 and 58

Page 13, Lincoln's message, as above, [Reel No. 19] page 2

Page 13; South Carolina information [page 181]taken from "Financial History of the United States" By Davis Rich Dewey; published in 1903 by Longmans Green & Company; reprinted 1968 by Augustus M. Kelley, New York. Page 181.

Congressional proceedings and documentary in Chapter One, pages 9 through 15, from Reels No.19 and 20; The Congressional Record, The

Library of Congress, The Jefferson Building. Lincoln's messages; reports to the Congress by Secretary Chase and cabinet members etc.

Historical Record Page 10, from the Saturday Evening Post, Philadelphia, June 15, 1861.

CHAPTER TWO Suspension of Specie The Greenbacks

Page 16, Galusha Grow, Hannibal Hamlin—37th Congress, 2nd Session, December 2nd 1861, from the Congressional record, micro-film reading room, Reel No. 20, Library of Congress, Jefferson Building, Globe Printing Co. Page 2

Page 17, Caleb B. Smith, as above Reel No. 20, Appendix, pages 11-15

Page 16, 17, 18 Lincoln's message, as above, Reel No. 20, Appendix, pages 1-4

Page 16, Civil war history, from "The Civil War" Day by Day, Published by Barnes and Noble; Brompton Books, 1989; Early engagements, The Trent Affair.

Page 17, 18 and 19; Chase's message, as above, Reel No. 20, Appendix, pages 23-27

Page 18, Chase, Jay Cooke, Madison Building, Library of Congress. O.B. Potter, from the Congressional Record, 72 Congress, Session 1, 1932; Reel 196, Page 9899

THE HOUSE

Page 19, The Loan bill, as above, Reel No. 20, page 522;

Page 20, Thadeus Stevens,—38th Congress, 2nd Session, February 28, 1865, from the Congressional Record, micro-film reading room, Reel No. 23, Library of Congress, Jefferson Building, Globe Printing Co., Page 1202

Page 21, Vallandigham, Reel 20, Pages 614,615, Appendix, pages 308, 309

Page 21, Conkling, Reel No. 20, page 615

Page 21 and 22, Spaulding, Reel No. 20, pages 523-526

Page 22, Crisfield, Reel No. 20, Appendix, pages 47-51

Page 23 and 24; Pendleton, Reel No. 20, pages 550-551

Page 23 and 24 Gouverneur Morris, James Madison; From the collection in the Manuscript Reading Room; Madison Bldg. The Library of Congers.

Pages 24, Spaulding, From Reel 20, pages 523-526

Page 24, 25 and 26, Pendleton's reference to Hamilton's Bank report to the Congress, from the Congressional Record in the Micro Film reading Room , Jefferson Building, Library of Congress. Reel No. 20 pages 550 551. Also "The Federalist Papers," Papers 23 and 34.

Page 24, Robert Morris, 1781-1784; From the collection in the Manuscript Reading Room, Madison Building, Library of Congress.

Page 26, The First Congress in 1789, Reel No. 1, The Public Credit, Congressional Record, Micro-film reading room, pages 1170-1264.

Pages 27, 28 and 29; Hooper, From Reel No. 20, pages 615-617

Page 27 and 28, Chase, From Reel 20, Page 618; Revolutionary War debt.

Page 28; Congressmen Vallandigham, Stevens, Pendleton, Spaulding, From Reel 20. Pages 630-635

Page 29; Congressmen Hooper and Morrill, From Reel 20 as above.

Pages 29 and 30, Conkling, From Reel No. 20, pages 633-635

Page 31, David Hume, "Essays on Economics," published in 1752; The Library of Congress, Room of Rare Books, Jefferson Building.

Pages 29 to 33; Bingham, From reel 20, pages 636-640

Pages 29, 30 and 32, Conkling, From Reel 20, page 640

Page 33, Sheffield, From Reel 20, pages 640-641

Page 33 to 36; Senator Carlile, From Reel 20, pages 642-643

Page 37, Spaulding, From Reel 20, page 665

Page 37, Edwards, From Reel No. 20, pages 682-686

Page 38 and 39; Stevens, From Reel 20, pages 687-688

Page 38, Kellogg, From Reel 20, pages 679-680

Page 39, Riddle, Pike, Alley, Wright, From Reel 20, pages 684, 685, 659, 662,663

Pages 39 and 40; Shellabarger, From Reel 20, pages 690-691

Pages 40 and 41, Stevens, From Reel 20, pages 687-688

Page 41; Morrill, Hooper, Conkling and Stevens, From Reel 20, pages 690-695

THE SENATE

Pages 42 to 45, Fessenden, Chase, From Reel 20, pages 705, 762-767

Page 45, 46 and 47; Collamer, Sherman, From Reel 20, pages 767-774

Page 47 and 48; Howe, From Reel 20, Appendix, pages 51-55

Pages 48 and 49; Doolittle, From Reel 20, Appendix, pages 56-58

Page 49 , Sumner, From Reel 20, pages 798-799

THE HOUSE

Page 49, 50 and 51; Stevens, From Reel 20, page 900

Page 51, Lincoln's Son, From Reel 20, page 910

Page 51, Lincoln signs bill 240, From Reel 20, page 976.

Congressional proceedings, documentary and summary in Chapter Two, pages 16 through 56, primarily from Reel 20 in the Micro-Film Reading Room; The Congressional record, the Library of Congress, The Jefferson Building.

CHAPTER THREE *The Legal Tender Greenbacks*

Congressional proceedings from the Micro-Film Reading Room;

Page 57 and 58, Lincoln from Reel 20.

THE HOUSE

Page 58, Certificates of indebtedness, From Reel 20, page 2767, Appendix, page 340

Page 58, Chase, From Reel 20, page 2665

Page 58; The polygamy bill, Reel 20

Page 58 and 59, Spaulding, From Reel 20, pages 2766-2768

Page 58; Spaulding presented Chase's message; from Reel No. 20, page 2768

Page 59, Thomas, Stevens, From Reel No. 20, page 2794

Pages 59 and 60, Baker, From Reel 20, pages 2880-2882

Pages 61 and 62; Hooper, From Reel No. 20, pages 2882-2883

Page 62, Watts, From Reel 20, page 2883

Page 62, Holman, From Reel 20, page 2883

Page 62 and 63; Morrill, Lovejoy, From reel 20, pages 2884, 2885

Page 63, Stevens, From Reel 20, pages 2886, 2887

Pages 64-66, Bill 187, From Reel 20, Laws of the United States

Congressional Proceedings in Chapter Three, Pages 57 through 66 was taken from Reel No. 20, micro-film reading room, Library of Congress, Jefferson Building.

CHAPTER FOUR   *The Credit Circulation*

Pages 67, 68, Lincoln's message to Congress, The Third Session, 37th Congress, December 1, 1862, Congressional record, micro-film reading room, Library of Congress, The Jefferson Building, Reel No. 21, Appendix, pages 1-5

Page 69; The Louisiana Purchase, From the Public Acts of Congress, First Session of the Eighth Congress, the Congressional Record in the Jefferson Bldg.; Pages 1245-1247, the Appendix Section in the Micro-Film Reading Room.

Pages 69, 70 and 72; Secretary Chase, as above, Reel 21, Appendix, pages 21-28

Pages 72, 73 and 74; The Uniform Currency Act; as above, Reel No. 21, Appendix, pages 189-194.

THE SENATE

Pages 74 and 75; Senator Sherman, as above, Reel No. 21, Pages 840-846, Appendix, pages 49-52

Pages 75 and 76; Senator Collamer, as above, Reel No. 21, Pages 869-874

Page 75, Referred to by Collamer, Reel No. 21; Montesquieu.

Page 76, Senator Sherman, as above, Reel No. 21, Pages 871-877

Pages 76, 77 and 78; Senators Sherman and Collamer, as above, Reel No. 21, Pages 871-877

Page 78, Senators Powell and Howard, as above, Reel No. 21, pages 878-879

Pages 78 and 79; Senator Carlisle, as above, Reel No. 21, page 879

Page 79, Senator Doolittle, as above, Reel No. 21, page, New Series No. 56.

Pages 79 and 80; Spaulding, as above, Reel No. 21, pages 1114-1117

Page 80 and 81; Congressman Love in the House [1810]; First Session, Eleventh Congress, Reel No. Five, 1810, From the Congressional Record, micro-film reading room, Library of Congress, Jefferson Building, Pages 1799-1800.

Page 81 and 82; Alexander Hamilton, In the Madison Building, Library of Congress, the Manuscript Reading Room. Hamilton's Bank Report.

Pages 82; "The Public Creditors," The First session, The letter to The First Congress, The Micro Film Reading Room, Jefferson Bldg. August 1789, Reel No. One, pages 822-824.

Page 84; Mr. Love, as above, Reel No. Five; 1810, Pages 1799-1800.

Page 84, Spaulding, as above, Reel No. 21, pages 1114-1117

Pages 82 and 83; The First Bank, from the Book of Statutes, Third Session of the First Congress, Chap. X; Pages 191 to 197, approved March 2, 1791.

Pages 84-90; Thomas Jefferson, letters of Thomas Jefferson to Eppes, The Second Bank; The Library of Congress, The Madison Building, the Writings of Thomas Jefferson, the collection in the Manuscript Reading Room.

Page 85, Benjamin Franklin, the Library of Congress, The collection in the Manuscript Reading Room,The Madison Building.

Page 87, Referred to by Jefferson, Buffon's Tables

Page 92, Secretary Dallas, Outline of Plan for National Bank By Treasury Secretary Dallas, First session of the 14 th Congress, Reel No. 6, Micro-film reading room, Congressional Record, Library of Congress, Jefferson Building; Pages 511-514, January 1816.

Page 89, Treasury Notes, the Act of Feb 25, 1813; the Act of March 4, 1814; the Act of Feb24, 1815, From the Statutes of the United States, Main Reading Room, Jefferson Building, Library of Congress.

Pages 89 and 90, Letter to John Adams from Thomas Jefferson, the works of Thomas Jefferson , the collection in the Manuscript Reading Room, Madison Bldg, Library of Congress.

Page 91; Seat of Government, Third Session, Thirteenth Congress, Reel No. 5, Micro-film reading room, Pages 312-324. Congressional Records, Library of Congress, Jefferson Building.

Page 91, Thomas Jefferson, as above, Reel No. 5, Pages 24 and 26.

Page 92; Second Bank, as above, Reel No. 6, Pages 511-514.

Page 93, Andrew Jackson's message to Congress, First Session of the 21st Congress, December 8, 1829. Congressional Record; Jefferson Building, Micro-Film Reading Room; Pages 3 to Page 19.

Page 92; The Second Bank, also from the Book of Statutes; April 10, 1816, 14th Congress; First Session; Chap. XLIV, Pages 266-277. The Law Library Room, the Madison Bldg, Library of Congress.

Page 93, 94 and 96; Senator Benton; From the Congressional Record, 2nd. Session, 22nd. Congress, in July 1832; The collection in the Manuscript Reading Room, the Madison Bldg, Library of Congress. The "Thirty Years View" D. Appleton And Company, New York,

1854.

Page 94, 95 and 98; Daniel Webster, First and 2nd Sessions of the 22nd Congress, Reel No. 6, in July 11, 1832; Pages 1221-1230, Library of Congress, The Micro-Film Reading Room, The Jefferson Building

Page 95, Mr. Cuthbert, First Session of the Fourteenth Congress, From Reel No. 6, February 1816, Congressional Records, Micro-film reading room, Library of Congress, The Jefferson Building. Pages 1091-1094

Page 97 and 98; Senator White refuted Daniel Webster's bank approval, July 1832, Reel No. 6, pages 1241, 1242

Page 98; Senator Thomas Ewing's positives and negatives, July 1832, Reel No. 6, Page 1249

Page 99, 100 and 101; President Jackson, December 5, 1836 Message to Congress, Second Session, 24th Congress, Reel No. Six, the Micro Film Reading Room, The Jefferson Bldg.; Appendix, Pages 1 through 10.

Page 99, The Deposit Act, The Specie Act; Session 2, 24 Congress, Pages 90-104;

25 Congress, First Session, Pages 66-67.

Page 100; Levi Woodbury's Treasury Report, From the 24 Congress, 2nd Session, December, 1836, the Appendix, Page 80. Webster, 20 million in silver; 22 Congress, First Session, July 1832, Reel 6, Pages 1221-1230. The national debt was paid off.

Page 100, The Sub-Treasury Act Of 1840, also Chapter Two, Reel No. 20 etc.

Page 100, Van Buren, The Sub Treasury Act in 1840; Volume I, 1840; The Book of Statutes, in the Madison Building, Room of International Law.

Pages 101, 102; Nicholas Biddle, From the Congressional Record, the Micro Film Reading Room, Jefferson Building; Reel 5, The 23 Congress, 2nd Session, Dec. 18, 1834; Pages 24-32.

Page 102, 103; "Manifest Destiny" American history, from the Congressional Record Louisiana Purchase, from the Congressional Records in Reel No. 4, Appendix, Acts of Congress, Pages 1245-1250, Microfilm Reading Room, Jefferson Building, Library of Congress. Also, from the Book on Treaties in the Main Reading Room, Jefferson Building. Jefferson's letter to Lewis and Clark, from the Writings of Jefferson as above. Trail of Tears from World Book, Internet. President Polk, From World Book.

Page 103 and 104; Treaty of Guadalupe Hidalgo; The Mexican Treaty of 1848. From the Book of Treaties in the Jefferson Building, Main Reading Room, Library of Congress.

Page 103, The Louisiana Purchase, from the Book of Statutes, covered earlier.

Page 104; The panic of 1857, from "The Complete Book of U. S. Presidents", Buchanan Presidency; William A. Degregorio, 1984, Wings Books; Random House. Also, "The Financial History of The United States" by Davis Rich Dewey, Chapter XI, Pages 262-263. Library of Congress.

Page 105, Spaulding, Baker, Alley, Hooper, as above, Reel 21, Pages 1141-1143, 1146-1147, 1148; President Lincoln signs the Bank bill, his remarks presented by Senator Frazier in 1927 debating the Branch Banking bill, 69 Congress, Session 2, Page 3946, Reel 175. The Micro-Film Reading Room, The Jefferson Bldg, Library of Congress.

Page 105; The Bank bill or the "Uniform Currency Act", Reel 21, The Appendix, Pages 189-194; also O.B. Potter, 72 Congress, Session 1, Reel 196, 1932, Page 9899.

Congressional Proceedings in Chapter Four, Pages 67 to 109, was taken from the Congressional Globe Records in Reel 21, the Third Session of the 37 Congress. Reel One, The First Session of The First Congress; Reel Five, the Third Session of the Thirteenth Congress; Reel Six, the First Session of the Fourteenth Congress, the First Session of the 22nd Congress. The Micro-Film Reading Room, Jefferson Bldg, Library of Congress.

CHAPTER FIVE The Gold Bill

All of Chapter Five from the Congressional Record, the Micro Film Reading Room in the Jefferson Building, Library of Congress.

Pages 111, 112 and 113; Lincoln's messages to the First and second Sessions of the 38th Congress, December 1863, and December 1864, Reels 22 and 23; From the Appendix, pages one to four in Reel 22 and pages one to five in Reel 23; Appendix pages 143 and 203; the micro-film reading room, The Congressional Globe, Jefferson Building, Library of Congress.

THE HOUSE

Page 114, The Gold Bill, John Kasson, From Reel 22, First Session of the 38th Congress, Micro-film reading room, Jefferson Building, Library of Congress, Pages 707, 738.

Page 114, 115; Mr. Pendleton, as above, Reel 22, Pages 731-732.

Page 115 and 116; James Garfield, as above, Reel 22, Pages 734-735

Page 116, Mr. Boutwell, as above, Reel 22, Pages 735-736

Page 115, 116; Mr. Brooks, as above, Reel 22, Page 733

THE SENATE

Page 117, 118; Senator Sherman, as above, Reel 22, Pages 1023-1024

Page 117, Senator Hendricks, as above, Reel 22, Pages 1023-1024

Page 117, Hendricks and Sherman, as above, Reel 22, Page 1048.

Page 118 and 119; The Gold Bill, as above, Reel 22, the Appendix, page 264

THE HOUSE

Page 119, Mr. Kernan, as above, Reel 22, page 1099.

Page 119, 120; Congressman Thadeus Stevens, as above, Reel No. 23, Pages 1202-1204

Page 118, 119; Loan Bill, as above, Reel No. 23, The Appendix, Page 128

THE SENATE

Page 120, 121; Senator Sherman, as above, Reel 23, page 1224

Page 121,; Senator McDougall, as above, Reel 23, Page 1225

THE HOUSE

Page 122; Congressman Thadeus Stevens, as above, Reel No. 23, Pages 1202-1204, in the Micro-Film Reading Room, Jefferson Bldg. Library of Congress.

CHAPTER SIX The Legal Tenders and The Supreme Court

Legal Tender Supreme Court decisions, From Supreme Court Cases, The Madison Building, Volume No. 37, Salmon Chase statement, pages 575, 576. Room of International Law.

Page 123, 124; Salmon Chase letter, From the Congressional Globe, Reel No. 21, Micro-Film reading Room, Jefferson, Library of Congress, Page 618.

Page 123, Supreme Court decision, First Bank of the United States, From Supreme court decisions, The Madison Building, From the Caxton Press of Philadelphia, Pages 528-682. Justice Strong delivered the opinion of the Court, January 1872.

Page 124 and 125; Madison and Gouverneur Morris and the Constitutional draft, from the Writings of James Madison, the collection in the Manuscript Reading Room, Madison Bldg, the Library of Congress.

Pages 126, 127, The Federal Reserve Act, Library of Congress, Micro-Film Reading Room, Congressional records, Jefferson Building, 63 Congress, First Session; November / December 1913. Pages 5991-6009.

Page 125; Amos Akerman, as above, Supreme Court Cases, Page 527.

CHAPTER SEVEN *The Nations Currency*

Pages 128, 129, 130, 131; Hugh McCulloch, 39th Congress, First Session, December 1865, The Globe Congressional Record, Micro-film reading room, The Jefferson Building, The Library of Congress. Appendix, Pages 34-44. National Banking System by McCulloch, as presented by Senator Glass, a report by the Attorney General; 72 Congress, Session 1, Reel 196, May 1932, Page 9899.

Pages 129, 130 131; First Session, 39th Congress, as above, Reel No. 25 , Appendix, Page 317, Ways and Means—Contraction of the Greenbacks. Micro-Film Reading Room in the Jefferson Bldg, Library of Congress.

Page 130, 131 and 132; the Act of April 12, 1866, re-funding the Treasury notes and contraction of the Greenbacks, as above, Reel No. 25 , Appendix, Page 317.

Pages 131, 132; Second Session, 39th Congress, January 1868, An Act to suspend the contraction of the Currency. The Globe Congressional

Record, Micro-film reading room, the Jefferson Building, Library of Congress. Reel No. 25 Appendix, page 317.

Page 131, Senator Sherman, in the Senate, in 1890, mentioned the savings to the people, the Greenback issue. Page 4239, in the congressional record, Micro-film Reading Room, The Jefferson Building, Reel No. 39, The first Session, 51Congress.

Page 132, The Act of July 14, 1870—Refunding the Debt, Second Session, 41 Congress, Micro-film reading room, Jefferson Building, Library of Congress, Reel No. 32, Appendix, Page 707.

Page 132; "Black Friday", Gould and Fisk,—Davis Rich Dewey, Page 369, Library of Congress.

Page 132, The last southern States to return members to Congress, The Manuscript Reading Room, The Madison Building, Library of Congress.

Pages 133 and 134; The Mint Act of 1873—the Demonitization of Silver. Third Session of the 42 Congress, Micro-film Reading Room, Appendix, Page 236. Jefferson Bldg, Library of Congress.

Page 134; The Act of 1869, Coinage for Bonds, 41 Congress, Congressional Globe Record, Micro-film Reading Room, Jefferson Building, Library of Congress, Reel No. 32 in the Appendix.

Page 133; Davis Rich Dewey on silver, "Financial History of the United States" Pages 403-405. General Grant and his ignorance of the law. Library of Congress.

Pages 133, 134; Bimettalism, Hamilton and Jefferson, In the House, by Congressman Kenna of West Virginia, The Micro-film Reading Room, The Jefferson Building, Library of Congress, First Session, 45 Congress, Reel No. 9, Page 884.

Pages 134, 135, The Private Debt, Davis Rich Dewey; Library of Congress.

Page 135, The panic of 1873, "The Complete Book of U.S. Presidents," Page 272, and Dewey—"The Financial History of the United States," Pages 370-372.

Pages 136 and 137; The "dishonored Silver Dollar", Congressman Voorhees speaking in the House, January 15, 1878, Reel No. 9, the 45 Congress, Pages 334 335 and 336, Micro-film reading room, Jefferson Building, Library of Congress.

Page 137, Foreign held debt, Government Bonds, Secretary McCulloch's message to the 40 Congress, Reel 30, Appendix, Page 12, Micro-film Reading Room, Jefferson Building, Library of Congress.

Pages 137, 138 and 139; The Resumption Act, 1875; to take place in 1879, Dewey, Page 372 , 375. Library of Congress.

Page 139, The Greenbacks, cancellation ended, by Act of 1878, the 45 Congress, as above Reel No.9

Pages 136, 137 and 138; Congressman Voorhees, as above, 45th Congress, Reel No. 9, Pages 330-338.

Pages 135,136; Solution to the Social Problem" by J H Proudhon of France, Vanguard Press, 1927, Page 25; Library of Congress.

Page 139; The Silver Dollar reinstated, The new Morgan Dollar, The Bland Allison Act of 1878, The 45 Congress, as above, Reel No.9, in the Appendix.

Page 139, 140; Uniform Currency in circulation, Secretary McCulloch's message to the 40th Congress, as above, Page 17.

Page 139, Circulation per capita; "The single standard", Currency per capita, Congressman Giddings, Reel No. 9, 45 Congress, Page 890, Micro-film reading room, Jefferson Building, Library of Congress.

Page 140 and 141; Greenbacks held by the Treasury, from Reel 39, Micro-film Reading Room, Jefferson Building, Library of Congress, Page 4238, First Session, 51 Congress, Senator Sherman.

Page 142,143 and144; Stopping the coinage of Silver, the credit circulation etc., the National Banking System, Secretary McCulloch's message to the 48th Congress, second Session, 1884, Madison Building; Room 201, The Room for International Law; Library of Congress. 1884 Annual Treasury Report by McCulloch. Davis Rich Dewey and the silver dollars, pages 403-407.

Page 141; President Chester Arthur's message to the 48th Congress, First Session, 1884 about the circulation and redemption of Bonds, Micro Film Reading, Jefferson Building, Library of Congress; Reel 24, Pages 19-24.

Page 146 and 147; President Grover Cleveland, messages to Congress in 1886, the Congressional Globe, Second Session, 49 Congress, Micro-film reading room, Jefferson Building, Pages 7 and 8.

Page 146; The Silver Act of 1890, From the Book of Statutes in the Jefferson Building, First Session 51 Congress, Chapter 708, Pages 289, 290. Also, Davis Rich Dewey, Chapter 19, pages 437-447, Library of Congress.

Pages 149, 150 and 151; Reducing the coinage of Silver, Congressman Henry Coffeen of Wyoming in the House of Representatives, 53 Congress, 3rd Session, 1894, Reel 55, in the Micro-film Reading Room in the Jefferson Building, Library of Congress, Appendix, Page 86.

Page 151; The Barings collapse; Davis Rich Dewey, Page 442. Library of Congress.

Page 151 and 152; The Gold Standard Act of 1900, From the Book of Statutes in the Jefferson Building, The Library of Congress, The Main Reading Room, March 14, 1900, The 56 Congress, First Session, Chapter 41, Page 45.

Pages 152 and 153; Gold and Silver Certificates, William Jennings Bryan, Micro-film Reading Room, The Jefferson Building, Library of Congress, Congressional Record, Reel 55, 3rd Session, 53 Congress, Appendix, Pages 144-145; page 148, Page 151.

Page 147, 148 and 149; The Carlisle Plan by Secretary of the Treasury Carlisle. 1894, State of the Finances, Annual Report, in the Madison Building, Library of Congress, Pages LXVII-LXXVIII. Grover Cleveland's message to Congress, December 1894, 3rd Session, 53 Congress, Reel 55, Pages 10 and 11, Micro-film Reading Room, Jefferson Building, Library of Congress

Page 158 and 159; "Currency Volume", 53 Congress, address by Congressman Henry Coffeen, in the Appendix, Reel 55, Pages 80-87, Page 103. Micro-film Reading Room, Jefferson Building, Library of Congress.

Page 151; Davis Rich Dewey, Pages 443-447; gold for trade, gold for export; Library of Congress.

Page 152; Thomas Jefferson, As above, Reel 55, Appendix, Page 144.

Pages 154 and 155; William McKinley, From the "Complete Book of U.S. Presidents," Pages 358-370.

Page 154, The Tariff Act of 1890, From the Book of Statutes, Jefferson Building, Chapter 647, Pages 209 and 210, also, From Davis Rich Dewey.

Page 154, The McKinley Tariff, Panic of 1893; Davis Rich Dewey, Page 445, The Library of Congress.

Page 154; The Tariff of 1894, Grover Cleveland; From the Complete Book of U.S. Presidents, Page 349.

Page 154 and 155; McKinley's message to the 55 Congress, Second Session, Reel 62, Pages 2 and 3, Micro-film Reading, Jefferson Bldg. Library of Congress.

Page 154; The Tariffs of 1894 and 1897, From the Book of Presidents, Pages 349 and 365, Also the Carlisle Plan from Dewey and the State of the Finances, 1894 Annual Report by Carlisle in the Madison Building pages 100 and 101. Dingley Tariff from Dewey, Page 464.

Pages 155, 156, 157 and 158; Congressman James McCleary, Reel 68, The Appendix, Pages 3-16, Micro-film Reading Room, Jefferson Building,

Page 158, Secretary Lyman Gage, from his Treasury report of 1897, Library of Congress, The Madison Building, Page XXXIV.

Page 158 and 159; Congressman Coffeen, Reel 55 as above, Pages 111, 112 and 110.

THE SENATE

Pages 160 and 161; The Senate in May, 1890, Senators Sherman and Aldrich, From the Micro-Film Reading Room, The Jefferson Building, Library of Congress, Reel 39, First Session, 51 Congress, Pages 4239-4241. Also Senators Reagan and Plumb.

Page 161; Sherman Anti Trust, From World Book, "Antitrust Laws, also the Complete Book of U.S. Presidents, page 339.

Page 162; The Gold Standard Act of 1900, From the Book of Statutes in the Madison Bldg; Fifty-Sixth Congress, Session 1; Page 45, Chapter 41.

Page 164, National and State Banks, From "Historical Statistics of the United States, Colonial Times to 1970." Main Reading Room, Jefferson Bldg., Library of Congress.

Page 164 and 165; The Government, business as usual, Postal Service, Pensions etc., from Grover Cleveland Message to Congress, Micro Film Reading Room in the Jefferson Building. December 3, 1894.

Page 165; The Treaty between The United States and Spain, signed on December 10, 1898, From the Book of Statutes at Large, Pages 1754-1762, Jefferson Building, Library of Congress. The Ways and Means Act of June 13, 1898, Statutes at Large, 55th Congress, Session II, Jefferson Building.

Page 165, Naval Ships, From McKinley's message to the 55 Congress, as above.

CHAPTER EIGHT *The Federal Reserve System*

Page 167, 168 and 169; Message to the First Session of the 56 Congress on December 3, 1900 by William McKinley, from the Congressional Records, Micro-film Reading Room, the Jefferson Building, Library of Congress, Reel 68, Pages 2 through 13; The Philippines, Cuba, Puerto Rico. The Boxer Rebellion. Imports and exports to Brazil; The Panama Canal; Exposition in Buffalo.

Page 169, The Huge Trusts, Senator Owen in the Senate, November 1913, Micro-Film Reading Room, Congressional Record, etc. Reel No. 114, Page 5993. Samuel Untermyer of New York.

Page 169, 170, 172 and 173 Congressman Burke, Appendix of the Congressional Record, Pages 290 and 291, September 17, 1913, in the House of Representatives; Banking and Currency Committee;

Page 171, The Wall Street Journal, October 22 and 23 of 1907, also, the New York Times of October 23, 1907

Page 171, Davis Rich Dewey; The Panic of 1907, New York and the money, Page 481. Library of Congress.

Page 171; Report of the Senate Finance Committee, Report 133, Part 2, 63 Congress, First Session, Micro-Film Reading Room, Jefferson Building, Page 6007, Interest Rates, the year 1907. Carter Glass, 72 Congress, Session 1, Page 9882, Vol. 196, May 10, 1932

Page 171, Congressman Adolph Sabath, Library of Congress, Micro-Film Reading Room, The Jefferson Building, Reel No. 114 Appendix, Pages 466-467.

Page 172, The Bank Act Of 1863, From the Book of Statutes at Large, Library of Congress, Madison Building, Volume 22 Chapter 290 Section 32 of the Revised Act, 1882. The Room of International Law

Page 173, Congressman Stephens, Appendix, Reel 114, Pages 327 and 328, September 18, 1913, in the House of Representatives. Also, Louis Fitzhenry of Illinois; Page 329, Banking and Currency.

Page 171, Congressman Burke, As above, Pages 290 to 296.

Page 171; Monies deposited in New York banks by Secretary Cortelyou, from the 1908 Annual Treasury Report. The Room of International Law, Madison Building, Library of Congress

Page 174, An Act to Amend the National Banking Laws, Aldrich-Vreeland, From the Book of Statutes at Large, Jefferson Building, Volume 1, Chapter 229, Pages 546-547.

Page 174, Senator Owen, 63 Congress, First Session, Reel No. 114, Page 6002, Micro-Film Reading Room, Jefferson Building.

Page 174; Glass-Owen Bill, HR 7837; From the Congressional Record, Senate Report 133, Part 1 and 2; 63 Congress, Session 1; read in the Senate, taken from the Appendix; pages 6002 to 6005 of the Congressional Record.

Page 174, Congressman Fess, 63 Congress, First Session, In the Appendix, Pages 282-284. Micro-Film Reading Room.

Page 175, The Amended Banking Act as above, and Congressman Charles Lindbergh Sr. 60 Congress, Session One, Reel 91, in the Appendix, Page 58; Micro-Film Reading Room, Jefferson Bldg .

Page 175, Wilson Hill, 60 Congress, Session One, Reel 91, Micro-Film Reading Room Jefferson Bldg; In the Appendix, Pages 70-71.

Page 177, Davis Rich Dewey, Emergency Currency, Page 482.

Pages 175, 176 and 177; Congressmen Sabath and Williams, "The Currency Crime", 60 Congress, Session One, Reel 91, as above, in the Appendix, Pages 366-367 and Pages 464-468.

Page 177, 178, 179,180 and 181; Senator Howe, The Currency Bill Report from the Finance Committee, Submitted to the Senate on Nov. 22, 1913, 63 Congress, Session 1, Congressional records, Micro-Film Reading Room, Jefferson Building, Library of Congress, Reel 114, Pages 5991-6009. Sherman Anti-Trust Act, From the Book of Statutes,

Madison Bldg. Library of Congress. Treasury 1912-1913 Financial Statements, Secretary MacVeagh, in the Madison Building, Room of International Law; 62 Congress, Session 3, page 75. President Roosevelt, from the Wall Street Journal of October 22, 1907. Also, James Sinclair, 67 Congress, on "Money and Credit," in the House, Page 8249, the Congressional Record, Micro-Film Reading Room, Jefferson Building.

Page 182 and 183; Chairman Carter Glass, Ways and Means, December 22, 1913, Conference Report, Congressional Records, Micro-Film Reading Room, Jefferson Building, Library of Congress, Reel 115, pages 1430-1439. Secretary of the Treasury MacVeagh, 1913 Treasury Report, As above the Madison Building, Pages 1, 2 and 3. Wilson Hill and asset currency again, as before.

Page 183, 184 and 185; Congressman Charles Lindbergh, the Conference Report, Reel 115 as above, Pages 1445-1446; Congressmen Platt and Carter Glass

Page 185, 186 and 187; Congressmen Morgan, Platt, Underwood, and Carter Glass, The Conference Report Reel 115 as above, Pages 1458 and 1459.

Page 187, Woodrow Wilson, Elected President, From World Book, From the Complete Book of U.S. Presidents, Page 417.

Page 187 and 188; Congressman Mann of Illinois, The Conference Report as above, Reel 115; also Congressman Glass of Virginia, Pages 1463, 1464.

Page 188, 189, 190, 191, 192, 193; The Federal Reserve Act, From the Book of Statutes. From the congressional record, the Micro-Film Reading Room; Senator Owen in the Senate, explaining the Obligation and the Acceptance, November 24, 1913; 63 Congress, First Session, Page 5996, also Pages 5991-6009; also the Statutes in the Jefferson Building, Main Reading Room, Pages 251-275; 63 Congress, Session 2.

Page 194, 195, 196, 197, From the Book, "The Federal Reserve Act" by C.W,. Barron; published in 1914—Boston News Bureau Company. The Library of Congress, Jefferson Building, Parts I and II, Pages 10-15

CHAPTER NINE   World War One

Pages 199, 200, 201 and 202; Woodrow Wilson elected to a second Term, from the Complete Book of U.S. Presidents, Pages 408, 428. 1915 message to the 64 Congress, First Session, December 7, 1915, From the Congressional Records, Pages 95 to 100, Micro-Film Reading Room, Jefferson Building, Library of Congress.

Page 200, 201, 202, 203, 204; Congressman William Bennet of New York and Congressman Simeon Fess of Ohio. From the Congressional Record, Micro-Film Reading Room, Jefferson Building, Library of Congress, Reel 131, In the Appendix, Pages 96-103, 64 Congress, 2nd Session, January 2, 1917. " The Wilhelmena"

Page 204, Declaration of War by the Congress, From World Book and the Complete Book of U.S. Presidents, pages 423-424.

Pages 204, 205, 206, 207, 208 ; Secretary McAdoo and his December 7, 1914 Treasury Report to the Congress, The Library of Congress, The Madison Building, Pages 1-35, Also, the Treasury Report of 1915, Pages 1-19.

Page 209; President Harding, 1921, Official end of the War with Germany, From the Complete Book of U.S. Presidents. Page 440.

Page 209 and 210; Congressman James Sinclair, From the Appendix, 67 Congress, Sessions 2 and 3, Page 13249.

Page 210 and 211; The Bolshevik; Congressman Fess, The 65 Congress, Session 3, Speech before the Indiana Editorial Assoc. From the Appendix; Page 8781, Micro-Film Reading Room, Jefferson Building, Library of Congress.

CHAPTER TEN   Readjustment

Pages 212, 213, 214; Secretary Carter Glass, Annual Treasury Report to the Congress, November 20, 1919; In the Madison Building, Library of Congress, The Room of international Law. Pages 1-4, 5

Page 213, 214; President Wilson; Messages to Congress, 1915, 1918 and 1919. From the Micro-Film Reading Room, The Jefferson Building, Library of Congress,

Page 214, Rental of the Railroads, stated by Senator Robert La Follette on December 20, 1919; In the Micro-Film Reading Room, The Jefferson Building, Library of Congress, 65 Congress, Session 3, Page 8746 in the Appendix.

Page 217, The Federal Reserve and all the Gold, C.W. Barron's Book, Page 99.

Page 219, The new Secretary of the Treasury D.F. Houston, The events of 1920 leading to the Depression of 1921; From the 1920 Treasury Report, the Madison Building, pages 1-4

Page 214, 215, 216, 217; Governor Harding's letter as part of Secretary Glass's Report of 1919; See above; Treasury Report of 1919, Pages 18-21.

Page 218; Congressman Fess's warning, 65 Congress, Session 3, in the House, Micro-Film Reading Room, Jefferson Bldg, in the appendix, Page 8780.

Page 219, 220; Congressman King; the Newell Report, 65 Congress Session 3, Micro-Film Reading Room, Jefferson Bldg; The Appendix, Pages 8915-8917.

Page 220; The Roaring Twenties, From World Book.

Pages 221, Secretary Houston, From his 1920 Annul Treasury Report.

Page 221 and 221; Congressman Edward King of Illinois, The Webb bill and the Edge Bill; From the Micro-Film Reading Room, The Jefferson Building, The Library of Congress, The 67 Congress, First Session, the Appendix, pages 8331-8337.

Page 221, 222, 223, 224, 225 Senator Ladd, speech on Dec. 15, 1921; before the Monetary Conference. The address was presented by Congressman Sinclair in the House; 67 Congress, Session 3; From the Appendix, pages 13249-13256; Micro Film Reading Room; The Jefferson Building, The Library of Congress.

Page 223 and 224; Congressman Platt, speaking in the House on the Webb bill, 66 Congress, Session One, Reel 145, Page 7855; Micro-Film Reading; The Jefferson Building, The Library of Congress.

Page 225; The Wall Street Journal, Contracting Federal Reserve Notes, July 1, 1921. Senator Smith

Page 226; Articles from the Wall Street Journal, July 1st, 1921, and July 14, 1921; Room 135, in the Madison Building, Library of Congress. Also, Henry Ford Article; Shifting the credit burden to the car dealers.

Page 226, 227; Speech by Gov. Harding; The Federal Reserve; The speech was presented by Congressman Barkley in the House, 67 Congress, Session 3; From the Appendix, Pages 13256-13258; The Jefferson Building, The Library Of Congress. 53 billion in resources, speech by Charles Sabin, January 17, 1921, Guarantee Trust Co. of NY. Library of Congress, Madison Bldg.

Page 227; World War One indebtedness, From debate in the House on the Edge bill, by Mr. McFadden, November 3, 1919, 66 Congress, Session One, Page 7900, Reel 145, Micro-Film Reading room, The Congressional Record, Jefferson Building, Library of Congress.

Page 228 229; World Trade, From a Report by The Federal Trade Commission, presented by Mr. Webb in the House on June 13, 1917; 65 Congress, Session One; Page 3576-3577, Micro-Film reading room, The Congressional Record, Jefferson Building, Library of Congress.

Page 229, National City Bank, by Congressman Platt, the Edge Bill, Nov. 1, 1919; as above the Congressional Record, 66 Congress, Session 1, Reel 145, Page 7855.

Page 229, Congressman Platt in the House, the Edge bill, November 1, 1919, 66 Congress, Session One, Micro-Film reading room; The Congressional record, Reel 145, Page 7856, The Jefferson Building, Library of Congress.

Page 229 and 230; Congressman Steagall in the House, Congressional Record, November 3, 1919, Reel 145, as above, Page 7900.

Page 230, Congressman Nelson in the House, Congressional Record, Nov. 3, 1919, Two kinds of Foreign Banks, Reel 145 as above, Page

Page 228, 229,230, 231 232, 233, 234, 235, 236, 237; Congressman King, the Edge bill, November 7, 1919, in the House, as above, the Congressional Record, Micro-Film reading room, 66 Congress, session One, Pages 7898 through 7900; Page 8084. Also the 67 Congress, Session 1, June, 1921, The Appendix, Pages 8331 through 8337.

Page 232, 233; The Wall Street Journal of Monday January 2, 1922. Gold shipments, Gold imports.

Page 235, 236; Congressman McFadden, 66 Congress, Session 1, November 3, 1919, from the Appendix, Pages 7898 through 7900.

Page 237 and 228; Senate Resolution 212, From the Book of Statutes, page 1084; and Senate bill 1915, Page 181, the Book of Statutes, War Finance Corporation

Page 238; George Bush and the New World Order.

Page 238; States admitted to the Union, From the Complete Book of US Presidents.

CHAPTER 11   The 1920's

Page 239, The Wall Street Journal, January 1, 1923.

Page 239, 240, 242; Secretary of the Treasury Andrew Mellon, Annual Reports of 1921, 1922 and 1923. The Library of Congress, The Madison Building, Room 201 of International Law.

Page 240, Population, From Mellon Treasury Report of November 1927.

Page 240, Motor Vehicles, from the Wall Street Journal, January 8, 1924

Pages 240, 241; The "Dole" from the Wall Street Journal, January 27, 1925

Page 241; President Harding, From the Complete Book of U.S. Presidents, Messages to the Congress, and the Congressional Record, Jefferson Building, Library of Congress, Micro-Film Reading Room.

Pages 241, 242; The Gold Report in the five Banks, from the Wall Street Journal

Page 242; The Foreign Debt Commission, From Mellon's 1922 annual Report, in the Madison Building, Library of Congress, Room 201, Room of International Law; Pages 24-26.

Page 243; French Budget in doubt, From the Wall Street Journal April, 1925.

Page 243; Private meeting; Harding and Bankers, From the Wall Street Journal, April 28, 1925.

Pages 243, 244, 245; Hjalmar Schacht and Montague Norman, Page 194, From Toland's Book, "Adolf Hitler" Doubleday & Company, Inc. Garden City New York. Also, From Confessions of "The Old Wizard," Pages 181-183, by Hjalmar Schacht, Houghton Mifflin, Cambridge, Mass.

Pages 244, 245, 246; "Confessions of the Old Wizard" By Schacht, Pages 179-197.

Page 246, Movement of Gold, From Mellon's 1924 Treasury Report, Madison Building, Room 301, Pages 69-75. American currency returning; Room of International Law

Pages 247, 1925 Annual Treasury Report, Gold was moving, Gold was going to Germany, Secretary Mellon. Madison Bldg, Room of International Law

Page 246; England returns to the Gold Standard, From the Wall Street Journal, April 29, 1925.

Page 246, The Fordney Tariff, From Davis Rich Dewey, Pages, 522 and 523.

Page 247 and 248; Hjalmar Schacht, The Retenmark, discount of; From Schacht's "Confessions" Pages 179-197

Page 248; "Allied Loans," From the Wall Street Journal, January 1, 1925.

Pages 249, 250; Secretary Mellon; 1922 and 1923 Annual Treasury Reports, refunding, surpluses showing the need for reduction in taxation. Pay down of the debt. Room of International Law, The Madison Bldg.

Pages 250, 251; Federal Reserve earnings, From the Wall Street Journal, January 1, 1924.

Pages 251, 252; Secretary Mellon's 1929 Report, taxation reform, as above

Pages 252 and 253; The movement of Gold, London to New York, From the Wall Street Journal, April 29, 1825.

Pages 253, 254; The McFadden Bill, H.R. 2, From the Congressional Record, the Micro-Film Reading Room in the Jefferson Building, Library of Congress. The 68 and 69 Congresses, 1925 through February 1926, Reels 167 and 168, Pages1563 1586 and pages 2825-2861.

Page 255, Congressman Nelson in the House; January 27, 1926; The Branch Bank Hook, from the Congressional Record, Reel 168; Page 2840; Micro-Film Reading Room, Jefferson Bldg; 69 Congress Session 1,

Page 256, Congressmen Stevenson and Fulmer; Branch Banking, From the Congressional Record, Micro Film Reading Room, Jefferson Bldg. Page 2849, Reel 168 as above.

Pages 256 and 257; Congressman Steagall, Branch Banking as above, Pages 2851-2854; January 23, 1926 Reel 168

Page 258; Congressman Kurtz, Branch Banking as above, Page 2855; Reel 168

Pages 258 and 259; Congressman Celler, Branch Banking as above, Pages 2859-2860; Reel 168

Pages 259, Congressman Black, Branch banking as above; February 3, 1926, Page 3238; Reel 168. Pages 165 though 167, From the Micro-Film Reading Room, Jefferson Bldg

Page 259 and 260; The Wall Street Journal, January 29, 1926; The small Unit Bank.

Page 260, The McFadden bill, February 25, 1927, Limitless Succession. From the Book of Statutes in the Madison Building, Room 201, the Room of International Law.

Page 261; The Wall Street Journal of February 24, 1927; Changes in the Federal Reserve System. Page 171, W,L. Harding, 69 Congress, Session 2, Reel 175, Micro-Film Reading Room, Pages 3848, 3849.

Pages 261 and 262; Senator Heflin, about WPG Harding, W "Poison Gas" Harding, same as above, Page 3850. Reel 175 in the Micro-Film Reading Room.

Pages 262, 263, 264; Dr. Commons of the University of Wisconsin before the Congressional Committee about the Federal Reserve System, February 4-15, 1927, the 69 Congress, Session 2, Pages 3835-3848. Micro-Film Reading Room, Jefferson Bldg.

Page 260; President Coolidge veto of the McNary-Haugen Bill, From the Congressional Record, the 69 Congress, Session 2, Reel 175, Page 4771, Micro-Film Reading Room

Page 265, Dr. Commons of Univ. of Wisconsin; "Managed" Gold, From the Congressional Record, 69 Congress, Session 2, Reel 175, Micro-Film Reading Room, Jefferson Bldg. Page 3839. Page 173, Senator Nye, Reel 175, Page 3830-3835.

Page 264, James Madison; Those "close to and within reach of Government," From the collection in the Manuscript Reading Room, Library of Congress, Madison Building.

Pages 265 and 266; Senator Wheeler, the Chronicle Article—Federal Reserve power with Gold and Federal Reserve Bank Notes, 69 Congress, Session 2, Reel 175, Page 3954.

Pages 266, 267, 268; The Federal Farm Loan Act of 1916, From the Statutes, Room 201 in the Madison Building. All information from the Annual Treasury Reports by Secretary Mellon—1916 through 1929

Page 270; The Gold Certificates made a Legal Tender, Senate bill 3458, From the Book of Statutes, December 24, 1919; Room of International Law, Madison Bldg.

Pages 268 through 271, The Varied Currencies, Economic condition of the country; Prohibition and Narcotics; All information taken from the Annual Treasury Reports by Secretary Mellon, Reports 1926 through 1929. Room of International Law, Madison Bldg.

Page 273, Bureau of Prohibition statistics From Secretary Mellon's 1929 Annual Treasury Report, Pages 199-200; The Madison Building, Room of International Law, Library of Congress

Page 273, Herbert Hoover and Alfred Smith; the 1928 presidential election, from The Complete Book of U.S. Presidents—Herbert Hoover, Pages 468-470.

Page 273; Federal Reserve Gold, From Mellon's 1930 Annual Treasury Report, Room of International Law, The Madison Bldg. Etc.

CHAPTER TWELVE The Crash

Page 275, Secretary Mellon's 1930 Annual Treasury Report, opening statement, Page 1; Room of International Law, The Madison Bldg.

Page 275, Total money, per capita money, Secretary Mellon's Annual Treasury Report, Pages 604 and 607; Room of International Law, Madison Building.

Page 276; 200 billion dollar debt, Volume 195, the 72 Congress, Session 1 in the Micro-Film Reading Room, Page 4225; Mr. King in the Senate, "obligations amounting to nearly $200,000,000,000 . . . ."

Page 277; President Roosevelt, from the Complete Book of U.S. Presidents, Pages 473, 479, also, devaluation of the dollar, Roosevelt's Prolcamation No. 2072, Statement from the White House by Franklin Roosevelt; the Manuscript Reading Room, the Madison Building, Library of Congress. Also from the Congressional Records, Micro-Film Reading Room; see below

Pages 277 and 278; The Hague Convention, from the Congressional Record; See 71 Congress, Session 2, Reel 187 in the Micro-Film Reading, Pages 4328-4336, The Jefferson Building, Library of Congress. The Wall Street Journal of January 22.

Pages 278 through 288; The Owen Young Plan, The Bank for International Settlements, The Dawes Plan, The Federal Reserve, J.P. Morgan & Co. et al; Montague Norman, Benjamin Strong, Federal Reserve Bank of New York, etc. as presented by Chairman McFadden—his Two Resolutions, 71 Congress, Session 2, Reel 187, as above, Pages 4328-4336. Also, Hjalmar Schacht and the BIS from his "Confessions"

Page 277; President Franklin Roosevelt; Devaluation of the Dollar, from the Congressional Records; in the Micro Film Reading Room, the Jefferson Bldg. Reels 204-206; 73 Congress, Session 2; January through May 1934. The "Public Works Administration," from the Complete Book of U.S. Presidents, Page 499.

Pages 278 and279; Chairman McFadden of Banking and Currency, Congressman Wingo, Gates W. McGarrah, G.L. Harrison, The New York Times, Hjalmar Schacht, Montague Norman, Parker Gilbert; the secret meeting of 1926, The Versailles Treaty, The State Department Policy of 1929, J.P. Morgan & Co., as above, Reel 187, Pages 4329, 4330

Page 280; American Policy on Reparations, as above, Reel 187, The Micro-Film Reading Room, Page 4330, Jefferson Bldg.

Page 283; Hjalmar Schacht signs the Young Plan, from his "Confessions" Pages 244-249. Also, Schacht and the BIS in Basel Switzerland.

Page 283 and 284; The London Economist, The German Reichstag, as above, Reel 187 in the Micro-Film reading Room, Page 4333

Page 284; Hjalmar Schacht, Reparations to Allied Governments, losses to private investors, from his "Confessions;" Pages 203-204, 218-219.

Page 284; Hoover's Moratorium, From Congressman McFadden's discourse, Pages 4328-4335, in the Micro-Film Reading Room, 71 Congress, February 1930.

Pages 283 and 284; McFadden, the Dawes and Young plans, referenced above.

Page 285; The New York Times of February 22, 1930.

Pages 286 and 287, John Kenneth Galbraith; Churchill, Norman, Schacht, Lionel Robbins; The Federal Reserve, Pages 14-17; From Galbraith's book "The Great Crash", The Riverside Press, Cambridge, Mass. Houghton Mifflin Company Boston, 1955.

Page 288; The Financial Chronicle, produced by McFadden in the House; Gold shouldn't be placed in the BIS by the Federal Reserve. In the Micro-Film Reading Room, Jefferson Bldg

Pages 288 and 289; Gold Accumulation, From the First Annual Report of the Federal Reserve Bank of New York, Page 19, The Adams Building, Fifth Floor, Library of Congress.

Pages 287, 288, 289, 290; Secretary Mellon, Credit Conditions, from the 1930 Annual Treasury Report; Pages 18 through 22. Room of International Law, The Madison Bldg.

Page 291 and 292; Wall Street Journal Article, Bankers Convention in June 1929

Pages 292 and 293; John Kenneth Galbraith, New York Banks, from his Book "The Great Crash" Pages 119 and 120.

Page 293 and 294; Senator Nye, from the Congressional Record, Resolution 144, 71 Congress, Session 1, Micro-Film Reading Room, Reel 186, Page 5004.

Page 290; President Hoover, Chamber of Commerce speech, From the 71 Congress, Reel 186, May 1930, Pages 8639-8641. presented by Julius Klein.

Pages 294, 295, and 296; Recoil in Washington, the Senate, Resolution 144, From the Congressional Record, 71 Congress, Session 1, Micro-Film Reading Room, Jefferson Building, Reel 186, Page 5004, Also, Senators Robinson, Senator Harrison, Senator Barkley; debating the Stock Market Debacle, pages 5004 and 5005; Pages 5063-5068. The Smoot-Hawley Tariff bill; assistant secretary of commerce Julius Klein.

Page 296; John Kenneth Galbraith, "Tight Money" from "The Great Crash," Page 174

Pages 296 and 297; Washington Post article of October 26, 1929, presented by Senator Barkley.

Page 297; The Baltimore Sun of November 1, 1929; presented by Senator Tydings of Maryland, presented in the Senate.

Page 297; President Hoover and the Smoot-Hawley Tariff, from the Micro-Film Reading Room as above, the congressional record, 71 Congress, Reel 186, Pages 5004-5068.

Pages 297 and 298; Secretary Mellon's 1931 Annual Treasury Report, The Credit Thing, The Room of International Law, The Madison Building, Library of Congress.

Page 298; Senator Trammell presented an editorial—The Deland Florida News—Judge John W. Dodge. Credit is more important than money.

Pages 298 and 299; Wall Street Journal Article on "Confidence," Sept. 18, 1931.

Pages 299, 300 and 301; The 72 Congress, Session 1; The Foreign Debt, The Moratorium, From Volume 190, in the Micro-Film Reading room, Jefferson Building, Library of Congress, December 1931, Pages 535-540. Senators Shipstead, Johnson, Copeland and Reed in the Senate, December 15, 1931.

Pages 301 through 305; the 72 Congress, Session 1, Vol. 190, as above, pages 603-607. Senator Copeland presented in the Senate for the record, The Saturday Evening Post article of December 12, 1931. The gold raid.

Page 302; The New York Times; Hoover-Laval Conference. October 26, 1931. All newspaper articles, Newspaper Room, First Floor in the Madison Bldg, Library of Congress.

CHAPTER THIRTEEN Depression

Pages 306, 307, 308, 309; Hoover's message, from Vol. 199, 72 Congress, 2nd Session; Micro-Film Reading Room, the Jefferson Bldg. Vol. 196, 72 Congress, Session 1, May 10, 1932, Senator Glass, Page 9891. Hoovers second message to Congress, January 4, 1932, from Senate Document No. 32, Pages 1,2 and 3; the Madison Bldg. Room 201.

Page 308; Acts of Congress, From the Book of Statutes in the Room of International law, Room 201, the Madison Building, Library of Congress; and the Congressional Record, the 72nd and 73rd Congresses, the Micro-Film Reading Room, the Jefferson Building, Library of Congress.

Page 307; Government salaries—$1400 / Year, 72 Congress Session 1, Reel 200, Page 3440, February 6, 1933, presented by Senator Cutting

Page 309; Secretary of the Treasury Ogden Mills; From the 1932 Annual Treasury Report, Page 1, Room of International Law, The Madison Building.

Pages 309 and 310; Franklin Roosevelt, 1932; From the Complete Book of U.S. Presidents, World Book, The London Times, The Wall Street Journal, The New York Times, The Congressional Record, Library of Congress. etc.

Pages 310 and 311; Smoot-Hawley Tariff, Congressman McFadden and the Banker's Manifesto, and Democratic bill H.R. 6662. "payroll robbery." From the Congressional record, Micro-Film Reading Room, Jefferson Bldg; 72nd Congress, Session 1, Reel 194, Pages 1636-1639.

Pages 311 and 312; Congressmen Sparks and Horr, the Tariff and H.R. 6662, 72 Congress as above; Reel 194, Pages 1639-1642.

Pages 312, and 313; Congressman Cochran; Chairman Steagall and the Reconstruction Finance Corporation, From the Congressional Record Micro-Film Reading Room; 72 Congress, Session 1, Reel 194, Page 1734; 1734-1744, Congressman Lambreth, Reel 195, 72 Congress, Session 1, February 15, 1932, Pages 3991-3993. Doctor Commons and the Federal Reserve

Page 313; The New York Bankers Association, From the Wall Street Journal Article of June 18, 1929; covered previously.

Page 314; Resolution from the State of Wisconsin; Revision of the Federal Land Bank Act. From the Congressional Record; 72 Congress, Session 1, Reel 194; the Micro-Film Reading Room, Jefferson Bldg; January 11, 1932; Page 1648, by Senator Blaine.

Page 315; The Emergency Banking Bill; H.R. 9203, From the Congressional Record, the Micro-Film Reading Room, Jefferson Bldg. Reel. 195, The 72 Congress, Session 1, Pages 4215-4335. Also, from the Book of Statutes; in the Madison Building, Room 201, the Room of International Law.

Page 315, Congressman Laguardia of New York, from the above record; 72 Congress, Session1, January 11, 1932; Reel 194, Pages 1742-1744. The Emergency bill, HR 9203.

Pages 316 and 317; Congressman McFadden; From the Congressional Record; Micro-Film Reading Room, Reel 195, the 72 Congress, Session 1, Pages 3986-3987. Also, from the Impeachment Process, Reel 203, 73 Congress, Session 1, Pages 4055-4058.

Page 316; Adam Smith, as referenced previously.

Page 316; Congressman Lindbergh, as referenced previously

Page 317 and 318; Alexander Hamilton, From the Federalist Papers, No. 34.

Page 316; Eugene Meyer—objection to the Emergency Bill, from the Congressional Record, 72 Congress, Session 1, February 19, 1932, Page 4327; letters presented by Senator Walsh of Massachusetts.

Page 319; Ogden Mills, Secretary of the Treasury, 1932 Annual Treasury Report, Page 1; The Madison Building, Room of International Law, Library of Congress.

Page 320; H. Parker Willis, Senator Kean, Carter Glass, Reel 196, the Congressional Record, Micro-Film Reading Room; 72 Congress, Session 1, Pages 9996-9998. Senate Hearings, Telegram reports to France by Willis.

Pages 320 and 321; Carter Glass, Federal Reserve System defended, from the Senate debate, January 16, 1922; "The Truth About the Federal Reserve System." In the Library of Congress—Jefferson Bldg, Reading Room; Book File No. HG2565 .G6

Page 321; Senator King of Utah—11 billion in gold in the world; Micro-Film Reading Room, Jefferson Bldg., Micro-Film Reading Room, Reel 196, Pages 9996-9998.

Page 321 and 322; Adolph Hitler, The Japanese, Benito Mussolini; as part of the World record, World War II. World Book etc.

Page 322; The Moratorium, Crisis in Germany, June 1931, From the New York Times, Thursday, July 7, 1932.

Page 323; Herbert Hoover, Credits in Europe first, then the United States, From the Congressional Record, Reel 194, Vol. 74; January 4, 1932; 72 Congress, Session 1; presented in the House by Congressman Sirovich of New York.

Page 323; President Roosevelt elected, From the London Times of March 6, 1933.

Pages 323, 324 and 325; President Roosevelt—The New Deal; The Welfare State, Russia recognized, from the Complete Book of U.S. Presidents, The World Book. The "ultraconservative" From the Congressional Record, Micro-Film Reading Room, Reel 195, 72 Congress, Session 1, February 19, 1932, presented by Congressman Walsh, Page 4327.

Pages 325 and 326; The 1932 Annual Treasury Report, in the Madison Building, Library of Congress, Room 201, Room of International Law.

Pages 326, 327, 328 and 329; The Lausanne Conference in Switzerland; From the New York Times of July 7; the front page article stated "ACCORD AT LAUSANNE BALKED BY PROPOSAL ERASING WAR GUILT" Times articles ran through July 10, 1932.

Page 328; Unauthorized loans, presented by former Congressman Charles Scott of Kansas, entered into the record by Senator Capper, 72 Congress, Session 1, Reel 195, Jefferson Building, Library of Congress, Pages 4219-4221. The Young Plan by Morgan et al; from McFadden in the House, July 6, 1932; 72 Congress, Session 1, Reel 198, 14706; the Micro-Film Reading Room.

Page 328; The Economy Act, From the New York Times of July 7, 1932.

Page 329; Von Papen, The Reichstag elections, Hitlerism, Dr. Joseph Goebbels, From the New York Times, July 10, 1932. German Debts owed the United States, From the New York Times. Dr. Schacht, from The same Times edition, July 10, the "Bravo" telegram.

Page 330; The European war debts—More than11 billion dollars, From the New York Times of July 9, 1932.

Page 330, Senatorial commentary in the New York Times, July 9, 1932; Senator Rainey, Senator Norbeck

Page 330, Senator Barkley of Kentucky, indebtedness of the United States in 1932, 72 Congress, Session 2, Reel 200, Page 3502, February 6, 1933; Micro-Film Reading Room, Jefferson Bldg.

Pages 330 and 331; Congressman Patman—Velocity of Money; February 11, 1933; 72 Congress, Session 2, Page 3892; Reel 200; Micro-Film Reading Room, Jefferson Bldg.

Page 340, Carter Glass radio address, from the Congressional Record, the Micro-Film Reading Room, The Jefferson Building; Reel 202, 73 Congress, Session 1, Pages 2462-2467.

Pages 331, 332 and 333; Doctor Arthur Adams address on February 1, 1932; presented in the Congress by Senator Gore of Oklahoma, From the Congressional Record, Reel 195, Pages 4234-4235; 72 Congress, Session 1, Micro-Film Reading Room, Jefferson Bldg.

Page 333; Congressman McFadden—"worthless European paper," From Congressional record; 72 Congress, Session 1, July 6, 1932, Reel 198, Micro-Film Reading Room, etc.

Page 333; Congressman Laguardia of New York; From the Congressional Record, 72 Congress, Session 1, Reel 195, Page 3970, Micro-Film Reading Room, etc.

Pages, 334, 335, 336, 338, 339; Senator Thomas of Oklahoma; presentation of barter in the United States, 72 Congress, Session 2; Reel 199, January 13, 1933, From the Micro-Film Reading Room, etc. Page 1735; Also Senator Glass and Senator Long of Louisiana Mr. Hiscoe, economist, devaluation of the dollar.

Page 337, Wall Street Journal, March 1, 1933; Editorial—Bank Deposits

Page 340; Secretary Stimson and Carter Glass, From the Congressional Record, 72 Congress, Session 1, Micro-Film Reading Room, etc.

Pages 340 and 341; President Roosevelt, From the Book of Statutes in the Madison Building, Room of International Law; The Emergency Act of March 9, 1933 [HR 1491] Closing the Banks, calling in the Gold; 73 Congress, Session 1, Reel 202, Pages 1 through 7; also in the Micro-Film Reading Room, Jefferson Bldg

Page 341; The Wall Street Journal of March 6, 1933; the listing of Cities across the United States on Banking holiday

Page 342; The Wall Street Journal of March 7, 1933; Editorial agreeing with Roosevelt's action—Banking holiday, calling in the Gold, the Gold shipping embargo.

Pages 342, 343, 344 and 345; The Wall Street Journal Articles of March 7, through March 11, 1933; The hoarders of the Gold, Treasury payment from the Statute, 35% of deposit example, etc. The North Dakota State Legislature authorized Scrip. Hudson Motor Co. and General Motors—payrolls in cash. Number of Banks in 1929 versus 1933

Page 346; Congressman McFadden and Congressman Steagall, the 73 Congress, Session 1, from the Micro-Film Reading Room, Jefferson Bldg, Reel 202, Pages 78-81. The Federal Reserve Bank Notes.

Page 347; Congressman Rankin and Congressman Patman, the Finance Corporation and "sink hole" money; Micro-Film Reading Room; Reel 202, Pages 202 and 206

Pages 347 and 348; Congressman Steagall—The new Federal Reserve Bank Note and the Government Obligation; Micro-Film Reading Room; Reel 202, Page 79

Page 348; Congressman McFadden, Micro-Film Reading Room; Reel 202, Page 79; Audit the Treasury and the Federal Reserve System for the Gold.

Page 351; The Wall Street Journal—The new currency—Federal Reserve Obligations; Monday morning March 13, 1933.

Pages 349 and 350; Senator Huey Long, and the Banking execution; Micro-Film reading Room; Reel 202, Pages 186 to 190

Pages 350 and 351; The Wall Street Journal, from March 7 through March 11, 1933. State Banks, Governor Lehman of New York—Resolution to the President, salvaging the death knell of State Banks.

Page 351, Huey Long, Micro-Film Reading Room, Reel 202, Page 188. Secretary Woodin and the 1933 Annual Report, Madison Bldg; Room of International Law.

Pages 351 and 352; The Wall Street Journal of March 13, 1933; the circulation of the new currency; also, Roosevelt radio address, Secretary Woodin and currency circulation, also, the phase out of the currency, the 1% tax, etc.

Page 352; Franklin Roosevelt, the Congress and the $500,000,000 budget cut. The Wall Street Journal of March 14, 1933.

Page 353; Congressman Patman discussing J.P. Morgan, From the Congressional Record, Reel 202 in the Micro Film Reading Room; 73 Congress, Session 1, Pages 206 and 207.

Pages 353 and 354; Congressman Lundeen, Micro-Film Reading Room, 73 Congress, Session 1, Pages 207 and 208, March 11. The Panic Stricken Patrioteers, from the Washington Times of March 10, 1933, presented in the Congressional record

Page 356; Roosevelt's message to Congress, presented by Congressman Britten, Micro-Film Reading Room; the 73 Congress, Page 210, March 11.

Page 355; Congressman Busby, the Gold "farce." From the Congressional Record, Micro-Film Reading Room; Reel 202, 73 Congress, Session 1; Vol. 77, Page 4058.

Page 356; "Maintenance of Credit, etc." the name of the Bill, from page 198, Micro-Film Reading Room; the 73 Congress, at the start of legislation.

Page 357; The New York Times and the Budget cuts, reported on March 21, 1933.

Pages 357 and 358; The Wall Street Journal Editorial of March 14, 1933

Pages 358 and 359; Congressman Busby and the Bankers' coercion of the German shutdown of 1931; it was the same as the Banks closing in the United States, etc. From the Congressional Record, the Micro-Film Reading Room, Reel 202, 73 Congress, Session 1, Vol. 77; Page 291.

Pages 359 and 360; Congressman Patman, From the Congressional Record; Micro-Film Reading Room; Pages 291-292. Also Patman and Mellon from the Congressional Record; 73 Congress, Session 2; Page 7089;

Page 360; The New York Times reported Hitler as Dictator of Germany, March 21, 1933. Also, the reported beginning of the persecution, and internment of German Jews.

Pages 360 and 361; Hjalmar Schacht, from his "Confessions;" Chapters 39 and 40; Pages 275-286.

Page360; Cyrus Adler and Alfred Cohen, the New York Times of March 21, 1933

Pages 361 and 362; Japan quits the League of Nations, Japanese aggression in China, from the Wall Street Journal of March 13, 1933

Page 362; The Wall Street Journal of March 17, 1933—Armed Camps, Impending War in Europe.

Page 362; Roosevelt and Social Security, from World book, from the Complete Book of U.S. Presidents, Pages 498-500. Congressional Hearings; from the Wall Street Journal, June 12, 1933. Almost four billion dollars in appropriations; from the 1933 Annual Treasury Report, Room of International Law, Madison Bldg, Pages 25-35.

Page 362; Banks re-opening, from the Wall Street Journal of March 15, 1933.

Page 363; The 1933 Annual Treasury Report by Secretary Woodin; Emergency Banking; Room of International Law, Madison Bldg

Pages 363 and 364; The Wall Street Journal of June 9, 1933; London's Free Market in Gold etc.

Pages 363, 364 and 365; The 1933 Annual Treasury Report by Secretary of the Treasury Woodin, Room of International Law. Madison Bldg, Pages 28-35; The Banking, Act Recovery Act, The NRA, The CCC, The Farm Mortgage Act, etc. From the Book of Statutes, Room of International Law, The Madison Bldg. The 73 Congress, Session 1

CHAPTER FOURTEEN

Page 367; The "New Deal," also, "The Modern Welfare State." From "The Complete Book of U.S. Presidents;" Franklin Roosevelt, page 498.

Page 369; The Wall Street Journal of July 7, 1933; the meeting between President Roosevelt and Governor Black of the Federal Reserve Board

Page 370; "The Emergency Farm Mortgage Act of 1933" From the Book of Statutes in the Madison Building; 73 Congress, Session 1; May 12, 1933; Page 51.

Pages 371 through 376; The Gold Reserve Act of January 30, 1934; From the Public Papers of Franklin Roosevelt; Room of International Law, Madison Bldg. The Advance of Recovery and Reform; the Proclamation from the White House [No. 2072], Also from the Book of Statutes in the Madison Building; 73 Congress, Session II, January 30, 1934;

Page 375; The Joint Resolution of June 5, 1933; Changing the status of gold; from the Book of Statutes; in the Madison Bldg; 73 Congress Session 1; pages 112-113.

Page 370; Senator Byrnes of South Carolina; repayment of public funds, from Vol. 78, Reel 204; 73 Congress, Session 2; from the Micro-Film Reading Room, the Jefferson Building, Library of Congress. The lawful money Greenbacks, Page 69

Page 369; John Maynard Keynes; From World Book

Page 370; Secretary Woodin and his 1933 Annual Treasury Report; Room of International Law, Madison Building, Pages 25 and 26, the Greenbacks; 3 billion issued.

Page 371; Hjalmar Schacht; From his "Confessions," Page 281.

Page 372; The Wall Street Journal of July 7, 1933; The big profit for the U.S. Also more debt.

Page 373; The Wall Street Journal of June 12, 1933; It was the London and the world's free market; all the countries were shipping their gold there and buying dollars.

Page 374; All currencies legal tender, from Woodin's 1933 Treasury Report, Page 26 and also from the Book of Statutes, the currencies made legal tender by the Joint Resolution of June 5, 1933; Room of International Law, the Madison Building.

Page 375; Congressmen Busby and Goldsborough—Gold was the "farce," and gold as the nemesis of the world; From the Congressional Record, the Micro-Film Reading Room in the Jefferson Building; Reel 203, 73 Congress Session 1; Pages 4523 and 4536.

Page 374; Amendments to the Federal Reserve Act, from the Book of Statutes; 73 Congress Session II, Page 338. Lawful money reserve for deposits.

Pages 376 and 377; The Silver Purchase Act of May 1934; From the Congressional Record, the Micro-Film Reading Room in the Jefferson Building, Library of Congress; Reel No. 207, the 74 Congress, 1st Session; June 18, 1934, Pages 12407-12408.

Pages 377 and 378; The Wall Street Journal of July 7, 1933; Roosevelt's three phase agenda; Andrew Carnegie, Millionaires in America.

Page 379; The "Temple"—Congressman Hoeppel, 73 Congress, Session 2; from the Congressional Record, the Micro-Film Reading Room, Vol. 78, Reel 204.

Page 378; The Depression period, "Human Suffering" World Book.

Pages 378 and 379; The Wall Street Journal of June 17, 1933; The London Economic Conference. The eventual elimination of economic nationalism.

Page 379; The Wall Street Journal of March 1, 1934; France and its lost gold.

Pages 380 and 381; The Wall Street Journal of May 15, 1934; The "Rescue Party;" Hugh Knowlton of Kuhn-Loeb Banking.

Page 380; Senator Byrne of South Carolina, from the Congressional Record, Vol. 78, Reel 204; 73 Congress, Session 2; January 1934, page 69; the Micro-Film Reading Room, Jefferson Bldg., Library of Congress.

Pages 381 and 382; The Congressional Acts of 1934; from the Congressional Record, the Micro Film Reading Room; 73 Congress, Session 2, Pages 12404-12407.

Page 382 ; Roosevelt's 37 Government Agencies; From the Complete Book of U.S. Presidents

Page 381; The Reconstruction Finance Corporation—acquisition of bank stock and Government ownership thereof.; From the Wall Street Journal, June 11, 1934. Number of operating banks.

Pages 382 and 383; Money and Population figures from the Treasury Annual Report of 1934 by Henry Morgenthau Jr.; Room 201, Room of International Law, the Madison Building, Library of Congress.

Page 383; The Wall Street Journal of June 5, 1934; Gold shipments to the U.S.

Pages 384 and 385; Prime Minister Chamberlain and his non-payment note to the United States. From the New York Times, of June 6, 1934. Also, Editorials from Newspapers across the Nation. Germany liked the non-payment note.

Page 385; President Roosevelt and the Navy in New York harbor. from the New York Times of June 1, 1934.

Pages 385 and 386 ; The Securities Act of 1934; From the Book of Statutes in the Madison Building, Room 201, The Library of Congress; 1934, Volume 1, Pages 881-909.

Pages 386 and387; The Stock Measure signed by Roosevelt, and Judge Landis; From the Wall Street Journal of June 7, 1934. The Securities Act of 1934

Pages 387-388; Newspaper Editorials, the New York Times of June 7,1934.

Page 387; The big banks and their affiliates, The New York Times of June 7, 1934.

Pages 387 and 388; Seven billion dollar bid on Government Bonds; From the New York Times, June 7, 1934.

Page 387; Banks called before the Senate Banking and Currency Committee; Kuhn Loeb JP Morgan, From the New York Times, June 7, 1934. The Dust Bowl in the Midwest.

Pages 388 and 389; New paper circulation; From the New York Times of June 7, 1934. The Dust Bowl in the Midwest. Roosevelt committed 500 million dollars to aid the stricken areas.

Page 387; J.P. Morgan Income Taxes, From the Wall Street Journal, June 12, 1933.

Page 390; Conditions in France, The Wall Street Journal of June 6, 1934. The "Old Deal" was the gold.

Page 390; Schacht and devaluation, The Wall street Journal of June 11, 1934.

Pages 391 and 392;Fiat credit and Capital credit; From the Wall Street Journal of June 7, 1934. Bernard Kilgore article.

Pages 392 and 393; Roosevelt's message to the Congress about Housing and Social Security; From the Wall Street Journal of June 9, 1934. Also, the Housing Act from the Book of Presidents, Page 499.

Pages 392 and 393; The mortgage debt and foreclosures; from the Wall Street Journal of June 9,1934.

Page 393; The Emergency legislation remained in place during Roosevelt's terms in Office; from the Book of Statutes, The Madison Building, Room 201; 1933 into the 1940's.

Pages 393 and 394; Roosevelt's second election; from the Complete Book of U. S. Presidents Page 490.

Pages 394, 395, 396, 397 and 398; Senator Owen's letter to the Congress; 75 Congress, Session 3; Reel 227, Vol. 83 in the Micro-Film Reading Room, Jefferson Bldg. Presented by Congressman Cartwright of Oklahoma.

Page 395; Senator Owen in the Senate, May 18, 1920, from the Congressional Record, the Micro-Film Reading Room, the Jefferson Building, Library of Congress. the 66 Congress, Session 2, Page 7200.

Page 396; Congressman Lemke, from the Micro-Film Reading Room, as above; Reel 227, Vol. 83; 75 Congress, Session 3, the Appendix, page 41.

Pages 399 and 400; Chairman Eccles and the Federal Reserve; From the Micro-Film Reading Room, as above; 75 Congress, Session 3, Reel 227, Vol. 83, Pages 134-136.

Pages 400 and 401; Credit and Money, the contraction of money by the Federal Reserve System; by Governor Harding of Iowa. As part of the testimony before the Banking and Currency Committee by Dr. Commons, From the Congressional record, February 15, 1927; 69 Congress, Session 2; Reel 175, Page 3849.

Page 401; The Money stock; the 1939 Annual Treasury Report by Henry Morgenthau, Jr. The Library of Congress; The Madison Building, Room of International Law, Room 201. The Report pages 502 ,507

Pages 401and 402; Radio address by Harold Ickes in 1938, From the Congressional Record, the Micro-Film Reading Room; 75 Congress, Session 3, Reel 227, Vol. 83; Pages 115-117.

Page 402; Nicholas Biddle, Andrew Jackson, the Specie Circular, Van Buren, the Panic of 1837, etc. references covered earlier in the Bibliography.

Pages 402, 403 and 404; The Christian Science Monitor of November 20, 1937, Msgr. Ryan. Presented in the House by Congressman Herman Koppleman of Connecticut on January 12, 1938. 75 Congress, Session 3; Reel 227, Vol.83; Pages 151 to 153.

Pages 404 and 405; The American Gunboat Panay sunk by Japanese Aircraft, The Ludlow Referendum, From the New York Times articles of December 20 through 22, 1937.

Pages 404-405; January 9, 1938; The New York Times; 14 Church leaders for the Ludlow Resolution.

Pages 405 and 406; Jane's Fighting Ships, from the New York Times of December 21 1937.

Pages 406 and 407; taken from Hjalmar Schacht's "Confessions," It was Schacht's "Conversion Fund and the Mefo Bills, Chapter 41, pages 287-293.

Page 407; The unemployment census, from the New York Times, January 2, 1938.

Page 407; President Roosevelt's five-month relief plan, from the New York Times, January 6, 1938

Page 407; Congressman Alexander, from the congressional record Appendix, Page 128, 76 Congress, Session 1, Reel 233, Volume 84; Micro-Film Reading Room, Jefferson Bldg.

Page 407 and 408; January 3, 1938; Social Security, Unemployment insurance rolls, Federal Labor Relations, The Supreme Court, from the New York Times;

Page 408; The Spanish Civil War, From World Book

Page 409; Letter exchange between Senator Byrd and Chairman Eccles, From the Congressional Record, Micro-Film Reading Room, Reel 233, Vol. 84; Pages 132-136, 76 Congress, Session 1, 1939.

Page 410 and 411; Letter from Senator Owen to Eccles by way of Senator Logan; From the Congressional Record as above, Reel 233, Pages 226-227.

Page 412; Chairman Eccles, 75 Congress Session 3; Reel 227, Vol. 83; Pages 234-236

Pages 411 and 412; Congressman Dornan of California—The "Deficit Dilemma;" From the Congressional Record in the Jefferson Bldg, in Alcove 3; the 96 Congress, Page 23119 Page 269; Chairman Paul Volcker, From the Congressional Record, in Alcove 3. 96 Congress, Pages 33210 to 33212.

Page 414; Congressman Patman; from the Congressional Record, the Micro-Film Reading Room in the Jefferson Bldg. The Library of Congress; the 88 Congress Session 1 Reel 450, pages 21193-21195.

CHAPTER FIFTEEN   World War II—Bretton Woods Agreement Act

Page 415; Adolf Hitler, News Broadcast, from the New York Times, September 1, 1939, the beginning of World War II

Page 415; Non-Aggression Pact, Germany and the Soviet Union, Page 4 of the New York Times, September 1, 1939.

Page 415; Alliance between Japan, Germany and Japan

Pages 415 and 416; Japan attacks Pearl Harbor, December 7, 1941; from the New York Times, December 8, 1941. Documentation from World Book, World War II

Pages 416 and 417; World War II, facts and figures from World Book

Page 417; Henry Morgenthau to Ambassador Winant—Roosevelt message, April 1944, In the Madison Building, Vol. 2 of Foreign Relations of the United States, 1944 and 1945, Pages 107-111

Pages 418 ,419 and 420; Henry Morgenthau address, from the 79 Congress, First Session, in the Jefferson Bldg. Main Reading Room, Library of Congress, Volumes containing Appendix, Pages A1223 and 1224.

Pages 420 and 421; Congressman Chenoweth and Congressman Smith on Bretton Woods and Keynes from the 79 Congress, First Session, in Alcove E in the Jefferson Bldg. Main Reading Room, Library of Congress, Appendix, Pages A424-A427.

Pages 421 and 422; The Annual Treasury Reports of 1944 and 1945, facts and figures on gold and currency in The United States, also amendments to the Federal Reserve act. Pages 74 and 96, in the

Madison Bldg., Library of Congress, Room 201, Room of international Law.

Pages 422 and 423; Albert Hawkes in the Senate presented the address by professor Kemmerer on Bretton Woods; from Alcove E in the Jefferson Bldg. In the Appendix as Pages A520 to Page 523. 79 Congress Session 1

Page 423; The Dumbarton Oaks conference, 79 Congress, Session 1, Alcove E, Page A1203.

Pages 423 and 424; Congressman Outland and the Bank Strategy on Bretton Woods, from the 79 Congress, First Session, in the Jefferson Bldg., Main Reading Room, Alcove E, Volumes of the Appendix, Page A1112.

Page 424; Congressman Sundstrom, 79 Congress, Session 1, from the Appendix, Alcove E, Page A538

Page 424 and 425; Congressman Noah Mason, 79 Congress, Session 1, from the Appendix, Alcove E, Jefferson Bldg., Pages A732 and A733.

Page 425 and 426; Congressman Reed, 79 Congress, Session 1, from the Appendix, Alcove E Pages A842 and A843.

Page 426; Congressman Grant, 79 Congress, Session 1; from the Appendix, Alcove E, Pages A1140 and A1141.

Pages 426 and 427; Congressman De Lacy, 79 Congress, Session 1, from the Appendix, Alcove E, Pages A1167 and A1168.

Page 427; Article by Samuel Grafton presented in the Congress by Francis Myers of Pennsylvania; the date was March 12, 1945; 79 Congress, Session 1, from the Appendix, Alcove E Pages A1203 and A1204.

Pages 427, 428, 429 and 430; Letter by Charles Binderup, presented in the House by Congressman William Lemke of North Dakota; 79 Congress, Session1, from the Appendix, Alcove E , Pages A1433 and A1434

Pages 430, 431, 432, and 433; Report by the American Bankers Association, presented in the House by Congressman Daniel Reed of New York. 79 Congress, Session 1, from the Appendix, Alcove E, Pages A2183 to 2185.

Page 433; Henry Morgenthau before the House Banking Committee in March, 1945; The 79 Congress, Session 1; Alcove E.

Pages 433, 434 and 435; Article by Paul Wohl from C.W. Barrons Financial Weekly, presented in the House by Congressman Howard Buffett of Nebraska, the 79 Congress, Session 1; from the Appendix, Page A2673. All of the above, found in Alcove E in the Jefferson Building, Main Reading Room, Library of Congress.

Pages 435 and 436; Article by Henry Hazlitt, presented by Daniel Reed in the House; the 79 Congress, Session 1; in the Appendix, Page A1142. Alcove E Page 436; President Roosevelt died; World War II ended, from World Book

Pages 436, 437 and 438; The Banking and Currency Committee Hearings—June 12, 1945; Bretton Woods; From the Main Reading Room in the Jefferson Building in the round file adjacent to main desk, Volume 85, Secretary Henry Morgenthau—pages 6-19. Lend-lease figures from Page 569.

Pages 438, 439 and 440; The Committee Hearings as above, Dean Acheson, Senator Murdock, Senator Taft, the gold thing, Volume 85, Pages 19-23.

Pages 441 to 449; Committee Hearings , Gertrude Coogan, economist from Chicago; as above Volume 85, Pages 432-440, and Pages 570-574.

Page 449; The Hearings ended; Vol 85, as above; see Page 588, Main Reading Room in the Jefferson Building.

Page 449; The Senate passed H.R. 3314 on July 19, 1945; See Vol 91, 79 Congress, Session 1, Page 7780. Micro Film Reading, Jefferson

Building, Library of Congress. Bretton Woods became law on July 31, 1945.

Pages 449, 450, 451 and 452; Senator Taft debates in the Senate, as above, Vol 91, 79 Congress, Session 1, Micro-Film Reading Room; pages 7563, 7564, 7566, 7567.

Pages 452 and 453; Chairman Wagner, as above; Vol 91, 79 Congress, Session 1, Pages 7558 and 7559. Micro-Film Reading Room

Pages 453 and 454; Gertrude Coogan and approved House bill H.R.3314; Section 8 [c]; from the bill as printed; See Vol 85, the Committee Hearings in the Main Reading Room; Jefferson Building, Pages 1-5, The Bretton Woods Act. Also, Section 6 removed.

Page 454; The Bretton Woods Act; from the Book of Statutes in the Madison Building, Room 201; 1945, Volume 1, Pages 512-517. The Articles of Agreement, International Agreements other than Treaties, Pages 1401 to 1480.

Pages 454 and 455; "Review and Outlook, From the Wall Street Journal, July 20, 1945. Also, Article about the New York Federal Reserve and European restrictions, August 1, 1945. C.W. Barron paper as covered previously.

Page 455; Editorial of the New York Times, July 20, 1945—Bretton Woods, Great Britain agreements.

Page 455, 456; The Anglo American Agreement, Attlee, Churchill, British socialism, from the Congressional record, the Micro-Film Reading Room in the Jefferson Building; 79 Congress, Session 1, Vol. 91; Pages 12152-12156.

Page 456; Congressman Celler of New York; the British loan, as above, the Congressional record, 79 Congress, Session 1; Vol 91; pages 11927-11928. The Micro-Film Reading Room

Page 456; Senator Brooks: The British loan, the Congressional record, 79 Congress, Session 1; Vol. 91, pages 12151-12156.

Page 456: The British Loan Agreement—From Secretary Snyder's 1947 Annual Treasury Report, Pages 51 and 52. Room of International Law, Madison Bldg,

Page 457; UNRRA—Senator Taft, as above, the Congressional record, Vol 91, page 12157; Also, Secretary Snyder, 1947 Annual Treasury Report, Pages 47-52; Room of International Law, Madison Bldg.

Page 457; The United Nations Charter, 1945, from World Book

Page 457; India critical of the UN. Charter, from the Chicago Tribune, July 16, 1945.

Pages 458, 459, 460; Secretary Snyder, from the 1947 Annual Treasury Report the International Monetary Fund and the Bank. The Fund and the Bank, started in 1947, Pages 47-52; The Advisory Council to Bretton Woods, The Export-Import Bank. Lend Lease and wartime obligations. Also, investments by the member banks in U.S. securities, same report, Pages 181 and 182. Also, the National Advisory Council, from Page 188. The 1948 Annual Treasury Report, page 45, stated that securities owned by the International Bank were sold in the capital market. Room of International Law, Madison Bldg.

Page 460: Member Banks bought International Bank securities, from the 1949 Annual Treasury Report, Page 97. Room of International Law, Madison Bldg.

Page 461; Russia was out of the Monetary Fund, from the California Mining Journal, March 1947; This article was presented in the Congressional record by Frederick C. Smith of Ohio, Congressional Record, Room of International Law; 80 Congress, Session 1; Madison Bldg.

Page 462; The 1948 Annual Treasury Report; Economic Assistance Program, and looted gold by Germany. United States and Russia took German scientists and technology; Pages 41 and 47. Room of International Law, Madison Bldg.

Page 462; Washington's farewell address, etc. from the Congressional Record, the Micro—Film Reading Room in the Jefferson Building, Library of Congress.

Page 463; The change in currency exchange rates in 1949, according to the 1950 Annual Treasury Report, page 47. Room of International law, Madison Bldg.

Page 463; International Bank lending, and total Treasury grants and loans, from the 1950 Annual Treasury Report, Page 48, pages 329 to 333. Room of International law, Madison Bldg.

Page 464; The Berlin airlift; occupied East and West Berlin; From the 1952 Annual Treasury Report by Secretary John Snyder, Pages 1-15; Pages 366-367

Pages 464 and 465; Secretary Snyder's 1952 Annual Treasury Report; the operations of the Bank for Reconstruction and Development. Room of International Law, Madison Bldg.

CHAPTER SIXTEEN *Bretton Woods Altered*

Page 467; President Nixon ends International monetary gold; Headlines of the New York Times and the Wall Street Journal; August 16, 1971.

Page 467; American aid—$18 billion dollars to Europe, from the 1947 Treasury Report by Secretary John Snyder, Page 42. Room of International Law, Madison Bldg.

Page 468; Gold reduction in the United States, From the 1972 Treasury Report by George P. Schultz. Page 244. Room of International Law, Madison Bldg.

Page 468; Gold to $38 per ounce, the 1972 Treasury Report, Page XXVI; Room of International Law, Madison Bldg.

Pages 468 to 472; From documented History of the United States from 1952 to 1972.

Page 472 and 473; The Recession of 1959-1960; Interest rates, tight money, etc., from the Micro-Film Reading Room, Reel 392, Page 6450; Senator Proxmire presented "Tight Money" by Silvia Porter. Also, Eisenhower and the 4 1/2 % interest rate ceiling; Reel 397, page 18885, and page 19982; Senator Byrd of Virginia; 86 Congress, Session 1. President Truman and Chairman Eccles. Jefferson Bldg, Library of Congress.

Page 473; 4.5 billion dollars to the IMF and the Bank, Micro-Film Reading Room; Reel 395, page 13766 by Senator Proxmire; 86 Congress, Session 1, Library of Congress.

Page 474; John Kennedy and deficit spending, From the Congressional Record, the 88 Congress, Session 1, the Micro Film Reading Room, Jefferson Building, Library of Congress, Volume 109, Reel 444, March 4, 1963, Pages 3394-3405.

Page 474; Henry Hazlitt—Gold and currency distribution, from Newsweek magazine, presented in the Congress. Vol 109, Reel 444; 88 Congress, Session 1; Micro-Film Reading Room, Jefferson Bldg.

Pages 475, and 476; Congressman Moorehead presented the study of the Euro-Dollar, as recorded by the Economist. From the Congressional Record, the Micro Film Reading Room, the 88 Congress, Session 1, The Appendix, Pages 5362-5363.

Page 472; The Wall Street Journal of September 1959, and the Congressional Record in the Micro-Film Reading Room, 86 Congress, Session 1, Vol 105, Reel 397, Pages 18884-18886. Article by Vermont Royster.

Pages 477 and 478; Congressman Patman of Texas-From the Micro-Film Room, the Congressional Record, Vol 113, Reel 502, Page 5419; Statement by Chairman Martin of the Fed. 90 th Congress Session 1; and the Washington Post editorial, Page 455.

Page 477; Secretary Snyder and the 1952 Annual Treasury Report, Page 2; Room of International Law, Madison Bldg.

Pages 476, 477, 478, 479; Congressman Patman, Federal Reserve interest rates, and John Kenneth Galbraith; from the Congressional Record, Micro-Film Reading Room, Jefferson Bldg; Reel 501, Vol 113, Pages 427-429. 90 th Congress Session 1

Page 480; Congressman Patman, comparing the Fed with the Politburo, Micro-Film Reading Room, Jefferson Bldg; Vol. 113, Reel 502, Page 5425; 90 Congress Session 1.

Page 480; FOMC minutes; new law regarding publication; from Serial Set collection, 13300; Room 201, Room of International Law, the Madison Building. The 96 Congress; Report No. 96-421, Pages 1 through 5.

Pages 481 and 482 Congressman Patman, Micro-Film Reading Room the Congressional Record, 45 billion dollars in securities should be removed from the public debt; Vol 113, Reel 510, Pages 27953-27963; 90th Congress, Session 1.

Page 483; House Resolution 1113, to extend the Amendment to Section 14 [b] of the Federal Reserve Act. Micro-Film Reading Room, Jefferson Bldg; Vol 114, Reel 521; Pages 8058-8062.

Page 483; Carter Glass and Treasury securities; the Federal Reserve Bank of New York; 72nd Congress, Session 1, Reel 196, in the Micro-Film reading Room in the Jefferson Bldg. Page 9885.

Page 484; Federal Reserve Act amended in 1942; buying securities direct from the Treasury; Section 14[b] was amended. The Book of Statutes [Vol 1, 1942], in Room 201. Room of International Law, The Madison Bldg.

Pages 483 and 484; Patman and the Federal Reserve Bank of New York—Investments on Wall Street; The purchase of Municipal bonds; currency to Europe, From the Congressional record, the Micro-Film Room, Jefferson Bldg; Reel 510, Vol. 113, Page 27954.

Page 484; Currency can't be retired; Patman; from the Congressional record, Micro-Film Room, Jefferson Bldg; Reel 510,Vol 113, October 5, 1967; Page 27963. The Bonds of 1884, gold and the currency, recorded prior.

Pages 485 and 486; The 1970 Report by Secretary Kennedy, Economic conditions, in the Madison Building, Room 201; Room of International Law, Pages XV to XXII; The Special Drawing Rights Act became law in 1970. Also on Pages 238 and 239, Currencies in circulation, Table 55.

Pages 486-495; Special Drawing Rights; From the Congressional Record, the Micro-Film Room, Reel 522, Vol 114; Pages 11551-11552; and Pages 12717-12737. Senator Fulbright introduced the bill in the Senate, Page 11551; President Johnson—Page 12722; Congressman Berry, Page 12717 and 12718; Mr. Patman, Page 12722-12738 The Statute—SDR and gold certificates, the Exchange Stabilization Fund, the Act as presented by Fulbright; Congressman Brock , Mr. McClory, Mr. Widnall, Pages 12725-12731; The Rio Conference—Vol 113, reel 510, Page 28243. $31 billion dollars in Europe, Page 12725—Mr. Conable; Mr. Reuss, Mr. Gross, Mr. Kyl, and others. Voting on the bill, Pages 12737-12738. Micro-Film Reading Room, Jefferson Bldg.

Pages 495 and 496; Secretary Schultz and the 1972 Treasury Report—Gold at $38 dollars an ounce, listed before. Room of International Law, Madison Bldg.

Page 495: U.S. trade imbalance and "drawing" purchases; From the 1972 Annual Treasury Report, pages 57 and 58; in the Madison Bldg, Room 201, Room of International Law, Madison Bldg.

Page 496; Federal Banking Agency Act, in 1978; From the 1978 Book of Statutes, Vol 1, Pages 1051-1053, Room 201, Room of International Law, The Madison Building; Auditing of the Federal Reserve Banks.

Page 497, 498 and 499; Congressman Binderup and the Credit Stabilization Fund; the purchase of gold by Morgenthau, "Financial gimmickry" by McChesney Martin; Reel 522, Volume 114, Page 12718 in the Jefferson Building, Micro-Film Reading Room.

The Special Drawing Rights Act; See Public law 95-435, Page 1051 in the Book of Statutes, for the year 1978; 95 Congress; The Madison Building, Room of International law, Room 201, The Library of Congress.

CHAPTER SEVENTEEN

Page 500; 1973-1979; the "Oil Embargo," King Faisal of Saudi Arabia, the Israel / Egypt confrontation, from World Book.

Page 500; the 1974-75 Depression, from the 1975 Annual Treasury Report Introduction, Page XXI. Room of International Law, Madison Bldg.

Page 500; The Oil Embargo and the IMF, from the 1975 Annual Treasury Report, Pages XXXIV and XXXV. Room of International Law, Madison Bldg.

Page 501; More Treasury money for the IMF, from the 1975 Annual Treasury Report, Pages XXXIV and XXXV. Room of International Law, Madison Bldg.

Pages 500, 501 and 502; The 1975 Annual Treasury Report, Pages 270-271, In the Madison Building, Room 201, Room of International Law.

Page 502; The Camp David Peace Accords, Sadat and Faisal Assassinations, Iran and the Shah, the Ayatollah Khomeini, the hostage crisis, the Iran/Iraq war; from World Book and the Complete Book of U.S. Presidents.

Page 502; the debt limit at 798 billion dollars, from the Serial Set in Room 201 in the Madison Bldg. Report No. 96-2, The House of Representatives, the Temporary Public Debt Limit, Accompanying HR 1894. Room of International Law, Madison Bldg.

Pages 502, 503 and 504; Reagan's debt limit. See Public Laws 97-270; 98-161; 98-475; and 99-177; 1982 to 1985; the limit was raised to 2.1 Trillion dollars; from the Books of Statutes, for the years 1982 to 1985; in the Madison Building, Room 201, The Library of Congress. President Reagan's address, from the Congressional Record, the 97 Congress

Session 1, Vol 127, Part 17, Page 2015.—Alcove 3 in the Jefferson Bldg. Events during the Reagan Presidency "tear down this wall" etc.; National Television. Hermit Kohl, from the Newspapers.

Page 503; Congressman Dornan, September 9, 1985, in the House, 99 Congress, Session 1, Page 23119 in the Congressional Record.—Alcove 3 in the Jefferson Bldg.

Page 504; Senator Proxmire and the private debt; November 22, 1985; Page 33210; 98 Congress, the Congressional Record, in Alcove 3, the Jefferson Building

Page 503; The Federal Finance Bank started in 1973, from the 1975 Treasury Report, Page 27.

Page 503; The Soviet "Evil Empire, " as voiced by Ronald Reagan via Television.

Page 504; The United States a debtor nation again; Japanese own 35% of the Treasury; September 16, 1985; From the Congressional Record, Chairman Gonzales, page 5458, Vol 140, Part 1; 103 Congress, Session 2, Room 201 in the Madison Bldg.

Pages 504 and 505; "Tear down this Wall." Ronald Reagan in Berlin, 1988. George Bush, Premier Gorbachev, and Boris Yeltsin, agreements ending the cold war, The Complete Book of U.S. Presidents, pages 692-696.

Pages 505 and 506; Congressman LaFalce of New York, 1990, from the Congressional records in the Madison Building, Room 201; Vol 136, Part 7; 101 Congress, Session 2, Page 9432.

Page 505; Senator Roth of Delaware; From the Congressional records in the Madison Bldg., Room 201, Vol 135, Part 21; 101 Congress, Session 1, 1989, Page 28382.

Page 506; The S and L collapse and bailout, from the Congressional Record, Vol. 136, Part 22; 101 Congress, Session 2, pages 25186-25187; Congressman Bruce Vento of Minnesota. Also, from the Wall Street

Journal, presented by Senator Dixon, June 22, 1990, from the Congressional Record, Vol 136, Part 11; 101 Congress, Session 2, in the Madison Bldg, Room 201, pages 15900-15901. Economist James Smith—University of North Carolina Business school, in the Congressional Record.

Page 506; The Continental / Illinois Bank collapse, From the Congressional Record, in the Madison Bldg, Room 201; Vol 140, Part 7; 103 Congress, Session 1; Page 10344, Chairman Gonzales.

Page 506; George Bush and no new taxes, from the Complete Book of U.S. Presidents, Page 689.

Page 507; Operation Desert Shield, the Gulf War, the Complete Book of U.S. Presidents, Pages 694, 695. The New World Order; George Bush

Page 507; Secretary Brady and the IMF, from the Congressional Records in the Madison Bldg; Room 201, Vol 137, Part 6, page 8090; and Vol 137, Part 14, page 18947; Also from the "Government Financial Highlights", 1992, page 23; and 1994, page 23. Source Information [The Adams Building] obtained in the Newspaper Room, Madison Bldg.

Pages 507 and 508; Average IMF loans, 1980-1991, from the Congressional record, Vol 137, Part 20, 102 Congress, Session 1, Page 29148; in the Madison Bldg. Room 201.

Pages 508 and 509; The Freedom Support Act; From the Congressional Record in the Madison Bldg, Room 201; Vol 138, Part 12; 102 Congress, Session 2; Pages 17434-17436. [The Commonwealth of Independent States.]

Page 509; Special Drawing Rights; From the 1992-1994 Government Financial Highlights, shown on the Balance Sheets, Page 23; in the Adams Bldg., Fifth Floor.

Page 509; Average loans to the IMF, from 1980-1991; From the Congressional Record in the Madison Bldg., Room 201; Vol 137, Part 20, Session 1; Page 12948.

Pages 509, 510 and 511; Chairman Gonzales and bill H.R. 28; the Federal Reserve Accountability Act.; From the Congressional Record, in The Madison Bldg., Room 201; Vol 140, Part 4, 103 Congress, Session 2 Pages 5457-5462; Vol 140, Part 5, 103 Congress, Session 2; Vol 140, Part 7, 103 Congress, Session 2, Pages 10341-10348.

Page 510; Alan Greenspan before the House Banking Committee on October 19, 1993; Page 84; From House Banking Committee meeting records in the Madison Bldg. Room 201, Library of Congress.

Page 511; Chairman Gonzales and derivatives; from the Congressional Records, in the Madison Bldg., Room 201; Volume 140, Part 5; March 24, 1994; 103 Congress, Session2; Page 6693. Also, discussion of Hedge Funds.

Page 511; Market Derivatives, From the Internet, Wikipedia source, June 2004, Page 1 of 2.

Page 512; The 2007 Sub-prime losses, from the Newspapers, the Wall Street Journal; bank trillions in assets, and losses of 10 billion, from the Newspapers; 131 billion in equivalent dollars in loans from the ECB to faltering banks, from the Wall Street Journal of November 6, 2007.

Pages 512 and 513; George Bush and the new world order, from the Complete Book of U.S. Presidents and The World Book. GDP listings of all the countries, from the Economist "Pocket World in Figures," 2006 Edition.

Page 512; Congressman Kasich and Congressman Obey, The World Bank, from the Congressional Record, Vol 139, Part 9; 103 Congress, Session 1; Pages 13157 and 13158; in the Madison Bldg.

Page 513 and 154; 1985, foreign money in the United States; From the Congressional Record, Vol 140, part 4; 103 Congress, Session 2, page 5459; in the Madison Bldg. Room 201. Congressman Gonzales.

Page 514; Foreign Banks in the United States, in New York's Federal Reserve district; From the Congressional Record; In the Madison Bldg., Room 201; 103 Congress, Session 1; Page 111.

Page 514; The World Economic Conference of 1933, listed previously, The Wall Street Journal, June 17, 1933.

CHAPTER EIGHTEEN Prophecy

Page 515; Alexander Hamilton from the Federalists Papers No. 34.

Page 516; The national debt, from the 2006 Government Financial Report, approaching 9 trillion dollars, and projected to 10 trillion by January, 2009. GDP of 14 trillion projected from a 12. 5 trillion product [the internet] in 2005. 2.1 trillion GDP shown previously, page 43 in the bibliography. One trillion circulation, estimated from 14 trillion GDP. GDP is now at least 15 trillion dollars, from the latest information—President George Bush, when he signed the stimulus package.

Page 517; Household wealth now 58 trillion dollars—Federal Reserve figures, found on the internet.

Page 516; American GDP is 2.5 times it's nearest competitor, from "The World in Figures" by the Economist.

Page 519; George Washington address; From the Congressional Record, the First Congress in 1791, the First Congress in th Micro-Film Reading Room, Jefferson Bldg; Hamilton's first bank, 10 million in gold to Europe from the Congressional Record, Congressman Love, the 11 Congress, Session 1, in 1810, Page 6; Micro-Film Reading Room, Jefferson Bldg.

Page 518; George Bush and the tax cuts, the Complete Book of U.S. Presidents, page 689. Clinton's reduction of the deficit spending from the 1995-1997 Government Consolidated Financial Reports. Source information, the Web Site, from the Newspaper Reading Room, Madison Bldg.

Pages 517, 518 and 519; 1980 to the present, 2008; deficit spending, GDP, increase in the debt, Total Federal debt projected to ten trillion, from the Congressional Reports, Newspapers, etc. Figures from the Wall Street Journal of October 2007; percentages of income in the United States.

Page 519; Oil at 142 dollars a barrel, from the Newspapers, the first week in January, 2008. The Baltimore Sun, The Wall Street Journal. The NYMEX, from the Wall Street Journal.

Pages 519 and 520; President Clinton and the reduction of the deficit and the debt from the Government Consolidated Financial Report Web Site: 1995-1997.

Page 520; The Mexican bailout and currency crisis as discussed by Chairman Gonzales in the House; from the Congressional Records in the Madison Bldg, Room 201; Volume 140, Part 7; 103 Congress, Session 2. Stabilization Fund; stated in the Wall Street Journal of Nov. 5, 2007.

Pages 519 and 520; President Clinton and the Mexican bailout; from the Congressional Record in the Madison Bldg. Room 201; Volume 141, Part 7; 104 Congress, Session 1; Pages 9849-9851

Page 521; Clinton reduction of the deficit; The gold statutory price 42.22 dollars an ounce, the market price etc. From the 1997 Government Consolidate Financial Report Web Site.

Page 521; IMF gold "hoard," from the Internet Wikipedia Encyclopedia.

Pages 521 and 522; America third in the World in mined gold, from the Economist "World in Figures." 2006.

Page 522; Alan Greenspan reprint from WSJ December 12, 2007, all rights reserved. Also Sub-prime problem, Global forces, Central Banks and their economies.

Page 524; The sub-prime debacle, Hedge Funds, from the Newspapers, the Wall Street Journal, The New York Times.

Page 524; Will Rogers and Wall Street as presented by Congressman Foley in the House, March 1, 1995; From the Congressional Record in Room 201 in the Madison Bldg. Volume 141, Part 5; 104 Congress, Session 1.

Page 525; President Mahathir Bin Mohamad of Malaysia and the Speculator, from the Wall Street Journal, September 23, 1997.

Page 525; The Economist, referenced previously, from the Congressional record.

Pages 525 and 526; Y2K, the Dow Jones collapse, from World Book.

Page 526; 911 and the Terrorist attack on the World Trade Center in New York, from the Newspapers, television, etc.

Page 526 and 527; President Bush and the tax cuts, the war in Iraq, the "lean army;" from the television, the Newspapers; 180 thousand contractors in Iraq from the Wall Street Journal; the Greenspan interview, from the television.

Page 527; John Kenneth Galbraith, "Keynes could be had by tax cuts." From the Congressional Record, the 90 Congress, Session 1; Vol 113, Reel 501, in the Micro-Film Reading Room, Page 427, January 12, 1967.

CHAPTER NINETEEN

Page 528; The 2008 Election year, the Wall Street write off, President Bush and the Stimulus package of 152 billion dollars; the deficit projection of 400 billion dollars—all from the latest reports in the Newspapers, Television.

Page 529; New Credit Rules, The Wall Street Journal, March 13, 2008.

Page 530; Wall Street Journal of May 21, 2008; FHA and 300 billion dollar housing bill; Fannie May and Freddie Mack overhaul.

Page 531; Super Highway through Texas, February, 2008, from CNN Television news

Pages 532 and 533; The credit circulation, from 1980 Treasury Combined Statement, and 2007 Federal Reserve on line figures—increase in circulation—500 %; Increase in money and GDP much greater than population increase.

Pages 533 and 534; Government Agencies, See Chapters 13 and 14. See Chapter 15, The Bretton Woods Agreement; Gertrude Coogan, etc.

Pages 535 and 536; A review of the IMF and World Bank schemes, Gertrude Coogan and the Statute, etc. covered previously,

Page 538; The Wall Street Journal article about "Global Ties," April 28, 2008

Page 539; The Wall Street Journal article about Central Banks of undeveloped countries.

CHAPTER TWENTY

Page 542: Alexander Hamilton's statement from his 1791 Bank Report. The Manuscript Reading Room in the Madison Building.

Page 543; European interest rates, France and England, taken from C. W. Barons writings, "The Federal Reserve Act," 1914. Boston News Bureau Company

Page 550 and 551; Fannie May and Freddie Mac—the bailout as covered in the Wall Street Journal, July 14, 2008, from Television coverage and local Newspapers.

Page 546: The gold in the Federal Reserve Bank of New York—160 billion dollars; from the Internet; Wikipedia, the free Encyclopedia.

Page 551 and 552; The 2007 Financial Report of the United States Treasury—2080 Public debt will be 600% of GDP.

Page 550: The Wall Street Journal, July 14, July 24, and July 27, 2008; the bailout and the Housing bill; Fannie / Freddie mortgage assistance. The debt limit raised to 10. 6 trillion dollars.

Page 553; From the Wall Street Journal of July 30, 2008; Geneva Trade Talks.

Page 551; Auction rate securities, from the Wall Street Journal, August 22, 2008.

Pages 555 and 556; From the Internet, The bailout and the credit circulation, the money supply in the U.S.?

Page 557: From the Wall Street Journal; "Warrants" to the Treasury for money by GMAC. December 30, 2008.

Page 556; More monies to the IMF, the October G-20 meeting in London.

Page 561; The "Phantom" economy from the internet; The "Sovereign Society;" cash behind notional amounts is 1 % or less. Notional amounts in the hundreds of trillions of dollars.

Pages 555, 556, 557 and 558; September 18 to November 22, 2008—The Wall Street crash and 700 billion dollar bailout , from the Wall Street Journal and Television Networks. Secretary Paulson, 290 billion dollars now; 410 billion dollars later—the Obama Administration. Chairman Bernanke and 540 billion dollars to the Mutual Fund Industry; Total monies approaching four trillion dollars and counting. The Wall Street Journal of November 18, November 25, October 22, 2008.

Page 561; The Wall Street Journal of November 26, 2008; 800 billion more dollars, more lending, investing by the Federal Reserve System.

Page 564: Proposed 825-900 billion dollar stimulus package—Obama administration from Television, the Newspapers.

SUMMARY

Pages 569-576; summary and conclusion.

IMPORTANT SOURCES

The following sources were most important in correlating and authenticating the history.

- "Financial History of the United States" by Davis Rich Dewey; first published in 1903, reprinted in 1934 by Longmans Green & Company; reprinted in 1968 by Augustus M. Kelly, New York. The work was Researched at the Library of Congress.

- The Wall Street Journal, New York. Researched at the Library of Congress; home delivery. WSJ reprints all rights reserved.

- The New York Times, New York. Researched at the Library of Congress; home delivery. New York Times reprints, all rights reserved.

- "The Great Crash" 1929 by John Kenneth Galbraith, The Riverside Press Cambridge, Houghton Mifflin Company, 1954, 1955. Researched at the Library of Congress. Houghton Mifflin reprints, all rights reserved.

- Confessions of "The Old Wizard" by Hjalmar Schacht; Houghton Mifflin, Cambridge, 1956. Researched at the Library of Congress. Houghton Mifflin reprints, all rights reserved.

- C.W. Baron "The Federal Reserve Act" 1914; Boston News Bureau Company. Researched at the Library of Congress.

INDEX

Meade, George, 111
Mefo Bills, 406–7, 623
Mellon, Andrew, 239–40, 242, 244,
    246–51, 253, 268, 271–73,
    287, 289–90, 293–94, 297–98,
    318, 322, 353, 359, 484
Mexico, 102–3, 168, 187, 200–201,
    204, 510, 520, 523
Meyer, Eugene, 316, 320, 611
Middle East, 433–34, 462, 468, 500,
    502, 507, 513–14, 516, 519,
    525, 529, 538, 546–47, 575
Milken, Michael, 529
Mills, Ogden, 305, 309, 353
Minot, Robert S., 170
Mississippi Scheme, 61, 63, 197
Mitchell, John, 471
Mohamad, Mahathir Bin, 525
money
    interests, 55, 72, 90, 102, 107–8,
        118, 126–28, 137–38, 145,
        153–54, 174–75, 312, 356,
        436, 516–18, 536–37
    supply, 21, 102, 107–8, 131,
        138, 142, 148, 153–54, 225,
        298–99, 378, 394, 396, 400,
        404, 414
Monroe, James, 91, 102, 156
Monroe Doctrine, 91, 168, 201
Montesquieu (Charles-Louis de
    Secondat), 75, 564, 583
Moorehead, William S., 475–76,
    525
Morgan (congressman), 185
Morgan, D. N., 150
Morgan, J. P., 166, 227, 233, 255,
    280, 282, 292, 310, 322–23,
    327, 347, 353, 362, 379, 387,
    534

Morgenthau, Henry, Jr., 349, 383,
    388, 397, 406, 417–20, 425,
    428–29, 433, 437–38, 440,
    498, 535, 545, 632
Morrill (congressman), 28–30, 41,
    63, 580, 582
Morris, Gouverneur, 23, 125
Morris, Robert, 24, 86, 99, 579
Murdock (senator), 439–40
Mussolini, Benito, 322, 611
Myers, Francis, 427, 625

N

Napoleon. *See* Bonaparte,
    Napoleon
National Advisory Council on
    International and Monetary
    Financial Problems, 460
National Bank Note, 63, 151, 159,
    271
National City Bank, 176–77, 223,
    227, 387, 430, 600
National Financial Weekly, 433
nationalism, 199–200, 379, 514,
    517, 538–39, 541, 545, 564,
    575
National Labor Relations Board, 382
Nelson (congressman), 230, 255
New Deal, 277, 325, 367–69, 426,
    461
Newell, V. F., 219–20
Newsweek, 474
new world order, 238, 323, 517,
    523, 532, 541, 546, 552, 563–
    64, 566, 571
New York Bankers Association,
    291–92, 299, 313, 318, 480,
    610

New York City, 36, 39, 79, 111,
172–73, 179, 226, 290, 293,
362, 385, 408, 526
New York Herald Tribune, 433
New York Stock Exchange, 172,
176, 272, 386, 511
New York Times, 170, 275, 279, 285,
329–30, 360, 384–88, 405,
407–8, 454–55, 609–10, 612–
13, 616, 620, 622–24, 642
Nicholas II (king), 210
Nixon, Richard, 467–68, 471, 475,
478, 485, 495, 499, 521,
545–46
Norbeck (senator), 330
Norman, Montague, 243–45, 279,
281–82, 287, 313, 322, 355–
56, 379, 418
North American Union, 523
NRA (National Recovery
Administration), 364
Nye (senator), 265, 293

O

Obama, Barack, 557, 559
Obey (congressman), 512
oil embargo, 500–501, 546
Operation Desert Shield, 507,
635
Operation Desert Storm, 507
Outland, George, 423–24
outsourcing, 200, 235, 513, 517,
537, 540–41
Owen, Robert, 169, 174, 182,
190–91, 225, 261, 333, 367,
394–95, 397–98, 410, 543

P

Panic of 1907, 140, 163, 169, 173–
75, 177, 179, 191, 220, 260
Patman, Wright, 330–31, 347, 353,
359, 396, 414, 427, 477–84,
493, 510, 534, 616, 631–32
Paulson, Henry, 555
Peace Dollars, 270, 346
Pendleton, George, 23–24, 28,
30–31, 114–15, 579, 587
Perry, Matthew, 405
Pershing, John Joseph, 201
Philadelphia Record, 427
Philippines, 165, 167, 416, 595
Pike (from Maine), 39, 580
Platt (congressman), 183–85, 223,
229, 597
Plumb (senator), 160
Pocket World in Figures, 522
Polk (senator), 14
Polk, James K., 103
Porter, Sylvia, 473
Potter, O. B., 18
pound sterling, 228–29, 244, 247–
48, 252, 280, 285, 304, 339,
379, 420, 423, 463, 558, 575
Powell (senator), 14, 78
Presley, Elvis, 469
Prohibition, 220, 240, 273, 319, 365
Proudhon, Joseph, 136, 144
　Solution of the Social Problem, 136
Proxmire (senator), 473, 490, 504
Pullman Strike, 147

Q

Quayle, Dan, 507

R

Rainey (congressman), 330
Randolph, Edmund Jennings, 23, 26, 515
Rankin (congressman), 347, 427
Rarick (congressman), 494
Raskob, John J., 294–96
Rayburn (chairman of the House Interstate Commerce Commission), 386
Reagan (senator), 160
Reagan, Ronald, 411, 478, 502–4, 506, 516, 532, 552, 565
Redfield (secretary), 231–32
Reed (senator), 300
Reed, Daniel, 425, 431, 626
Reichsbank, 243, 245, 247, 252, 284, 358, 361, 390, 406–7, 419
Renken (premier), 326
Rentenmark, 247
Republicans, 153, 155, 157–58, 174–75, 183–84, 187–88, 209–10, 294–97, 312, 348, 393–94, 516, 519–20, 527, 556–57, 560
Reserve Banks and the Money Market, The (Burgess), 190
Reuss (congressman), 492–93, 632
Reynolds, Jackson E., 281
Riddle (from Ohio), 39, 580
Rio Conference, 490, 632
Rist, Charles, 287
Robbins, Lionel, 287, 607
Robinson (senator from Arkansas), 294–96, 565
Robinson (senator from Indiana), 294, 296

Rockefeller, John, 169, 177
Rogers, Will, 311, 409
Rollins (from Missouri), 36
Roosevelt, Franklin, 176, 178, 259, 276–77, 308–9, 323, 339–41, 368–70, 385–86, 392–93, 397–98, 404–5, 429, 515, 557–58, 617
Roosevelt, Theodore, 168–69, 176, 178, 259, 324
Roth (senator), 505, 509
Rowen, Hobart, 490
Russia, 168, 199, 201, 209–10, 242, 247–48, 281, 325, 415–16, 460–61, 464, 468–69, 471, 505, 512–13, 538
Ruth, Babe, 240, 319
Ryan, John A., 403, 622

S

Sabath, Adolph, 171, 175, 207, 349
Sadat, Anwar, 502
San Francisco Conference, 457
Sarnoff, David, 361
Saturday Evening Post, 301, 303, 305, 577–78
savings and loan collapse, 506
Schacht, Hjalmar, 243–45, 247, 279, 282–84, 287, 313, 322, 327–29, 360–61, 384, 390, 406–7, 434–35
Confessions of "the Old Wizard", 244–45, 282–84, 327, 360, 390, 406–7, 438, 602, 606, 618, 623, 642
Schultz, George P., 468, 495–96, 629
Scott, Winfield, 17

Wilson, Woodrow, 178, 187, 192, 199–202, 204, 209–10, 213–14, 385
Winant, John Gilbert, 417–18
Wingo (congressman), 278
Wohl, Paul, 433, 435, 626
Woodbury, Levi, 100, 115
Woodin, William, 349, 351, 362–63, 370–71, 618
Works Progress Administration, 394
World Bank, 491, 501, 505, 509, 512, 534–36, 538, 545–46, 556, 560–61, 566
World Economic Conference, 377–79, 514, 637
World War, 208–10, 212, 227–28, 240–42, 248–49, 264, 280–82, 322–23, 355–56, 361–62, 404, 415–18, 421–23, 455–57, 475–78, 544–46
World War Foreign Debt Commission, 242

World War I, 163, 166, 168, 181, 194, 212, 217–18, 227–28, 232–33, 240–41, 248–49, 264, 280–81, 322–23, 355–56, 415–16
World War II, 165, 227, 245, 248, 308, 322, 328, 369, 404, 407–8, 410, 469–70, 472, 475–78, 483–84, 545
WPA (Works Progress Administration), 382, 394, 398, 403–4, 407
Wright (mister), 39
Wright brothers, 166
Writings on Economics (Hume), 31

Y

Yeltsin, Boris, 505, 634
Young, Owen, 278, 282, 328, 361
Young Plan, 278, 283, 285, 302, 327, 329–30, 406, 607, 612